Communication
Research
Statistics

For my children,

Ian Reinard, Jill Chiotti, Aaron Reinard, and Geoffrey Reinard

---

Building Block Formulae Box 5: Formulae for Correlations

If z scores are computed using σ, the following formula for population correlation may be used:

$$\rho = \frac{\sum z_x z_y}{N}$$

If z scores are computed using s, the following formula for sample correlation may be used:

$$r = \frac{\sum z_x z_y}{n - 1}$$

(from Chapter 5)

Building Block Formulae Box 6: Formulae for One-Sample z and t

$$z = \frac{\overline{X} - \mu}{\sigma_{\overline{X}}} \qquad\qquad t = \frac{\overline{X} - \mu}{s_{\overline{X}}}$$

(from Chapter 7)

Building Block Formulae Box 7: Formulae for Independent Samples t Test

$$t = \frac{\overline{X}_1 - \overline{X}_2}{s_p \sqrt{\frac{1}{n_1} + \frac{1}{n_2}}}$$

(from Chapter 7)

Building Block Formulae Box 8: Formula for F (ANOVA)

Conceptually, the formula for F is: $F = \dfrac{\text{between groups variance}}{\text{within groups variance}}$.

Computationally, the formula for F is: $F = \dfrac{n * s_{\overline{X}}^2}{s_p^2}$.

where: n is the number of events in each group;

$s_{\overline{X}}^2$ is the variance computed from the sample means; and

s_p^2 is the pooled variance, which is the average of the variances within each group;

if the number of events is unequal, the pooled variance is computed as

$$S_p^2 = \frac{(n_1 - 1)s_1^2 + (n_2 - 1)s_2^2 + \ldots (n - 1)s_n^2}{n_1 - 1 + n_2 - 1 + \ldots n_n - 1}$$

(from Chapter 8)

Communication
Research
Statistics

John C. Reinard

California State University, Fullerton

SAGE Publications
Thousand Oaks ▪ London ▪ New Delhi

For information:

 Sage Publications, Inc.
2455 Teller Road
Thousand Oaks, California 91320
E-mail: order@sagepub.com

Sage Publications Ltd.
1 Oliver's Yard
55 City Road
London EC1Y 1SP
United Kingdom

Sage Publications India Pvt. Ltd.
B-42, Panchsheel Enclave
Post Box 4109
New Delhi 110 017 India

Printed in the United States of America

Library of Congress Cataloging-in-Publication Data

Reinard, John C.
Communication research statistics / John C. Reinard.
        p. cm.
Includes bibliographical references and index.
ISBN 0-7619-2987-8 (pbk.)
    1. Communication—Statistical methods. I. Title.
P93.7.R45 2006
302.2′02′1—dc22   2005020161

This book is printed on acid-free paper.

06   07   08   09   10   9   8   7   6   5   4   3   2   1

Acquiring Editor:	Todd R. Armstrong
Editorial Assistant:	Deya Saoud
Production Editor:	Diane S. Foster
Copy Editor:	A. J. Sobczak
Typesetter:	C&M Digitals (P) Ltd.
Proofreader:	Scott Oney
Indexer:	John Roy
Cover Designer:	Bryan Fishman

CONTENTS

Preface

This book is designed for the communication student of the 21st century. It recognizes that, over the past few decades, some important things have changed for modern communication students. As the communication studies field developed into a sophisticated area of study, communication students faced some challenges. This book attempts a response to these practical and immediate needs of today's communication students. To be specific, here are the issues that gave rise to this work.

On one hand . . .	But . . .	So, they faced this dilemma:	Yet, this book . . .
the field's inevitable methodological advances require students to have statistical knowledge (often just to read the literature in their field).	students could not always find comprehensive communication statistics textbooks to meet their needs.	either students could be pawned off on classes in other disciplines (mostly in psychology, education, sociology, or mathematics), *or* students could rely on brief handbooks (not that there were many) requiring substantial supplements to treat popular methods in communication studies.	is a comprehensive treatment in communication.
today's students have to show computer literacy to be admitted to college.	no communication-oriented textbooks included computerized analyses of communication data (in fact, they usually were written for a precomputer age).	either they could ignore the computer information they were trained to handle, *or* they could buy separate books on statistics and others on computer applications.	integrates material on computer applications in Excel, SPSS, and Amos into the presentation of statistical analyses.
students needed to be exposed to many subjects such as modeling, multiple regression,	most statistics books used in communication research methods classes focused on the wide	either students could take several courses in advanced research methods, *or*	includes coverage of the statistics actually used most in modern

(Continued)

(Continued)

On one hand . . .	But . . .	So, they faced this dilemma:	Yet, this book . . .
measurement, and ANOVA.	scope of statistics, regardless of the tools that students actually needed.	they could try to supplement their textbooks with materials on advanced methods drawn from instructors, supplemental books, or the Internet.	communication research, along with a Web site with supplemental materials.
students needed full treatments of statistical tools they were likely to use and to encounter in their reading.	the most popular brief handbooks available did not include correct statistics, or they failed to cover all the major statistics that students were most likely to need.	either students could do without training in some critical statistics, *or* they could rely on limited books in communication that provided incomplete or sometimes erroneous information.	provides enough accurate information in enough detail to permit students to know what information may be reported in research.
many comprehensive volumes drawn from other fields often included materials that were not central to the presentation of data analyses in communication (e.g., probability, fractional factorial experiments, permutations, and combinations).	students seeking comprehensive treatments were forced to purchase books with sections that would not be featured in their own communication studies or the communication studies they would be likely to read.	students could buy comprehensive textbooks with sections that would be ignored, *or* they could rely on incomplete communication volumes.	provides a comprehensive treatment of statistics that are most prominent in communication research.

In sum, students who tried to study quantitative methods within the field could try to "tough it out" by relying on textbooks that were not designed for their needs, or they could rely on noncomprehensive treatments in communication-oriented volumes.

This book attempts a realistic view of things. Most statistical analyses are not done by hand these days. Such programs as Excel XP®,[1] SPSS 12®,[2] and Amos 5®[3] have taken the drudgery out of statistical analyses. But before this book, there was no communication statistics book that included computerized statistical analysis methods as a central part of its treatment. The guide to Excel XP in Appendix A and the guide to SPSS 12 in Appendix B can help you get "up and running" with these most popular tools. Starting with Chapter 3, the coverage of statistical tools includes information and examples on ways to use these tools as appropriate. Sometimes, extra spreadsheet systems have been drafted by the author to meet

---

[1]Excel XP is a registered trademark of Microsoft Corporation.

[2]SPSS 12 is a registered trademark of SPSS, Inc.

[3]Amos 5 is a registered trademark of Amos Development Corporation.

specific needs. Additional tools are available at the online Web site for this book, and tools for the use of Excel are supplemented in some detail. Because active researchers use computers to complete most of their research computations, it is odd—and perhaps absurd—not to encourage you (the introductory student) to use major computer applications for your own work. I join the instructors of your classes in the hope that once freed from the tedium of repetitive computations by hand (following initial simple examples to illustrate relevant concepts), you will develop a rapid appreciation for the satisfaction of conducting quantitative research and using statistics to help make decisions.

Assumptions About You. This book makes only a few assumptions about you. First, the book presumes that you are interested in communication studies. Thus, the textbook includes examples of applying statistics in such fields as mass communication, speech communication, and communicative disorders. Second, you are presumed to be a person with no particular background in statistics, except perhaps for a vague memory of some high school math. Hence, the approach of this book is not highly mathematical. Rather than pursue detailed mathematical operations and matrix algebra, useful though they are, this book sticks to the basics and focuses on applied communication research using statistics. Third, this book assumes that you are not interested in statistical tools for their own sake. Instead, the book presumes that you are concerned with using statistics properly because you may wish to improve your reading of quantitative research or because you may be preparing to complete your own research. In fact, after the first two chapters, most chapters follow initial comments with sections dealing with ways to conduct studies using the specific statistical tools.

Assumptions About Your Studies. You may be taking a class dealing with quantitative research methods in communication or statistical analysis of data. Hence, this book may be a core textbook or a supplement to use in preparing research projects. Whether you are reading this book to become a savvy consumer and critic of quantitative research, or whether you are trying to develop particular skills in statistical analysis, this book is for you. It takes the view that statistics can be understood best by preparing to carry out rudimentary work. This book is intended for undergraduate and graduate students of communication who are completing research methods courses. It is appropriate as a supplement to existing books in research methods, and it will be useful for those who need a brief primary volume introducing statistical analyses most commonly used for communication data. As such, the work is written to suit the practical needs of instructors and introductory students, although enough substantive material is covered to make the book suitable for use in some advanced courses as well. The presentation of material in this book begins with a brief treatment of a concept, followed by a complete example, and then a step-by-step description of how to use SPSS and (where appropriate) Excel software applications.

The learning process is not limited to this book alone. This book is part of a system that also includes a Web site of materials and exercises. Because this book does not try to cover *all* possible statistical tools that *could* be used in communication, additional materials are featured in electronic form. These Web materials include the following:

- A glossary of statistical terms
- An orientation to the study of statistics called "The Uses of Statistics" that includes a brief history of the subject and applications of statistical analysis

- Chapter-by-chapter supplements featuring detailed chapter outlines complete with definitions, supplemental materials and statistical tools, links to examples of various research models, and macros in Excel (and Visual Basic Excel®[4] applications) that may be downloaded and used by students to complete analyses not directly supported by built-in Excel functions
- Supplemental materials including additional examples, information in supplemental chapter form on content analysis, log-linear analysis, multiple discriminant analysis, and logistic regression

If you cannot find what you need in this book, you probably will find it (or a link to it) on the Web site.

The book itself is designed to include both content and examples to simplify your learning. It is divided into parts, so that most materials—following the first two chapters—may be taken in independent order as desired. When a chapter makes comments about information in another chapter, the specific location of that information is identified. The first part of the book is an "Introduction to Statistical Analyses." You will be guided through two chapters that introduce "Using Statistics to Conduct Quantitative Research" and "Collecting Data on Variables." This section provides an orientation needed to complete the rest of the book and to understand the ways in which data may reveal relationships. Though the first section is largely noncomputational, it introduces statistical vocabulary, such as variables, hypotheses, measurement, sampling methods, and data displays. These chapters also encourage you to look at the guides in Appendix A and Appendix B to get information (or refresh yourself) about the mechanics of using Excel XP and SPSS 12.

Part II presents "Descriptive Statistics." Beginning in this portion of the work, key "building blocks" of statistical formulae are presented. You will find that these basic formulae serve as the foundation for most other tools that follow. The section begins with Chapter 3, on "Central Tendency." In addition to identifying chief measures of central tendency, this chapter includes use of SPSS 12 and Excel XP to secure such information. This format is repeated in subsequent chapters throughout book. Chapter 4 deals with "Looking at Variability and Dispersion," including the interpretation of standard measures, distributions, and the standard normal curve. Chapter 5 is dedicated to "Correlations" and considers some detailed information on interpretation issues (including the binomial effect size, elements of correlations, matters jeopardizing interpretations of correlations, and major forms of correlations). Chapter 6 examines notions of measurement in a treatment titled "Ensuring Reliability and Validity." Because these methods rely on correlations to create reliability coefficients, the discussion of correlations is placed immediately before the treatment of reliability and validity.

Part III is composed of three chapters dedicated to examining "Inferential Statistics," with an emphasis on parametric statistical hypothesis testing. Though there is healthy controversy among scholars, the logic of this approach remains a major part of quantitative scholarship in communication, and the tools are used so frequently that modern students must be familiar with them. Chapter 7 begins this part with "Statistical Significance Hypothesis Testing When Comparing Two Means" and introduces statistical hypothesis significance testing in general. The logic of hypothesis testing is applied to two families of parametric

---

[4]Visual Basic and Visual Basic Excel are registered trademarks of Microsoft Corporation.

tests: z and t. Confidence interval computations also are considered, along with examination of the tenability of assumptions underlying the parametric tests. The next two chapters involve analysis-of-variance techniques. In particular, Chapter 8 considers "Comparing More Than Two Means: One-Way Analysis of Variance" and includes effect size computation, multiple comparison tests, and extensions of ANOVA to trend analysis and analysis of covariance. Chapter 9 examines "Factorial Analysis of Variance," including isolating and interpreting main and interaction effects, and the use of fixed, mixed, and random effects models, including treatment of repeated measures designs.

Part IV is dedicated to reviewing "Nonparametric Tests." This part includes two chapters. Chapter 10 explores "Nonparametric Tests for Categorical Dependent Variables." This chapter also deals with determining effect sizes and using immediate alternatives to chi-square testing, such as Fisher's exact test and testing of proportional data. Chapter 11 explores "Nonparametric Tests for Rank Order Dependent Variables," beginning with the one-sample runs test and continuing through the Friedman two-way analysis of variance. To help promote understanding, the ways that these tools often parallel parametric tests are discussed prominently.

In Part V, the last section of the book, "Advanced Statistical Applications" are covered. Six chapters compose this section. Though not particularly complicated from a statistical point of view, Chapter 12 deals with "Meta-Analysis," a research approach that has become very prominent as an alternative to traditional literature reviews. Chapter 13 examines "Multiple Regression Correlation," including examination of different models, steps in completing multiple regression studies, and checking on the adequacy of the regression model. Chapter 14 explores "Extensions of Multiple Regression Correlation," including using categorical predictors though dummy variable coding, contrast coding, and orthogonal coding of variables. Furthermore, ways to identify interaction effects and to explore nonlinear effects are described with examples. Chapter 15 presents a survey of "Exploratory Factor Analysis." Chapter 16 continues with "Confirmatory Factor Analysis Through the Amos Program" and introduces the Amos program. Chapter 17 is dedicated to "Modeling Communication Behavior." Because this area has grown in prominence over the years, two major tools (path modeling and structural equation modeling) are described, along with methods for testing their fit to data. The emphasis in this section is on interpretation rather than on computation.

The book has several features designed to help you understand these materials. Each chapter begins with an outline of the chapter topics. Enrichment materials are placed in "Special Discussion" boxes. Each time a key term is mentioned for the first time, it is indicated in boldface type and promptly defined. Wherever possible, tables and examples are used to help you find material you need at a glance, rather than requiring detailed plodding through pages of text. Finally, computer output is described with examples.

ACKNOWLEDGMENTS

Many people helped me develop this work. My sincere thanks must go to my own teachers of research methods. Some of those people were professors who provided instruction in empirical research methods and statistics. Others permitted me to spend a sabbatical leave studying multivariate statistics and structural equation modeling, changing my role from instructor to being a student in their classes. Yet others included colleagues who worked with me to develop some appreciation for the need to refine statistical tools, and who seriously tutored me in the development of my research and statistical analysis of communication data. My students over the years have influenced the selection of topics and treatment of materials more than they can know. I am very grateful to the scholars and teachers who reviewed drafts of this work and provided invaluable advice and support. Trenchant and constructive assistance in developing this work was provided by Bryan E. Denham, Clemson University; William Evans, University of Alabama; Kelby K. Halone, University of Tennessee, Knoxville; John Pollock, the College of New Jersey; and John Sumser, California State University, Stanislaus. A special thanks must go to Rodney Reynolds of Pepperdine University, who gave extensive advice and feedback, and who helped me consider areas of related work that have enriched this book. Of course, any shortcomings in the volume are mine and not theirs. I wish to thank the editorial staff at Sage Publications, especially Todd Armstrong, for his patient and encouraging effort in shepherding this book from its beginning through its publication. His support has been nothing less than outstanding. I must express heartfelt thanks to Editorial Assistant Deya Saoud, Project Editor Diane S. Foster, and Copy Editor A. J. Sobczak, who worked so hard to make this project a completed fact. Finally, I wish to thank my wife and family, who sacrificed so that this book and its Web site could be completed. If they had not supported my efforts, this project would not exist.

Part I

INTRODUCTION TO
STATISTICAL ANALYSES

Chapter 1

Using Statistics to Conduct Quantitative Research

Whether you are taking a class in empirical research methods, whether you are using this book to help prepare yourself to conduct research, or whether you just want help to understand some of the research you have read, this book is designed for you. The emphasis is on your practical use of statistical thinking to help make decisions. To this end, the first two chapters of this book will give you background and vocabulary to help you understand other sections of the book. In each subsequent section, you will find a brief introduction to the statistical tools of interest, including a description of ways computers have helped us make fast work of analyses (few people do major data analyses by hand anymore—why should you?). The descriptions here are short and sweet and designed to give *you*—not your instructors—immediate information to address issues of quantitative research methods. For further details on things suggested here, you may wish to refer to the Web site for this book or to examine an extensive reference book of statistical analysis of data.

A WORLD OF STATISTICS

Quantitative research uses statistical information to help make decisions to answer research questions. As innocent as it may sound, this statement often gets tied up with a lot of unpleasant associations that we probably should discard right away.

The Misleading Image of Statistics: A Bum Rap

Many people have some strange ideas about studying research statistics. Three of the major misperceptions are that the subject is boring, that you can prove anything with statistics, and that it is a subject for math majors. In each case, the charge is a bum rap.

A Technical, Unexciting Subject. Some people think that research statistics is a dry subject that involves deriving theorems and toiling over long columns of numbers. You may have chosen your major field of interest, in part, because you thought you were interested in content that had little to do with numerical information. But because so many interesting questions can be answered by looking at numbers, you may find yourself drawn to statistical analyses because there are topics that fascinate you. Actually, statistical analysis of data is just commonsense use of information to help explore meaningful research questions. As such, the statistical data analysis is as exciting and stimulating as the questions that it is being used to examine.

"You Can Prove Anything With Statistics." Some people suspect that most statistics are used to mislead us. Way back in 1954, Darrell Huff wrote a lighthearted guide with the wry title *How to Lie With Statistics*, to help readers evaluate statistical reports. The book was intended to prevent mischief in the use of statistics, but the book's title reinforced the image of statistics as a form of particularly untrustworthy information. But misleading statistics are no more prevalent than tricks used by deceitful people using any *other* sorts of information. In fact, statistics can only prove what data show. Most of the time, people cannot find statistics to prove their private views no matter how strangely they manipulate the numbers. Statistics are no more prone to deception than other forms of information. Indeed, one way to avoid being misled by deceptive use of statistics is to study a little about them. This guidebook may help you in this regard.

A Study for Mathematicians. The time is long past when methods of statistical analysis were the specialties only of mathematicians. But the stereotype remains. As this book will show you, statistical tools are available to anybody trying to answer research questions that invite quantitative methods. In reality, the statistical analysis is just a form of applied reasoning and logic. You do not need to have an extensive background in mathematics to understand the descriptions of tools in this book. Furthermore, computers have taken most burdens out of studying statistical reasoning. Hence, this guidebook reflects that convenience by showing you how to use and interpret these tools.

In reality, the study of statistics has at least as much of a link to politics, social relationships, and business as it does to mathematics. Early on, statistical analyses were completed for governments. In ancient Babylon before 3000 B.C.E., agricultural yields were regularly recorded on clay tablets. Before they began to build their pyramids, ancient Egyptians statistically analyzed their kingdom's population and wealth in the 31st century before the Common Era. The Chinese kept extensive statistical records before 2000 B.C.E. Both the ancient Greeks and Romans used census data to aid in collecting taxes. The Romans were the first to hire permanent "statists" ("status takers"—a term from which the word "statistician" is derived) shortly before the beginning of the Common Era. But the serious modern study of statistics did not take off until the 17th century, when it was desired to keep track of "vital statistics" (birth and death rates) for use by governments and insurance underwriters.

Unconcerned with politics, many people examined principles of probability to prosper in gambling. Soon the basic notions were applied to setting annuity prices for life insurance policies. Scientists explored such things as the notion of "least squares" and various distributions to help advance the study of astronomy. By the 20th century, social science work led large numbers of students to study statistics to keep up with the experimental and survey work being done in their fields. The communication field often is classified as a social science because so many scholars approach the discipline with empirical research interests.

Branches of Statistics: Descriptive and Inferential

Quantitative analyses of data involve two kinds of statistical tools. **Descriptive statistics** are "numbers that are designed to characterize some information in a data set" (Reinard, 2001, p. 434). In essence, these numbers are designed to help summarize some collection of information. These sorts of statistics are contrasted with **inferential statistics**, which, as the term suggests, are tools to help researchers use sample data to draw conclusions about populations. This process usually involves assessing the probability that samples were part of populations with particular characteristics. The term **population** refers to a universe of events (e.g., people, types of statements, numbers of newspaper articles, or the like) from which a sample is drawn. These populations are universes to which a researcher is interested in generalizing, but a population does not have to be enormous. A communication studies department chair may be interested in knowing what proportion of undergraduate majors tend to apply to graduate school. The population of interest would not include all college students in the world, but only those at one location. This population could be small because the department might have a modest number of students. The point is that populations are *defined* by the researcher. In statistics, a number that is "a characteristic of a population" (Vogt, 2005, p. 227) or computed from a population is called a **parameter**. Though in everyday conversation people sometimes use "parameter" as a synonym for "perimeter" or boundary, this meaning is not preferred, and you probably should avoid using it. Most parameters of interest to researchers have nothing to do with boundaries or limits. Many pieces of data are from **samples** or selections from a larger collection of events. Naturally, nearly all published research in communication and the social sciences involves sample data. When a number is derived or computed from a sample, it is called a **statistic**. Of course, if one had more than one sample statistic, they would be called "statistic*s*." Thus, the word "statistics" carries a double meaning. Statistics (a singular noun) *is* a subject that deals with analysis of quantitative information. Statistics (a plural noun) *are* numbers computed from samples of data. To help keep things straight, different symbols are used. When referring to population data (by observation or inference), Greek letters are used. When referring to sample data, the Roman alphabet letters that we use every day are employed.

WHY DO QUANTITATIVE RESEARCH?

The **quantitative methods** studied here are tools in which descriptions of observations are expressed in predominantly numerical terms. A reasonable person might wonder why it is necessary—or even desirable—to complete quantitative research. In part, the answer to this question stems from the fact that the tradition of quantitative research comes from efforts to apply the scientific method to explore vital research questions. Yet, this statement does not mean that something is scientific just because it uses numbers. The **scientific method** is described in many ways, but one widely accepted view is that, at the very least, it involves gathering data and advancing "a functional relationship among these data" (Bachrach, 1981, p. 4).

Not all research questions require quantitative research methods. For instance, some research questions may be answered by applying critical standards to speeches. Other research questions may be answered by looking at the development of ideas through the contributions of scholars over the years. These sorts of matters may be explored by use of **qualitative research methods**, which involve examination of predominantly nonquantitative data. In general, qualitative methods are used most often when researchers wish to *describe, interpret, or criticize phenomena* that typically are *not* summarized numerically.

Research questions invite use of quantitative analysis of data if they involve

Issues of the current status of things that can meaningfully be summarized numerically,

Prediction of values of variables from the occurrence of other variables, and

Development of research measures.

Such research questions involve phenomena that can be identified and measured. These methods allow us to *describe and predict* phenomena rather than gathering evidence to help make philosophic or individualistic judgments about communication.[1] The benefits of using quantitative tools include the following:

---

[1]Making statements of such a broad nature is difficult, because one can always find exceptions. For instance, scholars using quantitative methods are concerned with the philosophical meaning of their work, but to explore these matters, they find that they must use other than quantitative methods, which are the focus of this book.

- Emphasizing work where replication of results is possible;
- Using measurement that usually is strong;
- Permitting researchers to examine complex phenomena (both the nature of simple effects of variables and complex interactions may be explored directly) (first three benefits loosely adapted from the classic treatment by Dahle and Monroe, 1961, pp. 176–178); and
- Efficiently examining data when large numbers of events are involved (though such things as single subject experiments exist [Barlow & Hersen, 1984] and one may find quantitative reports in case studies).

Of course, these methods have their limits. First, quantitative tools are useful only when it is possible to secure numbers to describe the frequency or extent of the presence of variables. Second, quantitative methods are not particularly helpful when the phenomena cannot be repeated. Thus, communication studies use both qualitative and quantitative methods. Because this book is not focused on qualitative methods, if you are interested, you should consider reviewing dedicated reference books on these methods. Then you would be able to identify the unique advantages and disadvantages of specific qualitative tools such as criticism of texts, linguistic analysis, ethnography, discourse analysis, ethnomethodology, conversational analysis, and standard historical methods.

There are many ways to classify quantitative research, but such communication studies tend to use two major groups of methods: surveys (taken generally) and experiments. **Surveys** are sometimes called **descriptive empirical studies** and use questionnaires, rating forms, or interviews to characterize phenomena. These techniques allow researchers to draw conclusions about relationships and group differences, but they do not permit direct claims of cause-and-effect relationships.[2] There are at least three major types of these studies prominently used in communication studies:

- *Descriptive or observational surveys:* studies in which variables are not manipulated by researchers, though the methods of making observations and measurements may be carefully controlled. When researchers examine whether men or women have different rates of self-disclosure, for example, the type of study is descriptive because it is not really possible to manipulate the communicator's sex. On the other hand, self-disclosure may be measured with highly sensitive tools and under carefully controlled conditions.
- *Content analysis:* a collection of methods "used to describe and systematically analyze the content of written, spoken, or pictorial communication—such as books, newspapers, television programs, or interview transcripts" (Vogt, 2005, p. 59). Such techniques typically count the frequency or the extent of various characteristics of messages, such as the length of newspaper articles on a subject, the number of minutes

---

[2]Sometimes researchers can use survey information as circumstantial evidence for the existence of cause-and-effect relationships. Stiff (1994, pp. 36–37) explained that under some idealized conditions, researchers may satisfy Mill's canons of causality by use of non-experimental data. It should be mentioned, however, that in most circumstances, it is not possible to make claims of causality from survey research. Furthermore, it should be granted that cause-and-effect claims could be made from historical studies if one had the ability to establish long-term historical antecedents and consequents.

dedicated to television news, or the number of dysfluencies by speakers during impromptu speeches.

- *Opinion surveys:* surveys designed to identify how groups of people report their evaluations of various topics. Large-scale opinion polls of public reactions to the U.S. president following a State of the Union address are examples of such popular surveys.

Experimental methods study the effect of variables manipulated in situations where all other influences are held constant. Obviously, clever researchers may find it easy to manipulate variables, but the hard part comes in controlling all other influences. When the variation of some other variables mixes with the variation of the chief variables in a study, it is called **confounding**. When a study's experimental variables are confounded with other variables, it becomes impossible to tell if any results are due to the operation of experimental variables, the confounding variables, or some mix of them. In addition to efforts at direct control, researchers also randomly assign subjects to experimental and control groups. As the terms suggest, an **experimental group** is a collection of events exposed to the experimental variable. Contrariwise, a **control group** is a collection of events receiving comparable treatment as the experimental group except that the experimental variable is absent. The random assignment ensures that any extraneous variables will not introduce their influences systematically more in the experimental condition than in the control condition. The presence of these extraneous variables does not disappear, but the variables are controlled because their presence is deliberately mixed (in this case, deliberately confounded) with random variation. Their contributions show up as "background noise," or what researchers commonly call **error variance**. Though it takes some doing, if experimenters control all extraneous variables, they can claim to obtain direct evidence of cause-and-effect relationships. Thus, when researchers are interested in causal relationships and when they can manipulate (presumed) causal variables, the experimental approach is invited. As we will see elsewhere in this book, the concern for control sometimes invites researchers to prefer some statistical methods over others.

TYPICAL STEPS INVOLVED IN QUANTITATIVE RESEARCH

Completing a study involving quantitative methods involves many steps that lead to the analysis of data. Because these elements affect the ways statistics are used and how they are selected, it is worth a moment to pay some attention to them.

Isolating a Problem Question and Hypothesis

The first step in an empirical study is stating a research problem worth investigating. Problem questions tend to be stated either as direct questions (sometimes identified with the notation "RQ"), or as purpose or objective statements. These problem questions tend to satisfy a number of criteria. For instance, they tend to ask about at least two variables, though these days many problem questions deal with three or more variables of interest. Problem questions in empirical research are testable against some kind of observable data, usually in

Special Discussion 1.1

How to Select a Hand Calculator

Much data analysis can be completed with the aid of computers, but sometimes you have a task that requires entering only a little data and getting information to complete reports. Sometimes you will find that you want to complete operations that are not really supported conveniently in some of the programs available to you. Thus, it is inevitable: You will need to have a hand calculator. Unfortunately, lots of people spend large sums of money and get the wrong thing. This discussion contains a few considerations to guide your selection.

You will need to get a calculator that has built-in statistical functions. That fact means that you will not want to spend money on calculators that have extensive engineering functions (unless you are an engineer, of course). In fact, you probably can get a calculator with everything you need for somewhere between $10 and $20. A calculator that is called "scientific" tends to have the features you need. Inspect the function keys and make sure that there is a key for the mean and the standard deviation. Different manufacturers use different formats, so make sure the calculator has what you want. Most Texas Instruments and Sharp calculators, for instance, have separate keys for s (sample standard deviation) and σ (population standard deviation). Other manufacturers use different symbols. Some use σ_n for population standard deviation and σ_{n-1} or σ' for sample standard deviation. Other functions, such as those for correlations and analysis of variance, probably will not be used with large data sets. They may be considered luxuries that some researchers will like and others rarely will use.

A feature that is quite useful is parentheses and brackets. Some manufacturers provide both, and some provide only one. You should ask how deeply the parentheses may be embedded (how many parentheses within parentheses). Rarely are they limited only to one level. If you are interested in using single-subject experiments, you will need to have a key that returns the number of combinations of a larger set of data.

Some Web sites claim to have scientific calculators for your use. Two of the best at the time of the writing of this chapter are www.scientificcalculator.com/ and http://mypage.bluewin.ch/a-z/cusipage/scicalc.html. Yet, these resources are not really designed for students of statistical analyses. Eventually you will need to have your own calculator with dedicated functions.

A few final pieces of advice might bear mentioning. Avoid calculators that have so many buttons that the buttons are very small. Though the calculator may look nice, the small buttons may give you trouble unless you have very small fingers. Whatever you do, do not discard the instruction book. The need to reference the manual at a future time is almost guaranteed, and the failure to have the instruction guide may make the calculator of limited use. Sometimes instead of buying a calculator, a person is persuaded to borrow one from a friend. Unfortunately, each manufacturer does things a little differently from the others. So, if a friend also supplies the instruction manual, the gift may be generous, but if the manual is not available, it may prove frustrating to try to learn how to use the calculator at the same time one is doing work with it.

the form of numerical scores. Because our focus here is on quantitative methods of data analysis, our data of interest will be in the form of numerical information. Of course, problem questions should avoid making value judgments, because answering such questions requires moving beyond empirical research into ethical or political interpretations.

The Research Hypothesis. An answer to a research question is called a hypothesis. Stated precisely, a **hypothesis** is an expectation about events based on generalizations of the assumed relationship between variables. Hypotheses are abstract statements concerned with theories and concepts, whereas the observations used to test hypotheses are specific data based on facts (Tuckman, 1999, p. 74).

Unlike the commonly repeated palaver that a hypothesis is just an "educated guess," a hypothesis is the result of some inquiry and reasoning that leads to a possible answer to a research question. Hypotheses may be justified as extensions of past research or as applications for some theory or conceptual orientation. Occasionally you can read studies that have stated neither problem questions nor hypotheses. One wonders how the researchers knew when they were done with the research project.

Research hypotheses often are stated in ways that reflect the ways in which the research is designed. By the time researchers state hypotheses to answer research questions, they know if their research designs will ask about differences in proportions, difference between means, or magnitudes of correlations. Thus, the hypotheses are written in ways that reflect these choices. Researchers rarely use methods of statistical analysis to test research hypotheses directly. Instead, for the sake of argument, they posit **null hypotheses** that deny the existence of a relationship between two or more variables. By gathering data, researchers can show how improbable such a statement is, given the data that have been observed. If researchers get results that show the null hypothesis to be very improbable (such as 20 to 1 odds against it), support for the research hypothesis is claimed. Part III of this book deals with this notion of statistical hypothesis testing, referred to as inferential statistics.

Selecting Measures

Selection of ways to measure important variables is given great attention in quantitative research. The **reliability** of a measure is the degree to which it is consistent and stable. As such, a reliable measure gives results that tend to show little variation over time. The **validity** of a measure is the degree to which the measure can be shown to measure what it claims to measure. There are many techniques to demonstrate reliability and validity of measures. Thus, researchers regularly take time to explain evidence for the adequacy of their measures.

Sampling

Empirical research requires researchers to spend time focusing their attention on careful sampling of data from a population. Researchers often are interested in drawing conclusions that have something to do with populations. To do so requires them to show information about sampling adequacy. Two aspects of sampling are particularly important.

First, randomization often is required. **Random sampling** means that sampling is completed such that every event in the population has an equal chance of selection.[3] Not only do researchers frequently ensure randomization for the sake of their designs, but most inferential

---

[3]Mathematically, in an infinitely large universe of events, randomization would mean that the probability of any event following any other particular, chosen event would be 0. The accommodation to reality made here is widely accepted.

statistics tools also require that they use randomization in their studies (random sampling or random assignment of subjects to experimental conditions, at a minimum). This matter is so important that researchers are expected to produce some evidence to show that they actually accomplished the task. If a research article states that subjects were "randomly sampled" (or even "randomly assigned" to conditions), a protocol of sorts has emerged. Either researchers are expected to take the time to explain how they accomplished this task or they are expected to explain that they selected subjects at random using the method of random numbers. The random number method involves giving an identifying number to every event in the population or the sampling frame and then turning to a table of random digits (or a computer-generated selection system based on random digits) to select a sample of the desired size. If the method of random numbers is used to acquire a sample, the researchers are expected to identify the source of the random number table or the specific computer subroutine they used. If neither of these randomization methods is used, readers will not necessarily assume that complete steps toward random sampling were made.

Second, researchers should provide evidence to show that the sample was representative of the larger population to which they wish to generalize any results. **Representativeness** means that a sample is similar enough to the population that its characteristics correspond to those of the population. Researchers typically explain sample representativeness by describing the population of interest and reporting characteristics of the sample to show that the events in the study are compatible with those in the population. Sometimes some known characteristics of the population are contrasted statistically with sample data (e.g., age of subjects, education level, sex of subjects, race of subjects). Even with random sampling, occasionally a sample can prove to be unrepresentative of the population. Hence, researchers who do not report sample representativeness information are treated with some suspicion.

Design

The **design** of an empirical inquiry is "the plan that a researcher will follow when conducting a study" (Vogt, 2005, p. 87). This section of a research report usually specifies the type of experimental or nonexperimental approach. Then, any procedures and tasks to be completed by subjects are described in some detail. Control checks usually are explained in this section of a research piece. **Control checks** are additional measures used to provide evidence that nuisance variables are controlled. Such things as message language emotiveness, perception of source credibility, and the like might be measured to ensure that their influences do not add substantial uncontrolled influences in the study. One form of control check is called a **manipulation check**, which permits the researchers to have independent evidence that the chief variables in their studies were operating as planned. When researchers expose people to written messages, for instance, they often wish to have proof that respondents actually understand what they read. Thus, a manipulation check may be added to a study design to measure message comprehension.

Researchers also design studies to examine the influence of independent variables separately and in combination with others. In experiments and other studies, researchers use designs to explore main and interaction effects. **Main effects** are effects in dependent variables stemming from variation from independent variables separately. **Interaction effects** are effects in dependent variables stemming from variation from combinations of two or more independent variables.

Selection of Statistics

The selection of research statistics is, of course, a major part of this book. In fact, most of the book involves your selecting and using different forms of statistics. Yet, data analysis involves more than reporting on hypothesis tests. It also involves "data cleaning," in which the researcher goes through the data to determine if there are any "data entry" errors. Usually this process is simple enough. Researchers usually prepare a frequency distribution for all variables. For instance, if a researcher sampling college students discovers that someone's age is "05" (measured in years), the researcher knows to look at the original data and see where the error lies. After any corrections are made, hypotheses still cannot be tested until the reliability of the measures has been found to meet minimum standards. Finally, after the preliminary steps are completed, the researchers may examine the primary variables of interest in the study. Data analysis also involves assessing the reasonableness of assumptions that underlie statistical tests. Thus, this book takes some time describing some of these important steps.

Writing the Report

The job is not over until the paperwork is done. The last part of the research craft involves documenting the work. Naturally, research reports vary greatly in their depth and detail. Researchers attempt to write with enough detail so that others could replicate the project, if they wished. In addition, because research is an argument in which claims are made on the basis of evidence, researchers justify their choices and share the reasoning that leads them to their conclusions. Some areas involving the greatest amount of argument include the following.

Sample Information

The methods for selecting events for inquiry always take serious attention. Thus, individual researchers are expected to identify the size of the sample they selected and the reasons for that size. Often the choice is a compromise between expense and statistical ideals. The characteristics of the sample should be described, and any demographic information (i.e., information about the background of the subjects) should be revealed. The actual methods for collecting the data (e.g., using students in their classrooms, reliance on volunteers responding to a newspaper advertisement, or the ways in which a literature search was completed for a meta-analysis) should be described. The number of refusals or nonrespondents out of the original sample should be described and, to the extent possible, descriptions of their characteristics should be presented. If an argument can be made to suggest that the differences between the nonrespondents and the rest of the sample are only random differences, this location is the place where such an argument should be made. Any training of data collectors or interviewers should be described, and the methods for debriefing subjects should be identified. Of course, the approach used to obtain informed consent must be described when presenting information about the sample.

Measurement Adequacy Information

Though many researchers like to use measurement systems that have been successful in the past, modern practice requires that they also present some sort of information about the reliability of the measures. Validity information also is welcomed, but failure to present measurement reliability information is considered a flatly unacceptable practice. Researchers typically describe and justify the types of measurement scales and devices they employed. In addition, information is presented about the statistical adequacy of the measures. Methods to score the instruments and to derive single numbers from a collection of scale items should be described and, if necessary, justified (certainly, a failure to treat interrelated scales as one measure should be explained).

Manipulation Checks

If the study is an experiment, manipulation checks should be explained in enough detail that readers can tell whether the variables introduced into the study actually are operating as planned. For studies that do not have experimental manipulations, much sound research still features control checks along with explanations of the statistical information about such checks.

Check Hypothesized Results

The presentation of hypothesized results usually is advanced in a businesslike manner in a part of the research report dedicated to "Results." When reporting a test of a hypothesis, there is general agreement (see Tuckman, 1999, pp. 343–344) that (at minimum) one should

- Restate the hypothesis;
- Report descriptive statistics (usually a measure of central tendency and a measure of dispersion) for each group involved in the hypothesis;
- Identify the statistical tests used and the decision rules used when applying them;
- Show that the assumptions underlying the statistical tests are satisfied;
- Describe whether the hypotheses are supported or not, including reporting any relevant coefficients from the statistical tests; and
- Report the size of the relationship found, at least for those results that are "statistically significant."

This "Results" section does not interpret the theoretic or practical meaning of the findings. The "Discussion" arguments provide such interpretations.

It might be added that when communicating the hypothesis tests, one cannot logically claim that a hypothesis has been "confirmed" or "proven." In reality, a researcher may have found that a hypothesis has survived one additional test. In the future, the relationship could disintegrate in the light of other influences on it. Hence, the strongest claims that researchers make are that their hypotheses are "supported" or "found tenable."

Report Unhypothesized Results

Unexpected or "incidental" findings should be reported in enough detail to permit readers to understand their meaning. Because researchers usually discover *something* that was "unexpected," this section of a report may be among the most intriguing parts of a research project. These results often receive as much formal attention as if they were hypothesized findings.

Researchers usually review all of the variables in the study to determine if other relationships have (or have not) been found.

Interpret Results

The final discussion permits the researcher to make arguments from the research findings. The interpretations typically involve three areas of interest. First, the theoretic foundations used to develop research questions or hypotheses can be revisited. In some cases, findings support a theoretic orientation. In some other cases, the results challenge a theoretic orientation. Regardless of the impact, some argument relating the results to the underlying theoretic rationale is expected in the "Discussion" of results. Second, arguments about the significance— potential or actual—of the study results may be presented. Though researchers are supposed to base their comments on research findings, many writers let their thinking carry them beyond the specific evidence before them. Such opinions, however, may be no better than anybody else's. Thus, researchers are usually careful to ensure that their arguments satisfy general standards expected of any sound reasoning and appropriate use of evidence. Third, any suggestions for future research may be advanced. Sometimes researchers find mistakes to correct. Sometimes they suggest potential applications for their work. These suggestions constitute part of a research agenda for the future.

Special Discussion 1.2

Guidelines for Writing Research Arguments

Research is an argument; hence, the major steps involved in writing research require that the researcher make claims from information and evidence. The following list is a set of guidelines in question form regarding things to "do" or "don't" when writing a research report. Though not an exhaustive list (and, of course, different reports require different kinds of information), it may be helpful to give you topics to consider in a typical report.

QUESTION	COMMENT
Introduction and Problem	
What is the significance of the research topic?	Topics may be justified by showing how the new research would fill a gap in knowledge, solve a practical problem, or extend past research (Reinard, 2001, p. 76).
Does the research problem question meet the standards for useful problem questions?	Requirements: 1. Usually ask about two or more variables; 2. Testable; 3. Stated clearly and in terms of observable information and scores; 4. Should avoid making value judgments.
Are terms in problem question defined (either in this section or elsewhere in the report)? Are controversies related to proper definitions resolved?	

Context of Problem

Are relevant theories reviewed to help make a case for the merit of the research question?

Researchers usually reason that the variables in the problem may operate in ways that are similar to those expectations derived from the theory. Sometimes, however, researchers challenge theories.

Are all elements of theories or theoretic orientations clearly identified?

Researchers typically show that in isolation or other contexts, each variable in the study has exhibited interesting relationships to other variables.

Is a justification provided for looking at each of the principal variables in the problem question?

Researchers must use the literature review to show that that research question should be answered, but has not yet been.

Does the review of literature show that the research question has not already been answered?

Hypotheses

Is there a rationale leading up to each hypothesis?

Stating "based on the previously reviewed literature, the following hypotheses are advanced" is not a rationale. It must be specific. Typical rationales are based on expectations from past research or theories (or, at least, theoretic orientations). See Chapter 2.

Do the hypotheses clearly identify the independent and dependent variables?

Method

General Design

Is the general method suitable to the research problem question?

For instance, a problem question that asks about the "effect" or "impact" of one variable on another generally requires the use of an experiment, not a survey.

Is there sound evidence that the variables in the design actually were operating as planned?

Were manipulation checks included in the study?

Are there control checks on potential intervening variables?

Does the design reflect the hypotheses in terms of number of groups or treatment choices?

Measures and Manipulations

Are the measures reliable?
Are the measures described in detail?
Is full information presented about the means by which the data were collected?

Are questionnaires fully described, including instructions? In interviews, are the qualifications of the interviewers identified and are the steps to train interviewers described?

Are methods for scoring measures sound?
Are the measures valid?
Are any tasks and/or experimental manipulations of variables fully described?
Is there evidence that any tasks and/or experimental manipulations of variables did

Confounding of manipulated variables occurs when the treatment also inadvertently introduces

(Continued)

Special Discussion 1.2 (Continued)

not also introduce uncontrolled influences from other variables?

Sampling

Is there evidence of randomization in sampling?
In experiments, is there evidence of random assignment of subjects to experimental and control conditions?
Is there evidence of the representativeness of the sample?
Is the size of the sample justified?

Statistics

Is the appropriate set of descriptive statistics reported when presenting results? Are they appropriate ones?
Are any inferential statistics appropriately used?

Are the assumptions for the statistical tools satisfied?
Are the statistics reported completely?

Discussion and Interpretation

Are all conclusions based on research evidence found in the research project?
Were conclusions suitable to the data?

Are all results interpreted?
Is there evidence of how well the findings relate to the tradition of previous studies or theories?
Are limitations to the study completely described?
Are suggestions for future research reasonable and complete?
If necessary, does the researcher adequately account for finding that the independent variables account for only small proportions of variance in the dependent variables?
If necessary, does the research adequately account for alternative interpretations of study findings?
Is the significance of the study clearly demonstrated?

Ethical Choices

If relevant to the study design, is there evidence of informed consent from subjects?
Does the research project show high ethical conduct by the researchers?
Are procedures for debriefing provided?

changes in another variable (e.g., message length or language emotiveness in studies that add or subtract elements of messages).

See Chapters 3 through 5.

Is a justification offered for the selection of the statistical tools and for the decision rules that are employed when using them?
The assumptions are introduced in this book as the tools are introduced.

Claims of causality should not appear in survey studies. In addition, the language of the researcher reflects a tentativeness, such that the words "may" and "appear" are used frequently rather than unqualified claims.

Chapter 2

COLLECTING DATA ON VARIABLES

Empirical researchers often use questionnaires and interviews to collect data. The process of creating and using such measurement "tools" can be a study of its own. For our purposes, however, we need to understand the basics that are related to selecting and using other statistical tools. This chapter considers the role of variables and hypotheses. Then, the measurement of variables and techniques of sampling is considered.

VARIABLES AND HYPOTHESES

The types of variables and the ways they are measured determine which statistical tools researchers may choose. There are several ways in which variables and hypotheses play important roles for users of statistics.

Recognizing Research Variables

A **variable** is a characteristic to which numbers or values may be assigned (after Reinard, 2001, p. 444). The communication field has many variables that have defined it, such as the dimensions of source credibility, measures of communication apprehension, depth of self-disclosure, and levels of communication satisfaction. Though many variables are measured on some index or scale, others may involve simply identifying sample characteristics (such as which participants are male or female) or presenting participants with control or experimental treatments.

There is an important characteristic of variables that bears recognizing. Variables must, well, *vary*. If a variable has only one category or value, it is not called a "variable" at all. For instance, a researcher once suggested this problem question:

RQ₁: What is the relationship between married women who work outside the home and their satisfaction with the amount of communication in their marriages?

Though the research question raises an interesting social concern, it has only an output variable. "Married women who work outside the home" is only one "level" or category of the "location of work" variable. In fact, this study controls for the type of employment among women by holding it constant. It is not a variable at all, but the opposite of a variable, called a constant. A **constant** is a characteristic to which only one number or value may be assigned. Researchers often try to examine the relationships among some variables of interest while holding other variables constant.

Variables as Used in Hypotheses

In Chapter 1, a hypothesis was defined as "an expectation about events based on generalizations of the assumed relationship between variables" (Tuckman, 1999, p. 74). These hypotheses are suggested as potential answers to research questions. Hypotheses also help identify which research variables are inputs and which are outputs. The "input" variables in a hypothesis typically are called **independent variables**, which are "variables that can be used to predict or explain the values of another variable" (Vogt, 2005, p. 151). Some researchers like to reserve the term "independent variable" for input variables in experiments, and they prefer to call input variables "predictor variables" in all other research. Because most scholars find this distinction of only passing interest, this book does not emphasize this difference.

A second type of variable is the output or dependent variable. **Dependent variables** are variables whose values are predicted by independent variable(s), whether or not caused by them (after Vogt, 2005, p. 86). In experiments, the dependent variables actually are the measures on which effects are seen. Dependent variables appear in nonexperimental studies, too. Whether a variable is an independent or dependent variable is identified by the hypotheses in a study.

Special Discussion 2.1

Other Types of Variables

Sometimes researchers make use of other labels for some variables. Some of the most popular labels are listed here.

- *Moderator variable:* a type of independent variable that affects the ways in which the primary independent variables are related to the dependent variables.
- *Mediating variable:* "a variable that 'transmits' the effects of another variable" (Vogt, 2005, p. 190). Though the term often is used by researchers as a synonym for moderator variable, others view mediating variables as indirect influences that primary independent variables have on dependent variables.
- *Intervening variable:* "a factor that theoretically affects observed phenomena but cannot be seen, measured, or manipulated; its effect must be inferred from the effects of the independent and moderator variables on the observed phenomena" (Tuckman, 1999, p. 101). Others use the term as a synonym for mediating variables (Vogt, 2005, p. 158).
- *Control variable:* a "nuisance" variable that is held constant for the purposes of controlling its influence. Technically, calling something a control variable may be a contradiction in terms because a constant is the opposite of a variable.
- *Suppressor variable:* a "variable that conceals or reduces (suppresses) a relationship between other variables" (Vogt, 2005, p. 318). When such variables are present, the relationship between the independent and dependent variable is reduced.

Hypothesis Types

If there is more than one hypothesis, hypotheses may be numbered such as H_1, H_2, H_3, and so on. There are two broad types of hypotheses: research hypotheses and null hypotheses.

Research or "Alternative" Hypotheses

Although problem questions reflect the topic of the investigation, research hypotheses are stated in ways that reflect the design of the research. By the time researchers state research hypotheses to answer research questions, they know if their research designs will make comparisons of proportions, assess differences between means, or examine magnitudes of correlations. Thus, the hypotheses reflect these choices. Because the research hypotheses stand as alternatives to the null hypotheses, they sometimes are called "alternative hypotheses." There are several ways research hypotheses may be stated.

Comparisons of Dependent Variable Means: Sometimes researchers compare two or more groups of events and test for a difference in the means of the dependent variable measure. For instance, a hypothesis might state

H: During initial interactions, women engage in more self-disclosure than do men.

Men and women compose the two groups or levels of the independent variable. Self-disclosure is the dependent variable. As a matter of protocol, when researchers examine sample characteristics, they use symbols from the Roman alphabet (our As, Bs, and Cs). When describing or estimating population characteristics, they use symbols from the Greek alphabet. Though researchers usually deal with sample data, for conceptual purposes they hypothesize general relationships that may exist in the population as a whole. Hence, the symbol system in hypothesis testing uses Greek letters to represent population relationships. The standard abbreviation for the population mean is the lowercase Greek letter μ (mu). Hence, the hypothesis may be stated as

$$H: \mu_{women} > \mu_{men}.$$

The symbol ">" represents "greater than," and "<" stands for "less (or fewer) than." Thus, this hypothesis states, "the mean of women is greater than the mean of men." Because writing out "women" and "men" could be tiresome, numbers sometimes are used to keep the relationship straight (H: $\mu_1 > \mu_2$).

These types of hypotheses are called **directional hypotheses** because, logically enough, they state the direction of the difference in means (or, in a broad sense, they state the direction of the relationship). These sorts of hypotheses often define the ways in which researchers use distributions to engage in statistical hypothesis testing. In particular, the type of hypothesis determines whether researchers will use "one-tailed" (reflecting directional hypotheses) or "two-tailed" statistical tests.

Sometimes researchers look at variables where they expect a difference, but they do not have enough background information to guide them in a particular direction. They can only hypothesize that "something's got to give." Because this type of hypothesis states a relationship, but not its direction, it is called a **nondirectional hypothesis**. A nondirectional hypothesis may be represented as

$$H: \mu_1 \neq \mu_2.$$

The symbol "$\neq$" represents "is not equal to." Hence, the hypothesis states, "the mean of the first group is not equal to the mean of the second group." As an example of this sort of hypothesis, there has been controversy about whether a manager's high degree of predictability in communication leads to increased communication satisfaction among workers. One view is that managers whose communication is highly predictable are dependable and, hence, stimulate positive reactions among employees. Another view is that a manager whose communication is highly predictable makes employees think that there is little use discussing a new suggestion because "we already know what s/he's going to say." Given the contradictory reasoning, researchers might advance a nondirectional hypothesis

> H: Employees of managers whose communication is highly predictable have different levels of communication satisfaction in the organization than employees of managers whose communication is not highly predictable.

This sort of hypothesis suggests a difference in means in *either* a positive or a negative direction. Hence, statistically, testing it might require a two-tailed test (depending on the specific statistical tool employed).

Special Discussion 2.2

Lowercase Greek Letter	Uppercase Greek Letter	Equivalent Roman Letters
α alpha	A	A
β beta	B	B
γ gamma	Γ	G, N
δ delta	Δ	D
ε epsilon	E	E
ζ zeta	Z	Z
η eta	H	ē
θ theta	Θ	Th
ι iota	I	I
κ kappa	K	K
λ lambda	Λ	L
μ mu	M	M
ν nu	N	N
ξ xi	Ξ	X
o omicron	O	O
π pi	Π	P
ρ rho	P	R, rh
σ sigma	Σ	S
τ tau	T	T
υ upsilon	Y	Y, U
φ phi	Φ	Ph
χ chi	X	Ch
ψ psi	Ψ	Ps
ω omega	Ω	ō

Comparisons of Proportions. Sometimes researchers use hypotheses to speculate about percentages or proportions.[1] For instance, one might hypothesize

> H: The proportion of high communication apprehensive students with noticeable public speaking anxiety is lower for those given training in systematic desensitization than for those who are given lectures on the subject.

As a matter of protocol, a sample proportion is symbolized as p and the population proportion is symbolized as π (pi). So, one might abbreviate the hypothesis about proportions as

$$H: \pi_{\text{systematic desensitization training}} < \pi_{\text{lecture on public speaking anxiety}} \text{ or}$$

$$H: \pi_1 < \pi_2.$$

Of course, even though this example represents a directional hypothesis, researchers also could use nondirectional hypotheses with proportional data.

Examination of Correlations. Research hypotheses sometimes involve measures of **correlations**, which identify the degree of coincidence between variables (in numbers that usually range from −1 to 1). The abbreviation for the sample correlation is r (or some variation of r, including R), and the abbreviation for the population correlation is ρ (rho).[2] A nondirectional hypothesis stating that the actual correlation coefficient is different from no correlation at all could be symbolized as

$$H: \rho \neq 0.$$

A correlational hypothesis also could be directional as in these examples:

$$H: \rho > 0 \text{ or}$$

$$H: \rho < 0.$$

Sometimes researchers hypothesize that a correlation will be greater (or lower) under some circumstances than others. For example, a researcher could hypothesize that in classes where

---

[1]In the language used here, such data will be called "proportional" rather than "percentage" data. The reason is that proportional data are expressed as portions of a whole equal to 1.0. Percentages, on the other hand, move the decimal point (e.g., an advertisement that promises "10% off" the price of a product is not the same as one that promises ".10% off"). Because many computations require retaining the original decimal point, that language will be reflected here.

[2]Sometimes you can find statistics books that use ρ (rho) as the symbol for the Spearman rank order correlation. This convention, however, is not standard and will not be found in this volume. We will stay with the tradition of using Greek letters for population parameters and using the Roman alphabet for sample statistics. In this book, Spearman's rank order correlation is symbolized as r_s for the sample and ρ_s for the population.

exams are perceived as rigorous, there are lower correlations between the teacher's amounts of humorous communication and student satisfaction than when exams are not perceived as rigorous. Symbolized as a simple difference, the hypothesis would be

$$H: \rho_{\text{classes where exams are not perceived as rigorous}} > \rho_{\text{classes where exams are perceived as rigorous}}.$$

Null Hypotheses

Though research hypotheses are the chief interest of researchers, they are tested only indirectly. We cannot really take samples and *prove* whole population characteristics from them. We can, however, use statistics to identify how unlikely it would be for us to find data with such observed relationships as a result of random sampling error. To do so, researchers use a null hypothesis. The **null hypothesis** is a statistical hypothesis that states that there is no relationship between the variables presented in the research hypothesis. Researchers can determine how unlikely it is that they could find data such as observed in a study if the world of the null hypothesis were true. By this process, we can decide whether to reject the assumption that only random sampling error is at work, rather than an actual relationship between variables. Put in a nutshell, it is the null hypothesis—not the research hypothesis—that is really tested by researchers.

If researchers get results that show the null hypothesis is improbable, support for the alternative research hypothesis is claimed through a process of elimination. The null hypothesis, in essence, states that the variables are "presumed innocent" of having any nonrandom relationships. Then statistics may be used to help examine if the evidence makes holding this assumption very improbable. If researchers reject the null hypothesis, then the **alternative hypothesis**, the research hypothesis, is supported. When differences between the means of groups are hypothesized, the null hypothesis is stated as

$$H_0: \mu_1 = \mu_2.$$

The zero in the null hypothesis abbreviation "H_0" symbolizes that the null hypothesis states there is no difference between the groups.[3] This expectation is reasonable because stating $\mu_1 = \mu_2$ is equivalent to stating $\mu_1 - \mu_2 = 0$.

The logic here may be extended to other sorts of data situations. For instance, when dealing with proportional data, the null hypotheses may be stated as

$$H_0: \pi_1 = \pi_2.$$

For correlational hypotheses, the null hypothesis that there is "no correlation" is stated as $H_0: \rho = 0$. When comparing the sizes of two correlations, the null hypothesis would be

---

[3]For practical purposes, some volumes on statistics include all alternatives to the research hypothesis as part of the "null hypothesis." For instance, if the directional research hypothesis is H: $\mu_1 > \mu_2$, some state the null hypothesis as $H_0: \mu_1 \geq \mu_2$ because either finding no differences or finding differences opposite to the directional hypothesis would not permit the researcher to claim support for the research hypothesis.

H_0: $\rho_1 = \rho_2$. In reality, the null hypothesis may be used when exploring many other sorts of data such as whether variances among groups are unequal.

Researchers must watch their language when writing about hypotheses. One may "reject" the null hypothesis, but one cannot claim to "accept" or "support" a null hypothesis. One can accept a claim only if there is evidence for it. Because the null hypothesis denies the presence of any evident relationships, other language must be used. Researchers who do not reject the null hypothesis report only that they "failed to reject," "could not reject," or were "unable to reject" the null hypothesis. Similarly, as may be recalled from Chapter 1, those who find support for alternative research hypotheses do not claim to have "confirmed" or "proven" their hypotheses. They only have found that the hypotheses have survived additional testing. Instead, the hypotheses are "supported" by the data or "found tenable."

MEASUREMENT OF VARIABLES

In a general sense, **measurement** refers to systems by which numbers are associated with characteristics of interest. To make appropriate statistical choices, researchers need to know the levels of measurement involved for their chief variables.

Levels of Measurement

In some cases, numbers are used as classifications (Group 1, Group 2, and so forth). In other cases, the measures may tell a great deal about the details. It is important to distinguish among these matters because different sorts of computations are permitted for variables measured on different levels. As Figure 2.1 shows, four levels of measurement are regularly distinguished.

Nominal level measurement involves the use of numbers as simple identifications of variables (Reinard, 2001, p. 439). Debate team code numbers, identification of men as "Group 1" and women as "Group 2," and distinguishing between experimental and control groups in a study are examples of nominal level measurement. It is sometimes called the lowest level of measurement because it cannot be used to identify degrees of differences among categories. Though there may be some dispute, many researchers find it convenient to use the terms "qualitative measures" and "nominal level measures" interchangeably.

Ordinal level measurement employs rank order on some variable. Hence, the numbers indicate that there is a difference among the points on the measurements, but not the actual *degrees* of differences. For instance, if one ranked the speakers in a competitive event from the number one best, to number two best, and so forth, the ordinal level of measurement would be used.

Interval level measurement involves assignment of numbers to items as a matter of degree such that "the intervals between numbers are *equal* in size" (Cozby, 1989, p. 149). Unlike ordinal level measures, the degree of difference is identified in this approach. Additionally, the intervals are equal from one point to another adjacent point. Hence, if two people scored 12 and 13 on the "superior subordinate communication openness scale" (Jablin, 1978), their difference would have the same interval distance as two people who scored 26

Figure 2.1   Four Levels of Measurement

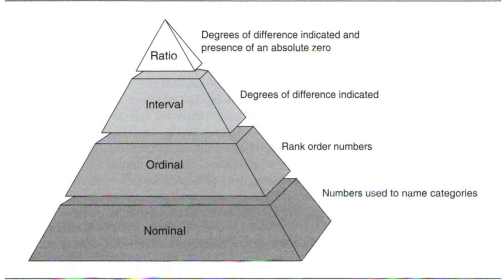

and 27 on the same test. Hence, it is acceptable to engage in addition and subtraction operations when dealing with interval level measures.[4] Most measures that use established scales in communication research are in the realm of interval level scales. When responses from several individual scale items are added together, the result sometimes is called an "index."

Ratio level measurement consists of assignment of numbers to items such that "any adjoining values are the same distance apart and in which there is a true zero point" (Vogt, 2005, p. 264). An absolute zero means that a score of zero would indicate the complete absence of the property being measured. If someone's income for the previous week were 0, it would

---

[4]This statement may be qualified somewhat. "Multiplication and division with interval scales are permissible only with respect to the *intervals* and not with respect to the scale values" (Nunnally, 1978, p. 20). Such scales may be subjected to transformations and multiplication and division by constants. Given three equally spaced scale points, *a*, *b*, and *c* (such as 2, 5, and 8), on an interval scale with equal intervals, it follows that

$$\frac{a - b}{b - c} = 1,$$

which illustrates the legitimacy of forming ratios of *intervals* on interval scales. As another example of the legitimate employment of multiplication and division with the intervals, the distance from *a* to *c* should equal twice the distance from *a* to *b* when calculated from the equalities stated in the definition of the scale. . . . Whereas the condition of invariance demonstrates why it is permissible to form ratios of the *intervals* (multiply and divided by one another), they also demonstrate why it is not permissible to form ratios among the *scale points* on an interval scale (Nunnally, 1978, pp. 21–22).

mean that that person had no income at all last week. If a speaker had 0 dysfluencies during a speech, then there were no dysfluencies at all. This property also means that the ratio of different scores could be identified. For instance, when looking at age, one might observe that a person who is 25 years old is half as old as one who is 50. Similarly, a person who is 80 is twice as old as someone who is 40 years old. The 2 to 1 ratios remain meaningful in ratio level data. But on a communicator competence scale (which has a range of scores from 12 to 84), it might not make sense to say that a person who scores 30 is twice as competent as a person with a score of 15. After all, we did not start at a zero point. In ratio level measurement, it also is permissible to use multiplication and division of scale values to examine ratios.

Naturally, one can reduce the measurement level to a lower level if desired. For instance, researchers could take 7-point attitude scales and rank the responses of individuals from the most positive attitudes to the least positive attitudes. Sometimes attitudes are measured as simple categories, such as counting the number of people who changed and did not change their attitudes on such measures as the "Woodward Shift of Opinion Ballot." Yet, unless researchers have special reasons, they generally avoid reducing their data measurement to lower levels because they prefer the sensitivity allowed by high levels of measurement. It might be mentioned that even though one could collapse the level of measurement to a lower level, it does not work the other way around.

Statistical Debates Regarding Measurement Levels

Scholars have engaged in arguments about measurement. Three of the most prominent issues include debates regarding interval scales, continuous and discrete variables, and variable and attribute data. There are honest differences of opinion on the matters, and I will give you only an idea of the arguments that are used.

- *Distinguishing between pure interval and ordinal scales:* Some statisticians doubt that many so-called interval scales used in the social sciences actually are interval or ratio scales. For instance, on a 10-item true-false test developed to measure recall of information contained in a speech, it is difficult to say that improving one's score from 4 to 5 is really the same as improving one's score from 9 to a perfect 10. Thus, some scholars believe that 7-point semantic differential–type scales and 5-point Likert-type scales really only tell *relative* differences among respondents. Unless there is clear evidence to the contrary, they recommend assuming that these scales are no better than ordinal measures. Yet, most research completed in the social sciences regularly treats these sorts of scores as interval scales. In fact, the consensus is that the importance of violating assumptions of pure interval measurement has been overstated. Indeed, some writers have explained that such scaled responses could be considered "quasi-interval, that is, close enough to interval to allow interval methods to be used" (Ender, 2003, ¶ 9; see also M. E. Cohen, 2001).
- *Distinguishing between continuous and discrete variables:* A **continuous variable** is a variable that can take any of a large number (often infinite) of values. These sorts of measures frequently include numbers with decimal points. In contrast, a **discrete variable** is "made up of distinct and separate units or categories" (Vogt, 2005, p. 92). That

Special Discussion 2.3

Rules on Rounding

Researchers are concerned with accuracy in their measurements, but nearly all data sets require some sort of rounding. If you asked the age of respondents to a survey, some might tell you how old they were in terms such as "$21\frac{1}{2}$ years" or "21 and 3 months." You probably would have to round the data to complete your work. There are some guidelines to follow both for rounding the original data and for reporting results. If you are associated with an organization that has a policy on the matter, your rounding decisions clearly would be guided by those choices. There usually has been a decision to consider the implications for local practices. If you are without such a policy, some other rules have been suggested over the years.

One approach holds that rounding should be made back to the original precision of the data. Hence, if the data are from a credibility scale with original scores ranging from 3 to 21, this view suggests that the final answers should be rounded to that original level of precision. If the sample group's mean rating of source credibility for a public figure is 16.2372, you should round the number to 16 because it is alleged to be a claim of false precision to carry computations further.

A second school of thought is that researchers should round results to two critical digits beyond the original precision of the data. So, assuming that the original data in our example had no decimal point, researchers would be permitted to go two additional decimal points to make decisions. Thus, a mean of 16.2372 would be rounded to 16.24.

One may wish to make a rounding decision based on communicating results to others. Sometimes newspapers report such statements as "approximately 45.3% of the eligible voters stayed away from the polls" when, of course, the word "approximately" should have made it clear that the results were rounded. The report probably should have stated "approximately 45% of the eligible voters stayed away from the polls." Such phrasing might enhance reading ease.

---

is, discrete variables are measured as categorical variables, and continuous variables are identified as interval or ratio level measures (though by our definition, not all interval or ratio measures are continuous variables, unless they have a large number of values [Vogt, 2005, p. 61]). But there is controversy regarding how many measures really are continuous. For instance, yearly income would seem to be a continuous variable, but because there is no division lower than one cent, the classification is limited by the way one decides to treat it statistically. Even though a variable may be individually discrete, most researchers have decided that it often makes sense to treat it as a continuous variable in further analyses.

- *Distinctions between attribute and variable data:* Some researchers like to draw a distinction between attribute and variable data. **Attribute data** are measured on the nominal or ordinal levels. Because they do not permit making interpretations of the degrees to which the variables are present, they serve primarily to identify "attributes" or qualitative characteristics of data. **Variable data,** on the other hand, are measured as true "variable data" or ratio measures that feature an absolute zero. Such a distinction is often found in statistics kept in industry and manufacturing, where different control charts depend on identifying the nature of the data and their measurement.

SAMPLING

Researchers must provide evidence of sound data sampling. To select statistics wisely, it is helpful to understand the importance of sampling, forms of probability and nonprobability sampling, and evidence for sampling adequacy.

The Importance of Careful Sampling

There are at least three reasons sampling is critical enough to report detailed information about it in research reports.

- Careful sampling is important to ensure a **representative sample**, which is a sample that adequately reflects the population from which it was drawn. To obtain a representative sample, researchers often take probability samples, so that the likelihood of capturing population characteristics (called population **parameters**) may be estimated.
- Careful sampling is required to avoid bias. In sampling, **bias** refers to systematic error that prevents the researcher from correctly identifying the population characteristic. In particular, a **biased estimator** occurs "when the expected value of a sample statistic tends to over- or underestimate a population parameter" (Vogt, 2005, p. 25). In essence, bias is a consistent under- or overestimate of the population characteristics. Sometimes bias is introduced when researchers take samples of convenience rather than random samples from the population. For instance, if you wanted to learn how college students felt about being required to take a course in public speaking, you could sample students in such classes. The samples, of course, would overrepresent those students who were no longer trying to postpone taking the course.
- Careful sampling is important because statistical tools often require certain forms of sampling. If you wish to use tools of statistical significance testing, random sampling (or at least random assignment) is required. If you do not use random sampling or assignment, you may restrict yourself to descriptive statistics alone.

Types of Sampling

There are two broad categories of sampling techniques. The first category involves probability sampling methods that employ some form of random sampling. The second category involves nonprobability sampling methods.

Probability Sampling

Sampling in which "each case that could be chosen has a known probability of being included" (Vogt, 2005, p. 248) is called **probability sampling**. In essence, this approach permits researchers to use sample statistics and related information to identify how close the population parameter and the sample statistics are likely to be. Though they all are related, a couple of forms often are distinguished.

Random sampling involves selecting data in such a way that each event "in the population has an equal chance of being chosen and . . . every combination of *N* members has an equal chance of being chosen" (Frankfort-Nachmias & Leon-Guerrero, 2002, p. 404).[5] The term "random" does not mean that it is a haphazard affair. Taking a random sample requires a lot of effort and it is not easy. There are at least two forms of random sampling.

- *Simple random sampling:* identifying all members of a population and then selecting events at random from this universe of events. Though researchers could identify a population of events and draw elements out of a hat, this method may not be practical for large samples. To sample a group of registered voters, researchers might find it most convenient to take the voter registration lists, assign a number to each registered voter, and then make a random selection by using a table of random numbers. It might be mentioned that to complete simple random sampling, the entire population first must be available. Sometimes this condition is difficult to satisfy. Sampling from telephone directories is particularly troublesome because not everyone has a telephone and large numbers of people have unlisted numbers; others have two telephones. Such researchers often rely on random digit dialing systems.

  Random sampling is not the same as **periodic** or **systematic** sampling, in which samples are taken at preset intervals (such as sampling every 10th event). This sort of sampling would not have the same characteristics as random sampling if there were any periodic cycles in the data. For instance, in a content analysis of the amount of children's programming on commercial television, if you selected every 7th day to collect data for a 2-month period, you would sample the same day of the week throughout the sample. If you started on a Saturday, where lots of children's programming is presented, you might conclude that there is a great deal of children's programming on commercial television—a finding that would not generalize to the broadcast week as a whole. Systematic sampling is really a compromise in random sampling, and unless researchers are very, very sure of the absence of any potential periodic effect, they might be advised to avoid taking this shortcut.

  In experimental studies, researchers are able to complete **random assignment** of events to experimental and control conditions. This approach means that individuals are not "intact" groups but are chosen to receive experimental or control treatments at random. This method promotes control because background differences among individuals are randomly distributed across conditions and, therefore, are no more likely to be present in the experimental than in the control group. It also is not random sampling for researchers to decide (at random) that one classroom of students will be exposed to the experimental treatment and the other to a control treatment. Random sampling presumes independence of observations rather than the use of "intact" groups.

- *Stratified random sampling:* After dividing the population into categories based on known proportions, simple random sampling is completed within each category to represent subjects with characteristics consistent with the population proportions. This method is regularly used by most national polling organizations. For instance, researchers who are interested in sampling national trends might wish to sample randomly so that they select 51% of the sample to be female and 49% to be male.

---

[5]As noted in Chapter 1, mathematical randomness would mean that the probability of any event following any other particular event would be 0. The accommodation made here is widely accepted.

Special Discussion 2.4

Using Random Number Tables

To eliminate human biases in sampling and to assure that samples are drawn at random, researchers often use tables of random numbers. Appendix C.2 includes a table of random numbers with three-digit numbers, but if you require two-digit or four-digit numbers, the table still could be used because the formatting of the numbers is arbitrary. That the numbers were arranged into columns is a matter of convenience. Even so, perhaps the most comprehensive list of numbers is found in a book called *A Million Random Digits With 100,000 Normal Deviates* (1955), prepared by the Rand Corporation to be used in some of its research. To use a table of random numbers to draw a random sample or to assign subjects randomly to experimental or control treatments, one follows a few steps.

1. Every element in the population must be given an identifying number.

2. A random location should be found to enter a table. Just pointing at the page while closing one's eyes is not recommended because the corner elements are effectively excluded as possible starting points. There are several ways to identify a starting location. One may cut cards or throw dice to determine row and column numbers on which to begin. Others (e.g., Leedy, 1989, pp. 154–155) have suggested asking people to give you social security numbers, checking the closing Dow Jones Industrial Average, or taking numbers from the serial number of a handy dollar bill. Regardless of the source, the researcher will let the first two numbers identify the column and the last two numbers identify the row on the random number table. For the sake of having an example, let us presume that we used a dollar bill with the serial number L 05385110 J. On the portion of the table shown here, we could go to column 5 and row 10. The number found here is 258. So, the first person in the sample would be the person who has number 258.

Random Numbers

127	275	054	576	974	438	900	773	118	682
796	457	043	782	012	309	372	298	196	698
095	455	550	524	819	058	014	199	949	847
228	863	271	236	910	833	700	573	719	231
842	383	636	766	831	864	542	183	042	796
674	678	109	730	366	215	433	586	153	534
653	827	572	299	517	272	659	733	673	206
542	623	153	786	346	447	217	030	590	711
761	710	300	306	807	246	310	961	636	478
596	175	814	445	258	601	440	767	143	951
238	926	598	917	871	951	353	221	534	385
790	882	297	397	417	204	838	593	615	127

3. To tell if numbers are to be "called" by moving to the right, to the left, up, or down, you might toss a coin twice. Two heads could mean that you use numbers to the right, two tails mean that you read numbers to the left, heads followed by tails could be that you read up the column, and tails followed by heads could mean that you read down the column. Let us suppose that we received two heads. In this case, our sample would include person (or event) 258 followed by 601, 440, 767, and so forth. At the end of the row, we could move to the next row and continue. The process would be repeated until complete random selection and/or assignment is completed.

- *Cluster sampling:* Groups or regions called "clusters" are identified and then, in at least two stages, a random selection is made from the groups or areas followed by a random sampling of events from them. Sometimes known as "multistage cluster sampling" or "area" sampling, the method adapts random sampling to situations in which there is no fixed list of population events and when the universe of events is widely scattered. For instance, in a national survey, a researcher might start by randomly selecting a number of states (using simple random sampling to do so). In a second stage, the researcher might randomly select a number of counties from those states. In a third stage, the researcher might randomly select cities in those counties. In a fourth stage, a number of residential neighborhoods could be selected at random from which (in a fifth stage) simple random sampling could be completed. Because this method uses probability sampling methods, it is often regarded highly for its ability to be applied to statistical assessment. But it might be remembered that this approach is not just one sampling process but a *number* of them, each one of which contributes its own sampling error to the total mix. For instance, in our hypothetical example there were five stages. If—using percentages just for conceptual ease—each sample stage had only a 5% chance of misidentifying population parameters, the overall probability of accurately identifying population parameters from the sample statistics would be 77.38%.[6] On the other hand, if researchers had 99% confidence in their samples at each level (and kept the margins for error the same as before), the overall probability of accurately identifying population parameters would be 95.099%, which probably would be acceptable for most sampling purposes.

Nonprobability Sampling

Sometimes it is impossible to sample events at random from a population. Indeed, when dealing with events that are illegal, socially deviant, or just very unusual, it is not realistic to define a population that could be sampled. So, researchers do the best they can with nonprobability samples. With these samples, it is not possible to apply tools that reveal how closely the samples probably represent various population characteristics. Yet, if researchers can advance good reasons to believe that a given sample is a fair representation of a population, they are free to share their reasoning. Of course, the burden of proof for such claims is great and, if possible, nonprobability samples should be avoided.

---

[6]In this example, the overall probability of accurately capturing population parameters would not be the simple averages from each stage. Instead, the question becomes: "What is the probability of accurately identifying the population parameter from the sample (within a certain range) at the end of the first stage $(1 - .05 = .95)$, AND what is the probability of also accurately identifying the population parameter from the sample (within a certain range) at the end of the second stage $(1 - .05 = .95)$, AND what is the probability of also accurately identifying the population parameter from the sample (within a certain range) at the end of the third stage $(1 - .05 = .95)$, AND what is the probability of also accurately identifying the population parameter from the sample (within a certain range) at the end of the fourth stage $(1 - .05 = .95)$, AND what is the probability of also accurately identifying the population parameter from the sample (within a certain range) at the end of the fifth stage $(1 - .05 = .95)$?" One multiplies .95 * .95 * .95 * .95 * .95, which results in an overall probability of .7738.

There can be as many nonprobability samples drawn as researchers might use their imaginations to develop. Four of the most prominent ones are identified here. The first two of these methods are widely disdained. The other methods may be required because researchers might have few other options.

- *Accidental or convenience sampling:* selecting events that are easy to obtain rather than those that are representative of the population. This approach takes a couple of forms. Researchers might nonrandomly sample students from classes that are conveniently available, or they might interview the first 50 people they encounter exiting a department store. Sometimes researchers will respond to the problem of using convenience samples by randomly assigning subjects to experimental and control conditions. Yet, sometimes convenience samples do not necessarily indicate a lack of research rigor. For instance, researchers might conduct a small pilot study to develop hypotheses for other studies to explore. Furthermore, they may use this approach when sample bias is not a substantial issue. "Studies of some basic physiological or nonconscious responses may be less susceptible to sample bias. Basic perceptual, reasoning, and memory processes may be so universal that sample bias is not a problem" (Watt & van den Berg, 1995, p. 102). Limitations on representativeness and defining the population of interest, however, still may remain.

- *Quota sampling:* Nonrandom sampling is completed to secure events matching known proportions of types of events within the population. In essence, this method involves stratified random sampling without the *randomness*. Hence, sometimes researchers call this form "stratified sampling" (note the absence of the word "random"). For instance, instead of randomly selecting samples of men and women to reflect their appearance in the population, researchers accept the first events that conveniently are available to fill the quota.

- *Known group sampling:* Also known as "purposive sampling," it involves collecting "a sample composed of subjects selected deliberately (on purpose) by researchers, usually because they think certain characteristics are typical or representative of the population" (Reinard, 2001, p. 293). For instance, if you wanted to study the levels of self-esteem among stutterers of different ages, a random sample of all people—stutterers and nonstutterers—would be wasteful. Instead, you might find a place where people known to stutter are located, such as a speech and hearing clinic. Then, a sample of different-aged stutterers could be drawn. Of course, the sample would not be composed of people who were completely independent of each other (after all, they had an interest in seeking therapy and the means to get to a clinic). One might consider taking a random sample of stutterers at a clinic. Some writers call such a technique taking a "quasi-random sample." But such a sample still would not represent those stutterers who were unaffiliated with a therapy center (either by personal motivation or finances) or who were not located in the urban geographic areas where clinics tend to be located. For studies with carefully limited populations defined by the researcher or studies for which known groups are required for other purposes (such as known groups used in predictive validity studies used to assess new measurement instruments), this sampling method may be chosen. For instance, focus groups have been popular tools in legal communication, advertising, and public relations. The purpose of these inquiries has been to explain behaviors among members of specific target populations. Hence, people who share characteristics in common with sitting jurors might be sampled for a focus group and asked to watch a trial. These samples are not random, but they are purposive samples designed to gain insights into key population groups.

- *Snowball sampling:* samples gathered from referrals from participants already in the sample. This method may be most useful when individuals are sampled from a population involved in socially deviant or even illegal activities. For instance, if researchers wanted to study the communication of social support that cross-dressers provide one another, it would not be possible to get a random sample. A researcher might interview one member of the group. Then, after building trust with that person, a request might be made for the names of others whom the researcher might interview. Eventually, the sample would "snowball" as one referral led to others, which led still to others. Of course, such a sample would not be random, and it certainly would not be independent, because the members of the sample groups knew each other directly or indirectly. Snowball sampling leads researchers to draw cautious conclusions, but it often is the only option available to researchers.

In passing, it might be mentioned that researchers often combine sampling methods. Thus, no list of sampling types can be exhaustive. Even so, some of the advantages and disadvantages of major approaches identified here are illustrated in Table 2.1.

Table 2.1   A Comparison of Sampling Methods

	Sampling Method	Advantages	Disadvantages
Probability	Simple random sampling	1. Tools of inference may be used to identify probable errors and to construct confidence intervals around population parameters 2. Avoids systematic bias	1. Ignores any information the researcher may have about the population 2. Requires enumeration of the population elements 3. May be time-consuming
	Stratified random sampling	1. Controls for sample subjects' background influences that may not be randomly distributed across a general population 2. Aids in meeting assumptions of statistics	1. Requires enumeration of the population elements, which may be time-consuming 2. Sometimes researchers overstratify variables such that excessive numbers of divisions lead to essentially unrepresentative samples 3. The stratification variables must be selected based on population knowledge that may be difficult to obtain 4. The addition of stratification variables requires the expense of substantially increasing the sample size

(Continued)

Table 2.1 (Continued)

	Sampling Method	Advantages	Disadvantages
	Cluster sampling	*In addition to the advantages listed above:* 1. Useful when the population is nearly infinite or widely scattered 2. Helpful when a large population has no list of members of the population 3. Characteristics of clusters can be estimated	1. Increased opportunity for bias because the method is actually a series of samples, each one of which has its own opportunities to introduce errors 2. Usually time-consuming and expensive 3. Requires ability to associate each event to only one cluster to prevent duplication or omission of events
Nonprobability	Accidental or convenience sampling	1. Readily available sampling 2. Usually less expensive than probability sampling methods 3. No defined sampling frame is required for convenience sampling	1. Unable to generalize the results of the sample to the population 2. Unable to ensure the randomization assumption underlying many statistical tests 3. Unable to compute sampling error and confidence intervals 4. Nature of sampling biases remains unknown
	Quota sampling	1. Reduces cost of sampling 2. Attempts to introduce some control by use of a limited stratification effect	*In addition to the disadvantages listed above:* 1. Potential bias introduced by researchers' classification into categories
	Known group sampling	1. Limits cost of sampling because events can be selected based on their frequent occurrences in groups 2. Particularly useful in studies where possession of some characteristics is required for admission to the sample group	*In addition to the disadvantages listed for convenience sampling:* 1. Requires the researcher to have *strong* evidence and knowledge of population characteristics
	Snowball sampling	1. Makes possible collection of samples dealing with illegal or socially deviant activity	*In addition to the disadvantages listed for convenience sampling:* 1. Usually is a time-consuming sampling method because referrals are nearly always contacted and sampled one at a time 2. Practicality of the sample requires that the researcher have skills necessary to create trust to secure referrals

Testing Sampling Adequacy

Every sample is representative of *some* population of events. Yet, nonprobability samples do not make it possible to use statistics to identify *which* populations actually might be represented by a particular sample. On the other hand, probability samples allow researchers to make statements about the probability that a sample's statistics have represented that population's characteristics. These matters will be considered next.

Sampling Error and Confidence Intervals

You probably have noticed that public opinion polls frequently describe results by saying something such as "the margin for error around these percentages is ± (plus or minus) 2%." These reports convey some information related to sampling and sampling error. The difference between the sample statistic and its corresponding population parameter is called **sampling error**. If we take a truly random sample, it is possible to identify how far the sample value probably is from the population value. Though we can complete estimates for all types of measures of interest, two of the most popular forms are for proportions (and percentages) data and for means.

To assess the degree to which a sample proportion differs from a population proportion, researchers also need to know the sample size. For instance, the following formula shows the formula for the "confidence interval" around a proportion.

$$\text{C.I.} = \text{observed sample proportion} \pm z * \sqrt{\frac{p * (1 - p)}{\text{sample size}}}$$

As you can see, the formula is composed of information found in the sample.

- "C.I." is the **confidence interval** one wishes to identify. This term refers to "a range of values of a sample statistic that is likely (at a given level of probability, called a **confidence level**) to contain" (Vogt, 2005, p. 55, bold added) the population characteristic that the researcher wishes to claim. The probability (such as "90% confidence," "95% confidence," or "99% confidence") is a percentage of the time that the relevant population characteristic falls within the confidence interval. The researcher is stating that he or she wishes to know at a certain probability that the population proportion is somewhere within a specified range (called the actual confidence interval or, in popular media, the "margin for error").
- p is the proportion of the total (expressed as a number with the decimal points included, rather than expressed as a percentage) found in the category of interest (e.g., the proportion favoring a political candidate, the proportion with a hearing problem, the proportion who have taken a public speaking class).
- z is a value that corresponds to a value under the standard normal curve associated with the probability of confidence to be claimed. Though the actual meaning of z as a unit under the standard normal curve will be explained in Chapter 4, for now it is

enough to state that the z value for a 90% confidence claim is 1.645, the z value for a 95% confidence claim is 1.96, and the z value for a 99% confidence claim is 2.58.

For example, suppose a researcher gathered a sample of 100 communication students and found that only 10% of them were planning to go to graduate school. The researcher might wonder how representative of the population this proportion is. The researcher might decide to construct a 95% confidence interval around this proportion. If this interval were relatively small, the sample proportion would appear to be identified quite accurately by the sample data. Inserting values into the formula, the researcher might obtain the following:

$$\text{C.I.} = \text{observed sample proportion} \pm z * \sqrt{\frac{p*(1-p)}{\text{sample size}}}$$

$$95\% \text{ C.I.} = .10 \pm 1.96 * \sqrt{\frac{.10*(1-.10)}{100}}$$

$$95\% \text{ C.I.} = .10 \pm 1.96 * \sqrt{\frac{.10*.90}{100}}$$

$$95\% \text{ C.I.} = .10 \pm 1.96 * \sqrt{\frac{.09}{100}}$$

$$95\% \text{ C.I.} = .10 \pm 1.96 * \sqrt{.0009}$$
$$95\% \text{ C.I.} = .10 \pm 1.96 * .03$$
$$95\% \text{ C.I.} = .10 \pm 1.0588$$

Thus, the researcher may claim to be 95% confident that the proportion of students who plan to attend graduate school is only 10%, plus or minus 5.88%. Put another way, the researcher is 95% confident that the proportion of students planning to attend graduate school is between 4.12% and 15.88%. Because the confidence interval covers such a wide portion of the reported area, the researcher might wish to keep collecting data before concluding that the sample percentage is a highly accurate identification of what is occurring in the population.

To compute a confidence interval around a mean, the formula is

$$\text{C.I.} = \text{observed sample mean} \pm z * \frac{\text{standard deviation of the sample}}{\sqrt{\text{sample size}}}.$$

As explained elsewhere (Chapter 4), the standard deviation is an effort to identify the average distance of scores from the mean. At this moment, it is important only to understand what this confidence interval formula tells about sampling adequacy. A researcher might ask 50 randomly selected people to complete a study on the impact of strong previews in a speech. After the message, the mean attitude score was 5.5, with a mean sample standard deviation of 0.5. To assess sampling adequacy for the posttest attitude score, the researcher might want to compute a confidence interval. A small confidence interval would indicate that the posttest sample mean probably is close to the population mean. A relatively large confidence interval would be taken as evidence that the sample is not as adequate as the researcher might wish. One may apply the formula for a 95% confidence interval to these sample data:

$$\text{C.I.} = \text{observed sample mean} \pm z * \frac{\text{standard deviation of the sample}}{\sqrt{\text{sample size}}}$$

$$95\% \text{ C.I.} = 5.5 \pm 1.96 * \frac{0.5}{\sqrt{50}}$$

$$95\% \text{ C.I.} = 5.5 \pm 1.96 * \frac{0.5}{7.0711}$$

$$95\% \text{ C.I.} = 5.5 \pm 1.96 * .0707$$

$$95\% \text{ C.I.} = 5.5 \pm .1386$$

According to this computation, the researcher would conclude that s/he is 95% confident that the posttest population mean is 5.5 units plus or minus .1386. Or the researcher could state that s/he is 95% confident that the posttest population mean is between 5.3614 and 5.6386. This modest range would make most researchers fairly comfortable with the sample.

Nevertheless, these examples illustrate some important characteristics of confidence intervals. First, when researchers state that they are 95% confident, that statement also means that there is a 5% chance that they are completely wrong. Yet, they may not have additional evidence beyond the sample alone to guide them. Second, as a quick look at the confidence interval formulae show, the sizes of confidence intervals decrease as sample sizes increase. This fact indicates that sampling error generally is reduced as sample size increases. Eventually, if a researcher sampled the entire population of events, there would be no sampling error at all. Third, to make claims with increased confidence, the researcher must either increase the sample size or must tolerate increasing the size of the confidence interval. These matters are the basis for many decisions that researchers make about sampling.

How Big a Sample Is Big Enough?

Inevitably, researchers have to decide how big a sample to draw from the population. Because sampling is time-consuming and sometimes expensive, this question actually translates into asking "How small a sample is permissible?" This question, of course, cannot be answered glibly. The type of research question, the types of measures, the effect sizes of interest, and the types of statistics to be used all affect the answer. Though there is no single answer that fits all situations, there are some fairly good guidelines.

In the absence of other considerations, one source has declared, "Now, the best rule of thumb is to get at least 25 people per group, per level of independent variable. This will permit you to calculate all of the common, inferential and statistical tests" (Sampling, 2003, ¶ 13). The reasoning behind this suggestion is that when one looks at tables used for testing statistical significance (such as the t table) at a frequently used level ($p < .05$), the critical values seem to round to the same numbers (at least to the nearest tenth) whether they come from samples of about 30 or an infinite sample size. Thus, the recommendation of 25 events makes a certain amount of sense. There is a catch, however. This reasoning assumes that the sampling is truly random. To the degree that imperfections have been introduced, increased sample sizes may be required so that researchers may use tools to help overcome and control such limitations. In manufacturing settings, others have suggested that sample sizes as small as 16 are reasonable to balance the risks of errors in hypothesis testing in experimental research. The advice for 25 or 30 randomly selected events for a study seems sensible. Nevertheless, some additional guidance also seems invited.

The type of study involved makes a difference. Here are some guidelines for these situations:

- *Pilot studies:* A sample of between 10 and 30 is recommended for pilot and exploratory studies (Isaac & Michael, 1981, p. 96). If the purpose is only to get feedback on wording of instructions or questionnaire items, small samples of under a dozen might be used.
- *Cross-validation studies:* For large studies that involve comprehensive examination of results across sample groups, the sample sizes should increase. Several hundred may be required. Because these studies typically involve tools such as multiple regression correlation and factor analysis, there should be at least 200 events. For the other statistical methods that often are found in such studies, the researcher is likely to need large samples. "N should be at least about 60, and preferably 100 or more, for this purpose" (Tatsuoka, 1969, p. 27). Thus, such studies should have samples as large as the researcher can afford to gather, but they should be in the hundreds at any rate.

The types of measures can affect the sample sizes required.

- *Physiological measures:* Small samples, often only 8 subjects, may be the norm in studies that use only physiological measures. In health research, where physiological measures are used, and in manufacturing, where destructive tests are used, such small samples are considered acceptable because there usually are few uncontrolled social and background variables. To determine if a medication has produced a change in the CAT scan of an autistic patient does not require the respondent to report his or her own condition, and the overall differences in subjects may be relatively minor. If individuals are asked to interpret their behavior, however, more than physiological measures are involved and a return to increased sample sizes may be required. Aside from some work in speech and hearing science, the use of physiological measures in communication studies is still in its infancy. Even so, such measures require fewer events in a sample than studies that must control for other individual response variables.

The size of the effects a researcher is interested in studying can influence the sample sizes chosen. If a researcher is interested in a rather large effect, a smaller sample might be acceptable. One influential writer (J. Cohen, 1992) has suggested that to balance risks in hypothesis testing,[7] detecting small effects[8] requires a minimum sample of 393, detecting medium effects requires samples of at least 64, and large effects could be determined with samples as small as 26. Yet, this general advice about effect size and samples probably has been extended beyond the intentions of the original thinking on the subject. A little common sense goes a long way. "Because practical significance depends upon the research context, only *you* can judge if an effect is large enough to be important" (Light, Singer, & Willett, 1990, p. 195). Because variables in social science research often have many causes, finding very large effects is rare. Thus, arbitrary statements about effect sizes probably should be considered only one of several sources of advice. Looking at a research tradition and examining effects found in the past may provide helpful lessons. If one knows a great deal about the population variance and various effect sizes one wishes to identify, it is possible to use a formula to identify the minimum sample necessary to detect differences of a particular size.[9] But such formulae also require that researchers know such things as population (or at least sample) standard deviations, which may not be available until after the proposed study has been completed.

The types of statistics researchers plan to use will influence required sample sizes. Though some measures, such as the *t* test for independent samples, may apply to very modest sample sizes, other tools require fairly large samples. In particular, in multivariate statistics "unless sample size is large relative to the number of variables the results will not be reliable—that is, they will not generalize" (J. P. Stevens, 2002, p. 12). Further related information is in Table 2.2.

---

[7]This standard involved setting statistical power (the probability of correctly rejecting null hypotheses) at .80.

[8]This matter of small, medium, and large effects can be somewhat complicated because Cohen identified both a formula and an interpretation guide. For instance, for the *t* test, he suggested that researchers complete a formula to identify a difference of interest:

$$d = \frac{(\mu_1 - \mu_2)}{\sigma}.$$

In this formula, σ is the standard deviation, and the μ_1 and μ_2 are means that the researchers find of interest. The result of this effort is to express how much of a difference (expressed in standard deviation units or *z* scores [see Chapter 4]) is of interest. A difference showing a change of .30 or below was considered small, .50 moderate, and .80 or above large. Not all writers have embraced these pieces of advice.

[9]One such formula, for instance, asks researchers who test statistical hypotheses to balance the probability of committing various errors against each other. Though the notions of alpha and beta risk and standard deviation will be covered in subsequent chapters, the terms are mentioned here without further explanation. In particular, for comparison of two means, the following formula may be used to compute a minimum sample size:

$$n = \left[\frac{(|z_0| + |z_1|)\sigma}{\mu_0 - \mu_1} \right]^2,$$

where *n* is the number of events to be sampled (rounding up any fraction), $|z_0|$ is the absolute value of the *z* value corresponding to the desired alpha risk for the study (for a one-tailed test, alpha risk of .05 is 1.645, for instance), $|z_1|$ is the absolute value of the *z* value corresponding to the desired beta risk for the study (for a one-tailed test, beta risk of .05 is 1.28), σ is the standard deviation of the population, and $\mu_0 - \mu_1$ is the minimum difference between means that the researchers wish to detect as statistically significant.

Table 2.2   Sample Sizes for Different Statistical Tools

Statistic	Recommended Sample Size	Related Sampling Concerns
Chi-square test of independence	Various advice: • No conditions in which "expected frequencies" are lower than 5. • No more than 20% of study conditions with "expected frequencies" are lower than 5 (Frankfort-Nachmias & Leon-Guerrero, 2002, pp. 515–516).	"The size of the calculated chi square is directly proportional to the size of the sample, independent of the strength of the relationship between the variables" (Frankfort-Nachmias & Leon-Guerrero, 2002, p. 515). If sample sizes are reduced in half, the chi-square value also is reduced in half.
Multiple regression correlation	At least 15 events for every predictor of independent variable (J. P. Stevens, 2002, p. 143).	The minimum sample size is affected by the size of the correlation. "For example, if $\rho^2 = .75$, then for three predictors only 28 subjects are needed, whereas 50 subjects were needed for the same case when $\rho^2 = .50$" (J. P. Stevens, 2002, p. 146).
Factor analysis	At least 10 events for each item included (Nunnally, 1978, p. 421).	
Multivariate analysis of variance	For adequate power (.7) with three to six dependent variables at alpha risk = .05, a medium effect size requires: • 42–54 events per group when comparing three groups • 48–62 events per group when comparing four groups • 54–70 events per group when comparing five groups • 58–76 events per group when comparing six groups (J. P. Stevens, 2002, p. 247).	For small effect size detection, the sample size more than doubles.

Illusions in Sampling

Sometimes researchers presume that samples are representative of the population even though there may be clear threats. Two of the biggest threats involve the casual use of volunteers and the assumption that large samples are representative ones.

Volunteers and Nonparticipants

Though, of course, for ethical reasons participation in any research project must be voluntary, the fact is that some studies involve respondents who invite themselves to participate. Indeed, many studies may ask for people to answer classified ads or to respond to a general call for participation over the Internet. The problem, of course, is that individuals who volunteer usually have reasons for doing so. These reasons—a desire for attention, an abnormal desire to meet new people, or a desire to have the chance to offer religious testimony—may make such volunteers different from other participants or systematically different from the population of interest. If volunteers can be randomly distributed across experimental and control conditions, their systematic influences may be reduced, but if people are asked to volunteer for a treatment (perhaps volunteering to take a class in intercultural communication awareness), they may not be like other people, who are less interested. Although the characteristics of volunteers can be an area of study all by itself, it seems reasonable to recognize that volunteers may bring substantial nonrandom influences that bear watching.

Confusing Sample Size With Representativeness

Sometimes researchers mistakenly think that a large sample is *necessarily* a representative one. After all, as sample size increases, sampling error decreases, even regardless of the size of the population. But such reasoning rests on a big assumption: that the sample was truly taken at random. There is an ugly truth in research, however: There rarely are truly random samples. Researchers may sample college students in one geographic region and then assume that the other regions also are similar. Though in experimental research, researchers might use random assignment to enhance representativeness, there are limits on the population to which samples can be generalized. One sometimes hears that there is strength in numbers, but there are contrary examples when it comes to sampling. A notorious example was the experience of a poll completed by the *Literary Digest*, a very popular magazine of the 1930s. In 1936, the magazine collected more than two million "ballots" in the largest public opinion sampling ever undertaken. The poll concluded that President Franklin Roosevelt would lose the election to Governor Alf Landon (Landon captured eight electoral votes). The sample was large, but it was unrepresentative of the national population because it drew sampling lists from people with telephones, people who had purchased new cars, and volunteers who wanted to send postcards to the magazine. The magazine went out of business shortly after the fiasco. In the U.S. presidential election of 2004, the MSNBC polls of individuals who telephoned in their opinions frequently had samples of more than 50,000 respondents, but because the political parties urged their party faithful to participate, the MSNBC "polls" rarely represented opinion in the nation as a whole. These examples remain object lessons in sampling: Bigness is not a substitute for randomness when one wants a representative sample.

Part II

DESCRIPTIVE STATISTICS

Chapter 3

CENTRAL TENDENCY

In the late 1990s, the American Psychological Association formed a Task Force on Statistical Inference to consider appropriate data analysis for research studies. Part of the report created a stir among social scientists by suggesting that descriptive statistics needed to be given extra attention by researchers (Task Force on Statistical Inference, 1996):

[W]e recommend that more extensive descriptions of the data be provided to reviewers and readers. This should include means, standard deviations, sample sizes, five-point summaries, box-and-whisker plots, other graphics, and descriptions related to missing data as appropriate. (¶ 6)

[T]he use of techniques to assure that the reported results are not produced by anomalies in the data (e.g., outliers, points of high influence, non-random missing data, selection, attrition problems) should be a standard component of all analyses. (¶ 8)

These comments suggested two important things. First, it is important to characterize data before taking further action. Second, such data summaries as measures of central tendency are vital to help understand what the data can reveal to researchers. This chapter surveys a family of statistical methods designed to describe the typical or average characteristics of data.

DOING A STUDY AND REPORTING DESCRIPTIVE INFORMATION

Though novice researchers often wish to test hypotheses immediately, as the APA Task Force on Statistical Inference suggested, it is important to describe the data first. Because typical readers may readily understand most data descriptions, this information may be among the most important parts of statistical analyses.

The first descriptive information to report involves sample characteristics. Though most researchers reveal the sample size, it is also helpful to report information on such matters as

- Proportions of nonrespondents and, if possible, evidence about ways they may differ from others may be identified. If researchers can show that the differences between the refusers and others are not substantial, then the occasional refusals might be acceptable. If there are large proportions of refusers, however, researchers may wish to make further investigations into the differences.
- Strategies used to handle missing data should be included. For instance, the SPSS statistical package permits researchers to substitute the mean for a missing variable, to exclude the response, or to exclude the entire case. Researchers should identify choices they have made.

The second part of the descriptive information is related to checking the accuracy of the data. Before exploring primary research questions, prudent researchers produce frequency distributions of data to identify any coding errors and any outliers that might throw off the estimates. If outliers can be explained as coming from another population of events (e.g., if the outlier comes from a respondent who did not speak the language of the measurement instrument), one may discard the item. If an outlier cannot be immediately explained, it may have to be retained.

Third, researchers need to report information to help readers understand the reasonableness of choices that are made. Though not an exhaustive list, some of the most important pieces of information include the following:

- Statistics may be reported about the degree to which the data meet the underlying assumptions for the statistical tools to be employed. For instance, many statistical tools require distributions around the means in different sample groups to be equal. Yet, if a researcher used 7-point scales and found an average score of 6, the data would have only one scale position to disperse above the mean, but many more below the mean. This dispersion probably would not equal that of groups with means of 4 or 5. Ultimately, the researchers also would want to examine the measures of dispersion, such as those covered in Chapter 4, to assess whether the distributions around the mean are unequal.
- Demographic variables such as age and sex of respondents should be reported. If helpful, charts may be used to summarize many such characteristics.
- Descriptive profiles of major variables in the study should be completed before other analyses. Then, it would be possible to determine the consistency of scores on one measure with those of another.

Though measures of both variability and dispersion need to be used, only measures of central tendency are considered in this chapter.

TYPICAL MEASURES OF CENTRAL TENDENCY

Everyone has heard people refer to "average" grades, "average" gas mileage, and "average" income. The term "average," however, is a very broad one (even though people often represent it with a number technically called the arithmetic mean).[1] For our purposes, **central tendency** will be defined as "any of several statistical summaries that, in a single number, represent the typical member in a group of several numbers" (Vogt, 2005, p. 41). What most people call "the average" actually is called the "arithmetic mean." Speaking very literally, all measures of central tendency are "averages" because they attempt to identify different notions of the center of a distribution. Though there are many ways to identify central tendency, only the most common one will be reviewed here.

---

[1]Perhaps this matter is more trouble than it is worth. Some sources call the arithmetic mean "the average" (Champion, 1970, p. 33). Most statistics books, however, use the term "average" as a broad synonym for central tendency measures rather than identifying it with the mean alone.

Special Discussion 3.1

How to Read a Statistical Formula Involving Summation

A little notation can summarize a lot of individual steps. Hence, it is important for you to know something about the ways that a statistical formula (especially for central tendency) is organized. It makes sense to review the symbols used and the use of the sigma ($\sum$) operator for summation.

Scores from continuous distributions typically are symbolized with the symbol X, which represents, cleverly enough, an X score. Other symbols often are enlisted as well. As a matter of convention, scores on levels of independent variables are identified as X variables, and scores on dependent variables are identified as Y scores. Sometimes researchers also encounter lowercase letters such as x and y, which indicates that they are not raw scores but numbers obtained when some operation is performed on them, such as subtracting them from their means. In a statistical formula, of course, we have more than one piece of data. So, to indicate this matter, subscripts are identified, such as X_1, X_2, X_3, and so forth. In most formulae, these subscripts would be very limiting. Hence, X scores are identified with a letter subscript, such as X_i or X_j. The symbols suggest that X_i is an "instance" of an X score (that "i" does not stand for "instance," but if it helps you understand what is happening in a formula, it doesn't hurt anything to suppose that it does stand for an "instance").

The Greek capital letter sigma ($\sum$) is a symbol that instructs one to sum or add whatever follows. If what follows is in parentheses or brackets, one performs those tasks prior to summing the results. Then, one goes to the next data point identified and repeats the process. In full form, the summation sign is as follows:

$$\sum_{i=1}^{n,1} X_i.$$

Actual numbers may be substituted for the symbols other than sigma. This formula means that one is to sum each instance (i) of an X score. The subscripts under sigma ($i = 1$) and the superscripts above the sigma (n, 1) give details about ways to perform the addition. The "$i = 1$" instructs us to start the summation with the i score that is first (number 1) in the data set. The "n" in the superscript indicates that the summation will finish with the nth score (by convention, "n" represents the last piece of data). The "1" following the "n" indicates that the summation is supposed to be completed by moving from the first data point to the end by intervals of one. This statement means that after we have included the first item to the running total, the number 1 should be added to the i value, and the summation may continue until one has cycled through the data. If one wanted to skip every other data point, one could replace the "1" with a "2."

You might think that the extra notation is a lot of work for most circumstances when you would be likely to add all the data in the sample. A lot of other people think the extra notation is often unnecessary. Hence, you often will see the summation sign in some form such as $\sum X_i$. The absence of the sub- and superscripts means that all instance of X scores are to be added.

Median

The **median** is the middle score in an ordered list of scores. This measure of central tendency reveals the center position of a set of scores that are ranked from lowest to highest (or just halfway through, actually). Hence, as should be obvious, the median can be used only for measures on the ordinal, interval, or ratio levels. Most people have a sense of the median because when they drive on a highway, they notice that there is median strip that divides one half of the road from the other. This use of the word "median" is not a metaphor, but a direct statement of the concept. The point that divides one half of the road from the other half is called the highway median. Similarly, the point that divides the top half of scores from the bottom half of scores is known as the statistical median. In the case of communication data, suppose 10 people completed Infante and Rancer's measure of argumentativeness (the tendency for people "to advocate positions on controversial issues and to attack verbally the positions which other people take on these issues" [Infante & Rancer, 1982, p. 72]). This measure has a possible range of scores from −40 to +40. Ranked from lowest to highest, their scores might be

−20 −10 5 10 10 10 12 14 20 29.

To find the median, we need only identify the middle score. Yet, with an even number of scores, there is no middle score. So, to identify the median, we must find the point halfway between the two scores surrounding the center. In our case, the fifth and sixth scores are both 10. Splitting the difference identifies a median of 10. This point separates the top 50% of scores from the bottom 50% of scores.

Advantages of the Median

The median is a highly useful number with at least three advantages.

- The median is not affected by extremely high or low scores in a data set, which makes it a stable summary statistic.
- The median may be a superior index of central tendency when distributions are skewed (not perfectly centered).
- The median still may be computed when distributions are open-ended. For instance, the number of disfluencies in spontaneous speech appears to have no upper boundary. Someone could always come along and add another "uh" or "um" more than the previous communicator. The overall trend in the data might be upward, but the median would not necessarily change because the middle data position might not necessarily change.

Disadvantages of the Median

There are two limitations on the use of the median that researchers should recognize.

- The median may be tedious to compute by hand if the data sets are large. This problem has been greatly reduced by the use of computer-assisted analyses, but the problem could be a limitation for those double-checking data against computerized output.
- The median is not used very often in inferential statistics, and its use for advanced statistical inquiry is limited.

Mode

The **mode** is the most frequently occurring score in a data set. The mode reports the most repeated score in the data set. In normal distributions, the mode is not only the most frequent score, but the one that also appears in the center of a distribution. Some have developed the notion of an **anti-mode** (Vogt, 2005, p. 11) to describe the least frequent score, but thankfully, in communication studies this term has not caught on. In the previously described data on argumentativeness, the most commonly occurring score was 10, a score that also was the median.

Advantages of the Mode

The mode has been a popular measure of central tendency because it carries three advantages, the first two of which it shares with the median.

- The mode is not affected by extremely high or low scores in a data set. Thus, it is useful to describe the center of greatest activity in the distribution.
- The mode is still meaningful when applied to open-ended distributions.
- The mode can be used for data measured on the nominal scale. Because it involves the most frequent occurrence, it can be used for both qualitative and quantitative data. This quality is so substantial that some have asserted that "it makes little sense to use the mode with a set of ordinal, interval, or ratio data" (Frey, Botan, & Kreps, 2000, p. 295). But, as we shall see, this statement overstates the situation.

Disadvantages of the Mode

There are two major limitations on the use of the mode.

- Sometimes data may not have a mode. Of course, such a condition also would mean that the data distribution is far from normal—information that would be useful for the researcher to know when using statistics that assume underlying normal distributions. Recognizing the absence of a mode would be more useful information than computing an arbitrary point of central tendency.
- Sometimes data may have more than one mode. When a distribution has two modes, it is called **bimodal**. When it has three modes, it is called **trimodal**. One could come up with fancy names for distributions with more than three modes, but they may be stated simply as **multimodal**. In multimodal distributions, the meaning of the mode may be difficult to determine and the mode may be a poor measure of central tendency. Unfortunately, most computerized statistical programs report only one mode anyway. Of course, especially for interval and ratio level data, an observed bimodal distribution can yield very meaningful information. A bimodal distribution often indicates that two qualitatively different populations have been combined into one distribution. For instance, a group of people used a scale ranging from 1 to 10 (with 10 indicating the most positive attitude toward the topic) to report their attitudes in responses to a speech on increasing financial guarantees to women's athletic programs.

A first glance at the diagram to the right, would make it appear that there is division of opinion and perhaps that the mode is not a useful index of central tendency. But if one were to look at the audiences who contributed to these responses, highly interesting materials might emerge. In this example, those who were negative tended to be men, and those who were positive tended to be women. A second diagram to the right shows that mixing the two populations actually created the bimodal distribution. As can be seen, far from being useless for such interval data, examining the modes reveals material of great value for researchers. The mode also is useful in exploring the nature of data distributions, as shall be seen elsewhere in this chapter.

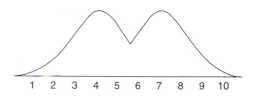

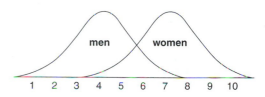

Mean

The **arithmetic mean** is the sum of a set of scores divided by the number of scores. As a matter of speech, when individuals refer to "the mean," it is presumed to be the arithmetic mean. This number is what most people commonly call "the average," though all measures of central tendency are forms of averages. The population mean is represented by the Greek letter *mu* (mew), μ. The symbol for the mean of the sample is $\bar{X}$, which is read "X bar." The bar above something means that the arithmetic mean is being taken of the item below it. Hence, $\bar{Y}$ indicates that the means of Y scores are taken. Similarly, $\bar{X}$ tells us that the arithmetic mean of a group of means is represented.

The formulae for the population and sample means are as follows:

Population Mean   Sample Mean

$$\mu = \frac{\sum X_i}{N} \qquad \bar{X} = \frac{\sum X_i}{n}$$

As can be seen, the two formulae bear much in common. Where they differ also is noteworthy, however. In the first place, the population formula uses a Greek letter, and the sample formula uses only the Roman alphabet. In the second place, the sum of population scores is divided by N to indicate the number of events in the population. On the other hand, the sum of the sample scores is divided by n to indicate the number of events in the sample. In other statistics in this book, the same sort of notation will be found.

Building Block Formula Box 1: Formulae for Population and Sample Means	
Population Mean	Sample Mean
$\mu = \dfrac{\sum X_i}{N}$	$\bar{X} = \dfrac{\sum X_i}{n}$

The mean of the sample is an unbiased estimator of the mean of the population. With an **unbiased estimator,** the expected value of a measure is equal to the population measure. In plain talk, an unbiased estimate is "a sample statistic that is free from any systematic error leading it to over- or underestimate the corresponding population parameter" (Vogt, 2005, p. 331). In the case of the sample mean, the expected value of $\overline{X}$ is equal to μ. This reasoning indicates that the sample mean is more likely to estimate accurately the population mean than any other sample measure we might choose. This property of unbiased estimation has a practical application for researchers. If we ever find ourselves with a formula that contains μ, and if we do not have the population mean, we may substitute $\overline{X}$. This fact makes the mean very helpful for researchers doing advanced work with statistics. These formulae are so foundational that they may be considered "building blocks" in statistics. That is, they are the foundation for other tools to follow. Thus, these formulae are the first of the building block formulae we will identify in special boxes.

To compute the mean for the argumentativeness data, one could follow the sample formula. Given the data, –20, –10, 5, 10, 10, 10, 12, 14, 20, 29, the following computations emerge:

$$\overline{X} = \frac{\sum X_i}{n}$$

$$\overline{X} = \frac{(-20) + (-10) + 5 + 10 + 10 + 10 + 12 + 14 + 20 + 29}{10}$$

$$\overline{X} = \frac{80}{10}$$

$$\overline{X} = 8$$

The mean of these data is 8, a number that is below the median and mode, both of which were 10.

Advantages of the Mean

There are several advantages of the mean beyond those already indicated.

- The mean is a commonly understood number. As such, it communicates its meaning effectively to others.
- All distributions have one mean reflecting all values. Hence, it is always possible to find a mean for a set of data. This statement does not claim that the mean is superior to other measures of central tendency under all circumstances, but it indicates that the mean can always provide a basis for comparing data.
- The mean usually is the measure of central tendency employed for computations in other statistical formulae. Thus, the mean tends to be a highly useful number. The reason for this fact is that the mean is suitable for receiving arithmetic and algebraic operations. Not all measures of central tendency can make this claim.
- The mean tends to be stable when taking random samples from a population. The mean actually shows less variability among successive samples than the median or mode. In short, the mean shows more resistance to sampling fluctuations than other central tendency measures (Minium, 1970, p. 64).

Special Discussion 3.2

Other Means—Geometric, Harmonic, Trimmed

There are occasions where simply computing the arithmetic mean will not do. For these special circumstances, there are alternative forms of means.

For instance, suppose you were driving a car to class and you traveled the first mile at 20 miles an hour, the next 4 miles at 40 miles an hour, and the last mile at 30 miles an hour. What was the average speed you were driving? To solve this problem, you could use the harmonic mean. The formula for the harmonic mean is

$$\frac{1}{H_x} = \frac{n}{\sum x_i^{-1}}.$$

In our example, n equals the 6 miles traveled. As a shortcut here, each x_i^{-1} is a fraction composed of the number of miles traveled over the speed. In this case, the formula turns into

$$\frac{6}{\frac{1}{20} + \frac{4}{40} + \frac{1}{30}} = \frac{6}{\frac{6}{120} + \frac{12}{120} + \frac{4}{120}} = \frac{6}{\frac{22}{120}} = \frac{6}{.1833} = 32.73 \text{ miles per hour.}$$

If one were concerned about comparing rates of growth, the geometric mean would be used. For instance, if you had a bank account that paid the going rate of interest (say 5% the first year, 4% the second year, 3% the third and fourth years, and 2% the fifth year), at the end of 5 years you might wonder what the average interest was. You could take the arithmetic mean, but this amount would be misleading because interest is compounded and interest is paid on the total amount in the bank. Instead, you would use the geometric mean. Technically, the geometric mean is the nth root of the product of the data elements. A standard formula illustrates this definition:

$$GM = \sqrt[n]{\prod x_i}$$

In practical terms, for small samples, this formula may be represented as

$$\overline{X}_G = \sqrt[n]{X_1 X_2 \ldots X_n}.$$

The X_1, X_2, and so forth represent the interest rates paid each year. The number of years is indicated by n. Entering the data into the formula, we would find:

$$\overline{X}_G = \sqrt[5]{5 * 4 * 3 * 3 * 2} = \sqrt[5]{360} = 3.25 \text{ percent interest.}$$

It should be mentioned that this sort of thing cannot really be done conveniently with negative numbers. To make such comparisons, you would have to subtract the proportion losses from 1 and make computations accordingly. Hence, a 5% loss would be .95 (= 1 − .05).

Other means also are available for special circumstances. For instance, the quadratic mean (also known as "root mean square" or RMS) is employed most often with data whose population mean

(Continued)

(Continued)

is zero. For instance, if one followed the positive and negative values of voltage ranges in U.S. businesses, a nearly perfect sine wave might be found and mean distances from zero could be identified by use of the quadratic mean computed by the formula

$$RMS = \sqrt{\frac{\sum x_i^2}{n}}.$$

Another specialized mean is the weighted mean. In this form, the average of differently weighted scores, such as grades (where a teacher may count a final exam as 40% and a midterm exam as 25%, with the remaining 35% dedicated to a term paper) are summed before the mean is taken. The formula is

$$\text{weighted mean} = \frac{\sum (w_i^* , x_i)}{\sum w_i}$$

where w_i are the weights and x_i are the scores to be weighted. The "combination mean" (Calkins, 2002, ¶ 16–17) is a variation in which the harmonic or geometric means may be weighted based on some decision by the researcher.

Because extreme scores, sometimes called "outliers," can abnormally affect arithmetic means, some have suggested "trimming" or "winsorizing" the data. Trimming the data "is calculated by arranging the terms in numerical order, taking away the first quarter and the fourth quarter of the values, and then finding the arithmetic mean of what remains" (Sternstein, 1994, p. 3). Rather than exclude the first and fourth quarters of the data, some researchers set a different proportion to trim, such as 5% or 10% of the data. An alternative to arbitrary trimming is the use of winsorizing. In this approach, the most extreme scores are replaced with the next available less extreme scores. The number of data points winsorized depends on the number of responses in the data set and the unit of evaluation. One guideline is to winsorize the highest 5% of the data scores and the lowest 5% of the data scores. Another guideline is that if four responses are received for a single respondent, four of the individual scores in the entire data set (the two highest and the two lowest) should be replaced with the next two highest and lowest scores. For example, all data below the 5th percentile are set equal to the value of the 5th percentile, and all data greater than the 95th percentile are set equal to the 95th percentile.

The replacement of outliers is controversial, of course. In general, researchers are warned to exercise care. In fact, researchers who winsorize data find that they lose an additional "degree of freedom" with this method (Dixon & Tukey, 1968), a fact that can affect tests of the statistical significance of the difference between means. If the outlier response can be explained as coming from a different population from the rest of the data, for instance, it makes sense to exclude it. If the outlier cannot be explained, it may be that the vagaries of data in the population make keeping it useful. One group warned journalists reporting statistical results, "Analysis can be biased (an obviously ethical issue) if trimmed means are not calculated correctly. You can't trim just the high values or just the low values to sway the data in any certain fashion. This needs to be strictly adhered to" (World at Work, 2000, ¶ 37). In addition, it should be noted that trimming and winsorizing are useful for description alone. Advanced statistical tools are not based on the use of trimmed or winsorized means.

Disadvantages of the Mean

The arithmetic mean has several limitations. Furthermore, the first two of these matters can greatly affect the meaning of this measure.

- The mean is affected by extremely high or low scores that may not reflect most of the distribution. For instance, in our example the mean was distorted by the very low scores of only a couple of respondents. Sometimes the results can be very troublesome. Suppose you were doing a study relating age to communicator competence. If 20 people in the sample were 18 years old and if 4 people were 66, the mean age would be 26. But nobody in the sample was 26. The mean produced a number that might be *unhelpful* to summarize the typical age of the sample group members.
- The mean may not be useful when distributions are open-ended. If scores representing infinity in either direction are possible, the mean cannot really be defined. Granted, this matter is more theoretical than practical, but it is a limitation of the use of the mean.
- The mean may be tedious to compute by hand. Computers have made this problem less significant than it used to be, but if hand computations are to be used, it can be a challenge.

Using SPSS and Excel to Obtain Central Tendency

Computer programs have made efficient work of computing central tendency. With both SPSS and Excel, subroutines are dedicated to central tendency statistics.

SPSS

To illustrate using SPSS, data will be used from a study completed about the news coverage of the September 11, 2001, terrorist attack on the United States. A portion of the numbers of stories broadcast by CNN for each half-hour period are listed here. The first column shows the time the story was broadcast, starting with the first half-hour period following the attack (9 a.m. EDT) through the period beginning at 8:30 p.m.

To get a frequency count to check accuracy of data entry, we may look at the menu item *Analyze* and select *Descriptives* from the drop-down menu. Then we would select *Frequencies*. In the dialog box that appears, the two variables would be selected and moved to the active "Variable(s):" field. We would make sure to check the box to "Display frequency tables."

	time	stories	var	var	var
1	9:00	6			
2	9:30	19			
3	10:00	7			
4	10:30	8			
5	11:00	11			
6	11:30	7			
7	12:00	11			
8	12:30	8			
9	13:00	5			
10	13:30	13			
11	14:00	13			
12	14:30	9			
13	15:00	8			
14	15:30	10			
15	16:00	9			
16	16:30	11			
17	17:00	11			
18	17:30	7			
19	18:00	6			
20	18:30	8			

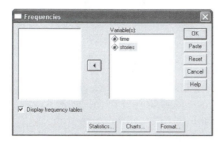

Clicking the *Statistics. . .* button would produce a dialog box of optional information. As seen below, we would want to check the boxes for the *Mean*, *Median*, and *Mode*.

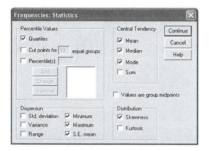

Following these selections, the researcher would click the *Continue* button followed by the *OK* button. The result in the output window would be

Frequencies

Statistics

		TIME	STORIES
N	Valid	24	24
	Missing	0	0
Mean		14:45	8.71
Std. Error of Mean		0:43	.690
Median		14:45	8.00
Mode		9:00ᵃ	8
Skewness		.000	1.099
Std. Error of Skewness		.472	.472
Minimum		9:00	3
Maximum		20:30	19
Percentiles	25	11:37	7.00
	50	14:45	8.00
	75	17:52	11.00

a. Multiple modes exist. The smallest value is shown.

As can be seen, the mean, median, and mode are identified for both variables, though, of course, the descriptive statistics for the "stories" variable are the only ones of particular interest

here. To check on the possible presence of keystroke errors or anomalies, the frequency table may be examined, as shown here. In this case, there is little to attract much attention.

STORIES

		Frequency	Percent	Valid Percent	Cumulative Percent
Valid	3	1	4.2	4.2	4.2
	4	1	4.2	4.2	8.3
	5	1	4.2	4.2	12.5
	6	2	8.3	8.3	20.8
	7	4	16.7	16.7	37.5
	8	5	20.8	20.8	58.3
	9	2	8.3	8.3	66.7
	10	1	4.2	4.2	70.8
	11	4	16.7	16.7	87.5
	13	2	8.3	8.3	95.8
	19	1	4.2	4.2	100.0
	Total	24	100.0	100.0	

From the *Analyze* menu, we may select *Descriptive statistics* followed by *Explore. . . .* On the dialog box that appears, we would select the variable of interest, "stories" on the "Dependent List."

To select additional statistics, we would click on *Statistics. . .* and check desired tools as shown on the dialog box below. Afterward, one may click on *Continue.*

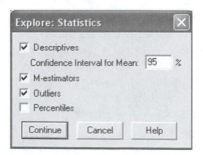

The output would appear as shown below.

Explore

Case Processing Summary

	Cases					
	Valid		Missing		Total	
	N	Percent	N	Percent	N	Percent
STORIES	24	100.0%	0	0%	24	100.0%

Descriptives

			Statistic	Std Error
STORIES	Mean		8.71	.690
	95% Confidence	Lower Bound	7.28	
	Interval for Mean	Upper Bound	10.14	
	5% Trimmed Mean		8.50	
	Median		8.00	
	Variance		11.433	
	Std. Deviation		3.381	
	Minimum		3	
	Maximum		19	
	Range		16	
	Interquartile Range		4.00	
	Skewness		1.099	.472
	Kurtosis		2.568	.918

The mean and median are fairly close to each other. The next chapter will consider other measures related to dispersion, though they might invite some additional attention for these data.

Excel

Descriptive analysis using Excel is rather direct. We can use the insert function key f_x to the left of the formula bar, or we may identify a location on the spreadsheet to place output and then use a combination of functions that have been prepared as a collection. The latter approach will be used

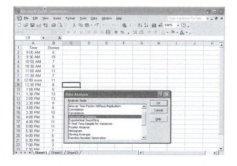

here. From the *Tools* menu, click to select *Data Analysis.* If this option does not appear, you will need to add in the Analysis ToolPak.[2] After selecting *Data Analysis*, select *Descriptive Statistics* from the *Data Analysis* dialog box. Click on *OK.*

In the dialog box that appears you will be prompted to identify an "Input Range," which is the location of the data. Click on 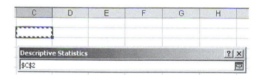 and proceed to highlight the data of interest (column B rows 1 though 24, in this instance).

Click on to complete your selection. On the dialog box, select the *Output Range* button and click on to open the window to identify a place for the output. Click on the cell where you wish to place the output.

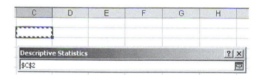

Click on to complete the selection. On the *Descriptive Statistics* dialog box, check the box to indicate that a variable label appears in the first row of the column. Then, select *Summary statistics.*

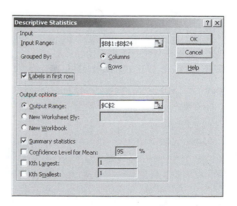

---

[2]To add the ToolPak, go to the *Tools* menu and click on *Add-Ins.* From the dialog box that appears, check the box to select the *Analysis ToolPak* and then click *OK.*

Click on *OK* to execute the operations. The following results will appear:

Mean	8.708333
Standard Error	0.6902
Median	8
Mode	8
Standard Deviation	3.381268
Sample Variance	11.43297
Kurtosis	2.567539
Skewness	1.039338
Range	16
Minimum	3
Maximum	19
Sum	209
Count	24

As can be seen, the output reveals mean, median, and mode, as well as a host of other measures that will be discussed in Chapter 4.

RELATIONS AMONG MEAN, MEDIAN, AND MODE

There may be controversy about which measure of central tendency is "best," but there is little doubt of the interpretations that such matters make possible. The measures of central tendency may reveal quite a bit about the nature of underlying distributions of data.

Relations Among Measures of Central Tendency for Symmetrical Distributions

When distributions are symmetrical, such as the one shown below, the mean, median, and mode are identical.

Of course, because of measurement imperfections and sampling error, we would not expect to find a *perfect* arrangement in actual data. Yet, for generally symmetrical distributions, we expect the mean, median, and mode to be fairly close. Since the normal distribution of data around a mean is an assumption underlying

many advanced statistical tools, it makes sense to look at these descriptive qualities before plunging into hypothesis testing.

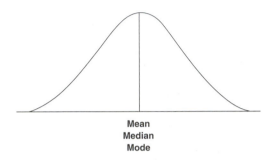

Mean
Median
Mode

Relations Among Measures of Central Tendency for Asymmetrical Distributions

Distributions are not always symmetrical. If data form patterns that are radically off center, such information would be important to know. Alternative statistical tools might be sought, changes in data collection could be explored, or transformations of data might be considered. An inspection of differences among measures of central tendency can reveal a lot. The example below, for instance, shows a severely troubled distribution that is far from symmetrical.

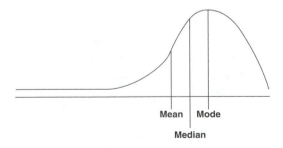

Mean | **Mode**
Median

When the data are far off center (**skewed**, as it is called) with most of the data to the right of the distribution, the mode will be higher than the median. In turn, the median will be higher than the mean.

If the distribution is off center with most of the data to the left, as in the example shown

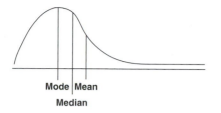

Mode | Mean
Median

here, the location of the various measures of central tendency also are affected.

The mode will have a lower score than the median, which will have a lower score than the mean. If the differences between any one of these measures and another are great, the distribution may invite additional attention before continuing. For purposes of this discussion, however, it is useful simply to know that looking at the measures of central tendency can identify the distribution's characteristics.

LOOKING AT VARIABILITY AND DISPERSION

Though measures of central tendency identify numbers to summarize typical or average characteristics of data, measures of variability satisfy our need to know how far from the center these data tend to be. This chapter identifies measures of dispersion and how they can be used to help understand the meaning of information.

ASSESSING DISPERSION

In a general sense, **measures of variability** or **dispersion** are statistics that describe how far from the mean events tend to be. If most of the data are close to the mean, we might say that the mean pretty much tells the whole story. But if the data tend to be spread out "all over creation," the mean may not be the most helpful way to get a sense of what the data are trying to tell us. Several tools are popular for measuring dispersion: the range, the absolute average deviation, the variance, and the standard deviation.

Range

The **range** is the distance between the highest and lowest scores. The range is computed by subtracting the lowest score in the data set from the highest score. For instance, the table on the next page shows the number of different news stories CNN broadcast on September 11, 2001, for each half-hour period beginning at 9:00 a.m. EST through the period beginning at 8:30 p.m.[1]

In this case, the range is

$$R = X_{largest} - X_{smallest}$$
$$R = 19 - 3$$
$$R = 16$$

This range may seem a little large. Three stories indicate that each story was covered for nearly 10 minutes, excluding station breaks. Nineteen stories translate into rapid review of slightly over a minute and a half each (roughly "headline-style coverage"). A prudent reader might ask why such differences existed. In this case, the early news accounts and "person in the street" reactions were replaced by extended interviews with experts during the evening hours.

The range is easily understood and lets readers understand the limits of the data. Furthermore, it is useful for researchers who wish to construct frequency distributions and histograms. It also has "expected" relationships to other measures such as the standard deviation and the standard error of the mean. In fact—to use terms that are explained elsewhere in this chapter—the standard deviation is approximately one fifth to one fourth of the range (Sternstein, 1994, p. 8). These facts have made this measure very popular in manufacturing, where it is the basis for constructing variable control charts used to keep production variability statistics for quality control purposes (see Grant & Leavenworth, 1996, esp. chap. 2). Yet, the range has a couple of limitations. The range is really suited for description of data measured on the interval or ratio levels. For ordinal data, the rankings can only identify that the

---

[1]The data for this example are part of a study completed by the author and a group of students (Reinard et al., 2002). It is available on http://commfaculty.fullerton.edu/jreinard/new_page_6.htm

Beginning Time Period	Number of Different News Stories Broadcast About 9/11 Attack
9:00 a.m.	6
9:30 a.m.	19
10:00 a.m.	7
10:30 a.m.	8
11:00 a.m.	11
11:30 a.m.	7
12:00 noon	11
12:30 p.m.	8
1:00 p.m.	5
1:30 p.m.	13
2:00 p.m.	13
2:30 p.m.	9
3:00 p.m.	8
3:30 p.m.	10
4:00 p.m.	9
4:30 p.m.	11
5:00 p.m.	11
5:30 p.m.	7
6:00 p.m.	6
6:30 p.m.	8
7:00 p.m.	3
7:30 p.m.	7
8:00 p.m.	8
8:30 p.m.	4

highest ranking was larger than another, but not how much. The greatest shortcoming of the range is that it can be thrown off wildly by the presence of atypical extreme scores. Thus, comparing ranges of different distributions can give unreliable estimates of variability.

Another use of the range relates to the interquartile range and centiles. The **interquartile range** avoids difficulties created by extreme scores by identifying the distance from the top 25% of the scores to the bottom 25% of scores. To accomplish this task, the data must be arranged in order from the lowest to the highest score. Then, the point that ends the first quartile (the lowest 25% of the scores) is subtracted from the point that ends the third quartile (the third set of 25% of the scores). In our example data above, if arranged from lowest to highest, we would get

Because the third quartile is 11 and the first quartile is 7, the interquartile range is 4 (third quartile – first quartile = 11 – 7). **Centiles** or "percentiles" report the proportion (percentage) of scores that fall below any given point. For instance, the median is the point where 50% of the scores fall below it, and the 10th percentile is the location that exceeds 10% of the distribution.

Absolute Average Deviation

Sometimes called the "average deviation," the **absolute average deviation** is the mean of the absolute differences between scores and their mean. The "absolute differences" are the actual distances of scores from the mean, ignoring the sign of the differences. Thus, all differences take on positive values. The vertical lines | | in the formula are meant to reveal the use of absolute values. Computing the absolute deviation involves one of these formulae, depending on whether the sample or population is used:[2]

Population Absolute Average Deviation

$$A.D. = \frac{\sum |X_i - \mu|}{N}$$

Sample Absolute Average Deviation

$$A.D. = \frac{\sum |X_i - \overline{X}|}{n}$$

For example, here are scores that five people received on a measure of conversational appropriateness, which is itself a set of 20 seven-point scales that measures the degree to which communicators believe that they tend to achieve their goals during conversations (Canary & Spitzberg, 1987). The possible range of scores is from 20 to 140.

Conversational appropriateness rating

X

80

80

90

100

100

To compute the absolute average deviation, we subtract the mean from each score and average the absolute differences. In this case, the mean of the sample data is 90. Applying the formula, the following answer is found.

Conversational Appropriateness Rating X	$|X_i - \overline{X}|$
80	$|80 - 90| = 10$
80	$|80 - 90| = 10$
90	$|90 - 90| = 0$
100	$|100 - 90| = 10$
100	$|100 - 90| = 10$
$\overline{X} = 90$	

$$A.D. = \frac{\sum X_i - \overline{X}}{n} = \frac{10 + 10 + 0 + 10 + 10}{5}$$

$$A.D. = \frac{40}{5} = 8$$

---

[2]Some formulae for the average deviation (e.g., Mason, 1970, p. 34) compare scores with the median rather than the mean.

The average absolute deviation often is used to describe simple data sets or to report deviations of a model's observed values from its predicted values. But this statistic is not an unbiased estimator of any population characteristic. Thus, other alternatives have been explored, particularly the variance and the standard deviation.

The Variance and the Standard Deviation

To understand these versatile tools of variability, it is instructive to use an example to illustrate the logic at work. Consider this sample of three scores from a short true-false test of student understanding of statistical analysis of communication data:

$$2, 5, 8$$

On the average, how far from the mean are the data? *Note: We are not asking which one* **is** *the mean—just how far the data are from the one that is the mean.*

When we examine how far the other data are from the one that is the mean, the answer is that the average distance of the other data is 3. This number is, in fact, the sample standard deviation. With so few pieces of data it is easy to "eyeball" the differences of scores from the mean point, but with large data sets it is helpful to have a formula.

<table>
<tr><td>The formula for the
standard deviation
of a entire *population* of events is</td><td>The formula for the
standard deviation
of a *sample* is</td></tr>
<tr><td>$$\sigma = \sqrt{\frac{\sum(X_i - \mu)^2}{N}}$$</td><td>$$s = \sqrt{\frac{\sum(X_i - \bar{X})^2}{n-1}}.$$</td></tr>
</table>

Though researchers sometimes work with entire populations of events, most analyses are based on samples. For this reason, the sample formula will be used in this example. As with any formula containing parentheses, it makes sense to start by examining the materials inside the parentheses.

First, we subtract the mean from each score.

X_i	$X_i - \bar{X}$	$(X_i - \bar{X})$
2	2 − 5	−3
5	5 − 5	0
8	8 − 5	3

We might be prone to add these differences and divide by the number of scores. Yet, adding –3, 0, and 3 would equal 0, a number that would suggest that scores do not vary from the mean at all. Thus, we must temporarily get rid of the minus signs. The absolute average deviation could be used but, as we have seen, it may lead us to a dead end. Another option would be to add a constant to the numbers (perhaps 3, in this case), which could be subtracted out from our final answer. But this approach is inelegant because a different number would have to be used for each new data set. An alternative suggested by the formula involves squaring each difference number (each "$(X_i – \bar{X})$"). Then, we could "unsquare" the final answer to get back to the cardinal numbers with which we began. This option will work, as the following computations show.

X_i	$X_i – \bar{X}$	$(X_i – \bar{X})$	$(X_i – \bar{X})^2$
2	2 – 5	–3	9
5	5 – 5	0	0
8	8 – 5	3	9
			$\sum(X_i – \bar{X})^2 = 18$

The number $\sum(X_i – \bar{X})^2$, which is equal to 18 in this case, is often called the **sum of squares** for short.

The natural next step would divide the sum of squares by the number of scores, and, if we were using the entire population, we would. But when we made our comparison of scores around $\bar{X}$ (the mean of the sample), we were only estimating the *likely* mean of the population (μ). The estimate was the best we could do, but it still was an estimate. So, the comparisons we have made around this point are imperfect. If we did not make some kind of adjustment, the measure of dispersion from these sample data would underestimate the actual amount of variability in the population. To correct for this problem, the sum of squares is divided by the number of scores minus one (for the sample mean used as an estimate of the population mean). The adjustment is based on the fact that in statistical analyses a **degree of freedom** is lost each time a population parameter is estimated from a sample statistic. These degrees of freedom reflect the actual degree to which individual data points could have taken different values. Even though—theoretically—all the data points could take on any values, for the mean to be reported as it is, the last data point could only take a single value. Hence, because we used the sample mean as a point of comparison, the degrees of freedom in the data were restricted. You may wonder why we do not lose a similar degree of freedom when computing the population standard deviation. The reason is that there is no *estimation* of any population characteristic. With the whole population as our sample, we can identify—rather than estimate—the mean. Because there is no *estimation* of the population mean, there is no chance to *under*estimate variability based on comparisons around the population mean.

The combination of squared differences from the mean (9 in this example) is called **the variance.** This number is called **the variance**. It is a formula widely used in statistical analyses. The sample variance is abbreviated with the symbol s^2 because, as can be seen, the

X_i	$X_i - \bar{X}$	$(X_i - \bar{X})$	$(X_i - \bar{X})^2$
2	2 – 5	–3	9
5	5 – 5	0	0
8	8 – 5	3	9

$$\sum(X_i - \bar{X})^2 = 18$$

$$s = \sqrt{\frac{\sum(X_i - \bar{X})^2}{n-1}}$$

$$s = \sqrt{\frac{18}{n-1}}$$

$$s = \sqrt{\left(\frac{18}{2} = 9 = s^2\right)}$$

$$s = \sqrt{9} = s^2 = 3$$

variance is the square of the standard deviation.[3] The raw variance, for all its usefulness, is a bit difficult to interpret since it is based on squared differences. So, a final step is taken to get back to the cardinal numbers with which we started, by taking the square root of the variance. The resulting number, 3, is the standard deviation, which you probably identified when you eyeballed these data. Though, as has been seen, the standard deviation is not the same as the average differences of scores from the mean, this number is a useful index of dispersion. The **standard deviation** is symbolized as *s* for the sample standard deviation and σ (sigma) for the population standard deviation.

Building Block Formula Box 2: Formulae for Population and Sample Variances

	Population	*Sample*
The Variance: the mean of squared differences of scores from their means	$\sigma^2 = \dfrac{\sum(X_i - \mu)^2}{N}$	$s = \sqrt{\dfrac{\sum(X_i - \bar{X})^2}{n-1}}$
The Standard Deviation: the average of the deviation of scores from their means (the square root of the variance)	$\sigma = \sqrt{\dfrac{\sum(X_i - \mu)^2}{N}}$	$s = \sqrt{\dfrac{\sum(X_i - \bar{X})^2}{n-1}}$

By using the proper formula, researchers create **unbiased estimators** for population parameters that avoid underestimating population dispersion. In particular, the sample standard deviation *s* is an unbiased estimator of the population standard deviation σ. Furthermore, the sample variance s^2 is an unbiased estimator of the population variance σ^2. These statements mean that the sample statistics are not likely to either over- or underestimate the population characteristics that they estimate. This fact also means that if researchers employ formulae that use the population standard deviation or variance, they may substitute the sample standard deviation and variance.

---

[3]It is wise not to confuse terms, such as "the variance," with words that sound similar, such as "the variation," or "the variability." "The variance" is used here to refer to the formula you have seen. "Variability" or "variation" are just general words referring to measures of dispersion.

Special Discussion 4.1

Alternative Measures of Variability

The *coefficient of variation* (also known as the coefficient of relative variation) is used only for data that are measured on the ratio level of measurement. It is computed by dividing the standard deviation by the mean of the distribution.

The *Gini coefficient* is a measure of variation that takes the mean difference between all pairs of scores and then divides by twice the population mean, μ. It sometimes is called a "coefficient of concentration." It often is used to identify so-called "inequalities" among scores of data, such as income figures for particular groups of people and occupations.

Mueller and Schuessler's *index of qualitative variation* is used when the data are simple categorical attributes. Hence, it is a useful measure of dispersion for nominal level data. The formula for this measure is

$$IQV = \frac{\text{total observed differences}}{\text{maximum possible differences}} * 100.$$

For instance, if a researcher had 90 communication students with 15 specializing in argumentation, 50 in interpersonal communication, and 25 in intercultural communication, one could determine the degree of variation by using the formula. Obviously, if students were equally divided among specialties, the maximum variation would have 30 students in each group. But there is less variation than this expectation would lead one to believe. To identify the total observed difference, the researcher would multiply each category of events with all the others: (15 * 25) + (15 * 50) + (25 * 50) = 2,375. To compute the maximum possible differences, one multiplies each of the groups' maximum difference numbers by all the others: (30 * 30) + (30 * 30) + (30 * 30) = 2,700. Substituting the numbers into the formula, one finds .8796 * 100 = 87.96%. This result means that there is nearly 88% of possible heterogeneity among the different specializations of communication majors.

The Standard Error

When researchers compute or estimate the size of the standard deviation of scores other than raw scores on variables, these numbers are the **standard errors** of the measure in question. Thus, the standard error is "the standard deviation of the sampling distribution of a statistic" (Vogt, 2005, p. 307). For instance, if we had a series of samples, computed their means, and then reported the standard deviation of these means, the result would be called the **standard error of the mean**, symbolized as $s_{\bar{x}}$. Because the mean of a large collection of sample means is likely to identify the population mean, the standard error of the mean indicates how far the sample mean is likely to differ from the population mean. "The standard error of the mean indicates how much the sample mean differs from the expected value (which is the mean of the sampling distribution of means). By so doing, it gives an answer to the question: How good an estimate of the population mean is the sample mean?" (Vogt, 2005, p. 307).

Researchers rarely compute the standard error of the mean by collecting repeated samples. Instead, they estimate it by applying the central limit theorem. The **central limit theorem** states that the sampling distribution of means tends toward a normal distribution with increased sample sizes regardless of the shape of the parent population. So, if you collected a host of samples of 3 events and plotted the means on a histogram, the histogram would tend to look about as normal as the underlying population. Yet, if you collected a host of samples of 30 events each and plotted their means on a histogram, the histogram would tend to look like a bell-shaped standard normal curve, even if the underlying distribution were severely nonnormal. This principle is the foundation of what is known as the law of large numbers. Because of the central limit theorem, the standard error of the mean may be computed by use of the following formula:

$$\sigma_{\bar{X}} = \frac{\sigma}{\sqrt{N}}.$$

Of course, one rarely knows the population standard deviation, σ. So, the formula for the standard error of the mean must rely on the following estimate from sample statistic substitutions:

$$s_{\bar{X}} = \frac{s}{\sqrt{n}}.$$

As in past notation, s is that standard deviation of the sample, and n is the number of events in the sample. This formula allows one to enter a distribution of means to help make decisions about the ways to compare means. It also lets us know how far from the sample mean the population mean is likely to be. In addition, this formula may be useful in computing confidence intervals around estimates of population means from knowledge of sample means.

Building Block Formula Box 3: Formulae for Standard Error of the Mean		
	Population	*Sample*
Standard Error of the Mean: the standard deviation of a distribution of means, indicating "how much the sample mean differs from the expected value (which is the mean of the sampling distribution of means)" (Vogt, 2005, p. 307)	$\sigma_{\bar{X}} = \dfrac{\sigma}{\sqrt{N}}$	$s_{\bar{X}} = \dfrac{s}{\sqrt{n}}$

Using SPSS and Excel to Compute Measures of Dispersion

Both SPSS and Excel have made analysis of dispersion increasingly efficient. In this example, the data from the table on the top of page 63 will be used as a case in point.

SPSS

After the data have been imported or entered, information about data dispersion can be completed by selecting *Analyze* on the menu bar, followed by clicking on *Frequencies* in the drop-down menu that appears.

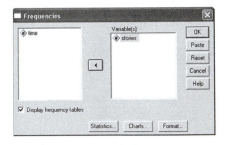

When the dialog box for "Frequencies" appears, one selects the variable(s) to be analyzed. In this case, we are interested in analyzing data for the number of stories broadcast by CNN during each half-hour period on September 11, 2001. Thus, in the left portion of the dialog box, you would click on the "stories variable" and use the arrow button to transfer the selection to the "Variable(s)" field at the right. Because data "snooping" often is helpful to examine distributions and to identify possible data entry errors, the box to "Display frequency tables" is checked.

To select the specific descriptive statistics, researchers click on the *Statistics* button. In the dialog box, many choices appear. Though in this chapter we are focusing on measures of dispersion, you normally would want to get most descriptive analysis completed in one pass. Thus, we will request all the information you would be likely to choose at one time. In this case, we have checked all measures of dispersion except the minimum and maximum scores (the

frequencies table will reveal this information for us). We also have requested the popular measures of central tendency and quartile information. Click on *Continue* and then *OK*.

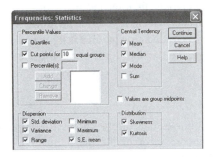

The output of the analysis appears in the output window. As can be seen, the first cell shows the descriptive statistics requested, along with a few others. The results show a standard deviation of 3.381 (standard error of the mean equal to 0.69) stories per half-hour period, with a range of 16 stories. Information about the distribution of the scores also is reported and will be referenced in a subsequent discussion.

STORIES

N	Valid	24
	Missing	0
Mean		8.71
Std. Error of Mean		.690
Median		8.00
Mode		8
Std. Deviation		3.381
Variance		11.433
Skewness		1.099
Std. Error of Skewness		.472
Kurtosis		2.568
Std. Error of Kurtosis		.918
Range		16
Percentiles	10	4.50
	20	6.00
	25	7.00
	30	7.00
	40	8.00
	50	8.00
	60	9.00
	70	10.50
	75	11.00
	80	11.00
	90	13.00

The frequencies table appears at the end of the output and shows the actual distribution of scores and the cumulative frequencies.

STORIES

		Frequency	Percent	Valid Percent	Cumulative Percent
Valid	3	1	4.2	4.2	4.2
	4	1	4.2	4.2	8.3
	5	1	4.2	4.2	12.5
	6	2	8.3	8.3	20.8
	7	4	16.7	16.7	37.5
	8	5	20.8	20.8	58.3
	9	2	8.3	8.3	66.7
	10	1	4.2	4.2	70.8
	11	4	16.7	16.7	87.5
	13	2	8.3	8.3	95.8
	19	1	4.2	4.2	100.0
	Total	24	100.0	100.0	

Excel

Once the data are placed into an Excel spreadsheet, measures of dispersion can be identified. The most direct way to find major measures of variability involves using a collection of functions prepared in Excel. From the *Tools* menu, one selects *Data Analysis*. From the dialog box that appears, the researcher selects *Descriptive Statistics* and clicks on the *OK* button.

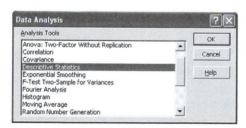

In the "Descriptive Statistics" dialog box, one uses the box marked "Input Range" to specify the location of the data. Clicking on the ▣ button identifies the range of cells in which the data are found. The following dialog appears:

In this case, the researcher could highlight cells B1 through B25 on the spreadsheet. Clicking on the ▣ button returns to the dialog box. Checking the box marked "Labels in first row" indicates that the first row does not contain data, but instead contains variable labels.

To enter a location for the output, one may click on the "Output Range" radio button. Clicking on the adjacent ▣ button, the researcher may then highlight column C. Clicking on the ▣ button returns to the "Descriptive Statistics" dialog box.

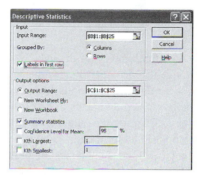

After returning to the "Descriptive Statistics" dialog box, the researcher should check the "Summary Statistics" box and click on the *OK* button. The results are shown below and include most measures of dispersion.

	A	B	C	D
1	Time	Stories	Stories	
2	9:00 AM	6		
3	9:30 AM	19	Mean	8.7083333
4	10:00 AM	7	Standard Error	0.6901984
5	10:30 AM	8	Median	8
6	11:00 AM	11	Mode	8
7	11:30 AM	7	Standard Deviation	3.3812677
8	12:00 noon	11	Sample Variance	11.432971
9	12:30 PM	8	Kurtosis	2.5675389
10	1:00 PM	5	Skewness	1.0989474
11	1:30 PM	13	Range	16
12	2:00 PM	13	Minimum	3
13	2:30 PM	9	Maximum	19
14	3:00 PM	8	Sum	209
15	3:30 PM	10	Count	24
16	4:00 PM	8		

One of the quickest ways to identify percentiles and the interquartile range involves selecting *Tools* from the menu list and then clicking on *Data Analysis*. Selecting *Rank and Percentile* and then clicking on the *OK* button causes the subroutine to become active.

A new dialog box will appear for "Rank and Percentile" (see p. 72). On the box marked "Input Range," one may click on the ▣ button to identify

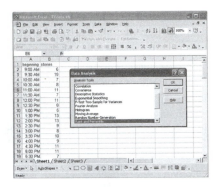

data point is involved (the first data point in the data, or the second, and so forth). The next column (column D) shows the rank ordered news stories data. The column marked "*Rank*" identifies the rank of the score from the highest value to the lowest. The last column provides the cumulative percentage ranking.

	A	B	C	D	E	F
1	Time	Stories	Point	Stories	Rank	Percent
2	9:00 AM	6	2	19	1	100.00%
3	9:30 AM	19	10	13	2	91.30%
4	10:00 AM	7	11	13	2	91.30%
5	10:30 AM	8	5	11	4	73.90%
6	11:00 AM	11	7	11	4	73.90%
7	11:30 AM	7	16	11	4	73.90%
8	12:00 noon	11	17	11	4	73.90%
9	12:30 PM	8	14	10	8	69.50%
10	1:00 PM	5	12	9	9	60.80%
11	1:30 PM	13	15	9	9	60.80%
12	2:00 PM	13	4	8	11	39.10%
13	2:30 PM	9	8	8	11	39.10%
14	3:00 PM	8	13	8	11	39.10%
15	3:30 PM	10	20	8	11	39.10%
16	4:00 PM	9	23	8	11	39.10%
17	4:30 PM	11	3	7	16	21.70%
18	5:00 PM	11	6	7	16	21.70%
19	5:30 PM	7	18	7	16	21.70%
20	6:00 PM	6	22	7	16	21.70%
21	6:30 PM	8	1	6	20	13.00%
22	7:00 PM	3	19	6	20	13.00%
23	7:30 PM	7	9	5	22	8.60%

the data set. Highlighting B1 through B25 identifies the range for the data. Clicking the ▣ button to return to the dialog box permits the researcher to check the box marked "Labels in first row." Specifying the location for the output is completed by clicking on the "Output Range" radio button. The researcher clicks the ▣ button and highlights column C. Clicking the ▣ button returns to the dialog box. Finally, the researcher clicks the *OK* button.

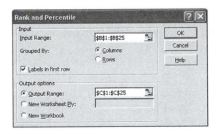

The output appears in the specified range. The column marked "*Point*" identifies which

To find the interquartile range, because there were 24 half-hour periods included, one need only look at the number of stories for the sixth-highest-ranked half-hour period (11) and the sixth-lowest-ranked half-hour period (7). Excel also has a function for determining the interquartile range, which is explained in detail in the Web site for this chapter.

THE RELATIONSHIP BETWEEN MEASURES OF CENTRAL TENDENCY AND VARIABILITY

How much variation is to be expected ordinarily? Fortunately, there are two guides to help answer this question. The first is called the empirical rule, and the second is called Chebyshev's inequality.

Using the Empirical Rule to Approximate the Frequency of Data in Distributions

Most communication data (as well as most data in the social sciences) tend to have distributions that form a sort of bell shape, with most data near the mean and fewer and fewer pieces of data found as one moves toward the extremes.

Special Discussion 4.2

Computing Total Variability With Multiple Independent Variables

If a researcher had variation from three variables expressed as standard deviations, one might imagine that it would be possible to identify the total variance by adding up the separate elements. Unfortunately, this approach would be a mistake, one that researchers are careful to avoid. Put another way, the total standard deviation σ_{total} created by three variables is not $\sigma_{variable\ 1} + \sigma_{variable\ 2} + \sigma_{variable\ 3}$. Similarly, the average standard deviation (sometimes called a pooled standard deviation) is not $(\sigma_{variable\ 1} + \sigma_{variable\ 2} + \sigma_{variable\ 3})/3$. This sort of arrangement would presume that there is some order of sequence and that variable 1 produces its contribution only, followed by variable 2 and the like. But, of course, in most cases, there is no such order effect claimed and, in fact, there is some overlap in the contributed variation.

   Thus, researchers learn not to sum or to average standard deviations, but to employ variances instead. Hence, σ_{total} is computed by $\sqrt{\sigma^2_{variable\ 1} + \sigma^2_{variable\ 2} + \sigma^2_{variable\ 3}}$. Similarly, the average or pooled standard deviation is based on variances, rather than averages of standard deviations directly.

Even with "imperfect" data, researchers generally find that the following so-called "empirical rule" can be used to estimate how much data exists at different distances from the mean:

the mean ± 1 (plus or minus 1) standard deviation contains approximately 68% of the measures;

the mean ± 2 standard deviations contains approximately 95% of the measures; and

the mean ± 3 standard deviations contains approximately all the measures.

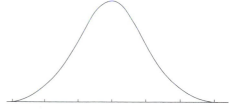

Such numbers allow researchers to identify which scores are within the "norm" (a term that usually means scores ranging within one standard deviation of the mean) and which ones are unusual and, hence, may invite special interpretation.

Using Chebyshev's Inequality to Determine the Mathematically Guaranteed Bound for the Frequency of Data in Distributions

   Not all data come from underlying standard normal distributions. Not all are lovely bell shapes. Yet, if there is only some sort of "mound shape" to the data, Chebyshev's (also spelled Chebycheff, Tchebechev, and Tchebycheff) inequality may give you a clue to the expected arrangement between the mean and the data.[4] The rule is stated as an inequality asserting that

the mean ± 2 standard deviations contain at least 75% of the measures, and

the mean ± 3 standard deviations contain at least 89% of the measures.

---

[4]Chebyshev actually discovered that at least a proportion $(1 - 1/k^2)$ of the data are distributed within k standard deviations from the mean. Hence, when $k = 3$, the formula becomes $1 - 1/9 = .8889$. When $k = 2$, the formula returns .75.

Because Chebyshev's inequality applies to any set of measurements, it is equally useful when researchers apply it to sample data or entire populations of data distributions. If the data show normal distributions, however, it makes most sense to rely on the empirical rule to obtain an understanding of the data.

EXAMINING DISTRIBUTIONS

Though some data can be understood in isolation, others are most easily understood by reference to some kind of distribution. Among the most popular have been normal curves that show what happens when there is random variation of scores around a mean. Such variables as communication apprehension, source credibility of public figures, and satisfaction with family communication all have underlying normal distributions around their means. By examining characteristics of such curves, we can logically compare the long-run pattern of things against some new data we might collect. Thus, the distribution can be very helpful to let researchers know if their data were what might have been expected often, or instead quite rarely, if only random variation were at work.

Normal Distributions

Actual scores or data distributions often are compared with **normal distributions**, which are continuous distributions that are symmetric and bell shaped (though, of course, there are many types of bells that are not shaped like a normal distribution). Though not the only characteristics that define normal curves, two important properties of normal distributions are symmetry and peakedness.

Symmetry

Symmetrical distributions are centered, with the distribution above the mean equal to that below the mean. The distribution illustrated in the top figure is clearly a normal distribution and, as one can see with the eye, the distribution is perfectly centered with an equal amount on each side. Because it is not off center, we may say that it is not **skewed**. To verify this condition, one may compute skewness by use of the following formula, though few people compute it by hand these days:

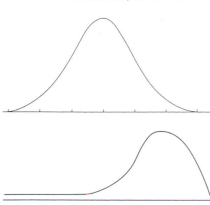

$$\frac{n}{(n-1)(n-2)} \sum \left(\frac{X_i - \overline{X}}{s} \right)^3.$$

If a distribution has no skew, the result of this formula is 0. If a distribution has a longer tail on the left than on the right, it is called (appropriately enough) "skewed to the left." The middle figure shows such a distribution.

The skew to the left means that the left side is where most of the data are *not* located. If the skewness formula were computed for such data, the coefficient would have a negative sign before it. In contrast, the bottom figure shows a distribution that is skewed positively. If the formula for skew were computed, the diagram would have a positive value.

One might wonder how severe skew would be before it would attract the special attention of the researcher. Theoretically, a skewness coefficient could range from $-\infty$ to $+\infty$. Though the particular research situation would guide interpretation, in most cases a skew that is within the range of -1 to $+1$ would be considered normal in an actual data set.

Peakedness

A normal curve has a noticeable peak at its center. A measure of **kurtosis** may be computed to identify the degree to which a distribution is peaked or flat. The way the formula for kurtosis is computed, 0 is taken as the value of an appropriately peaked distribution.[5] The computation of kurtosis involves the following formula that is used by both SPSS and Excel:

$$\left\{ \frac{n(n+1)}{(n-1)(n-2)(n-3)} \sum \left(\frac{X_i - \overline{X}}{s} \right)^4 \right\} - \frac{3(n-1)^2}{(n-2)(n-3)}.$$

When the distribution is appropriately peaked, it is called **mesokurtic**. A positive kurtosis coefficient indicates that the distribution is more peaked than in a normal distribution. For instance, the first distribution at the right has a kurtosis equal to 3. One might think that such a situation would indicate that something is troubled in the data. In many cases, however, researchers or practitioners may wish to have a distribution that shows such strong consistency of scores around the mean. When a distribution is so peaked, it is called **leptokurtic**. When a kurtosis coefficient has a negative value, it indicates that the distribution is flatter than expected for a normal distribution. For instance, the second distribution at the right has a kurtosis of -2. Such a flat distribution is also known as a **platykurtic** distribution. Because a negative value for kurtosis also means that there are many more events in the distribution's tails than normally are expected, this information often is evidence of a bimodal distribution.

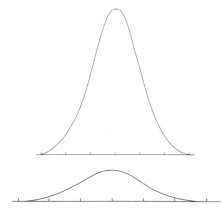

The Standard Normal Curve

The **standard normal curve** is a theoretic probability distribution that shows the distribution of events representing random variation around a mean. Though there are many normal distributions, the standard normal distribution is defined with specific theoretic values that make it unique. Its qualities are useful in letting us know what long-run expectations would be if there were only random variation around a mean of communication data (or any data, for that matter).

---

[5]At one time, the formula for kurtosis was not standardized at 0, but at 3. The reasoning was that the peak of the distribution also happened to be equal to a distance 3 sigmas wide. Thus, if you find an old statistics book, a normal distribution's kurtosis value might be identified as 3. You then might notice that kurtosis actually has the same formula as for the fourth derivative. The form of the kurtosis formula with kurtosis for a normal distribution equal to 3 is also known as *Pearson kurtosis*. The form of the kurtosis formula with kurtosis for a normal distribution equal to 0 is also known as *Fisher kurtosis*.

Special Discussion 4.3

A Short History of the Standard Normal Curve

Largely because of an interest in gambling and the need to set prices for life insurance policies, writers began studying the standard normal curve. Abraham de Moivre often is given credit for advancing the notion of the standard normal curve when he published the third edition of *Doctrine of Chances* in 1756, though he apparently discovered the formula for the normal curve in 1733. In this work, he observed outcomes in games of chance and ages at which people died. He found that such data tended to be distributed as normal curves. He completed a natural logarithm problem that permitted him to identify with great accuracy the area from the center of the distribution to one standard deviation from it.

Studying the standard normal curve was picked up by Karl Friedrich Gauss (1777–1855), a German mathematician and physicist, and the Marquis de Pierre Simon Laplace (1749–1827), a French astronomer and mathematician. Independently of each other, they developed the density function for the standard normal curve and then applied it to the study of the eccentric "wobbles" of the poles of planets in response to the influence of gravity of other celestial bodies. As a result of their work, this distribution was known as the "Laplace-Gaussian curve" or sometimes just the "Gaussian curve."

Though the standard normal curve remained valuable to astronomers and physicists, it began to be explored by people in the emerging social sciences when, in 1835, Lambert Adolphe Jacques Quetelet (1796–1874), a Belgian astronomer, gathered data on physical characteristics of French and Scottish soldiers. He found that both the measures were normally distributed and that the differences from the mean were distributed normally as a general "law of errors." When Karl Pearson (1857–1936) advanced his contributions to the study of statistics, he called this distribution the standard normal *curve* and was the first to use the term "standard deviation" in 1893. These names have stuck ever since.

Properties of the Standard Normal Curve

The standard normal curve is applicable to continuous measured variables. The standard normal distribution has several defining characteristics.

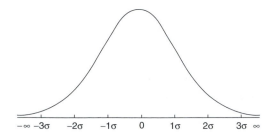

- The mean is defined with a value of 0. In fact, all measures of central tendency—mean, median, and mode—are at the same location and share the same zero value. Because the mean is 0, a negative sign for any value using the standard normal curve indicates that a location is below the mean. Similarly, a positive sign indicates a location above the mean.

- The numbers on the horizontal axis of the figure on page 76 indicate the standard deviations ranging from 3 below the mean to 3 above the mean. The value of one full standard deviation unit is equal to 1. As can be seen, the first standard deviation also is the location of the point of inflection where the curve changes from concave to convex.[6]
- The distribution stretches from negative infinity ($-\infty$) below the mean to plus infinity (∞) above the mean. This property makes the distribution what is called an **asymptotic distribution**, a term that means "a curve that gets closer to a line but never touches it" (Vogt, 2005, p. 15).
- As we have already seen, the standard normal curve has a skewness equal to 0, indicating the absence of skew.
- The kurtosis of the distribution is equal to 0 (as most current formulae compute it).

Areas Under the Standard Normal Curve

To make use of the standard normal curve to help make decisions, one needs to understand the proportions of the distributions that are located at different positions. In the standard normal curve, 68.26% of the area under the distribution lies from one sigma (standard deviation) below the mean to one sigma above the mean. As the figure to the right indicates, this distance is the center of the distribution and usually is considered the typical range of normal variation. The distance from two standard deviations below the mean to two standard deviations above the mean contains 95.44% of the total area. The range from three standard deviations below the mean to three standard deviations above the mean covers most (99.74%), but not all, of the area under the distribution.

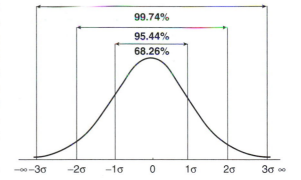

The density function has been summarized in tables that make easy work of using the standard normal curve. These tables have many uses. For instance, if your score on a measure of interpersonal immediacy puts you one standard deviation above the mean (+1.00 sigma), you might wonder how many people's scores you exceeded. To find that percentage, you could look at the table in Appendix C.1. A portion of that table is presented on page 78. The table shows the area (expressed as a proportion similar to a percentage) that extends from the mean up to that sigma value (identified here as a "z score"). To help understand things, there is a

---

[6]In 1893, Pearson wrote a letter to *Nature* magazine in which he described how the method of moments could be used to characterize binomial distributions. In it, he wrote, "Now the centre of gravity of the observation curve is found at once, also its area and its first four moments by easy calculation" (p. 616). Over the years, he returned to this notion of moments to characterize aspects of other sorts of distributions, including the standard normal distribution. He explained that the first central moment was a measure of central tendency known as the mean (in a standard normal curve, this value is 0). The second moment identified a measure of dispersion known as the variance (in a standard normal curve, this value is 1 and its square root, the standard deviation, also is 1). The third moment is a measure of skewness (in a standard normal curve, this value is 0). The fourth moment is a measure of peakedness called kurtosis (Pearson, 1905; in a standard normal curve, this value originally was computed to be 3, though the current practice is to use a formula that subtracts 3 from the original kurtosis value to produce a kurtosis of 0).

little drawing on the table in Appendix C.1 that illustrates that the table shows how much of the area exists *from* the mean to any point *above* the mean. To solve our example, we read down the column marked "*z*" until we find the first two digits in the standard deviation score we wish to interpret, 1.0 in our case. To find the second decimal point value, we read across the columns until we find .00 (to indicate that the second decimal point number also is 0). Thus, we find the value located at the intersection of the row for "1.0" and the column for ".00." The number from the table is .3413. Thus, 34.13% of the total area under the standard normal curve exists in the area ranging from the mean up to 1.00 standard deviation units. So, how many people scored below you (expressed as a percentage or proportion of the whole) on interpersonal immediacy ratings? You might be prone to double the observed area that you just found. But remember, your score was higher than *everybody's* scores who were below average. Thus, your score was higher that 50% of the population below average and *still* higher than 34.13% of those who scored above the mean (and median in the standard normal curve). Hence, .5000 + .3413 = .8413. Expressed as a percentage, your interpersonal immediacy rating was greater than that received by 84.13% of those completing the scale.

z	.00	.01	.02
0.0	.0000	.0040	.0080
0.1	.0398	.0438	.0478
0.2	.0793	.0832	.0871
0.3	.1179	.1217	.1255
0.4	.1554	.1591	.1628
0.5	.1915	.1950	.1985
0.6	.2257	.2291	.2324
0.7	.2580	.2611	.2652
0.8	.2881	.2910	.2939
0.9	.3159	.3186	.3212
1.0	.3413	.3438	.3461
1.1	.3643	.3665	.3686
1.2	.3849	.3869	.3888
1.3	.4032	.4049	.4066
1.4	.4192	.4207	.4222
1.5	.4332	.4345	.4357
1.6	.4452	.4463	.4474

To use the standard normal curve to interpret scores below the mean, the *z* values would have negative signs before them. Yet, you could use the same table because the areas above and below the mean have the same proportions of events. This fact is a result of the standard normal curve's quality of being perfectly symmetrical.

Using z Scores. Researchers rarely collect data that have a mean of zero and a standard deviation of 1. Even so, researchers can use the logic of the standard normal curve to help them make decisions. To do so, researchers have to transform their raw scores into *z* **scores** that represent what the scores would look like if they came from a distribution that had a mean of 0 and a standard deviation of 1. Sometimes *z* scores are called **standard scores** because they permit researchers to use the "standard normal curve" to interpret their scores. The formula for *z* is

$$z = \frac{X - \mu}{\sigma}.$$

The *X* is the score the researcher wishes to compare to the overall mean. For instance, scores on the popular Stanford-Binet IQ test are normally distributed with a population mean (μ) of 100 and a population standard deviation (σ) of 15.[7] Suppose you found a communication studies student who scored 118 on an IQ test. Even though we will not consider what these tests actually measure for the moment, you reasonably might wonder how many people this

---

[7]Though previous versions of the Stanford-Binet IQ test had standard deviations of 16, starting with the fifth edition in 2004, the scale adopted a standard deviation of 15. See *Stanford-Binet Intelligence Scales, Fifth Edition: Features* (2004).

student's scores surpassed. You already know that this score is above the mean, which tells you that this person's score is higher than 50% of the scores that are below average. But how many scores above average also are exceeded? The formula for z can be enlisted to provide this information. With the numbers inserted into the formula, the terms would become

$$z = \frac{118 - 100}{15}$$

$$z = \frac{18}{15} = 1.2$$

To interpret results, one could look at the table in Appendix C.1. A portion of that table appears here. As can be seen, you would begin by finding the row corresponding to "1.2." To find the second decimal point value, you would need to find the column marked ".00." This location reveals that the area extending from the mean to 1.2 standard deviation units includes .3849 or 38.49% of the total area under the standard normal curve. Thus, this IQ score of 118 exceeds 88.49% of IQ scores (it is higher than 50% of the scores that are below average and another 38.49% of the scores that are above average).

z	.00	.01	.02
0.0	.0000	.0040	.0080
0.1	.0398	.0438	.0478
0.2	.0793	.0832	.0871
0.3	.1179	.1217	.1255
0.4	.1554	.1591	.1628
0.5	.1915	.1950	.1985
0.6	.2257	.2291	.2324
0.7	.2580	.2611	.2652
0.8	.2881	.2910	.2939
0.9	.3159	.3186	.3212
1.0	.3413	.3438	.3461
1.1	.3643	.3665	.3686
1.2	.3849	.3869	.3888
1.3	.4032	.4049	.4066
1.4	.4192	.4207	.4222
1.5	.4332	.4345	.4357
1.6	.4452	.4463	.4474

Suppose you used a measure for which you did not have the population mean (μ) or the population standard deviation (σ). You could substitute the sample mean ($\overline{X}$) for population mean and substitute the sample standard deviation (s) for the population standard deviation. The reason you could make these substitutions is that $\overline{X}$ is an unbiased estimator of the population mean (μ) and s is an unbiased estimator (provided that the right formula was used for the sample standard deviation) of the population standard deviation (σ).

For all the usefulness that the standard normal distribution has, a word of caution might be added. Though you can transform your actual data into units under the standard normal curve, this step is actually appropriate only if the data have underlying normal distributions (or are distributions of means). Fortunately, statisticians have investigated other sorts of distributions to help make decisions about such data forms. These alternatives make it possible to handle interpretation issues for most distributions.

Building Block Formula Box 4: Formulae for z **Computed From Population and Sample Standard Deviations**		
	Population	*Sample*
z scores (a.k.a. "standard scores"): transformations permitting expression of scores as units under the standard normal curve	$z = \dfrac{X - \mu}{\sigma}$	$z = \dfrac{X - \overline{X}}{s}$

Alternative Standard Scores

There are other ways to interpret data scores. Three of the most popular ones can be seen here.

- **_T-scores_**: The _T_-score (named the "_T_-score" in honor of the influential psychologist of education E. L. Thorndike) sets the mean at 50 and the standard deviation at 10. Often used in educational research, there is an intuitively appealing characteristic to _T_-scores because the mean of 50 sounds much like the middle of a scale ranging from 0 to 100%. As it is computed, however, researchers first must identify the z score of an individual score. Then, they use the following formula to standardize this value with a mean of 50 and a standard deviation of 10: $T = 10z + 50$.

- **Stanines**: During World War II, researchers developed the nine-point scale (called the "standard nine" or "stanines" for short) with 9 equal to the highest rating. You may have heard people who are well dressed called "dressed to the nines," which is a reference consistent with this scaling system. The mean of the stanine is 5, and the standard deviation is 1.96. The stanines are actually ranges of scores in a population, rather than individual points along the distribution. For instance, the fifth stanine actually is bounded by the 40.13th percentile on the low side and the 59.87th percentile on the high side. The stanines and corresponding percentiles are found in the table below. In addition to use in the military, stanines often are reported on other presentations of results, such as school achievement tests and physiological rating scales.

Stanine	Low Percentile to High Percentile of the Stanine Range
9	95.99–100
8	89.44–95.99
7	77.34–89.44
6	59.87–77.34
5	40.13–59.87
4	22.66–40.13
3	10.56–22.66
2	4.01–10.56
1	0–4.01

- **Applied scores:** Some individual measures have their own standardized scoring systems. For instance, the Educational Testing Service has developed various tests called the Scholastic Aptitude Test, the Graduate Record Exam, and the Law School Aptitude Test, which frequently are taken by communication studies majors. These tests are standardized to have a mean of 500 and standard deviation of 100. The Wechsler IQ test has a mean of 100 and a standard deviation of 15. On the other hand, the developers of the scales composing the Minnesota Multiphasic Personality Inventory (the most popular personality test in the world) report results as simple z scores. Many other measures standardize results for convenience.

Using the Standard Normal Curve

As this chapter has indicated, the standard normal curve has many applications that are useful to researchers. First, the standard normal curve is useful in comparing scores to means. One might wonder why a researcher might want to make such a comparison. The reason is that finding the location of a score expressed as a number of units under the standard normal curve reveals quite of bit of information very quickly. The positive or negative sign of the z score identifies the general location of the score. Furthermore, the use of z scores to interpret standard errors of the mean permits researchers to learn how many standard deviations a score may be from the population mean. It also is easy to translate the z scores into percentiles that often provide an improved understanding of the meaning of a score.

Second, researchers often use the standard normal curve as a tool to help develop norms for measures and behaviors. By identifying a stable mean and the size of the standard deviation, researchers may identify the normal operating range of scores. Such a step allows others to identify the difference between typical and unusual scores.

Third, researchers often use the standard normal curve to help make predictions about what may be expected. For instance, suppose a teacher in a public speaking class notices that on days when a round of speeches begins, the time that the 25 students arrive for class is normally distributed with a mean of 5 minutes before the hour with a standard deviation of 5 minutes. The instructor likes to start class on time, but she wonders how many students will arrive late (after the official beginning of class). The standard normal curve could be used to estimate the numbers. The mean ($\overline{X}$) is −5 (5 minutes *before* the hour), and the standard deviation (s) is 5 minutes. Thus, in the formula

$$z = \frac{X - \overline{X}}{s},$$

X represents the arrivals *on the hour* (0 or "zero hour"). The question is how many people can be expected to arrive after 0 ("zero hour"). To solve the problem, we can run the numbers to find the appropriate z value:

$$z = \frac{X - \overline{X}}{s}$$
$$z = \frac{0 - (-5)}{5}$$
$$z = \frac{5}{5} = 1$$

When one looks up the z value in Appendix C.1, the answer is .3413 or 34.13%. How many students exist after this point? If half the distribution (50%) is above the mean, then the area above the point of interest is computed as 50% − 34.13%, which is 15.87%. Thus, the number of students likely to arrive late for the first day of a round of speeches is 15.87% of the 25 students, or 3.97 students (which, of course, rounds to 4 students). Using the standard normal curve in such a manner can help researchers make predictions that have very practical applications.

Special Discussion 4.4

Transformations of Data

Many times, researchers have data that are not normally distributed, either because of the sorts of measures that are used or because of some properties of the variables themselves. Thus, sometimes transformations of data are used to "normalize" scores before other analyses that assume normal distributions are undertaken. Some of the most popular of these transformations include the following.

Arcsin. Percentage data, especially when the percentages are very low or very high, are not normally distributed. Percentages are not free to vary because they cannot be lower than 0% or higher than 100%. An arcsin transformation will convert percentages into scores that are more centered than the raw percentages.

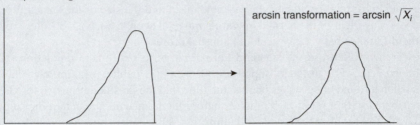

arcsin transformation = arcsin $\sqrt{X_i}$

A variation on this tool is the Anscombe standardization, which takes additional steps to secure an asymptotic distribution. Another transformation, called the *empirical Bayes standardization* (Assunçào & Reis, 1999), transforms raw proportional data into distributions with means of zero and standard deviations of 1.

Square Root. When the variances of the data are proportionate to the means, the effect can mask the existence of relationships in other statistical tests. When the data show moderate positive skew, a square root transformation will move the data to a normal distribution with most data close to the mean, as shown in the following diagram.

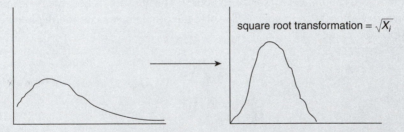

square root transformation = $\sqrt{X_i}$

If a skew in residuals still remains, some sources recommend using the cube-root ($\sqrt[3]{X_i}$) transformation. There also is a square root transformation to deal with moderate negative skew.

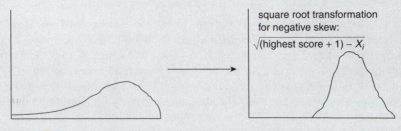

square root transformation
for negative skew:

$\sqrt{(\text{highest score} + 1) - X_i}$

Logarithm. When the data show strong skew and data from different comparison groups show heterogeneous variances, typically with different sample sizes, the volatility may be eliminated by the logarithmic transformation. When the heterogeneity increases with the scores on the dependent variable (showing positive skew), and when researchers are dealing with positive values, this transformation is most useful. In this transformation, some experts recommend using natural logarithms and other experts recommend base-10 logarithms.

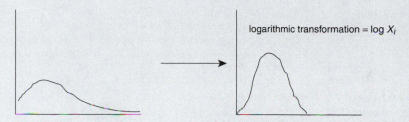

logarithmic transformation = log X_i

Reciprocal $\left(\frac{1}{X}\right)$ *or Inverse.* When the data show very large increases in variance after a specific threshold value is reached and also exhibit severe positive skew, the reciprocal or inverse transformation is invited.

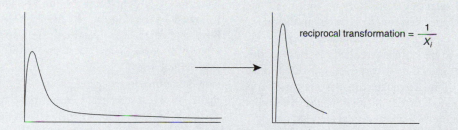

reciprocal transformation = $\dfrac{1}{X_i}$

Square. If the data show great negative skew and the variance decreases with increases in means, the square of the scores may be used to "linearize" the scores.

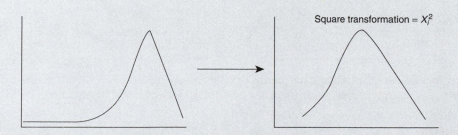

Square transformation = X_i^2

If one's data were not normally distributed, the use of these transformations is certainly easier than revising the statistical tools to be used. Yet, sometimes even transformations will not normalize a distribution. Thus, especially when the data continue to show more than one mode, the researcher should be very cautious about using statistical tests (such as analysis of variance or multiple regression correlation) that presume normal distributions (DeCoster, 2001, p. 12).

Using SPSS to Examine Distributions

One of the best ways to examine the nature of distributions of data is by use of charts and graphs. Though Excel permits creating histograms, it does not fit normal curves to data, create stem-and-leaf displays, or provide tests of the assumption of normal distribution. Hence, this discussion will focus on using SPSS.

An easy way to picture distributions of data is to use the *Histograms. . . Graphs* menu. Another way is to use the *Histograms* option from the *Frequencies* subroutine (though, in reality, the *Frequencies* option to create *Charts. . .* uses the *Graphs* subroutines). Yet another way to get information about distributions, outliers, and normality is to use the *Explore* subroutines. The *Graphs* and *Explore* approaches will be illustrated.

After selecting *Graphs* from the menu bar, the researcher selects *Histograms*. In the dialog box that appears, the researcher chooses the variable to be graphed (called "stories" in this case) and uses the arrow key to transfer it to the *Variable* field. To make sure that a normal curve line is added to the histogram, the researcher clicks on the "Display normal curve" box.

Clicking on the *OK* button causes the program to output a chart, such as the one at top right.

The chart shows the number of times that a given number of news stories was broadcast. Though far from perfect, the overall pattern shows a tendency toward a normal distribution. If a researcher wants to examine other characteristics of the data, such as checking for outliers, the *Explore* subroutine would be appropriate. After selecting *Analyze* from the menu bar, *Descriptive*

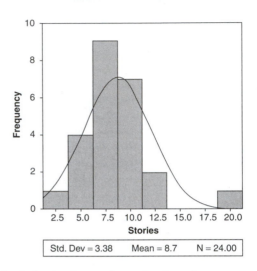

| Std. Dev = 3.38 | Mean = 8.7 | N = 24.00 |

Statistics is chosen from the drop-down menu, followed by *Explore. . . .* In the *Explore* dialog box, the researcher identifies the variable of interest ("stories") and uses the arrow key to transfer it to the "Dependent List:" field. No division according to independent variables is being made, so the researcher does not need to insert variables into the "Factor list:" field. In this case, the researcher has requested "Both" statistics and plots from the "Display" options.

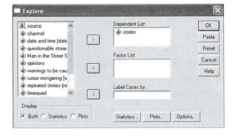

Clicking on *Plots. . .* produces an "Explore: Plots" dialog box. From this set of choices, the researcher may select both box plots and normality plots in addition to stem-and-leaf diagrams and histograms.

Clicking the *Continue* button returns the researcher to the "Explore" dialog box, from

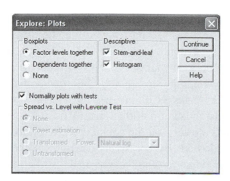

Descriptives

			Statistic	Std Error
STORIES	Mean		8.71	.690
	95% Confidence Interval for Mean	Lower Bound	7.28	
		Upper Bound	10.14	
	5% Trimmed Mean		8.50	
	Median		8.00	
	Variance		11.433	
	Std. Deviation		3.381	
	Minimum		3	
	Maximum		19	
	Range		16	
	Interquartile Range		4.00	
	Skewness		1.099	.472
	Kurtosis		2.568	.918

which the *Statistics. . .* button may be selected. From this set of choices, the researcher would wish to examine all such output. Afterward, one may click on *Continue* and then *OK*.

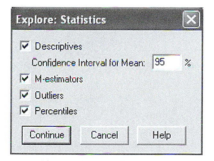

The output may reveal characteristics of interest to the researcher, especially of anomalies that emerge in the data. The first part of the output describes the numbers of present and missing data, as well as the basic descriptive statistics, as shown at the top of the next column.

This output joins other information that could help researchers. Some information deals with M-estimators of the mean. These elements are maximum-likelihood estimators of the mean given

different weights of data points. Those toward the extremes are given less weight than others. If the data come from distributions with very long tails, or if the data set has some extreme values, these alternative estimators of the mean usually are considered better identifications of central tendency than are the raw mean, the median, or the mode. The different estimators have their own forms but share a common approach of dealing with extreme scores.[8] Because the M-estimators are very close to the arithmetic mean, it seems that additional adjustments are not particularly indicated.

M-Estimators

	Huber's M-Estimator[a]	Tukey's Biweight[b]	Hampel's M-Estimator[c]	Andrews's Waved
STORIES	8.44	8.23	8.38	8.23

a. The weighting constant is 1.339.
b. The weighting constant is 4.685.
c. The weighting constants are 1.700, 3.400, and 8.500.
d. The weighting constant is 1.340*pl.

The output includes a list of the most extreme scores in the data set to aid in identifying outliers.

---

[8]Huber's M-estimator computes a coefficient, and standardized values below it receive a weight of 1, with larger absolute values receiving smaller weights as their extremity grows. Tukey's biweight estimator standardizes scores using the studentized distribution, gives zero to observations with values greater than 4.685, and assigns smaller weights to scores that are increasingly extreme. Hampel's redescending M-estimator involves three coefficients (*a*, *b*, and *c*). Standardized values greater than the *c* coefficient are effectively discarded, scores between zero and the *a* coefficient are retained, and scores falling between the *a* and *b* coefficients are given weights with values that decrease as their extremity increases. Andrews's wave uses a smooth curve (a sine wave) to determine weights to adjust data values. Scores above a certain point are effectively discarded.

Extreme Values

			Case Number	Value
STORIES	Highest	1	2	19
		2	11	13
		3	10	13
		4	16	11
		5	5	.[a]
	Lowest	1	21	3
		2	24	4
		3	9	5
		4	1	6
		5	19	6

a. Only a partial list of cases with the value 11 are shown in the table of upper extremes.

It also includes a histogram identical to the one already seen.

A stem-and-leaf plot also is included. The table shows that when the first digit in the data is 0, the next digit was 3 for one piece of data, 4 for the next piece of data, and so forth. This analysis also revealed that that one data point was identified "extreme" in comparison with the others. The associated diagram illustrates one extreme score that is shown as outside the range

```
        STORIES Stem-and-Leaf Plot

     Frequency          Stem & Leaf
       2.00          0 . 34
      14.00          0 . 56677778888899
       7.00          1 . 0111133
       1.00  Extremes    (>=19)

    Stem width:        10
    Each leaf:         1 case(s)
```

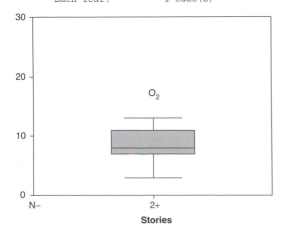

Stories

of the others. If attention is given to the causes for this unusual data point, it may be examined for possible deletion.

Checks on normal distributions for the data also were requested. The Q-Q normal probability plot contrasts the quintiles of the data distribution against those of a normal distribution. If the data points cluster near the line of predicted values (as they do here, except for the one outlier), the data are said to approximate a normal distribution.

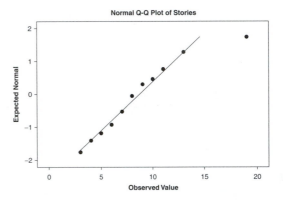

Tests for the normality of the distribution also are included. Though they involve statistical significance testing (a concept that has not yet been introduced), the tests are common parts of reports of dispersion and will be identified here. The Kolmogorov-Smirnov test examines the null hypothesis that the sample data do not differ from a normal distribution. Using a typical standard, a small number (usually .05 or smaller) in the "*Sig.*" column is taken as evidence that the data actually differ from a normal distribution. The Shapiro-Wilk test is reported when sample sizes are below 50 events. In both cases, the values in the "*Sig.*" columns are above .05. Hence, the assumption of an underlying normal distribution is *not* rejected.

Tests of Normality

	Komogorov-Smimov[a]			Shapiro-Wilk		
	Statistic	df	Sig.	Statistic	df	Sig.
stories	.166	24	.085	.926	24	.077

a. Lilliefors Significance Correction

Chapter 5

CORRELATIONS

Research questions often probe the relationships between variables by looking at simple associations. For instance, you might wonder about the relationship between the extent of public speaking experience you have and the amount of communication anxiety you feel. Researchers might ask if the speed at which a report of an international crisis is filed is linked to its likelihood of containing inaccuracies. Others might wonder how strong the relationship is between communicator competence and satisfaction in marriage. These sorts of matters invite using correlations. This chapter deals with the notion of a correlation, elements of the correlation, conditions that affect correlations, and forms of correlations.

THE NOTION OF CORRELATION

In simplest terms, a **correlation** is "the extent to which two or more things are related ('co-related') to one another" (Vogt, 2005, p. 64). Correlations simply identify the degree to which scores on different variables *coexist*. Whether the associations are causally related or not depends on the design of the study and is not directly measured by this statistic.

Interpreting Correlations

A correlation coefficient can have a value ranging from −1 to +1. Relationships at these extremes (sometimes called "unit relationships") are rare. Most of the time, researchers find correlations that take the form of decimal numbers, or fractions. The correlation coefficients themselves may indicate several types of relationships.

Direct Relationships

A **direct relationship** is indicated by a correlation coefficient with a positive sign (although, of course, a positive sign rarely is included; it is implied by the lack of a negative sign). This type of correlation shows that as one variable increases, so does the other. Such a

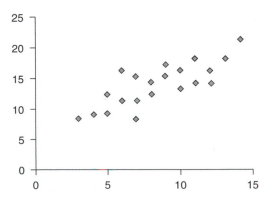

diagram as the one on the left reveals direct correlation (.79 in this example). One might imagine that the variable on the horizontal axis is a set of ratings of the amount of eye contact a speaker has with an audience, and the vertical axis is the perceived persuasiveness of the speaker. The positive sign (assumed, at least) of the coefficient indicates that the relationship is a direct one. The greater the correlation, the closer the data points are to an imaginary line that might be drawn through the center of the distribution.

One might wonder what a correlation of zero would look like. Aside from an unusual random pattern, there are two ways that a correlation coefficient of zero could be achieved. First, if one of the "variables" actually is a constant, then it has no variability, and the correlation would necessarily equal zero. At the top of the next page are two illustrations of this pattern.

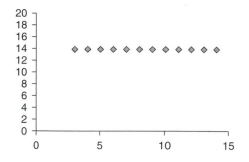

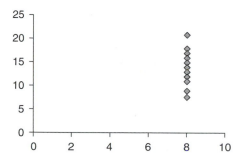

As can be seen, in each case there is no variation present in one of the two variables. The reduction or absence of variation is called range restriction and results in artificially diminished correlation coefficients.

Second, a zero correlation could be found if a symmetrical pattern in all directions from the center were found, such as shown in the diagram on the right. A perfect circle also would produce a correlation of zero.

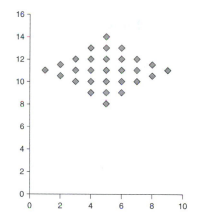

Inverse Relationships

Correlation coefficients preceded by negative signs indicate that the relationship is **inverse**, which means that as one variable increases, the other one decreases. The negative sign indicates the direction of the slope, not subtraction. Hence, a negative sign does not indicate that the magnitude of a correlation coefficient is "less than" that of another correlation coefficient. For instance, the diagram below and to the right shows a correlation that is −.79, which is a high correlation, though it is inverse. In particular, the variable on the horizontal axis might be communication apprehension and the variable on the vertical axis might be the ratings of communication responsiveness. The scatterplot indicates that the more communication apprehensive a person is, the lower is one's rating of communication responsiveness.

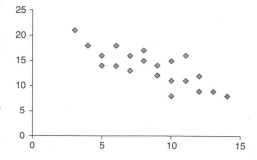

Curvilinear Relationships

Relationships can form curves in the data. If the relationships show such curves, they may be called **curvilinear** as a matter of shorthand. The exact nature of the curves, however, can be very different.

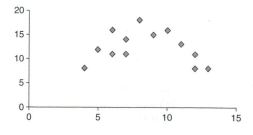

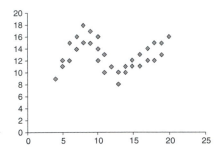

Sometimes, curves may have one or more points of inflection, where the curve changes direction. For instance, the curvilinear scatterplot to the left indicates that the two variables increase together until a point is reached (around a level of 9 of the X variable) where an increase in one variable is associated with a decrease in the other. After another point (around a level of 14 of the X variable), increases in one variable are again associated with corresponding increases in the other.

Doing a Correlational Study

Completing a correlational analysis takes some doing. First, a correlational study begins with a hypothesis (or at least a problem question) that probes the association between variables. Rather than asking if there is a simple difference between the means of two or more groups, correlational hypotheses probe whether there is a variation in one variable as another variable changes its values. For instance, researchers might suggest the hypothesis that "there is a direct relationship between students' perceptions of a teacher's source credibility and the amount of nonverbal immediacy behaviors," or they might advance the notion that "there is an inverse relationship between the amount of jealousy communicated in messages between romantic partners and the length of their relationships." In short, a correlational hypothesis asks if there is an association between one set of scores and another.[1]

Second, to examine correlations, researchers must gather data on two measures (and sometimes more than two measures) to permit examination of the "co-" relationship under study.

Third, not only do researchers look at the relationships between two variables, but they also take steps to consider the potential influences of other variables on the relationship. Either by reviewing literature or theory, or through personal observation, researchers prepare "short lists" of other intervening variables that might influence relationships. Then, these individual variables can be controlled or, at least, measured in the research study so that they may be studied and statistically explained.

Fourth, once researchers decide to use correlations, they must check the assumptions that underlie using the specific correlational tool. Naturally, the assumptions for different types of correlations are different. Before researchers can complete correlation studies, they must examine and report the evidence that assumptions underlying the use of the statistics have been met. As the tools identified in this chapter are considered, their assumptions will be identified.

Though all these steps are important, under most circumstances, researchers do not usually spend time in the final report sharing the details of their reasoning about the first two matters listed. The remaining items, however, must be discussed and handled in the research report.

---

[1]One could say that hypotheses that express differences also ask whether there is a change in one variable as another variable changes its values. Indeed, the argument can be made—and has been made—that correlational methods may be applied to the same data that researchers examine when testing for differences between means. Indeed, Kelly, Beggs, and McNeil (1969) argued that the correlational approach could be applied to data tested for mean differences, with the same substantive results.

Indeed, the final item, providing evidence that the assumptions underlying the statistical tests have been satisfied, must be covered in appropriate parts of the report dedicated to methods and results of statistical analyses. Finally, after these steps are completed, the researchers are in a position to complete the correlation itself.

ELEMENTS OF THE CORRELATION

There is more to a correlation than a formula. To get a sense of what is involved, a little dissection would be in order.

Components of Correlations

Three of the most essential elements of correlation are the line of "best fit," the intercept, and the slope. Though interrelated, these elements have separate meanings and roles.

Line of "Best Fit" (Line of Regression)

If one were to plot the data to be correlated, it would be possible to send a line through the middle of them. This line (often called a line of regression) would show the general relationship that exists, despite natural variation from one data point to another. This line would be drawn to represent the minimum possible distance of the line from the data points. Constructed using a method known as the "least squares," this line would be a good approximation of the overall relationship.[2]

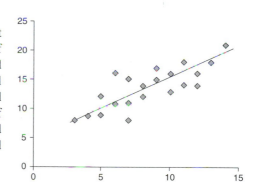

The Intercept

The line of "best fit" goes through data points, but it could be extended across the vertical axis. The **intercept** is the value of the line of "best fit" at the point at which it intersects the vertical axis (also called the *y*-axis or the ordinate). The intercept, thus, is "the expected value of the dependent variable when the value of the independent variable is zero" (Vogt, 2005, p. 155). There also can be a horizontal intercept, but it need not be discussed in this introductory treatment. Furthermore, although predictor variables can have negative values, for ease of explanation here, we will consider examples where variables have positive values. The value of

---

[2]The least squares line is drawn to minimize the sum of squares error term, $\sum e^2$. In turn, $\sum e^2$ is the sum of squared differences between the predicted and the actual values of the dependent variables $(Y - \hat{Y})$. The predicted value of the dependent variable, $\hat{Y}$, is computed by the linear regression equation $\hat{Y} = a + bX$. Constructing the line of best fit involves identifying a combination of the intercept a and the slope of the regression line b that produces the smallest $\sum e^2$. To compute b, the researcher divides the covariance of the X and Y variables by the standard deviation of the X or predictor variable. To compute a, the researcher uses the formula $a = \bar{Y} - b\bar{X}$. To draw the line of best fit, the researcher computes the predicted value for two points and draws a line with this slope through all the data points. Because this sort of work is done electronically these days, we will not cover this process further.

the intercept can be tested to determine if it is statistically significantly different from zero. Correlations permit predictions to be made *after* the point of the intercept. For a direct correlation, below the point of intercept, the correlation does not inform our predictions. For inverse correlations, of course, above the point of intercept, the correlation does not inform our predictions.

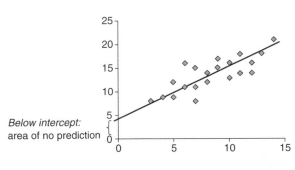

Below intercept: area of no prediction

For instance, suppose a researcher asked employees to rate their satisfaction with their jobs (the dependent variable on the vertical axis) on a scale ranging from 1 to 11. The researcher might find that there is a positive association between job satisfaction and the predictor variable, the amount of communication feedback received from managers. If the intercept were 3.0, this finding would indicate that the correlation does not apply to the prediction of job satisfaction scores below 3.0. Of course, as measurement becomes increasingly sophisticated, the slope of the line of best fit might lead to lower and lower intercepts. Then, the correlation would apply to a wider and wider range of dependent variable scores.

Slope

The **slope** of the line of "best fit" is its angle. These slopes may have positive or negative values that indicate the slope's direction. Thus, a direct correlation has a positive slope, and an inverse relationship is indicated by a negative slope.

Avoiding Confusion Between Correlation and Causation

A nonzero correlation does not mean that a causal relationship has been established. A correlation coefficient is only a measure of how much the variables coincide with each other. If there were a causal relationship between variables, we would expect to observe a strong correlation, but it is not the case that a strong correlation alone means that a cause-and-effect relationship exists. Other possibilities may explain high correlations.[3]

---

[3]Identifying a causal relationship often is viewed as an example of logic, rather than statistics, because claims about causal relationships between variables have been based traditionally on the fulfillment of the Humean criteria, as elaborated for the social sciences by Paul Lazarsfeld and his coworkers (see Hyman, 1955):

1. There exists a nonzero association between X and Y.

2. X precedes Y.

3. The relationship between X and Y is not spurious. (Snuder & Hagenaars, 2001, p. 4)

Though there are some different views of causality, there are three major ways that the notion is used in social science research.

Cox and Wermuth (1996) distinguished between three interrelated senses of causality: first, an association that cannot be explained away by other variables; second, as an inferred consequence of some intervention; third, as the first and the second, but then augmented by some understanding of a process or mechanism accounting for what is observed (pp. 219–228). They actually favored the third sense of causality. We fully agree. (Snuder & Hagenaars, 2001, p. 8)

- A third factor may explain high correlations. For instance, until the virtual elimination of polio, there was a strong correlation between the per capita amount of ice cream consumed during a month by North Americans and the number of polio cases. Casual observers wondered if something in ice cream might have contributed to susceptibility to polio. Of course, the reason for the high correlation was that polio was a disease with its highest incidence during the warm summer months. Naturally, ice cream sales tended to increase during the summer months as well.

- Sometimes the causal relationship exists, but it is in the opposite direction presumed by individuals. For instance, it was observed that the greater the number of small appliances one owned, the fewer children one tended to have. This information seemed to suggest a new breakthrough in family planning: sending small appliances such as toasters and hair dryers to places where the population was exploding. Of course, the causal relationship was not in the direction implied by the statement; it was in the opposite direction. If you had few children, you could afford to buy small appliances for yourself, but if you had many children, you might not have spare money to buy many small appliances.

- Sometimes correlations seem to advance causal relationships when the research methods used did not permit drawing causal claims. For instance, survey research (Wheeless, 1978) showed a high correlation between one's amount of self-disclosure, trust, and interpersonal solidarity ("feelings of closeness between people that develop as a result of shared sentiments, similarities, and intimate behaviors" [Rubin, 1994, p. 223]). But the survey measured all these matters at the same time. Identifying a clear starting point may not really be possible. The survey method may show an association among variables, but not which variable may trigger any effects.

In sum, then, to draw causal conclusions, researchers need to use research designs (such as experiments and long-term historical studies) that may assess these matters directly. Correlations alone cannot ensure that a causal relationship has been identified.

The Correlation Coefficient

The sample correlation coefficient is symbolized with some variation of the letter r. For population correlations (and in many conceptual discussions), the equivalent of r in the Greek alphabet, ρ (*rho*, pronounced "roe"), is used. Yet, it is a fact that notation in different statistics books is not always standard. Some statistics books do not distinguish population from sample correlations. In fact, some statistics texts even reserve *rho* to identify the Spearman rank order correlation. In this work, traditional notation is used.

Interpreting the Magnitude of Correlation Coefficients

A correlation coefficient may be difficult to assess just by looking at the coefficient itself. Helpful aids, such as those found in Table 5.1, suggest initial ways to interpret the meaning of a correlation coefficient. Nevertheless, to understand "whether a correlation coefficient is large or small, you have to know what is typical" (Jaeger, 1990, p. 68). In a study of the persuasive effects of evidence, a correlation of .40 would be considered quite high, but a correlation of .50 between two measures of communicator competence would be considered

Table 5.1   Typical Correlation Interpretation Guidelines

Overall Correlations Regardless of Signs	Koenker (1961, p. 52)		Losh (2004, citing G. Lutz)		J. Cohen (1988)	
	r	*Verbal Interpretation*	*r*	*Verbal Interpretation*	*r*	*Verbal Interpretation*
1.0			1.0	"Perfect"		
.95		"Highly dependable relationship"				
.90	.80 to 1.00					
.85			.76 to .99	"Very strong"	"Large"; *r* = .371 corresponds to a difference *d* of .8 standard deviation units or more, which Cohen labeled as a large difference (p. 25)
.80						
.75		"Moderate to marked relationship"			above *r* = .371	
.70	.60 to .79					
.65						
.60			.51 to .75	"Strong"		
.55		"Fair degree of relationship"				
.50	.40 to .59					
.45						
.40						
.35		"Slight relationship"	.26 to .50	"Moderate"	.243 and above but under .371	"Medium"; *r* = .243 corresponds to a difference *d* of .5 standard deviation units or more, which Cohen labeled as a medium difference (p. 25)
.30						
.25	.20 to .39					
.20		"Negligible or chance relationship"	.11 to .25	"Weak"	·10 *or* above and under .243	"Small"; *r* = .100 corresponds to a difference *d* of .2 standard deviation units or more, which Cohen labeled as a small difference (p. 25)
.15						
.10	.00 to .19					
.05			.01 to .10	"Very weak"		
0						
			0	"No relationship"		

quite low. Thus, above all else, the researcher should consider the research situation when interpreting correlation coefficient sizes. Nevertheless, all other things being equal, Table 5.1 provides some guidelines to help researchers translate their numbers into the initial languages of interpretation of results.

The Coefficient of Determination

Students sometimes think that correlations indicate *percentages* of variability. It is important *not* to make this mistake. For instance, the following picture shows what a rela-
tionship might look like if the variables represented by the two circles had a correlation of .77. The shaded area shows the co-relationship shared by the two variables. Even though the association is strong, you can see that there is a part of each variable that is not at all associated with the other variable. The total of the two circles represents the total variability. To find the percentage of variability in one variable explained by a knowledge of the other alone, researchers traditionally have been encouraged to square the correlation (which would yield a coefficient of .59 in this case). This number is called the **coefficient of determination** and may be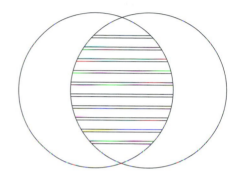
interpreted as a percentage. Typically, researchers would claim that 59% of the variation in one variable may be explained (or determined) by a knowledge of the variation in the other variable alone.

It must be mentioned, however, that the coefficient of determination has been the object of some serious criticism. When two variables are correlated with each other *and* "some latent variable [an underlying factor or construct] underlies scores on both measures . . . the latent variable is responsible for the covariance between the measured variables. In this model, the correlation coefficient itself provides the appropriate coefficient of determination" (Ozer, 1985, p. 312).[4] Though some scholars have disagreed with aspects of this conclusion (Steiger & Ward, 1987), there is little doubt that using the coefficient of determination may "grossly underestimate the magnitude of a relation" (Ozer, 1985, p. 307). In cases involving categorical data, the *unsquared* coefficients of association may produce interpretations that are more intuitively meaningful than coefficients of determination (D'Andrade & Dart, 1990). Furthermore, Beatty (2002) explained that "in general, squaring correlations and other measures of association has been unjustified in the social sciences. These incorrect calculations produced gross underestimates of effects, followed by misleading evaluations of research and theory" (p. 609).

---

[4]A distinction often is drawn between percentages of "variance" and percentages of "variation." Instead of looking at the variance, which is based on squared differences from means, D'Andrade and Dart (1990) urge researchers to rely on correlation coefficients that report "accurate estimate[s] of the proportion of variation (not variance) accounted for" (p. 50).

Special Discussion 5.1

Misleading Correlation Magnitudes and the Binomial Effect Size

Communication researchers sometimes despair over disappointingly small correlation and effect sizes. One survey (Hemphill, 2003) found that fewer than 3% of all studies in social psychology had correlations above .50. Yet, finding modest effect sizes can be of some value. The concept of the "binomial effect size display" is useful (Rosenthal, 1983; Rosenthal, Rosnow, & Rubin, 2000; Rosenthal & Rubin, 1982a, 1982b).

Here is the reasoning. Suppose that the results of a correlational analysis could be reduced to a dichotomous situation, such as pass or fail, or persuaded or unpersuaded. For instance, researchers might study whether trial lawyers influence verdicts when they ask questions to achieve rapport during the jury selection process. The outcome would be "guilty" or "not guilty" verdicts that might be identified as an overall "probable guilt" rating. In such a study, Reinard and Arsenault (2000) found an effect size correlation of .176. If the probability of guilt in the minds of jurors were divided evenly, .50 and .50 (the same as if they decided by randomly guessing at the probability of defendant guilt), a small correlation of .176 might not be sniffed at. To compute the "binomial effect size display," the correlation is split in half (.176 divided in half becomes .088). This amount may be added to or subtracted from the .50-.50 random split to reveal something very interesting. When added to 50, the result is .588 or 58.8%. Subtracted from .50, the result is .412 or 41.2%. These numbers mean that if there were an initial .50-.50 split in the jury judgment, failure to use the questions to build rapport would be associated with a guilty verdict 58.8% of the time. Using such questions would be associated with a probability of guilt reduced to 41.2%. Put another way, the proportion of the time that using this communication strategy would move subjects from decisions of guilty to not guilty would represent a 58.8% to 41.2% shift. Such numbers suggest the practical value of even modest effect sizes.

COMPUTING THE PEARSON PRODUCT-MOMENT CORRELATION

The oldest formula for computing a correlation was developed by Karl Pearson and, not surprisingly, bears his name. This correlation may be used when one wishes to correlate two variables that are measured on the interval or ratio level.[5] There are two major ways to compute the Pearson product-moment correlation, though they all give the same result. To emphasize the logic of the correlation, the original method, which uses z scores, will be presented first. Then, the alternative popular computational approach will be described.

Conceptual Notions of Correlational Formulae

The earliest approach to the correlation involves taking the averages of the products of z scores for each variable. As a first step, the raw data must be transformed into z scores. These z scores permit researchers to represent data as if the scores were units under the standard normal curve. Then, the correlation will be computed by the following formula:

---

[5]There are, however, ways to apply this correlational method to other forms of data, including nominal level measures. In fact, the correlation methods developed for other levels of measurement really involve adaptations of the Pearson product-moment correlations.

$$\rho = \frac{\sum z_x z_y}{N}.$$

In this formula, z_x represents each respondent's z score of the X variable. The z_y represents each respondent's z score of the Y variable. The N represents the total number of subjects in the population. Though it may be obvious from this formula, it should be mentioned that with population characteristics, it is presumed that z scores were computed using the formula for z that includes *population* data:

$$z = \frac{X - \mu}{\sigma}.$$

If *sample* data are used, computing the Pearson product-moment correlation is a little different from the population formula. This new formula is

$$r = \frac{\sum z_x z_y}{n - 1}.$$

In this formula, $n - 1$ is used to indicate the number of events in the sample minus one (for estimating the population intercept from knowledge of sample data alone). The values z_x and z_y represent each respondent's z scores on the X and Y variables, respectively. Because sample characteristics are used, it is understood that the z scores were computed using the sample data, as in the formula

$$z = \frac{X - \overline{X}}{s}.$$

Building Block Formula Box 5: Correlation

If z scores are computed using σ, the following formula for population correlation may be used:

$$\rho = \frac{\sum z_x z_y}{N}.$$

If z scores are computed using s, the following formula for sample correlation may be used:

$$r = \frac{\sum z_x z_y}{n - 1}.$$

To illustrate how this formula would work, consider the example in Table 5.2. This example shows a sample from six individuals on two measures related to communication in business settings. The researcher wants to know if there is a relationship between a person's "communication satisfaction" at work (measured by Hecht's [1978] scales) and the perception of active teamwork on the job (measured by the "teamwork" subscale of the Organizational Culture Survey [Glaser, Zamanou, & Hacker, 1987]). The communication satisfaction measure has a possible range of scores from 16 to 112, and the teamwork scale has a possible range from 8 to 40. As can be seen, by transforming the data into z scores, it is quick work to identify a correlation coefficient.

Table 5.2   Computing the Pearson Product-Moment Correlation Using the z Score Method

H: There is a direct correlation between communication satisfaction and perceptions of the extent of teamwork on the job.

Applying the data from two measures drawn from each of six employees, one finds:

Subject	Communication Satisfaction X	$X_i - \bar{X}$	$z = \dfrac{X - \bar{X}}{s}$	Teamwork on the Job Y	$Y_i - \bar{Y}$	$z = \dfrac{Y - \bar{Y}}{s}$	$z_x * z_y$
Tom	100	29	1.44	23	2	0.28	0.40
Dick	80	9	0.45	32	11	1.56	0.70
Harry	76	5	0.25	20	−1	−.14	−0.04
Larry	70	−1	−0.05	21	0	0	0
Moe	40	−31	−1.54	10	−11	−1.56	2.40
Curly	60	−11	−0.55	20	−1	−0.14	0.08
Mean:	$\bar{X} = 71$		$\bar{Y} = 21$				$\sum z_x * z_y = 3.54$
Standard deviation:	$s = 20.15$		$s = 7.04$				

Applying the formula for a correlation based on sample data reveals

$$r = \frac{\sum z_x z_y}{n - 1}$$

$$r = \frac{3.54}{6 - 1}$$

$$r = .708 = .71$$

Thus, a direct correlation was found. To interpret it using the guidelines provided here would suggest that it is a "marked," "strong," or "large" correlation coefficient.

It is usually a good idea to plot the data. In this case, the relationship is clearly a direct one. As one variable increases, so does the other.

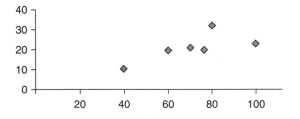

Computation of the Pearson Product-Moment Correlation From Raw Scores

Though the formula for computing correlation coefficients from z scores is simple and clearly shows the logic of correlations, there is another way to compute correlations from raw scores. To save a couple of steps, the same answers may be obtained by using this formula:

$$r = \frac{\text{Covariance}\,(X, Y) \text{ or } s_{xy}}{s_x s_y}.$$

To compute the covariance, you need to multiply the difference between each score and its mean for each of the two variables to be correlated. This formula (including its division by $n - 1$, because we are dealing with sample statistics—indicated by the s_x and s_y) is:

$$\text{Covariance } (X, Y) \text{ or } s_{xy} = \frac{\sum \left[(X_i - \overline{X}) * (Y_i - \overline{Y}) \right]}{n - 1}.$$

Though the brackets probably are not necessary, they are included here to keep the order of the arithmetic clear. Mathematically, of course, this formula is equivalent to the z score method. Because the covariance has some uses in other advanced statistics, it makes sense to show the computation of this element separately. Table 5.3 shows what happens when the raw score formula is applied to the same data used in the z score example in Table 5.2.

Table 5.3   Computing the Pearson Product-Moment Correlation Using the Raw Score Method

H: There is a direct correlation between communication satisfaction and perceptions of the extent of teamwork on the job.

Applying the data from two measures drawn from each of six employees, one finds:

Subject	Communication Satisfaction X	$X_i - \overline{X}$	Teamwork on the Job Y	$Y_i - \overline{Y}$	$(X_i - \overline{X}) * (Y_i - \overline{Y})$
Tom	100	29	23	2	58
Dick	80	9	32	11	99
Harry	76	5	20	−1	−5
Larry	70	−1	21	0	0
Moe	40	−31	10	−11	341
Curly	60	−11	20	−1	11
Mean:	$\overline{X} = 71$		$\overline{Y} = 21$		$\sum [(X_i - \overline{X}) * (Y_i - \overline{Y})] = 504$
Standard edeviation:	$s = 20.15$		$s = 7.04$		

Applying the formula for covariance produces

$$\text{Covariance } (X, Y) \text{ or } s_{xy} = \frac{\sum [(X_i - \overline{X}) * (Y_i - \overline{Y})]}{n - 1}$$

$$\text{Covariance } (X, Y) \text{ or } s_{xy} = \frac{504}{6 - 1} = 100.8$$

When inserted into the formula for correlation, the appropriate computations become

$$r = \frac{\text{Covariance } (X, Y) \text{ or } s_{xy}}{s_x s_y}$$

$$r = \frac{100.8}{20.15 * 7.04}$$

$$r = \frac{100.8}{141.86} = .711 = .71$$

Depending on the interpretation guide used, this correlation coefficient may be called a "marked," "strong," or "large" one.

MATTERS AFFECTING CORRELATIONS

Correlations can be distorted by unequal dispersion around the line of "best fit" and the presence of outliers. These conditions also can lead researchers to draw misleading conclusions. Researchers who use correlations often overlook these factors, but they should be identified, and steps should be taken to deal with the situation.

Homoscedasticity

Correlations can be affected by the presence of unequal variation around the line of "best fit" and problems with variability. For correlations to be meaningful across the range of scores, they must have "equal scatter" or **homoscedasticity**. This condition means that variability in scores of one variable is stable through the entire range of the other variable.

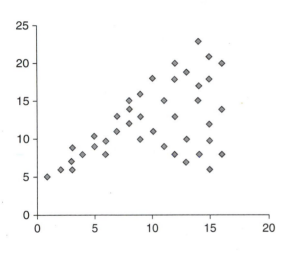

The reasoning is simple: Correlations provide shorthand to help predict the value of one variable from the knowledge of another. The accuracy of the shorthand depends on the consistency of variability across the range of data. For instance, the scatterplot to the left shows what might happen with data reflecting a correlation of .54. As can be seen, the correlation applies quite nicely to the data that are on the left side of the distribution, but the wide spread to the right indicates that the correlation does not apply well to all of the distribution.

The absence of equal scatter, called **heteroscedasticity**, does not completely invalidate a study, but it weakens the conclusions one may draw. Researchers may use transformations to eliminate statistical influences of heteroscedasticity, but the fundamental question remains: Why do data show unequal scatter? In addition to random sampling, there are three possibilities: (a) at least one variable in the correlation with a nonnormal underlying distribution, (b) the presence of indirect relationships between variables, or (c) the unexpected side effect of using a data transformation (after Wulder, 2002, ¶ 2). Thus, when researchers find heteroscedasticity, they should investigate sources of influence other than simple randomness that may be responsible. Though inspecting the scatterplot should be sufficient to identify this difficulty, sometimes researchers also like to check **residuals,** a process that will be covered as a standard step in multiple regression analyses.

Outliers

Outliers are extreme scores that do not fit the overall pattern of the data. When researchers produce plots of data, they may find that outliers are present. If these data points can be explained as coming from another population of events, they may be deleted from the study. For instance, if a researcher inspects the data and finds that an outlier score came from a respondent who was interrupted during the middle of completing a research questionnaire, the outlying response would seem to come from another population of events, one in which the survey respondents were distracted from the task. Such a "traumatic" instance might be deleted from the final sample. But if the researcher cannot identify a special circumstance that causes a piece of data to be defined as coming from a population other than the one from which the rest of the sample came, the outlying data point must be retained.

The effect of outliers can be surprising. For instance, the diagram on the right shows a correlation of .29. If outliers were present, the correlations could be affected dramatically. The set of four diagrams below shows what would happen if outliers were placed at different locations.

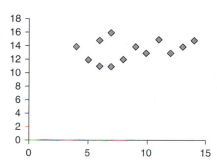

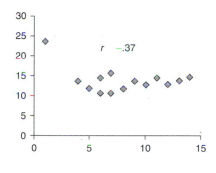

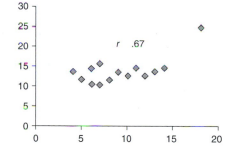

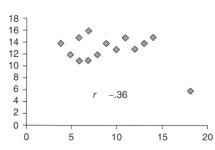

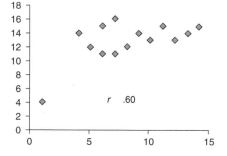

Even if a strong correlation were observed in the data, an outlier could prevent researchers from recognizing the relationships. For instance, the plot to the right indicates a correlation coefficient of .83. One outlier could cause coefficients to change greatly, as the diagrams below illustrate.

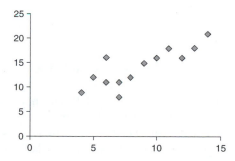

The diagram below, on the left, reveals a correlation coefficient of .10, and the diagram on the right shows a correlation of .07. In sum, the correlation coefficient is not an accurate summary of relationships if there are outliers. Hence, researchers need to plot data before making interpretations of correlations.

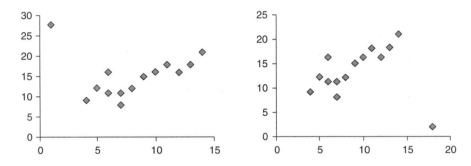

The overall variability in data affects the size of reported correlations. In general, the lower the variability among data values, the smaller the obtained correlation. Indeed, if a variable actually is held constant, the observed correlation is zero. In addition, though plots of bivariate normal relationships tend to look like the shape of a football, some distributions do not. The distribution below, on the left, shows what happens when a correlation of .72 is present. But if the middle-range values were missing, as shown in the diagram on the right below, the correlation would tend to jump artificially. In fact, the diagram to the right has a coefficient of correlation of .91.

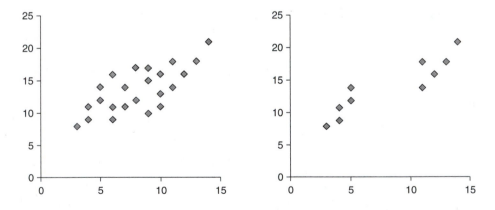

As you can see, it is more than helpful to look at charts of correlational output. It becomes essential if researchers are to avoid drawing the wrong conclusions.

METHODS OF CORRELATIONS

Though the Pearson product-moment correlation is the foundation for all measures of correlation, there are others that often are used in research. Four of the most commonly employed will be described here: the Spearman rank order correlation, the contingency coefficient, the point biserial correlation, and Kendall's coefficient of concordance.

A Comment on Nonlinear Correlation

One of the forms of correlation is, of course, curvilinear. But the Pearson product-moment correlation is actually the Pearson product-moment *linear* correlation, a term that means that this correlation method attempts to determine how well a *straight* line identifies data arranged on two axes representing variables. Another way to examine curved relationships with correlational methods involves an application of multiple regression correlation.[6] This approach, which is mentioned in Chapter 14, involves creating variables to represent quadratic and cubic functions and checking on changes in overall correlation coefficients.

Spearman Rank Order Correlation

When variables are measured on the ordinal level, an alternative correlation method may be suggested.[7] The Spearman rank order correlation considers two sets of ranks and then identifies the correspondence between the two sets. The formula for this correlation is

$$r_s = 1 - \frac{6 * \sum D^2}{n(n^2 - 1)},$$

where D^2 refers to the differences between the ranks on the
two variables of interest that have been squared;
n refers to the number of events in the sample.

Sometimes slightly different symbols are offered for the population correlation. The change to a population correlation instead of a sample correlation uses ρ_s for r_s and N for n.

Table 5.4 illustrates how this formula works. Suppose a researcher were interested in knowing the correlation between job applicants' ranking by personnel directors following screening interviews and the applicants' extent of previous communication training. Rankings could be made of the most trained applicant, the second most trained applicant, the third most trained applicant, and so forth. Of course, one could count the number of communication classes an applicant took in college, but rankings might give a convenient measurement. Similarly, the personnel directors could identify whom they perceived to be the "number one" best candidate, the "number two" best candidate, and so on.

As the example in Table 5.4 shows, sometimes there are ties in the ranks, and the Spearman rank order correlation does not have difficulty with this fact. One simply gives every item with a tied rank the average of the ranks for that measure (even if the average ranking requires including a decimal point). The Spearman rank order correlation is so simple to compute that it traditionally has been a popular tool among researchers who were involved in initial "data snooping."

---

[6]To test a correlation involving a curved relationship, we may use the correlation ratio, also known as η (eta). But this approach actually is merely a step in the application of trends analysis, an application of analysis of variance. Because computers have made quick work of such materials, it no longer is necessary to rely on the general tool, eta alone, except as a measure of effect size to follow analysis of variance.

[7]As another mildly irritating variation in the nomenclature of research statistics, some writers reserve the term "correlation" for measures that are on the interval or ratio level and refer to correlations for other measures as coefficients of "association."

Table 5.4   Spearman Rank Order Correlation

A researcher explored the following hypothesis.

> H: There is a positive correlation between job applicants' rank by personal directors following screening interviews and the applicants' communication training.

Six applicants for a job were ranked from best (1) to worst (6) of the candidates for the position. In addition, they were ranked according to the number of communication classes they took. The applicant who completed the greatest number of classes was ranked number 1, and the one with the fewest communication classes was ranked 6. Two candidates tied in the number of classes, and they were given the midpoint for the second and third rankings (2.5). The data appear below, along with computations for the Spearman rank order correlation.

Applicants	Rank by Personnel Directors	Ranks According to Number of Communication Classes Taken	D	D^2
Chasen	1	1	0	0
Ciro	2	4	−2	4
Lawry	3	5	−2	4
Wolfgang	4	2.5	1.5	2.25
Emeril	5	2.5	2.5	6.25
Perrino	6	6	0	0
				$\sum D^2 = 16.5$

$$r_s = 1 - \frac{6 * \sum D^2}{n(n^2 - 1)}$$

$$r_s = 1 - \frac{6 * 16.5}{6(36 - 1)}$$

$$r_s = 1 - \frac{99}{210}$$

$$r_s = 1 - .47 = .53$$

Thus, the correlation shows a "fair," "strong," or "large" direct relationship.

Using SPSS and Excel to Obtain Pearson and Spearman Correlations

Computing correlations is rarely done by hand these days. The availability of computers has made the work both increasingly efficient and accurate. To illustrate this process, data will be used from a study first introduced in Chapter 3. This inquiry dealt with CNN's news coverage of the September 11, 2001, terrorist attack on America. The data listed the number of stories broadcast by CNN for each half-hour period following the attack (9 a.m. EDT) through the period beginning at 9:30 p.m.

SPSS

To see if there is an association between the time of day and the number of news stories presented, a Pearson product-moment correlation may be used because the time of day is an interval measure and the number of stories presented is a ratio level measure. To compute the correlation, one begins by choosing *Correlation* from the *Analyze* menu. From the drop-down menu, one selects *Bivariate. . . .* From the *Bivariate Correlations* dialog box, click to select the variables and use the arrow key to transfer the variable list into the "Variables:" field. Check the box marked "Pearson" to choose the Pearson product-moment correlation. If the researcher wishes to use the Spearman rank order correlation method, the "Spearman" box should be checked. One may check the "two-tailed" box on the *Test of Significance* field to produce a *t* test exploring whether the observed correlation is statistically significantly different from zero. For practical purposes, the smaller the probability of this significance test, the lower is the probability that the observed correlation would be found if the population correlation were equal to zero.

Click on the *Options. . .* button. In the new dialog box, one checks the "Means and standard deviations" box to select reporting of these statistics. Checking the "Exclude cases pairwise" option selects a method for dealing with missing values.

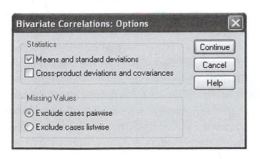

Clicking *Continue* and then *OK* produces the following output.

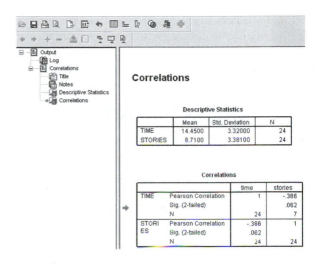

The observed correlation between these variables is −.386. This correlation would be interpreted as a "slight," "moderate" or "medium" inverse relationship depending on the interpretation guides used. The test of significance showed that the probability that this correlation coefficient differs from zero by random sampling error is .062, a result usually not enough to reject the null hypothesis that there is no relationship between the variables.

To check assumptions and examine the data, it is important to secure a plot of the data. To obtain this plot, one chooses the *Graphs* menu, followed by selection of *Scatter. . . .* From the *Scatterplot* dialog box, one selects *Simple* and then clicks on the *Define* button.

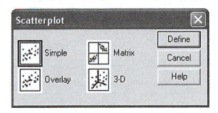

On the *Simple Scatterplot* dialog box, identify the variable to be placed on the *y*-axis (or vertical axis) and click the arrow to place it in the "Y Axis:" field. Then select the variable to be placed on the *x*-axis (or horizontal axis) and click the selection arrow to transfer this variable to the "X Axis:" field. As a matter of routine, the dependent variable is placed on the vertical axis and the independent variable is located on the horizontal axis. Then, click *OK*.

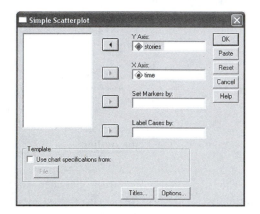

The results of the analysis appear in the SPSS Output Window.

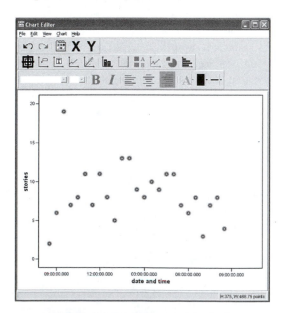

To add a line of best fit to the scatterplot, one double-clicks on the chart and opens the SPSS Chart Editor. Clicking on a data point in the grid

activates the chart. From the *Chart* menu, select *Add Chart Element,* followed by *Fit Line at Total.* This step calls up the *Properties* dialog box at the *Fit Line* tab. For a line of best fit, the *linear* radio button may be used. For *Quadratic* and *Cubic* functions, those options may be selected on separate presentations. In this case, only the method for fitting a linear line of best fit is illustrated. Clicking on *Apply* fits the line to the scatterplot.

Closing the *Chart Editor* produces the scatterplots with the lines of best fit included. The first diagram on page 107, on the left, shows an R^2 of .044, equivalent to a correlation coefficient of .21. The curvilinear trend in the diagram on page 107 on the right reports an R^2 of .19, equivalent to a correlation coefficient of .44. Even without further testing, it seems clear that the curvilinear pattern is an improved fit to the data. The distributions may show some difficulty with homoscedasticity, but it would be helpful to wait to see if any outliers are present before assessing whether the heteroscedasticity is great enough to warrant further attention.

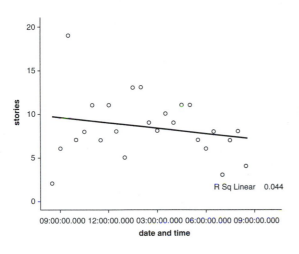

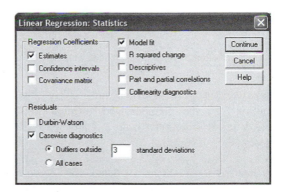

Some assumptions may be checked by looking at related subroutines in SPSS. Though examining residuals will be covered in Chapter 13, the identification of outliers will be described here. From the *Analysis* menu, the researcher selects *Regression* from the drop-down menu, followed by *Linear Regression*. In the *Linear Regression* dialog box, one selects stories as the dependent variable and time as the single independent variable. When there is only one predictor variable in multiple regression, it is equivalent to simple linear correlation. To check assumptions, special statistics should be selected. Hence, researchers click on the *Statistics. . .* button.

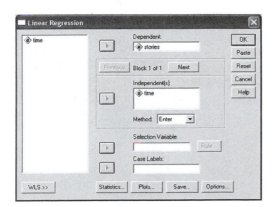

In the *Statistics* dialog box, the researcher checks the boxes for "Model fit," "Estimates" under *Regression Coefficients*, and "Casewise

diagnostics" under *Residuals*. This latter category permits identification of outliers. In particular, any outliers beyond a certain point will be recognized. In this case, the default is used to identify outliers that are at least three standard deviations from the mean.

After the researcher clicks the *Continue* and *OK* buttons, the output appears, including the following portions (see top of p. 108).

The Regression output begins with descriptive output. Other tables in the output reveal information about other assumptions underlying the use of correlations. The output was to include a list of any data points that might have been outliers falling more than three standard deviations from the mean. Because there were no such examples in the data, however, no list of such outliers appears in the output. If there were

Model	R	R Square	Adjusted R Square	Std. Error of the Estimate
1	.209(a)	.044	.002	3.568

Model Summary(b)

a Predictors: (Constant), date and time

b Dependent Variable: stories

any outliers, they would be identified by their case number in the data set.

To check whether the assumption of a bivariate normal distribution has been met, a plot of a variable's cumulative proportions against some other test distribution might be examined. For these data, a "P-P plot" may be requested by clicking on the *Plots* button from the *Linear Regression* dialog box.

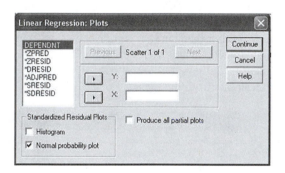

By checking the "Normal probability plot" option from the "Standardized Residual Plots" field, a researcher may secure a chart such as the following illustration.

Normal P-P Plot of Regression Standardized Residual

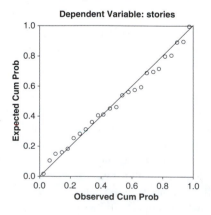

If the assumption is not met, the points for the dependent variable will tend to differ from the expected distribution represented by the straight line. As can bee seen here, however, the dispersion is very close to the line representing a normal distribution. Hence, the assumption of an underlying bivariate normal distribution seems reasonable.

Excel

To compute a Pearson product-moment correlation with Excel, one needs to make sure that the measures are clearly identified as interval or ratio. In Excel, the data are in a spreadsheet with columns marked A, B, C, and so forth. Thus, the "time" data must be transformed into numeric format data. One begins by highlighting the column of data to be transformed. In this case,

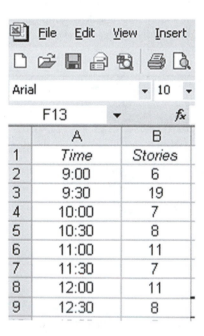

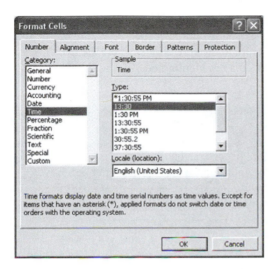

one goes to Column A (where the time of day variable is located) and clicks on "A" to make the whole column active. From the *Format* menu, the researcher clicks on *Cells...* from the drop-down menu that appears. In the dialog box that appears, the researcher makes sure the *Number* tab is chosen and that *Time* is selected from the "Category:" field. To transform the time from text characters, click on "13:30" to indicate the format in which the time data are to be represented.

From the *Tools* menu, the researcher selects *Data Analysis...* from the drop-down menu. Then, "Correlation" is selected from the dialog box.

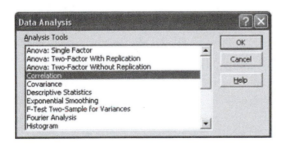

In the *Correlation* dialog box, the researcher clicks the *Columns* option for the "Grouped By:" radio button. Then the researcher clicks on ![icon], which appears next to the "Input

Range:" field. This step returns the researcher to the spreadsheet. Highlighting all the data starting in the first row of the first column and stopping in the last row of the second column produces the range identified in the *Correlation* range box.

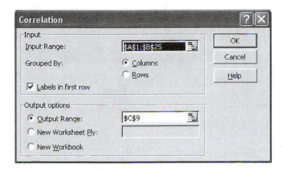

Clicking the ![icon] button returns to the *Correlation* dialog box.

Checking the box marked "Labels in first row" instructs Excel that the first row consists of variable names, not actual data values. The researcher then selects the "Output Range:" radio button from the "Output options" field. Clicking on ![icon] selects an empty cell where the output may begin to be placed. After finding a location on the spreadsheet, the researcher clicks the cell and then the ![icon] button to return to the *Correlation* dialog box. Clicking the *OK* button produces the results shown below. This correlation coefficient was −.386.

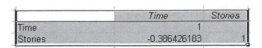

	Time	Stories
Time	1	
Stories	-0.386426183	1

Excel also can produce charts. From the *Insert* menu or from the toolbar, the researcher selects *Chart...* by clicking on this choice from the drop-down menu or by using the toolbar button. This step launches a "Chart Wizard" that guides the researcher through steps to create displays. This step activates a dialog box with a "Chart type:" field where display formats may be chosen. The researcher may select "XY (Scatter)" for a simple scatterplot.

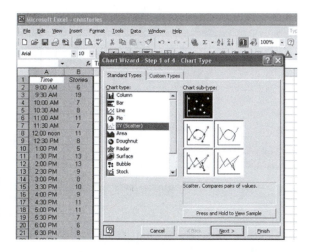

After the researcher clicks on the *Next* button, the Chart Wizard instructs the researcher to identify "Chart Source Data." The researcher selects the "Columns" radio button from the

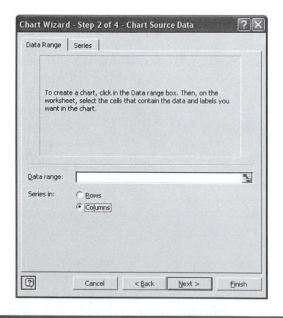

"Series in:" field. Then, the researcher clicks on the ▦ button in the "Data range:" field to return to the spreadsheet where the two columns of data are highlighted.

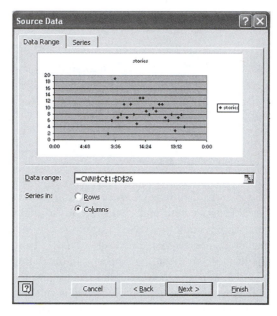

When this process is completed, the researcher clicks on the ▦ button on the *Chart Source Data* range box. Assuming no changes are required in the display options, researchers may click *Finish* on the Chart Wizard. The chart below appears on the spreadsheet.

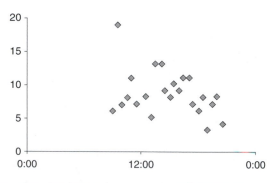

Special Discussion 5.2

Levels of Measurement for Variables	Form of Correlation
Both nominal measures	*Asymmetric lambda (λ):* used when comparisons are made between the number of events in the mode and one variable is identified as an independent variable
	Contingency coefficient (C): an application of chi-square that may be used when there are two or more categories for a variable
	Cramer's V: used when there are two or more categories for each variable
	Phi (ϕ) coefficient: an application of chi-square that is used when there are two categories for each variable to be correlated
	Symmetric lambda (λ): used when comparisons are made between the number of events in the mode (identification of which variable is the independent and which the dependent variable is relatively unimportant)
	Tetrachoric correlation: used when the two variables are false dichotomies that have been reduced into two nominal groupings
	Yule's Q: used if the two correlated variables have two levels each
One nominal and one interval or ratio	*Biserial correlation (r_{bis}):* used when one variable is an artificial dichotomy and the other variable is continuously distributed
	Point biserial correlation (r_{pbis}): used when one variable is a true dichotomy and the other variable is continuously distributed
Both ordinal measures	*Goodman and Kruskal's gamma (γ):* used when data are organized in tables of any size
	Kendall's tau a (τ_a) and tau b (τ_b): used when large numbers of tied ranks are involved
	Kim's d: used when large numbers of tied ranks are involved
	Somers's d: used when one variable is identified as the independent variable and the other is treated as a dependent variable
	Spearman rank order correlation (r_s): used when data are from two ordinal measures that may or may not have tied ranks
One ordinal and one interval or ratio	*Jaspen's coefficient of multiserial correlation:* used when data measured on the ordinal variable are reduced to this level of measurement from an originally normally distributed interval variable

(Continued)

Special Discussion 5.2 (Continued)

Levels of Measurement for Variables	Form of Correlation
Both interval or ratio	*Mayer and Robinson's* M_{yu}: used when the ordinal variable is composed of ordered levels from an underlying interval or ratio level variable
	Eta (η): (sometimes called the correlation ratio) an adaptation of analysis of variance that attempts to provide an estimate of nonlinear relationships
	Pearson product-moment correlation (r): used to identify linear correlations between variables

ALTERNATIVE FORMS OF ASSOCIATION

Other forms of correlation coefficients may be computed when data are not interval or ratio level measures. Three of the most common are the contingency coefficient, the point biserial correlation, and Kendall's *W.*

Contingency Coefficient

When both variables are presented as nominal categories, the contingency coefficient may be used to determine the size of the association. This measure requires researchers first to compute the chi-square (χ^2) test. Since this matter is covered elsewhere (Chapter 10), a computational example will not be presented until that point. It is worth noting that the formula is simply a variation of the chi-square statistic:

$$C = \sqrt{\frac{\chi^2}{\chi^2 + N}}.$$

The maximum possible value of the contingency coefficient is limited by the number of categories in the levels of the groups.

Point Biserial Correlation

Sometimes researchers need to examine associations between a continuous variable and a true dichotomous (nominal) variable. For instance, suppose a researcher in forensics education wonders if losing or winning competitive debates is associated with delivery, a factor sometimes measured on debate ballots with 5-point scales. The dichotomous variable identifies one category (in this case, a loss in a debate round) as the "lower subgroup" and another category (a win) as the "higher subgroup." Each group has a .5 chance of occurring if wins and losses are random. Table 5.5 illustrates the use of the point biserial correlation.

Table 5.5 Point Biserial Correlation

A researcher wished to examine this hypothesis:

H: There is a positive association between academic debaters' ratings of delivery and winning debates.

Based on results from a random sample of 10 debaters from different debate teams competing in preliminary rounds at a forensics tournament, data on delivery and win-loss records were obtained. The "higher subgroup" mean $\overline{X}_p$ consisted of the mean delivery ratings for the debaters winning their debates. The "lower subgroup" mean $\overline{X}_q$ consisted of the mean delivery ratings for the debaters losing their debates. The s_t represents the standard deviation of delivery ratings.

Debater	*Rating on Delivery Scale*	*Win-Loss in Debate Round (Win p; Loss q)*
Manny	3	Loss
Moe	2	Loss
Jack	4	Loss
Parnelli	3	Loss
Tim	3	Loss
Lucy	4	Win
Jeanine	4	Win
Jon	4	Win
Robert	3	Win
Larry	5	Win
	$s_t = .85$	

$$r_{pis} = \frac{\overline{X}_p - \overline{X}_q}{s_t}\sqrt{p * q}$$

$$r_{pis} = \frac{4 - 3}{.85}\sqrt{.50 * .50}$$

$$r_{pis} = \frac{1}{.85}\sqrt{.25}$$

$$r_{pis} = 1.18 * .5 = .59$$

Thus, the hypothesis was supported with a coefficient showing a "fair," "strong," or "large" relationship (depending on the interpretive guidelines used by the researcher).

Kendall's Coefficient of Concordance

When there are ranks of more than two variables (sometimes representing different raters), the coefficient of concordance is used. In fact, the method often is used with interval level data that are reduced to ranks for the purposes of the computation. It is very popular in many assessments of reliability among different raters. The formula for this correlation is

$$W = \frac{S}{(1/12)k^2(n^2 - n)},$$

where S is the sum of the squares of the observed deviations from the expected sum of ranks, k is the number of items ranked, and n is the number of individuals ranked in the sample.

Suppose a person wondered if there were a correlation between a competitive speaker's ratings for organization, delivery, and use of evidence in a speech. That is, if a speaker is good in one skill area, is he or she generally good in all these factors? Table 5.6 shows such a

Table 5.6   Kendall's Coefficient of Concordance

A researcher wishes to examine the following hypothesis:

> H: Agreement exists among ratings of the speaker's organization, delivery, and use of evidence in a competitive speech.

To compute Kendall's W, the researcher collected the following data set.

Speaker	Ranking of Speech Organization	Ranking of Speech Delivery	Ranking of Evidence Use	Rank Sum
Patty	1	2	1	4
Maxine	2	4	4	10
Laverne	3	1	5	9
Rita	4	3	3	10
Susan	5	6	2	13
Rock	6	5	6	17
$N = 6$				$\sum$ Rank Sum = 63

$$W = \frac{S}{(1/12)k^2 (n^3 - n)}$$

To calculate S, we begin by computing the expected rank sum (or mean rank sum). This amount is computed by dividing the $\sum$ *Rank Sum* by the number of items given rankings. In this case, the expected sum ranks would be 63/6, which is 10.5. S is computed by taking the sum of the squared differences between the each rank sum and the expected rank sum, or

$$S = \sum (\text{rank sum}_i - \text{expected rank sum})^2.$$

In this case it is $S = (4 - 10.5)^2 + (10 - 10.5)^2 + (9 - 10.5)^2 + (10 - 10.5)^2 + (13 - 10.5)^2 + (17 - 10.5)^2 = 89.5$. Inserting the numbers, the formula becomes

$$W = \frac{89.5}{(1/12)3^2(6^3 - 6)}$$

$$W = \frac{89.5}{(1/12)9(216 - 6)}$$

$$W = \frac{89.5}{.75(210)} = \frac{89.5}{157.5} = .568 = .57$$

computation. You also could substitute three raters instead of three variables and see how much agreement exists among raters who assess the same things. In such a case, the coefficient of concordance would measure overall reliability among raters. As can be seen, the coefficient of concordance has only positive values. Thus, it is an assessment of agreement and cannot identify inverse relationships.

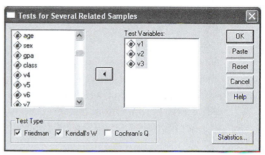

Kendall's coefficient of concordance may be computed in SPSS. The researcher begins by choosing *Nonparametric Tests* from the *Analyze* menu. Then, the researcher chooses *K Related Samples. . . .* In the dialog box that appears, the variables that constitute the three or more observations to be associated are highlighted and moved to the "Test Variables:" field. Then the researcher selects "Kendall's W" from the *Test Type* section.

After clicking *OK,* the output found to the right appears. In addition to descriptive information, the report of the test statistics is provided. In this case, a small correlation of .076 is found to be statistically significantly different from 0 (as indicated by a small probability in the significance report).

Test Statistics

N	864
Kendall's W[a]	.076
Chi-Square	131.538
df	2
Asymp. Sig.	.000

a. Kendall's Coefficient of Concordance

Chapter 6

ENSURING RELIABILITY AND VALIDITY

To use statistical tools, researchers must have sound measurements of variables. To help explore these matters, researchers present arguments based on a combination of statistics and artistic reasoning to show that their measures are acceptable ones. This chapter reviews some of the major forms of statistics that are used to measure the acceptability of measures.

THE NOTION OF MEASUREMENT ACCEPTABILITY

Researchers present information about the consistency and accuracy of measures *before* assessing major research questions and hypotheses. There are three major reasons for this state of affairs.

- First, to do a sound empirical study, all variables must be operationally defined. An **operational definition** is "a description of the way researchers will observe and measure a variable" (Vogt, 2005, p. 220). The soundness of the operational definitions must be identified before researchers can know that the research variables actually were *operating* their inquiries. For measured variables, statistical tools may be used as direct evidence of the adequacy of measures. For manipulated or experimental variables, however, a **manipulation check** may be used to assess the accuracy of the assumption that the variables were operating in the study.
- Second, measurement adequacy underlies the very ability to use statistical tools. Imperfect measurement limits the size of relationships that can be found. Thus, when computing statistics, measurement inconsistencies decrease the chances of observing relationships among variables, even if they really exist.
- Third, inadequate measurement prevents capturing the true value of a variable. A **measured value** is equal to the true value of the variable plus measurement error. To the extent that measurement error is increased, researchers are kept from identifying the true value of the variable measured.

Sound measurement is not just a nicety. Researchers who wish to make progress in answering related research questions must show evidence of accurate measurement.

HOW TO DO A STUDY OF MEASUREMENT ADEQUACY

The communication field's major publications require researchers to report measurement reliability as a standard part of empirical research. To get such information, researchers could design a study dealing with measurement issues alone, but researchers rarely have resources to do a second measurement study. So, taking a calculated risk, researchers typically select or develop tentative measures, complete their studies, and then examine the measures (discarding measures that failed to pan out).

Isolating Measurements and Securing Baselines

In many experiments, participants are pretested, exposed to some experimental materials, and then posttested on the same measures used in the pretest. To obtain baseline data, pretest measures are preferred. Sometimes posttest measures are artificially stable because respondents gain experience from their pretesting. Nevertheless, measures can be only as adequate as the consistency of responses from inexperienced participants. With specialized gauges such as oscilloscopes or voice analyzers, researchers need to recalibrate the gauges *before* initial use to get a stable baseline measurement.

There also is a somewhat technical reason for preferring baseline measures before influences of independent and experimental variables have their impact. The overall amount of random error around a mean tends to increase as the mean does (W. G. Hopkins, 2000b, p. 3; Nevill & Atkinson, 1997). Similarly, if an experiment is designed to lower the dependent variable mean, *both* the mean and the variance will tend to *decrease*. Because measurement adequacy assessment tools rely on the variance in one form or another, using posttest scores to compute reliability will produce an inaccurate assessment of reliability, sometimes overestimating reliability and sometimes underestimating reliability. Of course, researchers often have only posttest scores available. Under these circumstances, they must do the best they can with the available data. Yet, it may be wise for the researchers to add limiting comments that the reported reliability coefficients (and any related validity coefficients) may have been affected by changes in sizes of random variation as a function of mean size.

Ensuring Consistency of Measurement Applications and Instructions

Instructions must be given to study participants who complete questionnaire items, who rate observed behavior, or who use gauges. In general, the more detailed the instructions, the more consistent the measures tend to be and, in many cases, the more trustworthy or valid they may be. Naturally, when reporting a study's measurement adequacy, it is vital to share the information about instructions.

Though this difficulty may emerge in any empirical study, using inconsistent instructions is notorious in some interview studies. During face-to-face interviews, respondents often make comments or ask questions of the interviewer. A researcher might be asked, "How should I answer if I don't know much about the topic?" One interviewer might respond, "Just give your first impression," but another might say, "Just say you neither agree nor disagree." On another occasion, an interviewer might be asked to define words in a question. Very different definitions of varying accuracy might be provided. If interviewers have been trained to respond in the same way, the data may have consistent meaning. But if every interviewer is left to his or her own ingenuity, differences in answering questions might increase instability in the data. This circumstance would not necessarily mean that the study is unsound, though the populations to which one could generalize results would be difficult to identify. It would mean, however, that the reported reliability would be troubled by larger background or error variance than otherwise if people were responding consistently to the measure.

Securing Consistent Data With Consistent Measurement Elements

Researchers must assure that the data examined for measurement adequacy are from the target population used in the full study. If the study sample and the measurement sample are not the same, it is vital to show that characteristics of the sample—such as sample sources and demographic characteristics—are the same as those in the actual research study.

Sample size also must be big enough to justify the use of statistical tools. Insufficient sample sizes can seriously affect the meaning of reliability coefficients. For instance, if you have only two events and use what is known as "test-retest reliability," the coefficient (a correlation, actually) would be 1.0 or −1.0. Small samples tend to inflate reliability coefficients. W. G. Hopkins (2000b, p. 4) explains:

> The values of the limits of agreement depend on the sample size of the reliability study from which they are estimated. In statistical terms, the limits are biased. The bias is <5% when there are more than 25 degrees of freedom (e.g., >25 participants and two trials, or >13 participants and 3 trials), but it rises to 21% for 7 degrees of freedom (8 participants and 2 trials).

Thus, it makes sense to have an adequate sample size. The tools to be used also may affect the choice of samples to be included. Chapter 2 describes some sample sizes required for different sorts of studies and statistics.

Assessing Reliability and Validity While Looking for Signs of Abnormal Variability

Some researchers try to avoid the trouble of verifying the adequacy of their measures by using measures that others have previously validated. An extensive treatment of such measures may be found in such volumes as *Communication Research Measures: A Sourcebook*, edited by Rubin, Palmgreen, and Sypher (2004).

A problem with failing to revalidate an existing measure is that it may be a "misconception" to suppose that "if Researcher A uses a test that Researcher B built a year ago and documented as being reliable, then Researcher A can use the test today and have full confidence that it will be reliable for him/her too" (Huck, 2003, ¶ 3). Indeed, the American Psychological Association Task Force on Statistical Inference explains:

> If a questionnaire is used to collect data, summarize the psychometric properties of its scores with specific regard to the way the instrument is used in a population. Psychometric properties include measures of validity, reliability, and any other qualities affecting conclusions. If a physical apparatus is used, provide enough information (brand, model, design specifications) to allow another experimenter to replicate your measurement process. . . .

It is important to remember that a test is not reliable or unreliable. Reliability is a property of the scores on a test for a particular population of examinees (Feldt & Brennan, 1989). Thus, authors should provide reliability coefficients of the scores for the data being analyzed even when the focus of their research is not psychometric. Interpreting the size of observed effects requires an assessment of the reliability of the scores. (Wilkinson & Task Force on Statistical Inference, 1999, p. 596)

This standard reminds researchers that each time they use measures, they are obligated to show that the measures are sound (Thompson, 1994b).

RELIABILITY

Reliability of a measure occupies more concern and effort among researchers than other aspects of measurement. In general terms, **reliability** is "the internal consistency of a measure" (Reinard, 2001, p. 441). If you took a measure of communication apprehension and scored 80 and then took the same measure a day later and got an 80, you would conclude that the measure is reliable for you because it is stable and gives consistent results. If you scored 80 one day and then—without any significant changes in your life—you scored 78 the next day, the measure would not necessarily show perfect reliability. But people are not machines; even with sound measures, there would be some inconsistency.

To identify the extent to which a measure is reliable, a statistical tool called a **reliability coefficient** is used. This measure is a form of correlation coefficient "that measures the degree of consistency of a measure" (Reinard, 2001, p. 441). These coefficients are a bit different from other correlations, however. They range in value from 0, indicating no reliability, to 1.0, indicating perfect reliability. Indeed, the square root of the reliability coefficient "is the correlation of a test with true scores" (Nunnally, 1978, p. 220). Ideally, reliability coefficients should be as close to 1.00 as possible, but interpretations often are based on guidelines such as the following:

.90 and above: highly reliable

.80–.89: good reliability

.70–.79: fair reliability

.60–.69: marginal reliability

under .60: unacceptable reliability

Some publications set minimum standards for reliability of reported measures of variables. The author is unfamiliar with any publication that regularly accepts reporting results of measures with reliability coefficients below .60.

Sources of Unreliability

Reliability coefficients can be affected by several factors. Among these sources of unreliability are the four listed here.

Uncontrolled Variation in the Test Setting or Instrument (Repeatability)

If the testing situation is filled with distractions and disruptions, scores obtained on any kind of measurement instrument may be inconsistent. This problem is essentially a set of flaws that introduce the problem of repeatability of measures. Thus, in measurement studies, researchers take care to keep the testing situation as free of contaminating influences as possible.

Differences Among Respondents or Raters (Reproducibility)

Individuals respond in wildly different ways to measures. This problem is called a defect of **reproducibility** among different participants or raters. Sometimes it occurs because the researcher has accidentally sampled individuals from very different populations. In many circumstances, researchers find—especially in the case of questionnaire items—that the language of the measurement items is understood by some, but not by others. A related source of unreliability involves the use of different raters. Their different experience, training, or moods can produce great inconsistencies.

Lack of Precision in the Measurement Tool

Sometimes the measurement instrument does not have precise degrees and individuals have a difficult time giving responses. "**Precision** refers to how finely an estimate is specified" (Helberg, 1995, ¶ 30, bold added). Early thinking was that measures with few scale intervals were most reliable because they were believed to minimize response set (Cronbach, 1946, 1950), especially when respondents were uncertain about the content of the scale items and about their knowledge of how to answer. But lack of precision actually tends to increase item difficulty. Thus, it reduces overall reported reliability coefficients by a combination of enhancing background variation and reducing variation that may show increased correlation coefficients.

In recent decades, researchers have found that increasing the number of scale intervals improves scale sensitivity.[1] This sensitivity enhances abilities of individuals to register

---

[1] The evidence is generally supportive of this statement, though for different reasons. One inquiry found that moving from a 5-point to a 7-point scale enhances sensitivity (Diefenbach, Weinstein, & O'Reilly, 1993). Some argue that reliability is maximized as the number of scale items is minimized, especially if it is not greater than two intervals (Bardo & Yeager, 1982a, 1982b; Bardo, Yeager, & Klingsporn, 1982). But if a measure has limited variability restricted by a very small number of scale items, this lack of variability will be reflected in the artifact of increased reliability; it also means that the measure minimizes identification of relationships with other variables. Other studies have found that actual Likert scale reliability increased as intervals changed from 2 to 5 points (Lissitz & Green, 1975) but no more than 5 points. But other large scale Monte Carlo simulation studies have found that as measures are increased beyond 5 to 7 points, interrater reliability and accuracy of judgment increases (Cicchetti, Showalter, & Tryer, 1985; Jenkins & Taber, 1977). Yet others have suggested that there was no reduction in test-retest and internal reliability when scales moved from 2 to 19 intervals (Matell & Jacoby, 1971), or from 5 to 100 points (Diefenbach et al., 1993). Cummins and Gullone (2000) found that studies that have suggested the advantages of reduced numbers of scale items were either misinterpretations of results (i.e., the McKelvie [1978] study), or were based on interpreting some reliability coefficients and ignoring others (i.e., the Chang [1994] study).

differences in their degrees of positive and negative ratings. A meta-analysis of 131 market-ing studies found that reliability of measurement increases as the number of scale items increases (Churchill & Peter, 1984). Yet, some categories—especially "sometimes" and "occasionally," on 7-point scales to measure satisfaction—increase variation on the items, indicating that participants do not consistently understand the meaning of the words used to describe the scale positions (Cummins & Gullone, 2000). This condition means that respon-dents have only two "positive" scale positions on 5-point scales to indicate degrees of posi-tive attitudes. Cummins and Gullone recommend the use of 11-point scales (zero to 10) to overcome this deficiency. In addition to adding degrees of precision, 11-point scales are equally as reliable as scales containing fewer intervals. Weng (2004) found that reliability increases when the number of scale categories is increased along a range from 3 to 9 points and when verbal labels for each of the scale positions are included (as opposed to labeling just the end points). Of course, there may well be a point where adding scale points does not help sensitivity much. Yet, it is clear that limiting a measure's precision generally reduces reliability.[2]

Length of the Measure

Short tests tend to be less reliable than long ones. In short tests, differences in item variances cannot really be expected to "balance out" in the long run. This degree to which the length of a measure is affected by measurement length is predictable from the Spearman-Brown prophecy formula. This formula states that

$$r_n = \frac{nr}{1 + (n - 1)r},$$

where r is the original reliability, n is the number of items on the new test divided by the number of items on the original test, and r_n is the reliability of the test when composed of n times the number of items on the original test.

Suppose that you had a 40-item test with a reliability of .80, but you wanted to have a 20-item short version of the test. Because 20 items randomly selected from the full test is

---

[2]Though only occasionally used, there is a correction for the range restriction on reliabilities coefficients

$$r_{XX} = 1 - \left[\frac{\sigma_x^2}{\sigma_X^2} (1 - r_{xx}) \right],$$

where r_{xx} and σ_x are the reliabilities and standard deviation of the original group, σ_X is the standard deviation of the unrestricted group, and r_{XX} is the corrected reliability.

one half of 40 items, the value of n would be $\frac{1}{2}$. Applying the formula, one would be able to predict the reliability of the shorter measure accordingly:

$$r_n = \frac{nr}{1 + (n-1)r}$$

$$r_n = \frac{\frac{1}{2} * .80}{1 + (\frac{1}{2} - 1).80}$$

$$r_n = \frac{.40}{1 + (-.5).80} = \frac{.40}{1 + (-.4)} = \frac{.4}{.6} = .67$$

Of course, making a test small or large is not always simple. Two experts in research methods explain:

> The formula assumes that when we change the length of the test, we do not change its nature. Extreme increases in test length, however, introduces [*sic*] boredom and may reduce reliability. Added items or added periods of observation may not confer the same behavior or ability as the original test.
>
> *Note:* An increase in test length has a great effect on reliability but a much smaller effect on validity. (Isaac & Michael, 1981, p. 174)

Methods to Determine Reliability

"Studying the reliability of a measure is a straightforward matter of repeating the measurement a reasonable number of times on a reasonable number of individuals" (W. G. Hopkins, 2000b, p. 2). Thus, all methods of attempting to determine reliability share many of the same underlying concepts. Some of the most common reliability approaches will be mentioned here.

Test-Retest Reliability

This approach involves administering a measure twice and reporting the correlation between scores. The most obvious way to do a test-retest reliability measure is to employ a simple Pearson product-moment correlation between two tests. Unfortunately, if researchers use small sample sizes (under 15, for instance), the Pearson product-moment correlation will tend to be inflated. Thus, the **intraclass correlation coefficient** may be preferred. It also can be used when more than two tests are used (W. G. Hopkins, 2000a, ¶ 18). The formula for the intraclass coefficient requires the researcher to compute analysis of variance for repeated measures first:

$$ICC = \frac{F - 1}{F + k - 1}$$

$$\text{where } k = \frac{\text{number of observations} - \text{number of tests}}{\text{number of subjects} - 1}$$

If there are no missing values in the data set, the number of observations is equal to the number of tests times the number of participants. F is the observed ratio derived from the analysis of variance in which the dependent variable is the measure and the "between subjects" source of variance corresponds to the number of times the tests were applied to the participants.

For instance, suppose that a measure of marital communication satisfaction were given to 40 respondents and then given again 2 weeks later. This condition means that there were two tests on 40 participants. Because there were no missing values, the value of k is 2. In this case, the observed F ratio was 8. Thus, the formula for the intraclass correlation becomes:

$$ICC = \frac{F - 1}{F + k - 1}$$

$$ICC = \frac{8 - 1}{8 + 2 - 1} = \frac{7}{9} = .778$$

The observed test-retest reliability coefficient of .778 would be considered "fair" given the standard interpretation offered in this chapter.

As with all reliability estimates, test-retest reliability can be greatly affected by the sample. Furthermore, if the sample size is small and multiple trials or measures are involved, the correlation will be affected greatly by just a few extreme responses. The measure also is influenced by the length of time between tests. In general, researchers in the social sciences make retests within approximately 2 weeks after the initial test. Much delay beyond that point can increase the chance that nonrandom factors in the environment can significantly interfere with the test-taking behaviors.

Alternate Forms Reliability

This method consists of constructing different forms of the same test from a common pool of measurement items. Then, one takes two (or three) forms, administers them to the same individuals (varying the order of presentation), and computes the correlation between the two measures, or the intraclass correlations in the case of more than two measures. This approach assumes that because the tests consist of items drawn at random from the same pool of items, any differences in scores should be random. If the correlation among the measures is low, then the items in the pool would be identified as inconsistent with each other. In short, low reliability means that the test items do not measure the same content with any real consistency.

Split-Half Reliability

This method to determine a measure's reliability consists of dividing a test into two parts after giving it to a group of people, scoring the two parts separately, and checking consistency between the two scores. This measure emphasizes the homogeneity of the items a researcher is using to measure a concept. It might be mentioned that one does not casually score the two halves of a test. Instead, researchers usually score all the odd items as one test and the even items as another. Sometimes, if a pattern of content is detected in the items, researchers make a selection of one half of the test by selecting items at random as if they were drawing a random sample from a population.

To compute the measure, researchers take the correlation between the separately scored test parts. Because the correlation reflects the relationship between two "shorter" tests rather than the reliability of the full measure, researchers apply the Spearman-Brown prophecy formula to produce a final reliability estimate. In the case of the split-half method, the formula is simplified to

$$r_{sb} = \frac{2r_{xy}}{1 + r_{xy}},$$

where r_{xy} is the observed correlation between the two halves of the measure.

Item to Total Reliability

This method involves taking the average correlation of items with the total test score. The reasoning is simple. If you "pass" an item on a test, you should earn a higher total test score than someone who fails the item. Thus, each test item should score highly with the total test score. Sometimes, however, an item is not reliable. An item could correlate inversely with the total, which is clear evidence of its unacceptability. In another pattern, if everyone gets the same score on an item, it correlates 0 with the total test score. By use of Pearson product-moment correlations, point biserial correlations, or other shortcuts, the researcher may assess item reliability. As you can see, this form is often used to complete an "item analysis" of a measure.

Intercoder Reliability

This method of reliability involves determining the consistency of different raters who respond to the same events by using some sort of check sheet. Researchers may listen to the types of contributions made by people in a group discussion and then use a coding sheet to identify what types of comment each person made and how often. Similarly, a speech therapist could listen to the types of articulation errors a person made during spontaneous speech. These matters involve the use of some form of coding sheet applied to communication phenomena. In content analysis studies, such coding sheets are significant matters described in some detail. To determine reliability, one usually has several different raters (also known as "coders") examine a number of examples for evaluation.

There are several ways to compute such reliability information. Some methods involve simply counting the number of agreements in ratings of different "coders," but this strategy produces rather crude estimates. Instead, using a reliability formula that adjusts for the number of categories and the frequency of their use enhances accurate assessments. If a measure has three categories to code, reliability might be artificially high. For instance, if one were coding the types of physical violence in cartoon shows, one might use the categories of slaps, kicks, eye pokes, hits with objects, and other. Researchers may use either Cohen's kappa (κ; J. Cohen, 1960) or Scott's pi (π; Scott, 1955). But suppose that in our sampling of cartoons there were no eye pokes, and hits with objects constituted 75% of the examples of physical violence. Given the dominance of one category and the presence of infrequently used categories, Cohen's kappa would exaggerate the degree of reliability. On the other hand, Scott's pi adjusts for the frequency with which categories may be used (what is called the degree to which agreement would be expected by chance). Table 6.1 illustrates the ways that Scott's pi may be computed. If one has more than two raters, Scott's pi may be extended using an approach found by Fleiss (1971).[3]

---

[3]In the notation in the article introducing this method, Fleiss refers to it as κ. Because of this statement, some writers mistakenly think that it is an actual extension of *Cohen's* kappa when, in fact, inspection of the formulae reveals it to be an extension of Scott's pi.

Table 6.1   Computation of Scott's pi

The formula for Scott's pi in the case in which two raters are used is[†]

$$\pi = \frac{\text{proportion of observed agreement} - \text{proportion of expected agreement}}{1 - \text{proportion of expected agreement}}.$$

The "proportion of observed agreement" is computed by:

$$\text{proportion of observed agreement} = \frac{\text{number of raters} * \text{number of same ratings made}}{\text{total number of rating by all raters}}$$

$$\text{proportion of expected agreement} = \sum \text{proportions in each category}^2$$

Identifying the "number of same ratings made" is a simple task of looking at the ratings made by individual raters and counting the total number of times that they agreed on rating the same event with the same coding category.

Example: Consider the case of two coders rating the frequency of examples of each type of cartoon violence (slaps, kicks, eye pokes, hits with objects, other). The overall observed agreement is .90. To compute Scott's pi, one needs to examine the proportions. Then, Scott's pi may be computed as seen below:

Category	Observed Proportion	Squared Observed Proportions
Slaps	.05	.0025
Kicks	.12	.0144
Eye pokes	0	0
Hits with objects	.75	.5625
Other	.08	.0064
		Sum: .5689

$$\pi = \frac{\textit{proportion of observed agreement} - \textit{proportion of expected agreement}}{1 - \textit{proportion of expected agreement}}$$

$$\pi = \frac{.90 - .5689}{1 - .5689}$$

$$\pi = \frac{.3311}{4311}$$

$$\pi = .768$$

Thus, the reliability of the ratings using the coding sheet is .768, which is "fair" reliability.

For Fleiss's adaptation with more than two raters, the following formula may be used.

$$\frac{\overline{P} - \overline{P}_e}{1 - \overline{P}_e}, \text{ where}$$

$$\overline{P} = \frac{1}{Nn(n-1)} * \left(\sum_{j=1}^{k} n_{ij}^2 - Nn \right) = \overline{P} = \frac{1}{20 * 6 * (6-1)} * [(1^2 + 1^2 + 6^2 + 4^2 \ldots 1^2) - (20 * 6)],$$

[†]You may notice that the formula states that the "proportions" are used (with the decimal points included in their original locations) rather than percentages. If you use percentages as some textbooks mistakenly instruct when explaining this formula, the decimal points will be in the wrong locations and you will get the wrong answers.

(Continued)

Table 6.1 (Continued)

where N is the number of events to be classified;

n is the number of ratings per participant (number of raters completing ratings for the participant); and

n_{ij} is the number of raters who assigned the ith participant to the jth category.

$$\overline{P}_e = \sum_{j=1}^{k} p_j^2,$$

where p_j is the proportion of ratings in each of j categories.

Example: Consider the case of six raters identifying the frequency of four types of violence (slaps, kicks, eye pokes, and hits with objects) in "Three Stooges" films. Twenty examples were presented to coders. The data appear as follows:

Communication Event to Be Coded	Slaps $j = 1$	Kicks $j = 2$	Eye Pokes $j = 3$	Hits With Objects $j = 4$
1			6	
2		1		5
3		1		5
4	1		1	4
5	1	5		
6	6			
7	4			2
8		2	4	
9	1		5	
10	2			4
11		5	1	
12		1	5	
13			6	
14		5		1
15	6			
16				6
17		1		5
18	5		1	
19		6		
20	4		1	1
Totals	30	27	30	33
p_i	0.25	0.225	0.25	0.275

$$\overline{P} = \frac{1}{Nn(n-1)} * \left(\sum_{j=1}^{k} n_{ij}^2 - Nn \right) = \overline{P} = \frac{1}{20 * 6 * (6-1)} * [(1^2 + 3^2 + 6^2 \ldots 1^2)$$
$$- (20 * 6)]$$

$$\overline{P} = \frac{1}{600} * (546 - 120) = \frac{1}{600} * 426 = \frac{426}{600}$$
$$= .71$$

$$\overline{P}_e = \sum_{j=1}^{k} p_j^2 = .25^2 + .225^2 + .25^2 + .275^2$$

$$= .2513$$

With these pieces of information, the final formula for pi becomes

$$\frac{\overline{P} - \overline{P}_e}{1 - \overline{P}_e} = \frac{.71 - .2513}{1 - .2513} = .6127.$$

The reliability coefficient shows marginal reliability. It should be noted, however, that the correction for expected proportions makes this test deliberately conservative. This measure of reliability might seem a bit burdensome to compute. The Web site for this chapter of this book contains an Excel spreadsheet that may be used to automate the computation of Scott's pi with the researcher's own data.

Sometimes the question involves the degree to which a set of items is ranked by different evaluators. For instance, a researcher might have three judges rank a set of speeches. To determine their overall consistency, Kendall's coefficient of concordance (W) might be employed. This formula is found in Chapter 5 and is illustrated with an example in Table 5.5. Of course, sometimes researchers may wish to reduce their data to rank order data to compute such reliability, but unless it is necessary to use rankings, other methods would seem preferable.

Other Statistical Shortcuts

Conceptually, reliability methods should be equivalent (because they all are estimates of True Scores + Measurement Error) in practice, their results often are not. Some statistical shortcuts are popular because they seem to combine some of the best characteristics of other methods (especially alternative forms, split-half, and item to total correlation methods) into fairly simple formulae.

Cronbach's Coefficient Alpha

Coefficient alpha is a measure of the "consistency of items in an index" (Vogt, 2005, p. 71). In essence, coefficient alpha is an average of the correlations of pairs of items on a measure. Cronbach (1951) explains that coefficient alpha is equal to the average of all possible split-half reliabilities. Yet, this assertion is "true only when all the split-half coefficients are computed using r^2 (Feldt & Brennan, 1989) or in the unlikely event that all the test items are classically parallel" (Charter, 2001, p. 693). Nevertheless, coefficient alpha is a highly regarded and efficient way to measure reliability. Coefficient alpha is most appropriately used when the items are equivalent and have been combined into an index of many items (see Table 6.2). Because coefficient alpha may be computed after the study data actually have been completed, it has been a popular way that researchers simply "double-check" reliability.

Table 6.2   Coefficient Alpha

The formula for Cronbach's coefficient alpha is

$$\alpha = \frac{k}{k-1} * \left(1 - \frac{\sum \sigma_i^2}{\sigma_X^2}\right),$$

where k is the number of items on the measure, σ_i^2 is the variance of each individual item on the index; and σ_X^2 is the variance of the total of all items on the index.

If a researcher does not have population variances (for instance, σ_i^2 and σ_X^2) with which to work, corresponding sample statistics variances (s_i^2 and s_X^2) may be substituted as unbiased estimators.

(Continued)

Coefficient alpha is most popularly used when researchers have measures that do not have "right or wrong" answers to the items on a measure. So, such matters as attitudes, beliefs, or perceptions of communication behavior seem most appropriately involved. There also are adaptations of coefficient alpha to include multiple response categories that are identified according to ability or difficulty distributions of participant responses (Shojima & Toyoda, 2002).[4]

Research on coefficient alpha has shown it to be a versatile tool. Researchers can construct confidence intervals around coefficient alpha reliability estimates (Duhachek & Iacobucci, 2004). Furthermore, different coefficient alpha measures may be compared to see if they differ by more than would be expected to occur by random sampling error alone (Alsawalmeh & Feldt, 1994; Feldt, 1969, 1980; Feldt, Woodruff, & Salih, 1987; Hakstian & Whalen, 1976;

---

[4]Sometimes researchers think that a high coefficient alpha shows that a dimensionality of a measure has been accurately identified. Thus, they reason that there is little reason to complete additional validation work, including applications of factor analysis, where appropriate. But coefficient alpha does not measure the dimensionality of measures (Schmitt, 1996). This thinking treats measures and participants in what sometimes is called type 12 sampling. In this approach,

> components of a test (these components referred to as *conditions*—e.g., items, test forms, subtests, occasions, or raters) arose from a random sampling of subjects and of conditions from their respective populations . . . (Lord, 1955). We note here that we are using the word "test" in the broadest possible sense, to mean any measurement process having a number of component sources of data (conditions), scores on which are aggregated to yield a total. If Type 12 sampling is assumed, it is appropriate to make statements and inferences about the construct the test was designed to measure. (Hakstian & Barchard, 2000, p. 428)

Yet, when this type of sampling is used, coefficient alpha shows great biases when there are violations of the assumption of parallel form of items (Barchard & Hakstian, 1997). On the other hand, if the researcher is simply using coefficient alpha as way to measure the reliability of the particular items on the measure, coefficient alpha is a suitable and robust measure.

Table 6.2 (Continued)

Example: A researcher wanted to determine the reliability of an index designed to measure general satisfaction with patient-physician communication. The measure was composed of eight 7-point semantic differential–type scales. The variances for each of the items were 3.1, 2.5, 2.9, 3.7, 3.2, 3.4, 2.8, and 3.6, and the variance for the total test score was 70.

$$\alpha = \frac{k}{k-1} * \left(1 - \frac{\sum \sigma_i^2}{\sigma_X^2}\right)$$

$$\alpha = \frac{8}{8-1} * \left(1 - \frac{3.1 + 2.5 + 2.9 + 3.7 + 3.2 + 3.4 + 2.8 + 3.6}{70}\right)$$

$$\alpha = \frac{8}{7} * \left(1 - \frac{25.2}{70}\right)$$

$$\alpha = 1.14 * (1 - .36)$$

$$\alpha = 1.14 * .64 = .73$$

Thus, the overall reliability of this measure is only fair.

Woodruff & Feldt, 1986). It also is robust to violations of underlying assumptions. Even when data show nonnormal distributions, coefficient alpha seems to produce relatively unbiased reliability estimates (Sideridis, 1999).

Yet, coefficient alpha has some limitations. First, though it is robust to moderately heterogeneous data, when heterogeneity is large, it may underestimate (Osburn, 2000), overestimate, or both under- and overestimate (Raykov, 1998) reliability. Second, it may be imprecise when sample sizes are small (Bonnett, 2003). Third, if the items do not measure a single dimension with homogeneous true score variances (called the assumption of **essential tau-equivalence**), coefficient alpha may be inflated (Shevlin, Miles, Davies, & Walker, 2000) and the maximum possible value will not be 1 (Shojima & Toyoda, 2002). But if the violation is only moderate, coefficient alpha remains a robust measure (Feldt & Qualls, 1996; Zimmerman, Zumbo, & Lalonde, 1993). Fourth when measurement error terms are correlated, coefficient alpha is inflated (Komaroff, 1997). Fifth, because coefficient alpha is computed from ratios of variances, and it measures more than internal consistency of a scale (Streiner, 2003b), it shares this limitation with the measure of average intercorrelation (S. B. Green, Lissitz, & Mulaik, 1977).

The basic approach of coefficient alpha may not apply to all types of indices. For instance, where items are lists of symptoms (often called "effect indicators") or stressful life events, the presence or absence of events may not be highly correlated with each other. Yet, the presence of one or two symptoms or life stress events permits a researcher to make a reliable assessment even though the items do not have to associate strongly with all the other "effect indicators" (Streiner, 2003a). Under such circumstances, using approaches that assume a normal distribution may lead to systematic bias in sample coefficient alpha (Yuan, Guarncaccia, & Hayslip, 2003). This fact is not unique to coefficient alpha; it applies to all other reliability measures that attempt to identify high intercorrelations among items.

Using SPSS to Compute Coefficient Alpha. This is the most popular option among communication researchers today. To illustrate how to produce coefficient alpha, data will be used from a study completed about measuring attitudes toward persuasive messages. In this undertaking, an index of sorts was formed from four 7-point semantic differential–type scales to measure attitudes: wise-foolish; good-bad; positive-negative; and beneficial-harmful. In preparation for this analysis, all the scale items were scored so that the highest scores indicated positive ratings. In actual data collection, researchers routinely vary the poles of the scales to help prevent response set bias.

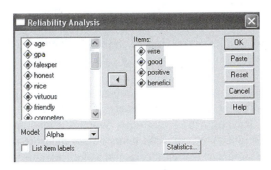

From the *Analyze* menu, the researcher chose *Scale* and then *Reliability Analysis. . . .* In the dialog box that emerged, the researcher selected the variables to be treated as scale items.

A model also was selected from the drop-down list at the bottom of the dialog box. In this case, the researcher chose *Alpha* to obtain Cronbach's coefficient alpha. The researcher also could have used dichotomous data (items that may be scored "correct" or "incorrect") for the scale items. The resulting coefficient alpha would have been equivalent to use of Kuder-Richardson 20 (K-R 20). Other models that could have been chosen include reliability information for *Split-half* models, *Guttman* models, and *Parallel* and *Strictly Parallel* models.

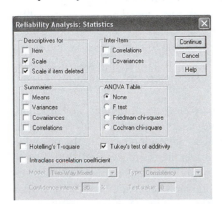

By clicking on the *Statistics. . .* button, the researcher opened the "Reliability Analysis: Statistics" dialog box. Under the *Descriptives for* field, boxes were checked to report statistics for the "Scale" and "Scale if item deleted." As can be seen, many other statistics also might be requested.

Clicking on the *Continue* button and then on the *OK* button on the *Reliability* dialog box resulted in the following output. As can be seen, scale reliability is high for these standard scales.

```
R E L I A B I L I T Y   A N A L Y S I S   -   S C A L E   (A L P H A)

                              Mean        Std Dev       Cases

    1.    WISE              5.5000         1.3061        52.0
    2.    GOOD              5.2885         1.3768        52.0
    3.    POSITIVE          5.3077         1.5280        52.0
    4.    BENEFICI          5.1731         1.4914        52.0

                                                      N of
    Statistics for      Mean    Variance   Std Dev  Variables
          SCALE       21.2692   25.5732    5.0570       4

    Item-total Statistics

                     Scale         Scale      Corrected
                     Mean         Variance      Item-           Alpha
                    if Item       if Item       Total          if Item
                    Deleted       Deleted    Correlation       Deleted

    WISE            15.7692       15.9849       .7547           .8943
    GOOD            15.9808       14.2545       .9064           .8407
    POSITIVE        15.9615       14.8612       .7111           .9120
    BENEFICI        16.0962       14.2063       .8132           .8732

    Reliability Coefficients

    N of Cases =      52.0                   N of Items =   4

    Alpha =     .9079
```

Using Excel to Compute Coefficient Alpha. This calculation in Excel does not feature the use of any built-in functions. Yet, on the Web site for this chapter is an Excel worksheet identified as "Coefficient Alpha" (COALPHA.XLS) that permits you to take your data and compute coefficient alpha. If dichotomous data are used, the results will be the same as K-R 20. In this worksheet shown at the top of page 134, you simply copy your data to replace the data in the worksheet with your own (following the instructions contained on the spreadsheet). As you can see, with the same data as used in the SPSS reliability example, the results are the same.

Kuder-Richardson 20

K-R 20 is used when items have responses scored as "passing" or "not passing."[5] This formula is actually equivalent to coefficient alpha for nominal data (Feldt, 1980), and the

---

[5]There is another formula, called Kuder-Richardson 21, which is less time-consuming to compute if one is completing reliability analyses by hand. It is not as accurate as the formula listed, but it sometimes appears nonetheless. It takes the form

$$\text{K-R } 21 = \frac{k}{k-1} * \left(1 - \frac{\overline{X}(k - \overline{X})}{ks^2}\right),$$

where k is the number of items on the measure, $\overline{X}$ is the mean for the test, and s^2 is the variance for the total test.

| | File | Edit | View | Insert | Format | Tools | Data | Window | Help | | | coefficient alpha |

	B	C	D	E	F	G	H	I	J
56									
57	Select the columns that you want as the variables of interest.								
58	Copy them into the shaded space below replacing the data that is there below.								
59		You must have the same space as is necessary to paste the data.							
60		So, insert any rows and columns within the grid that may be necessary.							
61		If you need to eliminate and rows or columns, do so from the center							
62		of the rows or columns array (do not delete the items in the exterior							
63		columns and rows).							
64	Answer the question in the shaded box to indicate the number of scale items.								
65									
66									
67		How many items on the scale?				4			
68							SUMS		
69			7.00	7.00	7.00	7.00	28.00		
70			6.00	6.00	7.00	6.00	25.00		
71			7.00	7.00	7.00	7.00	28.00		
72			4.00	5.00	5.00	5.00	19.00		
73			5.00	5.00	5.00	6.00	21.00		
74			4.00	3.00	4.00	4.00	15.00		
75			7.00	7.00	7.00	7.00	28.00		
76			4.00	4.00	4.00	4.00	16.00		
77			6.00	4.00	4.00	4.00	18.00		
78			1.00	1.00	1.00	1.00	4.00		
79			7.00	7.00	7.00	7.00	28.00		

118			7.00	7.00	7.00	7.00	28.00	
119			6.00	6.00	6.00	6.00	24.00	
120			7.00	3.00	5.00	2.00	17.00	
121		Variance	1.705882	1.895551	2.334842	2.224359	25.57315	
122								
123		Coefficient Alpha =		0.907854				
124								

precise computation is illustrated in Table 6.3. Both coefficient alpha and K-R 20 permit rapid interpretation of the internal consistency of measures. Hence, they have become dominant reliability coefficients of preference, perhaps promoted by their support in major data analysis programs.

Attenuation in Measurement Reliability

The lack of perfect reliability reduces the size of relationships that can be observed. This effect is called *attenuation* and consists of "a reduction in a measure of association caused by measurement errors" (Vogt, 2005, p. 15). Indeed, unreliability of a measure always works against a researcher finding a statistically significant relationship—it never increases the chances of finding one. The reason is that "no test can correlate more highly with a criterion

Table 6.3   Kuder-Richardson Formula 20

The formula for K-R 20 is

$$\text{K-R 20} = \frac{k}{k-1} * \left(1 - \frac{\sum P_i * Q_i}{\sigma_X^2} \right),$$

where

k is the number of items on the measure;

P_i is the proportion who answered the item "correctly";

Q_i is the proportion who did not answer the item "correctly"; and

σ_X^2 is the variance of the total of all items on the index.

The sample variance (s_X^2) may be substituted as an unbiased estimator of the population variance of the total test score.

Example: A researcher designed a six-item true-false test to measure comprehension of a speech's content. After the test was given to 60 respondents in a study, the variance for the total test was found to be 3.6. The proportion who passed the first item was .75 (equivalent to 75% passing the item, but we retain the decimal point), and the proportion not passing was .25. The proportion passing the second true-false item was .80 (not passing = .20); the proportions for the other items were third item, .65 (not passing = .35), fourth item, .70 (not passing = .30), fifth item, .20 (not passing = .80), and last item, .55 (not passing = .45). K-R 20 would be computed as follows:

$$\text{K-R 20} = \frac{k}{k-1} * \left(1 - \frac{\sum P_i * Q_i}{\sigma_X^2} \right)$$

$$\text{K-R 20} = \frac{6}{6-1} * \left(1 - \frac{(.75 * .25) + (.80 * .20) + (.65 * .35) + (.70 * .30) + (.20 * .80) + (.55 * .45)}{3.6} \right)$$

$$\text{K-R 20} = \frac{6}{5} * \left(1 - \frac{.1875 + .16 + .2275 + .21 + .16 + .2475}{3.6} \right)$$

$$\text{K-R 20} = 1.2 * \left(1 - \frac{1.1925}{3.6} \right) = 1.2 * (1 - .3313) = 1.2 * .6687 = .8022$$

than the square root of its reliability" (Towers, 2003, ¶ 7). So, researchers who use unreliable measures may miss identifying relationships that really are there because of the effects of the cloud of unreliability. The correction for attenuation often is suggested to prevent misreporting the size of effects that really are observed. The formula (Nunnally, 1978, p. 220) for the correction for attenuation is

$$\frac{r_{xy}}{\sqrt{r_x} * \sqrt{r_y}},$$

Special Discussion 6.1

Misguided Use of "Gain Scores"

Researchers often find that they are interested in testing hypotheses that involve a pretest followed by a posttest. But then, the question emerges: What should be done with such data? Common sense would lead one to think that subtracting the pretest from the posttest would be most appropriate. This approach is known variously as using "difference scores" or "gain scores" (even when there is no gain in the size of the measurement values at all).

Regardless of the name one uses, and the common sense behind it, this option is a dangerous one. In the first place, difference scores are less reliable than the scores on which the differences were computed. In the second place, the reliability of the difference scores depends not just on the reliability of the pretest and the posttest; the correlation between the two tests affects reliability of change scores. In fact, to the extent that such scores are highly related, the reliability of the change scores declines.

So, what should researchers do with pretest and posttest scores? One suggestion is to analyze the posttest scores and use a method called analysis of covariance (with pretest scores as covariates) to adjust the posttest scores based on the pretest score ratings. Then, in essence, a method of statistical control has permitted analysis of posttest scores after the scores have first been "equalized" by the covariate adjustment. Another suggestion has been that data should be transformed into z scores before the degree of change is computed. This approach, however, would seem to normalize the distributions (often on occasions when normality may not have been an issue) without necessarily overcoming the limited reliability that would be created by using change scores in the first place.

---

where r_{xy} is the observed correlation between variable x and variable y, r_x is the reliability for measurement of variable x, and r_y is the reliability for measurement of variable y.[6]

This computation is not really a "correction" as much as it is an estimate. The formula estimates the correlation between variables if measurement reliability had been perfect. This tool is very popular in studies that involve meta-analyses and modeling communication behavior.

VALIDITY

In addition to reliability matters, researchers are expected to argue for the validity of their measures. Unlike the case for reliability, there are few special statistical tools that are designed for validity. Instead, most validity questions involve using standard tools such as correlations to present evidence that a measure is valid.

---

[6]An alternative formula sometimes is suggested for reliability of restricted range scores. It is

$$r_{XY} = \frac{\sigma_X r_{xy}}{\sqrt{\sigma_x^2(1 - r_{xy}^2) + \sigma_X^2 r_{xy}^2}},$$

where r_{XY} is the corrected correlation, r_{xy} is the uncorrected correlation, σ_X is the standard deviation of the unrestricted group scores, and σ_x is the standard deviation of the unrestricted group scores.

The **validity** of a measure is "the consistency of a measure with a criterion (the degree to which a measure actually assesses what is claimed)" (Reinard, 2001, p. 444). To present an argument for measurement validity, researchers must share evidence that relates a measure to other behaviors or measures. Validity assessments permit researchers to identify any biases that would prevent ever identifying what is actually being measured. **Bias** in estimating population characteristics is "when the expected value of a sample statistic tends to over- or underestimate a population parameter" (Vogt, 2005, p. 25). This definition sounds as if it addresses sampling issues, but it also applies to measurement invalidity. For instance, if researchers attempted to measure the amount of previous communication training received by people in a sample, it would be a simple matter to ask respondents to list the number of classes they have had in the subject. But if a researcher asked participants to list only classes taken in colleges and universities, then courses taken in high school, during service in the military, or in business would be omitted. The measure would be biased. The observed measures would keep the researcher distant from the true value of interest. Similarly, there sometimes is debate about whether standardized tests such as the SAT are biased, particularly in favor of Anglo and Asian groups. These attacks claim that bias keeps the measures from being valid ones.

Methods to Determine Validity

To show that a measure is valid, researchers conduct supplementary tests to help identify whether the measure is acceptable. In reality, the types of validity information are limited only by the researchers' creativity. In practice, however, several validity methods are most prominent.[7]

Face Validity

"**Face validity** is the practice of examining the content of measurement items and advancing an argument that, on its face, the measure identifies what is claimed" (Reinard, 2001, p. 435, bold added). Researchers make arguments about the degree to which they believe that the content of the measure is related to the concepts being measured.

Expert Jury Validity

Expert jury validity (or just **jury validity**) involves "having a group of experts in the subject matter examine a measurement device to judge its merit" (Reinard, 2001, p. 435). Researchers actually make a point of asking for advice to revise the measure before it finally is used. Thus, expert juries actually interact with the researchers to develop measures.

---

[7]This statement is complicated somewhat by the fact that different labels often have been given to the forms of validity. Nunnally (1978) explains:

> Predictive validity [known as group validity] has been referred to as "empirical validity," "statistical validity," and more frequently "criterion-related validity"; content validity [face and jury validity] has been referred to as "intrinsic validity," "circular validity," "relevance," and "representativeness"; and construct validity has been spoken of as "trait validity" and "factorial validity." (p. 111)

Sometimes researchers provide jurors with scales to rate how well the content of the measure identifies the concept under inquiry. Jurors may rate each item on a 4-point scale ranging from "an irrelevant item" to "an extremely relevant item," such as the following:

| 1 | 2 | 3 | 4 |

an irrelevant item   an extremely relevant item

When this step is done, researchers sometimes use the Content Validity Index to reveal agreement. This formula is simply the number of items on a measure that received a 3 or 4 rating from all raters divided by the number of items on the measure:

$$CVI = \frac{\text{number of items receiving positive ratings of content relevance from all raters}}{\text{total number of items on measure}}.$$

This method sometimes is known as "content validity." In theory, presenting such an argument should be thorough and should include "how representative or adequate the content of the measure is: Are all aspects of the construct (substance, matter, topic) represented in the measure?" (Rubin et al., 2004, p. 2). Of course, these arguments are the same as those made for face validity. Indeed, the distinction between jury and face validity has been difficult to draw based on content information provided for validity. But one writer attempted to make a distinction based on practical research steps, rather than fundamental methods or issues that are addressed:

[F]ace validity concerns judgments about an instrument *after* it is constructed. . . . [C]ontent validity more properly is ensured by the plan of content and the plan for constructing items. Thus face validity can be considered as one aspect of content validity, which concerns an inspection of the final product to make sure that nothing went wrong in transforming plans into a completed instrument. (Nunnally, 1978, p. 111)

Face, jury, and content validity have been attacked. Pedhazur and Schmelkin (1991) argue that content validity, in particular, is not really a form of validity because it concerns the content of the instrument, and validity refers to arguments made about test scores. Even so, these methods are among the most commonly used ways to present arguments for measurement validity.

Criterion Validity

Though face validity and jury validity present artistic arguments to suggest that the measure really measures what is claimed, **criterion** (or **criterion-related**) **validity** presents an argument for validity by showing that it is related to some critical outside criterion.

Concurrent validity involves correlating a new measure with a previously validated measure of the same thing (Reinard, 2001, p. 434). Sometimes researchers update a measure because popular language changes or because previously identified measures are incomplete in some way. To show that the measure is valid, both the new and old measures are given to the same people. Then, a correlation (known as a **validity coefficient**) is computed between the two. Though the correlation should be high, it would not be perfect because the new measure is not a simple repeat of the old one. It might be mentioned that the argument for the concurrent validity of the new measure can be only as strong as the evidence was for the validity of the previous measure.

Predictive validity is the degree to which a measure predicts known groups in which the construct must exist (Reinard, 2001, p. 440). This validity form takes a measure, identifies a known group that must score highly on the measure, and compares it with at least one other group that is not known to score highly on the characteristic. A researcher developing a measure of satisfaction with marital communication might administer the scale to a group of people receiving conciliation services ordered by family and divorce courts. One would expect that these people should score much lower than a randomly selected group of married people who are not involved in conciliation services. If the measure failed to predict the known group, then the measure would be judged invalid.

Construct Validity

Construct validity involves studying the relationships between a new measure of a construct and its known properties in regard to another measure. This sort of undertaking usually is in the form of a full-blown study of construct validity, rather than as a part of another study. In construct validity, researchers correlate "a measure with at least two other measures, one of which is a valid measure of a construct that is known conceptually to be directly related to the new measure, and another one of which is a valid measure of a construct that is known conceptually to be inversely related to the new measure" (Reinard, 2001, p. 433). Researchers often talk about evidence of convergent and discriminant validity. An expert in measurement, Anne Anastasi (1968), explained these terms:

> In a thoughtful analysis of construct validation, D. T. Campbell (1960) pointed out that, in order to demonstrate construct validity, we must show not only that a test correlates highly with other variables with which it should theoretically correlate, but also that it does not correlate with variables from which it should differ. In an earlier article, Campbell and Fiske (1959) described the former process as convergent validation and the latter as discriminant validation. (p. 118)

Thus, researchers who do content validation studies review the literature to determine what other constructs are known to be highly related to the construct measured by the new test. Then, they determine constructs known to be inversely related (that is, as one variable increases, the other decreases). Finally, although many leave out this step, they identify constructs that are known to be unrelated to the construct measured by the new test. Researchers then find valid measures of each of the constructs they have selected and administer them to study subjects, along with the new measure. If the new measure is valid, *all* relationships should emerge exactly as the theoretically known characteristics of the constructs demand. Such studies are rigorous and demanding of the researchers. Thus, the claims of validity for such successful inquiries are treated with considerable respect in the research community. Of course, such studies may lead to great changes in research. For instance, Timothy Levine and his associates (Levine, Bresnahan, et al., 2003) produced strong evidence that when researchers rely on respondents to report their "self-construals" of themselves in cross-cultural research, the "measures of self-construals lack convergent validity [and] . . . catastrophic validity problems exist in research involving the use of self-construal scales in cross-cultural research" (p. 210). Prudent researchers have been compelled to seek new sorts of measures.

THE RELATION OF VALIDITY TO RELIABILITY

Statistically, there is an obvious relationship between reliability and validity. A reliable measure may not be valid, but a valid measure must be reliable. An analogy might help explain this matter. If you wanted to build a stairway to second-floor bedrooms of a house, you would need to ensure that the stairway was stable—in short, that it was a reliable stairway. If it wobbled and shook each time you tried to use it, you would never really get anywhere.

But if the stairway were built so that it could be used because it had great stability, it would be a reliable structure. Similarly, a test that is stable and repeatable has reliability.

But suppose that you used this stairway and found that it did not lead to the second floor bedrooms, but to an attic over a garage. The stairway would be pointed in the wrong direction and you would never get where you were supposed to go. The stairway would not be a valid stairway to the second-floor bedrooms. Similarly, a measure, even if is reliable, may not be valid if it is pointed in the wrong direction. Obviously, a valid stairway to the second-floor bedrooms must be reliable first, but it can be reliable without being valid. Statistically, the same pattern exists. If a measure is unreliable, it will add additional error variance to computations and will militate against researchers finding statistically significant relationships.

Some authors of communication research methods books have suggested that a measure could be valid even though it may be unreliable. Here is the reasoning: When qualitative methods are used, reliability may be weak even though people have great confidence in their assessments. For instance, Moss (1994) argues that when qualitative judgments are used to decide who should be hired as a new faculty member, clear standards may be missing. Despite unreliable evaluations, Moss believes that the data may be valid (though stubbornly challenging to define). In a technical argument, Salvucci, Walter, Conley, Fink, and Saba (1997) submitted that reliability is actually "invariance" and validity is a degree of "unbiasedness." Yet, because an unreliable sample has a high variance, it may be more likely to capture a population parameter than a sample that has a low variance with an expected value far from the corresponding population parameter. Such reasoning often has employed the analogy of a target. Consider the two diagrams below. The diagram to the left shows an ideal situation in which measures are both reliable (consistent) and valid (on target). The diagram to the right shows a situation that most writers would identify as "neither valid nor reliable" (Delaware Student Testing Program, 1999, ¶ 11).

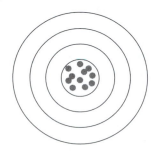
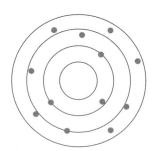

Special Discussion 6.2

Using Gauges in Research

Though many measures in communication studies involve responses to scales or open-ended questions, sometimes specialized gauges are used. For example, oscilloscopes may be used to assess vocal variety of speakers. In fact, gauges often are used when researchers want to assess actual behaviors rather than asking about perceptions and sentiments.

Conducting Repeatability and Reliability Measures. To begin the process of making assessments, it is important to secure information about repeatability as a component of overall reliability. Repeatability, in essence, is the variation in measurements when the same rater makes repeated measures of the same events. To interpret gauge adequacy, the researcher needs to identify how much variability is due to differences among raters and how much is variation within the gauge.

The following steps may be used:

1. Researchers must recalibrate the gauge before beginning the gauge capability study.

2. Design an efficient check sheet to keep track of the data. (The Web site for this book contains an example check sheet.)

3. Have at least two different individuals make at least two different ratings of the same events (in this case, several speech examples) that have been placed in random order.

4. Complete general assessments of overall variance attributable to equipment variation (reproducibility) and the variance from rater variability (repeatability).

To assess the capability of the gauge, the researcher needs to know the operating range within which the gauge needs to be capable of providing meaningful measurements. For instance, the range of normal hearing of different pitches would constitute the range in which the gauge must be capable. Just for the sake of an example, if the expected operating range of normal hearing were from 20 to 20,000 Hz (20 cycles/sec to 20,000 cycles/sec), the total operating range would be 19,800 Hz. If the total variance from reproducibility and repeatability were 990 Hz, the final gauge capability reliability estimate would be equal to 1 minus the proportion of the required operating range occupied by total equipment and rater variance. In this case, the proportion of the operating range occupied by combined sources of unreliability would be .05 (= 990/19,800). Thus, the overall gauge capability estimate would be .95 (= 1 − .05).

But some have tried to argue that the target on the right indicates a situation in which measures are unreliable but still valid. They assert that "you seldom hit the center of the target but, on average, you are getting the right answer for the group (but not very well for individuals)" (Trochim, 2002, ¶ 3). Such thinking does not reflect any mathematical relationships. As such, this alternative view is not endorsed here.

Part III

INFERENTIAL STATISTICS

Chapter 7

STATISTICAL SIGNIFICANCE HYPOTHESIS TESTING WHEN COMPARING TWO MEANS

To understand the logic of statistical hypothesis testing, which underlies many other tests, it makes sense to begin with comparisons of two groups. Furthermore, comparisons of two groups (e.g., men and women, people with high communication apprehension and people with low communication apprehension, people who listen to a speech with evidence and people who listen to the same speech without any evidence) on some output measure of interest is common in communication research.

DOING A STUDY THAT TESTS A HYPOTHESIS OF DIFFERENCES BETWEEN MEANS

Researchers often ask research questions about the means of two groups on some measure of interest. These two groups usually are categories or levels of an independent variable that is measured on the nominal level. To understand this process, it helps to grasp what studies using these tools look like and the general process of hypothesis testing.

Design of a Study That Compares Two Conditions

Researchers who wish to compare the means of two groups usually are involved in completing experiments or some form of survey research. A **survey** is an "empirical study that uses questionnaires or interviews to discover descriptive characteristics of phenomena" (Reinard, 2001, p. 225). On the other hand, an **experiment** is "the study of the effects of variables manipulated by the researcher, in a situation in which all other variables are controlled, and completed for the purpose of establishing causal relationships" (Reinard, 2001, p. 256). Unlike the work in surveys, in experiments researchers introduce variables that were not already present in the situation (to participants called an "experimental group"), and they withhold those variables from others (participants in a "control group"). For instance, an experimenter might expose one group of people to a message with climax order and another group to a message with anticlimax order. Then, the researcher would compare the dependent variable mean scores of participants from the two groups. In surveys, researchers do not manipulate variables, and they often find that independent variables already are organized into two groups, such as participant sex (men and women), type of cultural background (individualistic or collectivist cultures), or age (old and young). Some of these variables originally were continuous variables, but they have been broken into levels called **variable factors** or just factors.

Once variables are divided into two categories, researchers may posit hypotheses to be tested. For comparisons between means, research hypotheses take the form of comparing the means of two groups, symbolized as

H: $\mu_1 > \mu_2$ (the dependent variable mean of the first group is higher than the mean of the second group),

H: $\mu_1 < \mu_2$ (the dependent variable mean of the first group is lower than the mean of the second group), or

H: $\mu_1 \neq \mu_2$ (the dependent variable mean of the first group is not equal to the mean of the second group).[1]

The first two examples are called directional hypotheses because, not surprisingly, they assert a direction to the differences between means. The last hypothesis is a nondirectional hypothesis because it asserts a difference between groups but not the nature of that difference. In contrast to these research hypotheses is the null hypothesis that states that there is no difference between groups: H_0: $\mu_1 = \mu_2$. As will be seen, this null hypothesis is actually what is tested statistically. In the case of a directional hypothesis, rejection of the null hypothesis would have to be accompanied by a finding of mean differences in the predicted direction.

Some, therefore, have suggested that the null hypothesis for the first hypothesis actually be stated as H_0: $\mu_1 \leq \mu_2$ and that the null hypothesis for the second hypothesis should be stated as H_0: $\mu_1 \geq \mu_2$. Though it sometimes may sound curious at first, researchers investigating material hypotheses typically want to *reject* opposing null hypotheses. The approach that includes "directions" in null hypotheses attempts to take account of all relationships that would not support a researcher's material hypotheses.

Before testing the hypotheses, researchers must examine whether the assumptions underlying the use of the statistics have been satisfied. Finally, after the assumptions have been checked, the primary statistical tools may be employed.

Applying the Logic of Hypothesis Testing

You might think that testing a research hypothesis is a simple matter of checking to see if the means are in the direction suggested. But because we collect data in samples and try

---

[1]As was explained in Chapter 2, though researchers typically deal with sample data, for conceptual purposes they hypothesize general relationships that may exist in the population as a whole. Hence, hypothesis notation uses Greek letters to represent population characteristics. The standard abbreviation for the population mean is the lowercase Greek letter μ (mu). For sample data, the ordinary Roman alphabet (the ABCs) is used. Sometime in the future, statistics books may not use the Greek alphabet notation for hypotheses, but until the change becomes universal, it is helpful to learn the typical notation so that you can understand the meaning of specific concepts you may wish to investigate from other sources in statistics.

to make inferences about populations, this approach might not be very helpful. One could imagine a researcher and a skeptic discussing the matter:

Researcher: I have confirmed my research hypothesis that a speech with internal organizers is more easily recalled than a speech without internal organizers.

Skeptic: In the first place, you do not *confirm* or *prove* hypotheses. You can "support" them or find them "tenable," but that's it. In the second place, even if we assume that your research design actually manipulated internal organizers without confounding them with other variables, such as language vividness and message length, you still do not have evidence of the impact of internal organizers because you used *sample* data. I'd bet that if you sampled the entire population, you would find no difference at all in recall of the message.

Researcher: But I used random sampling to ensure that my samples would be representative of the population.

Skeptic: That's just the point. If you used random sampling—and I would like you to tell me how you developed a large enough sampling frame to pull off that trick—then most of the time you would tend to get samples that mirrored the population characteristics of interest.

Researcher: See!

Skeptic: Not exactly. If you sampled at random, in addition to getting results that might reflect the population, you occasionally would get samples that represented extreme results. You do not really know whether your study results reflected the effects of sampling error or whether they identified a real relationship that exists in the population.

Researcher: OK, if you don't believe that internal organizers increase recall of a message, where is your proof?

Skeptic: Whoa! I don't have the burden of proof here. You do. Those who assert things must prove them. Besides, how could I be expected to prove a null hypothesis?[2]

Researcher: I guess I've wasted my time.

---

[2]Sometimes, though not in this example, you can prove a null hypothesis, but doing so requires two things. First, what is identified must be equally recognized by everyone in a position to make observations, rather than being a matter of personal preference or subjective judgment. Second, the universe must be limited, so that a complete search is possible. So, if a dentist tells you, "You do not have any new cavities," the dentist is asserting the truth of a null hypothesis. What constitutes a cavity is recognized as the same by everybody with dentistry training (we hope), and the universe in which to search (the teeth in your mouth) is limited. This situation is rare in everyday life. Thus, under most circumstances, it is not possible to prove a null hypothesis.

There is another way.[3] The rest of this chapter will explain this logic of hypothesis testing. Because it underlies all the other tests of significance, it is useful to be sure to be comfortable with this logic before proceeding to specific tests.

Reasoning From Reverse: The Logic of Testing the Null Hypothesis

Rather than trying to prove the point directly, researchers may use a *process of elimination* to support a hypothesis. Just for the sake of argument, you could assume that the null hypothesis of the skeptic is true. Then, you could ask how improbable it would be to find a difference as large as observed as a result of random sampling error. If random sampling could produce a sample such as yours quite often, then you would decide that the evidence is not good enough to reject the doubts of the skeptic (in other words, you would fail to reject the null hypothesis). Yet, if your sample could be found *quite rarely* due to sampling error, then you would decide that it is unlikely that your sample came from a population described by the null hypothesis. Now you have two options:

1. Decide that your results are, in fact, just the kind of occurrence that happens at random once in a while, even though it is admittedly unlikely—and conclude that this occurrence is one of those random sampling oddities, or

2. Decide that it is so improbable that your results could be found at random from a population defined by the null hypothesis that the null hypothesis must be untrue.

You do not *prove* that your research hypothesis is true. Instead, you show how *improbable* an explanation the null hypothesis is for your results. If the null hypothesis is improbable, what's left? The properly stated research hypothesis is the only alternative. Statistics cannot prove that your research hypothesis is true, but you can use the statistics that follow to show how long the odds are against skeptics who would posit a null hypothesis. As you can see, the null hypothesis is actually the one that researchers test. If they can reject it as improbable, they use a process of elimination to conclude that the research hypothesis is "supported."[4]

---

[3]There actually is more than one other way. The approach presented here is a standard treatment of significance testing, but you should know that serious scholars have suggested other ways to approach hypothesis testing. Relying on Bayesian probability theory, many are exploring alternatives to the "process of elimination" approach taken here.

[4]The logic of hypothesis testing is not a metaphor. The conditional syllogism is used throughout the process. For instance:

Major premise: If the null hypothesis is true, then no statistically significant differences will be found.

Minor premise: Statistically significant differences were found.

Conclusion: Therefore, the null hypothesis is untrue.

This form of reasoning is known as *modus tollens*. You may notice that finding no significant differences would not prove the null hypothesis to be true. In such a case, the minor premise "no statistically significant differences were found" would commit the fallacy of affirming the consequent. Even with formal logic, it is difficult to make a valid argument to prove a null hypothesis.

Steps in Hypothesis Testing

To test a statistical hypothesis, researchers follow several steps. Each will be considered in turn.

- *Determining a decision rule to reject the null hypothesis* is the starting point for assessing a hyothesis. This decision rule is called setting a level of **alpha risk** (α risk). The researcher announces alpha risk before the research is completed, and it is the decision rule under which null hypotheses are to be rejected. The decision rule (or "alpha" for short) is usually set at a probability of .05 for research in communication studies. So, if a set of results could have been found by random sampling error from a distribution defined by the null hypothesis no more than 5 times out of 100, the researcher agrees to reject the null hypothesis explanation. Of course, this level means that 5 times out of 100 (or 1 time out of every 20 tests), when the researcher claims to have found a significant difference, the effect *really is* just attributable to random sampling error. To make the test understandable, it often is useful to state the null hypothesis explicitly (though in published research, such a feature is rare).
- *Computing a test statistic* is the result of using a statistical formula. In this chapter, the statistics of interest are z and t, but many others are available.
- *Finding the critical value* to interpret the meaning of the test statistic requires researchers to look at distributions and tables. Then, based on adjustments for sample sizes and parameters estimated from samples, researchers look at distributions to identify critical regions of interest. The **critical region** of a distribution represents

> values that are "critical" to a particular study. They are critical because when a sample statistic falls in that region, the researcher can reject the null hypothesis. (For this reason, the critical region also is called the "region of rejection." (Vogt, 2005, p. 70)

Researchers look at a distribution for their type of data and then identify the proportion that corresponds to their decision rule for rejecting the null hypothesis. For instance, if a researcher were using the standard normal curve as the underlying probability distribution, and using an alpha risk of .05 as the decision rule to reject the null hypothesis, then 5% of the standard normal curve would have to be identified as the critical region.

If the research hypothesis is a directional hypothesis, 5% of the distribution that is the critical region would be on one side of the distribution. In the case of the standard normal curve, the last 5% of the distribution begins at 1.645 standard deviations.[5] But which side of the distribution is the location of the critical region? It depends on the hypothesis.

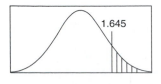

- o If the directional hypothesis is stated as H: $\mu_1 > \mu_2$, the 5% of the distribution that is the critical region is on the right side, as shown in the diagram on the left.

---

[5]Though it appears in Table C.1 in this book, the value of 1.645 does not appear in most tables of the standard normal curve and must be interpolated from the surrounding z values.

○ If the directional hypothesis is stated as H: $\mu_1 < \mu_2$, the 5% of
the distribution that is critical region is on the left side, as
shown in the diagram on the right.

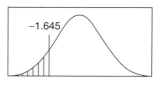

○ If the research hypothesis is a nondirectional hypothesis,
the 5% of the distribution that is the critical region would
be divided, with half on one side of the distribution and half
on the other side. Hence, for a null hypothesis such as
H: $\mu_1 \neq \mu_2$, 2.5% of the distribution that is part of the critical region is on the right side, and the remaining 2.5% of
the distribution that is part of the critical region is on the
left side. Because the last 2.5% of the distribution starts at
± 1.96 standard deviations, the critical regions can be identified as in the diagram
shown in the right.

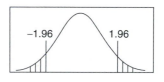

- *Rejecting or failing to reject the null hypothesis* is the final step in statistical hypothesis
testing. If the test statistic falls in any critical region for the particular hypothesis, the
researcher applies the decision rule to reject the null hypothesis, and a real relationship
or "statistically significant" difference is claimed. The term **statistical significance**
is often defined as a relationship that is beyond what might be expected to occur by
chance alone, but "statistical significance means that the result was unlikely due to
chance; if the null hypothesis is true, an improbable event has occurred" (Johnson,
1995, p. 1999). Either the improbable event can be dismissed, or it can be taken as
evidence that the null hypothesis explanation is unpersuasive. Researchers usually
claim statistical significance with such claims as "statistically significant differences
were found ($p < .05$)." The *p* in this statement symbolizes the probability that observed
differences could have been found if the null hypothesis were true. In short, the smaller
this probability is, the more potent the evidence is against the null hypothesis—and, by
a process of elimination, the more tenable is the alternative research hypothesis. It is
important to remember

> that a p-value merely indicates the probability of a particular set of data being
> generated by the null model—it has little to say about size of a deviation from that
> model (especially in the tails of the distribution, where large changes in effects size
> cause only small changes in p-values). (Helberg, 1995, ¶ 28)

Of course, the decision a researcher makes to reject a null hypothesis is a "yes" or "no"
option. Sometimes these choices will prove—in the long run—to be sound decisions, and
sometimes they will be mistaken. When completing a study, researchers play the odds, but
they cannot know for sure that they have decided correctly. The options are found in
Table 7.1.

The "Actual Situation" is not known to the researcher at the time of a study, of course.
But there are two options: The null hypothesis could be true, or it might be false. In addition, researchers might look at statistical analyses completed and decide that the odds seem
to be against the null hypothesis explanation of the data, that the null hypothesis should be
rejected.

Table 7.1

		Actual Situation	
		H_0 is false	H_0 is true
Researcher's Decision Based on Statistical Testing Decision	Reject H_0	Correct decision Power	Type I error α risk
	Do not reject H_0	Type II error β risk	Correct decision

If the researcher decides to reject the null hypothesis and the null hypothesis is false, the researcher has made a correct decision. Of course, at the time of the study, the researcher could not know for sure, but the researcher can compute the probability of correctly rejecting the null hypothesis. Called **statistical power**, this term refers to "the probability of rejecting the null hypothesis when it is false—and therefore should be rejected" (Vogt, 2005, p. 242). Of course, if a researcher rejects the null hypothesis and it turns out that the null hypothesis is true, then the researcher has made an incorrect decision. This type of mistake is known as **Type I** error.[6] One cannot know whether a Type I error has occurred at the time the data are first analyzed statistically (though in the long run, researchers usually find out). But researchers can identify the probability that a Type I error might occur. This probability of incorrectly rejecting the null hypothesis is known as **alpha (α) risk.** Many students find it useful to think of Type I error as a researcher producing a "false positive" claim of support for the research hypothesis. The researcher thought there was a predicted relationship, but it was a false positive finding.

The researcher could fail to reject the null hypothesis. If the null hypothesis were false— if there actually were differences that went undetected—the researcher would have made a mistake. This type of error is called **Type II error**. Though at the time the study is conducted, the researcher cannot know if Type II error has occurred, the probability that the error might have occurred can be identified as **beta (β) risk**. Students sometimes find it useful to think of Type II error as a researcher producing a "false negative" claim about the research hypothesis. Though the data *seemed* to suggest the absence of a relationship, it actually was a false negative finding. In general, researchers control beta risk by using large enough sample sizes for statistics to detect relationships in the data. Of course, if the researcher fails to reject the null hypothesis that is true, the decision is a correct one. As you might expect, $1 - \beta$ is the power of a statistical test.

In passing, it might be mentioned that researchers must have a hypothesis before using these steps of statistical hypothesis testing. It is not appropriate to compose a hypothesis after the data are examined. Similarly, it is not appropriate to set a decision rule after a test statistic has been computed.

---

[6]One might wonder why they are called Type I error and Type II error (to be discussed later). The reason appears to go all the way back to Aristotle, who identified two types of errors: to say about that which is true that it is untrue, and to say about that which is untrue that it is true.

Special Discussion 7.1

Troubled Language Use in Hypothesis Testing

Reasoning by a process of elimination often has created difficulties for researchers in reporting their findings. One writer (Thompson, 1994, p. 6) explains:

> Many of the problems in contemporary uses of statistical significance testing originate in the language researchers use. Several names can refer to a single concept (e.g., "SOS (BETWEEN)" = "SOS(EXPLAINED)" = "SOS(MODEL)" = "SOS(REGRESSION)"), and different meanings are given to terms in different contexts (e.g., "univariate" means having only one dependent variable but potentially many predictor variables, but may also refer to a statistic that can be computed with only a single variable).
>
> Overcoming three habits of language will help avoid unconscious misinterpretations:
>
> – Say "statistically significant" rather than "significant." Referring to the concept as a phrase will help break the erroneous association between rejecting a null hypothesis and obtaining an important result.
> – Don't say things like "my results approached statistical significance." This language makes little sense in the context of the statistical significance testing logic. My favorite response to this is offered by a fellow editor who responds, "How did you know your results were not trying to avoid being statistically significant?"
> – Don't say things like "the statistical significance testing evaluated whether the results were 'due to chance'." This language gives the impression that replicability is evaluated by statistical significance testing.

ASSUMPTIONS IN PARAMETRIC HYPOTHESIS TESTING

When comparing two means, a family of statistical tests called parametric tests is used. **Parametric statistics** are methods that "make assumptions about populations from which the samples were drawn" (Reinard, 2001, p. 341). Four major assumptions underlie the use of parametric tests:

- Interval or ratio level measurement of dependent variables;
- Randomization in sampling and any assignment of events to experimental and control conditions;
- Normal probability distribution of dependent variables; and
- Equal (homogeneous) variances of the dependent variable in the population (and the corresponding requirement that sample variances remain equal within the limits of sampling error).

Many of these assumptions are not about sample data; they are inferences about population elements. For instance, the one assumption states that the populations have normal probability distributions. But because population characteristics rarely are known to the researcher, unbiased sample statistics are taken as the next best indicator of these characteristics.

Researchers, therefore, look at sample data to get evidence about whether the assumptions have been met in the population as a whole.

Effects of Violating Parametric Assumptions

Naturally, scholars are interested in what happens if the assumptions underlying these parametric tests are not satisfied. Some matters, such as the required level of measurement and randomization, seem fairly firm. If one wishes to ask how rarely one's study results could be found by random sampling error, it is vital for researchers to reference distributions with randomness in mind. Though there may be controversy regarding whether many measures used in communication research really are interval level measures, regardless of the way the researcher comes down on the issue, using at least quasi-interval measurement is presumed.[7]

Univariate parametric tests seem to be resistant to the effects of violating the assumption of normality (see classic studies by Boneau [1960] and Hsu and Feldt [1969]). When the sample sizes are at least 15 in each condition, the actual number of Type I errors tends to be off by an average of only ±1%. If the sample sizes are under 6 per condition, a skewed distribution can lead to more Type I errors than the ±1% range limit. If there is a nonnormal distribution, researchers may want to know why. According to the central limit theorem (Chapter 4), distributions of means will tend toward normality as sample sizes used to compute the means are increased. Hence, if one still finds nonnormal distributions, it may be that some uncontrolled variables are introducing nonrandom influences that should be isolated and studied. What should researchers do if the distributions are nonnormal and sample sizes do not permit one to believe that assumptions have been satisfied? One option is to use nonparametric test alternatives. This approach, however, frequently reduces statistical power (Hodges & Lehmann, 1956; Tanizaki, 1997) and introduces bias when multiple violations of assumptions exist (Zimmerman, 1998).

Another option is to use transformations of nonnormal data. Yet another option is to employ a "robust" statistic, such as *Yuen's t* (Yuen, 1974).[8] The ideal solution, of course, involves taking steps to avoid the problem of nonnormal distributions—by use of adequate sample sizes and control of extraneous variables when sampling.

Studies of the assumption of homogeneous variances of the dependent variable in the population have revealed that the effect of violating this assumption usually is trivial if sample sizes are equal in comparison groups (Glass, Peckham, & Sanders, 1972). If sample sizes are not equal, the impact still is not great unless the ratio of the largest to the smallest sample size is more than 5 to 4. If the variances are unequal and the largest variance comes from the group with the

---

[7]As was mentioned in Chapter 2, there is some controversy regarding whether most measures in communication studies and the social sciences are interval or quasi-interval data. Over the years, Monte Carlo simulation studies have revealed that the effects of true intervality are relatively unimportant for the sorts of data typically found by social science researchers (Baker, Hardyk, & Petrinovich, 1966; Borgatta & Bohrnstedt, 1980). For a review of this controversy, see Velleman and Wilkinson (1993).

[8]This method involves trimming data to compute means and winsorizing data to compute a measure of within-groups variance (see Chapter 3). Though it has some effect on overcoming the problem of heterogeneous variances, Yuen's t primarily addresses the difficulties of nonnormal distributions. Yet, the method suffers criticisms of winsorizing and trimming generally, including the charge that it may give misleading results because it arbitrarily dismisses actual unexplained variability that probably should not be dropped arbitrarily. Furthermore, methods using trimmed means often have lower power than methods that use standard nonparametric techniques (Keselman & Zumbo, 1997).

largest sample size, Type I error actually would be lower than the announced alpha risk. So, researchers would think that they were rejecting the null hypothesis at the .05 level when they really were rejecting it at the .04 or .03 level. Thus, the test would be increasingly conservative. If the largest variance comes from the group with the smallest sample size, the resulting Type I error would be greater than the announced alpha risk. So, researchers would claim rejecting null hypotheses at the .05 level when, in fact, they were rejecting null hypotheses at a .06, .07, or greater probability level. In other words, the test would be increasingly likely to reject null hypotheses erroneously. It might be mentioned that if the heterogeneity in variances accompanies other violations, the violations could be increasingly important (Lix & Keselman, 1998).

Testing the Assumptions

There are formal ways to test assumptions of normal distributions and homogeneous variances. These two matters will be examined.

Testing for Normal Distributions

The assumption of an underlying normal probability distribution in the population is often checked by looking at a plot of sample data. Examining skewness and kurtosis statistics may be all that is necessary. Yet, there are other ways to check on such information. The Lilliefors modification of the Kolmogorov-Smirnov one-sample test (often called the **Lilliefors test** for normality) may be used to test the assumption of normality (Lilliefors, 1967). The Lilliefors test transforms data into z scores. Then, the cumulative frequency distribution of the data is compared to the cumulative frequency distribution that would be expected based on the z values. For instance, suppose there were 10 scores on a measure of interpersonal solidarity: 5, 10, 14, 6, 8, 8, 7, 11, 9, 12. Arranging the scores from the lowest to highest z scores produces the following:

Scores	5	6	7	8	8	9	10	11	12	14
CFD	0.1	0.2	0.3	0.5	0.5	0.6	0.7	0.8	0.9	1
z score	−1.43	−1.08	−0.72	−0.36	−0.36	0	0.39	0.72	1.08	1.79

The CFD is the cumulative frequency distribution of scores (expressed as proportions—with 10 scores, each score is one tenth of the total or 0.1). Because there were two people with scores of 8, they both share the same location on the cumulative distribution. The method involves looking at the discrepancy between the cumulative frequency distribution for the raw and z scores. The researcher needs to compute the sample mean and standard deviation for the raw data (in this case, the mean is 9 and the standard deviation is 2.79). Then, the researcher looks at the table of the standard normal curve and identifies the proportion of the area that is to the left of the particular z score. For instance, the score of 5 corresponds to a z score of −1.43:

$$z = \frac{X - \bar{X}}{s} = \frac{5 - 9}{2.79} = -1.43.$$ Checking the table of the standard normal curve reveals that this z score

identifies the location of the area under the standard normal curve that exceeds .0764 of all scores. As the figure below shows, this value is placed in the row identified as "area below z." Differences in cumulative frequency distributions are inserted in a separate row in the table of comparisons.

Scores	5	6	7	8	8	9	10	11	12	14
CFD	0.1	0.2	0.3	0.5	0.5	0.6	0.7	0.8	0.9	1
z score	−1.43	−1.08	−0.72	−0.36	−0.36	0	0.39	0.72	1.08	1.79
Area below z	0.08	0.14	0.24	0.36	0.36	0.5	0.64	0.76	0.86	0.96
Difference	0.02	0.06	0.06	0.14	0.14	0.1	0.06	0.04	0.04	0.04

The largest difference is .14. The critical values are found in Appendix C.12. For alpha risk of .05, the minimum critical difference is .258. Because the test statistic is smaller than this critical value, the assumption of a normal distribution continues to be tenable. The Lilliefors test has been shown to be powerful, especially when detecting "heavy-tailed" distributions (Young & Seaman, 1990).

To use SPSS to produce such a test, the researcher selects *Descriptive Statistics* from the *Analyze* menu. On the drop-down menu, the researcher then selects *Explore. . . .* On the dialog box that appears, the researcher moves the dependent variable into the "Dependent List:" field. In this case, the same data from the example above are used. Hence, the "solidarity" variable is moved by use of the arrow button. The box for both plots and statistics is checked, though the researcher might choose only the statistical analysis if desired.

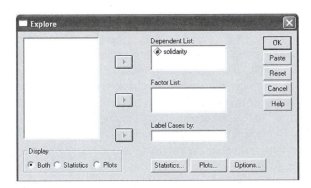

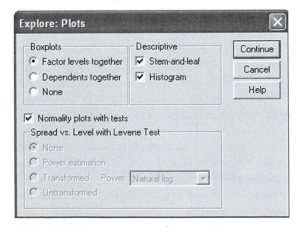

Clicking on the *Plots. . .* button produces a dialog box in which the specific "Normality plots with tests" choices may be checked.

Among other things, the results of the analysis include the following table. The Kolmogorov-Smirnov value is .14, which corresponds to the results produced in our calculations above. This value is associated with a probability value of .20, which is well above the standard of .05 used to identify statistically significant deviations from normality. Hence, this test did *not* suggest that the assumption of an underlying normal distribution was untenable.

Tests of Normality

	Kolmogorov-Smirnov[a]			Shapiro-Wilk		
	Statistic	df	Sig.	Statistic	df	Sig.
solidarity	.140	10	.200*	.979	10	.962

*This is a lower bound of the true significance.
a. Lilliefors Significance Correction.

A popular alternative is the *Shapiro-Wilk test*, which remains powerful even when sample sizes are as small as 20 (Wilk, Shapiro, & Chen, 1965). This test examines the null hypothesis that the sample distribution is normal. Hence, a statistically significant difference means that the distribution is not normal. In this case, the probability associated with this test was .962, a value suggesting that the assumption of a normal distribution remained tenable for these data.

Another choice is the Anderson-Darling test for normality (T. W. Anderson & Darling, 1954).[9] Though involving more complicated computations, the Anderson-Darling test is more powerful than the Lilliefors modification of the Kolmogorov-Smirnov test (Crown, 2000; Spinelli & Stephens, 1987; Stephens, 1974). Computer programs have been developed for this test (Calzada & Scariano, 2002), and a link to one can be found on this chapter's Web site.

Testing for Homogeneous Variances Among Two or More Groups

To test the equality of variances, there are several options. One of the most popular is the F test (sometimes called F_{max}) for the equality of two variances. The null hypothesis to be tested is H_0: $\sigma_1^2 = \sigma_2^2$. This formula (sometimes known as F_{max})[10] takes the largest variance and divides it by the smallest variance:

$$F = \frac{\sigma_{largest}^2}{\sigma_{smallest}^2}.$$

Though popular, this measure tends to exaggerate the chances of finding heterogeneous variances as sample sizes increase. An alternative formula is *Levene's test*, which subtracts each score from its cell mean and then performs a test called analysis of variance on the difference scores. Other tests often are suitable options for different sorts of data.[11] In each case, a distribution is referenced to see if the test statistic falls in the critical region corresponding

---

[9]The discrete Anderson-Darling test statistic is

$$A^* = \left\{ \frac{-1}{n} \left[\sum_{i}^{n} (2i - 1)[ln(p_i) + ln(1 - p_{n+1-i})] \right] - n \right\} \left(1 + \frac{.75}{n} + \frac{2.25}{n^2} \right).$$

In this formula, p_i is the cumulative probabilities for each value of the variable (transformed into z scores). To estimate the significance of the test statistic, the following formula may be used: $\alpha \approx 3.6789468 e^{-\frac{A^*}{.1749916}}$ (see Nelson, 1998).

[10]Another related test, sometimes called Hartley's H, is, in fact, the F test for which there are equal cell sizes and for which the table of critical values has been simplified.

[11]For instance, when sample sizes are unequal and when any of the variances is very small, Cochran's C often is indicated.

to the decision rule the researcher sets. If the test statistic is located in the critical region, the null hypothesis (of equal variances) is rejected. If not, the assumption continues to "hold."

For the data found in the two-sample test in the example found in Table 7.4 (in the section "Conducting the Hypothesis Test for the Difference Between Two Sample Means," pp. 165–166), a test of the assumption of heterogeneous variances is included using the F test. The test statistic of 1.68 is smaller than the critical value of F (2.95 with 17 and 14 degrees of freedom at the assigned alpha risk). Hence, the assumption of homogeneous variances cannot be rejected.

The test can be completed by Excel. After the data have been placed in separate columns (perhaps labeled "explicit" and "no explicit" as shown on page 166), the researcher selects *Data Analysis. . .* from the *Tools* menu. In the "Data Analysis" dialog box, the "F-Test Two-Sample for Variances" is highlighted. Then the researcher clicks on the *OK* button.

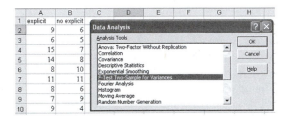

"The F-Test Two-Sample for Variances" dialog box (above right) includes fields into which the researcher must identify the location of the scores for each of the groups. The step is accomplished by clicking on the ▨ symbol in the "Variable 1 Range:" field. This step puts the researcher on the spreadsheet where data are located. By clicking on the first cell in which data appear for the first group of scores and highlighting the remaining data in that row (by holding down the left mouse button), the cell range in which the first group's data are found can be input. Clicking on the ▨ symbol on the drop-down menu returns the researcher to the main dialog box. Then, the process of highlighting the cell range may be completed for the second group of data scores. If the researcher has highlighted cells that contain variable or group labels, the "Labels" box should be checked to prevent attempts to analyze group variable names as data. The researcher also must specify a location in which the output is to be placed. In this case, the researcher has identified the "Output Range:" to begin at cell D13. Clicking the *OK* button causes the output to be produced. As can be seen on the left, the observed F statistic of 1.67 has an accompanying probability level ("P(F < = f) one-tail") that is larger than the standard .05 (or smaller) probability necessary to reject the null hypothesis. Hence, the researcher concluded that the assumption of homogeneous variances continues to hold.

F-Test Two-Sample for Variances		
	Variable 1	Variable 2
Mean	9.625	8
Variance	8.383333	5
Observations	16	15
df	15	14
F	1.676667	
P(F<=f) one-tail	0.170421	
F Critical one-tail	2.463004	

SPSS also provides ways to examine the assumption of homogeneous variances. Regularly provided as part of the *t* test, for independent samples, SPSS reports Levene's test. Because getting this output will be covered in the section on using SPSS for the two-sample *t* test, the individual steps to get this output will not also be presented here. Because Levene's test is robust to violations of the assumption of

		Levene's Test for Equality of Variances	
		F	Sig.
attitude	Equal variances assumed	.030	.863
	Equal variances not assumed		

normal distributions, it often is preferred for tests of computing homogeneous variances. In this case, the Levene test produced an *F* ratio of .03, which produced a very high significance "Sig." value. Thus, the null hypothesis of equal variances in the two groups could not be rejected. If the Levene test had indicated statistically significant differences, the researcher would have been invited to use the *t* test computation method in which "equal variances [are] not assumed."

Aside from the desire to determine if heterogeneous variances have affected actual risk levels in hypothesis testing, there is another reason to look at heterogeneous variances. Two categories of influences can be responsible for unequal variances. First, there may be **ceiling or floor effects** in the data. In other words, it may be that there are conditions where the means are so high (or low) that there is not enough room left in the measurement range for the scores to show normal spread.[12] By looking at the means and checking that the cells with the means near the top of their measurement range also have low variances, a ceiling effect may be identified. Similarly, looking at the cells with means near the low end of the measurement range and checking that they also had small variances would reveal floor effects. If more than two groups are compared, a correlation between the cell means and variances could be computed. A high inverse correlation would point to a ceiling effect, and a high direct correlation would suggest a floor effect. Of course, the actual means have to be examined to tell if the ceiling or floor effect actually is present.

Second, if there is no ceiling or floor effect, the heterogeneous variances indicate the presence of **participants by treatments interactions**. This condition suggests that there is at least one other additional variable—and perhaps many more than one—that is mixing nonrandom variation with the chief variables in the study. Thus, there are uncontrolled variables affecting the observed relationships. Researchers would be encouraged to reconsider their studies and to look for additional variables that should be included in future research.

COMPARING SAMPLE AND POPULATION MEANS

Comparisons of samples with some population mean—such as a historical standard or simply a defining characteristic—can be completed under two conditions. First, the population standard deviation may be known. Second, sample standard deviations may be substituted for population standard deviations.

When the Population Standard Deviation Is Known

Under many circumstances, if a researcher wishes to compare a mean from a sample against characteristics of a well-defined population, the *z* test (using the standard normal curve) would be an appropriate option. In addition to requiring that population means and

---

[12]As Paul R. Cohen (1995) explains:

> Technically, a ceiling effect occurs when the dependent variable, *y*, is equal in the control and treatment conditions, and both are equal to the best possible value of *y*. In practice, we use the term when performance is nearly as good as possible in the treatment and control conditions. Note that "good" sometimes means large (i.e., higher accuracy is better) and sometimes it means small (e.g., low run times are better), so the ceiling can be approached from above or below. A ceiling thus bounds the abstract "goodness" of performance. Floor effects occur when performance is nearly as bad as possible in the treatment and control conditions. Again, poor performance might involve small or large scores, so the "floor" can be approached from above or below. (p. 80)

standard deviations be known, the use of z requires fairly large samples, at least 30 events. The formula for z is

$$z = \frac{X - \mu}{\sigma}.$$

To adapt to a comparison with means instead of X scores, one might imagine that one could simply use the following modification:

$$z = \frac{\overline{X} - \mu}{\sigma}.$$

Using this formula would be *incorrect*. The scores compared in the numerator and denominator of the formula are not the same types of data. The sigma (σ) score in the denominator is the standard deviation of raw scores, but the numerator does not compare *scores*, but *means*. A distribution of means has a much smaller standard deviation than a distribution of scores. The reason is found in the central limit theorem, which was introduced in Chapter 4. This theorem states that a sampling distribution of means tends toward a normal distribution with increased sample sizes regardless of the shape of the parent population. As a result of the central limit theorem, the standard deviation of means ($\sigma_{\overline{X}}$, called the "standard error of the mean") could be computed as

$$\sigma_{\overline{X}} = \frac{\sigma}{\sqrt{N}}.$$

So, a new sample could be compared with a population mean, but the following formula is required:

$$z = \frac{\overline{X} - \mu}{\sigma_{\overline{X}}},$$

where

$$\sigma_{\overline{X}} = \frac{\sigma}{\sqrt{n}}.$$

In this case, the size of the new sample (n) is substituted for N, the number of events in the population.

The z test also can be used to determine how often a set of findings might occur at random. For instance, one might wonder how unusual it would be to find a sample of 50 people with a mean of 70 or higher from a population in which the mean on a measure of communication apprehension is 65.6 and the standard deviation is 15.3. Inserting these numbers into the formula reveals these results:

$$z = \frac{\overline{X} - \mu}{\frac{\sigma}{\sqrt{n}}} = \frac{70 - 65.6}{\frac{15.3}{\sqrt{50}}} = \frac{4.4}{2.16} = 2.04.$$

Looking up the value on the z table (a portion of which is shown below on the left) reveals that the area from the mean to a z score of 2.04 includes .4793 of the total area. Thus, only .0207 lies above that point. So, we may say that in the population, only 2.07% of the time will one find a random sample of 50 with a mean score of 70 or above. An example of the z test of statistical significance is found in Table 7.2.

z	.00	.01	.02	.03	.04
0.0	.0000	.0040	.0080	.0120	.0160
0.1	.0398	.0438	.0478	.0517	.0557
2.0	.4772	.4778	.4783	.4788	.4793

Table 7.2   The One-Sample z Test

The Personal Report of Communication Apprehension has a known population mean (from studies of 52 university samples including more than 25,000 participants) of 65.6 and a standard deviation of 15.3 (see McCroskey, Beatty, Kearney, & Plax, 1985). Yet another study of 64 pharmacy students found an initial communication apprehension mean of 62.14 (Berger & McCroskey, 1982).

The one-sample z test may be used to test the null hypothesis that there is no difference between the sample mean and the population mean, H_0: $\mu_{\text{pharmacy students}} = \mu_{\text{population}}$.[13] If the null hypothesis is tested with a two-tailed (nondirectional) test featuring an alpha risk of .05, the critical value of z (the point where the critical region begins) would be ± 1.96. The test statistic would be computed as follows:

$$z = \frac{\overline{X} - \mu}{\frac{\sigma}{\sqrt{n}}}$$

$$z = \frac{62.14 - 65.6}{\frac{15.3}{\sqrt{64}}} = \frac{-3.46}{1.91} = -1.81$$

Thus, the null hypothesis would not be rejected. One would conclude that there is no significant difference in the mean communication anxiety of pharmacy students and the general population.

---

[13]The null hypothesis sometimes is stated as H_0: $\mu = \mu_0$. In this case, μ_0 represents a particular assigned population value for purposes of comparison.

When the Population Standard Deviation Is Unknown

Researchers often have only sample data. Thus, they cannot always use the z test, because they may not know the population standard deviation. An alternative is to substitute the sample standard deviation, s, an unbiased estimate of the population standard deviation, σ.

But the z test also requires sample sizes of at least 30. So, if either the population standard deviation is not known or the sample size is below 30, using t (or Student's t)[14] is required. By either design or accident, the symbol in the t distribution emphasizes that the t test focuses on testing the difference between *t*wo means.[15]

The t distribution shares many characteristics with the standard normal curve. In fact, as an inspection of the table of critical values of t will reveal (Appendix C.4), with an infinite sample size, the standard normal curve and the t distribution are identical. But as sample sizes get

---

[14]The Student t distribution has nothing to do with educational research. William Sealy Gosset trained as a mathematician at Oxford University and worked for the Guinness Brewery in Dublin, Ireland. Guinness is the same organization responsible for Guinness Stout Malt Liquor and the famous book of world records. While doing experiments related to temperature, he developed the t distribution and the t test. Because Guinness had a policy that prevented employees from publishing under their own names, he published his discovery under the pen name "Student" (1908), and the label has stuck.

[15]There is a song ("Tea for Two") from a 1924 musical called *No, No, Nanette*. Aside from constituting a way for modern students to remember the purpose of the t test, it has nothing to do with Student's t test.

smaller and smaller, the t distribution tends to flatten out. To use the t distribution, one must identify the **degrees of freedom**, which is calculated as the number of events in a sample minus the number of parameters estimated from sample statistics. By looking at the formula for the test statistic, one may identify the number of X-bars ($\overline{X}_s$) used to estimate population means.

The t test making comparisons of a sample mean and a population mean uses the following formula:

$$t = \frac{\overline{X} - \mu}{\frac{s}{\sqrt{n}}},$$

where $s_{\overline{x}}$ is equal to $\frac{s}{\sqrt{n}}$. This formula differs from the z test by the use of the *sample* standard deviation, s, instead of the *population* standard deviation, σ. Thus, the t test is actually one more building block formula that follows a basic pattern of statistical uses that were identified earlier in this text.

Building Block Formula Box 6: One-Sample z and t

$$z = \frac{\overline{X} - \mu}{\sigma_{\overline{X}}}$$

$$t = \frac{\overline{X} - \mu}{s_{\overline{X}}}$$

Because the one-sample t formula includes only one $\overline{X}$ in the numerator, degrees of freedom are equal to $n - 1$. These degrees of freedom may be used to enter the table found in Appendix C.4 to find critical values of t. (A portion of this table is reproduced below.)

| degrees of freedom | .10 | .05 | .025 | .01 | .005 | ← Alpha risk for *one-tailed* tests |
	.20	.10	.05	.02	.01	← Alpha risk for *two-tailed* tests
1	1.078	6.314	12.706	31.821	63.657	Degrees of freedom are
2	1.886	2.920	4.303	6.965	9.925	computed by taking the
. . .	. . .					number of events in the study
19	1.328	1.729	2.093	2.539	2.861	and subtracting the

In addition to testing the difference between a sample mean and a standard or a historical mean, the one-sample t test also is useful when a researcher wishes to examine whether a sample is representative of the population. In particular, researchers may use this test when they wish to tell if the population and sample means actually are from the same populations.

Table 7.3   The One-Sample t Test

The population mean for class grades of undergraduates at a university is 2.59 (possible range: 0 to 4). A researcher noticed that a group of 17 students taking courses in Intercultural Communication had the following grades in that class: 4, 3, 2, 2, 2, 2, 1, 1, 1, 4, 3, 2, 2, 2, 1, 1, and 1.

The mean of this sample is 2, and the standard deviation is 1.0. One may wonder if this sample is unrepresentative of the ordinary population of students. Using the one-sample t test, the researchers may test the null hypothesis H_0: $\mu_1 = \mu_0$, which states that the mean grade of the sample of students taking Intercultural

Table 7.3 (Continued)

Communication classes is equal to the population mean of 2.59 (in fact, the null hypothesis could have been written as H_0: $\mu_1 = 2.59$). With a sample of 17, degrees of freedom are $n - 1$ or 16. Using a two-tailed t test with alpha risk at .05, the critical value of t is 2.120. Using the one-sample t test, one would find:

$$t = \frac{\overline{X} - \mu}{\frac{s}{\sqrt{n}}}$$

$$z = \frac{2. - 2.59}{\frac{1}{\sqrt{17}}} = \frac{-.59}{\frac{1}{4.1231}} = \frac{-.59}{.2425} = -2.433.$$

Because the test statistic is greater than the critical value (remember, the negative value does not mean subtraction, but a location on the t distribution), the null hypothesis would be rejected. One would conclude that the sample is not representative of the population. Thus, researchers would want to determine why and explore possible explanations.

Using SPSS for the One-Sample t

Though Excel does not have built-in functions that permit the direct computation of the one-sample t test, SPSS has such an option. To use the SPSS package for this application of the t test, the researcher starts by clicking on the *Analyze* menu followed by selecting *Compare Means* from the drop-down menu that appears. Then, the *One-Sample T Test. . .* option is selected. In the "One-Sample T Test" dialog box, the researcher selects the sample measure of interest and uses the arrow key to move it to the "Test Variable(s):" field. As an example, we may use the same data as employed in Table 7.3, in which case the variable "gpa" is selected for analysis. In this example, the population mean against which comparisons are made is 2.59. Hence, this value is entered into the "Test Value:" field. To execute the program, the researcher clicks the *OK* button.

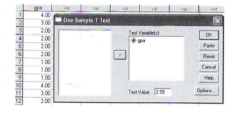

The output shows that the probability of finding a difference such as that observed here by random sampling error is only .027, or 2.7 chances out of a hundred.

One-Sample Statistics

	N	Mean	Std. Deviation	Std. Error Mean
gpa	17	2.0000	1.00000	.24254

One-Sample Test

	Test Value = 2.59					
					95% Confidence Interval of the Difference	
	t	df	Sig. (2-tailed)	Mean Difference	Lower	Upper
gpa	−2.433	16	.027	−.59000	−1.1042	−.0758

Because this probability is below the .05 usually employed as a decision rule, most researchers would reject the null hypothesis and conclude that there is a difference between this sample mean and the traditional population mean.

COMPARING THE MEANS OF TWO SAMPLE GROUPS: THE TWO-SAMPLE *t* TEST

Researchers often do not have a population standard against which to make comparisons, but they often have control groups to help them draw conclusions. If researchers wish to compare two sample groups, the two-sample *t* test is appropriate.

Using *t* as a Sampling Distribution of Mean Differences

To make this comparison, the null hypothesis takes the form H_0: $\mu_1 = \mu_2$, which tests that the dependent variable mean of the first group is equal to the mean of the second group. Actual alternative research hypotheses may be directional or nondirectional.

In addition to the assumptions of parametric statistics generally, the two-sample *t* test also assumes **independence**. This assumption means that the events in the sample are unaffected by each other. In many cases, this sort of thing is quite reasonable, but in some cases, it is not. For example, some researchers sample college classrooms. If these classes are required in an academic major, students probably interact with each other and may discuss things that happen in their classes, such as a new teaching approach or a study in which are they participating. Thus, the samples of student responses from such classes may not be completely independent.

Conducting the Hypothesis Test for the Difference Between Two Sample Means

To examine a hypothesis about two means, such as H_1: $\mu_1 > \mu_2$, the researcher must state a null hypothesis for direct testing. Then, it is useful for the researcher to test the assumption of homogeneous variances before computing the actual *t* test statistic. As we have seen:

- If sample sizes are equal in the two groups, the result of heterogeneous variances on Type I error rate is negligible. If variances are equal (within the limits of sampling error), the so-called pooled standard deviation (s_p) or "equal variances" model may be used.
- But if sample sizes are unequal, a significant heterogeneity in variances requires the researchers to use the "separate variance" (also called unequal variances *t*) method of conducting the independent samples *t* test. Using the pooled standard deviation when assuming equal variances, the formula for *t* is

$$t = \frac{\overline{X}_1 - \overline{X}_2}{s_p \sqrt{\frac{1}{n_1} + \frac{1}{n_2}}}.$$

The formula looks a lot like the one-sample *t* test formula. With equal sample sizes, the pooled standard deviation (s_p) is simply the square root of the average of the variances. With unequal sample sizes, the following formula for the pooled standard deviation is used:

$$s_p = \sqrt{\frac{(n_1 - 1)s_1^2 + (n_2 - 1)s_2^2}{n_1 - 1 + n_2 - 1}}.$$

Because there are two sample sizes, instead of dividing the standard deviation estimate by $\sqrt{n}$, the pooled standard deviation is multiplied by the sum of the square root of the fractions $\frac{1}{n}$ (equivalent to dividing a term by n).[16] An alternative formula for t with unequal variances is the separate variance estimate in which the variance for the control group is used as the measure of variance in the denominator of the t statistic. In addition, the following is a popular formula (used in Excel, for instance) employed when the variances are unequal:

$$t' = \frac{\overline{X}_1 - \overline{X}_2}{\sqrt{\dfrac{s_1^2}{n_1} + \dfrac{s_2^2}{n_2}}}.$$

To determine if a statistically significant difference exists between the two means, researchers enter the t distribution with degrees of freedom that adjust sample sizes for the number of population parameters estimated from sample means.

- If the variances are equal between the two groups, degrees of freedom are equal to $n - 2$ (because there are two sample means in the numerator of the t formula).
- If the variances are significantly different, the formula for degrees of freedom is:

$$d.f. = \frac{\left(\dfrac{s_1^2}{n_1} + \dfrac{s_1^2}{n_1}\right)^2}{\dfrac{\left(\dfrac{s_1^2}{n_1}\right)^2}{n_1 - 1} + \dfrac{\left(\dfrac{s_2^2}{n_2}\right)^2}{n_2 - 1}}.$$

This formula usually yields a number with a decimal point. So, the result must be rounded to a whole number.

Building Block Formula Box 7: Independent Samples t Test

$$t = \frac{\overline{X}_1 - \overline{X}_2}{s_p\sqrt{\dfrac{1}{n_1} + \dfrac{1}{n_2}}}$$

Table 7.4 Independent Samples t Test

A researcher wondered whether it would be more persuasive for a speaker to include an explicit statement of the advocated position even when the audience was initially hostile to the topic. Thus, as part of a pilot study, a randomly selected group of 16 individuals was given a message with an explicit statement of the persuasive proposition. A control group of 15 individuals was given the message with the explicit statement omitted. The chief dependent variable was attitude toward the topic, measured on a set of interval level scales with possible scores ranging from 3 (most negative attitude) to 21 (most positive attitude).

The study hypothesis was H: $\mu_{\text{explicit statement of proposition}} > \mu_{\text{no explicit statement of proposition included}}$. The null hypothesis was H$_0$: $\mu_{\text{explicit statement of proposition}} = \mu_{\text{no explicit statement of proposition included}}$. The researcher tested the null hypothesis with alpha risk of .05.

(Continued)

---

[16]Multiplying a value by the fraction $\frac{1}{n}$ produces the same result as dividing a value by n.

Table 7.4 (Continued)

The following data were collected:

Explicit Statement Group	No Explicit Statement Group
9	6
6	5
15	7
14	8
8	10
11	11
8	6
7	9
9	4
10	8
9	7
10	12
9	8
4	10
12	9
13	
Mean = 9.63	8
Variance = 8.38	5

- Using a one-tailed t test, with $n - 2$ degrees of freedom $(31 - 2 = 29)$, the critical value of t is 1.699.

Test the assumption of homogeneous variances.

- Testing $H_0: \sigma_1^2 = \sigma_2^2$ at alpha risk of .05:

$$F = \frac{S_{largest}^2}{S_{smallest}^2}$$

$$F = \frac{9.63}{5} = 1.68$$

- Critical value:

$$d.f. := \frac{n_{largest} - 1}{n_{smallest} - 1} = \frac{15}{14}$$

$$\text{Critical } F_{(15,14) \text{with } \alpha/2}: 2.949$$

Therefore, no significant heterogeneity of variances was claimed, and the assumption of homogeneous variances was maintained. (When Excel computes this test, it uses a one-tailed probability, in this case involving a critical value of 2.463.)

- Computing t assuming equal variances, the following computations are made:

$$t = \frac{\overline{X}_1 - \overline{X}_2}{s_p \sqrt{\frac{1}{n_1} + \frac{1}{n_2}}}$$

$$t = \frac{9.63 - 8}{2.6 \sqrt{\frac{1}{16} + \frac{1}{15}}}$$

$$t = \frac{1.63}{2.6 \sqrt{.13}}$$

$$s_p = \sqrt{\frac{(n_1 - 1)s_1^2 + (n_2 - 1)s_2^2}{n_1 - 1 + n_2 - 1}}$$

$$s_p = \sqrt{\frac{(16 - 1)8.38 + (15 - 1)5}{16 - 1 + 15 - 1}}$$

$$s_p = \sqrt{\frac{195.7}{29}} = \sqrt{6.75} = 2.6$$

$$t = \frac{1.63}{2.6 * .36} = \frac{1.63}{.94} = 1.73$$

Because 1.73 is greater than the critical value (1.699), the null hypothesis is rejected.

- To determine the effect size in terms of a correlation, the following formula is used:

$$r = \sqrt{\frac{t^2}{t^2 + \text{degrees of freedom}}}.$$

Inserting the information from this pilot study, the following computations may be completed:

$$r = \sqrt{\frac{2.99}{2.99 + 29}} = \sqrt{.09} = 0.3.$$

Thus, using the interpretation guides for correlations found in Chapter 5, this degree of relationship is equivalent to a "slight," "moderate," or "medium" relationship.

Using SPSS and Excel to Compute the Two-Sample *t*

Computers have made easy work of completing statistical hypothesis testing for comparing two sample means. The methods in both SPSS and Excel will be reviewed here.

SPSS

For the pooled standard deviation and separate standard deviation methods, the *t* test can be completed in one step. From the *Analyze* menu, select *Compare Means*. Several alternative *t* tests are provided: *Means...* includes descriptive statistics and various ways of testing the equality means; *One-Sample T Test...*; *Independent-Samples T Test...*; *Paired-Samples T Test...*; and *One-Way Anova....* To illustrate the use of the program here, the choice of an "Independent Samples T Test" will be made. In the dialog box that emerges, the researcher highlights the dependent variables of interest and transfers them to the fields marked "Test Variable(s):". Separate *t* tests will be completed for each of the variables listed as a test variable.

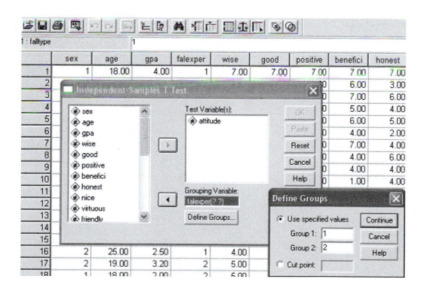

To identify the two groups, a categorization variable is highlighted and then transferred to the box marked "Grouping Variable:". It is assumed that the two groups are identified by taking such values as 1 or 2 in this variable. But sometimes researchers want to use grouping variables that originally had three or more groups. After the *Define Groups...* button is clicked, another dialog box opens and the researcher indicates the values used to identify group one and group two. Sometimes researchers take a continuous variable and break it down into two categories or groups. For instance, a researcher might want everyone with an IQ score equal to or below 100 to be in the first group and all those with higher scores in the second group. In such a case, the researcher would have clicked on the "Cut Point" radio button and entered a number in the field that became active. Participants with scores above that point are placed in the first group, and the rest are identified as members of the second group.

Group Statistics

	FALEXPER	N	Mean	Std. Deviation	Std. Error Mean
ATTITUDE	1.00	23	19.8696	6.0250	1.2563
	2.00	29	22.3793	3.8952	.7233

After the researcher is done, the *Continue* and *OK* buttons are clicked and the following output at the left appears. The first portion of the output provides simple descriptive statistics about the sample.

The next section of the output provides information about the Levene test of homogeneous variances. A "Sig." value of .05 or smaller for the Levene test is taken as evidence that the two samples did not have equal variances. If such is found, then the *t* test that is based on "Equal variances not assumed" is used. The *t* test in the example below shows no significant difference in the means at the .05 level (.075 is found). Of course, these results are for a two-tailed *t* test. If a one-tailed test were used, then the results would have been statistically significant (.075 divided by two would have produced a probability of .0375).

Independent Samples Test

		Levene's Test for Equality of Variances		t-test for Equality of Means					95% Confidence Interval of the Difference	
		F	Sig.	t	df	Sig. (2-tailed)	Mean Difference	Std. Error Difference	Lower	Upper
ATTITUDE	Equal variances assumed	3.606	.063	−1.817	50	.076	−2.5097	1.3812	−5.2839	.2844
	Equal variances not assumed			−1.731	35.903	.092	−2.5097	1.4498	−6.4500	.4305

Excel

To compute the *F* test for homogeneous variances, researchers using Excel select *Data Analysis. . .* from the *Tools* menu. In this example, we will illustrate the use of the *t* test when unequal variances are present. Thus, the effort begins with the *F* test of differences in variances. In the dialog box that appears, one may select *F-Test Two-Sample for Variances* and click *OK*. Using the highlighting tools, the researcher selects data for the first variable and second variable (indicated in the "Variable 1 Range:" and the "Variable 2 Range:" fields).

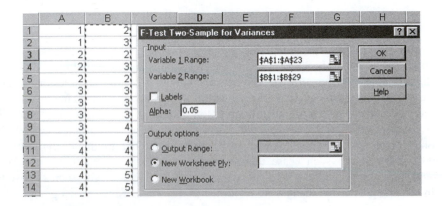

Clicking on the *OK* button reveals the following output.

	A	B	C
1	t−Test: Two−Sample Assuming Unequal Variances		
2			
3		*Variable 1*	*Variable 2*
4	Mean	19.86957	22.37931
5	Variance	36.3004	15.17241
6	Observations	23	29
7	Hypothesized Mean Difference	0	
8	df	36	
9	t Stat	−1.73129	
10	P(T<=t) one−tail	0.045982	
11	t Critical one−tail	1.688297	
12	P(T<=t) two−tail	0.091964	
13	t Critical two−tail	2.020091	

As can be seen, the output reveals the results of the *F* test of the difference between variances. Because there is a statistically significant difference in the variances (indicated by a *p* value smaller than .05), the researchers would be invited to use a *t* test for unequal variances.

To use Excel to compute an independent samples *t* test, select *Data Analysis* from the *Tools* menu and then choose *t-Test Two Sample Assuming Unequal Variances*. In the dialog box that appears, select ranges to indicate the scores for variables 1 and 2.

After identifying the variable ranges, click on *OK* to complete the analysis. The result is found on output such as that on page 170. As can be seen, the one-tailed probability level is less than .05, which would indicate a statistically significant difference. If researchers had chosen a two-tailed test, however, the difference would not be statistically significant by usual standards.

	A	B	C
	File Edit View Insert Format Tools Data Window Help		
	Courier ▾ 8 ▾ **B** *I* <u>U</u> ≡ ≡ ≡ ▦ $ %		
	D18 ▾ *fx*		
1	F-Test Two-Sample for Variances		
2			
3		*Variable 1*	*Variable 2*
4	Mean	19.8695652	22.37931034
5	Variance	36.3003953	15.17241379
6	Observations	23	29
7	df	22	28
8	F	2.39252605	
9	P(F<=f) one-tail	0.01524807	
10	F Critical one-tail	1.93487182	

Effect Size Computations

Statistical significance really tells us only how improbable the null hypothesis is when it comes to explaining sample results. But a statistically significant effect may be large or small. To learn if the results are substantial or not, it is useful to look at the size of relationships. To use the language of correlation, researchers may take information from a *t* test by use of this formula:

$$r = \sqrt{\frac{t^2}{t^2 + \text{degrees of freedom}}}.$$

Squaring this number reveals the proportion of variance in one variable that may be explained by knowledge of variation in the other alone.

Confidence Intervals for Mean Differences

To say that a mean difference of five points on a scale is beyond what might have been expected to occur by sampling error tells only part of the story. The mean difference is only a single best estimate of the difference, called a **point estimate** because it is a single number. But the true population difference may lie within an interval around the observed differences. An alternative way of using these data employs a **confidence coefficient** or **degree of confidence** followed by an interval (called, not surprisingly, a **confidence interval**) into which the population difference is likely to fall. As shorthand, researchers often report such confidence intervals with such brief statements as "the 90% confidence interval of the differences in means is 3.5 to 6.5." The numbers 3.5 and 6.5 are known as the lower and upper **confidence bounds** (or **confidence limits**). The statement indicates that the researcher is 90% "confident" that the difference in means lies somewhere between 3.5 and 6.5 on the measure in use. To be precise, however, a 95% confidence interval means that if a large number of random samples were drawn and confidence intervals were computed, 95% of them would include (or capture) the mean difference parameter of interest. The fact that a 95% confidence interval has been drawn, however, also means that there is a 5% chance that the report made by the researcher is *way off*, not even close.

To compute a confidence interval for differences in means, such as the study found in the independent samples *t* test example in Table 7.4, the following formula may be used:

$$95\% \ C.I. = \overline{X}_1 - \overline{X}_2 \pm (t_{(\alpha/2, \text{d.f.})} * s_{\bar{x}_1 - \bar{x}_2}),$$

where $\overline{X}_1 - \overline{X}_2$ is the difference in means, $t_{(\alpha/2, d.f.)}$ is the critical value of *t* found in the *t* table (the α corresponds to the announced confidence interval [e.g., $1 - \alpha$ of .05 corresponds to a 95% degree of confidence]), the $\alpha/2$ term means that the critical value should be two-tailed (in this case, the two-tailed critical *t* value with alpha risk of .05 and 29 degrees of freedom is 2.045), and $s_{\bar{x}_1 - \bar{x}_2}$ is the standard error of the mean differences and includes everything in the denominator of the *t* test formula

$$\left(s_p \sqrt{\frac{1}{n_1} + \frac{1}{n_2}} \right).$$

For the example, the confidence interval may be identified:

$$95\% \ C.I. = 163 \pm (2.045 * .94)$$
$$95\% \ C.I. = 1.63 \pm 1.92$$

In other words, the researcher is 95% confident that the difference between means is somewhere between $-.29$ and 3.55. Because the confidence interval includes zero, one would conclude that the mean difference is not significantly different from zero. But the example found a significant difference between the groups. How can this situation exist? The test in the example was a one-tailed test, but the confidence interval was a two-tailed test.

One-tailed confidence intervals can be constructed. One could imagine a person asking only about one side of the confidence interval, such as "what is the *minimum* mean difference improvement that can be expected if the controversial proposition is stated explicitly?" Such a person would not care to know the upper limit, just the *least* improvement to be expected. The difference in the formula is that a one-sided critical *t* value (1.699) is used, such as:

$$95\% \ C.I. = \overline{X}_1 - \overline{X}_2 \pm (t_{(\alpha/1, d.f.)} * s_{\bar{x}_1 - \bar{x}_2})$$
$$95\% \ C.I. = 1.63 \pm (1.699 * .94)$$
$$95\% \ C.I. = 1.63 \pm (1.59)$$

In other words, the researcher is 95% confident that the difference between means is at least 0.04. This number might be taken as the smallest difference for which one might be confident.

COMPARING MEANS DIFFERENCES OF PAIRED SCORES: THE PAIRED DIFFERENCE t

Researchers often give people a pretest, followed by some treatment, and then a posttest. The "before and after" designs gather sample data from every person twice; thus, the samples are not independent. A way to deal with such data is to use the t test for paired differences.

Conducting the Hypothesis Test for Paired Differences

Instead of dealing with mean differences among groups, researchers using the paired differences t test subtract the posttest from the pretest and examine the size of these differences. The null hypothesis in the paired samples t test is H_0: $\mu_{\text{difference}} = 0$. Because the same sample is examined twice, the degrees of freedom for the t test are based on the number of events, not the number of scores. The degrees of freedom are equal to $n - 1$.

The formula for the paired samples t test is a bit different from those for the other t tests:

$$t = \frac{\overline{X}_{diff}}{\frac{s_D}{\sqrt{n}}},$$

where $\overline{X}_{diff}$ is the mean difference between the paired scores (often pretest and posttest; when the research hypothesis speculates that the posttest scores will be higher than the pretest scores, the difference would have a negative sign before it; if the research hypothesis speculates that the posttest scores will be lower than the pretest scores, the difference would have a positive value), s_D is the standard deviation of the difference scores, and n is the number of events in the sample (not the number of total scores).

Table 7.5 Paired Difference t Test

A researcher explored the hypothesis that students who go through a unit of instruction on communication styles have higher posttest scores on a measure of perceived comfort in communication with difficult people (possible range: 3 to 21) than they did on a pretest. A sample of 19 people was collected, and following the pretest, sample members were given instruction and then posttested. Because the researcher predicted that the posttest scores would be higher than the pretest scores, a negative value is predicted in the one-tailed hypothesis: H: $\mu_{\text{difference}} < 0$. The null hypothesis is

H_0: $\mu_{\text{difference}} = 0$.

Degrees of freedom are $n - 1$ or $19 - 1 = 18$.

The critical value of t (one tailed) with alpha risk of .05 is -1.734.

The following data were collected:

Table 7.5 (Continued)

Pretest	Posttest	Difference
3	5	−2
12	11	1
7	9	−2
20	18	2
18	19	−1
16	18	−2
14	17	−3
15	18	−3
16	18	−2
17	19	−2
7	6	1
8	10	−1
18	17	1
10	14	−4
12	15	−3
14	15	−1
13	15	−2
15	16	−1
16	17	−1

Mean =   −1.37
Standard Deviation =   1.61

$$t = \frac{\overline{X}_{diff}}{\frac{S_D}{\sqrt{n}}}$$

$$t = \frac{-1.37}{\frac{1.61}{\sqrt{19}}} = \frac{-1.37}{\frac{1.61}{4.36}} = \frac{-1.37}{.37} = -3.7$$

The null hypothesis would be rejected because the test statistic (−3.7) is beyond the critical value of −1.734. (It is helpful to remember that the negative sign is not a symbol for subtraction but instead a way to identify the place where the critical region begins. In this case, the critical region starts at −1.734 and extends out to −∞. For these data, the test statistic of −3.7 falls into the critical region.)

Using SPSS and Excel to Compute the Paired Differences *t*

Both SPSS and Excel include ways to conduct the paired differences *t* test. The basic format remains relatively unchanged from that which has been described previously. Hence, only the chief differences will be examined in this brief treatment.

SPSS

From the *Analyze* menu, researchers select *Compare Means* from the drop-down menu, followed by *Paired-Samples T Test...* from the subsequent menu that appears. In the dialog box that appears, two separate variables for each participant must be selected and transferred into the "Paired Variables:" field by highlighting them and moving them with the arrow key.

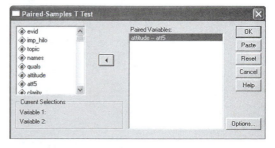

Clicking the *OK* button causes the program to execute. The output produced by this process is a little different from the previous example. In addition to a set of descriptive statistics, a measure of correlation between the two measures appears. This correlation is not a measure of effect size, but a measure of association between the two sets of scores.

Paired Samples Correlations

		N	Correlation	Sig.
Pair 1	ATTITUDE & ATT5	66	.843	.000

Paired Samples Test

		Paised Difference							
					95% Confidence Interval of the Difference				
		Mean	Std. Deviation	Std. Error Mean	Lower	Upper	t	df	Sig. (2-tailed)
Pair 1	ATTITUDE - ATT	−.67	3.788	.466	−1.60	.26	−1.430	65	.158

A regular feature of the *t* test in SPSS is the presentation of confidence intervals. If the confidence interval contains zero, then no statistically significant difference between the means is revealed. In this case, because the 95% confidence interval extends from −1.6 to 0.26, it includes zero, which indicates no statistically significant difference.

This correlation should be reasonably large when there is no statistically significant difference between two sets of scores. If the difference between the pairs scores is large and the correlation is low, researchers may wish to consider whether they really wished to use the independent samples *t* test instead. As can be seen in the output, there was no statistically significant difference in the paired scores.

Excel

The paired samples *t* test also may be computed with Excel. The researcher begins by selecting *Data Analysis. . .* from the *Tools* menu. Then, on the drop-down menu that appears, the researcher chooses *t-Test: Paired Two Sample for Means* option. In the "t-Test: Paired Two Sample for Means" dialog box, the researcher clicks the symbol in the "Variable 1 Range:" field and highlights the cells where the first set of data scores are located. Clicking on the symbol on the drop-down menu returns the researcher to the main dialog box. Then, the same process can be followed to identify the "Variable 2 Range:" of data.

The "Labels" box should be checked if the researcher has highlighted any cells with variable or group labels. Before clicking on the *OK* button, the researcher also will want to select a location for the placement of output in the "Output Range" field.

The output differs from that of other *t* tests by including a measure of correlation between the two measures. In this case, the correlation is quite high, so any differences between the two sets of scores should be modest (exactly the situation found in this case).

```
File   Edit   View   Insert   Format   Tools   Data   Window   Help
```

Courier   ▼ 8 ▼   **B** *I* U   ≡ ≡ ≡ ⊞ $ % ,   ⁺⁰

E10   ▼   *fx*

	A	B	C
1	t–Test: Paired Two Sample for Means		
2			
3		*Variable 1*	*Variable 2*
4	Mean	17.4545455	18.1212121
5	Variance	44.5902098	19.4927739
6	Observations	66	66
7	Pearson Correlation	0.84346902	
8	Hypothesized Mean Difference	0	
9	df	65	
10	t Stat	−1.4297963	
11	P(T<=t) one–tail	0.07878232	
12	t Critical one–tail	1.66863629	
13	P(T<=t) two–tail	0.15756465	
14	t Critical two–tail	1.99713668	

Confidence Intervals for Paired Differences

A confidence interval may be constructed around mean paired differences using the formula

$$95\% \ C.I. = \overline{X}_{diff} \pm (t_{(\alpha/2, d.f.)} * \frac{s_D}{\sqrt{n}}),$$

where $\overline{X}_{diff}$ is the mean paired differences,

$t_{(\alpha/2, d.f.)}$ is the critical value of *t* (with α corresponding to the announced confidence interval; e.g., $1 - \alpha$ of .05 corresponds to a 95% degree of confidence),

$\alpha/2$ means that the critical value should be two-tailed, and

$\frac{s_D}{\sqrt{n}}$ is the standard error of the mean paired differences and includes everything in the

denominator of the paired *t*-test formula.

For the example of the paired *t* test, a 95% confidence interval would be computed as follows:

$$95\% \ C.I. = -1.73 \pm (-1.734 * .37)$$
$$95\% \ C.I. = -1.73 \pm (-.64)$$

Thus, the researcher would claim 95% confidence that the difference between the pretest and posttest is somewhere between −1.09 and −2.37.

ASSESSING POWER

Statistical power is "the probability of rejecting the null hypothesis when it is false—and therefore should be rejected" (Vogt, 2005, p. 242). Some writers recommend that researchers routinely compute power before they complete studies. This step may help researchers select appropriate sample sizes. Furthermore, when researchers propose a new study, it makes sense to compute power to decide if there are enough possible data to make a study feasible.

There are many ways to increase the power of a statistical significance test. First, the researcher may decide to examine only large differences. Large differences are more easily detected with statistical significance tests than are small differences. A popular rule of thumb has been Cohen's (J. Cohen, 1988) effect size guidelines. He suggests that an effect size difference of below 0.2 standard deviations is small, up to a 0.5 standard deviation difference is medium, and 0.8 standard deviations or greater is large. For correlations, he suggests that associations below $r = .1$ are small, in the range of $r = .3$ are medium, and above $r = .5$ are large. Yet, these guidelines and the use of "after the fact" power analyses have been questioned in recent years, especially when used as a basis for trying to balance power and sample size issues (see Lenth, 2001). Second, researchers may exercise control to minimize the size of the population standard deviation. Third, the researcher could raise the alpha risk. If alpha risk were raised from .05 to .10, for instance, more null hypotheses are likely to be rejected than when the decision rule is kept at .05. Finally, of course, researchers may increase sample size.

This last option is the one researchers have given their greatest attention (probably because the first three options are difficult to apply). They often wonder how large their sample sizes would have to be for statistical significance to be claimed. They identify the level of power desired, typically .80 or .90; the alpha risk to be used in the statistical significance test; and the smallest size for an effect they would be interested in reporting. Once done, the researchers may use formulae and occasionally tables to determine the power of a test. The power of a test is computed as $1 - \beta$ where

$$\beta = P\left(Z < \frac{C - \mu_1}{\sigma/\sqrt{n}}\right)$$

and C = upper confidence limit, such as

$$95\% \ UL = \mu_0 + \left(1.645 * \frac{\sigma}{\sqrt{n}}\right).$$

Suppose you were doing a study on the trustworthiness of television news anchors. On scales ranging from 5 to 35 points, the traditional mean has been 22 with a standard deviation of 16. You have a sample size of 100 and wish to identify differences in trustworthiness ratings of 25 in comparison with the traditional mean (22) in trustworthiness ratings. What would be the power of a one-tailed test?

Special Discussion 7.2

The Treachery of After-the-Fact Power Analyses

Sometimes researchers compute power *after* they have completed their studies and analyzed most of their data, but such an approach is generally not advised. In the first place, computing power after the fact does not reveal anything that the probability level of the hypothesis test does not (Hoenig & Heisey, 2001). In fact, after-the-fact power statistics are simply proportional to alpha risk: The smaller the alpha risk, the greater the power. In the second place, the effort to show high power in the absence of statistical significance probably is misleading because it often is a veiled effort to "prove" a null hypothesis. When advertisers state that "no product has been shown superior to the ingredients contained in [their product]," they are asserting the truth of a null hypothesis, generally in the absence of evidence. The use of power analyses, however, cannot prove that a null hypothesis is true.

As a superior alternative, some writers have suggested reporting confidence intervals (S. N. Goodman & Berlin, 1994; M. Levine & Ensome, 2001). If one computes a confidence interval around a mean difference (or around a correlation) and finds that the confidence interval is very small, then the failure to find support for a research hypothesis may have some practical value (because it would indicate that only trivial effects remained undetected). A broad confidence interval might indicate a need to increase sample sizes and reduce background variation in future research. Indeed, the National Center for Educational Statistics of the U.S. Department of Education developed a program of statistical standards for researchers in which it stated that one of the preferred options when a null hypothesis is not rejected is to "use a 95% confidence interval to describe the magnitude of the possible difference or effect" (National Center for Educational Statistics, 2002, Standard 5-1-5: 7).

Using the formula on page 176, one would find the following:

$$C = \mu_0 + \left(1.645 * \frac{\sigma}{\sqrt{n}} \right)$$

$$= 22 + \left(1.645 * \frac{16}{\sqrt{100}} \right) = 22 + (1.645 * 1.6) = 22 + 2.63 = 24.63$$

$$\text{Power} = 1 - \beta$$

$$\text{Power} = 1 - P \left(Z < \frac{C - \mu_1}{\sigma/\sqrt{n}} \right)$$

$$= 1 - P \left(Z < \frac{24.632 - 25}{16/\sqrt{100}} \right) = 1 - P \left(Z < \frac{-.368}{1.6} \right) = 1 - P(Z < -.23)$$

To compute this beta, we look at the z table and ask how much area exists below the point identified. On the z table, the area from 0 to -0.23 standard deviations includes .091 of the total area. The area *below* that point includes .50 (50% of the distribution) minus .091, which comes out to .409. Thus, power is computed as follows:

$$\text{Power} = 1 - .409 = .591.$$

This estimate means that a new mean as large as that identified with such a sample and such population characteristics will be detected as statistically significant 59.1% of the time.

Chapter 8

COMPARING MORE THAN TWO MEANS

One-Way Analysis of Variance

$\mathbf{R}$esearchers often have more than two means to compare. In a typical case, the independent variable consists of more than two nominal categories and the dependent variable is an interval measure whose means are compared. This chapter deals with the use of analysis of variance (abbreviated ANOVA) for this situation. In the next chapter, we will extend this tool to situations where there is more than one independent variable to consider.

HYPOTHESIS TESTING FOR MORE THAN TWO MEANS

When comparing more than two means, the t test is not appropriate. The reason is that the t test for independent means is designed for two groups. If three means are involved, a problem is created. Consider a study of the levels of self-esteem of people with low, moderate, and high communication apprehension (CA). Using the t test would require three tests (low CA vs. moderate CA, low CA vs. high CA, and moderate CA vs. high CA). But if *each* test of significance were completed with an alpha risk of .05, the *total* experimentwise alpha risk would be well above .05.[1] This situation sometimes is called the Bonferroni inequality (Upton & Cook, 2002, p. 43). This value states that the actual Type I error rate is somewhat less than .05 multiplied by the number of comparisons made. As an alternative, the one-way analysis of variance uses one test to compare more than two groups.[2]

Doing a Study That Involves More Than Two Groups

A researcher comparing more than two groups often needs to have a test of the statistical significance of the difference between the means of the study groups. If there are three groups to compare, the research hypothesis takes the form H: $\mu_1 \neq \mu_2 \neq \mu_3$. As can be seen, analysis of variance makes an "omnibus statistical significance test" of the difference among group means.

Researchers choose conditions based on some thinking about relevant variables. The groups may be different categories, such as people who are Republicans, Democrats, or Independents. Sometimes continuous variables, such as ratings of communicator assertiveness, are broken down into levels, such as "lowly assertive," "moderately assertive," and "highly assertive." Selection of the ways to create such levels sometimes is done arbitrarily. For instance, researchers often call the people with the lowest third of scores "low," the next third of participants "moderate," and the final third "high." But if researchers look at the actual scores, most of the people in the sample might come from objectively high ranges. Thus, dividing samples into thirds might not be an accurate way to set levels. Instead, researchers should have some reasoning behind the choices they make to select the variable levels.[3]

---

[1]For the actual Type I error rate with alpha risk of .05, one computes $1 - 0.95^{\text{the number of comparisons}}$. For three tests, the value is $1 - .95^3 = 0.142625$.

[2]Analysis of variance could be applied to comparisons of two groups. In such circumstances, the value of F is the same as the value of t^2.

[3]So-called "nominalizing" a variable that is conceptually and operationally an interval level measure may be inappropriate for two reasons. First, nominalizing interval concepts may encourage thinking that may not fit with theory. Second, nominalizing interval measures usually educes the statistical power of tests.

To conduct a research study involving analysis of variance, the researchers must do the following:

- State a hypothesis. Analysis of variance is invited if the hypothesis is a statement about expected differences on an interval level dependent measure across different groups defined by one or more nominal level independent variables.
- After the hypothesis is stated and after data have been collected, the researcher should screen data by looking for outliers, after which they may be deleted or the data may be transformed.
- Though often ignored, researchers should check the assumptions underlying the tests.
- Examine if distributions are normal by checking kurtosis, skewness, and tests of normality such as the Lilliefors test modification of the Kolmogorov-Smirnov one-sample test and the Shapiro-Wilk test (see Chapter 7). If sample sizes are large (such as 30 or greater), deviations from such abnormality may not greatly affect statistical significance testing with analysis of variance. But if samples are small, difficulties with normality may have to be adjusted by transformations before further analyses.
- Check on homogeneity of variances by such tests as F_{max} or Levene's test. If variances are unequal, steps should be taken to determine if the data show ceiling or floor effects (see Chapter 7). This process can be completed by examining the means and variances and even computing a Pearson product-moment correlation between the means and variances. If means and variances are highly directly correlated, the data may show a **"floor effect."** This circumstance means that as means become lower and lower, variances become artificially "compressed" as the lower bound of the measurement range is reached. Similarly, a **"ceiling effect"** would be found if the variances became "compressed" because the conditions with the highest means approached the upper boundary of the measurement range.[4] A significant inverse correlation may indicate that a ceiling effect exists. Even without ceiling or floor effects, it may be that the means and variances are correlated. As one source put it:

> One instance when the *F* statistic is very misleading is when the means are correlated with variances across cells of the design. . . . The reason why this is a "dangerous" violation is the following: Imagine that you have 8 cells in the design, 7 with about equal means but one with a much higher mean. The *F* statistic may suggest to you a statistically significant effect. However, suppose that there also is a

---

[4]This conception is not the only view of ceiling and floor effects. Sometimes the "compression" is not caused only by limits on the measurement range, but also by a measurement range beyond what respondents use. For example, on teaching evaluations, there may be both a floor (students do not want to be too negative) and a ceiling (students do not want to be too positive) effect even though an additional possible range of values is available on the scale. Expanding the explanation for the compression effects might lead to definitions of ceiling effects as compression of data at the top of a distribution due to limits on the highest score possible or actually used, and floor effects as compression of data at the bottom of a distribution due to limits on the lowest score possible or actually used. (Thanks to Dr. Rodney A. Reynolds for this input.)

much larger variance in the cell with the highest mean, that is, the means and the variances are correlated across cells (the higher the mean the larger the variance). In that case, the high mean in the one cell is actually quite unreliable, as is indicated by the large variance. However, because the overall F statistic is based on a pooled within-cell variance estimate, the high mean is identified as significantly different from the others, when in fact it is not at all significantly different if one based the test on the within-cell variance in that cell alone.

This pattern—a high mean and a large variance in one cell—frequently occurs when there are outliers present in the data. One or two extreme cases in a cell with only 10 cases can greatly bias the mean, and will dramatically increase the variance. (StatSoft, 2003a, ¶51–52)

- The analysis of variance is completed as any other hypothesis test. The alpha risk is set, and the relevant critical value is identified on that table of critical values of F (Appendix C.5). If the test statistic is greater than the critical F value, a statistically significant difference may be claimed.

- Because the analysis of variance only reveals that there is a difference *somewhere* among the means, other tests must be completed to learn *where* the differences come from:
  - If the groups are from an underlying continuum—such as low, moderate, and high communication apprehensive individuals—**trend analysis** may be used to explore a possible curvilinear relationship with the dependent variable.
  - If researchers have a measure of another variable that is believed to be a nuisance, such as the degree to which respondents try to answer survey questions in "socially desirable" ways, **analysis of covariance** may be used to control for the influence of such contaminating variables.
  - If researchers wish to "snoop" through the means by comparing them to each other, **multiple comparison tests** may be used. Such tests as Tukey's, Dunn's, and Scheffé's permit comparisons between groups while keeping Type I error rates under control.

Assumptions Underlying Use of Analysis of Variance

Because it also is a parametric test of statistical significance, the analysis of variance shares the same assumptions as the t test. There are four such assumptions:

1. Interval or ratio level measurement of dependent variables;

2. randomization in sampling and any assignment of events to experimental and control conditions;

3. normal probability distribution of dependent variables; and

4. equal (homogeneous) variances of the dependent variable in the population (and the corresponding requirement that sample variances remain equal within the limits of sampling error).

Another assumption is made for analysis of variance:

- that the numerator and denominator in the formula used to compute the F ratio are independent (this assumption means that in the formula used to compute analysis of variance,

$$F = \frac{\text{variance between groups}}{\text{variance within groups}} \, ,$$

the terms in the top and the bottom of the fraction are truly separate sources of variation).

In the **fixed-effects analysis of variance**, the levels for the independent variable are, well, fixed. The levels are chosen to cover a range of variation of interest to the researcher. Thus, in addition to the previous assumptions, the "fixed-effects model" here assumes that (Kirk, 1982, pp. 74–75)

- the elements in the model reflect the sum of all the elements that affect the dependent variable;
- the experiment contains all treatment levels of interest; and
- the error effects are independent and normally distributed.

As a result, another assumption—**independence**—also is included.[5] This assumption is that the samples are independent. Hence, knowing an individual's score on some measure does not either predict that degree of that individual's error or predict any other individual's responses.

Many of these supplementary assumptions are true by definition. For example, the assumption that the error terms are normally distributed quickly boils down to assuming that the dependent variable is normally distributed. Similarly, the assumption that error terms are normally distributed also implies that any error terms have mean and variance equal to zero. But such a statement is a simple reflection of the way an error effect ε is defined.[6]

---

[5]One could list additional assumptions, of course, but they also tend to exist as consequents of other assumptions or conditions for the fixed-effects model. For instance, the assumption may be made that the numerator and denominator of the F statistics "are estimates of the same population variance," σ_ε^2 (Kirk, 1982, p. 74). But "this assumption corresponds to the null hypothesis. It is advanced in the hope that it can be rejected" (Kirk, 1982, p. 76). Similarly, the assumption that the elements in the fixed-effects model contain all treatment levels that predict the dependent variable is simply another way of defining the fixed-effects model.

[6]As mentioned, analysis of variance assumes that error terms "over repeated observations will have a normal distribution with a population mean (expectation) of 0 and variance of σ_ε^2" (Glass & Hopkins, 1984, p. 351). But "since for each level of the factor $\varepsilon_{ij} = X_{ij} - \mu - \alpha_j$, and μ and α_j are constants, ε_{ij} is a linear transformation . . . of X_{ij}; thus the ANOVA assumption regarding the distributions of ε_{ij} and X_{ij} are synonymous" (Glass & Hopkins, 1984, p. 350). The way the error term is defined makes this condition so, as shown in this proof (Kirk, 1982, p. 77):

$$\varepsilon_{i(j)} = Y_{ij} - \mu_j - \alpha_j$$
$$= Y_{ij} - \mu_j$$
$$\text{and } E(Y_{ij} - \mu_j) = E(Y_{ij}) - \mu_j$$
$$= \mu_j - \mu_j = 0.$$

One might wonder what would happen if these assumptions were violated. In fact,

At the outset it should be observed that for real data some of the assumptions will always be violated. For example, the underlying populations from which samples are drawn are never exactly normally distributed with equal variance. The important question then is not whether the assumptions are violated, but rather whether violations have serious effects on the significance level and the power of the F test. (Kirk, 1982, p. 75)

With large and equal sample sizes in each condition, the analysis of variance is very *robust* to violations of the underlying assumptions. Thus, researchers probably should try to design studies featuring equal numbers of events in each condition. At one time, it was believed that violations of the assumptions were never important issues, but such a claim exaggerates things. Certainly, randomization is assumed as a foundation for entering distributions to determine how often a set of results could have been found due to random sampling error. Furthermore, the assumption of independence is fundamental for those who use the fixed-effect model of analysis of variance. For situations in which the samples are not independent, a different model (such as repeated measures ANOVA) may be required. Yet, with reasonably large samples and equal sample sizes in the conditions being compared, violations of the assumptions of normality and homogeneous variances are trivial on true Type I error rates. In fact, in one study, the use of a dichotomous dependent variable, instead of one measured on the required interval or ratio level, produced observed statistical significance levels that were quite close to named significance levels—provided sample sizes were equal across conditions (Lunney, 1970). When sample sizes are approximately equal, moderate heterogeneity of variances appears to have relatively insubstantial impact (Hsu & Feldt, 1969). But when sample sizes differ, often by ratios of 2 to 1 or greater, the effect on Type I error can be very great (Glass, Peckham, et al., 1972). In general:

- If the largest variance comes from the condition with the *largest* sample, true Type I error will be *lower* than the level announced by the researcher. That is, if researchers state that they are rejecting the null hypothesis at .05, the actual Type I error rate may be .03 or below. Of course, if the null hypothesis is rejected, the researcher's decision is unaffected by this limitation. Yet, if the null hypothesis is not rejected, the researcher might have some reason for concern.
- If the largest variance comes from the condition with the *smallest* sample, true Type I error will be *greater* than the level announced by the researcher. That is, if researchers state that they are rejecting the null hypothesis at .05, the actual Type I error rate will be above that level. Hence, researchers would erroneously reject more null hypotheses in error than they had announced by their alpha risk.

The Null Hypothesis for Analysis of Variance

If there are three groups, the null hypothesis is

$$H_0: \mu_1 = \mu_2 = \mu_3.$$

This statement is read "The mean on the dependent variable for the first group is equal to the mean for the second group, which is equal to the mean of the third group." Clearly, this null hypothesis states that there are no differences among the groups. Of course, the analysis of variance could be used for any number of groups greater than one.

THE ANALYSIS OF VARIANCE HYPOTHESIS TEST

Given its name, you might imagine that "analysis of variance" is a method to test differences among variances of groups. But the null hypothesis to be tested shows that *means*, not variances, are compared. So where does the analysis of *variance* language come in? The answer is that analysis of variance uses the variance to detect if there is a difference among the means of several groups. In the example on the right, for instance, your eyes can see that the means of the groups are different from each other. If you used the means of each group to compute a variance, there would be a positive number of some sort.

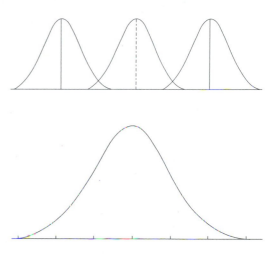

If all the means were the same, the three groups' distributions of scores would look like the diagram on the right. You probably do not see three distributions of data. The reason is that they are all on top of each other. If we computed a variance from these three means, there would be no variance at all, and the resulting coefficient would be 0 (zero). This expectation would be consistent with the null hypothesis.

Sources of Variation

There are two families of variances to be compared in analysis of variance. The first source is **between-groups variance**. A variance is computed from the means and then adjusted for sample sizes. Researchers often measure a continuous variable such as source credibility ratings, communicator competence, or communication apprehension. To create groups, a researcher may divide the continuous variable into levels or factors. In fact, the term **factor** refers to taking a variable and breaking it down into levels or categories. The **levels** of each variable are the categories of the factor, such as "low," "moderate," and "high" levels of such continuous variables as source credibility ratings, communicator competence, or communication apprehension.

The second source of variance is **within-groups variance**. This source also is known by the names "error variance," "within-treatments," and "within-replicates" variance. This source is the average of the variances within the samples (provided that equal sample sizes are used in the groups). This variance is computed by using the formula for the **pooled variance**, s_p^2. This term is identical to the computation for the pooled standard deviation s_p used in the t test. The pooled variance is an estimate of background variation that occurs ordinarily when only random variation around a mean is involved.

Conceptually (not computationally), the formula for analysis of variance is

$$F = \frac{\text{variance between groups}}{\text{variance within groups}}.$$

As can be seen, the analysis of variance uses the F distribution to help make decisions about rejecting the null hypothesis. In addition, because the pooled variance shows how much random variation might be expected within groups, researchers might expect at least as much variation between groups as there is random background variation. In short, the F statistic should be greater than 1.0, but researchers often find that observed F statistics are lower than 1.0. Because such a finding is not very sensible (and can never be statistically significant), experienced researchers usually report simply that they found $F < 1$.

Computing One-Way ANOVA

When only one independent variable is included, the ANOVA is called **one-way analysis of variance**. Computationally, analysis of variance is slightly more complicated than the conceptual formula. *Conceptually,* the formula states that

$$F = \frac{\text{variance between groups}}{\text{variance within groups}} \quad \text{or} \quad \frac{s_{\bar{X}}^2}{s_p^2}.$$

But the term in the numerator $(s_{\bar{X}}^2)$ is a variance based on a distribution of *means*. On the other hand, the term in the denominator (s_p^2) is a variance based on a distribution of *raw scores*. These two distributions are not comparable. In short, they are not on the same playing field. As stated in Chapters 4 and 7, a distribution of means has a much smaller standard deviation than a distribution of raw scores. The reason is due to the **central limit theorem**, which states that a sampling distribution of means tends toward a normal distribution with increased sample sizes regardless of the shape of the parent population. As a result of the central limit theorem, the standard deviation of means ($\sigma_{\bar{X}}$, called the "standard error of the mean") could be computed as

$$\sigma_{\bar{X}} = \frac{\sigma}{\sqrt{N}}.$$

Taking information from this theorem, it is possible to transform the data from the numerator into numbers comparable to the ones in the denominator. This step is completed by multiplying the term in the numerator $(s_{\bar{X}}^2)$ by the number of events in each sample (n).[7]

---

[7]To show how the transformation would be made, consider this statement from the central limit theorem applied to sample data:

$$s_{\bar{X}} = \frac{s}{\sqrt{n}}.$$

To transform this statement into related variances, each side of the equation may be squared:

$$(s_{\bar{X}})^2 = \left(\frac{s}{\sqrt{n}}\right)^2$$

$$s_{\bar{X}}^2 = \frac{s^2}{n}$$

To transform data into the same distribution of scores, each side of the equation may be multiplied by n.

$$n * s_{\bar{X}}^2 = \frac{s^2}{n} * \frac{n}{1};$$

the ns cancel out each other, leaving

$$n * s_{\bar{X}}^2 = \frac{s^2}{1} * \frac{1}{1}.$$

The result is $n * s_{\bar{X}}^2 = s^2$. Thus, to transform the numerator term in the conceptual F formula, the n numerator should be multiplied by n.

This adjustment assumes that the number of events in each group is the same. If, on the other hand, the number of events is different in conditions, then an alternative method to compute effects is used. In sum, for situations in which equal numbers of events exist in each condition, the formula for analysis of variance is

$$F = \frac{n * s_{\bar{X}}^2}{s_p^2}.$$

In most data analysis programs, the number in the numerator is called between-groups "mean square," and the number in the denominator is called "within-groups mean square." In other words, "mean square" is just another way of saying "variance." If unequal numbers of events are included in each group, the long formula for the pooled variance is required:

$$s_p^2 = \frac{n_{(1}-1)s_1^2 + (n_2 - 1)s_2^2 + \ldots (n - 1)s_n^2}{n_1 - 1 + n_2 - 1 + \ldots n_n - 1}$$

As can been seen, the formula for ANOVA is a fraction. The top and the bottom of the fraction have their own degrees of freedom.

- For the numerator, degrees of freedom are equal to the number of groups minus one.
- For the denominator, the degrees of freedom are equal to the number of events in the study minus the number of groups.

Once the F statistic is computed, one compares the observed value with the critical value that is found in the F table. Based on the decision rule (alpha risk of .05) the researchers set, the critical value from the F table (Appendix C.5) must be exceeded to claim that a difference has been observed that is beyond the limits of random sampling error. As can be seen by the diagram below, researchers use only one side of the F distribution to test statistical hypotheses.[8] To illustrate this method, an example is found in Table 8.1 on page 188.

between groups variance degress of freedom
within groups variance degress of freedom

		1	2	3	4
22	.05	4.301	3.443	3.049	2.817
	.025	5.786	4.383	3.783	3.440
	.01	7.945	5.719	4.817	4.313
23	.05	4.279	3.422	3.028	2.796
	.025	5.750	4.349	3.750	3.408
	.01	7.881	5.664	4.765	4.264
24	.05	4.260	3.403	3.009	2.776
	.025	5.717	4.319	3.721	3.379
	.01	7.823	5.614	4.718	4.218

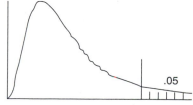

.05

[8]The computation of ANOVA makes it "inherently nondirectional with respect to means" (T. R. Levine & Banas, 2002, p. 136). Even so, some researchers have noticed that the tables of F indicate that two-sample comparisons are the equivalent of two-tailed t tests. To return to "directional ANOVA tests," they have begun to use critical F values that are associated with an alpha risk of .10, rather than the traditional .05. This approach has been the target of strong criticism. Levine and Banas submit that it leads researchers to claim statistical significance "that would not be considered statistically significant according to the critical values presented in standard F-tables" (p. 132). Furthermore, for a host of reasons, Levine and Banas recommend "that future researchers should most often avoid one-tailed F's . . ." (p. 132).

Table 8.1   One-Way ANOVA Example

A researcher wanted to discover if there were a difference in the persuasiveness of messages containing no evidence, statistical evidence, or narrative evidence. Nine students were randomly assigned to read messages with these three treatments. The attitude scores on a scale ranging from 3 (negative attitude) to 21 (positive attitude) are displayed in the table shown here.

	No Evidence	Statistical Evidence	Narrative Evidence
	12	15	16
	15	16	15
	14	16	17
	13	13	19
	14	17	16
	12	15	15
	17	18	18
	13	16	14
	16	15	20
$\bar{X} =$	14	15.6667	16.6667
$s^2 =$	3	2	4

The research hypothesis was that the means of the three conditions were not equal. Hence, the null hypothesis was H_0: $\mu_{\text{no evidence}} = \mu_{\text{statistical evidence}} = \mu_{\text{narrative evidence}}$.

The researcher wished to test this null hypothesis using an alpha risk of .05. The computational formula for analysis of variance is

$$F = \frac{n * s_{\bar{x}}^2}{s_p^2}$$

$$F = \frac{9 * 1.8149}{3} = \frac{16.3341}{3} = 5.444$$

In this case, initial means and variances are carried out to four places and the final answer is carried out three decimal places to be consistent with SPSS and Excel computations to be exhibited shortly in this chapter. The critical value of F at alpha risk of .05 (d.f.: 2, 24) is 3.403. Because the observed F statistic is greater than the critical value, the null hypothesis was rejected. A researcher would report this finding in the text of a research paper with the following expression: $F(2, 24) = 5.44$, $p < .05$, $\eta^2 = .31$. The last term here is explained elsewhere in the chapter.

Determining Effect Sizes

Analysis of variance reveals whether differences are statistically significant, but the F statistic does not reveal how big the statistically significant difference is. Of course, one could (and should) look at means, but it also is useful to compute a measure of effect size that reports a percentage of variance in one variable explained by a knowledge of the other variable. This number is equivalent to the coefficient of determination described in Chapter 5. One popular measure is known as eta squared (η^2). This measure takes the between-groups sums of squares and divides it by the total sums of squares. Sums of squares are the mean square values (the final values in the numerator and denominator of the F ratio) multiplied by their degrees of freedom. One needs to be careful about using computer programs such as SPSS to produce eta. As T. R. Levine and Hullett (2002) notice, SPSS does not report eta squared, but a liberal measure called "partial eta squared." Although current versions of SPSS accurately identify this form of eta squared, researchers who wish to use the appropriate measure still must compute eta squared by hand.

For the example in Table 8.1, between-groups variance (between-groups mean squares) is 16.3341. Thus, between-groups sums of squares would be 2 degrees of freedom times 16.3341, which is 32.6682. Within-groups sums of squares would be 24 degrees of freedom times 3, which would be 72. Total sums of squares would be 104.6682. To compute eta squared, the following formula is used:

$$\eta^2 = \frac{\text{between-groups sums of squares}}{\text{total sums of squares}}.$$

Substituting the information from the example reveals:

$$\eta^2 = \frac{32.6682}{104.6682} = .3121.$$

Thus, one could claim that 31.21% of the variation in one variable may be explained by knowledge of variation in the other variable. This effect size is equivalent to a correlation of .559.

Using Excel to Compute One-Way ANOVA

To complete the analysis of variance using Excel, the researcher should select *Data Analysis.* . . from the *Tools* menu. From the drop-down menu that appears, the researcher selects *ANOVA: Single Factor* and then clicks *OK*. In the dialog box, the researcher identifies the columns of data corresponding to groups involved. In the field identified as "Input Range:" the researcher clicks the button to highlight the cells in which the data appear.

Special Discussion 8.1

The Relationship Between t and F

Analysis of variance is recommended when the means of more than two groups are compared. But one *could* use analysis of variance to compare just two group means. Under such circumstances, the numerator of the F ratio would have one degree of freedom (the number of groups minus one). For instance, as Appendix C.5 shows, if there were 10 events in each of two groups, degrees of freedom would be equal to 1 and 18. The corresponding critical F ratio for alpha risk of .05 would be 4.414.

In contrast, if a researcher used the two-sample t test to assess the difference between the means of two groups, the degrees of freedom would be 18. The critical value for t would be 2.101 (two-tailed). Even though only one side of the F distribution is used to test hypotheses, the analysis of variance uses variances to identify differences between group means. Because the variance increases in value regardless of the direction of the mean differences, analysis of variance may be taken as a "two-tailed" test when two means are compared. Thus, it is clear that when comparing two groups, F is equal to t^2.

After the data range is specified, the researcher clicks the ▣ button to return to the dialog box. Then, the researcher identifies the location on the spreadsheet where output data are to be placed. In addition, the "Labels in First Row" choice should be checked because these data have variable labels identified in the first row of the spreadsheet. The radio buttons marked "Columns" and "Rows" are used to specify whether the data for a group are contained on each column or each row. After the researcher clicks *OK*, the following output appears:

14	SUMMARY						
15	Groups	Count	Sum	Average	Variance		
16	noev	9	126	14	3		
17	statev	9	141	15.666667	2		
18	narrev	9	150	16.666667	4		
19							
20							
21	ANOVA						
22	e of Vari	SS	df	MS	F	P-value	F crit
23	Between (	32.66667	2	16.333333	5.4444444	0.0112277	3.4028318
24	Within G	72	24	3			
25							
26	Total	104.6667	26				

For these data, there is a statistically significant difference as revealed by the "P-value" lower than .05. For multiple comparisons and trend analyses, one must use additional macros that are not in the standard Excel package. Similarly, there are no current subroutines to analysis of covariance in the Excel standard set of statistical tools. Nevertheless, a guide to some of these macro elements and some useful attachments may be found in the Chapter 8 materials on the Web site for this book.

WHAT AFTER ANOVA? MULTIPLE COMPARISON TESTS

Analysis of variance reveals if there are differences among several means, but it does not reveal *where* the differences are. Thus, researchers also follow a significant F statistic by use of a multiple comparison test to compare individual means.

Spreading Alpha Risk to Make Additional Comparisons

Researchers may set one alpha risk for their tests, but if they follow their tests by comparing their means one pair at a time, they may increase the overall alpha risk far beyond their announced alpha risk. Of course, researchers could reduce the individual alpha risk for their tests of significance, but another alternative would be to use **multiple comparison tests** that "spread out" the alpha risk across all possible contrasts.

The Notion of Contrasts

Researchers want to know if a contrast between means shows a statistically significant difference. A **contrast** is "the mean difference between two subsets of means" (Glass & Hopkins, 1984, p. 337). In its simplest form, a contrast compares one mean to another, such as $\mu_1 - \mu_2$. But there is another way to show this contrast, often symbolized by the Greek letter ψ (*psi*; pronounced "sigh"). One could multiply each mean by a contrast coefficient and then just add the results. For instance, a contrast between two means could be computed as $\psi = (1)\mu_1 + (-1)\mu_2$. For **pairwise contrasts**, which are simply the mean differences between two treatment means, one could subtract one mean from another and be done with it. But the notion of contrast becomes valuable when complex contrasts are involved. **Complex or compound contrasts** are the differences between subsets of means involving more than two treatment means. For instance, if researchers want to compare the means of two groups to the means of three other groups, a compound contrast would be involved. The contrast would be

$$\psi = \frac{1}{2}\mu_1 + \frac{1}{2}\mu_2 + (-\frac{1}{3}\mu_3) + (-\frac{1}{3}\mu_4) + (-\frac{1}{3}\mu_5).$$

The fractions are called **contrast coefficients**. As can be seen, each set of contrasts adds up either to 1 or –1. Another way to represent these matters is to let c symbolize a contrast. Then, the formula for a contrast is

$$\psi = \sum_j^J c_j \mu_j.$$

(Because in this book we have used i to represent each instance of an X score from a continuous distribution, in this case we will use j to represent each instance of a mean.) If we were to substitute sample means as estimates for population means (as we normally do), the basic formula would become

$$\psi = \sum_j^J c_j \overline{X}_j.$$

The Use of Multiple Comparison Tests

Any one of several multiple comparison tests could be used. Each is dedicated to specific situations. A distinction is often drawn between *a priori* comparisons, where a hypothesis is advanced about the differences that are predicted, and *a posteriori* comparisons, where comparisons are made without a hypothesis to guide initial research. Both the *t* test and analysis of variance might be taken as forms of *a priori* tests, but there are others that may be used as well. Though both families of tests are common in communication studies, the flexibility and power of *a priori* contrasts have made them favored alternatives of modern researchers. Tables 8.2 and 8.3 show such lists. Some of the most useful tools will be described here.

Popular Multiple Comparison Tests

A Priori *Comparisons*

Though one may use planned *t* tests or analysis of variance to explore the difference among means, sometimes researchers wish to make repeated comparisons of some groups to others. Two very popular tests are used in these circumstances.

The **Dunn-Šidák multiple comparison test** (*tDS*) is employed when small numbers of planned comparisons are to be made. In essence, this approach determines the number of contrasts to be completed, reduces the size of alpha risk for each pairwise test,[9] and runs *t* tests at these levels. This method uses a formula for Dunn's test that is really an adaptation of the *t* test:

$$tDS = \frac{\sum c_j \overline{X}_j}{\sqrt{MS_{\text{within groups}} \sum \frac{c_j^2}{n_j}}}.$$

This test uses within-groups variance ($MS_{\text{within groups}}$).[10] Then the test statistic is compared with the critical value found in Appendix C.6. If the test statistic is greater than the critical value, the null hypothesis of no difference between means is rejected. Most multiple comparison tests (including the Dunn-Šidák test) are available in computer data analysis packages such as SPSS, so the computation details are deleted here because you are unlikely to conduct the tests by hand.

Dunnett's multiple comparison test is widely employed when a control group is compared against a collection of experimental means. The formula for the Dunnett's method is

$$tD' = \frac{\overline{X}_j - \overline{X}_{\text{control}}}{\sqrt{MS_{\text{within groups}} \left(\frac{1}{n_j} + \frac{1}{n_{\text{control}}}\right)}}.$$

If this test statistic is greater than the critical valuable found in Appendix C.7, the contrast is statistically significant. Of course, the formula can be solved to reveal a minimum difference that also would be statistically significant.

---

[9]The formula for determining the experimentwise alpha risk is $\alpha = 1 - (1 - \alpha')^k$, where α' is the pairwise alpha risk and k is the number of pairwise tests conducted. To solve for α' (the pairwise alpha risk that would be required to maintain experimentwise alpha risk at the specified level), the following formula would be used: $\alpha' = 1 - (1 - \alpha)^{\frac{1}{k}}$

[10]In the one-way analysis of variance and in the fixed-effects analysis of variance, $MS_{\text{within groups}}$ and MS_{error} are the same. Hence, that simple language is used in this chapter. In some other designs involving random or mixed effects, MS_{error} is not the same thing as $MS_{\text{within groups}}$.

Table 8.2   *A Priori* Multiple Comparison Tests

Test	Uses	Assumptions and Power	Characteristics
1. Trend analysis	Fit underlying linear and nonlinear trends to data	1. Standard assumptions for fixed effect analysis of variance 2. Continuum underlies the levels of the factors of the independent variable 3. Very powerful	Applies orthogonal polynomials to "weight" means
2. Multiple F or t (with Behrens-Fisher and Welch procedures used for t when variances are heterogeneous)	Test of hypothesized comparisons between means with orthogonal (nonoverlapping) comparisons	1. Standard assumptions for t and analysis of variance 2. If variances are heterogeneous, the Behrens-Fisher and Welch procedures are used to compute t' 3. Powerful test overall	Recomputes t to account for heterogeneous variances and unequal sample sizes
3. Dunn's tD test, also known as the Bonferroni inequality test (in SPSS called Bonferroni)	Used to make a small number of nonorthogonal (overlapping) contrasts among pairs of means or as part of compound comparisons	1. Standard assumptions for t and analysis of variance 2. Sample sizes need not be equal and variances must be homogeneous 3. Powerful, though less than trend analysis, multiple Fs or ts, Fisher's *LSD*, Duncan's multiple range test, and Newman-Keuls test	Makes t tests of pairwise contrasts but controls alpha risk by reducing each test's alpha risk to the experimentwise alpha risk divided by the number of tests (the Bonferroni inequality)
4. Dunn-Šidák tDS (in SPSS called Sidak)	Same conditions as Dunn's test; there are fairly large numbers of planned contrasts	1. Same as Dunn's test 2. Powerful, though less than trend analysis, multiple Fs or ts, Fisher's *LSD*, Dunn's test, Duncan's multiple range test, and Newman-Keuls test	Similar to Dunn's test, but uses the specific testwise alpha required to equal the alpha risk level for the omnibus ANOVA effect (results in tighter bounds than Dunn's test)
5. Dunnett's tD'	Comparisons of a single control group with a number of experimental groups	1. Standard assumptions for t and analysis of variance 2. Sample sizes need not be equal and variances must be homogeneous (except if a modification to the method is employed [Dunnett, 1964]) 3. Less powerful than multiple ts, Fs, Fisher's *LSD*, Duncan's multiple range test, and Newman-Keuls test, but more powerful than Dunn's test and Dunn-Šidák	It is not necessary to complete a test of overall significance prior to using Dunnett's test; unlike the Dunn and Dunn-Šidák methods, this approach is exact, rather than an estimate of the upper bound of experimentwise alpha risk

Table 8.3   *A Posteriori* Multiple Comparison Tests

Test	Uses	Assumptions and Power	Characteristics
Pairwise comparisons • **Requiring homogeneous variances**			
6. Fisher's *LSD* (Least Significant Difference; called LSD in SPSS)	Makes all pairwise comparisons (usually not advised by modern statisticians)	1. Standard assumptions for *t* and analysis of variance 2. Most powerful *a posteriori* multiple comparison test	Equivalent to running a number of *t* tests, with a resulting increase in the probability of Type I error above testwise alpha risk
7. Newman-Keuls (called SNK in SPSS)	Makes pairwise comparisons in situations where researchers wish different critical values for different comparisons	1. Standard assumptions for *t* and analysis of variance 2. Powerful *a posteriori* multiple comparison test for initial contrasts and reducing power for subsequent contrasts	Under the assumption that an omnibus test reveals that the most extreme differences are most likely to be statistically significant, comparisons are made using a stepwise order of comparisons using the Studentized Range statistic; means are ordered from highest to lowest, and extreme differences are tested first
8. Duncan's multiple range test	Makes pairwise comparisons that feature a stepwise order of comparisons (uncertain statistical properties of the test have made it a controversial choice)		Similar to Newman-Keuls test (uses the Studentized Range statistic), but it establishes an error level for the total collection of tests, rather than an error rate for individual tests
9. Tukey's *HSD* (Honestly Significant Difference; called Tukey HSD in SPSS)	Makes pairwise comparisons	1. Standard assumptions for *t* and analysis of variance 2. Considered one of the most powerful *a posteriori* multiple comparison tests	Uses Studentized Range statistic to make the experimentwise Type I error rate the error rate for all pairwise comparisons
10. Tukey b (called Tukey b in SPSS), also sometimes known as Tukey's *WSD* (Wholly Significant Difference)	Makes pairwise comparisons	1. Standard assumptions for *t* and analysis of variance 2. Attempts to achieve power by use of a combination of methods used in Newman-Keuls and Tukey's *HSD* tests	Relying on the Studentized Range statistic, the critical value is the average of the values for Tukey's *HSD* and the Newman-Keuls test

Test	Uses	Assumptions and Power	Characteristics
11. Spjøtvoll-Stoline T'	Makes pairwise comparisons when sample sizes are unequal	1. Standard assumptions for t and analysis of variance 2. Slightly more conservative than Tukey's *HSD*	Modification of *HSD* useful when sample sizes are somewhat unequal
12. Tukey-Kramer *TK*	Makes pairwise comparisons when sample sizes are very unequal	1. Standard assumptions for t and analysis of variance 2. More conservative than Spjøtvoll-Stoline T'	Adaptation of *HSD* when sample sizes are very unequal but other assumptions are sound
13. Gabriel's (called Gabriel in SPSS)	Makes pairwise comparisons when sample sizes are somewhat unequal	1. Standard assumptions for t and analysis of variance 2. Generally more powerful than Hochberg's *GT2* but may become excessively liberal when cell sizes differ greatly	An application of a distribution called the Studentized maximum modulus statistic
14. Ryan-Einot-Gabriel-Welsch test (called R-E-G-W F in SPSS)	Makes pairwise comparisons when sample sizes are equal	1. Standard assumptions for t and analysis of variance 2. Generally more powerful than R-E-G-W *Q*	Multiple stepdown procedure based on an *F* test similar to Tukey's *HSD*
15. Ryan-Einot-Gabriel-Welsch test (called R-E-G-W Q in SPSS)	Makes pairwise comparisons when sample sizes are equal	1. Standard assumptions for t and analysis of variance 2. Generally more powerful than Hochberg's *GT2*	Multiple stepdown procedure based on the Studentized Range similar to Tukey's *HSD*
16. Hochberg's *GT2* (called Hochberg's GT2 in SPSS)	Pairwise comparisons	1. Standard assumptions for t and analysis of variance 2. Not as powerful as competing tests in this category of tools designed for pairwise contrasts requiring equal variances	A multiple comparison and range test that uses the Studentized maximum modulus statistic; similar to Gabriel's test
• For unequal variances			
17. Games-Howell's *GH* (called Games-Howell in SPSS)	Pairwise comparisons in situations where sample sizes are or are not equal	1. Standard assumptions for t and analysis of variance except for homogeneous variances 2. Slightly more powerful than Tamhane procedure 3. Occasionally may be too liberal in controlling Type I error	Uses the Studentized Range distribution statistic and the Behrens-Fisher statistic to compute the standard error of the contrast

(Continued)

Table 8.3 (Continued)

Test	Uses	Assumptions and Power	Characteristics
18. Tamhane's $T2$	Pairwise comparisons in situations where sample sizes are or are not equal	1. Standard assumptions for t and analysis of variance except for homogeneous variances 2. Slightly less powerful than Games-Howell procedure 3. Keeps experimentwise Type I error rate below announced alpha risk	Comparisons based on use of the t distribution along with the Behrens-Fisher statistic to compute the standard error of the contrast
19. Dunnett's $T3$ (called Dunnett's $T3$ in SPSS)	Pairwise comparisons Scheffé's test	1. Standard assumptions for t and analysis of variance except for homogeneous variances 2. Somewhat conservative when variances are equal, similar to Tamhane's $T2$	Comparisons based on Studentized maximum modulus statistic
Compound comparisons • **Equal variances assumed**			
20. Scheffé's test (called Scheffe in SPSS)	Though may be used for pairwise contrasts, it is most recommended for compound or complex contrasts; may be used in situations where sample sizes are or are not equal	1. Standard assumptions for t and analysis of variance 2. Keeps experimentwise Type I error rate below announced alpha risk 3. Though not powerful in making pairwise comparisons, Scheffé's test is quite powerful for compound comparisons; though other multiple comparison tests may be adapted for this use, Scheffé's test is designed for this purpose	Uses F distribution to examine all possible linear combinations of group means and is not restricted to pairwise comparisons
• **For unequal variances**			
21. Brown Forsythe BF	Used for compound comparisons when the variances are not equal; may be used in situations where sample sizes are or are not equal	1. Standard assumptions for t and analysis of variance except for homogeneous variances 2. Conservative when used to make pairwise comparisons and more conservative than Scheffé's test	Modification of Scheffé's test when variances unequal; makes use of the Behrens-Fisher statistic to compute the standard error of the contrast

A *Posteriori* Comparisons

There are many occasions when researchers have examined research hypotheses but still have other effects that may be explored. These types of *a posteriori* comparisons are unhypothesized, or "follow-up," contrasts. These tests sometimes are called *post hoc* analyses, although they surely should not be because *post hoc* means "after this" and is easily confused with the shorthand used to identify the fallacy of the false cause, *post hoc ergo propter hoc* ("after this, therefore because of this"). Though there has been an explosion of such tests, especially in recent decades, two "data snooping" methods remain most prominent, Tukey's *HSD* and Scheffé's *S*.

Tukey's *HSD* (Honestly Significant Difference) test is appropriate to make comparisons among all pairs of means. The method not only is among the most powerful tests for this purpose but also is among the most popular tests. Tukey's *HSD* uses a distribution called the Studentized Range statistic, which takes into account the fact that as the number of contrasted means increases, the differences between the largest and smallest means will appear to increase. Thus, unlike Student's *t* distribution, the critical value for the Studentized Range statistic is affected by the number of means compared. The formula for comparing any two means using Tukey's *HSD* is

$$HSD = \frac{\overline{X}_j - \overline{X}_{j'}}{\sqrt{\frac{MS_{\text{within groups}}}{n}}}.$$

The researcher enters the table of critical values of the Studentized Range statistic (Appendix C.8) with a chosen alpha risk for testing statistical significance of the difference for each pair of means. The appropriate column is found for the number of means involved. The appropriate row corresponding to the number of degrees of freedom for the within-groups variance term is found. If the observed test statistic is equal to or greater than the number in the table, a significant difference is claimed.

In practice, researchers find it most useful just to ask what the minimum difference between means would have to be for a statistically significant difference to be claimed. In such a case, if researchers know the Studentized Range statistic critical value, they may solve the formula to find the size of the minimal difference between means. The critical value of the Studentized Range statistic is multiplied by the quantity

$$\sqrt{\frac{MS_{\text{within groups}}}{n}}.$$

This revised formula is

Minimum statistically significant difference between pairs of means (often symbolized ψHSD)	=	Critical value from Studentized Range statistic	*	$\sqrt{\dfrac{MS_{\text{within groups}}}{n}}$.

This "minimum difference" value is, in fact, what is most often presented in computerized data analysis programs.

To illustrate this method, we may use the example found in Table 8.1. There were three means to compare: no evidence = 14; statistical evidence = 15.67; narrative evidence = 16.67. Each mean was based on nine events in each group. The within-groups variance (mean square error) was 3. With alpha risk of .05, the critical value from the Studentized Range statistic (with three groups compared and 24 degrees of freedom for the within-groups variance term) was 3.90. Inserting these elements into the formula for the minimum mean difference required for statistical significance using Tukey's *HSD*, the following computations emerge:

Minimum statistically significant difference between pairs of means ψ *HSD*	$= 3.90 * \sqrt{\dfrac{3}{9}}$	$= 3.90 * .57$	$= 2.25$

Thus, any difference as large as 2.25 would be statistically significant. Because the participants exposed to no evidence and the participants exposed to narrative evidence differed by 2.67, the difference was statistically significant. No other differences were statistically significant.

Using this tool makes the basic assumptions that also underlie analysis of variance (normal distribution, homogeneity of variance, etc.), but it also assumes that sample sizes are equal in the groups that are compared. If sample sizes are not equal, and if variances are not homogeneous, then alternative tests identified in Table 8.3 should be used (such as the Tukey-Kramer modification).

Scheffé's *S* is invited when complex comparisons are made, such as one mean versus two others. In these situations, Tukey's *HSD* is inappropriate. If the assumptions for ANOVA have been met, Scheffé's *S* method may be used to make tests. The formula for Scheffé's method is

$$F = \frac{\left(\sum c_j \overline{X}_j \right)^2}{MS_{\text{within groups}} \sum \dfrac{c_j^2}{n_j}}.$$

The critical value is F', which uses information from the F table. It is computed by the formula $F' = (\text{number of means} - 1) * F_{a, d.f. \text{ in numerator, } d.f. \text{ within groups}}$.

An example might help show how this tool works. Using the data from Table 8.1, suppose the researcher wanted to see if the single "no evidence" condition were significantly different from the combination of the "statistical" and "narrative" evidence conditions. The three conditions from samples of nine participants each are as follows:

$$\overline{X}_1 (\text{no evidence}) = 14.00$$
$$\overline{X}_2 (\text{statistical evidence}) = 15.67$$
$$\overline{X}_3 (\text{narrative evidence}) = 16.67$$

The contrasts would look like

$$\overline{X}_1 - \frac{(\overline{X}_2 + \overline{X}_3)}{2}.$$

To represent these elements, the contrast coefficients would be

$$1 - \left(\tfrac{1}{2} + \tfrac{1}{2}\right).$$

Substituting information into the formula, one finds:

$$F = \frac{\left(\sum c_j \overline{X}_j\right)^2}{\text{MS}_{\text{within groups}} \sum \frac{c_j^2}{n_j}}$$

$$F = \frac{\left([1 * 14] + \left[-\tfrac{1}{2} * 15.67\right] + \left[-\tfrac{1}{2} * 16.67\right]\right)^2}{3 * \left(\frac{1^2}{9} + \frac{\left[-\tfrac{1}{2}\right]^2}{9} + \frac{\left[-\tfrac{1}{2}\right]^2}{9}\right)}$$

$$F = \frac{(14 - 7.84 - 8.34)^2}{3 * (.11 + .03 + .03)}$$

$$F = \frac{(-2.18)^2}{3 * (.17)} = \frac{4.75}{.51} = 9.31$$

The critical value for this test is

$$F' = (\text{number of means} - 1) * F_{\alpha, d.f.\text{ in numerator, } d.f.\text{ within groups}}.$$

In this case, the number of means is three. With alpha risk of .05 and two degrees of freedom in the numerator (three groups minus 1) of the original ANOVA and 24 degrees of freedom (27 events minus three groups) associated with within-groups degrees of freedom, the critical F is 3.403. When inserted into the formula, $F' = 2 \times 3.403$, which is 6.806. Because the observed F value in Scheffé's S method is greater than F', the difference between the no evidence mean and the complex combination of the remaining conditions is statistically significant.

Though Scheffé's method can be used for pairwise comparisons, it tends to produce conservative results that often keep real differences from being detected. Of course, nearly all multiple comparison tests can be criticized for this problem. It sometimes occurs that multiple comparison tests reveal no statistically significant differences between means, even though the overall F was significant under analysis of variance. The reason is that the ANOVA is equivalent to making a test that *some* contrasts are significant. These elements may be compound contrasts (e.g., $\frac{(\overline{X}_1 + \overline{X}_2)}{2} - \overline{X}_3$), however, rather than simple pairwise analyses. Thus, wise researchers try to choose methods that are as initially powerful as possible.

EXTENSIONS OF ANALYSIS OF VARIANCE

One of the reasons ANOVA is so popular is that there are many things researchers can do with it. Two such applications are trend analysis and analysis of covariance.

Trend Analysis

Trend analysis is an application of analysis of variance used to identify linear and non-linear effects produced by an independent variable whose levels form a continuum arranged from "lowest" to "highest." For instance, if one completed a study of the influence of no evidence, two pieces of evidence, four pieces of evidence, and six pieces of evidence (none, low, moderate, and large amounts of evidence), the independent variable would have an underlying continuum ranging from "low" to "high."[11] This method presumes that the levels are separated by equal intervals and that the sample sizes on which the means are based are equal.

Isolating Underlying Trends in Factor Level Effects

Means may show differences that reveal underlying linear and nonlinear trends. The use of trend analysis helps reveal the nature of the patterns themselves. The simplest trend is a **linear** one in which a straight line is the best fit to the pattern of means. As the examples (not an exhaustive set of pictures, by the way) on the left show, the linear trend shows that the means are arranged in roughly a straight line.

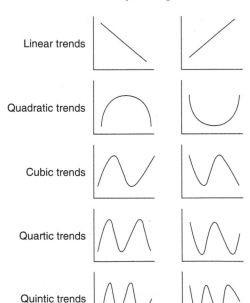

A **quadratic trend** shows one curve, such as a U or an inverted-U. A **cubic trend** is represented by a curve that shows both a concave and a convex curve. Hence, it is said to have one point of inflection. A point of inflection is a location where the curve begins to move in a new direction. A **quartic trend** forms a curve with two points of inflection. A **quintic trend** forms a curve with three points of inflection. As you might expect, linear trends are quite common, quadratic trends are not as frequent, cubic trends are relatively infrequent, quartic trends seldom are found, and quintic trends are very rare.

Use of Orthogonal Polynomials as Weights

To conduct a trend analysis of the means, and to determine whether the trend is linear or nonlinear, a researcher must use orthogonal polynomials. An **orthogonal polynomial** contains more than one term and expresses the powers of a variable. These orthogonal

---

[11]Of course, creative applications can be made of trend analysis. If one wished to contrast one condition against another that had a difference from another condition that, in turn, is predicted to be different from a third condition, trend analysis may be used even if the underlying continuum is not organized from "low" to "high."

polynomials are an efficient way to identify the nature of an underlying trend. A table of these orthogonal polynomials is found in Appendix C.9. A portion of that table is reproduced below.

Number of Group Means	Type of Trend	Coefficients (c_j) for Each Mean												$\sum c_j^2$
		1	2	3	4	5	6	7	8	9	10	11	12	
3	Linear	−1	0	1										2
	Quadratic	1	−2	1										6
4	Linear	−3	−1	1	3									20
	Quadratic	1	−1	−1	1									4
	Cubic	−1	3	−3	1									20

These polynomials may be multiplied by the means of the groups as a step to "weight" means according to various underlying trends. For instance, if one had a set of three means, the means would be multiplied by the values −1, 0, and 1 to detect a linear trend. To identify a quadratic trend, the means would be multiplied by 1, −2, and 1.

Computing Trend Analysis

To compute trend analyses, researchers provide separate assessments of means by using the polynomials for each related effect. For instance, if one examines trends among three means, a linear and a quadratic trend could be tested. If there are four groups, means could be examined for linear, quadratic, and cubic trends. Each trend is tested for significance using one degree of freedom for the trend effect tested. As the example in Table 8.4 shows, the significance of the trend is examined by computing an *F* ratio with a **mean square** (between-groups variance) for the trend divided by the mean square error (within-groups variance).

Table 8.4   Trend Analysis Example

A researcher exposed three randomly assigned groups of audience members to persuasive speeches containing two, four, or six pieces of opinion evidence. In each case, after listening to the speeches, respondents indicated their attitudes toward the topic on a set of three 7-point semantic differential–type scales, resulting in a possible range of scores of 3 to 21. The researcher observed the following means: two pieces of evidence = 14, four pieces of evidence = 15, and six pieces of evidence = 18. In this example, the following ANOVA table was produced:

Source of Variation	d.f	MS	F	
Between groups	2	20.82	4.16	*
Within Groups	27	5		
	p < .05			

To explore linear and quadratic trends, a table of means and contrasts may be used, as shown below. The linear contrast coefficients are drawn from the table of orthogonal polynomials for three means found in Appendix C.9.

(Continued)

Table 8.4 (Continued)

	Two Pieces of Evidence	Four Pieces of Evidence	Six Pieces of Evidence	$\sum c_j^2$
Mean	14	15	18	
Linear Contrast Coefficients c	−1	0	1	2
Quadratic Contrast Coefficients c	1	−2	1	6

- To compute the mean square (between groups) for each trend, researchers use the following formula:

$$MS_{trend} = \frac{\left(\sum c_j \overline{X}_j\right)^2}{\frac{\sum c_j^2}{n}}.$$

For the linear trend for the data in this study, this formula becomes

$$MS_{linear} = \frac{([-1*14]+[0*15]+[1*18])^2}{\frac{2}{10}} = \frac{(4)^2}{.2} = \frac{16}{.2} = 80.$$

For the quadratic trend, this formula becomes

$$MS_{quadratic} = \frac{([1*14]+[-2*15]+[1*18])^2}{\frac{6}{10}} = \frac{(2)^2}{.6} = \frac{4}{.6} = 6.67.$$

- To test if the difference is statistically significant, these mean square effects are divided by the mean square within groups. The resulting F statistics are tested for significance with one degree of freedom in the numerator and the within groups degrees of freedom for the denominator. The resulting ANOVA table would be expanded to report:

Source of Variation	d.f.	MS	F	
Between groups variance	2	20.82	4.16	*
Linear	1	80	16	**
Quadratic	1	6.67	1.33	
Within Groups Variance	27	5		

* $p < .05$ (critical F, d.f.: 2,27 = 3.35)
** $p < .05$ (critical F, d.f.: 1,27 = 4.21)

Hence, for these data there is a significant linear trend, but no evidence of a significant nonlinear quadratic trend. The best fit of a line to the means would be a straight line.

Using SPSS to Compute One-Way ANOVA and Trend Analysis

A one-way analysis of variance can be completed with ease by selecting the *Analyze* menu followed by *Compare Means. . .* and *One-Way ANOVA. . . .* In the dialog box, the dependent variable is highlighted and placed in the "Dependent List:" and the independent variable is similarly identified for the "Factor:" list.

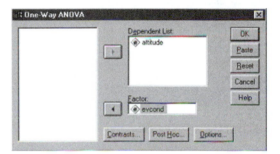

In some data that will be analyzed here, there are three levels of the independent variable. By clicking on the *Options. . .* button, the researcher may select descriptive statistics and homogeneity of variance tests. After these elements are included, the researcher may click on *Continue* and then *Contrasts. . .* from the *One-Way ANOVA. . .* dialog box.

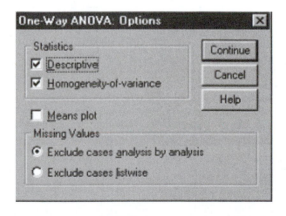

This step permits researchers to complete trend analysis for the experimental data. In the

One-Way ANOVA: Contrasts dialog box, one may check the "Polynomial" box to indicate that orthogonal polynomials are to be fit to the means. The "Degree:" box includes levels to be tested. The highest trend effects should be selected. Other low-level effects also will be tested. In this case, because there are three means, a quadratic effect may be selected.

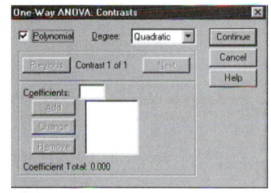

The researcher clicks on the *Continue* button and then the *Post Hoc. . .* button. The *One-Way ANOVA: Post Hoc Multiple Comparisons* dialog box provides a host of multiple comparison tests. In this case, the selection will be made to include the Tukey *HSD* test to compare means.

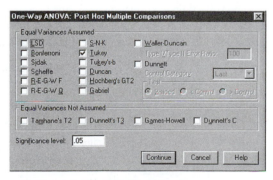

Following this work, the researcher would click on *Continue* and then *OK*. The results emerge in the output window.

Descriptives

ATTITUDE

	N	Mean	Std. Deviation	Std. Error	95% Confidence Interval for Mean		Minimum	Maximum
					Lower Bound	Upper Bound		
1	9	14.00	1.73	.58	12.87	15.33	12	17
2	9	15.67	1.41	.47	14.58	16.75	13	18
3	9	16.67	2.00	.67	15.13	18.20	14	20
Total	27	15.44	2.01	.39	14.65	16.24	12	20

To test the assumption of homogeneous variances, the Levene statistic is referenced. In this example, the results are not significant. Thus, the assumption of homogeneous variances is not rejected.

Test of Homogeneity of Variances

ATTITUDE

Levene Statistic	df1	df2	Sig.
.846	2	24	.442

The analysis of variance table below reveals a statistically significant difference between groups. Then, the trends were identified in separate passes through the data. In this case, the major trend in the means is linear, rather than quadratic.

ANOVA

ATTITUDE

			Sum of Squares	df	Mean Square	F	Sig.
Between Groups	(Combined)		32.667	2	16.333	5.444	.011
	Linear Term	Contrast	32.000	1	32.000	10.667	.003
		Deviation	.667	1	.667	.222	.642
	Quadratic Term	Contrast	.667	1	.667	.222	.642
Within Groups			72.000	24	3.000		
Total			104.687	26			

The follow-up examination of means is completed by use of Tukey's *HSD*, which compares means a pair at a time. As the table below shows, the only statistically significant difference (indicated by asterisks) is between the means of groups one and three.

Multiple Comparisons

Dependent Variable: ATTITUDE
Tukey HSD

(I) EVCOND	(J) EVCOND	Mean Difference (I-J)	Std. Error	Sig.	95% Confidence Interval	
					Lower Bound	Upper Bound
1	2	−1.67	.82	.124	−3.71	.37
	3	−2.67*	.82	.009	−4.71	−.63
2	1	1.67	.82	.124	−.37	3.71
	3	−1.00	.82	.451	−3.04	1.04
3	1	2.67*	.82	.009	.63	4.71
	2	1.00	.82	.451	−1.04	3.04

*The mean difference is significant at the .05 level.

To explore this difference, a table of homogeneous subsets also is presented. Each column identifies a subset that includes no differences in means. By a process of elimination, a researcher can figure out where differences exist. For compound comparisons, this presentation of contrast results is most useful. As can be seen in this example, the first subset shows that groups one and two do not differ (though, of course, group three differs from those two). Similarly, the second subset of means shows that groups two and three do not differ (though group one differs from the common set). The actual probabilities associated with the statistical significance tests for these contrasts are reported at the bottom of each subset column.

ATTITUDE

Tukey HSD[a]

EVCOND	N	Subset for alpha = .05	
		1	2
1	9	14.00	
2	9	15.67	15.67
3	9		16.67
Sig.		.124	.451

Means for groups in homogeneous subsets are displayed.
a. Uses Harmonic Mean Sample Size = 9.000.

As can be seen, using a standard significance test with alpha risk of .05, no differences emerge. Thus, the overall differences seemed restricted to the differences between the group one and group three means alone.

Control for Additional Variables: Analysis of Covariance (ANCOVA)

A very creative use of analysis of variance is **analysis of covariance** (often abbreviated ANCOVA), which combines methods from correlation analyses with ANOVA to control for other measured nuisance variables. This method adjusts dependent variable scores to reflect what they would be if all participants were equivalent on the third "nuisance" variable of interest. Though this approach can reduce the influence of extraneous variables, it cannot be expected to eliminate all sources of bias. Instead, one or two moderator variables are used to adjust the scores of primary dependent variables for control purposes.

An example might be helpful to illustrate the logic of using analysis of covariance. A researcher might study the retention of information contained in speeches with internal organizers (summaries and previews of main points along with full transitions between main points) and without internal organizers. The researcher might also believe that the listening abilities of audience members would affect whether they retained different levels of information. In fact, given the differences in the sample groups, the researcher may decide to collect information about the listening ability of respondents. Then, analysis of covariance may be used to provide statistical control of this third nuisance variable.

The reasoning behind this notion is related to the meaning of correlations. The square of a correlation is the degree to which variation in one variable may be explained from knowledge of variation in the other alone. If one subtracts this amount from 1.0, the result is a **coefficient of alienation**, which reveals how much variation in one variable is *not* explained by knowledge of the other variable alone. So, if researchers correlate the within-groups variance scores on the dependent variable with scores on some nuisance variable, subtracting the square of this correlation from 1 would reveal what proportion of the within-groups variance is unassociated with the nuisance variable. In the example in Table 8.5, one notices how this coefficient of alienation is used to reduce the size of the unadjusted within-groups and total sums of squares. Then, the size of the association between the nuisance variable and the dependent variable is used as

Table 8.5   Analysis of Covariance Example

A researcher gave speeches containing technical materials to two randomly selected groups of participants. The experimental condition of the speech included prominent use of internal organizers (transitions, previews, and internal summaries). In the control condition, the internal organizers were omitted. Participants were tested by examining scores on a 10-item true-false test dealing with content of the message. The researcher first analyzed data by using one-way analysis of variance, which yielded the following results:

Source of Variation	Sums of Squares	d.f.	Mean Square	F
Between Groups	12.8	1	12.8	10.97*
Within Groups	21	18	1.17	
Total	33.8	19		

$$*p < .05$$

On reflection, the researcher decided that respondents' basic listening abilities should be included as a covariate. A measure of listening ability was obtained for each person in the sample.

- To begin, the researcher needed to know the correlation between the nuisance variable and the dependent variable. In this case, the correlation was found to be .605. Other related computations are found in the data table that follows.

Participants Not Given Messages With Internal Organizers					Participants Given Messages With Internal Organizers				
Test of Listening Ability X	Compre- hension Test Score Y	$(X - \bar{X}_0)^2$	$(Y - \bar{Y}_1)^2$	$(X - \bar{X}_1)$ * $(Y - \bar{Y}_1)$	Test of Listening Ability	Compre- hension Test Score	$(X - \bar{X}_2)^2$	$(Y - \bar{Y}_2)^2$	$(X - \bar{X}_2)$ * $(Y - \bar{Y}_2)$
100	7	4	.49	−1.4	110	8	4.84	.01	.22
100	7	4	.49	−1.4	115	9	51.84	1.21	7.92
90	6	144	.09	3.6	109	9	1.44	1.21	1.32
100	5	4	1.69	2.6	101	7	46.24	.81	6.12
120	8	324	2.89	30.6	97	6	116.64	3.61	20.52
95	7	49	.49	−4.9	99	8	77.44	.01	−.88
108	6	36	.09	−1.8	115	8	51.84	.01	.72
102	6	0	.09	0	125	9	295.84	1.21	18.92
101	4	1	5.29	2.3	106	7	3.24	.81	1.62
104	7	4	.49	1.4	101	8	46.84	.01	−.68
$\bar{X}_1 = 102$	$\bar{Y} = 6.3$	$\sum(X - \bar{X}_1)^2$ = 57.0	$\sum(Y - \bar{Y}_1)^2$ = 12.1	$\sum(X - \bar{X}_1)$ * $(Y - \bar{Y}_1)$ = 31.0	$\bar{X}_2$ = 107.8	$\bar{Y}_2 = 7.9$	$\sum(X - \bar{X}_2)^2$ = 695.6	$\sum(Y - \bar{Y}_2)^2$ = 8.9	$\sum(X - \bar{X}_2)$ * $(Y - \bar{Y}_2)$ = 55.8

- To compute the pooled correlation coefficient between the independent and dependent variables, one uses the following formula:

$$r_w = \frac{\sum (X - \bar{X}_j) * (Y - \bar{Y}_j)}{\sqrt{[\sum(X - \bar{X}_j)^2] * [\sum(Y - \bar{Y}_j)^2]}}.$$

Substituting the data from the table reveals the following:

$$r_w = \frac{55.8 + 31}{\sqrt{[570 + 695.6] * [8.9 + 12.1]}} = \frac{86.8}{\sqrt{[1265.6] * [21]}} = \frac{86.8}{\sqrt{26577.6}} = \frac{86.8}{163.0264}$$
$$= .5324.$$

- To adjust the sums of squares to account for the correlation of the nuisance variable with the dependent variable, the researcher uses the following formulae:

$$\text{Adjusted Sums of Squares}_{total} = \text{Unadjusted Sums of Squares}_{total} * (1 - r^2_{total})$$
$$= 33.8 * (1 - .605^2) = 33.8 * (1 - .366) = 21.43$$

$$\text{Adjusted Sums of Squares}_{within} = \text{Unadjusted Sums of Squares}_{within} * (1 - r^2_{within})$$
$$= \{[\sum(Y - \bar{Y}_1)^2 = 12.1] + [\sum(Y - \bar{Y}_2)^2 = 8.9]\} * (1 - .5324^2)$$
$$= 21 * (1 - .2834) = 15.05$$

$$\text{Adjusted Sums of Squares}_{between\ groups} = \text{Adjusted Sums of Squares}_{total} - \text{Adjusted Sums of Squares}_{within}$$
$$= 21.43 - 15.05 = 6.38$$

When these elements are inserted into the ANCOVA table, the result is as follows:

Source of Variation	Sums of Squares	d.f.	Mean Square	F
Between Groups	6.41	1	6.41	7.25
Within Groups	15.02	17	.88	
Total	21.43	18		

- To adjust the means,[12] the researcher first must compute a term known as the regression coefficient between the nuisance variable and the dependent variable symbolized "b_w," which is an estimate of β_w, the regression coefficient indicating the population slope. This term is computed as

$$b_w = \frac{\sum(X - \bar{X}_j) * (Y - \bar{Y}_j)}{\sum(X - \bar{X}_j)^2}.$$

In this example, $\sum(X - \bar{X}_j) + (Y - \bar{Y}_j)$ is 31.0 for the first group and 55.8 for the second group, for a total of 86.8. The term, $\sum(X - \bar{X}_j)^2$ for each group is 570 + 695.6, which equals 1265.6. Inserted into the formula for b_w, the terms become:

$$b_w = \frac{86.8}{1265.6} = .0686.$$

---

[12]Though this example shows the process of adjusting means, it should be mentioned that this example uses a shortcut by going directly to adjusted means. In fact, the scores upon which the means are computed may be adjusted (in SPSS, this step is exactly what is done, which explains slight deviations due to summing and averaging rounded adjusted numbers), and in essence, the individual scores always are adjusted to permit comparison of adjustment means. To adjust individual scores, the formula takes the form $Y'_{ij} - Y_{ij} - b_w(X_{ij} - \bar{X}...)$. Such individual adjustment is particularly helpful for researchers facing participants by treatments interactions indicated by the presence of heterogeneous variances (at least heterogeneity that cannot be explained by ceiling or floor effects). If a nuisance variable measure is included as a covariate, adjusted scores may be examined to determine if insignificant heterogeneity were found when the covariate was included.

(Continued)

Table 8.4 (Continued)

- To adjust the means, the formula used is: $\overline{Y}_j = \overline{Y}_j - b_w(\overline{X}_j - \overline{X}.)$ In this formula, "$\overline{X}$." symbolizes the grand mean (the mean across all conditions) of the nuisance variable. For our example, $\overline{X}$ is 104.9.

To adjust the mean for the first group of participants, the computations become:

$$\overline{Y}_1 = \overline{Y}_1 - b_w(\overline{X}_1 - \overline{X}.) = 6.3 - .0686\,(102 - 104.9) = 6.3 - (-.1989) = 6.3 + .1989 = .6.4989.$$

To adjust the mean for the second group of participants, the computations become:

$$\overline{Y}_2 = \overline{Y}_2 - b_w(\overline{X}_2 - \overline{X}.) = 7.9 - .0686\,(107.8 - 104.9) = 7.9 - .1989 = 7.7011.$$

a step to adjust the scores of participants on the dependent variable. These procedures result in holding constant the nuisance variable by adjusting the dependent variable scores to what they would be if all individuals had the same grand mean score on the nuisance variable.

The process of selecting potential covariates to control is something of an art. Even so, a couple of guidelines may be used. First, it is common for studies to use pretest scores as covariates when assessing posttest scores. This approach, in fact, is much preferred over the use of "change scores" produced simply by subtracting pretest scores from posttest scores. As may be recalled from Chapter 6, these "difference" scores may have lower reliability than the scales involved in the computation of the differences. Second, researchers may read literature reviews and research reports to identify potential mediating variables. Of course, respondents may be interviewed in pilot studies to discover other sources of influence that may affect responses to primary independent variables under investigation. In subsequent research, these variables could be measured for potential inclusion as covariates. Communication researchers often have found that personality variables are useful sources for potential covariates. What people bring to the communication encounter often affects their responses in fairly systematic ways.

The effects of analysis of covariance go beyond controlling nuisance variables alone. The method also increases statistical power. Because the adjustment process also reduces the size of the within-groups variance, existing mean differences are increasingly likely to be detected as statistically significant.

Additional Assumptions of ANCOVA

In addition to the assumptions underlying any parametric tests (randomization, interval or ratio level measurement of the dependent variable, normal distribution of the dependent variable, and homogeneous variances), analysis of covariance makes three additional assumptions:

- A linear relationship exists between the covariate and the dependent variable.
- "The regression slopes for a covariate are homogeneous (i.e., the slope of the regression line is the same for each group)" (Mertler & Vannatta, 2002, p. 97).
- "The covariate is reliable and measured without error" (Mertler & Vannatta, 2002, p. 97).

The first new assumption means that if nonlinear relationships exist between the covariate and the dependent variable, the method will not permit complete adjustments of dependent scores to be made (Tabachnick & Fidell, 1996). As a result, interpretations of results could be highly misleading. Though one could look at diagrams of the correlation between the covariate and the dependent variable, an increasingly precise method examines plots comparing the predicted values and the standardized residuals for the dependent variable. If there were curvilinear patterns evident in the plot, this assumption would not be sound and the researchers would need to look into transformations of data before continuing with analysis of covariance.

The second new assumption is often called **homogeneity of regression** and means that the slopes of the lines of best fit between the covariate and the dependent variable are the same for each group. Because covariate adjustment is based on one adjustment function, it is important to assume that there is a predictable relationship between the covariate and the dependent variable. If the slopes of the lines of best fit are not equal, it must mean that there is no consistent covariate-dependent variable slope or that the covariate is interacting with an independent variable. The most direct way to examine this matter is to look at the interaction between the covariate and the independent variables. If a significant interation effect exists, there is no way to complete analysis of covariance.

The third assumption is that the covariate actually is a reliable and valid measure of the variable of interest. Researchers generally present evidence of such measurement adequacy as part of presenting their study methods. To some extent, this requirement is essential for all quantitative inquiries. But for analysis of covariance, the lack of reliability would greatly reduce the power of the statistical tests.

Using SPSS to Compute ANCOVA

From the *Analyze* menu, the researcher selects *General Linear Model* and then *Univariate*. . . . In the dialog box, the researcher identifies the dependent variable, the independent variable, and the covariate of interest.

Clicking on the *Options. . .* button reveals a number of choices for researchers. The display of adjusted means is requested by highlighting the

variables for which dependent variable means are to be reported. In addition, the researcher often finds it valuable to make initial tests of assumptions by examining homogeneity of variance and residual plots. Thus, these options are checked on the appropriate boxes. After these steps are taken, the *Continue* button is clicked, followed by the *OK* button.

The output analysis appears as shown below. The descriptive statistics show the means, the standard deviations, and sample sizes. These numbers are based on the original scores in the data, rather than covariate-adjusted scores. Yet, the Levene's test of homogeneity of variance is based on covariate-adjusted scores and shows that the assumption of homogeneous variances could not be rejected.

Descriptive Statistics

Dependent Variable: COMPREHE

ORGANIZ	Mean	Std. Deviation	N
1	6.3000	1.1595	10
2	7.9000	.9944	10
Total	7.1000	1.3338	20

Levene's Test of Equality of Error Variances[a]

Dependent Variable: COMPREHE

F	df1	df2	Sig.
2.092	1	18	.165

Tests the null hypothesis that the error variance of the dependent variable is equal across groups.
a. Design: Intercept+LISTENIG+ORGANIZ

The ANCOVA table appears below. In this case, the first row shows the sources of variation. The intercept test of the difference between the intercept (the point where a line of best fit crosses the *y*-axis) and zero was statistically insignificant. The covariate was identified by name and was tested to determine if the covariate adjustment were significant. In this case, the probability level of .019 indicated that the covariate adjustment was significant. With this element controlled, the impact of the message organization variable was included. It was found to be statistically significant.

Tests of Between-Subjects Effects

Dependent Variable: COMPREHE

Source	Type III Sum of Squares	df	Mean Square	F	Sig.	Eta Squared
Corrected Model	18.753[a]	2	9.377	10.594	.001	.555
Intercept	1.021E-03	1	1.021E-03	.001	.973	.000
LISTENIG	5.953	1	5.953	6.726	.019	.283
ORGANIZ	6.379	1	6.379	7.207	.016	.298
Error	15.047	17	.885			
Total	1042.000	20				
Corrected Total	33.800	19				

a. R Squared = .555 (Adjusted R squared = .502)

Lack of Fit Tests

Dependent Variable: COMPREHE

Source	Sum of Squares	df	Mean Square	F	Sig.	Eta Squared
Lack of fit	11.380	13	.875	.955	.579	.756
Pure Error	3.667	4	.917			

A test of fit for the adjusted model was completed. A significant effect reveals that the current model with its main and interaction effects cannot adequately represent the relationship between the predictor variables and the dependent variable. As can be seen, the lack of a significant F suggests the adequacy of the ANCOVA.

The presentation of adjusted means is presented, providing information on the impact of covariate adjustment. Inspection of the means will show how controlling the covariates altered the final means.

To check the additional assumptions, some additional examination of data must be made. To check the assumption that the relationship between the covariate and the dependent variable is linear, the researcher may look at the plot of the predicted by values standardized residuals for the dependent variable, as shown below on the left.

Estimated Marginal Means

1. Grand Mean

Dependent Variable: COMPREHE

Mean	Std. Error	95% Confidence Interval	
		Lower Bound	Upper Bound
7.100[a]	.210	6.656	7.544

a. Evaluated at covariates appeared in the model: LISTENIG = 104.90

2. ORGANIZ

Dependent Variable: COMPREHE

ORGANIZ	Mean	Std. Error	95% Confidence Interval	
			Lower Bound	Upper Bound
1	6.499[a]	.307	5.851	7.147
2	7.701[a]	.307	7.053	8.349

a. Evaluated at covariates appeared in the model: LISTENIG = 104.90

Dependent Variable: COMPREHE

In this case, this specific plot shown below on the right does not show signs of curvilinearity. Thus, the assumption that a linear relationship exists between the covariate and the dependent variable remains tenable. To determine if the assumption of homogeneity of regression is satisfied, one must use the SPSS alternative of a custom univariate model involving an interaction between the covariate and the independent variable. To do so, the researcher goes to the *Model* dialog box and clicks on the *Custom* radio button. The factor and covariates are highlighted and transferred to the *Model:* list. Then, the researcher clicks on the

Model: Intercept + Listenig + Organiz

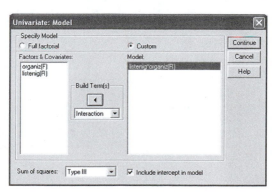

Continue button and then *OK*. The following output appears, including a test of the requested interaction. As can be seen, the interaction between the covariate and the independent variable is significant. This condition shows that the analysis of covariance cannot, in fact, be employed with these data because there is no consistency in the dependent variable-covariate slope in the cells in the design. Thus, the covariate adjustment would have to be considered misleading, and the use of analysis of covariance would have to be abandoned.

Tests of Between-Subjects Effects

Dependent Variable: COMPREHE

Source	Type III Sum of Squares	df	Mean Square	F	Sig.
Corrected Model	18.898[a]	2	9.449	10.779	.001
Intercept	1.057E-04	1	1.057E-04	.000	.991
ORGANIZ*LISTENIG	18.898	2	9.449	10.779	.001
Error	14.902	17	.877		
Total	1042.000	20			
Corrected Total	33.800	19			

a. R Squared = .559 (Adjusted R Squared = .507)

Chapter 9

FACTORIAL ANALYSIS OF VARIANCE

When researchers have more than two groups to compare, they use analysis of variance, which is commonly called "ANOVA." When they have more than one independent variable as well, the comparison of means is called "*factorial* analysis of variance."[1] This chapter explains the ways researchers may apply this versatile tool. The steps involved in completing

---

[1]It is important not to confuse factorial analysis of variance with factor analysis, which is a method to examine intercorrelations among variables to determine the number and nature of any underlying dimensions.

any factorial ANOVA study will be examined. Then, the use of standard factorial ANOVA will be followed by applications for random, mixed, and repeated measures applications.

DOING A STUDY THAT INVOLVES MORE THAN ONE INDEPENDENT VARIABLE

When researchers explore differences among more than two means from two or more variables, several processes are required as minimums. Five major steps are most prominent.

1. *Stating a Hypothesis for Factorial ANOVA.* A research hypothesis for a factorial analysis of variance deals with the differences among means. A hypothesis where ANOVA is an appropriate test has one or more independent variables measured at the nominal level and a dependent variable measured at the interval level. For instance, a researcher might wish to compare the communicator competence ratings of students who receive a combination of case study readings and classroom instruction on responsive listening. The students could be randomly assigned to receive (or not to receive) classroom instruction in responsive listening. At the same time, they could be asked to read sets of interpersonal communication case studies involving people in low, moderate, or high intimacy relationships. The researcher might state hypotheses for each independent variable (degree of classroom instruction in responsive listening and relationship intimacy levels of case studies read).

   - The researcher might hypothesize that students receiving classroom instruction in responsive listening have higher communicator competence scores than students not receiving classroom instruction in responsive listening. The hypothesis would be

     $$H: \mu_{\text{students receiving classroom instruction in responsive listening}} > \mu_{\text{students not receiving classroom instruction in responsive listening}}.$$

     The null hypothesis tested statistically would be

     $$H_0: \mu_{\text{students receiving classroom instruction in responsive listening}} = \mu_{\text{students not receiving classroom instruction in responsive listening}}.$$

     Because there are only two levels for this variable, if the null hypothesis were rejected and the means were as predicted, the research hypothesis would be supported.

   - For the relationship intimacy levels of the case studies variable, the researcher might predict that students reading case studies with high relationship intimacy would have significantly higher mean communicator competence scores than students reading case studies with moderate relationship intimacy, who would also have higher mean communicator competence ratings than students reading case studies with low relationship intimacy. The hypothesis would be

     $$H: \mu_{\text{reading high relationship intimacy case studies}} > \mu_{\text{reading moderate relationship intimacy case studies}} > \mu_{\text{reading low relationship intimacy case studies}}.$$

     Yet, analysis of variance is an omnibus test of the null hypothesis that there simply is no difference among the means. The null hypothesis would be

     $$H_0: \mu_{\text{reading high relationship intimacy case studies}} = \mu_{\text{reading moderate relationship intimacy case studies}} = \mu_{\text{reading low relationship intimacy case studies}}.$$

Special Discussion 9.1

Special Statistical Notation for Factorial Designs

Though there is no rule requiring it, most researchers dealing with factorial experiments use a fairly consistent notation form. The letter j is used to represent a variable represented on the rows. The letter k is employed to represent the variable on the columns. As typically is the case, i is used to reference an instance of a particular data point. Thus, a researcher might state $\sum X_{ijk}$ to indicate a desire to sum each instance of a score from each row and column cell.

Dots also are used in factorial experiments to represent a collection of events that go all the way through the total. For instance, a researcher would use the notation $\bar{X}_{1.}$ to refer to the mean of the first row computed from all the instances of data in the row.* Similarly, researchers who see $\bar{X}_{.2}$ know that the symbol refers to the mean of the second column and is computed from all the data through the column. Similarly, $\bar{X}_{..}$ may refer to the grand mean, but the symbols $\bar{\bar{X}}$ or $\bar{\bar{\bar{X}}}$ often are used instead.

---

*Though using $\bar{X}$ to indicate the mean is the most common, many research reports use M to symbolize means. This notation may be complicated by the fact that some communication researchers also use M to refer to the number of messages included in a research study.

Rejecting the null hypothesis could mean many things. Therefore, researchers who wish to speculate that there is a difference between one group and a collection of others must follow up with specific comparisons involving contrasts between specific combinations of means. Researchers using ANOVA also can present hypotheses that deal with combinations of variable levels. Such research hypotheses could look something like:

$$H: \mu_{\text{highly intelligent}} > (\mu_{\text{moderately intelligent}} + \mu_{\text{lowly intelligent}})/2,$$

for which the null hypothesis would be

$$H_0: \mu_{\text{highly intelligent}} = (\mu_{\text{moderately intelligent}} + \mu_{\text{lowly intelligent}})/2.$$

Obviously, researchers would need to use tools to make specific comparisons in addition to the general ANOVA test.

- Hypotheses about interactions also may posit specific combinations of levels of two variables that would be distinguished from others. For instance, researchers might speculate that highly intelligent women would have higher communication competence than any other combination of levels. Such specific hypotheses would have to be followed by individual contrasts.

2. *The Selection of Levels and Conditions.* Researchers must select variable levels with some care. When researchers can justify selecting variable ranges to reflect the scope of the independent variable of interest, then researchers can state that they are concerned with **fixed effects**. These levels generally are expected to cover the range in which the variable operates normally. If the researcher has a primary variable of interest, a hypothesis usually will accompany the selection of the variable and its levels. Sometimes researchers attempt to identify—roughly speaking—a random selection of variable levels to determine if the variable produces effects in general. Researchers who take this approach are said to explore **random effects**.

3. *Inclusion of Additional Variable Suspected of Interacting With Other Predictors.* The first set of variables may not tell the whole story. In addition to considering adding other variables that would produce important effects one at a time, researchers often include other variables that might be involved in interactions with the primary variables of interest.

4. *Organizing the Conditions and Coding Data.* Researchers must prepare study conditions, collect data, and score measures. For instance, researchers might design an experiment composed of two independent variables, source credibility (low and high) and use of humor in a message (without jokes and with jokes). Researchers would need to prepare all possible combinations of these variable levels. In this case, every participant who happened to be exposed to a message without jokes could receive a code of 1 for a variable called "Humor." Those exposed to a message with jokes could receive a code of 2 for the "Humor" variable. Similarly, those exposed to the message attributed to a source with little credibility could receive 1 for a variable called "Credibility," and those exposed to the message attributed to a highly credible source could receive 2 for the variable.[2] Table 9.1 illustrates the possible interactions of these two variables.

Table 9.1

		Humor	
		Without Jokes	*With Jokes*
Source Credibility	Low		
	High		

5. *Testing Assumptions.* When completing factorial analysis of variance, researchers regularly test assumptions underlying the statistic itself. These tests affect the how analyses may be completed and, hence, will be considered for different forms of ANOVA (fixed, random, mixed, and repeated measures designs) covered in this chapter.

TYPES OF EFFECTS TO TEST

A major reason to complete a factorial analysis of variance study is to identify effects from variables taken separately and in combinations. Each of these effect types will be considered.

Isolating Main Effects

Because factorial designs involve more than one independent variable, researchers naturally care whether these variables produce effects one at a time. Called a **main effect**, this type of

---

[2]Researchers sometimes find that credibility manipulations are difficult. When made the object of a manipulation check, some "low credibility" conditions turn out to be moderately credible. In some cases, the low credibility induction creates a strong positive violation of expectations (e.g., a high school student talking intelligently about the International Monetary Fund).

result is "the effect of an independent variable uninfluenced by other variables" (Vogt, 2005, p. 183). Because they are main effects, their contributions to total variation in the dependent variable are additive. That is, the factors do not interact, and they produce effects that may be added to other effects to determine the overall impact of variables.

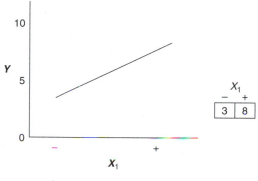

In the figure on the right, the numbers inside the 1×2 grid indicate mean scores on the dependent variable, and the identifiers outside the cells show independent variable levels. If only one independent variable is present, as in the case here, the main effect may be identified by looking at a simple line graph, such as shown on the diagram. The dependent variable is indicated on the vertical axis (also known as the y-axis or the ordinate). Though bar charts often are used to report research data, line graphs, rather than bar charts, traditionally are employed to identify different sorts of effects on dependent variables.

In this case, the diagram shows that when one moves from the low level of the independent variable (symbolized X_1) to the high level, the dependent variable scores show an upward slope. Indeed, main effects are indicated for the variable on the horizontal axis (also known as the x-axis or abscissa) by the existence of line(s) with some slope. A flat line, running parallel to the horizontal axis, would reveal the absence of a main effect. Such a flat line would mean that as one moves from one level to another on the independent variable, there is no change in the dependent variable. If there is a difference in the numbers, there is a main effect. The bigger the difference, the bigger is the effect.

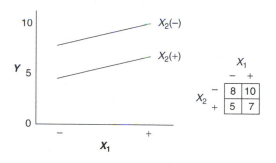

When two independent variables are included, the researcher runs out of available axes on a two-dimensional figure. Thus, separate lines are drawn to represent levels of the second dependent variable, as shown in the diagram on the right. Separate lines have been drawn to show the effects of the levels of variable 2.[3] To reveal whether there is a main effect from the independent variable on the horizontal axis, the researcher looks at the average dependent variable score when the independent variable is at each of its levels (often placing an imaginary dot on these positions). When an imaginary line connecting these means shows slope, a main effect is claimed. In this case, as shown in the diagram on the right, the dotted line shows "imaginary line" and, because it has slope, a main effect exists from independent variable 1.

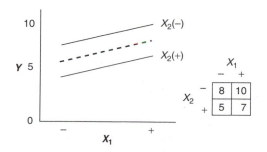

---

[3]References to "high" and "low" levels refer only to the levels of the independent variables, not what impact these variables have on the dependent variable.

To detect a main effect from the variable for which separate lines were drawn, the researcher looks at the average of each line and looks for a difference in the dependent variable scores. In short, the researcher looks for space between the middles of the lines. In the case of the example shown here on the left, the middle of each line is indicated by a circle, and there clearly is space between these points. Thus, in this example the researchers would identify a main effect from variable 2.

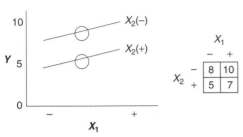

	X_1	
	−	+
X_2 −	8	10
X_2 +	5	7

Isolating Interaction Effects

In addition to main effects, researchers often are interested in exploring the effects of special combinations of levels of variables. **Interaction effects** are the "joint effect[s] of two or more independent variables on a dependent variable" (Vogt, 2005, p. 154). Whereas main effects are additive effects, interactions are multiplicative. In other words, the interactions are more than just the result of main effects moving in concert. Instead, they are contributions to overall effects that go beyond the addition of main effects alone. A direct way to identify the nature of interactions is to look at the diagrams of means. In general, interaction effects are revealed when the lines are *nonparallel*. In fact, they may be so nonparallel that they cross (but it is not necessary for lines to cross for an interaction to be present). As we shall see, however, the type of interaction found greatly affects the sorts of interpretations that can be made of the study results.

Two types of interactions regularly are identified in research reports. **Uncrossed or ordinal interactions** are dependent interaction effects that are in the same direction as the main effects of the variables involved (Reinard, 2001, p. 439). On the other hand, **crossed or disordinal interactions** are dependent interaction effects that are *not* in the same direction as the main effects of the variables involved (Reinard, 2001, p. 435).

In essence, ordinal interactions indicate the presence of a sort of "bonus effect" when levels of independent variables are put together. The interaction is in the same direction as the main effects, just more (or less) so. The diagram on the left reveals a slight tendency toward non-parallel lines. Obviously, it would be nice to know if such interaction effects contribute variation that is beyond random sampling error alone. Factorial analysis of variance provides such information and will be described shortly. In this example, the main effects reveal lowest dependent variable scores when variable X_1 is low and also when variable X_2 is low. When these two levels are combined, however, the effect goes beyond a simple average of the main effects. Hence,

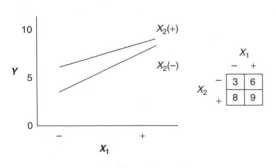

	X_1	
	−	+
X_2 −	3	6
X_2 +	8	9

the effect is not additive. By the way, in this case the so-called "bonus effect" is in a negative direction—the dependent variable scores are reduced greatly by the combination of variable levels.

A variation of this type of ordinal interaction involves finding what some researchers call a "magic cell" in which only one combination of conditions produces dependent variable scores that are different from the others. The diagram on the right illustrates such a situation, in which the only time that a different dependent variable score is observed is when independent variable X_2 is set at its low level and independent variable X_1 is set at its high level. It is important to remember, however, that the "high" and "low" levels of independent variables refer only to *their* settings, not the predicted scores on dependent variables.

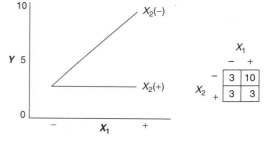

Another ordinal interaction form occurs when levels of one variable eliminate the contributions from the other variable. For instance, in the diagram below on the right, when variable X_1 is low, the different levels of variable X_2 influence the dependent variable scores. But when variable X_1 is high, different levels of variable X_2 have no influence on the dependent variable. One might wonder if this interaction is ordinal or disordinal, because the lines touch. The answer is that the interaction is *ordinal* because the lines do not cross. One might speculate that the interaction could be disordinal if the lines were extended further. Yet, interpretations are based on the actual levels and "operating ranges" selected by the researchers. If it is assumed that independent variable levels are set on the basis of some logical reasoning, it does not matter that the lines might cross if somebody else did a differ-

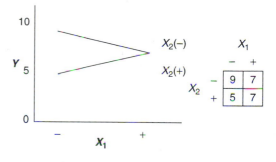

ent study using different levels of independent variables. In fact, if the levels were simple categories, such as whether the respondents were male of female, it would not make any sense to wonder what a "higher" level of the variable would be. Furthermore, the researcher does not really know that the lines might not have retreated in he opposite direction if the levels of the independent variable had been extended.

It is important for researchers to check alternative ways of drawing charts. For instance, if the data from the last example were graphed by switching which variable appears on the horizontal axis, the results would be very different. The diagram to the right shows this condition. The diagram now reveals a disordinal interaction. So, an inquiring mind might wonder, is the interaction actually ordinal or disordinal? The answer is that if the lines cross under any circumstance, the interaction is disordinal, even though

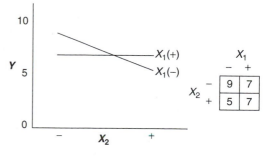

the disordinal interaction may have been "disguised" in one drawing. Though under most circumstances, disordinal interactions do not hide themselves, wise researchers should draw diagrams in more than one fashion before making final interpretations of interactions.

The reason identifying interactions is vital lies in the fact that the interpretations of results are completely different. When there is a disordinal or crossed interaction,

- researchers are not permitted to interpret the main effects involved in the interaction; and
- researchers acting on such information must look at the settings of two variables at once, rather than independent variables one at a time.

The reason for these rules may be obvious. With a disordinal interaction, each main effect from independent variables would accurately predict output about half the time. The rest of the time, results would not be as initially predicted from the main effects.[4] In short, interpreting the main effects would be misleading when there are disordinal interactions. Yet, this fact does not mean that the impact of the main effect is dropped from the study. The contribution to the total percentage of variance explained is retained. By the way, this requirement to avoid interpreting main effects for variables involved in disordinal interactions does not apply to *other* independent variable main effects that are *not* part of the disordinal interaction. If researchers had three independent variables, any main effect from the third variable could be interpreted provided it were not part of a disordinal interaction involving the first two variables.

If researchers wish to act upon their research findings, identifying the presence of disordinal interactions is very important. If there is an ordinal interaction, then it is possible to take action on one variable at a time, because the interaction is in the same direction as the main effects. On the other hand, if there is a disordinal interaction, researchers know that they cannot look at one independent variable at a time. If action is to be taken, one variable cannot be left to operate at random while the other is fixed.

COMPUTING THE FIXED-EFFECT ANOVA

The fixed-effect analysis of variance is "a model where the levels of the factor under study (the treatments) are *fixed* in advance. Inference is valid only for the levels under study" (Aczel, 1989, p. 379). In this approach, sometimes called the "Type I model" of analysis of variance, a serious choice is made of the levels of the independent variables, and the conditions are generally considered exhaustive of the variable. For instance, researchers might examine whether lengthy or brief speeches delivered by male or female speakers differ in their comprehensibility. Both the factors of speech length and sex of the speakers are composed of fixed levels that cover the researcher's range of interest. Most communication studies using factorial analysis of variance employ the fixed-effect model.

The fixed-effect model ANOVA makes four major assumptions that must be checked:

- Measurement of the dependent variable on the interval or ratio level
- Randomization
- Normal distribution of the dependent variable. Researchers may explore this matter by examining the kurtosis and skewness of the distributions. As shown in Chapter 4, researchers also could consider using the Kolmogorov-Smirnov or Shapiro-Wilks statistics to test the null hypothesis that the sample data do not differ from a normal

---

[4]For instance, in the previous example, there is a main effect from variable X_2 (though not from variable X_1). The main effect indicates that the dependent variable scores are highest when X_2 is set at its low level, but this effect will occur only if variable X_1 is low. If variable X_1 is high, then the dependent variable effects will be reduced when X_2 is at its high level.

distribution. With large sample sizes, the factorial analysis of variance is relatively robust to modest violations of normality. But if sample sizes are small (much below 30), researchers may wish to transform variables before continuing with analyses.

- Homogeneous variances. Researchers examine variances to detect if the variances are within the limits of sampling error and may use such tools as the F test (or F_{max}) of variances or Levene's test. If variances are unequal, researchers may look for ceiling or floor effects (by correlating means and variances). If heterogeneous variances exist in the absence of ceiling and floor effects, researchers have evidence of events by treatments interaction, and they should continue the search for moderating variables to include in the research effort.

The first two of these assumptions are matters that must be considered by researchers in their design or research. The third and fourth assumptions may be considered by examining data.

As mentioned in Chapter 8, the fixed-effect model also assumes these elements that are dependent on the research design choices and presumptions made by researchers:

- The elements in the model reflect the sum of all the elements that affect the dependent variable.
- The experiment contains all treatment levels of interest.
- The error effects are independent and normally distributed.
- The samples are independent, which means that knowledge of an individual's score on some measure neither predicts the degree of that individual's error nor affects the probability of predicting any other individual's responses.

Assessing Effects

Main effects for factorial analysis of variance are rather easy to compute. Researchers start by looking at the "between-groups variances" for each input variable separately. Table 9.2 shows such an example. To compute main effects mean squares is a relatively simple task because it uses the same formula as one-way analysis of variance, $n * s_{\bar{X}}^2$. Degrees of freedom for this term are the number of groups minus one. The process is repeated for the other main effects as well.

To compute interactions from levels of independent variables, researchers take each cell value and then subtract away the mean that would be expected by the row and column means (and means of "slices," in the case of three-way ANOVAs). Then, the contribution is contrasted by adding the grand mean (only once in the case of two-factor analysis of variance). Any remaining variation is attributable to interaction effects beyond influences of main effects alone. The degrees of freedom for interaction effects are simply the product of the degrees of freedom for each main effect involved in the interaction.

Within-groups variance (also known as error variance) is the same as a pooled variance s_p^2 introduced in Chapter 8. If sample sizes are equal, the pooled variance is simply the mean of the variances within each cell group. If the sample sizes are unequal, a formula that adjusts for sample sizes is used.

(Text continues on page 225)

Table 9.2   Example of a Two-Way Analysis of Variance

A researcher was interested in student's perceptions of their teachers' overall verbal communication and nonverbal immediacy with students (measured on a set of 18 seven-point "communication satisfaction" scales, with a possible range for the total of 18 to 126). The researcher thought that female students might report greater communication of teacher immediacy than male students generally. The researcher also suspected that students who were highly individualistic by nature (measured by a standard scale and then divided into "high" and "low" groups based on their scores) might report greater communication of teacher immediacy than would students who were low on individualism. The hypothesis for the sex of student was H_1: $\mu_{women} > \mu_{men}$. The hypothesis about individualism predicted H_2: $\mu_{highly\ individualistic\ students} > \mu_{lowly\ individualistic\ students}$. The researcher had a number of male and female students complete scales to rate their individualism and their perceptions of teacher verbal and nonverbal communication of immediacy. Their scores are found in the grid below, along with a list of means ($\overline{X}$) and variances (s^2). To compute the sources of variation, researchers must examine two main effects and an interaction effect.

		Sex of Student		
		Male	Female	
Individualism	Low	102, 103, 95, 80, 95, 110, 109, 102, 94, 98, 90, 101, 108, 105, 90, 96, 90, 93, 111, 95, 88, 81, 87, 91, 85, 89 $\overline{X}_{11} = 95.69$ $s_{11}^2 = 76.30$	97, 86, 104, 95, 92, 82, 91, 99, 74, 106, 90, 109, 89, 104, 101, 102, 71, 86, 89, 112, 90, 94, 94, 86, 107, 94 $\overline{X}_{12} = 94.00$ $s_{12}^2 = 102.80$	$\overline{\overline{X}}_{.1} = 94.85$
	High	114, 105, 104, 110, 76, 87, 84, 105, 85, 96, 91, 109, 95, 98, 101, 83, 99, 75, 103, 113, 101, 93, 102, 116, 104, 103 $\overline{X}_{21} = 98.15$ $s_{21}^2 = 125.42$	76, 101, 112, 104, 100, 109, 104, 99, 100, 116, 108, 106, 90, 111, 90, 110, 105, 102, 103, 92, 98, 114, 85, 104, 89, 94 $\overline{X}_{22} = 100.85$ $s_{22}^2 = 91.74$	$\overline{\overline{X}}_{.2} = 99.50$
		$\overline{\overline{X}}_{.1} = 96.92$	$\overline{\overline{X}}_{.2} = 97.43$	$\overline{\overline{X}} = 97.18$

- The mean square for individualism is computed as $MS_{individuals} = n$ in the row $* s_{\bar{X}}^2$ or, equivalently using the computational formula with j as the rows (individualism), k as the columns (sex of subjects), and i as instances of scores:

$$\left(\frac{\sum\limits_{j}\left(\sum\limits_{k}\sum\limits_{i} X_{ijk} \right)^2}{n_{j\cdot}} - \frac{\left(\sum\limits_{k}\sum\limits_{j}\sum\limits_{i} X_{ijk} \right)^2}{n_{\cdot\cdot}} \right) / \text{degrees of freedom.}$$

Using the conceptual formula, one may substitute scores as $MS_{individuals} = n$ in the row $* s_{\bar{X}}^2$. The equation then can be shown:

$$= 52 * \frac{\sum\left(\bar{X}_j - \bar{\bar{X}} \right)^2}{j - 1}$$

$$= 52 * \frac{(94.85 - 97.18)^2 + (99.5 - 97.18)^2}{2 - 1}$$

$$= 52 * \frac{5.43 + 5.38}{1}$$

$$= 52 * 10.81$$

$$= 562.12$$

- The mean square for sex of participants are computed as $MS_{sex\ of\ participants} = n$ in the column $* s_{\bar{X}}^2$ or, equivalently using a computational formula with j as the rows (individualism), k as the columns (sex of participants), and i as instances of scores:

$$\left(\frac{\sum\limits_{k}\left(\sum\limits_{j}\sum\limits_{i} X_{ijk} \right)^2}{n_{\cdot k}} - \frac{\left(\sum\limits_{k}\sum\limits_{j}\sum\limits_{i} X_{ijk} \right)^2}{n_{\cdot\cdot}} \right) / \text{degrees of freedom.}$$

Using the first formula, one may substitute scores as $MS_{sex\ of\ participants} = n$ in the column $s_{\bar{X}}^2$ to get the following equality:

$$= 52 * \frac{\sum\left(\bar{X}_k - \bar{\bar{X}} \right)^2}{k - 1}$$

$$= 52 * \frac{(96.92 - 97.18)^2 + (97.43 - 97.18)^2}{2 - 1}$$

$$= 52 * \frac{.07 + .06}{1}$$

$$= 52 * .13$$

$$= 6.76.$$

(Continued)

Table 9.2 (Continued)

- The mean square for the interaction between individualism and sex of subjects in this case is computed as $MS_{interaction} = (n$ in each cell condition $* \sum$ [cell mean − row mean − column mean + grand mean]^2) / degrees of freedom or, equivalently using the computational formula with j as the rows (individualism) k as the columns (sex of subjects), and $\overline{\overline{X}}$ as the grand mean:

$$\left(n_{jk} * \sum_j \sum_k \left(\overline{X}_{jk} - \overline{\overline{X}}_{j.} - \overline{\overline{X}}_{.k} + \overline{\overline{X}} \right)^2 \right) /\text{degrees of freedom.}$$

Substituting the scores, one finds:

$$= \left(26 * \left[\begin{array}{l} (95.69 - 94.85 - 96.92 + 97.18)^2 + (94 - 94.85 - 97.43 + 97.18)^2 + \\ (98.15 - 99.5 - 96.92 + 97.18)^2 + (100.85 - 99.5 - 97.43 + 97.18)^2 \end{array} \right] \right) /1$$

$$= (26 * [1.21 + 1.21 + 1.19 + 1.21])/1 = 125.32.$$

- Within groups variance (also known as error variance) is the same as a pooled variance s_p^2. If sample sizes are equal, the pooled variance is simply the mean of the variances within each cell group. If the sample sizes are unequal, the following formula that adjusts for sample sizes is used

$$s_p^2 = \frac{(n_1 - 1)s_1^2 + (n_2 - 1)s_2^2 + \ldots (n - 1)s_n^2}{n_1 - 1 + n_2 - 1 + \ldots n_n - 1}.$$

For these data, the pooled variance is 99.07. This term is the mean square, not the sums of squares. When entered into the ANOVA table, the numbers are revealed as:

Sources of Variation	Sums of Squares	Degrees of Freedom	Mean Square	F	Eta Squared
Individuality	562.12	1	562.12	5.67*	.05
Sex of participants	6.76	1	6.76	<1	
Individuality x sex of subjects	125.32	1	125.32	1.26	
Within-groups variance	9907	100	99.07		
Within-groups variance	9907	100	99.07		
Total	1,0601.2	104			

*$p < .05$.

- The degrees of freedom for each main effect are the number of levels of the variable, minus one. The degrees of freedom for the interaction effect are determined by multiplying the main effect degrees of freedom for each variable involved in the interaction. Hence, in this case, degrees of freedom for the interaction term equal one ($1 * 1 = 1$). The within-groups degrees of freedom are the total number of events minus the number of groups in the study. In this case, there were 104 events, minus four sample groups of cells. Thus, degrees of freedom equal 100.
- To test the statistical hypothesis of "no difference" with an alpha risk of .05, the researcher finds the critical value of F with the numerator degrees of freedom from the effect and degrees of freedom in the denominator equal to the number of degrees of freedom for the within-groups (or "error") term. In this case, with 1 and 100 degrees of freedom, the critical F ratio is 3.936. Thus, the main effect from individualism was statistically significant.
- To identify the source of differences from the main effect, one need only look at the marginal means (because there are only two levels). Those with high individualism showed the highest ratings communication immediacy. This effect was associated with 5% of the total variance.
- In this case, there was no statistically significant interaction effect. Yet, if a statistically significant interaction had been found, the researcher would want to examine diagrams of the specific interaction patterns.
- To investigate whether the assumptions underlying the analysis of variance held, the homogeneity of variance was tested. In this case, the F test was

$$F = \frac{\text{largest } s^2}{\text{smallest } s^2} = \frac{102.90}{76.30} = 1.35.$$

The critical $F_{(d.f.:\ 25,25)}$ with α at .025 was 2.23. Thus, the assumption of homogeneous variance held.

After the factorial analysis of variance is completed, researchers would be well advised to determine the size of each significant effect. The formula for eta squared (η^2) used for the one-way analysis of variance may be used here. The formula is

$$\eta^2 = \frac{\text{between-groups sums of squares}}{\text{total sums of squares}}.$$

In each case, the "between-groups sums of squares" are the sums of squares associated with each individual statistically significant effect, whether a main or interaction effect. This convenient formula permits the researcher to determine the share of total variance that is contributed by each individual source that produces a significant difference.

Using SPSS for Fixed-Effect ANOVA

As an illustration of a fixed-effect factorial analysis of variance, data from a study of perceived teacher immediacy will be considered. From the *Analyze* menu, the researcher would choose *General Linear Model* and then *Univariate*. . . . The dependent variable "immediacy" would be identified and moved to the "Dependent Variable:" field. The two independent variables, "sex" and "indhilo" (individualism) of the respondents, are highlighted and transferred to the "Fixed Factor(s):" field.

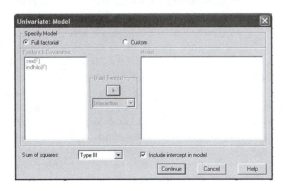

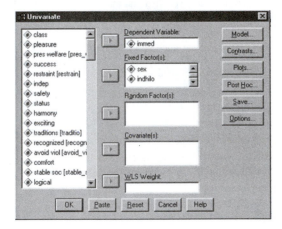

The researcher then would click on the *Model...* button to specify the "Full factorial" option (if it has not already been identified). The dialog box also includes the method to be used to compute sums of squares. The default is Type III, which includes a full factorial with no missing data cells. This reference to Type III refers only to the sums of squares, *not* the type of factorial design. Afterward, the researcher would click on the *Continue* button. (See illustration on the top right column.)

The researcher then clicks on the *Options* to identify the effects to be tested. In this case, the researcher requests displays of means for all effects by transferring the effects from the "Factor(s) and Factor Interactions:" field to the "Display Means for:" field. In addition, boxes

are checked to obtain "Descriptive statistics," "Estimates of effect size," and "Homogeneity [of variance] tests." Afterward, the researcher clicks the *Continue* button.

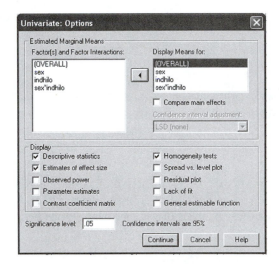

To obtain a plot of the results, the researcher would click on the *Plots...* button. Because it is wise to include two diagrams with different variables placed on the horizontal axis, two plots are requested. The first plot, "sex*indhilo," places "sex" on the horizontal axis. The second plot, "indhilo*sex," places "indhilo" on the horizontal axis. The researcher would click on *Continue* and then *OK*. (See illustration on the top of left column on p. 227.)

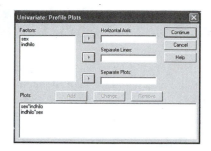

The ANOVA table indicated that the individualism variables produced a significant difference and that no significant interaction effect was present. In the estimated marginal means, those with high mean ratings of individualism (Group 2) reported greater perceptions of the teacher immediacy than others (Group 1).

Levene's test was not statistically significant. Hence, the researcher would conclude that the assumption that the variances were the same could not be rejected.

3. INDHILO

Dependent Variable: IMMED

INDHILO	Mean	Std. Error	95% Confidence Interval	
			Lower Bound	Upper Bound
1	94.846	1.380	92.108	97.585
2	99.500	1.380	96.762	102.238

Univarlate Analysis of Variance

Levene's Test of Equality of error Variances

Dependent Variable: IMMED

F	df1	df2	Sig.
.503	3	100	.881

Tests the null hypothesis that the error variance of the dependent variable is equal across groups.

a. Design: Intercept+ SEX+INDHILO+SEX*INDHILO

These steps would produce the following results:

Although the ANOVA showed that that interactions were not statistically significant, it is interesting to note that the type of interaction would have been disordinal because when the chart was drawn with individualism on the horizontal axis, the result was crossed interaction, as shown in the second chart below.

Descriptive Statistics

Dependent Variable: IMMED

SEX	INDHILO	Mean	Std. Deviation	N
1	1	95.69	8.74	26
	2	98.15	11.20	26
	Total	96.92	10.02	52
2	1	94.00	10.14	26
	2	100.85	9.58	26
	Total	97.42	10.36	52
Total	1	94.85	9.41	52
	2	99.50	10.41	52
	Total	97.17	10.15	104

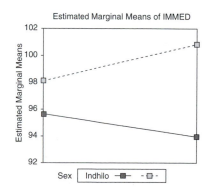

Tests of Between-Subjects Effects

Dependent Variable: IMMED

Source	Type III Sum of Squares	df	Mean Square	F	Sig.
Corrected Model	694.577ᵃ	3	231.526	2.337	.078
Intercept	962031.115	1	982031.115	9913.190	.000
SEX	6.500	1	6.500	.066	.798
INDHILO	563.115	1	563.115	5.684	.019
SEX*INDHILO	124.962	1	124.962	1.261	.264
Error	9906.308	100	99.063		
Total	992632.000	104			
Corrected Total	10600.885	103			

a. R Squared = .066 (Adjusted R Squared = .037)

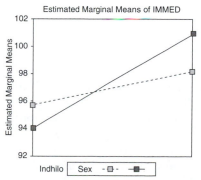

Using Excel for Fixed-Effect ANOVA

When completing a "two-way" or two-factor analysis of variance, Excel requires that each level of one independent variable should be identified by separate columns. The rows must group the levels of the dependent variable. So, the data must be arranged in a way similar to the one shown below. In addition, the rows must group the scores of the dependent variable.

	A	B	C
1		Low Individualism	High Individualism
2	Male	102	114
3		103	105
4		95	104
5		80	110
6		97	76
7		110	87
8		109	84
9		102	105
10		94	85
11		98	96
12		90	91
13		101	109
14		108	95
15		105	98
16		90	83
17		96	99
18		90	75
19		93	103
20		111	113
21		95	101
22		88	101
23		81	93
24		87	102
25		91	116
26		85	104
27		89	103
28	Female	97	76
29		86	101
30		104	112

To complete the two-way ANOVA, the researcher selects *Data Analysis* from the *Tools* menu. From the dialog box that appears, the researcher selects "Anova: Two-Factor With Replication" and then clicks the *OK* button. In the box that appears, the researcher clicks on

and then highlights the location on the spreadsheet where the data begin through the location where the data end.

The researcher clicks on ⊡ to return to the dialog box. To select a location to place output, the researcher clicks on the "Output Range:" window and goes to an available location such as one starting at cell A55. After making a selection, the researcher clicks on ⊡ to return to the dialog box. In the dialog box, the researcher must specify a desired alpha risk for use in significance testing (.05 in this case). In addition, the researcher identifies the "Rows per sample:" a number that corresponds to the sample size in each cell.

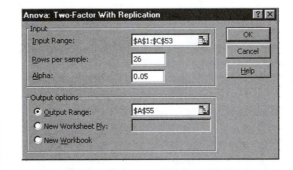

After clicking on the *OK* button, the following output appears. Inspecting the column marked *P-value* makes it clear that the only significant effect was a main effect for the column variable, individualism. A look at the means of the high and low individualism groups reveals that the highest ratings (dependent variable: immediacy) were from the high individualism group participants. Excel does not have built-in functions for designs involving more than two independent variables, but this chapter's Web site includes references to other add-in programs that help fill these additional needs.

Anova: Two-Factor With Replication						
Summary	Low Individualism	High Individualism	Total			
Male						
Count	26	26	52			
Sum	2488	2552	5040			
Average	95.69230769	98.15384615	96.92307692			
Variance	76.30153846	125.4153846	100.4253394			
Female						
Count	26	26	52			
Sum	2444	2622	5066			
Average	94	100.8461538	97.42307692			
Variance	102.8	91.73536462	107.3076923			
Total						
Count	52	52				
Sum	4932	5174				
Average	94.84615385	99.5				
Variance	88.52488689	108.2941176				
ANOVA						
Source of Variation	*SS*	*df*	*MS*	*F*	*P-value*	*F crit*
Sample	6.5	1	6.5	0.06561476	0.798358302	3.936150961
Columns	563.1153846	1	563.1153846	5.684412418	0.019002603	3.936150961
Interaction	124.9615365	1	124.9615385	1.261434051	0.264069015	3.936150961
Within	9906.307692	100	99.06307692			
Total	10600.88462	103				

RANDOM- AND MIXED-EFFECTS DESIGNS

Though in "fixed-effects" analysis of variance designs, the levels of a variable are *fixed* to include the full range of levels that a researcher considers important, there are times when researchers take random draws of examples from populations as variable levels. There also are times when the same participants are measured repeatedly.[5] This discussion will consider each of these approaches.

Understanding Random-Effects Designs

In analysis of variance, the **random effects model** is an experimental design in which the levels of the factor are random, in the sense that they are drawn at random from a population of levels rather than fixed by an investigator. Also called "variance components model" and "Model II ANOVA design,"

> [t]he random-effects model is used when there is a large number of categories or levels of a factor. For example, say researchers in a survey organization wanted to see whether different kinds of telephone interviewers get different response rates. Because there are [*sic*] potentially a very large number of categories (difference in accent, quality of voice,

---

[5]This is not meant to equate random effects with repeated measures. Whereas random-effects testing involves further partialing of the within-subjects error term, random effects do not require repeated measures designs.

etc.), perhaps as many as there are individual telephone interviewers, a sample is chosen randomly from the population of interviewers, which is also, in this case, a population of levels. On the other hand, if the survey organization were interested only in, say, the difference in response rate between male and female interviewers, they would use a fixed-effects model. (Vogt, 2005, pp. 260–261)

In this model, the researcher attempts to make an inference about the meaningfulness of an entire population of a variable. If a researcher finds that that variable fails to produce statistically significant effects, the researcher may have some reason to move to other variables that actually might produce different effects in the dependent variable. For most research in communication studies, the random-effects model is not used; instead, either a fixed- or mixed-effects model is employed.

For the random-effects model, several assumptions must be made in addition to the ones typically required of any parametric tests (i.e., interval or ratio level measurement of the dependent variable, randomization, normal distribution, homogeneity of variances). In particular, this model assumes that the error terms are independent and normally distributed. This assumption means, among other things, that knowing the factor level would not allow one to predict whether an error term was above or below zero.

Computationally, a one-factor fixed-effects model and the one-factor random-effects model are equivalent, but they differ in the additional assumption (independent and normally distributed error terms) and the interpretation of the meaning of an effect. The existence of a statistically significant effect means that the variable from which random selections of levels were made produces significant effects on the dependent variable. Hence, the variable bears further inquiry to determine fixed levels that produce predictable outcomes. It is, therefore, a variable "screening" exercise. It should be added that the computation of statistical significance for the random-effect variable does change when two-factor mixed-effect designs are involved. These highly useful designs are considered next.

Use of Mixed-Effects Designs

Sometimes researchers employ one or more fixed effects and one or more random effects. The mixed-effects ANOVA (also known as "Model III ANOVA") combines (mixes) between-subjects factors and within-subjects factors.

The Logic of Combining Fixed and "Random" Effects

One might wonder why communication researchers would want to complete studies where some variables are fixed and others are treated as randomly selected examples of variable levels. For example, suppose a researcher presented participants with four messages with or without emotional language (the fixed effect). Furthermore, suppose the researcher used messages on two different topics. If the researcher were interested in these specific messages, the message topics would be a fixed effect. If instead the researcher were interested in the influences of messages in general, the message topics would be a random effect. Statistically, if one uses a completely fixed-effect ANOVA, the "between-groups variance term" includes both the treatment and reactions to the specific message "replications" used. Some scholars have recommended that researchers who study message characteristics should include at least two examples of message and more than one topic (Clark, 1973; Jackson, Brashers, & Massey, 1992; Jackson & Jacobs, 1983; Jackson, O'Keefe, & Jacobs, 1988; Jackson,

O'Keefe, Jacobs, & Brashers, 1989).[6] A remaining controversy is whether the effect should be treated as a random selection of a variable level from the population of theoretic possibilities, or whether the effect should be considered a fixed effect and studied as any other primary variable of interest. If a rationale can justify the use of a fixed-effect approach, that method probably should be used. But if the researcher is using multiple messages simply for the purpose of control, the mixed-effect ANOVA is a particularly appropriate tool.

In the mixed-effects model, the fixed effect and interaction mean squares are identified the same way they are for the fixed-effect model. But for the computation of the *F* statistic, things change. In the mixed-effects model, each main effect mean square is divided by the *interaction* mean square between the fixed-effect variable and the random-effect variable. The use of the interaction mean square allows the shared contribution of the random influence to be controlled in estimates of the primary fixed effects of interest. For the interaction term itself, the within-groups mean square is used to compute the *F* value. Naturally, the degrees of freedom are computed differently depending on whether the within-groups mean square or the interaction mean square is used as the divisor:

- For the fixed effect, the degrees of freedom are

$$\frac{\text{[for the numerator] number of levels in the fixed effect} - 1}{\begin{array}{c}\text{[for the denominator] degrees of freedom in the interaction term} \\ \text{(number of levels in the fixed effect} - 1) * \text{(number of levels} \\ \text{in the random variable} - 1)\end{array}}.$$

- For the random effect, the degrees of freedom are

$$\frac{\text{[for the numerator] number of levels in the random effect} - 1}{\begin{array}{c}\text{[for the denominator] degrees of freedom in the interaction term} \\ \text{(number of levels in the fixed effect} - 1) * \text{(number of levels} \\ \text{in the random variable} - 1)\end{array}}.$$

- For the interaction effect, the degrees of freedom are

$$\frac{\begin{array}{c}\text{[for the numerator] (number of levels in the fixed effect} - 1) * \\ \text{(number of levels in the random variable} - 1)\end{array}}{\begin{array}{c}\text{[for the denominator] degrees of freedom in the within-groups} \\ \text{term (number of events in the study} - \text{number of groups)}\end{array}}.$$

---

[6]At one time, communication researchers routinely studied message variables by presenting participants with one example of a message and a message topic. Critics suggested that it often was difficult to know if the results could be generalized beyond the specific message and the specific topics. This position is controversial. Though admitting the value of replications, some have disagreed that using single messages is a flawed approach (especially when a series of studies across many topics has been completed) (Burgoon, Hall, & Pfau, 1991). Furthermore, some argue that insisting on multiple message replications may be an unfair demand that may drive out most worthy message-effects research. Settling the matter is not within the purview of this book. Yet, this chapter accepts the view that all researchers must shoulder a burden of proof and present arguments and reasons to support the proposition that the message examples they study are representative of some meaningful class of messages.

As can be seen, if there is a great interaction between the fixed effect and the random effect, the chances of finding a statistically significant fixed effect are reduced. But if the interaction is modest, the test can be quite powerful. Table 9.3 shows the steps involved in such a mixed-effects study.

Table 9.3   Example of Mixed-Effects Model

A researcher wanted to know if a message using deliberate ambiguity would produce more attitude change among initially hostile audiences than messages with clear language. The hypothesis was

H_1: $\mu_{ambiguous} > \mu_{unambiguous}$.

But the researcher wanted to determine if the strategies, rather than the particular topic of the messages, were responsible. So, the use of the message strategies was the fixed effect, and three different messages were designed with and without the ambiguous language used.

	Message Topic 1	Message Topic 2	Message Topic 3	$\bar{X}_{j.}$	$\bar{X}_{j.} - \bar{\bar{X}}$
Unambiguous language	29, 20, 22, 33	36, 23, 25, 24	38, 26, 21, 27	$n = 12$	
$\bar{X}_{1k}$	26	27	28	27	−3.165
s^2_{1k}	36.67	36.67	51.33		
Ambiguous language	42, 32, 25, 29	31, 45, 27, 37	31, 31, 25, 45	$n = 12$	
$\bar{X}_{2k}$	32	35	33	33.33	3.165
s^2_{2k}	52.67	61.33	72		
$\bar{X}_{.k}$	$n = 8$	$n = 8$	$n = 8$		
	29	31	30.5	30.165	
$\bar{X}_{.k} - \bar{\bar{X}}$	−1.165	.835	.335		

These messages were approximately the same length and had human interest quotients of nearly the identical levels. Computing sources of variation involves both fixed and random effects:

$$\text{Mean Square}_{\text{fixed effect}} = \frac{n_j * \sum \left(\bar{X}_j - \bar{\bar{X}} \right)^2}{j - 1},$$

where

n_j is the number of events in each level of the fixed effect and

j is the number of levels for the fixed effect.

In this case, the numbers are

$$\text{Mean Square}_{\text{fixed effect}} = \frac{12 * (-3.165^2 + 3.165^2)}{2 - 1} = \frac{12 * 20.03}{1} = 240.41$$

$$\text{Mean Square}_{\text{random effect (messages)}} = \frac{n_k * \sum \left(\overline{X}_k - \overline{\overline{X}}\right)^2}{k - 1},$$

where

n_k is the number of events in level of the random effect and

k is the number of levels for the random effect.

In this case, the data entry yields

$$\text{Mean Square}_{\text{random effect (messages)}} = \frac{8 * (-1.165^2 + .885^2 + .335^2)}{3 - 1} = \frac{8 * 2.165}{2} = 8.66$$

$$\text{Mean Square}_{\text{interaction effect (messages)}} = \frac{n_{jk} * \sum \left(\overline{X}_{jk} - \overline{X}_{j.} - \overline{X}_{.k} + \overline{\overline{X}}\right)^2}{(j - 1) * (k - 1)},$$

where

n_{jk} is the number of events in each cell,

j is the number of levels for the fixed effect,

k is the number of levels for the random effect,

$\overline{X}_{jk}$ is the mean of each individual cell,

$\overline{X}_{j.}$ is the mean of the corresponding level of the fixed effect,

$\overline{X}_{.k}$ is the mean of the corresponding level of the random effect, and

$\overline{X}$ is the grand mean.

In this case, the data entry yields

$$\text{Mean Square}_{\text{interaction effect (messages)}} = \frac{4 * [(26.67 - 27 - 29 + 30.165)^2 + \ldots (33 - 33.33 - 30.5 + 30.165)^2]}{(2 - 1) * (3 - 1)}$$

$$= \frac{4 * 2.33}{2} = \frac{9.32}{2} = 4.66$$

$$\text{Mean Square}_{\text{within groups}} = \frac{\sum s_{jk}^2}{j * k},$$

(Continued)

Table 9.3 (Continued)

where

s_{jk}^2 is variance within each cell,

j is the number of levels for the fixed effect, and

k is the number of levels for the random effect.

In this case, the data are

$$\text{Mean Square}_{\text{within groups}} = \frac{36.67 + 36.67 + 51.33 + 52.67 + 61.33 + 72}{2 * 3} = \frac{310.67}{6} = 51.78.$$

The ANOVA table for this effect is

Source	SS	d.f.	MS	F
Ambiguity (fixed)	240.41	1	240.41	51.59
Messages (random)	17.32	2	8.66	1.86
Interaction	9.32	2	4.66	.09
Within groups	9.32	18	51.78	

To compute the F ratios for both the fixed and random effects, the mean squares are divided by the interaction mean square. Therefore, the degrees of freedom to identify critical F values are for the fixed and random effects in the numerator and the interaction term for the denominator. Thus, the degrees of freedom for ambiguity are 1 in the numerator and 2 in the denominator. With alpha risk of .05, the critical F ratio is 18.5.

For the random effect, degrees of freedom are 2 for the numerator and 2 for the denominator. The critical F ratio is 19 with alpha risk at .05.

For the interaction term, the within-groups mean square is used in the denominator to compute the F ratio. Thus, the degrees of freedom are 2 and 18. This critical F ratio is 3.55.

In addition to the assumption of parametric statistics generally (interval or ratio level measurement of the dependent variable, normal distribution, randomization, and homogeneity of variance), the mixed effects ANOVA also assumes the following:

- Random effects, error effects, and interaction effects are normally distributed.
- Compound symmetry is made. This assumption holds that the covariance matrices for the levels of the "between factor" are homogeneous. Though a test for this assumption is available (Box, 1950), trusting routine testing for this assumption is not widely recommended (Kirk, 1982, p. 503). In addition, though violating this assumption slightly increases true Type I error, the effects tend to be small (Collier, Baker, Mandeville, & Hayes, 1967).

Using SPSS for Mixed-Effects ANOVA

In an example of a mixed model, Table 9.3 shows a study involving a researcher who examined whether use of deliberately ambiguous language in two sample speeches presented to initially hostile audience members would produce more positive attitudes than would the use of clear statements. The three messages would be random factors, and the strategic message ambiguity would be the fixed factor. To complete such analysis in SPSS, a researcher would select *General Linear Model* from the *Analyze* menu followed by *Univariate*. In the dialog box that appears, the researcher would transfer the appropriate dependent, independent, and random factors. The researcher clicks on the *Model...* button to specify the "Full Factorial" option (if it has not already been identified). Then the researcher clicks on the *Continue* button.

The results appear in the output window. As can be seen by the results below, the test of homogeneous variances was not statistically significant. Thus, the assumption of homogeneous variances was considered tenable.

Descriptive Statistics

Dependent Variable: ATTITUDE

AMBITG	MSSTOPIC	Mean	Std. Deviation	N
unambig	1	26.00	6.06	4
	2	27.00	6.06	4
	3	28.00	7.16	4
	Total	27.00	5.89	12
ambig	1	32.00	7.26	4
	2	35.00	7.83	4
	3	33.00	8.49	4
	Total	33.33	7.24	12
Total	1	29.00	6.97	8
	2	31.00	7.76	8
	3	30.50	7.75	8
	Total	30.17	7.22	24

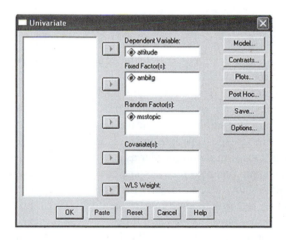

In the *Univariate* dialog box, the researcher clicks on the *Options...* button. The researcher highlights all the effects and transfers them to the "Display Means for:" field. To complete the report, the "Descriptive statistics" and "Homogeneity tests" boxes should be checked. The researcher then clicks on the *Continue* and *OK* buttons.

Levene's Test of Equality of Error Variance's

Dependent Variable: ATTITUDE

F	df1	df2	Sig.
.103	5	18	.990

Tests the null hypothesis that the error variance of the dependent variable is equal across groups.

a. Design: Intercept+AMBITG+MSSTOPIC+AMBITG *MSSTOPIC

The ANOVA table revealed a statistically significant main effect from the deliberate ambiguity fixed effect. The previously presented means showed that the unambiguous messages produced less favorable attitudes toward the topic than the deliberately ambiguous messages. As the researcher hoped, the random effect "msstopic" was not statistically significant, indicating that the effects were related to the message strategy across the selection of message examples.

Tests of Between-Subjects Effects

Dependent Variable: ATTITUDE

Source		Type III Sum of Squares	df	Mean Square	F	Sig.
Intercept	Hypothesis	21840.667	1	21840.667	2520.077	.000
	Error	17.333	2	8.667[a]		
AMBITG	Hypothesis	240.667	1	240.667	51.571	.019
	Error	9.333	2	4.667[b]		
MSSTOPIC	Hypothesis	17.333	2	8.667	1.857	.350
	Error	9.333	2	4.667[b]		
AMBITG * MSSTOPIC	Hypothesis	9.333	2	4.667	.090	.914
	Error	932.000	18	51.778[c]		

a. MS(MSSTOPIC)

b. MS(AMBITG * MSSTOPIC)

c. MS(Error)

The Repeated Measures Design

An interesting application of the mixed model design is called the **repeated measure ANOVA**, in which each experimental unit (person or item) is assigned to all treatments of at least one fixed factor. Then, several different observations are made of them. For instance, researchers could take communication apprehension measures from students in a public speaking class several times during the semester. Then, the repeated measures could be referenced. Similarly, researchers could expose people to three or more message treatments (with and without evidence, for instance) in random order as part of a counterbalanced design. The order in which the same people received the message could be tracked as a repeated measure. If there were any significant fatigue effects, they might be studied directly. In short, communication scholars may use this method in very creative ways.

For conceptual purposes, it makes sense to imagine a simple case. If people were surveyed at different times, shifts in their measured scores could be explained over time. Statistically significant differences could be tracked as repeated measures. The repeated measure is, in fact, treated as a fixed effect. The participants themselves would be used as a random effect because they would be selections of people from the larger population. If the fixed effect were diagrammed in a column and the random effect (the different participants) assigned to individual rows, there would be only one participant in each of the cells. It would not really be possible to determine a within-groups variance. Thus, just as with a mixed-effect design, the researcher could enlist the interaction term to substitute for the within-groups variance. Special Discussion 9.2 shows an example of this repeated measure design.

Special Discussion 9.2

Counterbalanced Designs

There are many times that participants in a study must be exposed to a series of treatments. They may be presented with three or more messages with different persuasive appeals or language treatments. These exposures could stimulate change in subjects even though the fixed effects may not be responsible. There are several ways that it may occur:

- Subjects may become "testwise" by the end of the study rather than remaining relatively "naive" as they were at the beginning.
- Subjects may grow fatigued over time.
- Cumulative exposure to content may make a subject increasingly sensitive to message elements by the end of the study.

There are several ways to deal the problem, such as lengthening the time between exposures to treatments or reducing the numbers of treatments subjects receive. Another option involves counterbalancing, which presents "conditions (treatments) in all possible orders to avoid order effects" (Vogt, 2005, p. 67). In short, the researcher randomly assigns subjects to receive the treatments in random order. A variation of this form is called the Latin square design, which is "a method of allocating subjects, in a within-subjects experiment, to treatment group orders. So called because the treatments are symbolized by Latin (not Greek) letters" (Vogt, 2005, p. 169). For the Latin square, the number of rows and columns must be equal (a square). For instance, researchers might counterbalance four treatments (A, B, C, and D) in the following fashion.

	Order of Presentation			
Person 1	A	B	C	D
Person 2	B	C	D	A
Person 3	C	D	A	B
Person 4	D	A	B	C

This method ensures that the order effects are "balanced" so that order biases do not affect reactions to one treatment any more than any other. The influence of order does not disappear, but it is mixed (confounded) with measures of error variance.

Alternatively, the data may be analyzed (and usually will be) by use of a mixed-effects model ANOVA. This analysis of data can grow increasingly complex as the researcher interprets the meaning of the independent variable as a within-groups variable and may include the counterbalancing sequence as an added between-subjects factor. Thus, in a mixed-effects design, the number of effects to examine may increase.

The repeated measures ANOVA embodies several assumptions. In addition to interval or ratio level measurement of the dependent variable, normal distribution, randomization, and homogeneity of variances, two other assumptions are featured prominently. The first of these is the independence of observations. There is no way to test the matter. Instead, the researcher must use a sound experimental design with a different person for each "row" in the random effect.

A second assumption is sphericity. The notion is related to the requirement of compound symmetry in mixed-effect designs. One scholar explains:

> For many years it was thought that stronger condition, called uniformity (compound symmetry), was necessary. The uniformity condition required that the population variances for all treatments be equal and also that all population covariances are equal. However, Huynh and Feldt (1970) and Rouanet and Lepine (1970) showed that sphericity is an exact condition for the F test to be valid. Sphericity requires that the variances of the difference for *all* pairs of repeated measures be equal. (J. P. Stevens, 2002, p. 500)

Of course, if a matrix has compound symmetry, it will meet the sphericity assumption by definition.

Sphericity is the assumption "of independent observations with a constant variance" (Upton & Cook, 2002, p. 344). For instance, if a researcher took listening ability measures of interpersonal communication students for three consecutive weeks, there would be a difference between Week 1 and Week 2 and between Week 2 and Week 3. In essence, two new variables would be created for analysis. If these new variables were uncorrelated with each other, sums of squares would equal zero. The matrix of such data would be called **orthonormal**. When a matrix of the new variables and the covariance of the original variables are compared, then (using the language of matrix operations) "the sphericity assumption says that the covariance matrix for the new (transformed) variables is a diagonal matrix with equal variance in the diagonal. . . . Saying that the off diagonal elements are 0 means that the covariance for all transformed variables are 0, which implies that the correlations are 0" (J. P. Stevens, 2002, p. 501). If this assumed sphericity is not present, then the F test statistic tends to be inflated. In other words, researchers will mistakenly reject null hypotheses more often than their announced alpha risks.

To test for sphericity, Mauchly's test usually is involved. This test is given by

$$W = \det(\mathbf{S}) \left(\frac{k+1}{\mathrm{tr}(\mathbf{S})} \right)^{k+1},$$

where

S is a $k \times k$ sample covariance matrix,

det(S) is the determinant of the $k \times k$ covariance matrix, and

tr(S) is the trace of the $k \times k$ covariance matrix.

Because this formula is mildly complicated, no computation example will be shown here. Instead, this test will be revisited in the section on using SPSS to help analyze data. After the W is computed, the "chi-square" (χ^2) distribution may be used to assess whether the data show a statistically significant difference from sphericity. If the observed chi-square value is greater than the required critical value at the specific alpha risk set by the researcher, the null hypothesis of sphericity is rejected.

This measure reports if there is a correlation between pairs of repeated measures. If the observed statistic for Mauchly's test is statistically significant and the underlying distributions are normal, then the assumption of sphericity is rejected and an adjustment will be necessary. It may be useful to switch to the multivariate form of repeated measures ANOVA in which sphericity is not assumed. It should be mentioned that although Mauchly's test is a popular tool, it has been criticized for its inaccuracy when multivariate normality cannot be assured (Keselman, Rogan, Mendoza, & Breen, 1980; Rogan, Keselman, & Mendoza, 1979). Thus, prudent researchers need to be careful about mechanical use of this test. It makes sense to check the underlying normality of the distributions of data (and the transformed variables tracking the differences between each pair of repeated measures) before relying on the Mauchly test.

If sphericity is not an assumption the researcher is prepared to make, a novice researcher probably should suspend analyses until help is found to determine what elements are troubling the data set. For an experienced researcher, it may make sense to use a statistical adjustment. A value known as epsilon (ε) is identified (Greenhouse & Geisser, 1959)[7] under these circumstances. Epsilon may range from 0 to 1. If sphericity is perfectly met, $\varepsilon = 1.0$. If sphericity is not met, then epsilon will be lower than 1.0 (the worst case would be a number equal to $\frac{1}{k-1}$, where k is the number of treatment conditions or repeated measures). To adjust the analysis of variance, the Greenhouse-Geisser estimator multiplies the numerator and denominator degrees of freedom by ε. Though this approach tends to keep true Type I error close to the announced alpha risk (Collier et al., 1967; Stoloff, 1967), when the value of ε is greater than .7, an alternative called the Huynh-Feldt estimator is recommended (Huynh, 1978; Huynh & Feldt, 1976).[8] Otherwise, the Greenhouse-Geisser approach will tend to

---

[7] $\hat{\varepsilon}$ is computed as

$$\hat{\varepsilon} = \frac{k^2 (\bar{s}_{ii} - \bar{s})^2}{(k-1)\left(\sum\sum s_{ijs}^2 - 2k\sum_i \bar{s}_i^2 + k^2\bar{s}^2\right)},$$

where

  $\bar{s}$ is the mean of all the entries in the covariance matrix $\mathbf{S}$,

  $\bar{s}_{ii}$ is the mean of entries on the main diagonal of $\mathbf{S}$,

  $\bar{s}_i$ is the mean of all entries in row i of $\mathbf{S}$, and

  $\bar{s}_{ij}$ is the ijth entry of $\mathbf{S}$.

[8] When the value of ε is greater than .7, Huynh and Feldt (1976) recommend that the computation of epsilon be adjusted as follows:

$$\bar{\varepsilon} = \frac{n(i-1)\hat{\varepsilon} - 2}{(i-1)[(n-1) - i - 1)\hat{\varepsilon}]}.$$

produce unacceptably conservative tests of statistical significance. For this reason, the method sometimes is known as the "Greenhouse-Geisser conservative F test" or sometimes just "the conservative F test." Unfortunately, using the Huynh-Feldt estimate of epsilon often may overestimate ε and, hence, will tend to increase the chances of committing Type I error. Hence, if sphericity is a problem, researchers are advised to look at *both* the Greenhouse-Geisser and the Huynh-Feldt formulations and to assume that the true F ratio lies somewhere between the two values. Kirk (1982, p. 261) recommends a three-step approach:

1. Check to see if the F statistic would be significant if sphericity were assumed (if not, stop the analysis, because there is little reason to believe that a statistically significant difference is present).

2. Use the Greenhouse-Geisser conservative F test (if the test is significant, claim a difference and stop).

3. Use the Huynh-Feldt method to see if the observed test statistic exceeds the critical value (if so, a difference is claimed as statistically significant).

Table 9.4 shows an example of such an analysis.

Table 9.4   Repeated Measures Example

A researcher was interested in learning if students changed their attitudes toward a topic that simply was mentioned but not explained in another speech. The attitudes about the "Simpson Environmental Protection Act" were taken for six people at 2, 4, and 6 weeks following their hearing a speech that mentioned the nonexistent act.

Subject	Time 1	Time 2	Time 3	Mean
1	4	5	8	5.67
2	1	2	5	2.67
3	2	3	5	3.33
4	5	4	8	5.67
5	1	3	6	3.33
6	5	7	10	7.33
Mean	3	4	7	Grand mean = 4.67

Computation:

$$\text{MS}_{\text{Time(a.k.a. within subjects)}}(\text{columns}) = n * s^2_{\bar{X}_k} = 6 * 4.33 = 26,$$

where n is the number of events measured at each time

$$\text{MS}_{\text{(Subjects)}}(\text{rows}) = k * s^2_{\bar{X}_{j.}} = 3 * 3.33 = 10,$$

where k is the number of repeated measures (times each event is measured)

$$\text{Interaction SS}: \sum \left(\bar{X}_{jk} - \bar{X}_{j.} - \bar{X}_{.k} + \bar{\bar{X}} \right)^2$$
$$= [(4 - 5.67 - 3 + 4.67)^2 + \dots (10 - 7.33 - 7 + 4.67)^2] = 4$$

Degrees of freedom for the time (a.k.a. within subjects) (columns) effect are the number of levels minus one.

Degrees of freedom for the subject (rows) effect are the number of levels minus one.

Degrees of freedom for the interaction effect are degrees of freedom for each of the main effects in the interaction multiplied by each other.

Because there is only one event in each "cell," within-groups variation is impossible to compute, but as with other mixed-effects designs, researchers may use the interaction mean square to get the job done. The following ANOVA table shows the results of the repeated measures analysis. As can be seen, the results show that the within-subjects "column" produced a statistically significant effect. Thus, the treatments evinced different effects on the dependent variable. Of course, because the subjects were different, it is not surprising that they showed some differences from each other as well, even though it is a matter of secondary interest here.

Source	Sums of Squares	d.f.	Mean Square	F
Columns (time)	52	2	26	65
Rows (subjects)	50	5	10	25
Interaction error	4	10	0.4	

These results show a repeated measures analysis assuming sphericity and with no adjustments made. Given the complexity involved in completing Mauchly's W by hand, the application of this test to these data is covered in this chapter's section on using SPSS. For these data, the sphericity assumption was tenable and the Mauchly's test was not statistically significant.

Using SPSS for Repeated Measures ANOVA

In the repeated measures design, the repeated measure sequence on which participants differ from one occasion to another is called the "within-subject factor." To run a repeated measures ANOVA, the researcher selects *General Linear Model* from the *Analyze* menu. Then, the researcher selects *Repeated Measures....* In the *Repeated Measures Define Factor(s)* dialog box, the researcher assigns a name to the "Within-Subject Factor" on which the repeated measures were taken. As a default, the name "factor1" is used as a starting point. The researcher specifies the "Number of Levels," or times that the repeated measure was taken. The researcher clicks on the *Add* to include this repeated measure variable in analyses.

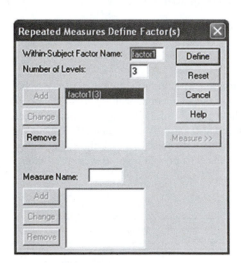

Then, the researcher clicks on the *Define* button to list the variables that have been used to identify each of the measurement occasions. For instance, in this case, the researcher measured the dependent variable three times for each person. The first time the variable was identified as "time1," the second time was called "time2," and the third time was "time3." In the *Repeated Measures* dialog box on the top of the right column, the researcher highlights the three variable "times" and then transfers them to the field marked "Within-Subject Variables (factor1):". Because the term "Subject" is simply a variable identifying the code number for the participants, it is not treated as another fixed variable.

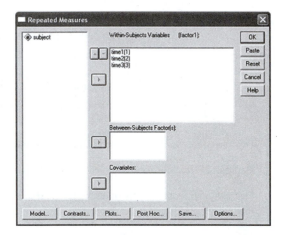

Clicking the *Options...* button offers analysis tools of interest. The mean effects to be reported are highlighted and transferred to the field "Display Means for:", and the box to display descriptive statistics is checked.

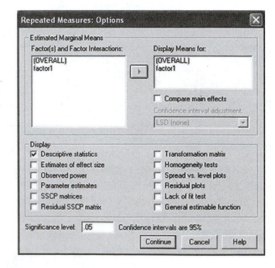

After clicking the *Continue* button, the researcher clicks the *Contrasts* button. In the dialog box, "factor1" may be selected for a contrast. Because there are three levels, a linear and a quadratic effect could be examined. Afterward, the researcher would click *Continue* and then *OK*.

The first set of results shows the means, standard deviations, and sample size for each dependent variable scored at each time.

Descriptive Statistics

	Mean	Std. Deviation	N
TIME1	3.00	1.90	6
TIME2	4.00	1.79	6
TIME3	7.00	2.00	6

This output also includes the results of multivariate tests of significance. In this case, all tests have the same *F* ratios. As will be seen below, these *F* ratios are identical to the *F* ratio found for the test of the linear effect of the within-subjects effect. The multivariate option is used when there are additional main effects to test and/or when the assumption of sphericity is not tenable.

Multivariate Tests[b]

Effect		Value	F	Hypothesis df	Error df	Sig.
FACTOR1	Pillai's Trace	.981	102.000[a]	2.000	4.000	.000
	Wilks' Lambda	.019	102.000[a]	2.000	4.000	.000
	Hotelling's Trace	51.000	102.000[a]	2.000	4.000	.000
	Roy's Largest Root	51.000	102.000[a]	2.000	4.000	.000

a. Exact statistic
b. Design: Intercept
Within Subjects Design: FACTOR1

As can be seen here, the Mauchly's *W* was not statistically significant. Thus, the sphericity assumption was tenable, and the univariate repeated measures approach could be retained.

Mauchly's Test of Sphericity[b]

Measure: MEASURE_1

| | | | | | Epsilon[a] | | |
Within Subjects Effect	Mauchly's W	Approx. Chi-Square	df	Sig.	Greenhouse-Geisser	Huynh-Feldt	Lower-bound
FACTOR1	.667	1.622	2	.444	.750	1.000	.500

Tests the null hypothesis that the error covariance matrix of the orthonormalized transformed dependent variables is proportional to an identity matrix.

a. May be used to adjust the degrees of freedom for the averaged tests of significance. Corrected tests are displayed in the Tests of Within-Subject Effect table.
b. Design: Intercept
Within Subjects Design: FACTOR1

The major test of the repeated measures ANOVA is reported on page 243. Because the sphericity assumption was reasonable, the standard ANOVA was employed and no adjusted tests were required. The "sphericity assumed" test showed a statistically significant *F* ratio. To identify the location of the differences, the researcher called for a trend analysis for the means, as reported on the "Tests of Within-Subject Contrasts" found on page 244.

Tests of Within-Subjects Effects

Measure: MEASURE_1

Source		Type III Sum of Squares	df	Mean Square	F	Sig.
FACTOR1	Sphericity Assumed	52.000	2	26.000	65.000	.000
	Greenhouse-Geisser	52.000	1.500	34.667	65.000	.000
	Huynh-Feldt	52.000	2.000	26.000	65.000	.000
	Lower-bound	52.000	1.000	52.000	65.000	.000
Error(FACTOR1)	Sphericity Assumed	4.000	10	.400		
	Greenhouse-Geisser	4.000	7.500	.533		
	Huynh-Feldt	4.000	10.000	.400		
	Lower-bound	4.000	5.000	.800		

Tests of Within-Subjects Contrasts

Measure: MEASURE_1

Source	FACTOR1	Type III Sum of Squares	df	Mean Square	F	Sig.
FACTOR1	Linear	48.000	1	48.000	120.000	.000
	Quadratic	4.000	1	4.000	10.000	.025
Error (FACTOR1)	Linear	2.000	5	.400		
	Quadratic	2.000	5	.400		

As shown here, a linear and a nonlinear (quadratic) effect were found. Thus, the presence of statistically significant effects when using higher-order polynomials would reveal that the best fit to the means is a curvilinear one. This effect is revealed by examining the means, which showed that the third condition was substantially above (higher than) the remaining means.

Using Excel for Repeated Measures ANOVA

To complete a repeated measures design, the researcher selects *Data Analysis* from the *Tools* menu and then chooses "Anova: Two-Factor Without Replication." After making this selection, the researcher clicks the *OK* button.

The data on the spreadsheet must be arranged in a particular way. The occasions for measuring the dependent variable are placed in columns, and the participants from whom repeated measures are taken are arranged as separate rows. The researcher selects the data by highlighting the cells in which the data are located.

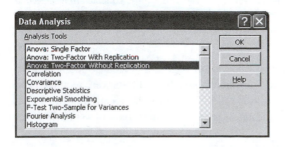

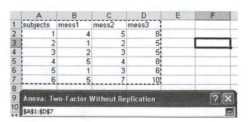

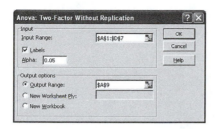

Following the selection, the researcher clicks 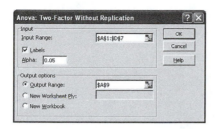 to return to the dialog box. In the dialog box, the researcher must specify a desired alpha risk for use in significance testing (.05 in this case). In addition, the researcher specifies a location for the output (starting at cell A9 in this case) and then clicks *OK*.

The output appears as shown below. The analysis assumes sphericity but does not test for it. In addition, the alternative significance testing tools are not included. Overall, however, the major results are that a statistically significant difference was found from the repeated measures. Because this matter is the chief independent variable, it is the critical element for the researcher's hypotheses.

Anova: Two-Factor Without Replication

SUMMARY	Count	Sum	Average	Variance
1	3	17	5.666667	4.33333
2	3	8	2.666667	4.33333
3	3	10	3.333333	2.33333
4	3	17	5.666667	4.33333
5	3	10	3.333333	6.33333
6	3	22	7.333333	6.33333
mess1	6	18	3	3.6
mess2	6	24	4	3.2
mess3	6	42	7	4

ANOVA

Source of Variation	SS	df	MS	F	P-value	F crit
Rows	50	5	10	25	2.37771E-05	3.325837
Columns	52	2	26	65	1.85934E-06	4.102816
Error	4	10	0.4			
Total	106	17				

Part IV

NONPARAMETRIC TESTS

Chapter 10

Nonparametric Tests for Categorical Variables

Most statistics identified in other chapters in this book are used with at least one continuous measure, for which characteristics of underlying populations may be assumed. There are, however, occasions when researchers do not have data measured on some continuum and for which they cannot assume major characteristics of underlying populations. This chapter deals with the family of nonparametric statistics that may be used to help make decisions with categorical data.

THE NOTION OF "DISTRIBUTION-FREE" STATISTICS

In contrast with parametric tests that make assumptions about characteristics of underlying populations, nonparametric statistics make few such assumptions. For instance, the assumption of a normal distribution of events in the population does not play a role in this branch of statistics. There is a different set of assumptions that need to be met when using nonparametric statistics.

Characteristics of Nonparametric and Parametric Statistics

One assumption is shared by parametric and nonparametric statistics. **Randomization** is the requirement that events are drawn from populations at random. In experimental designs, this requirement also means that the events are randomly assigned to conditions. After all, in any statistical significance testing, researchers compare what is expected to occur at random against what actually is observed. To play that game fairly, the researchers must have entered the population at random.[1]

Conditions That Invite the Use of Nonparametric Tools

Several circumstances invite the use of nonparametric tools. In fact, if a researcher faces at least one of the following conditions, nonparametric tools are strongly indicated (after Aczel, 1989, p. 738):

- The dependent variable consists of data that are simple frequency counts.
- The dependent variable consists of data that are rankings (material to be covered in Chapter 11).

---

[1]In most cases, practical randomization is not identical with mathematical randomization. Though ideal randomization is very difficult, and one might wonder how great an assumption it really is with nominal level data, it should be understood that randomization is an approximation, which is all that is usually required for the successful operation of the statistical tools described here. For generalization of study results to entire populations, of course, researchers must pay increased attention to evidence that the random sampling used was sufficient to represent the population.

- The hypotheses and methods do "*not deal with specific population parameters* such as μ or σ" (Aczel, 1989, p. 738).
- The researcher cannot make assumptions about population characteristics, especially such assumptions as those of normal distributions and equal variances.

Many researchers use these tools when evidence from samples suggests that assumptions of measurement and distributions have been violated.

It might be mentioned that nonparametric tests often seem so convenient that researchers sometimes reduce interval data to rank order or categorical data just so that they can use the nonparametric methods. For instance, to find out if people increase positive impressions of the sponsors of positive or negative political ads, the researcher probably could measure the amount of attitude change following participants' hearing the messages. Yet, some researchers might decide to categorize data into the number of people who change their minds toward the source in a positive direction and those who do not. Thoughtful researchers resist unnecessary reduction in the level of measurement of their variables. One major reason is that the reduction of levels of measurement results in significant loss of statistical power.

In addition to making fewer assumptions, because a nonparametric test often uses less information than may have been present in the original data, it sometimes is said to be "*an approximate solution to an exact problem*" (Aczel, 1989, p. 737). In contrast, if a parametric test meets all assumptions for appropriate use, it is said to be "*an exact solution to an approximate problem*" (Aczel, 1989, p. 737). Naturally, the nonparametric tests tend to be less powerful than their parametric alternatives, but with large samples, differences in power between parametric and nonparametric tests often become insubstantial.

CONDUCTING A STUDY THAT REQUIRES NONPARAMETRIC TESTS OF CATEGORICAL DATA

If a researcher finds that the data under examination are categorical data, nonparametric tests are indicated. The steps involved in conducting such a study are similar to those for any hypothesis testing.

Hypotheses Dealing With Frequencies and Proportions

The dependent variables in these comparisons are simple counts of events. Thus, a research hypothesis in this set of circumstances deals with frequencies or probabilities. As will all hypotheses, the research hypotheses state that variables are related in a certain fashion in the population. For instance, a researcher might hypothesize H_1: The frequencies with which men and women buy tickets to love story movies are not equal.

The hypothesis could be symbolized as asserting that the frequencies are not equal, such as H_1: $f_{men} \neq f_{women}$.[2] The symbol f represents the frequency. The null hypothesis would be

---

[2]There is another way of stating this hypothesis in terms of probabilities, which will be considered in the section on the one-sample chi-square test.

$H_0: f_{men} = f_{women}$, which asserts that the frequencies with which men and women buy tickets to love story movies are equal. An alternative is to compare proportions as the key concerns and to use the equivalent Greek letter π to indicate these proportions. In this case, the research hypothesis would be $H_1: \pi_{men} \neq \pi_{women}$. This hypothesis states that the proportion of men who buy tickets to love story movies is not equal to the proportion of women who buy tickets to love story movies. Naturally, the null hypothesis would be $H_0: \pi_{men} = \pi_{women}$.

The use of the test of independence involves the use of **contingency tables**, which are tables in which all the levels of one variable cross the levels of the other variable. To be **independent** means that the two variables involved in the classification are unrelated to each other.[3] The hypothesis for a test of independence states that the two variables in the contingency table are not independent of each other. Suppose a researcher is interested in testing whether students who took classes in public speaking or interpersonal communication would recommend that class to a fellow student. The research hypothesis would be

H_1: There is a relationship between taking a public speaking or interpersonal communication class and rates of recommending that class to a fellow student.

The null hypothesis would be

H_0: There is no relationship between taking a public speaking or interpersonal communication class and rates of recommending that class to a fellow student.

Conducting the Test

To complete testing, researchers need to do three things.

- First, the researcher needs to state the null hypothesis, which is the statistical hypothesis that actually is tested. If this null hypothesis can be shown to be highly improbable, the researchers may decide that an actual (nonrandom) relationship exists.
- Second, the researcher must select a decision rule or alpha risk to guide decisions. Typically in communication research (and most behavioral sciences), the default alpha risk is .05, which means that the researchers agree to reject the null hypothesis if results such as they observe could have been found at random (as a result of random sampling error) no more than 5 times out of 100. Sometimes researchers have reasons to set their alpha levels more conservatively than .05. For instance, if the result of a decision would

---

[3]This concept means a bit more than this important initial definition. First, "When two variables are statistically independent, their percentage distributions of the dependent variable within each category of the independent variables are identical" (Frankfort-Nachmias & Leon-Guerrero, 2002, p. 506). Second, "because statistical independence is a symmetrical property, the distribution of the independent variable within each category of the dependent variable will also be identical. That is, if gender and fear were statistically independent, we would also expect to see the distribution of *gender* identical in each category of the variable *fear*" (Frankfort-Nachmias & Leon-Guerrero, 2002, p. 506). Third, "Two events, A and B, are independent if the probability of their joint occurrence is equal to the product of their marginal (i.e., separate) probabilities" as indicated by the equation "A and B are independent if $P(A \cap B) = P(A)P(B)$" (Aczel, 1989, p. 797).

involve the commitment of a lot of time and money, an alpha risk of .01 might be set. If health and safety are involved, a .001 alpha risk might be chosen.[4]

- Third, the researcher must decide on a test statistic. In this chapter, the emphasis is on the analysis of categorical data.

  - Use the one-sample chi-square test if there is one categorical variable (regardless of the number of levels of the categorical variable) and if no categories have zero events. When there are more than two categories, this test should not be used if any category has "expected value" (a concept to be explained shortly) lower than one, or if more than one fifth of the categories have "expected values" lower than five (Cochran, 1954). When examining proportions from single samples, the binomial probability or binomial z may be used.
  - Use the chi-square test of independence when categorical data are arranged in contingency tables. As with the one-sample chi-square test, this tool should not be used if any expected frequencies are below one or if more than one fifth of the expected frequencies are below five.
  - Use Fisher's exact test if the data in any 2×2 contingency table cell is zero or if more than one fifth of the expected frequencies are below five.
  - Use the McNemar test if the data in a 2×2 contingency table include one categorical variable whose levels are not independent. For instance, if one variable is a "before" and "after" measure, each person in the study is measured twice. If samples are very small, the data may be collapsed and the binomial test should be used. If there are more than two related samples, the Cochran's Q test may be used. The binomial test is mentioned in the section "Using SPSS and Excel" later in this chapter.

After computing the appropriate test statistic, researchers find the critical value that must be exceeded to reject the null hypothesis. This value, adjusted for appropriate degrees of freedom, permits the researcher to identify how unlikely it is to find the observed data if the null hypothesis explanation for the observed data were true. When the null hypothesis is rejected as improbable, the alternative research hypothesis is found tenable.

Checking Assumptions

To examine the tenability of the assumptions underlying the tests, the researchers must make some checks. First, there must be some evidence that random selection, or at least random assignment, has been involved in the study. The details of this information typically are reported in a research article. Second, for the test of independence, the researchers must take care that the events are not "before" and "after" measures or otherwise related measures. Third, the researchers must look at test data to see if the assumptions of the use of the tool are satisfied. For the one-sample chi-square test, the chi-square test of independence, the researchers check that all "expected frequencies" are greater than one and that no more than 20% of the conditions have expected frequencies lower than five.

---

[4]Curiously, some researchers report the output of computer programs (which usually report exact probabilities) while failing to interpret the result as evidence sufficient to reject the null hypothesis. The application of the decision rule is important.

THE CHI-SQUARE TEST

There are several applications of the chi-square distribution for statistical significance testing. After describing some characteristics of the chi-square distribution, some popular chi-square test forms will be reviewed.

The Chi-Square Distribution

As the name suggests, the chi-square distribution is, in essence, a distribution of squared differences. In fact, with one degree of freedom, the chi-square distribution is equal to z^2. As a result, the distribution has a point where it touches a point of origin called a zero point. All chi-square values are positive values that begin with 0 and move on out to infinity. As the three diagrams below show, the chi-square distribution is a somewhat skewed distribution with skew becoming less and less pronounced as the number of degrees of freedom increases.[5] For instance, with 3 degrees of freedom, the chi-square distribution looks like distribution A. With 10 degrees of freedom, the distribution looks like distribution B. When degrees of freedom equal 50, the chi-square distribution resembles a normal distribution, as illustrated by distribution C.

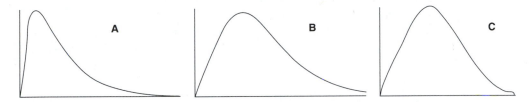

Forms of the Test

Though chi-square tests are used when the variables are nominal level measures, there are several different forms of chi-square tests. Two major methods will be described.

One-Sample Tests

Researchers often wish to interpret data in one sample. For instance, researchers might want to know whether men or women are more likely to be academic debaters, whether people have a preference among three leading news magazines, or whether professional public speakers rely on extemporaneous or memorized presentation techniques. To determine if there is a difference in proportions beyond what would be expected to occur by random sampling error, researchers may state the following research hypothesis: "The proportion of professional speakers who use the extemporaneous delivery method is not equal to the proportion of professional speakers who use the memorization delivery method." Expressed symbolically, the hypothesis is $H_1: \pi_{\text{extemporaneous delivery}} \neq \pi_{\text{memorization delivery}}$. The null hypothesis

---

[5]With one degree of freedom, chi-square is simple z^2. The chi-square distribution is defined as $f(x) = \{1/[2^{v/2} * \Gamma(v/2)]\} * [x^{(v/2)-1} * e^{-x/2}]$, where v represents the degrees of freedom, Γ(gamma) is the Gamma function, and e is the base of the natural log, also known as Euler's e (2.71828 . . .).

to be tested statistically states that "the proportion of professional speakers who use the extemporaneous delivery method is equal to the proportion of professional speakers who use the memorization delivery method," or H_0: $\pi_{\text{extemporaneous delivery}} = \pi_{\text{memorization delivery}}$.

The test statistic for this analysis is

$$\chi^2 = \sum_{i=1}^{k} \frac{(O_i - E_i)^2}{E_i},$$

where

O_i = observed number of cases categorized in the ith category and

E_i = expected number of cases in the ith category.

The sigma ($\sum$) sign's subscripts and superscripts mean that the researchers should add these differences across all categories. The "observed" numbers of cases are the actual events collected. The "expected" numbers of cases are what would be expected if a null hypothesis were true. In this case, if the null hypothesis were true, half the professional speakers should use each type of delivery method. It might be mentioned that what is expected should be informed by theory. If relative expected frequencies are calculated from sampling frequencies alone, the chi-square test could become largely meaningless in the presence of sampling error problems.

There are some requirements for use of this chi-square analysis. If no categories have zero events and if no more than one fifth of the cells have expected values below five, the chi-square method may be used. If these requirements are not satisfied, the chi-square test will not yield reliable results (Cochran, 1954). The approach of assuming that the proportions in each category are equal if the null hypothesis is true is called use of the **equal probability hypothesis**.

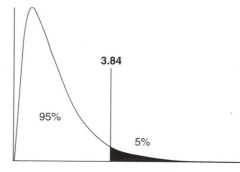

After a researcher has computed the test statistic, it is important to compare the test statistic with a critical value for chi-square. If the test statistic exceeds this critical value, the difference between the expected and observed frequencies is considered to be statistically significant.

Degrees of freedom for the one-sample chi-square test are the number of conditions minus 1. In this case, there were two categories, so the degrees of freedom are equal to $2 - 1$, which equals 1. As a portion of Appendix C.10 shows (below), with an alpha risk of .05, the critical chi-square value required to reject the null hypothesis is 3.84.

		Alpha Risk Identifying the Proportion of the Chi-Square Distribution to the Right of the Listed Critical Value							
Degrees of Freedom	.99	.95	.90	.10	.05	.025	.01	.005	.001
1	0.0002	0.0039	0.0158	2.71	3.84	5.02	6.63	7.88	10.88
2	0.0201	0.1026	0.2107	4.61	5.99	7.38	9.21	10.6	13.82

To illustrate the method involved in such an approach, an example using the "equal probability hypothesis" is found in Table 10.1.

Table 10.1   One-Sample Chi-Square Using the Equal Probability Null Hypothesis

A researcher was interested in finding out if voters reported relying most on newspapers, magazines, VHF and UHF television, cable television, or Internet news sources for information about the major political candidates. The researcher sampled 200 people at random, and the following data were found.

	Newspapers	Magazines	VHF and UHF Television	Cable Television	Internet News Sources
Observed frequency	20	25	65	55	35

The null hypothesis to be tested at alpha risk of .05 was that there would be no difference between the observed frequencies and what would be expected to occur by chance, or $H_0: f_1 = f_2 = f_3 = f_4 = f_5$.

Degrees of freedom for the chi-square test are the number of groups (columns) minus one. In this case, the degrees of freedom are $5 - 1 = 4$. With 4 degrees of freedom, the critical value of chi-square is 9.49. If the observed chi-square value is greater than 9.49, the null hypothesis will be rejected.

With only one sample, expected frequencies may be derived from an "equal probability hypothesis" in which each of the groups would be expected to be represented in equal proportions. If the sources were used equally, then $200 \div 5$ news sources would yield 40 people relying most on each news source. This notion is represented as follows:

	Newspapers	Magazines	VHF and UHF Television	Cable Television	Internet News Sources
Observed frequency	20	25	65	55	35
Expected frequency	40	40	40	40	40

To compute the one-sample chi-square test, the researchers would substitute the values into the formula

$$\chi^2 = \sum_{i=1}^{k} \frac{(O_i - E_i)^2}{E_i},$$

as in

$$\chi^2 = \left(\frac{(20-40)^2}{40} \right) + \left(\frac{(25-40)^2}{40} \right) + \left(\frac{(65-40)^2}{40} \right) + \left(\frac{(55-40)^2}{40} \right) + \left(\frac{(35-40)^2}{40} \right)$$

$$\chi^2 = \left(\frac{400}{40} \right) + \left(\frac{225}{40} \right) + \left(\frac{625}{40} \right) + \left(\frac{225}{40} \right) + \left(\frac{25}{40} \right)$$

$$\chi^2 = 10 + 5.625 + 15.625 + 5.625 + .625 = 37.5.$$

Because this chi-square value is greater than the critical value, a statistically significant difference may be claimed among the most frequently used news media sources.

Because this type of chi-square test compares observed with theoretically expected values, it sometimes is called a "goodness-of-fit" test. But this label has become widely applied to many chi-square tests that do not have these applications. Sometimes a theoretically unbiased null hypothesis must be substituted for the equal probability hypothesis. For instance, many researchers have been interested in whether one's location in a small group is associated with who talks the most. In one study (after Baxter, 1975), the researcher randomly assigned people to different conditions and watched who talked the most and who emerged as a dominant figure. One might think that if seating position made no difference, people in every position should talk to others an equal amount of the time. But as the figure below shows, the problem is somewhat complicated (after McCroskey, 1975).

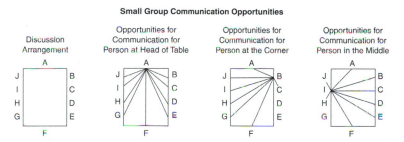

To communicate with others, it is vital to get eye contact to pick up invitations to contribute and to extend the discussion. People at the head or foot of the table can see the other nine people (100% of the others). But the people at the corners could communicate actively only with seven of the other people (78% of the others). Individuals in the middle can communicate actively only with eight of the other people (89% of the others). So, some adjustment had to be made in null hypothesis probabilities. The researcher wisely followed up analyses by using a different null hypothesis pattern. One could imagine another similar study of 100 group discussions, exploring which person spoke to others the most. Hypothetical observed frequencies are shown in Table 10.2.

Table 10.2

	Person Communicating the Most at Each Position									
	A	*B*	*C*	*D*	*E*	*F*	*G*	*H*	*I*	*J*
Observed frequency	17	6	6	13	7	15	6	12	13	5

- What do we use for expected frequencies? Ordinarily, the expected frequencies would be 10 each (100 events in the sample divided by 10 seating positions). Researchers could figure the total opportunities for communication and compute the proportion of contributions each person would make to the discussions if every seating position were equally represented. In any discussion, the positions allowed a total of communication with 78 other people who could be seen. Persons A and F could communicate with nine others each, which means that their expected share of opportunities to communicate with others was 11.54% ($9 \div 78 = .11538 \approx 11.54\%$). The number of opportunities for persons A and F to communicate with others would be 11.54 of 100 small group discussions. For persons B, E, G, and J, the number of opportunities to communicate with others would be

8.97 (7 ÷ 78 = .08974 ≈ 8.97%). For persons C, D, H, and I, the number of opportunities to communicate with others would be 10.26 (8 ÷ 78 = .10256 ≈ 10.26). Including these adjusted expected frequencies reveals the expected frequencies in Table 10.3.

Table 10.3

					Person Communicating the Most at Each Position					
	A	B	C	D	E	F	G	H	I	J
Observed frequency	17	6	6	13	7	15	6	12	13	5
Expected frequency	11.54	8.97	10.26	10.26	8.97	11.54	8.97	10.26	10.26	8.97

- The resulting chi-square value was 11.3. Because the critical value for chi-square with nine degrees for freedom is 16.92, the results do not suggest a difference with an alpha risk of .05. By the way, if the inappropriate "equal probability" hypothesis had been used, the coefficient would have been 17.8, which would have led the researcher to reject the null hypothesis erroneously.

Because this application can be used to compare observed categories with theoretically expected values, some researchers have found it useful to determine whether the underlying data resemble a normal distribution. For instance, if a teacher claimed to "grade on the curve," the relative proportions of A, B, C, D, and F grades might be compared to the expectations from a normal distribution. A significant difference would indicate that the grades are not distributed normally.

Tests of Independence

Researchers often have at least two variables that they wish to examine. The chi-square test that may be used in this circumstance is called a **test of independence** because it tests the null hypothesis that the two variables operate independently from each other. If this null hypothesis is shown to be an improbable explanation, the researcher concludes that the variables are dependent on each other.

Few assumptions underlie the chi-square test of independence, and some of them are satisfied by the nature of the research design and the measurement of the variables. The first assumption is randomization. The second assumption is that the data are from a **multinomial distribution**, in which more than one outcome is possible and for which the probabilities of the categories of the variables equal 1.[6] In essence, if two or more categories are to be used, they must cover all the probabilities of occurrence within the analyses to be completed. Usually this circumstance is a result of the categories to be used. In fact, in a contingency table, observed frequencies can be free to vary in only (rows − 1) ∗ (columns − 1) of the cells. "When these are filled the frequencies in the remaining cells are automatically determined. This distribution of

---

[6]This description is not a full definition. The multinomial distribution actually is an extension of the binomial distribution for more than two categories in which responses may be classified as dichotomies. The probabilities of the classes are given as follows, with X_j symbolizing the number "in a sample size n, that are in class j, for $j = 1, 2, \ldots, m$. The random variables $X_1, X_2, \ldots, X_m$ have a multivariate distribution given by

$$P(X_1 = N_1, X_2 = n_2, \ldots, X_m = n_m) = \frac{n!}{n_1! n_2! \ldots n_m!} p_1^{n_1} p_2^{n_2} \ldots p_m^{n_m}, \ldots, n_m \leq n, \text{ with}$$

$\sum_{j=1}^{m} n_j = n$" (Upton & Cook, 2002, p. 242).

the N observations among the cells is then multinomial . . . " (Keeping, 1995, p. 316). The third assumption is that "the observations constituting the sample are independent" (Keeping, 1995, p. 251). When a score on one variable is independent of another score, the measure is said to be unaffected by another's score. The assumption of independence means that the data should be separate pieces of information.[7] If one were to count the number of wins and losses of debate teams in academic debate tournaments, each event would be one debate.

The null hypothesis states that there is no difference between the observed frequencies and what would be expected to occur by chance. This matter could be symbolized as $H_0: \pi_1 = \pi_2 = \pi_3 = \ldots = \pi_{ij}$.[8] This statement asserts that the proportions are equal (what would be expected to occur by chance). If this test is rejected, the alternative hypothesis would be tenable. The researcher would conclude that the two variables are not independent and that there is a relationship between the variables.

The test statistic for the chi-square test of independence is

$$\chi^2 = \sum_{i=1}^{r} \sum_{j=1}^{k} \frac{(O_{ij} - E_{ij})^2}{E_{ij}},$$

where

O_{ij} is the observed frequency in the ith row and the jth column (in each cell taken one at a time);

E_{ij} is the expected frequency, assuming the null hypothesis, in the ith row and the jth column (in each cell taken one at a time); and

$\sum_{i=1}^{r} \sum_{i=1}^{k}$ means that the researcher starts with the first row and completes the computation for each of the columns (the cells) in that row, then the researcher turns to the next row and repeats the process until the rth row (the last row) of data has been examined.

To illustrate the use of this formula, an example is provided in Table 10.4 (see page 260).

When expected values in a 2×2 table are below five, a traditional recommendation has been to apply **Yates' correction for continuity**. This adjustment subtracts 0.5 from the absolute value (ignoring the minus signs of the differences) of each difference between the observed and expected values. The corrected coefficient is shown as

$$\chi^2 = \sum \sum \frac{(|O_{ij} - E_{ij}| - .5)^2}{E_{ij}}.$$

The requirement may seem to be a bit restrictive, but it makes sense to remember that the χ^2 distribution is based on the standard normal distribution, sometimes symbolized with z values. Furthermore, the use of the z test for differences between means is useful only with sample sizes of approximately 30 or more. Thus, it would not be surprising that chi-square probability values would be stable with expected sample sizes smaller than 30—and

(Text continues on page 262)

---

[7]"Because statistical independence is a symmetrical property, the distribution of the independent variable within each category of the dependent variable will also be identical" (Frankfort-Nachmias & Leon-Guerrero, 2002, p. 506).

[8]Another popular way of stating the null hypothesis with a contingency table is $H_0: \pi_{ij} = (\pi_i^r)(\pi_i^c)$, where (π_i^r) represents the probability for the row category and (π_i^c) is the probability for the column category. Thus, the alternative research hypothesis is $H_0: \pi_{ij} \neq (\pi_i^r)(\pi_i^c)$ for at least one pair (Pfaffenberger & Patterson, 1977, p. 459).

Table 10.4   The Two-Sample Test of Independence

Using an alpha risk of .05, a researcher was interested in testing the following hypothesis:

H_1: There is a relationship between taking a public speaking or interpersonal communication class and rates of recommending that class to a fellow student.

The null hypothesis would be

H_0: There is no relationship between taking a public speaking or interpersonal communication class and rates of recommending that class to a fellow student.

The researcher decided to collect a random sample of 90 students taking public speaking classes and 110 taking interpersonal communication classes. Reports of whether they would or would not recommend the class to a fellow student were gathered. The samples were independent and were organized into a 2×2 contingency table. The data were as follows.

	Students Taking Public Speaking Classes	Students Taking Interpersonal Communication Classes	
Students who would recommend the class to others	70	70	140
Students who would not recommend the class to others	20	40	60
	90 (45%)	110 (55%)	200

There are two ways to compute the expected frequencies for each cell of data.

- One may observe that 45% of the students took public speaking classes and 55% took interpersonal communication classes. Hence, of the 140 students who would recommend the class to others, 45% (or 63) should be from public speaking classes and 55% (77) should be from interpersonal communication classes. Similarly, of the 60 students who would not recommend the class to others, 45% (or 27) should be from public speaking classes and 55% (33) should be from interpersonal communication classes.
- For each cell, one may multiply the column total by the row total and divide by the total number of events in the design, or

$$\frac{\text{number in column} * \text{number in row}}{\text{total number in sample}}.$$

For instance, looking at students who took public speaking and would recommend the class the others, the total number of students who took public speaking classes in that column was 90, and the number who would recommend the class to others was 140. The total number of events in the study is 200. Thus, the formula for that expected frequency is

$$\frac{\text{number in column} * \text{number in row}}{\text{total number in sample}} = \frac{90 * 140}{200} = \frac{12,600}{200} = 63.$$

When the expected frequencies are inserted in the design (in parentheses), the following results

	Students Taking Public Speaking Classes	*Students Taking Interpersonal Communication Classes*	
Students who would recommend the class to others	70 (63)	70 (77)	140
Students who would not recommend the class to others	20 (27)	40 (33)	60
	90 (45%)	110 (55%)	200

Using the formula

$$\chi^2 = \sum_{i=1}^{r} \sum_{j=1}^{k} \frac{(O_{ij} - E_{ij})^2}{E_{ij}},$$

we have

$$\chi^2 = \frac{(70 - 63)^2}{63} + \frac{(70 - 77)^2}{77} + \frac{(20 - 27)^2}{27} + \frac{(40 - 33)^2}{33}$$

$$= .78 + .64 + 1.81 + 1.48 = 4.71.$$

To compare the test statistic with the minimum critical value required to reject the null hypothesis, one must identify the degrees of freedom used to enter the chi-square distribution. Degrees of freedom are equal to (rows − 1) * (columns − 1), which are (2 − 1) * (2 − 1) = 1. As can be seen below, the critical value with alpha risk of .05 is 3.84.

Because the test statistic is greater than 3.84, the researcher would reject the null hypothesis.

Alpha Risk Identifying the Proportion of the Chi-Square Distribution to the Right of the Listed Critical Value

Degrees of Freedom	.99	.95	.90	.10	.05	.025	.01	.005	.001
1	0.0002	0.0039	0.0158	2.71	3.84	5.02	6.63	7.88	10.88
2	0.0201	0.1026	0.2107	4.61	5.99	7.38	9.21	10.6	13.82

To examine the size of the effect, the researcher would apply a measure of effect size such as Cramér's *V*, which is computed by

$$V = \sqrt{\frac{\chi^2}{(N)Min(r - 1, c - 1)}} = \sqrt{\frac{4.71}{200 * 1}} = .15.$$

Special Discussion 10.1

Comparing Sample Variances With Historical Variances

Though most of the time, researchers are interested in comparing means, sometimes they want to know if a sample shows greater or less variance than previously has been the case in the population. For instance, one of the effects of training in communication may be to reduce uncontrolled variability in behavior, such as amounts of self-disclosure during initial interactions or the amount of communication apprehension in a class. If researchers know that the typical variance of self-disclosure amount in the population is 4.2 on a 7-point scale, they might look at a sample of 20 students whose variance is 2.5 following their taking a course in "Building Interpersonal Relationships Through Communication." Using an alpha risk of .05, the researcher would predict that one effect of the class may be to reduce the variance in the amounts of self-disclosure. Of course, researchers also would look at shifts in mean self-disclosure, but we are dealing only with variation here. The research hypothesis would be $H_1: \sigma_1^2 < \sigma_0^2$, which states that the variance observed in the sample group is lower than the population as a whole. This hypothesis is, of course, a directional hypothesis. Other hypotheses could be explored by researchers, including $H_1: \sigma_1^2 > \sigma_0^2$, or the nondirectional hypothesis $H_1: \sigma_1^2 \neq \sigma_0^2$. The null hypothesis of no difference would be $H_0: \sigma_1^2 = \sigma_0^2$.

Because this hypothesis is directional, only one side of the chi-square distribution is used. The hypothesis states that the new sample variance is *smaller* than the historical population standard. Furthermore, the arrow on the research hypothesis points to the left. Thus, the left side of the distribution is used to test the hypothesis. With degrees of freedom equal to $n - 1$ in the new sample (20 − 1 = 19 in this case), the chi-square value corresponding to the 5% of the chi-square distribution on the left has a corresponding value of 10.12. This value is found by looking at Appendix C.10 and noticing that with 19 degrees of freedom, 95% of the chi-square distribution lies to the right of the chi-square value of 10.12. If the test statistic is *smaller* than this value, the null hypothesis would be rejected and the researcher would claim that the new sample variance is smaller than the traditional population variance. In this case, the test statistic is

$$\chi^2 = \frac{(n-1)s^2}{\sigma^2} = \frac{(19)2.5}{4.2} = \frac{47.5}{4.2} = 11.31.$$

Because the test statistic is not smaller than 10.12, the researcher does not conclude that the new sample variance is smaller that the population variance.

certainly expected values of 5 are considerably low ones. Some researchers have found that the chi-square test with expected values as low as 2 seem robust (Camilli & Hopkins, 1978, 1979; Conover, 1974; Roscoe & Byars, 1971). Hence, if researchers faced with 2 × 2 tables are concerned about low sample sizes and low expected values, they probably are advised to use an alternative such as Fisher's exact test.

Studies of the effects of Yates' correction have not consistently supported its use (see Camilli & Hopkins, 1978). Simulation studies with different sorts of data have found that when sample sizes are small, Yates' correction makes chi-square "so conservative as to be almost useless" (Grizzle, 1967, p. 28). When the marginal values are not fixed, the correction factor decreases "the accuracy of probability statements" (Camilli & Hopkins, 1978, p. 163). In this book, Yates' correction is not used.

Using SPSS and Excel

Both SPSS and Excel have ways to analyze categorical and proportional data. This discussion will show how to complete chi-square using each set of tools.

SPSS

SPSS provides a chi-square test from both the *Nonparametric Tests* and *Crosstabs* subroutines. For this presentation, the second of these procedures is used, though both approaches lead to the same analyses. As an example, we will use the case of a researcher exploring the relationship between the sex of a person and his or her probability of renting action-oriented videos and DVDs. From the *Analyze* menu, the researcher selects *Descriptive Statistics* followed by *Crosstabs.* . . . In the *Crosstabs* dialog box below, the researcher may click and move the "sex" variable to the "Row(s)" box and move "choosvid" to the "Column(s)" box.

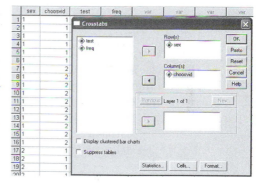

The researcher might then click on the *Statistics* . . . button and click to select the chi-square statistic and various effect size statistics to be covered in another section of this chapter. The researchers should click the *Continue* button, followed by clicking on the *Cells.* . . button. In the *Cross-tabs: Cell Display* dialog box on the left, the researcher should click on the boxes to select expected and observed counts, as well as row and column percentages.

Then the researcher would click on the *Continue* and *OK* buttons. The resulting output includes the following descriptive information.

SEX CHOOSVID Crosstabulation

			CHOOSVID		
			1	2	Total
SEX	1	Count	12	20	32
		Expected Count	16.4	15.6	32.0
		% within SEX	37.5%	62.5%	100.0%
		% within CHOOSVID	31.6%	55.6%	43.2%
	2	Count	26	16	42
		Expected Count	21.6	20.4	42.0
		% within SEX	61.9%	38.1%	100.0%
		% within CHOOSVID	68.4%	44.4%	58.8%
Total		Count	38	36	74
		Expected Count	38.0	36.0	74.0
		% within SEX	51.4%	48.6%	100.0%
		% within CHOOSVID	100.0%	100.0%	100.0%

Chi-Square Tests

	Value	df	Asymp. Sig. (2-sided)	Exact Sig. (2-sided)	Exact Sig. (1-sided)
Pearson Chi-Square	4.330[b]	1	.037		
Continuity Correction[a]	3.408	1	.085		
Likelihood Ratio	4.371	1	0.37		
Fisher's Exact Text				.060	.032
Linear-by-Linear Association	4.272	1	.039		
N of Valid Cases	74				

a. Computed only for a 2 × 2 table

b. 0 cells (0%) have expected count less than 5. The minimum expected count is 15.57.

The chi-square analysis also is reported. In this analysis, the Pearson chi-square is statistically significant. In fact, the chi-square tests are significant except for the estimate corrected for continuity. The likelihood ratio (sometimes called G^2) approximates "chi-squared distributions when the model under test is a correct description of the data" (Upton & Cook, 2002, p. 201).

The linear-by-linear association coefficient (also called the Mantel-Haenszel chi-square test) measures association between the row and column variables. For true nominal level variables, interpreting this statistic is inappropriate. Both assessments of probabilities of proportions and chi-square analyses may be completed with Excel.

Excel

Producing Tests of Proportions. One-sample tests sometimes are completed by researchers using the binomial test. For instance, if researchers know that the probability of finding a boy who stutters is .05 (5%), they might wonder what the odds would be of finding 1 person who stutters out of a sample of 10. The binomial probability can be computed by inserting a function.[9] After selecting a cell to place the results, researchers select *Function. . .* from the *Insert* menu. Then, from the *Insert Function* dialog box, the researchers select "BINOMDIST" and click the *OK* button.

In the *Functional Arguments* dialog box, researchers place the number of events

hypothesized in the "Number_s" field (1 stutterer in this case). In the "Trials" field, the researchers identify the sample size in question (10 in this case). In the "Probability_s" field, the researchers indicate the probability of finding one person in the group in question (in this case, about 5% of boys suffer from stuttering). The last line ("Cumulative") asks if researchers are interested in finding the probability that the number specified in the hypothesis actually is found (that the hypothesis is "TRUE") or that the hypothesis does not apply to the sample (that the hypothesis is "FALSE"—for example, speculating how likely it is that 1 person in a sample of 10 will not be a stutterer).

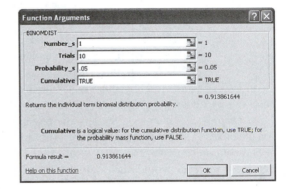

After *OK* is clicked, the answer appears in the specified field on the spreadsheet. In this case, the answer is $p = 0.913861644$, which means that the chances of finding exactly 1 person who stutters out of the sample of 10 is .91. Though statisticians do not prefer to speak of probabilities as percentages, this finding is equivalent to the everyday notion that there is a

---

[9]The formula for binomial z is

$$\frac{n!}{x!(n-x)!} * (p^x * q^{n-x}),$$

where

n is the number in the sample,

x is the run or number of observed events in the category,

p is the probability of observing an event in the category of interest, and

q is $1 - p$.

91% chance that 1 person out of a sample of 10 will be a stutterer.

Using Excel for Chi-Square Tests of Independence. To complete the chi-square test of independence, the researcher highlights a cell on the spreadsheet where the output is to be located. Then, the researcher selects *Function. . .* from the *Insert* menu. From the list of statistical functions, the researcher highlights "CHITEST" and clicks the *OK* button to select it.

This statistical function compares a matrix of actual frequencies with another matrix of expected frequencies, which must be supplied by the researcher. In the example shown below, the data from Table 10.4 are used.

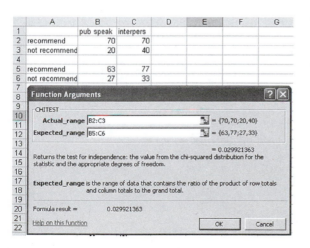

The researcher clicks on 🔲 in the "Actual_range" field and uses the cursor to highlight the spreadsheet cells in which the observed frequencies are found. After clicking 🔲, the range of cells appears. After moving to the field labeled "Expected_range," the researcher clicks on 🔲 and highlights the spreadsheet cells in which the expected frequencies are found. After clicking 🔲, the specific cells are identified in the "Expected_range" field. As can be seen, the "Formula result" displays a number, in this case .029921363. Clicking the *OK* button locates this number in the cell selected to receive the output. This number is not the chi-square value, but the probability of finding as such differences between observed and expected frequencies by random sampling error alone. A probability value below .05 (such as that found here) is normally taken as evidence that results in the researcher's rejecting the null hypothesis.

To find the actual chi-square value, the researcher selects *Function. . .* from the *Insert* menu. Then, from the list of statistical functions, the researcher highlights "CHIINV" and clicks the *OK* button to select it.

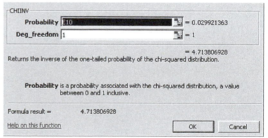

The spreadsheet cell in which the probability for the chi-square test is located (or the raw value itself) is placed in the field labeled "Probability." Degrees of freedom are identified as the number of rows minus one times the number of columns minus one. These degrees of freedom are entered into the "Deg freedom" field. The result of this process is a chi-square value of 4.71.

Producing the Chi-Square Statistic. Though, as you have seen, a chi-square test of independence using Excel can be completed in two steps, an alternative is available. The Web site for this book, in the link to Chapter 10, has a spreadsheet in the section "Excel Format for Chi-Square." You may substitute your data for a 2 × 2 table into this spreadsheet. As can be seen here, this format provides both the chi-square value and probabilities.

	A	B	C	D
1	Chi Square test of independence.			
2	Insert your own data into the 2 x 2 matrix.			
3				
4				
5		Category A	Category B	marginals
6	Group A	70	70	140
7	Group B	20	40	60
8	marginals	90	110	200
9				
10	Chi square value =	4.713804714		
11	Probability =	0.029921363		

Determining Effect Sizes

Though the chi-square test reveals that there are differences that are beyond what might be expected by chance alone, the test does not reveal the size of the differences. To supply this information, it is important to include a measure of effect size. It might be mentioned that although "effect" implies some causal relationship, in this context the label "effect size" is used to indicate relationship sizes, regardless of whether cause-and-effect claims are made. For categorical variables, there are several options.

The Phi (Φ) Coefficient

Phi is a measure of association that may be used for two nominal variables for which there are two levels each, as in Table 10.5. Inserting some data, one might have something like Table 10.6.

Table 10.5

		X_1	
		−	+
X_2	−	A	B
	+	C	D

Table 10.6

		X_1	
		−	+
X_2	−	20	40
	+	30	20

The formula for Φ is

$$\Phi = \frac{(AD - BC)}{\sqrt{(A+B)(C+D)(A+C)(B+D)}}.$$

When applied to the data above, the coefficient is –.2667. If a researcher is interested in knowing the percentage of variation in one variable that is explained from knowledge of the other, it is necessary to square the phi coefficient. The phi coefficient also may be computed from χ^2 as

$$\Phi = \sqrt{\frac{\chi^2}{N}}.$$

This second computation formula, of course, can only reveal positive values (.2667, in this case). In an effect size estimate incapable of taking negative values, an effect close to zero indicates the absence of a relationship and a coefficient close to 1.0 suggests a very strong association. The direction of the association, however, is not revealed by such coefficients.

The Contingency Coefficient

This effect size statistic may be used when there are more than two levels for each variable. The formula for C is

$$\sqrt{\frac{\chi^2}{\chi^2 + N}}.$$

Although chi-square values increase greatly as samples grow, this formula adjusts the chi-square for the sample size to avoid this inflation. The contingency coefficient is most suitable for the examination of tables that go beyond the 2×2 designs. In fact, C is affected greatly by the number of categories.

> Technically, associations range from 0 to 1.0 (positive values only), but C is restricted by the number of columns and rows, so that the upper end of the continuum has a lower ceiling than 1.0. For example for a 3×3 table, its upper limit is .82, not 1.0. Interpretation is often difficult. (Ahlgrim-Delzell, 2001, ¶ 5)

Because the formula is based on the chi-square test, its coefficients have positive values only. For the data listed above, the contingency coefficient is .2577.

Cramér's V

This measure of association adjusts for both sample size and the numbers of columns and rows. This fact makes it generally preferable to the contingency coefficient, particularly when the sizes of the tables are small. Regardless of the number of rows or columns, Cramér's V has values ranging between zero and 1, with zero indicating no association between the row and column variables and values close to 1 indicating a high degree of association between the variables. V is computed by

$$V = \sqrt{\frac{\chi^2}{(N)Min(r - 1, c - 1)}},$$

where $Min(r - 1, c - 1)$ is the smaller of the number of the rows minus one or the number of columns minus one. For the data listed above, the coefficient is .2667.

Lambda (λ), or Guttman's Coefficient of Predictability

Lambda may be used if researchers have categorical variables that are not restricted to two levels. Lambda is known as a **proportional reduction of error**, meaning that it reveals how much one "can reduce the error in the prediction of one variable by knowing the value of another variable" (Vogt, 2005, p. 250).

To understand the so-called symmetrical and nonsymmetrical forms, it is helpful to explore the logic behind the proportional reduction in error. One might imagine a study in which people with "high" and "not high" communication apprehension were compared with whether they were international students or national students. For instance, one might have the data shown in Table 10.7.

Table 10.7

| | Communication Apprehension | | |
	Not High	High	Total
National students	20	40	60
International students	30	20	50
Total	50	60	110

- If we pretended (for the moment) *not* to know if any particular student were an international student or not, we could make a best guess whether students did or did not have high communication apprehension. If we took the largest category (the mode), composed of 60 students without high communication apprehension, and just assumed that all the students were in that category, we would make 50 prediction errors (45.45% incorrect—hence, the probability of an incorrect classification would be $P_{(1)} = .4545$). That pattern is not very good.
- Perhaps we could "reduce" this "proportion of error" in classification by taking into account the students' national backgrounds. If we just classified everyone according to the largest "mode" national category, we could classify everyone as a national student. There would be 45.45% errors.
- If the two ideas were put together, the correct predictions would occur at the combination of national students who had "not high" communication apprehension and (by a process of elimination) international students with high communication apprehension. The remaining cells (circled in the figure below) are the smallest frequencies in each row and represent incorrect or "erroneous" predictions. In this case, the errors in prediction are $20 + 20 = 40$. This number represents 36.36% incorrect classifications, or $P_{(2)} = .3636$.

| | Communication Apprehension | | |
	Not High	High	Total
National students	⃝20	40	60
International students	30	⃝20	50
Total	50	60	110

Thus, the researcher could take these proportions of errors in predictions and compute lambda by subtracting the probability of the second source of prediction error from the first, as in the formula[10]

$$\lambda = \frac{P_{(1)} - P_{(2)}}{P_{(1)}} = \frac{.4545 - .3636}{.4545} = \frac{.0909}{.4545} = .20.$$

This lambda indicates that by knowing the background of the students, accuracy in predicting their levels of communication apprehension improved by 20%. Similarly, the proportional reduction in error of prediction is 20%.

Lambda asymmetric is used when one wishes to specify one variable as the independent variable and another as the dependent variable. For this work, using the column variable as the independent variable, the asymmetric lambda is

$$\lambda = \frac{\sum f_i - F_d}{n - F_d},$$

where

f_i is the largest frequency within each level of the independent variable,

F_d is the largest frequency found for the totals of the dependent variable levels, and

n is the number of events in the study.

For the data listed above, the lambda coefficient with the columns variable viewed as the independent variable is .20. When the variable in the rows variables is viewed as the independent variable, the formula remains the same as above, but the independent and dependent variables are switched. For the data listed above, the lambda coefficient with row variable

---

[10]Lambda also is computed as

$$\lambda = \frac{\sum f_r + \sum f_c - (F_r + F_c)}{2n - (F_r + F_c)},$$

where

f_r is the largest frequency in a row of data,

f_c is the largest frequency in a column of data,

F_r is the largest total in a row of data,

F_c is the largest total in a column of data, and

n is the number of events.

For the data listed above, this formula becomes

$$\lambda = \frac{\sum f_r + \sum f_c - (F_r + F_c)}{2n - (F_r + F_c)} = \frac{(40 + 30) + (30 + 40) + (60 + 60)}{(2 * 110) - (60 + 60)} = \frac{20}{220 - 120} = .2.$$

viewed as the independent variable is also .20. Sometimes the coefficients can differ greatly. For instance, in the matrix

10	20
40	30

the overall lambda (symmetric) is .125. Yet, lambda asymmetric for the variable in the columns serving as the independent variable is 0. Lambda asymmetric for the variable in the rows serving as the independent variable is .2.

Goodman and Kruskal's Tau[11]

This form is another measure of association that may be interpreted as a proportional reduction in error. Computationally, though lambda uses the mode to make predictions, tau uses marginal proportions to measure the reduction in the proportion of incorrect predictions that occur when one uses the row and column probabilities instead of the row marginal probabilities alone. With Y treated as the dependent variable, the formula for tau is

$$\hat{\tau}_{Y|X} = \frac{n \sum_{i=1}^{I} \sum_{j=1}^{J} \frac{n_{ij}^2}{n_i} - \sum_{J=1}^{J} n_{.j}^2}{n^2 - \sum_{j=1}^{J} n_{.j}^2},$$

where

n is the number of events in the study,

n_i is the number of events in the column,

n_j is the number of events in the row,

n_{ij} is the number of events in each cell,

I is the total number of columns, and

J is the total number of rows.

An example shows the operation of this tool. In this case, a researcher was interested in learning if there were a relationship between the sex of a person and his or her likelihood of renting action-oriented videos and DVDs. The data are shown in Table 10.8.

Table 10.8

Sex	Preferences for Choosing Videos and DVDs		Total
	1: Non-Action Movies	*2: Action Movies*	
1: Male	12	20	32
2: Female	26	16	42
Total	38	36	74

[11]Other measures also use *tau* as their symbols (e.g., Kendall's tau, tau-b, and tau-c). Thus, it is important not to confuse Goodman and Kruskal's tau with others that are not suited to analyze categorical data.

To complete computation of tau, the formula is entered with the numbers from the table:

$$\hat{\tau}_{X|Y} = \frac{n \sum\limits_{i=1}^{I} \sum\limits_{j=1}^{J} \frac{n_{ij}^2}{n_{i.}} - \sum\limits_{J=1}^{J} n_{.J}^2}{n^2 - \sum\limits_{j=1}^{J} n_{.j}^2}$$

$$= \frac{74 * \left(\frac{12^2}{38} + \frac{26^2}{38} + \frac{20^2}{36} + \frac{16^2}{36} \right) - (32^2 + 42^2)}{74^2 - (32^2 + 42^2)}$$

$$= \frac{74 * (39.8012) - (2,788)}{5,476 - (2,788)} = \frac{2,945.2888 - 2,788}{2,688} = \frac{157.2888}{2,688} = .059$$

As the next formula indicates, when the remaining variable is treated as the dependent variable, the formula stays largely the same, but the row and column indicators are reversed:

$$\hat{\tau}_{X|Y} = \frac{n \sum\limits_{i=1}^{I} \sum\limits_{j=1}^{J} \frac{n_{ij}^2}{n_{.j}} - \sum\limits_{i=1}^{I} n_{i.}^2}{n^2 - \sum\limits_{i=1}^{I} n_{i.}^2}$$

In this case, the result of the calculation ($\tau = .059$) remains the same for both versions of tau. Because τ relies on marginal frequencies, it tends to be more conservative than lambda.

The Uncertainty Coefficient

This measure of association uses the proportional reduction in error when values of one variable are used to predict values of the other variable. Unlike lambda, which emphasizes comparisons with the mode, and tau, which emphasizes marginal totals, the uncertainty coefficient uses the entire distribution of data to make comparisons.

$$\hat{U}_{Y|X} = \frac{\sum\limits_{i=1}^{I} \sum\limits_{j=1}^{J} n_{ij} \ln \left(\frac{n n_{ij}}{n_{i.} n_{.j}} \right)}{\sum\limits_{j=1}^{J} n_{.j} \ln \left(\frac{n_{.j}}{n} \right)}$$

where

  n is the number of events in the study,

  $n_{i.}$ is the number of events in the column,

  $n_{.j}$ is the number of events in the row,

  n_{ij} is the number of events in each cell,

I is the total number of columns, and

J is the total number of rows.

Using data from Table 10.8, this formula reveals

$$\hat{U}_{Y|X} = \frac{\displaystyle\sum_{i=1}^{I}\sum_{j=1}^{J} n_{ij}\ln\left(\frac{nn_{ij}}{n_{i.}n_{.j}}\right)}{\displaystyle\sum_{j=1}^{J} n_{.j}\,\ln\left(\frac{n_{.j}}{n}\right)}$$

$$= \frac{\left(12 * \ln\left[\dfrac{74*12}{38*32}\right]\right) + \left(26*\ln\left[\dfrac{74*16}{38*42}\right]\right)\left(20*\ln\left[\dfrac{74*20}{36*32}\right]\right)\left(16*\ln\left[\dfrac{74*16}{36*42}\right]\right)}{\left(32*\ln\left[\dfrac{32}{74}\right]\right) + \left(42*\ln\left[\dfrac{42}{74}\right]\right)}$$

$$= \frac{(12 * \ln[.7303]) + (26 * \ln[1.2055]) + (20 * \ln[1.2847]) + (16 * \ln[.7831])}{(32 * \ln[.4324]) + (42 * \ln[.5676])}$$

$$= \frac{(12 * -.3143) + (26 * -.1869) + (20 * -.2505) + (16 * -.2445)}{(32 * -.8384) + (42 * -.5663)}$$

$$= \frac{-3.7716 + 4.8594 + 5.01 + (-3.912)}{-26.8288 + (-23.7846)}$$

$$= \frac{2.1858}{-50.6134} = -.043.$$

Because the uncertainty coefficient is a proportional reduction in error measure, only the absolute value is interpreted. In this case, the error in predicting video choice error is reduced by 4.3% when sex of the person is known.

When the remaining variable is treated as the dependent variable, the formula stays largely the same, but the row and column indicators are reversed:

$$\hat{U}_{Y|X} = \frac{\displaystyle\sum_{i=1}^{I}\sum_{j=1}^{J} n_{ij}\ln\left(\frac{nn_{ij}}{n_{.j}n_{i.}}\right)}{\displaystyle\sum_{i=1}^{I} n_{i.}\,\ln\left(\frac{n_{i.}}{n}\right)}$$

In this case, the uncertainty coefficient does not change when the dependent variable is changed.

Obviously, this measure tends to be more conservative than lambda and even more conservative than tau. As a result, it is not as widely used as alternative tools.

So, when do we use the different methods? The "V is better than C, especially for small tables. Φ [phi] is only useful for 2×2 tables. Λ [lambda] is best except if the data . . . [are] badly skewed, then use V instead" (Ahlgrim-Delzell, 2001, ¶ 11). Tau is useful as a conservative estimate of proportional reduction in error. The uncertainty coefficient is most helpful when cautious researchers wish to use an especially conservative estimate.

Using SPSS to Assess Relationship Sizes

Though Excel does not include functions that automatically compute effect sizes, SPSS has a host of them. These tools are accessed from the chi-square subroutine. For the example involving men's and women's preferences for renting action movie videotapes and DVDs, the researcher first conducts a chi-square test of independence. Thus, as previously shown, the researcher selects *Descriptive Statistics* from the *Analyze* menu. Then, the *Crosstabs. . .* option is selected and the researcher moves the variables into appropriate locations (in this case, "sex" becomes the variable in the "Row(s)" and "choosvid" becomes the variable in the "Column(s)." To get effect size statistics, the researcher would click on the *Statistics. . .* button to open the *Statistics* dialog box. From the choices available, the researcher might select the contingency coefficient, phi and Cramér's *V*, lambda, and the uncertainty coefficient. Then, of course, the researcher would click on the *Continue* and *OK* buttons.

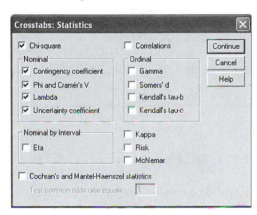

In the output that appears, the measures are divided into tables for directional and nondirectional measures. As can be seen in this example, the relationship sizes are small.

Directional Measures

			Value	Asymp. Std. Error[a]	Approx. T[b]	Approx. Sig.
Nominal by Nominal	Lambda	Symmetric	.176	.142	1.165	.244
		SEX Dependent	.125	.175	.669	.504
		CHOOSVID Dependent	.222	.139	1.434	.152
	Goodman and Kruskal tau	SEX Dependent	.059	.055		.039[c]
		CHOOSVID Dependent	.059	.055		.039[c]
	Uncertainty Coefficient	Symmetric	.043	.040	1.061	.037[d]
		SEX Dependent	.043	.041	1.061	.037[d]
		CHOOSVID Dependent	.043	.040	1.061	.037[d]

a. Not assuming the null hypothesis.
b. Using the asymptotic standard error assuming the null hypothesis.
c. Based on chi-square probability approximation.
d. Likelihood ratio chi-square probability.

None of the lambda coefficients was statistically significant, even though previous analyses revealed a significant chi-square for these data. Most important, using video selection as the dependent variable, $\lambda = .222$. The Goodman and Kruskal tau estimates and the uncertainty coefficient were substantially smaller. The uncertainty coefficient estimates the proportional reduction in error in predicting the dependent variables from a knowledge of the independent variable. Unlike some other formulae that place emphasis on the mode, this formula considers the entire distribution. In this case, the coefficient with video choice as the dependent variable is .043, which means that error in predicting viewer video preferences is reduced by 4.3% when the sex of the viewer is known.

Other symmetrical estimates are reported on another table of output. The size of these correlations (consistent with the lambda coefficients) suggests that they may be best understood as symmetrical, rather than asymmetrical, relationships.

Symmetric Measures

		Value	Approx. Sig.
Nominal by	Phi	−.242	.037
Nominal	Cramer's V	.242	.037
	Contingency Coefficient	.235	.037
N of Valid Cases		74	

ALTERNATIVES TO CHI-SQUARE FOR FREQUENCY DATA

There are times when researchers need alternatives to chi-square analyses.[12] This section considers two of them in some detail: Fisher's exact test and log-linear analysis.

Fisher's Exact Test

Fisher's exact test is used when sample sizes are so low that expected values are near zero. If any cell observed value *is* zero, this test must be used. This method is limited to 2×2 tables where the categories for each variable are dichotomies, such as male vs. female, win vs. loss, or experimental vs. control group. The assumption is that the data are independent random samples.

As an example, suppose a researcher attempts to learn if academic debate teams composed of members of the opposite sex have superior win-loss records in comparison to teams composed of members of the same sex. The null hypothesis would be

$$H_0: \pi_{\text{opposite-sex teams}} = \pi_{\text{same-sex teams}},$$

which states that the proportion of wins and losses for academic debate teams composed of members of the opposite sexes is equal to the proportion of wins and losses for academic debate teams composed of members of the same sex. The research hypothesis would be

$$H_1: \pi_{\text{opposite-sex teams}} > \pi_{\text{same-sex teams}},$$

Table 10.9

	Loss	*Win*
Same-sex debate teams	5	3
Opposite-sex debate teams	0	8

or that the proportion of wins and losses for academic debate teams composed of members of opposite sexes is greater than the proportion of wins and losses for academic debate teams composed of members of the same sex. Using an alpha risk of .05, the researcher might analyze data from 16 debates during preliminary rounds, as shown in Table 10.9.

---

[12]One test not covered here is Cochran and Mantel-Haenszel's statistic, which tests for independence of dichotomous variables when taking into account a set of "control variables" as covariates.

These cells may be identified by letters as in Table 10.10.

Table 10.10

	Loss	*Win*
Same-sex debate teams	A	B
Opposite-sex debate teams	C	D

The test statistic is

$$p = \frac{(A+B)!(C+D)!(A+C)!(B+D)!}{N!A!B!C!D!},$$

where N is the total number of events. You may recall that the exclamation point indicates a factorial; hence, $N!$ means that the researcher will multiply the number of debates by decrements of 1 until reaching 1. In other words, in this example of 16 debates, 16! is equal to $16 * 15 * 14 * 13 * 12 \ldots * 4 * 3 * 2 * 1$.

Inserting the data, the formula becomes

$$p = \frac{(5+3)!(0+8)!(5+0)!(3+8)!}{16!5!3!0!8!}$$

$$= \frac{40,320 * 40,320 * 120 * 39,916,800}{20,922,789,888,000 * 120 * 6 * 1 * 40,320}$$

$$= \frac{7,787,140,507,238,400,000}{607,396,959,564,595,000,000} = .01.$$

If any of the cells contains 0, this step ends computing Fisher's exact test. In this case, the probability of finding these results by chance is lower than the alpha risk of .05. Thus, the researcher would reject the null hypothesis.

If one of the cells does not contain a 0, the researcher must continue analyses. Aside from the observed cell values, there are even more extreme cell combinations that are consistent with the marginal totals that are present. Hence, the researcher must consider even more extreme arrangements for data that could produce the marginal totals. The reason is that the "statistical test of the null hypothesis asks: What is the probability under H_0 of such an occurrence *or of one even more extreme?*" (Siegel, 1956, p. 98). The probabilities for each of these "more extreme" arrangements must be computed and added to the total.

Consider these alternative data shown in Table 10.11. Using Fisher's exact test, the result for this analysis is $p = .03668$.

Table 10.11

	Loss	*Win*	*Total*
Same-sex debate teams	6	3	9
Opposite-sex debate teams	2	9	11
Total	8	12	20

To identify even "more extreme" examples that would add to the same totals, the researcher would add 1 to each of the two largest frequencies and subtract 1 from each of the lowest frequencies. The new matrix is shown in Table 10.12. The p value computed from these data is .00314.

Table 10.12

	Loss	Win	Total
Same-sex debate teams	7	2	9
Opposite-sex debate teams	1	10	11
Total	8	12	20

One last pass through the data completes the process. The researcher adds 1 to each of the two largest frequencies and subtracts 1 from each of the lowest frequencies—keeping the marginal totals the same. These revised data are found on the matrix in Table 10.13. The resulting probability observed from this arrangement is .00007. Because there now is a zero in one cell, the researcher has found the final extreme cell frequency combination that could be reflected in the marginal totals. Hence, the researcher may stop.

Table 10.13

	Loss	Win	Total
Same-sex debate teams	8	1	9
Opposite-sex debate teams	0	11	11
Total	8	12	20

When the probabilities are added (.03668 + .00314 + .00007), the final probability of finding such a relationship between sex composition of debate teams and win-loss records is .03989. Because this value has a lower probability than the alpha risk of .05, the researcher may reject the null hypothesis and decide that a relationship exists.

When tables go beyond 2 × 2 designs, the Freeman-Halton test (sometimes called the Fisher test 2) may be used to extend Fisher's exact test. It is based on computing the number of "re-randomizations" that will produce the row and column totals. Unfortunately, the test coefficients are not directly interpretable as the exact test. Thus, the test is not considered strictly equivalent to Fisher's exact test.

Using SPSS and Excel for Fisher's Exact Test

Though SPSS has built-in Fisher's *Exact test* functions, Excel does not. Yet, the author has prepared a spreadsheet format that will permit researchers to perform the *Exact test* for their data. Thus, both SPSS and Excel alternatives may be included here.

SPSS

To illustrate the *Exact test*, the same example will be used here that was used for illustrating SPSS for the chi-square test of independence. Only a subset of the original data will be used to illustrate this technique. To assess the matter, one selects *Descriptive Statistics* from the *Analyze* menu. Then, the researcher selects *Crosstabs*. . . . Using the same dialog boxes as used in the chi-square example above, the researcher moves "sex" and "choosvid" to fields that identify variables in rows and columns. After clicking on the *Statistics* button, the researcher selects chi-square and any nominal level effect size estimates desired. Then, the researcher clicks the *Continue* and *Cells* buttons. In the *Crosstabs: Cell Display* dialog box, the researcher chooses "observed" and "expected" counts and "row" and "column" percentages. Then, one may click on *Continue* and *OK*. The results begin with the descriptive statistics shown on page 277, top left column.

SEX * CHOOSVID Crosstabulation

			CHOOSVID		
			1	2	Total
SEX	1	Count	5	0	5
		Expected Count	2.5	2.5	5.0
	2	Count	3	8	11
		Expected Count	5.5	5.5	11.0
Total		Count	8	8	16
		Expected Count	8.0	8.0	16.0

The actual exact test is produced in the table of "Chi-Square Tests." In this case, the two-tailed probability is .026. The Fisher's *exact test* produces exact probabilities, not test statistics that must be referenced on a table of critical values.

Chi-Square Tests

	Value	df	Asymp. Sig. (2-sided)	Exact . Sig. (2-sided)	Exact Sig. (1-sided)
Pearson Chi-Square	7.273[b]	1	.007		
Continuity Correction[a]	4.655	1	.031		
Likelihood Ratio	9.290	1	.002		
Fisher's Exact Test				.026	.013
Linear-by-Linear Association	6.818	1	.008		
N of Valid Cases	16				

a. Computed only for a 2 × 2 table
b. 2 cells (50.0%) have expected count less than 5. The minimum expected count is 2.50

Thus, in this case, the researcher would conclude that there is an association between sex of the viewer and rates of selecting action videos. Because one of the cells has a zero, the other chi-square values should not be interpreted.

Excel

You can find a template for Fisher's *Exact test* by going to the Web site for this book, clicking on the link to Chapter 10, and selecting the "Excel Format for Fisher's Exact test" link. As can be seen below, the template provides places for you to enter your own data. The result of this work is a single test. Hence, if the data do not have a zero in any cell, the researchers must repeat the process for more extreme cell values, until an arrangement is found that includes a zero for one cell.

Tests of Related Samples

Sometimes researchers measure groups of people more than once. In such a way, each person serves as his or her own control. For categorical data, presuming that cell sample sizes are at least five, there are some tests that could be used, the most popular of which include McNemar's test for significance of changes and Cochran's Q test for related samples.

McNemar's Test for Significance of Changes

Often, the use of "before" and "after" designs requires such statistics. Suppose a researcher were interested in learning if students practiced responsive listening skills before and after taking a course in effective listening. Researchers start by arranging a 2 × 2 table such as Table 10.14.

Table 10.14

		X_1	
		−	+
X_2	−	A	B
	+	C	D

The A and D cells are supposed to include the conditions in which *change* is identified. So, in this case, it is possible that those who did not practice responsive listening skills would change to use those skills after the course. Unfortunately, some students might have practiced the skills before the course but stopped after taking the course. Thus, the data would be inserted into the design illustrated in Table 10.15.

Table 10.15

		Listening Skill After Taking a Course	
		Practicing Responsive Listening Skills	Not practicing Responsive Listening Skills
Listening skill before taking a course	Not practicing responsive listening skills	Cell A: 22	Cell B: 6
	Practicing responsive listening skills	Cell C: 10	Cell D: 5

The statement of the research hypothesis affects the test. In this case, the researcher might hypothesize:

H$_1$: For those participants who change their responsive listening behavior, more participants will change from not practicing responsive listening to practicing responsive listening than those who change from practicing responsive listening to not practicing responsive listening.

Clearly, this research hypothesis is a directional hypothesis that requires the use of one side of the probability distribution. The null hypothesis states:

H$_0$: For those participants who change their responsive listening behavior, the probability that participants will change from not practicing responsive listening to practicing responsive listening is equal to the probability that participants will change from practicing responsive listening to not practicing responsive listening.

The formula for this statistic is

$$\chi^2 = \frac{(|A - D| - 1)^2}{A + D},$$

which computes as

$$\frac{(|22 - 5| - 1)^2}{22 + 5} = \frac{(17 - 1)^2}{27} = \frac{256}{27} = 9.48.$$

At alpha risk of .05, the degrees of freedom are (rows − 1) * (columns − 1). In this case, the degrees of freedom are (2 − 1) * (2 − 1) = 1. The critical value is 3.84 for a nondirectional (two-tailed) test. Hence, a significant test of changes has been found. If researchers wished to use a one-tailed test, they would *halve* the probabilities, such that .10 on the chi-square table nondirectional (two-tailed) test would be used for a one-sided test at .05.

Cochran's Q Test for Related Samples

An extension of McNemar's test to deal with more than two samples for each event in the sample is Cochran's Q. Assuming a reasonable sample size with no cell frequencies lower than five, this statistic allows researchers to extend their analyses beyond two conditions. The formula for Q is

$$Q = \frac{(k-1)\left[k\sum_{j=1}^{k}G_j^2 - \left(\sum_{j=1}^{k}G_j\right)^2\right]}{k\sum_{i=1}^{N}L_i - \sum_{i=1}^{N}L_i^2}$$

where

G_j is the number of positive or "yes" responses for each of k samples, and

L_i is the number of favorable responses for each set of individuals.

For instance, a researcher might want to examine whether people would be willing to sign petitions calling for abolition of capital punishment after being exposed to a month-long persuasive campaign consisting of three messages using an inductive strategy. Willingness to sign a petition would be scored as "1" indicating a "yes" response. The research hypothesis would be

H$_1$: The probability of signing a petition against capital punishment will differ across the three occasions following exposures to messages in a persuasive campaign advocating the abolition of capital punishment.

The null hypothesis would be

H$_0$: The probability of signing a petition against capital punishment will not differ across the three occasions following exposures to messages in a persuasive campaign advocating the abolition of capital punishment.

Collecting data from the same 15 people following their viewing each of the three persuasive messages would be reflected in the data grid shown in Table 10.16.

Table 10.16

Set	Petition Signing Following Exposure to the First Message in the Campaign	Petition Signing Following Exposure to the Second Message in the Campaign	Petition Signing Following Exposure to the Third Message in the Campaign	L	L^2
1	0	1	1	2	4
2	1	1	1	3	9
3	0	0	1	1	1
4	0	1	1	2	4
5	1	1	1	3	9
6	1	1	1	3	9
7	0	0	0	0	0
8	0	0	0	0	0
9	0	1	1	2	4
10	0	0	1	1	1
11	1	0	1	2	4
12	0	1	1	2	4
13	1	1	0	2	4
14	0	0	0	0	0
15	1	1	1	3	9
	$G_1 = 6$	$G_2 = 9$	$G_3 = 11$	$\sum_{i=1}^{N} L_i = 26$	$\sum_{i=1}^{N} L_{i_i}^2 = 62$

Inserting the data, the formula becomes

$$= \frac{(3-1)\{[3(6^2 + 9^2 + 11^2)] - 26^2\}}{3(26) - 62} = \frac{2[(3 * 238) - 676]}{16} = \frac{38}{16} = 2.38.$$

	Alpha Risk Identifying the Proportion of the Chi-Square Distribution to the Right of the Listed Critical Value							
Degrees of Freedom	.99	.95	.90	.10	.05	.025	.01	.005	.001
1	0.0002	0.0039	0.0158	2.71	3.84	5.02	6.63	7.88	10.88
2	0.0201	0.1026	0.2107	4.61	5.99	7.38	9.21	10.6	13.82
3	0.1148	0.3519	0.5844	6.25	7.81	9.35	11.34	12.84	16.27

Degrees of freedom are $k - 1$, or the number of conditions minus one, or $3 - 1 = 2$. With a nondirectional test, the critical value is 5.99. As previously mentioned, if researchers wished to use one-tailed tests, they would *halve* the probabilities, such that .10 on the chi-square table nondirectional (two-tailed) test would be used for a one-sided test at .05.

Though Cochran's Q is a convenient test, it also tends to be so conservative that fairly large differences are required to detect statistical significance.

Chapter 11

NONPARAMETRIC TESTS FOR RANK ORDER DEPENDENT VARIABLES

The last chapter dealt with statistics that compare groups of nominal level data. This chapter covers similar tests focusing on dependent variables measured on the ordinal scale. Because we still are concerned with information that deals with nonparametric statistics, there are few assumptions for these tests, and since the assumptions were examined in Chapter 10, they need not occupy a great deal of attention here.

DOING A STUDY INVOLVING ORDINAL DEPENDENT VARIABLES

Researchers often deal with dependent variables that rank things. Speakers may be ranked in competitive forensics competition, employees may be asked to rank the importance of different benefits they are offered, or communicators may rank others with whom they would most like to work. In many cases, researchers start with ratings for which they are not sure of interval qualities. Then, they reduce data to a level that consists of ranks. Yet, when data are clear rankings, these tools are most invited. There are four general elements in completing such a study.

1. *Hypotheses.* Research hypotheses for ordinal level dependent data may deal with mean or median ranks. In such a case, the null hypothesis takes the form H_0: the mean (μ) or median (Md) rank of one group is equal to that of the other(s). This hypothesis also could be cast in the form of H_0: $\mu_{\text{rank of Group 1}} = \mu_{\text{rank of Group 2}}$, or H_0: $Md_{\text{rank of Group 1}} = Md_{\text{rank of Group 2}}$. Researchers also could compare the distribution of one set of data with the distribution of another. Such inquiries examine hypotheses such as H_0: The two distributions do not differ. The research hypothesis suggests the alternative that the two distributions differ. As in all statistical significance testing, researchers examine whether the null hypothesis is so improbable that it should be rejected.

2. *Measurement of Dependent Variables.* Though the dependent variable data originally may have been interval or quasi-interval data, the actual form of the data analyzed involve some form of rank order data (ordinal level measurement).

3. *Conducting the Test.* As with most test statistics, researchers begin by stating the null and research hypotheses. Then, a decision rule for rejecting the null hypothesis is chosen. The most typical guideline suggests rejecting the null hypothesis if the probability of obtaining results such as those observed could have been found by random sampling error no more than 5 times out of 100 (setting alpha risk at $p \leq .05$).

   Selecting the appropriate test statistics is not always simple. Nonparametric tests often reveal information about more than one characteristic of interest to the researcher. For instance, the Mann-Whitney U test and the Kolmogorov-Smirnov two-sample test examine whether distributions differ, but they could differ by their means, by their shapes, or by their variances (D. R. Anderson, Sweeney, & Williams, 2003, p. 772; StatSoft, 2003b, ¶ 14). So, researchers sometimes are advised "to run different nonparametric tests; should discrepancies in the results occur contingent upon which test is used, one should try to understand why some tests give different results" (StatSoft, 2003b, ¶ 14).

4. *Checking Assumptions.* Though there are few assumptions underlying nonparametric tests (which makes them very convenient), occasionally some assumptions must be checked, such as the requirements for randomization and the requirement that samples are related to each other (as in the case of the Friedman two-way "analysis of variance." Similarly, the Kolmogorov-Smirnov one-sample test assumes that there is some sort of theoretically specified cumulative frequency distribution of ranks. Researchers are wise to investigate whether the limited assumptions are reasonable.

COMPARING RANKS OF ONE GROUP TO PRESUMED POPULATION CHARACTERISTICS: ANALOGOUS TESTS TO ONE-SAMPLE *t* TESTS

Researchers often wish to determine if their rank order data have characteristics that are consistent with expectations about other distributions. Though it is not accurate to say that these statistics make inferences about populations, these tools allow researchers to get evidence that bears upon whether sample data show signs of randomization and how they compare with theoretically expected distributions. Two tools in this category will be described.

The One-Sample Runs Test

The **one-sample runs test** examines the randomness of a set of observations. In fact, it also may be used to check on the randomness of responses received during sampling in studies using parametric statistical tests. This test assumes that researchers are able to track the order of occurrence of observations. Though this matter is included here in the analysis of rank order data, this statistic frequently is applied to nominal level data, such as the number of men and women who arrive in order at the beginning of a class.

The major question involves whether researchers have taken observations that show randomness. For instance, researchers may mail questionnaires to people of different voting precincts and wish to keep track of whether people responded in sequence or at random over a period of 30 days of data collection. The runs test permits researchers to keep track of whether nonrandom *runs* of responses from some precincts occurred, or whether responses showed random responses.

Though the test may apply to very small samples (fewer than 20 events in the whole study), most social science research includes sample sizes that are greater than 20. Thus, the example provided in Table 11.1—as do most examples in this chapter—deals with a sample size greater than 20 to illustrate how the test statistics typically are computed.

Table 11.1   Runs Test Example

A researcher studied assertiveness levels of 42 pairs of students participating in discussions after half of them were randomly assigned to receive special training in managing conflict communication. The students were drawn from the same small-group communication classes, and the researcher removed the students from the classes to participate in the study over a period of a month. The researcher was concerned that the students who already had participated in the study discussions might talk with other students and influence their assertiveness levels and affect the independence of observations. Fortunately, the researcher kept records of the order in which data were collected in the discussions. As is seen in the data shown in the table, the assertiveness scores for each pair above the median are identified with plus signs, and those below the median are identified with minus signs. The data are arranged in the specified sequence. In this case, data are listed in the order that pairs of students were removed from their classes to participate in the study.

Order of Participation	Scores for Assertiveness	Above (+) or Below (−) the Median	Order of Participation	Scores for Assertiveness	Above (+) or Below (−) the Median
1	50	+	22	30	−
2	60	+	23	28	−
3	20	−	24	70	+
4	30	−	25	31	−
5	28	−	26	25	−
6	70	+	27	40	−
7	31	−	28	35	−
8	25	−	29	55	+
9	40	−	30	56	+
10	35	−	31	52	+
11	55	+	32	20	−
12	56	+	33	38	−
13	52	+	34	50	+
14	20	−	35	36	−
15	38	−	36	33	−
16	50	+	37	70	+
17	36	−	38	65	+
18	33	−	39	66	+
19	70	+	40	68	+
20	65	+	41	80	+
21	66	+	42	70	+

Median = 45
Number of uninterrupted runs: 17

The researcher examined the tenability of the null hypothesis:

   H_0: The order of pluses and minuses is random.

Rejecting this null hypothesis would support the research hypothesis:

   H_1: The order of pluses and minuses is not random.

Supporting the research hypothesis would indicate that some events are dependent on others in the sequence. In short, it would reveal that the responses of some scores are influenced in nonrandom ways by others in the distribution of scores.

The test statistic uses the z distribution to determine how rarely such a pattern of runs would be found by chance alone. A run is an uninterrupted series of plus or minus signs in the sequence. In this case, there were 9 runs of plus signs and 8 runs of minus signs. If a researcher used an alpha risk of .05 (two-tailed), the following formula could be used:

$$\mu_r = \frac{2n_1 n_2}{n_1 + n_2} + 1,$$

where

μ_r is the mean of the runs,

n_1 is the number of scores above the median (the number of pluses), and

n_2 is the number of scores below the median (the number of minuses).

The standard deviation of the runs, σ_r, is computed as

$$\sigma_r = \sqrt{\frac{(2n_1 n_2) * (2n_1 n_2 - n_1 - n_2)}{(n_1 + n_2)^2 * (n_1 + n_2 - 1)}}.$$

To use the z distribution, the researchers may use the formula

$$z = \frac{r - \mu_r}{\sigma_r},$$

where r is the number of uninterrupted runs of events above or below the median. Substituting the terms, the computational formula becomes

$$z = \frac{r - \left(\dfrac{2n_1 n_2}{n_1 + n_2} + 1\right)}{\sqrt{\dfrac{(2n_1 n_2) * (2n_1 n_2 - n_1 - n_2)}{(n_1 + n_2)^2 * (n_1 + n_2 - 1)}}}$$

$$= \frac{17 - \left(\dfrac{2 * 21 * 21}{21 + 21} + 1\right)}{\sqrt{\dfrac{(2 * 21 * 21) * ([2 * 21 * 21] - 21 - 21)}{(21 + 21)^2 * ([21 + 21] - 1)}}}$$

$$= \frac{17 - \left(\dfrac{882}{42} + 1\right)}{\sqrt{\dfrac{882 * (882 - 21 - 21)}{1,764 * (42 - 1)}}} = \frac{17 - (21 + 1)}{\sqrt{\dfrac{740,880}{72,324}}} = \frac{-5}{\sqrt{10.2439}} = \frac{-5}{3.2006} = -1.5622.$$

As Appendix C.1 shows, for the observed value to be statistically significant, the value of z must be below -1.96 or above 1.96. Because, in this case, the test statistic was not in either of these critical regions, the researcher did not reject the null hypothesis and concluded that the order of pluses and minuses was random.

Using SPSS to Conduct the One-Sample Runs Test[1]

Though Excel has no built-in programs for most of the statistical tests covered in this chapter, SPSS supports most of them. For instance, to complete a runs test, the researcher chooses *Nonparametric Tests* from the *Analyze* menu. Then, *Runs. . .* is selected from the drop-down menu. In the dialog box that appears, the researcher places the test variable for analysis in the "Test Variable List:" box.

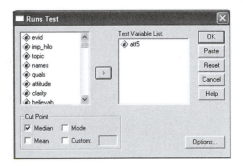

The researcher selects a division point from one of the *Cut Point* choices: the median (the standard option for the runs test), the mean, the mode, or some other "custom" dividing point. Clicking the *Options. . .* button permits researchers to request descriptive statistics, reports of quartiles, and decisions about missing data. Some of the essential output of the runs test includes the information below. The median is reported as the "test value," and the number of cases above and below the median is included.

Runs Test

	ATT5
Test Value[a]	20.00
Cases < Test Value	418
Cases >= Test Value	446
Total Cases	864
Number of Runs	342
Z	–6.171
Asymp. Sig. (2-tailed)	.000

a. Median

In this example, the fact that the numbers of events above and below the median are not equal tells the researcher that some events are located on the median. The division was made by comparing the number of events below the median to all others. The z value and probability are reported. The low probability ($p < .05$, reported as .000) means that the researcher would conclude that the data are not randomly ordered.

Kolmogorov-Smirnov One-Sample Test

The **Kolmogorov-Smirnov one-sample test** is designed to examine whether sample values agree with a theoretical distribution. The "theoretic distribution" is identified by the researcher and may represent either a historical pattern (such as the proportions of stutterers among a population of boys) or an "equal probability" null hypothesis. In either set of circumstances, the theoretic distribution represents the null hypothesis expectation. This test is distinctive for its use of a cumulative frequency distribution. A **cumulative frequency**

---

[1]Excel does not include data analysis routines for the rank order nonparametric tests, but this fact does not mean that researchers are completely left to their own devices. First, the Web site for this chapter includes Excel worksheets for the use of the Mann-Whitney U test, the Wilcoxon Matched Pairs Signed Ranks Test, and the Kruskal-Wallis H test. Researchers may substitute their own data and use these worksheets to complete their own analyses. Second, there are comprehensive add-on programs that include such tests. For instance, *StatistiXL* includes the Wald-Wolfowitz Runs Test, the Mann-Whitney U test, the Wilcoxon Matched Pairs Signed Ranks test, the Kruskal-Wallis H test, the sign test, and the extension of the median test for more than two samples. None of the single-sample measures is included.

distribution is a running total of all the events through each interval or class. Technically, a cumulative frequency distribution is not a standard normal curve, but sometimes the standard normal curve is used to define a cumulative distribution observed in data. Hence, this test is often used to check on the normal distribution of responses.

This test assumes randomization and a theoretically based cumulative frequency distributions of ranks. This latter assumption means that there must be an underlying continuum for the data under examination. Without making such assumptions, comparisons with actual ranks cannot be completed. Sometimes the test is used for variables that are simple dichotomies. When dichotomies are involved, the Kolmogorov-Smirnov one-sample test is especially conservative (L. A. Goodman, 1954).

This test is generally considered more powerful than the one-sample chi-square test, especially when samples are small. This test is said to have high power efficiency. **Power efficiency** refers to the power a test has relative to the sample sizes used (Plonsky, 1997, ¶ 2). Because the Kolmogorov-Smirnov one-sample test uses detailed information about the distribution of ranked responses, it does not have the disadvantage of losing information about available data.

Table 11.2   Kolmogorov-Smirnov One-Sample Test Example

A researcher wanted to know if rankings of students' communication competence scores reflected an equal distribution across five categories. Ten students were scored on a standard measure, and they were found to have the rankings shown below.

	Communicator Competence Rankings				
	1 (low)	*2 (moderately low)*	*3 (neither high nor low)*	*4 (moderately high)*	*5 (high)*
Rankings of 10 students	0	1	3	4	2

The null hypothesis was

H_0: There is an equal distribution of students across communicator competence rankings.

Rejecting this null hypothesis would indicate the tenability of the research hypothesis:

H_1: There is not an equal distribution of students across communicator competence rankings.

To test the statistical hypothesis, the cumulative frequency of actual data is compared with a theoretically expected distribution. If past research or an underlying distribution is known, such distributions may be used to identify the expected values. In this case, the researcher may presume a random use of the categories. Thus, each category should have $\frac{N}{k}$ students, which is $\frac{10}{5} = 2$. The test statistic identifies the maximum absolute difference between the observed and expected cumulative frequency distribution values and divides by N.[†] The test statistic is identified as

$$D = \text{maximum} \left| \frac{F_o - S}{N} \right|,$$

[†]Another formula transforms data into proportions before beginning computations (see Siegel, 1956, pp. 47–50).

(Continued)

Table 11.2 (Continued)

where

F_o is the cumulative observed frequency value for each ranking level,

S is the cumulative expected frequency value for each ranking level, and

N is the number of events in the study.

The notation | | refers to the absolute value of the term contained within the vertical lines. Absolute values ignore whether the values are positive or negative.

	Communicator Competence Rankings				
	1 (low)	2 (moderately low)	3 (neither high nor low)	4 (moderately high)	5 (high)
Frequency of students providing each ranking	0	1	3	4	2
Expected frequency of students	2	2	2	2	2
Cumulative observed frequencies (F_o)	0	1	4	8	10
Cumulative expected frequencies (S)	2	4	6	8	10
Absolute difference between cumulative observed and cumulative expected frequencies/ N|$(F_0 - S)/N$|	.2	(.3)	.2	0	0

In this case, the maximum value is .3. To interpret the D value, researchers reference Appendix C.11, a portion of which appears below. If the test statistic D is greater than the critical value in the table, the null hypothesis is rejected at the chosen alpha risk.

Table of Critical Values of the Kolmogorov-Smirnov One-Sample Test

	Minimum D Values Associated With Alpha Risk		
N	**.10**	**.05**	**.01**
2	.776	.842	.929
3	.642	.708	.829
4	.564	.624	.734
5	.510	.563	.669
6	.470	.519	.617
7	.438	.483	.576
8	.411	.454	.542
9	.388	.430	.513
10	.368	(.409)	.489

Because the observed D value is only .3, the null hypothesis is not rejected. The researcher concludes that the scores are normally distributed.

Using SPSS to Conduct the Kolmogorov-Smirnov One-Sample Test

To illustrate the use of the one-sample Kolmogorov-Smirnov test using SPSS, we will consider the case of a researcher examining a distribution of grade point averages (GPAs) from 864 alumni of a college's communication program. The grade point averages seem to include large numbers of grades in the high range. The researcher wants to know if the distribution happens to differ from an underlying uniform distribution.

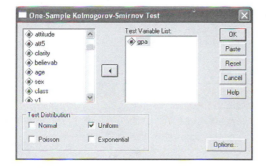

From the *Analyze* menu, the researcher selects *Nonparametric Tests*, followed by choosing *1-Sample K-S* from the *Nonparametric Tests* drop-down menu. Then, the researcher highlights the test variable for analysis and uses the arrow button to move it to the "Test Variable

List:" box. The cumulative frequency distribution is compared with another distribution.

The uniform distribution generally is selected because it reflects the null hypothesis of equal distribution of responses. The **uniform distribution** is defined by the observed minimum and maximum values that define the range. The output reveals the maximum and minimum values of the observed as well as the absolute difference between the cumulative frequency distribution of the observed data and the theoretic distribution. A small probability (usually $p \leq .05$) means that the observed distribution is not consistent with the theoretical distribution. In this case, the significance test probability is so small that the null hypothesis is rejected.

One-Sample Kolmogorov-Smirnov Test

		gpa
N		864
Uniform Parameters[a,b]	Minimum	1.8
	Maximum	4.0
Most Extreme Differences	Absolute	.156
	Positive	.156
	Negative	−.147
Kolmogorov-Smirnov Z		4.590
Asymp. Sig. (2-tailed)		.000

a. Test distribution is Uniform.
b. Calculated from data.

COMPARING RANKS FROM TWO SAMPLE GROUPS

Researchers often compare two sample groups, such as experimental and control groups. On other occasions, researchers wish to examine scores from the same people at different times. Comparisons of rank order data for different groups or pairs are considered next.

Independent Groups: Analogous Tests to Two-Sample *t* Tests

Independent groups are separate categories of events or data. Nonparametric tests that deal with such conditions include the median test, the Wald-Wolfowitz runs test, the Mann-Whitney *U* test, and the Kolmogorov-Smirnov two-sample test.

Table 11.3   Median Test Example

A researcher wished to examine if subjects from individualistic cultures are more willing to initiate conversations with strangers than are subjects from collectivist cultures. Samples were obtained from international students from collectivist and individualistic cultures. Their scores on the willingness to initiate conversations scale also were obtained. The comparison was made using the median and setting a decision rule to reject the null hypothesis at alpha risk of .05. The null hypothesis was that there is no difference between median willingness to initiate communication scores of subjects from individualistic and collectivist cultures. Put another way, the null hypothesis was

$$H_0: Md_{\text{individualistic cultures}} = Md_{\text{collectivist cultures}}.$$

The research hypothesis was that subjects from individualistic cultures have higher median willingness to initiate conversations scores than subjects from collectivist cultures:

$$H_1: Md_{\text{individualistic cultures}} > Md_{\text{collectivist cultures}}.$$

The median test is based on use of a 2 × 2 table comparing the number of scores above and below the median for each group.

	Group I	*Group II*
Number of events above the median	A	B
Number of events below the median	C	D

The researcher inserts the number of events into each cell:

	Individualistic	*Collectivist*
Number of events above the median	18	4
Number of events below the median	9	13

(Continued)

Median Test

The **median test** examines whether two different sample groups have been drawn from a population with the same median. Hence, this test explores differences in central tendency. The major assumption of this test is that the dependent variable is measured on an ordinal scale. Even so, the median typically is computed from data that actually are on the interval or ratio level. An example of the way that researchers may test statistical hypotheses with the median test is found in Table 11.3.

There are some limitations on the use of the median test. First, when samples are quite small, such as conditions where the total number of events is under 20, or when any expected frequency is under 5, researchers should use the Fisher's exact test rather than the median test. Second, if any data points fall exactly on the median, the researchers must make some

Table 11.3 (Continued)

The test statistic is

$$\chi^2 = \frac{N * \left(|AD - BC| - \dfrac{N}{2} \right)^2}{(A + B) * (C + D) * (A + C) * (B + D)}.$$

In this case, the computation is

$$\frac{44 * \left(|234 - 36| - \dfrac{44}{2} \right)^2}{22 * 22 * 27 * 17} = \frac{44 * (198 - 22)^2}{222,156} = \frac{44 * 30,976}{222,156} = 6.1351.$$

The critical value is identified by entering the chi-square value with

$$p = \frac{\alpha \text{ risk}}{2}$$

and one degree of freedom ([rows – 1] * [columns – 1]). As Appendix C.10 shows, the critical value for chi-square $\left(\dfrac{\text{alpha risk}}{2}; \dfrac{.05}{2} = .025 \right)$ is 5.02. Because the test statistic is greater than the critical value, the researcher rejected the null hypothesis and concluded that subjects from individualistic cultures are more willing to initiate conversations with strangers than are subjects from collectivist cultures.

adjustments. If researchers have large samples, they might delete the data points falling on the median. Alternatively, the researchers might change the research hypothesis to explore the number of events that are above the median (as normally is the case) in comparison with those that *do not fall above the median* (as opposed to exploring a comparison with those that are *below the median*). Though not actually a limitation of the method, it might be mentioned that computation of the median test is not supported by SPSS or Excel.[2] Hence, researchers must use their own spreadsheet computations to employ this tool.

Wald-Wolfowitz Runs Test

The **Wald-Wolfowitz runs test** attempts to determine if two samples come from the same population. Of course, many statistical significance tests could be described in the same way. The chief purpose of this test is to detect any difference between sample groups. These

---

[2]Yet, SPSS includes the median test for more than two samples. Because the extension of the median test is not as power efficient as the Kruskal-Wallis *H* test, this chapter has not covered it.

differences may involve central tendency, variances, skewness, or any other distribution pattern. Hence, the researchers ask if the two samples are so similar on some characteristics of distributions that they must be assumed to have come from the same population. The major assumptions of the test are randomness and that the dependent variable initially was a continuous measure. The basic approach of this test uses a pattern of runs to isolate differences in distributions. A run is an uninterrupted series of similar scores. The label stems from the fact that the researcher counts the number of times several scores from the same group "run together."

This test is an extension of the runs test to identify differences between groups. If data are not already expressed as ranks, they are ranked to identify the series of runs. Table 11.4 illustrates the use of the Wald-Wolfowitz runs test. Although there are tables that permit researchers to identify the statistical significance when there are small samples (no sample group above 20 events), this example illustrates the use of the underlying formula.

Table 11.4   Wald-Wolfowitz Runs Test Example

Assume a researcher was interested in comparing sets of scores from a group of Democratic and Republican voters. In particular, the researcher wanted to know if the two groups differed in their responses to negative campaign advertisements. Participants were shown examples of negative ads attacking the opposing party's candidate. Then they completed rating scales evaluating the fairness of the advertisements (the possible range of scales ratings was 12 to 60). The data are shown in the table here:

Group 1: Republicans	Group 2: Democrats
40	20
50	28
60	35
25	23
45	27
46	30
39	31
42	29
48	32
36	

The hypotheses were as follows:

H_0: There is no difference between the ratings of fairness of negative advertisements by Republicans and Democrats.

H_1: There is a difference between the ratings of fairness of negative advertisements by Republicans and Democrats.

The research hypothesis was a two-tailed test that the researcher wanted to test at alpha risk of .05.

To examine runs, the ratings were placed in rank order from the lowest to the highest. Then, the group from which each ranked score was taken was identified.

$$20, 23, 25, 27, 28, 29, 30, 31, 32, 35, 36, 39, 40, 42, 45, 46, 48, 50, 60$$

Group: 2 2 1 2 2 2 2 2 2 2 2 1 1 1 1 1 1 1 1

RUNS: 1   2   3   4

The number of uninterrupted runs of ranked scores from the same group was four. The test statistic uses the areas under the standard normal curve to make decisions. The test statistic formula is

$$z = \frac{\left| r - \left(\dfrac{2n_1 n_2}{n_1 + n_2} + 1 \right) \right| - .5}{\sqrt{\dfrac{(2n_1 n_2) * (2n_1 n_2 - n_1 - n_2)}{(n_1 + n_2)^2 * (n_1 + n_2 - 1)}}},$$

where

r is the number of runs,

n_1 is the number of events in the first group, and

n_2 is the number of events in the second group.

The computation for these data occurs as follows:

$$\frac{\left| 4 - \left(\dfrac{2*9*10}{9+10} + 1 \right) \right| - .5}{\sqrt{\dfrac{(2*9*10)*((2*9*10)-9-10)}{(9+10)^2 *(9+10-1)}}} = \frac{\left| 4 - \left(\dfrac{180}{19} + 1 \right) \right| - .5}{\sqrt{\dfrac{(180)*(180-9-10)}{19^2 * 18}}} = \frac{|4 - (10.4737)| - .5}{\sqrt{\dfrac{28,980}{6,498}}}$$

$$= \frac{5.9737}{2.1118} = 2.8287$$

For a two-tailed test, any value lower than –1.96 or greater than 1.96 would be statistically significant with alpha risk of .05. Looking up the test statistic in Appendix C.1 reveals .4977, which means only .0023 of the area under the standard normal curve lies above that point. Therefore, for a *two-tailed* test, the probability of finding such results by chance is .0046. Hence, the researcher rejected the null hypothesis and claimed support for the research hypothesis. In this example, the researcher noted that Republicans rated the fairness and accuracy of negative political advertisements higher than did Democrats.

Though the Wald-Wolfowitz runs test is versatile and permits comparisons of groups with different sample sizes, it has some limitations. First, the test merely identifies that there is a difference in the two compared samples. The statistical significant test does not reveal whether any effects are related to differences in means or difference in the dispersion of data. Researchers need to examine other clues to find the sources of differences. Second, unless all the tied ranks are from members of the same groups, the number of runs may not be correctly identified. There is no standard solution to this difficulty.

Using SPSS to Conduct the Wald-Wolfowitz Runs Test

To compute this test, the researcher selects *Two-Independent-Samples* from the *Nonparametric* drop-down menu. In the dialog box, the researcher highlights the dependent variable moves it to the "Test Variable List:" field.

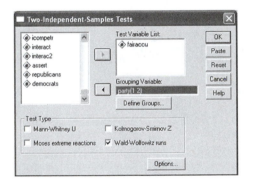

To define the groups, the researcher highlights a variable and moves it to the "Grouping Variable:" field. Clicking on the *Define Groups. . .* button moves the researcher to a dialog box that prompts the researcher to list the values that identify groups (1 and 2 in this case). After selecting

the "Wald-Wolfowitz runs" test, clicking the *OK* button executes the analysis.

Frequencies

	party	N
fairaccu	1.00	9
	2.00	10
	Total	19

Test Statistics[b,c]

		Number of Runs	Z	Exact Sig. (1-tailed)
fairaccu	Exact Number of Runs	4[a]	−2.829	.002

a. No inter-group ties encountered.
b. Wald-Wolfowitz Test
c. Grouping Variable: party

This example uses the same data as the example in Table 11.4 and includes output of both descriptive data and the Wald-Wolfowitz runs test. If the test of significance shows a small *p* value, as is the case here, the researcher concludes that there are differences between the two distributions.

Test for Large Samples: Mann-Whitney U Test

Also known as the "Wilcoxon rank sum test," this test is a popular alternative to the *t* test. When researchers find that data distributions do not permit making the assumptions underlying the *t* test, many researchers use the Mann-Whitney *U* test. This book previously discussed the controversy regarding whether such a need really exists based on sample data. When the original data are rank order scores, of course, the use of this method may be vital. This test is an extension of the runs test to identify differences between groups. The Mann-Whitney

U test assumes randomization and that the underlying data are from a continuous distribution, even though the test uses only the continuum of ranks.

The purpose of the Mann-Whitney *U* test is to test the equality of two distributions, though it is most often used by researchers who are interested in comparing differences between means of two groups. The method is a more powerful option than the Wald-Wolfowitz runs test and is not plagued by difficulties related to tied ranks. Furthermore, the Mann-Whitney *U* test is useful when the underlying population distributions are not normal. In fact, this test may be used even in the case of bimodal distributions. With small samples, tables exist to check on effects. In the example in Table 11.5, the standard use of the Mann-Whitney *U* test is illustrated for increasingly large samples. With large sample sizes, this test uses *z* scores that allow the researcher to use the logic of the standard normal curve to examine hypotheses.

Large numbers of tied ranks tend to make the Mann-Whitney *U* test very conservative. If a correction is made to account for the tied ranks, this bias may be eliminated. Instead, of the computational formula

$$z = \frac{U - \frac{n_1 n_2}{2}}{\sqrt{\frac{(n_1 n_2) * (n_1 + n_2 + 1)}{12}}},$$

the following formula is used:

$$z = \frac{U - \frac{n_1 n_2}{2}}{\sqrt{\left(\frac{(n_1 n_2)}{N(N-1)}\right)\left(\frac{N^2 - N}{12} - \sum T\right)}},$$

where

N is the number of events in both groups, and

$$T \text{ is } \frac{t^2 - t}{12},$$

when *t* is the number of scores that are tied at a given rank (see Siegel, 1956, pp. 124–126).

It should be mentioned that the Mann-Whitney *U* test examines distributions. These differences in independent samples could stem from differences in shape as well as from differences in locations. "Theoretically, in large samples the Mann-Whitney test can detect differences in spread even when the medians are very similar" (Hart, 2001, p. 391). Hence, when reporting results, researchers should report the features of the data (medians and shapes) as well as significance statistics. Simply assuming that this test identifies differences in central tendency can be misleading.

Table 11.5   Mann-Whitney U Test Example

A researcher was interested in comparing whether male and female students receive different rankings of public speaking competence ratings from students. The null hypothesis was

H_0: Males' and females' distributions of public speaking competence ratings do not differ.

The alternative research hypothesis was

H_1: Males' and females' distributions of public speaking competence ratings differ.

The researcher wished to test this hypothesis at an alpha risk of .05. As part of a round of speeches, students completed ratings of all the other student speakers. Using a rating scale with a possible range of 10 to 100, data were collected. The mean ratings for each student are shown below.

Group 1: Men	Rankings	Group 2: Women	Rankings
80	13	77	16
78	15	96	1
75	18	82	12
73	20	87	8
90	5	71	21
88	7	83	11
93	2	74	19
91	4	79	14
85	10	92	3
89	6	86	9
		76	17
$N_1 = 10$	$R_1 = 100$	$N_2 = 11$	$R_2 = 131$

H_1: The two distributions differ.

The test statistic is the larger of the two following formulae:

$$U = n_1 n_2 + \frac{n_1(n_1+1)}{2} - \sum R_1 \text{ and}$$

$$U' = n_1 n_2 + \frac{n_2(n_2+1)}{2} - \sum R_2,$$

where

n_1 is the number of events in the smaller group and

n_2 is the number of events in the larger group.

In this case, the test statistics are:

$$U = n_1 n_2 + \frac{n_1(n_1+1)}{2} - \sum R_1$$
$$= (10 * 11) + \frac{10(10+1)}{2} - 100 = 110 + \frac{110}{2} - 100 = 65 \text{ and}$$
$$U' = n_1 n_2 + \frac{n_2(n_2+1)}{2} - \sum R_2$$
$$= (10 * 11) + \frac{11(11+1)}{2} - 131 = 110 + \frac{132}{2} - 131 = 45.$$

The significance test requires that the researcher take the larger of U or U' to complete the z formula:

$$z = \frac{U - \frac{n_1 n_2}{2}}{\sqrt{\frac{(n_1 n_2) * (n_1 + n_2 + 1)}{12}}}$$

$$= \frac{65 - \left(\frac{10 * 11}{2}\right)}{\sqrt{\frac{(10 * 11) * (10 + 11 + 1)}{12}}} = \frac{65 - 55}{\sqrt{\frac{(110) * (22)}{12}}} = \frac{5}{\sqrt{\frac{2,420}{12}}} = \frac{20}{14.2009} = 1.4084$$

For a two-tailed test, any value lower than –1.96 or greater than 1.96 would be statistically significant at alpha risk of .05. Looking up this value in Appendix C.1 reveals .4207, which means .0793 of the area under the standard normal curve lies above that point. Because the probability of the z value does not fall in the critical region, the researcher did not reject the null hypothesis. Thus, the researcher concluded that the two distributions were equal.

Using SPSS to Conduct the Mann-Whitney U Test

A researcher explored whether men or women differed in their perception of the clarity of information conveyed in Internet advertising. To analyze these data using SPSS, the researcher selects *Nonparametric Tests* from the *Analyze* menu. Then, the researcher selects *Two-Independent-Samples* from the drop-down menu. The test variable is highlighted and moved to the "Test Variable List:" field. Selecting the *Define Groups. . .* button permits the researcher to identify the values that constitute the two groups for analysis (1 and 2 in this case). The *Mann-Whitney U* test is checked for the *Test Type.* Clicking on the *OK* button produces descriptive output including a list of the mean ranks of each group.

Ranks

	sex	N	Mean Rank	Sum of Ranks
clarity	1	324	459.38	148838.00
	2	540	416.37	224842.00
	Total	864		

The statistical significance test is reported along with the Wilcoxon *W.* Though these tests show the same results, the Wilcoxon *W* statistic test uses the sum of the ranks for the smallest group in its critical computations. Because the probability value of .014 is smaller than the typical decision level set in communication research ($p \le .05$), the researcher would reject the null hypothesis.

Test Statistics[a]

	clarity
Mann-Whitney U	78772.000
Wilcoxon W	224842.0
Z	–2.461
Asymp. Sig. (2-tailed)	.014

a. Grouping Variable: sex

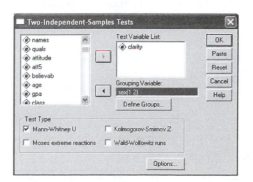

Test for Small Samples: Kolmogorov-Smirnov Two-Sample Test

The **Kolmogorov-Smirnov two-sample test** extends the Kolmogorov-Smirnov one-sample test to apply to two independent samples. By using cumulative frequency distributions of ranks, this test examines whether two sample distributions are the same. This test assumes that the data are measured on the ordinal level from an underlying continuous distribution. An example of this test is found in Table 11.6.

Table 11.6   Kolmogorov-Smirnov Two-Sample Test Example

A researcher was interested in learning if men or women exposed to a persuasive message appealing to common values would be different in willingness to sign petitions that differed in order of difficulty (based on a modified liberalism scale). Subjects were asked to identify the one petition out of five that they would be most willing to sign. The researcher wanted to make a two-tailed test at alpha risk of .05. The general null hypothesis was that the two samples are drawn from the same population. In this case, the specific null and research hypotheses were that

H_0: The difficulty levels of petitions men are willing to sign do not differ from the difficulty levels of petitions women are willing to sign.

H_1: The difficulty levels of petitions men are willing to sign differ from the difficulty levels of petitions women are willing to sign.

	Petition 1 (most difficult)	Petition 2	Petition 3	Petition 4	Petition 5 (least difficult)
Men (n_1)	5	11	16	5	23
Cumulative frequency proportion	.0833	.2667	.5333	.5883	1.0
Women (n_2)	2	3	3	17	10
Cumulative frequency proportion	.0571	.1429	.2286	.7143	1.0
Absolute difference	.0262	.1238	.3047	.126	0

Though there are tables for small samples, they require equal sample sizes. Furthermore, Siegel (1956, pp. 134–135) showed that an approximation of chi-square works well even for small samples. This underlying test statistic is

$$\chi^2 = \left(4 * [D]^2\right) * \left(\frac{n_1 * n_2}{n_1 + n_2}\right),$$

where

D is the largest absolute difference between cumulative frequency distributions, and

n_1 and n_2 are the number of events in the first and second groups.

Applied to these data, the computation becomes

$$\chi^2 = \left(4 * [.3047]^2\right) * \left(\frac{60 * 35}{60 + 35}\right) = (4 * .0929) * \left(\frac{2,100}{95}\right) = .3716 * 22.1053 = 8.2143.$$

For the two-sample test, the degrees of freedom for chi-square are equal to two. In this case, the chi-square critical value in Appendix C.10 is 5.99 with two degrees of freedom (one-tailed). Because a two-tailed test is involved, the p value of .05 is halved to .025, which yields a two-tailed critical value of 7.38. Because the test statistic of 8.21 was greater than the critical value, the researcher rejected the null hypothesis. The researcher concluded that the difficulty levels of petitions men were willing to sign were greater than the difficulty levels of petitions women were willing to sign.

Though in many ways this test resembles the chi-square test, when small samples are involved, it is more powerful than the chi-square test of independence. The Kolmogorov-Smirnov two-sample test also is more powerful than the median test. When compared with the two-sample t test, the Kolmogorov-Smirnov two-sample test has relatively high power efficiency for small samples (Dixon, 1954). This power efficiency declines as sample sizes increase. Though it has greater power efficiency than the Mann-Whitney U test when applied to small samples, the Mann-Whitney U test has superior power efficiency with large samples. Hence, researchers generally are advised to use the Kolmogorov-Smirnov two-sample test when the total sample size is 40 or fewer events. When the total sample size is greater than 40, other nonparametric statistical tools such as the Mann-Whitney U test are invited.

Special Discussion 11.1

Detecting Outliers by Use of the Moses Test

Most researchers, but especially those conducting experiments, expect that there are differences between two groups, one of which is called an experimental group and one of which is called a control group. Yet, a difficulty that plagues much research is the presence of outliers that introduce deviant data points that are not part of the standard population of interest. The Moses test attempts to examine the influence of outliers by conducting analyses of all data and comparing them to situations in which outliers are "trimmed" from the data set.

The Moses test assumes that the two groups affect the dependent variable by moving in different directions. When other simple differences are examined, Moses (1952) observed that this test may be used, but it is not as powerful as the Mann-Whitney U test for examining mean differences.

To illustrate this test, consider the following data:

Control Group: 8, 9, 10, 11, 14, 16, 20

Experimental Group: 5, 6, 12, 21, 25, 13, 23

(Continued)

Special Discussion 11.1 (Continued)

These scores may be ranked from lowest to highest and identified as coming from the control (C) or experimental (E) group:

Score	5	6	8	9	10	11	12	13	14	16	20	21	23	25
Group	E	E	C	C	C	C	E	E	C	C	C	E	E	E

The span of the control group scores (s') is computed by counting the number of cases or ranks extending from the lowest control group rank through and including the highest control group rank. In this case, the span starts with the third lowest ranked score (8) and extends through the fourth highest ranked score (20). This distance includes a span of nine ranks. Thus, s' equals 9. The Moses test examines whether the control group span (s') is "too small a value to be thought to have reasonably arisen by chance if the E's and C's are from the same population" (Siegel, 1956, p. 147).

Because the range traditionally is considered to be unstable, Moses recommends adjusting the scores by trimming a number of scores (called h) from the data set. In SPSS, h is set at 5% (rounded up to the next whole case) of the scores at each end of the control group span. The truncated span (s_h) is the span after the trimming has occurred in the control group. In this case, if h is 1, the range of ranks starts with score 9 and goes through score 16, a span that covers 7 ranks. The test statistic is

$$p(s_h \leq n_c - 2h + g) = \frac{\sum_{i=0}^{g} \left(\frac{(i + n_c - 2h - 2)!}{i! \left([i + n_c - 2h - 2] - i! \right)} \right) * \left(\frac{(n_e + 2h + 1 - i)!}{(n_e - i)! \left([n_e + 2h + 1 - i] - (n_e - i) \right)!} \right)}{\frac{(n_c + n_e)!}{n_c! \left([n_c + n_e] - n_c \right)!}},$$

where g is the amount that s_h is greater than $n_c - 2h$. In this case, $s_h - (n_c - 2h) = 7 - (7 - [2 * 1]) = 2$. In our example, one must sum the numerator terms for $i = 0$, $i = 1$, and $i = 2$.

The process may be speeded by use of SPSS. From the *Analyze* menu, the researcher selects *Nonparametric Statistics* followed by *Two-Independent-Samples...* from the submenu. In the *Two-Independent-Samples Tests* dialog box, the researcher selects "Moses extreme, reactions" from the *Test Type* section. The dependent variable is highlighted and moved to the "Test Variable List:" field. Then, the independent variable group is identified and the levels are defined. The first level is presumed to be the control group, and the second level is presumed to be the experimental group. Upon clicking the *OK* button, the output represented here is visible.

The output shows the results before and after trimming outliers. Before the trimming, the significance test produced a probability of .051, barely missing the standard requirement for rejecting the null hypothesis. After trimming one outlier from each end of the control group range, however, the significance test produced a probability of .296. Thus, when extreme cases are removed, the two groups clearly do not differ. By comparing these two results, it is possible to assess whether outliers contribute greatly or insubstantially in the analysis of results. Such a test may be useful to assess outlier effects in other data sets involving comparisons of two groups.

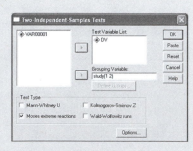

Test Statistics[a,b]

	DV
Observed Control Group Span — Sig. (1-tailed)	9
	.051
Trimmed Control Group Span — Sig. (1-tailed)	7
	.296
Outliers Trimmed from each End	1

a. Moses Test

b. Grouping Variable: study

Using SPSS to Conduct the Kolmogorov-Smirnov Two-Sample Test

From the *Analyze* menu, the researcher chooses *Nonparametric Tests*. In this drop-down menu, *Two-Independent-Samples Tests* is chosen. In the dialog box, the researcher selects the dependent variable as the test statistic in the *Test Type* field. To identify the dependent variable, the researcher moves the selected variable to the "Test Variable List:" field. The "Grouping Variable:" defines the values representing the categories of the independent variable.

After clicking the *OK* button, the analysis is completed and reported in the output window. The major analysis in the output window reports the largest absolute difference in the cumulative frequency distributions for the compared groups. As well, the largest positive and negative differences are reported. The significance probability reveals if the two groups differ in their location of measures of central tendency, or in their shape. In this case, because the probability value is below the decision rule standard of $p \leq .05$, the null hypothesis is rejected and the researcher concludes that the two distributions differ.

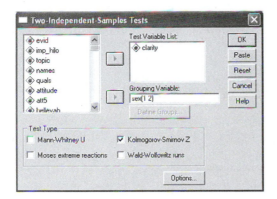

Test Statistics[a]

		CLARITY
Most Extreme	Absolute	.136
Differences	Positive	.136
	Negative	−.036
Kolmogorov-Smirnov Z		1.933
Asymp. Sig. (2-tailed)		.001

a. Grouping Variable: SEX

Dependent (Matched) Groups

Researchers often compare scores that are not independent. These dependent scores may be "before and after" tests from the same people, or they may reflect situations where researchers deal with groups of people who may have influenced others' responses. When dealing with rank order dependent variables, researchers have a couple of options. One test is called the *sign test*. Another test is the *Wilcoxon Matched Pairs Signed Ranks test*. Unlike the sign test, which simply compares the signs of matched pairs of scores, the Wilcoxon Matched Pairs Signed Ranks test assesses the sizes and directions of the ranked differences. For this reason, the Wilcoxon Matched Pairs Signed Ranks test is a more power efficient test than the sign test. In fact, this test is versatile and may be used to test whether the mean or median of a single population is equal to any given value. Hence, in this chapter Wilcoxon Matched Pairs Signed Ranks test is recommended in preference to the sign test.

Wilcoxon Matched Pairs Signed Ranks Test

An example of the Wilcoxon Matched Pairs Signed Ranks test is illustrated in Table 11.7.

Table 11.7   Wilcoxon Matched Pairs Test Example

A manager wanted to know if employee morale improved after a new communication hotline system was implemented in the company. Before and after the hotline was implemented, a random sample of employees completed morale scales. The data listed below seem to indicate that the communication hotline was associated with increased morale scores. The manager wished to make a one-tailed test at alpha risk of .05.

Morale Before Communication Hotline Implemented	Morale After Communication Hotline Implemented	D: Difference in Scores (After – Before)	Absolute Rank of Difference D (multiplied by sign of difference)	Ranks for Changes With Least Frequent Signs
40	30	−10	−14.5	−14.5
29	30	1	1.5	
50	52	2	3	
50	30	−20	−25.5	−25.5
40	49	9	13	
60	73	13	18	
55	72	17	22	
45	65	20	25.5	
57	62	5	8	
55	48	−7	−10.5	−10.5
35	56	21	27	
45	60	15	20	
50	69	19	24	
39	42	3	4.5	
48	47	−1	−1.5	−1.5
40	58	18	23	
67	71	4	6.5	
50	66	16	21	
56	66	10	14.5	
51	48	−3	−4.5	−4.5
66	72	6	9	
50	64	14	19	
44	56	12	17	
54	50	−4	−6.5	−6.5
48	55	7	10.5	
55	63	8	12	
40	51	11	16	
$n = 27$				$T = -63$

The null hypothesis tested was

H_0: There is no difference between the morale scores of individuals before and after implementation of the communication hotline.

(Continued)

The alternative research hypothesis is

H_1: There is an increase in the morale scores of individuals from before and after implementation of the communication hotline.

The test statistic uses the z distribution:

$$z = \frac{T - \dfrac{n(n+1)}{4}}{\sqrt{\dfrac{n(n+1)(2n+1)}{24}}},$$

where T is the smaller sum of ranks with the same sign. To identify this term, the researcher subtracts the pretest scores from the posttest scores. Then, these differences (in the column marked "*D:* Difference in Scores (After – Before)" are ranked from the lowest to the highest (ignoring for the moment whether the values are positive or negative values). In the case of ties, the mean of the tied ranks is assigned to all the tied examples. Hence, in this example, two scores tied for the smallest difference between employee morale ratings before and after implementation of the communication hotline. The tie was broken by assigning each score the average rank of 1.5. Once these ranks are determined, the sign of the difference (– or +) is applied to the ranked differences (and put in the column identified as "Absolute Rank of Difference *D* [multiplied by sign of difference]"). Next, the researcher looks at the differences and determines which sign (positive or negative) is *least frequent*. In this example, there are only six examples of ranks with negative signs. Thus, to compute T, these differences are added together in the column marked "Ranks for Changes With Least Frequent Signs." These steps lead to the test statistic as

$$z = \frac{T - \dfrac{n(n+1)}{4}}{\sqrt{\dfrac{n(n+1)(2n+1)}{24}}} = \frac{63 - \dfrac{27(27+1)}{4}}{\sqrt{\dfrac{27(27+1) * ([2*27]+1)}{24}}} = \frac{63 - \dfrac{756}{4}}{\sqrt{\dfrac{756 * 55}{24}}} = \frac{63 - 189}{\sqrt{\dfrac{41,580}{24}}}$$

$$= \frac{-126}{\sqrt{1,732.5}} = \frac{-126}{41.62} = -3.03.$$

The negative sign indicates that *fewer* individuals *did not* improve morale following implementation of the communication hotline. To see if this difference is greater than would have been expected by chance, the researcher looks at the z table (Appendix C.1) and finds that for alpha risk of .05 (one-tailed), the critical value is –1.645. Because the test statistic of –3.03 is further into the critical region than –1.645, the null hypothesis is rejected. In this example, the manager concluded that the dependent variable morale scores significantly increased following implementation of the communication hotline.

There are some assumptions underlying this test. First, because the magnitude of differences is to be assessed, the Wilcoxon Matched Pairs Signed Ranks test assumes that the dependent variable originally was measured on the interval or quasi-interval scale. Second, this test assumes that the two sets of scores are related in some way, such as testing subjects before and after some treatment, using subjects as their own controls. Third, the test assumes that "the distribution of differences between the two populations in the pairs, two-sample case is symmetric" (Aczel, 1989, p. 770). Among other things, in a symmetrical distribution, the mean and median are the same. Hence, this assumption means that the test comparing means and medians would be comparable. As a result, the comparison of this test with the *t* test for related samples is quite strong.

The actual null hypothesis test involves contrasting the distributions of two populations. Technically, then, the null hypothesis is

H_0: The distributions of the two populations are not different.

The alternative research hypothesis is simply

H_1: The distributions of the two populations are different.

If one assumes that differences between the two population distributions involve the locations of the mean and median, the researcher may make a directional hypotheses (Aczel, 1989, pp. 765–766). Because the assumption of symmetrical distributions has been made, this extra interpretation usually is sensible.

Though tables exist to permit researchers to look up results when sample sizes are lower than 25, the formula using samples of size above 25 is used in the example here. This formula uses the standard normal curve to help make decisions. Even when applied to small samples, the results of this test are an "excellent approximation" (Siegel, 1956, p. 79) of the small sample test statistic that is based on computing binomial probabilities.

Using SPSS to Conduct the Wilcoxon Matched Pairs Signed Ranks Test

To employ SPSS to complete the Wilcoxon Signed Ranks test for analysis of two related or matched groups, the researcher selects *Nonparametric* from the *Analysis* menu. Then, the *Two-Related-Samples Tests. . .* choice is made. In the dialog box, the researcher selects the related samples by clicking on the arrow button to move the two variables to the "Test Pair(s) List:" field.

Selecting *Wilcoxon* and clicking the *OK* button produces the analysis. Descriptive statistics (if requested from *Options. . .*) include the results found below.

Descriptive Statistics

	N	Mean	Std. Deviation	Minimum	Maximum
V1	864	5.40	1.30	1	7
V4	864	4.84	1.49	1	7

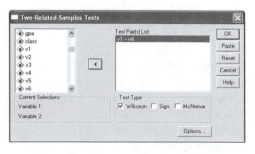

Ranks

		N	Mean Rank	Sum of Ranks
V4-V1	Negative Ranks	427[a]	276.37	118008.50
	Positive Ranks	116[b]	255.93	29687.50
	Ties	321[c]		
	Total	864		

a. V4 < V1
b. V4 > V1
c. V1 = V4

The lists of positive ranks (where the posttest is greater than the pretest) and negative ranks (where the pretest is greater than the posttest) are reported. As can be seen, the greatest number of shifts are negative rank differences. For the pairs with the least frequent sign, the reported sum of the ranks is standardized.

The actual Wilcoxon matched pairs signed ranks test is reported in a "Test Statistics" box. The large z coefficient and the small significance value show that the distributions differ. Thus, the researcher rejects the null hypothesis that the distributions are the same.

Test Statistics[b]

	V4-V1
Z	−12.615[a]
Asymp. Sig. (2-tailed)	.000

a. Based on positive ranks

b. Wilcoxon Signed Ranks Test

COMPARING RANKS FROM MORE THAN TWO SAMPLE GROUPS: ANALOGOUS TESTS TO ONE-WAY ANOVA

To compare more than two groups, nonparametric tools exist for both independent samples and related samples. The tools that may be used include the Kruskal-Wallis H test and the Friedman two-way analysis of variance.

Kruskal-Wallis H Test

The purpose of the **Kruskal-Wallis H** test is similar to that of one-way analysis of variance. The H test is designed to examine whether two or more independent samples differ. Of course, sometimes the test may be used for only two sample groups. In such a case, the Kruskal-Wallis H and the Mann-Whitney U test are the same. As with the Mann-Whitney U test, the Kruskal-Wallis H test examines the null hypothesis

H_0: The distributions of the populations are not different.

The alternative research hypothesis is simply

H_1: The distributions of the populations are different.

Rejecting the null hypothesis means that the researcher claims that at least two of the population distributions of ranks are different. As is the case with the Mann-Whitney U test, this statistic deals with differences in the distributions, one characteristic of which is the mean or median.

In addition to randomization, the Kruskal-Wallis H test assumes that the groups are independent groups of data. Furthermore, the method assumes that the dependent variable data are measured on an ordinal scale, though scores are presumed to represent data from a continuous distribution that originally may have been on the interval scale. Because this test does not assume that there is an underlying normal distribution to the data, it has become a popular tool for researchers who are uncomfortable assuming normal distributions or homogeneity of variances in their data sets.

Table 11.8   Kruskal-Wallis One-Way Analysis of Variance Example

A researcher wanted to know if executives, middle managers, or supervisors had different levels of workplace communication satisfaction. For a pilot study, the researcher sampled 8 executives, 10 middle managers, and 12 supervisors. The researcher hypothesized that the supervisors would have the lowest communication satisfaction. A significance test was planned with alpha risk of .05. The null hypothesis was

H_0: The distributions of ranks of workplace communication satisfaction among executives, middle managers, and supervisors are not different.

The alternative research hypothesis was

H_1: The distributions of ranks of workplace communication satisfaction among executives, middle managers, and supervisors are different.

The study data were as follows:

Executives	Ranks	Middle Managers	Ranks	Supervisors	Ranks
55	26.5	30	3	41	13
48	20	52	24	33	6
55	26.5	49	21	45	17.5
40	12	56	28	32	5
35	7	42	14	28	2
60	30	47	19	45	17.5
53	25	58	29	39	11
51	23	38	10	43	15
		44	16	26	1
		50	22	37	9
				31	4
				36	8

$n_1 = 8$ $R_1 = 170$ $n_2 = 10$ $R = 186$ $n_3 = 12$
$R_3 = 109$

Because there were more than five events in each condition, the alternative test statistic was used for such situations (Siegel, 1956, pp. 186–188):

$$H = \frac{12}{N(N+1)} \sum_{j=1}^{k} \frac{R_j^2}{n_j} - 3(N+1),$$

(Continued)

The procedure for the Kruskal-Wallis H test uses the chi-square distribution to examine differences. When tests compare three small sample groups of five or fewer events, tables are available to identify statistical significance of different combinations of rankings. When sample sizes are greater than five, the Kruskal-Wallis H test statistic must be computed in full. The example in Table 11.8 shows this approach. This test statistic uses the chi-square distribution with degrees of freedom equal to the number of groups minus one.

where

N is the number of events in the study,

k is the number of groups,

n_j is the number of events in each group j, and

R_j is the sum of the ranks in each group.

This test may be influenced by tied ranks, especially if the number of ties exceeds 25% of the data points. Thus, the researcher needs to divide the H statistic by the following formula to correct for the number of tied ranks:

$$1 - \frac{\sum T}{N^2 - N},$$

where T is the number of ties squared (t^2) minus the number of ties (t), and N is the number of events in the study.

Though the number of tied ranks is small, the use of the full formula including the adjustment for tied ranks will be used for purposes of illustration. In this case, there are two situations where there are tied ranks. Two individuals had ratings of 45 with tied ranks of 17.5 (thus, $T = t^3 - t = 2^3 - 2 = 8 - 2 = 6$). Two respondents had ratings of 55 and tied ranks of 26.5 (thus, $T = t^3 - t = 2^3 - 2 = 8 - 2 = 6$).

The test statistic for H is

$$H = \frac{\dfrac{12}{N(N+1)} \sum\limits_{j=1}^{k} \dfrac{R_j^2}{n_j} - 3(N+1)}{1 - \dfrac{\sum T}{N^2 - N}} = \frac{\left(\dfrac{12}{30(30+1)}\right) * \left(\dfrac{170^2}{8} + \dfrac{186^2}{10} + \dfrac{109^2}{12}\right) - [3 * (30+1)]}{1 - \dfrac{(2^3 - 2) + (2^3 - 2)}{30^2 - 30}}$$

$$= \frac{24.26}{1 - .0138} = \frac{24.26}{.9862} = 24.5994.$$

H is distributed as chi-square with degrees of freedom equal to the number of groups minus 1. In this case, the chi-square table is entered with 2 degrees of freedom. At alpha risk of .05, the critical value is 5.99. Because the test statistic is greater than the critical value, the researcher rejected the null hypothesis and concluded that the distributions of ranks of workplace communication satisfaction among executives, middle managers, and supervisors were different.

There are some challenges when using the Kruskal-Wallis H test. First, it directly explores differences located in the distributions, but any differences may stem from different medians, means, modes, and/or *shapes* of the distributions. Thus, researchers cannot automatically assume that a statistically significant difference is attributable solely to a mean or median difference. Hence, wise researchers report characteristics of distributions of ranks in addition to this significance test alone. Second, this test identifies that there is at least one difference among populations, but not *where* differences are located. Because most statistical computer packages fail to provide such follow-up work, researchers must add comparisons on their own (see Aczel, 1989, pp. 775–776). To compute this set of comparisons, researchers conduct the following steps.

The mean rank of the entire sample and of each sample group is computed using the formulae

$$\bar{R}_i = \frac{\sum R_i}{n_i} \text{ and } \bar{R}_j = \frac{\sum R_j}{n_j},$$

where

R_i is each instance of a rank in the initial group to be compared with another,

n_i is the number of ranks in the initial comparison group,

R_j is each instance of a rank in the next group to be compared with the initial group, and

n_i is the number of ranks in the next group to be compared with the initial group.

These formulae identify the mean ranks for each group. To test for differences, researchers compute $D = |\bar{R}_i - \bar{R}_j|$ to identify the difference in ranks between each pair of groups. In this case, the mean ranks were executives = 21.25, middle managers = 18.6, and supervisors = 9.08. The differences were executives vs. middle managers, $D = 2.65$; executives vs. supervisors, $D = 12.17$; and middle managers vs. supervisors, $D = 9.52$.

To test if these differences are statistically significant, the researcher computes the following test statistic:

$$C_{KW} = \sqrt{\left(\chi^2_{\alpha,k-1}\right) * \left[\frac{N * (N + 1)}{12}\right] * \left(\frac{1}{n_i} + \frac{1}{n_j}\right)},$$

where

$\chi^2_{\alpha,k-1}$ is the critical value of chi-square at the specified α (alpha risk) and degrees of freedom equal to $k - 1$ (number of sample groups minus one)—in this case, the chi-square value with alpha risk of .05 and 2 degrees of freedom is 5.99,

N is the number of events in the study,

n_i is the number of events in the initial group in the comparison, and

n_j is the number of events in the second group in the comparison.

For the comparison between executives and managers, the test statistic is

$$C_{KW} = \sqrt{\left(\chi^2_{\alpha,k-1}\right) * \left[\frac{N * (N + 1)}{12}\right] * \left(\frac{1}{n_i} + \frac{1}{n_j}\right)},$$

$$C_{KW} = \sqrt{5.99 * \left[\frac{30 * (31)}{12}\right] * \left(\frac{1}{8} + \frac{1}{10}\right)} = \sqrt{5.99 * 77.5 * .222} = 10.22.$$

Because the D value of 2.65 is lower than the critical C_{kw} value, this difference is not statistically significant.

For the comparison between executives and supervisors, the test statistic is

$$C_{KW} = \sqrt{5.99 * \left[\frac{30 * (31)}{12}\right] * \left(\frac{1}{8} + \frac{1}{12}\right)} = \sqrt{5.99 * 77.5 * .208} = 9.83.$$

Because the D value of 12.17 is greater than the critical C_{kw} value, this difference is statistically significant.

For the comparison between middle managers and supervisors, the test statistic is

$$C_{KW} = \sqrt{5.99 * \left[\frac{30 * (31)}{12}\right] * \left(\frac{1}{10} + \frac{1}{12}\right)} = \sqrt{5.99 * 77.5 * .183} = 9.22.$$

Because the D value of 9.52 is greater than the critical C_{kw} value, this difference is statistically significant. Overall, it appears that the first-line supervisors had lower workplace communication satisfaction ratings than the others on the management team.

Using SPSS to Conduct the Kruskal-Wallis *H* Test

To compare several independent groups with ordinal level dependent variable measures, the researcher begins by selecting *Nonparametric Tests* from the *Analyze* menu. Then, the researcher chooses *K Independent Samples. . .* from the drop-down menu. In the dialog box, the researcher selects the dependent variable by highlighting a variable and using the arrow button to transfer it to the "Test Variable List:" field. To identify the groups compared, the researcher selects a variable and moves it to the "Grouping Variable:" field. Then, the researcher clicks the *Define Range. . .* button and identifies the range of values that represent the groups (in this case, groups 1 through 4 are used).

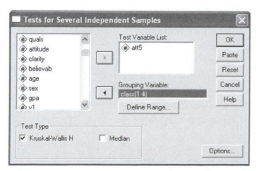

After selecting "Kruskal-Wallis H" from the *Test Type* field, the researcher clicks the *OK* button. Descriptive statistics (if requested from *Options*) include the mean ranks. The actual test statistic using the chi-square distribution also is reported.

Ranks

	CLASS	N	Mean Rank
ATT5	1	582	447.61
	2	72	379.56
	3	158	406.05
	4	52	417.08
	Total	864	

Test Statistics[a,b]

	ATT5
Chi-Square	7.392
df	3
Asymp. Sig.	.060

a. Kruskal Wallis Test
b. Grouping Variable: CLASS

In this case, the test statistic had a significance test coefficient of .06. Because this value is greater than the typical test decision rule at a set alpha risk, the researcher would not reject the null hypothesis that the groups differ. Though, as we have seen, there is a multiple comparison test option for the Kruskal-Wallis *H* test, SPSS currently does not support it, and researchers must compute it on their own. Nevertheless, a guide to using the Excel spreadsheet to compute this test is available on the Web site for this chapter.

The Friedman Two-Way Analysis of Variance

The **Friedman Two-Way Analysis of Variance** is a nonparametric alternative to the mixed-effects analysis of variance design. Despite its name, this test is *not* a two-way ANOVA for two fixed effects. It does not test directly for interaction effects. It actually is a randomized block (mixed-effects design) for rank order data. It often is used when the same person has been given all the experimental treatments in some order, when subjects have been matched with others, or when repeated measures within the same block of responses have been made. The purpose of the Friedman two-way analysis of variance is to test whether two or more dependent samples differ.

This test makes a few assumptions. First, it assumes that samples are related to each other in some way. Frequently, the same sample groups are sampled under each of the different fixed conditions. On other occasions, the same people may be sampled repeatedly. Second, the Friedman two-way analysis of variance assumes that the dependent variable is measured on the ordinal level. Though data could be reduced to rank order scores from initially higher levels of measurement, the test is not useful for categorical data. When the researcher cannot assume normal distributions of the dependent variable population or is faced with difficulties with the interval quality of measures, this tool can be helpful.

The procedure actually is an extension of the Wilcoxon Matched Pairs Signed Ranks test for situations where there are more than two groups of scores to be examined. As the example in Table 11.9 shows, to use the Friedman two-way analysis of variance, the data from each subject are rank ordered in a table in which the columns represent levels of an independent variable (the fixed effect) and the rows represent each subject (or matched subject, or otherwise related sample). Then, the chi-square distribution is checked to see if the ranks of each group differ from what might be expected by chance. A significance test statistic indicates that there is a difference somewhere among the groups compared. Multiple comparison tests currently are not available to determine the locations of the differences among more than two groups.

Table 11.9   Friedman Two-Way Analysis of Variance Example

A training and development director wanted to learn if skills taught in a course in "Communication Styles in Management" actually persisted over time. The course taught 10 competencies that could be rated on a self-report of perceived competencies. The researcher randomly sampled 10 people who were scheduled to take the course. They completed the competency ratings before taking the course, at the end of the course, and 1 month following the course. The director recognized that skills probably would decline somewhat, but she hoped that the delayed test still would show improvements in self-reported skill levels. The researcher wished to make a test with alpha risk of .05. The null hypothesis was

H_0: The distributions of ranks of communication style competencies before, immediately following, and 1 month after taking a course in communication style are not different.

The alternative research hypothesis was

H_1: The distributions of ranks of communication style competencies before, immediately following, and 1 month after taking a course in communication style are different.

For each person, the researcher identified which score ranked the highest (indicated by a rank of 1), which ranked the second highest (indicated by a rank of 2), and which ranked the third highest (indicated by a rank of 3). The data are found in the table below. For each time that competency measures were drawn, the ranks were summed.

Person	Precourse Rating	Ranks	Immediate Postcourse Rating	Ranks	Delayed Post-course Rating	Ranks
1	30	3	40	1	35	2
2	15	3	37	1	34	2
3	36	2	41	1	33	3
4	33	2	40	1	32	3
5	36	2	38	1	34	3
6	20	3	37	1	30	2
7	23	3	45	1	35	2
8	36	3	47	1	41	2
9	21	3	29	2	36	1
10	28	3	39	1	31	2
$N = 10$		$R_1 = 27$		$R_2 = 11$		$R_3 = 22$

The test statistic for the Friedman two-way analysis of variance is

$$\chi^2 = \left(\frac{12}{Nk(k+1)} * \sum_{j=1}^{k} R_j^2 \right) - [3N * (k+1)],$$

where

N is the number of events in the study,

k is the number of groups, and

R_j is the sum of the ranks in each group.

Inserting the appropriate scores, the computation becomes

$$\chi^2 = \left(\frac{12}{10 * 3 * (3+1)} * (27^2 + 11^2 + 22^2) \right) - [3 * 10 * (3+1)]$$

$$= \left(\frac{12}{120} * (729 + 121 + 484) \right) - 120 = (.1 * 1,334) - 120 = 133.4 - 120 = 13.4.$$

This test statistic is distributed as chi-square with $k - 1$ degrees of freedom. Because there were three groups, $k - 1$ equals 2 degrees of freedom. The critical value was 5.99. Because the test statistic of 13.4 is greater than the critical value of 5.99, the training and development director rejected the null hypothesis and concluded that the three distributions of competency ranks were different. Inspection of scores suggested that the competency rankings increased immediately after the course before showing a decline.

Using SPSS to Conduct the Friedman Two-Way Analysis of Variance

To employ SPSS for this test, the researcher begins by choosing *Nonparametric Tests* from the *Analyze* menu. Then, *K Related Samples. . .* is selected from the *Nonparametric* drop-down menu. In the dialog box, the researcher selects "Friedman." The related samples are highlighted and transferred into the "Test Variables:" field.

It might be noted that this dialog box permits the researcher to obtain Kendall's coefficient of concordance (*W*), which is a correlation among more than two groups. Though this dialog box permits computing Cochran's *Q*, this statistic deals with dichotomous data only and will not be described here. Clicking the *Statistics* button permits the researcher to obtain descriptive information such as the output provided below.

The Friedman test results include a significance test with a probability coefficient of .000, which is considerably smaller than the typical alpha risk level of $p \leq .05$. Hence, the researchers would reject the null hypothesis and conclude that at least one of the related groups differs from the others. Careful inspection of the means would be required to identify the specific differences. Even so, it appears that there was a steady decline from the first observation through the last measure made.

Descriptive Statistics

	N	Mean	Std. Deviation	Minimum	Maximum
V1	864	5.40	1.30	1	7
V2	864	5.25	1.43	1	7
V3	864	5.07	1.40	1	7
V4	864	4.84	1.49	1	7

Test Statistics[a]

N	864
Chi-Square	299.565
df	3
Asymp. Sig.	.000

a. Friedman Test

Part V

ADVANCED STATISTICAL
APPLICATIONS

Chapter 12

META-ANALYSIS

A popular approach to summarizing empirical research has been meta-analysis, a quantitative alternative to interpretive literature reviews. This chapter will share information about the method and describe some of the major issues raised by this approach.

META-ANALYSIS: AN ALTERNATIVE TO ARTISTIC LITERATURE REVIEWS

Literature reviews summarize research by making arguments based on reasonable interpretations of past research. There are several ways to gather evidence to make arguments about the status of past research.

Standard Methods of Approaching Research Information

There are several ways to determine the nature of a relationship empirically. One way is called **primary analysis**, which is "the original analysis of data in a research study" (Glass, 1976, p. 3). Most of the statistics described in this book involve tools to complete such data-based studies. Yet, despite their great value, single studies rarely provide conclusive answers to major research questions. Another way to identify relationships is by **secondary analysis**, which is "the re-analysis of data for the purpose of answering the original research question with better statistical techniques, or answering new questions with old data" (Glass, 1976, p. 3). This approach often is used when researchers take data from past researchers and complete advanced analyses. For instance, Franke and Kaul (1978) took the data from the Hawthorne studies completed in the 1920s and 1930s (which allegedly found that tangible rewards were not great motivators of workers) and subjected them to their first statistical analysis. These researchers found that the major conclusions drawn by the original writers were not, in fact, supported by the data. Such factors as changing lighting levels in the work area, paying bonuses for productive work, and firing unproductive workers made a big difference in productivity. In communication studies, Miller, Boster, Roloff, and Seibold (1977) took data from Marwell and Schmitt's (1967) research project and—subject to many additional limitations they subsequently added—found that use of compliance-gaining message strategies differed by the situation and by whether the persuasive effects involved short-term or long-term behaviors. But it is not always useful to review past data sets with different statistical tools. Furthermore, in many cases, original data may not be available for analysis at some later time.[1]

A third approach uses **narrative reviews** of literature. These reviews are nonquantitative assessments of the status of research related to a research topic. Narrative reviews carry several advantages. First, unlike most meta-analyses, these reviews typically include strong arguments about definitions and conceptual issues. Second, narrative summaries often point to new theories and suggest priorities for additional research. Third, narrative reviews help to

---

[1]Meta-analysis has grown in popularity also because institutional review boards that must approve research projects often discourage the storage of original data because of the remote risk that participants (individually or in aggregate) subsequently might be identified by a secondary analysis.

unearth patterns of inconsistencies among studies and to give weight to studies with strong designs. These lines of argument make narrative reviews considerably more than simple "counts" of studies that show a relationship minus "counts" of studies that fail to show a relationship. Fourth, narrative reviews are not limited to reviews of quantitative studies.

Narrative reviews also carry limitations. First, the quality of narrative reviews depends on the reviewer's clear thinking. Although many scholars reason very soundly to reach conclusions about research data, there is no guarantee that all reviews reflect such sound reasoning. Of course, most published reviews are peer-reviewed, and mistakes in reasoning are likely to be identified. Even in these cases, there is no guarantee that sound reasoning will win out over any mistaken conventional wisdom. Second, narrative reviews may draw conflicting conclusions. Then readers are stuck. Deciding which scholar to believe may be based more on social pressures than on the actual research. Third, narrative reviews may rely on misreadings of the literature or reflect strong personal biases. Scholars may rely on intuition to guide their interpretations and steer them in directions they believe are important. For several reasons, then, there is difficulty with relying on narrative literature reviews alone.

Meta-Analysis

Meta-analysis is a method of combining quantitative results from many studies to reveal the nature of relationships that exist among variables. It is a collection of tools to combine and analyze the results of different studies. This alternative to narrative literature reviews uses quantitative methods to give reviewers another set of tools to avoid biases along the way. We should not overstate matters here. Although meta-analysis is an alternative to conclusion-drawing based on single studies, without continuing primary analysis studies, there is little material upon which to base meta-analyses. In fact, a good meta-analysis often leads researchers to complete primary research projects of their own.

Advantages and Disadvantages of Meta-Analysis

Meta-analysis has several **advantages**. First, in combining the literature, meta-analysis attempts to employ methods to enhance statistical exactness. Second, meta-analyses may be replicated by others. Though narrative reviews rely on sound reasoning, which ensures a certain amount of replication by others, the use of statistical methods and meta-analytic procedures permits others to find the same results when dealing with the same data. Third, this method attempts to give weight to different studies based on the size and stability of their samples. In narrative literature reviews, although researchers may comment on sample sizes, study findings are contrasted study by study. Of course, some meta-analysts disagree on the desirability of "weighting" study findings by sample sizes, but this method is common in meta-analysis.

There are some **disadvantages** of meta-analysis. First, some researchers ignore the fact that the underlying conceptual definitions of terms and the validity of their operationalizations must be understood before meta-analysis is completed. If researchers compare studies on the reciprocity of self-disclosure during initial interactions, for example, it is helpful to know that researchers defined self-disclosure and reciprocity in approximately (or tolerably) the same ways. Meta-analyses generally do not involve definitional and conceptual matters (though these matters may inform the tenability of various theories). Furthermore, meta-analysis is not just a way to combine rambling set of studies with multiple and divergent methods. There should be some conceptual basis for choosing some variables and for combining studies. If the conceptual foundations of the meta-analysis are troubled, there may not be much benefit in completing it.

Second, meta-analysis is limited to reviewing quantitative studies, even though qualitative research also may inform aspects of a research issue. Hence, this restriction limits researchers' abilities to make research arguments based on theoretic or conceptual grounds.

Third, meta-analysis conclusions may conflict if different studies are sampled or excluded for different reasons. In short, researchers can secure an unrepresentative sample. It should be observed that, as with all statistical methods, meta-analysis is a tool to gather evidence to make a reasoned argument. It neither supplants nor guarantees good reasoning. Thus, high-quality meta-analyses can enhance intelligent discussion of critical issues, but they do not replace it. Poor meta-analyses and poor narrative reviews are equally troubling.

There are other criticisms that sometimes are waged against meta-analysis, such as that the method ignores study quality or that it mixes studies that include very different variables. These criticisms are not necessarily weaknesses of sound meta-analyses, but to understand these matters, it is important to understand some tools involved in this method. Hence, such criticisms will be revisited in Special Discussion 12.2 near the end of this chapter.

Objectives of Meta-Analysis

In addition to providing an alternative to narrative reviews, meta-analysis has some other objectives. These objectives reflect research questions that meta-analysts probe.

- Meta-analysts may ask about the overall *strength of relationships* between variables studied across many research efforts. A research question might ask: "What is the size of the relationship between source trustworthiness and perceptions of similarity?" Such questions are relatively exploratory, because only one issue (the size of the effect) is examined.
- Meta-analysts may ask about *sources of variability* in study effect sizes. Researchers may ask which factors explain why effect sizes in one set of studies are larger than those in the others. For instance, a researcher could pose the problem question, "What is the relationship between the sex of students and the effect sizes of studies dealing with the association between a teacher's violations of students' personal space and measures of learning?"
- Meta-analysts may compare the *strength of relationships from studies using different designs and variables*. Comparisons may be made between studies involving interactions with other variables, differences in study design, or changes in sampling methods. These elements may be coded, and such studies may be contrasted. Researchers could advance this problem question: "What is the relationship between the effect sizes of survey or experimental studies and the association between and amount of talking in group discussions and rates of leadership emergence?"
- Meta-analysts may check if evidence casts light on the *tenability of theories*. Because studies designed to explore different theories may produce different effect sizes, the meta-analyst often can learn if some theories are more sound than others.

For the most part, the researchers wish to know if there is a relationship between two variables at a time, but sometimes problem questions explore addition interaction effects.

Though meta-analyses may be a fad used by some researchers who give up on collecting original data for themselves, Lipsey and Wilson (2001) remind researchers that "if the full data sets for the studies of interest are available, it will generally be more appropriate and informative to analyze them directly using conventional procedures rather than meta-analyze summary statistics" (p. 1).

Assumptions of Meta-Analysis

Several assumptions underlie meta-analysis. These matters deal with requirements involved in treating research studies as elements in a common data pool.

- First, it is assumed that empirical studies are reported in enough detail to permit retrieving sufficient information about effects. The quality of incompletely reported studies is presumed to be randomly distributed. There may be some reasons to accept this secondary assumption because, at one time, high-quality published communication studies were not required to report measurement reliability or effect sizes (aside from occasional reports of means).
- Second, it is assumed that study samples are independent. Because the same researchers at the same institutions tend to complete studies that repeatedly dip into the same populations, it may be difficult to find studies where samples really are independent.
- The findings must be *exchangeable*, which means that within groups, they must be comparable in significant ways, such that their results may be interpreted directly. This assumption may be difficult to make if researchers use different constructs and methods.

> In many meta-analytic applications, the simplifying assumption of exchangeability (de Finetti, 1930/1981) is simply untenable—studies differ too much in their designs, subject selection criteria, or other details for any analysis that ignores these differences to be convincing. One approach would be to quantify how similar the different studies are to each other (Draper, Hodges, Mallows, & Pregibon, 1993) or how similar they are to the target circumstances, and exclude or discount in ad hoc ways those studies regarded as too dissimilar (Wolpert & Mengersen, 2004, p. 2).

This assumption may be tested by using diffuse tests of significance and by coding studies for qualitative differences that may be examined with focused comparisons.

CONDUCTING THE META-ANALYSIS STUDY

After isolating problem questions for research, researchers may complete meta-analyses. Major steps will be listed here, and appropriate statistics described in each section.

Step 1: Collect Past Studies

Because the "data" in a meta-analysis are the quantitative studies related to a topic, researchers must take care to collect them in full. Representativeness is difficult to ensure because, of course, some studies add variables that others do not. Researchers should include all these studies, while making particular note of their differences.

Locating Quantitative Studies

It helps to have solid library research skills to locate relevant quantitative studies, but there are some other matters that researchers should address. For a study to be included, it must meet some clear criteria:

- Studies must report information that is necessary to compute relationship sizes or mean differences. Editorial boards now routinely demand that researchers report measures of effect sizes when they find statistically significant relationships, but not all pieces of research are so complete. At a minimum, the researcher must be able to find the sample size actually used for the analyses (as opposed to the initial sample size before events were deleted) and actual test statistics.
- Studies should be comparable in major ways. Included studies should deal with common dependent variables, and study conditions should be clearly described. For instance, in many experiments, a "control condition" is included in which no experimental treatments are presented. In some other experiments, no separate control condition is present. To make meaningful contrasts, the types of groups compared must be similar in essential ways.
- Studies included from a single research project should be limited. Researchers often report two, three, or more studies in the same research article even though studies in meta-analyses are assumed to be independent. Moreover, studies using the same experimental materials tend to show less variability than studies using different treatments. But researchers cannot be expected to stop researching topics with methods and materials they have found to be useful, so the assumption of independence must be treated with a certain amount of leeway. A general rule is to include no more than two or three studies from a single project.

One gets the impression that studies may be omitted rather capriciously, but researchers must use some careful reasoning to justify deleting studies from the final sample. They cannot be omitted because they are inconvenient or just because they have extreme effects. Meta-analysts should be able to make arguments that omitted studies are not from the population to which the other studies belong.

Obtaining Published and Unpublished Studies

To find all relevant studies, researchers need to search for both published and unpublished work. Researchers must establish criteria in advance. Of course, sometimes criteria have to be added as needed. Then, the search may begin in earnest. Published work may be found by looking at standard indexing resources. The Web site for this chapter provides guides to such research pieces. Searches in the social sciences can be promoted by looking at such guides as *SSCI* (the *Social Science Citation Index*). This resource identifies publications that cite a particular source, typically a "classic" study. Of course, researchers also can find resources by examining reference lists from the articles and papers that are included in the data set.

There is controversy about the exclusive reliance on published research. On one hand, relying on published research from peer-reviewed journals may ensure that the quality of the included studies is fairly strong. On the other hand, considerable work shows that professional journals have a bias in favor of publishing studies with statistically significant results

(Ashenfelter, Harmon, & Oosterbeek, 1999; DeLong & Lang, 1992; Fagley & McKinney, 1983; Givens, Smith, & Tweedie, 1997). Studies failing to support hypotheses do not tend to get submitted or published, so meta-analysts must "beat the bushes" to find such research studies.

In communication studies, researchers also will want to look to unpublished doctoral dissertations and master's theses, by checking *Dissertation Abstracts International* and *Masters Abstracts International.* In addition, many unpublished pieces of communication research, such as working papers and convention presentations, are listed in *Resources in Education* (ERIC, short for Education Resource Information Clearinghouse). There also are ways to get unpublished convention papers by checking the archives of the National Communication Association and International Communication Association conventions. The latter source has also made papers of recent conventions available electronically. Even if a presentation does not seem to be available, completing an Internet search with an author's name as a reference can reveal Web pages from which additional resources may be obtained.

To explore the possible influence of publication bias, meta-analysts regularly report estimates of the file drawer effect problem. The **file drawer effect** is the tendency for studies that fail to find significant relationships to remain unpublished and become abandoned in file drawers. There is more than one approach to this matter; some of the most prominent are listed here.

- *Computing a Fail-Safe Number* (see Gleser & Olkin, 1996). This value reveals the number of additional studies showing a zero effect that would have to exist to reverse the reported relationship size pattern. When using exact probabilities of significance tests as the unit of analysis, the fail-safe number is computed by the formula[2]

$$X = \frac{\left(\sum z_j\right)^2}{z_p^2} - N_L,$$

  where

  z_j is the z score associated with the one-tailed probability value for each study j,

  z_p^2 is the square of the one-tailed value from the standard normal curve used for alpha risk (in most cases alpha risk is set at .05, which corresponds to a one tailed z value of 1.645), and

  N_L is the number of studies located by the researcher.

  When applied to the data on Table 12.1 with a meta-analyst setting alpha risk at .05, the fail-safe number is 223.191. Because there cannot be a fraction of a study, the fail-safe number is 224 studies.

---

[2]This number may be calculated (using the Stouffer method of combining probabilities) from the equation

$$X = \frac{\left(\sum z_i\right)^2}{2.706} - N_L,$$

where z_i is the z score associated with the one-tailed p value for study i, and N_L is the total number of located studies.

Table 12.1

r	n	Population r	z_r	z_j	t	p	z
.28	60	.28	.288	2.174	2.221	.0303	1.876
.40	50	.40	.424	2.907	3.024	.0040	2.652
.35	60	.35	.365	2.756	2.845	.0061	2.506
.45	56	.45	.485	3.531	3.703	.0005	3.291
.20	100	.20	.203	1.999	2.021	.0460	1.685
.25	60	.25	.255	1.925	1.966	.0541	1.606
.32	76	.32	.332	2.837	2.906	.0048	2.590
.22	80	.22	.224	1.966	1.992	.0499	1.646
.33	50	.33	.343	2.352	2.422	.0193	2.068
.34	60	.34	.354	2.673	2.753	.0079	2.414

When one is dealing with comparisons involving effect sizes, this number may be calculated as

$$X = \frac{\left(\sum Z_j\right)^2}{z_p^2} - N_L,$$

where

$$Z_j = Z_{rj}\sqrt{N_j - 3},$$

Z_{rj} is Fisher's Z-transformed correlation coefficient for the relationship between the two variables of interest for sample j,

Fisher's Z transformation is $Z_r = \frac{1}{2}\ln\left(\frac{1+r}{1-r}\right)$,

N_j is the sample size,

z_p^2 is the square of the value from the z table that corresponds to the one-tailed probability level of the significance tests (p usually is .05 in communication research, and the one-tailed z value corresponding to 95% of the area is 1.645), and

N_L is the number of studies located by the researcher.

As a rule of thumb, Rosenthal (1979) suggests that if the fail-safe number is at least $5N_L + 10$, the meta-analyst may be comfortable assuming that the sample of studies is not likely to be overwhelmed by a future influx of studies with no significant relationships. Table 12.2 shows a fail-safe number computation in a small meta-analysis involving effect sizes.

Table 12.2   The Fail-Safe Number

To illustrate computing a fail-safe number for effect sizes, consider what happened when a researcher completed an analysis with 10 studies with sample sizes ranging from 50 to 100. Using the Excel spreadsheet "FAILSAFE.xls" available from the Web site for this chapter, the researcher inserted the correlation for the two-variable association into Column A (for the moment, we will not concern ourselves with whether these correlations are corrected for reliability attenuation). The researcher also inserted the sample size in Column C. The spreadsheet automatically computed the remaining elements.

	A	B	C	D	E	F	G
1	r	Zr	n	Zj			
2	0.28	0.29	60	2.171952		(Sum Zj)^2	630.456
3	0.4	0.42	50	2.904391		Zp^2	2.706025
4	0.35	0.37	60	2.75904			
5	0.45	0.48	56	3.528671		Fail Safe Number	222.9823
6	0.2	0.2	100	1.996684			
7	0.25	0.26	60	1.928324			
8	0.32	0.33	76	2.833594			
9	0.22	0.22	80	1.962574			
10	0.33	0.34	50	2.350312			
11	0.34	0.35	60	2.67334			

Computationally, the process involved including the elements of the formula

$$X = \frac{\left(\sum Z_j \right)^2}{z_p^2} - N_L,$$

where

$$Z_j = Z_{rj} \sqrt{n_j - 3},$$

Z_{rj} is Fisher's Z-transformed correlation coefficient for the relationship between the two variables of interest for sample j,

Fisher's Z transformation is $Z_r = \frac{1}{2} \ln \left(\frac{1+r}{1-r} \right)$,

N_j is the sample size for sample j,

z_p^2 is a one-tailed value from the standard normal curve used for alpha risk (typically 1.645^2), and

N_L is the number of analysis units.

(Continued)

Table 12.2 (Continued)

In this case, the formula (with computations rounded to the nearest thousandth) becomes

$$X = \frac{\begin{array}{l}([.29 * \sqrt{60-3}] + [.42 * \sqrt{50-3}] + [.37 * \sqrt{60-3}] + [.48 * \sqrt{56-3}] \\ + [.2 * \sqrt{100-3}] + [.26 * \sqrt{60-3}] + [.33 * \sqrt{76-3}] \\ + [.22 * \sqrt{80-3}] + [.34 * \sqrt{50-3}] + [.35 * \sqrt{60-3}])^2\end{array}}{1.645^2} - 10$$

$$= \frac{25.10888^2}{2.706025} - 10 = \frac{630.456}{2.706025} - 10 = 232.9823 - 10 = 222.9823 \approx 223 \text{ studies.}$$

The standard interpretation guide holds that if the fail-safe number is at least 5K + 10 (which is [5 * 10] + 10 = 60 in this case), the researcher is relatively safe in concluding that the number of conflicting studies is so large that it may continue to be reasonable to assume that the "file drawer problem" is not a substantial difficulty.

The fail-safe number has not been without criticism. For instance, fail-safe numbers seem to assume that the unpublished studies in the "file drawer" are relatively unbiased when, of course, there is no proof of this claim. Furthermore, different approaches to computing fail-safe numbers give different results. Moreover, "if studies go unlocated because they reported results contrary to those in located studies, the 'true' fail-safe number is smaller than that based on an average effect of zero in unlocated studies" (Møller & Jennions, 2001, p. 584). Furthermore, Rosenberg (2005) observed that using a weighting system (particularly when using the inverse variance weight) improves the quality of the estimate of a fail-safe number and reduces perceived upward bias in the number of estimated "file drawer" studies.

- *Direct Computation of Publication Bias.* Assuming that a bias exists in favor of publishing research that reports statistically significant relationships, more small-sample studies with positive effects (whether significant or not) should have been published than small-sample "studies showing a negligible or negative effect" (Wolpert & Mengersen, 2004, p. 33). Hence, meta-analysts suspecting publication bias might expect effect sizes to decrease as sample sizes increase. Begg and Mazumdar (1994) developed a nonparametric rank-order correlation test between effect sizes and sample sizes. This method is "fairly powerful for large meta-analyses with 75 studies, but only moderately so with 25 studies, requiring caution of interpretation" (Møller & Jennions, 2001, p. 584).

Another alternative involves computing publication bias by taking into account that studies with large samples also have high t ratios. Card and Krueger (1995) suggest computing a regression coefficient between the logarithm of the absolute value of t on the logarithm of the square root of the degrees of freedom. "This suggests a straightforward test for publication bias, namely, estimate the said regression and examine the size of the coefficient" (Görg & Strobl, 2001, p. 732). If there were no publication bias, no significant relationship would be found between the standard error and the coefficient in question. "But if publication bias is present, a t ratio will have to exceed (roughly) 2 in absolute value, in which case there may be a positive relationship between the coefficient and the standard error (since t = b/SE)" (Görg & Strobl, 2001, p. 733).

- *Trim and Fill Methods.* These methods have received positive attention in recent years (Duvall & Tweedie, 2000a, 2000b). This approach combines both graphic and statistical tools to account for publication bias. Researchers start with a funnel plot of the natural logarithm of the sample size against the effect size. The method assumes that there is a symmetrical distribution of effect sizes around a true value. This distribution forms a funnel plot, such as found in the figure to the right.

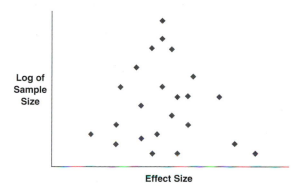

  The funnel suggests that there is much greater variability in effect sizes when sample sizes are small than when the sample sizes grow. Thus, the trim and fill approach starts by trimming or removing the extreme positive studies and rechecking for symmetry around the new average effect size. The process is repeated until the average stabilizes around a presumed "true" value. Then, estimates of the unpublished extreme negative effect sizes are added into the collection of studies by using a "mirror image" of the trimmed extreme positive effect sizes (by computing the absolute differences of the trimmed studies from the true mean and subtracting these absolute differences from the true mean). As might be expected, the trim and fill method results in finding that the number of missing studies needed to reverse the reported effects is smaller than the fail-safe number.

- *Other Methods.* Scholars continue to investigate ways to deal with the file drawer effect. Givens et al. (1997) advance a way to estimate excluded studies by using a model based on Bayesian statistics. Copas (1998) suggests a "sensitivity analysis" based on a regression analysis. Others have reviewed using weighted distribution theory and have suggested constructing linear models to study the matter directly (Song, Eastwood, Gilbody, Duley, & Sutton, 2000, esp. pp. 46–47).

Step 2: Compute Relationship Sizes

To compare effects from different studies, researchers must decide what data to examine. These choices will be considered next.

Selecting a Common Measure

In routine application of meta-analyses in communication studies, there are three options. Yet, the field's researchers have shown a strong preference.

Comparisons of significance level effects are possible, though they are rare in communication research. The reason is that significance testing reveals how unlikely a set of results is to have occurred from random sampling error. But with increasing sample sizes, sampling error automatically is reduced. So, testing whether there were statistically significant differences with the sort of large samples collected from a series of studies is rarely instructive. Random sampling error may be shown to be an unlikely explanation for the observed effect sizes, but with the kinds of samples collected in meta-analyses, such a fact is almost true by definition. If researchers wish to use such a method, they need to translate their test statistics into z scores that may be the basis of further analysis. Table 12.3 shows the formulae that may be used for this effort.

Table 12.3   Transformation of Significance Tests Into z Scores

Test Statistic	Formula for Translating Test Statistics
t	$$z = \sqrt{df * \log\left(1 + \frac{t^2}{df}\right)} * \sqrt{1 - \frac{t^2}{df}}$$
$F_{(1,\ df)}$ (one degree of freedom in the numerator)	$$z = \sqrt{df * \log\left(1 + \frac{F}{df}\right)} * \sqrt{1 - \frac{F}{df}}$$
$\chi^2_{df=1}$ (one degree of freedom)	$$Z = \sqrt{\chi^2}$$
r	$$z = \sqrt{df * \log\left(1 + \frac{\left[\frac{r^2(n-2)}{1-r^2}\right]}{df}\right)} * \sqrt{1 - \frac{\left[\frac{r^2(n-2)}{1-r^2}\right]}{df}}$$
Because $t = \dfrac{r\sqrt{n-2}}{\sqrt{1-r^2}}$, then	$$t^2 = \frac{r^2(n-2)}{1-r^2}$$

Comparisons of group differences in means may be completed by transforming mean differences. As Table 12.4 shows, there are different ways to compute this difference. One might imagine that researchers just divide a difference by the appropriate standard deviation term. Unfortunately, this approach creates a biased estimator of the population difference. Hence, it is useful to correct this difference by use of Hedges's *d*. The resulting difference between means is expressed as a difference in standard deviation units, so a *d* of +1.0 tells the researcher that the difference between the experimental and control mean is equal to one full standard deviation unit.

Researchers may face situations when they need to contrast two means from a design including more than two conditions. Thus, contrasts must be completed for the key comparison.[3] For mixed-effects or within-subjects models, the formula for the difference is

$$g = \frac{\overline{X}_e - \overline{X}_c}{s_{e-c}}.$$

---

[3]With more than two means, the use of contrasts is recommended to tease out the differences in means that should be contrasted (DeCoster, 2005, p. 16) using the formula $L = \sum c_j \overline{X}_j$. The pooled standard error is

$$s_p = \sqrt{\frac{\sum s_j^2 c_j^2 (n_j - 1)}{\sum c_j^2 (n_j - 1)}}.$$

To calculate the effect size as g, the formula is $g = \dfrac{L}{s_p}.$

Table 12.4   Transformation of Statistical Information Into Standardized Differences

Test Statistic	Formula for Translating Test Statistics	Comments
Cohen's Standardized Mean Differences	$g = \dfrac{\overline{X}_e - \overline{X}_c}{s_p}$, where $\overline{X}_e$ is the mean of the experimental group, $\overline{X}_c$ is the mean of the control group, and s_p is the pooled standard deviation $s_p = \sqrt{\dfrac{s_e^2\,(n_e - 1) + s_c^2\,(n_c - 1)}{n_e + n_c - 2}}$	• Expresses differences as units from a distribution with a mean difference of zero and a standard deviation of 1 • g is a biased estimator of population differences, especially with small sample sizes • The pooled standard deviation may be estimated from $\sqrt{\text{Mean Square Error}}$ in an analysis of variance
Hedges's d	$d = g * \left(1 - \dfrac{3}{(4 * [n_e + n_c]) - 9}\right)$, where n_e is the number of events in the experimental group and n_c is the number of events in the comparison group	• Adjustment of g to create an unbiased estimator of population differences
t	$g = t * \sqrt{\dfrac{1}{n_e} + \dfrac{1}{n_c}}$	• Used as a computational alternative to Cohen's g formula above
$F_{(1,\,df)}$ (one degree of freedom in the numerator)	$g = \sqrt{\dfrac{F\,(n_e + n_c)}{n_e * n_c}}$	• Used for the fixed-effects ANOVA
$\chi^2_{df=1}$ (one degree of freedom)	$g = \sqrt{\dfrac{\chi^2(n_e + n_c)}{n_e n_c}}$	
z score differences	$g = z * \sqrt{\dfrac{n_e + n_c}{n_e n_c}}$	
r	$g = \sqrt{\dfrac{4r^2}{1 - r^2}}$	

To identify the standard error of the contrast (s_{e-c}), researchers start with mean square error terms, but in a mixed-effects design, there are different mean square error terms to be used. Hence, the researcher needs to find the appropriate mean square error value, which then may be used to compute the standard error of the contrast using the formula $s_{e-c} = \sqrt{2 * \text{MEAN SQUARE}_{\text{WITHIN ERROR}}}.$

Comparisons of correlations are the most popular approaches for meta-analysts in communication studies. Because effect sizes are regularly reported in today's research journals, they are easily obtained. Even so, it is helpful to recognize that sample correlations are not unbiased estimators of population correlations (ρ). In fact, sample correlations tend to be slightly higher than population correlations. Hence, to correct for this bias, the following formula may be used:

$$G_{(r)} = r + \frac{r(1 - r^2)}{2(n - 3)}.$$

If researchers wish to complete meta-analyses with unbiased correlations, the correction $G_{(r)}$ should be used. There are, of course, different ways to identify correlations from different sorts of data. Many of these options are shown in Table 12.5.

The sampling distribution of a correlation coefficient is somewhat skewed, especially when the population correlation is large. Therefore, it is conventional in meta-analysis to convert correlations to z scores using Fisher's transformation:

$$Z_r = .5 * \ln\left(\frac{1 + r}{1 - r}\right).$$

The term *ln* represents the natural logarithm function. After the transformations, the meta-analytic calculations are performed. In the case of correlations corrected to create unbiased estimators of population correlations and/or corrected for measurement attenuation, Fisher's Z transformation should be made after these corrections have been made.

Weighting Observed Relationships for Sample Size

Because studies with increased sample sizes have reduced sampling error, most researchers find it sensible to "weight" their results according to the sizes of the samples used in individual studies. But there is an argument that can be made against giving weight to studies based on sample sizes. First, weighting studies may give unintended preferences to some research approaches over others (Mullen & Miller, 1991, p. 442). Because different studies may be viewed as a selection from all the possible studies that could be completed, some argue that the fairest approach should use an unweighted analysis. So, what are researchers to do? One popular method has involved reporting the results of both weighted and unweighted results, but there is another way to make this decision. There is a difference in the interpretation of statistics with each method. "Weighted analyses provide information about the covariation of conditions by subject, while unweighted analyses provide information about the covariation of conditions by study" (DeCoster, 2005, p. 37). So, if the researcher is most interested in drawing conclusions about groups of individuals in samples, the weighted analysis is preferred. If the researcher wishes to emphasize comparisons among studies and their traditions, the unweighted analysis is invited.

Table 12.5   Transformation of Statistical Information Into Correlations

Test Statistic	Formula for Translating Test Statistics
Adjustment for bias in sample correlations	$G_{(r)} = r + \dfrac{r(1 - r^2)}{2(n - 3)},$ where n is the number of events in the sample and r is the sample correlation
t	$r = \sqrt{\dfrac{t^2}{t^2 + n_e + n_c - 2}},$ where n_e is the number of events in the experimental group and n_c is the number of events in the comparison group
$F_{(1, df)}$ (one degree of freedom in the numerator)	$r = \sqrt{\dfrac{F}{F + n_e + n_c - 2}},$ where F is the F ratio from the chief independent variable of interest, n_e is the number of events in the experimental group, and n_c is the number of events in the comparison group
Two-way analysis of variance*	$r = \sqrt{\dfrac{F_a * d.f._a}{(F_a * d.f._a) + (F_b * d.f._b) + (F_{ab} * d.f._{ab}) + d.f._e}},$ where F_a is the main effect F ratio from the chief independent variable, $d.f._a$ is the number of degrees of freedom from the chief independent variable, F_b is the F ratio from the second independent variable in the study, $d.f._b$ is the number of degrees of freedom from the second independent variable in the study, F_{ab} is the F ratio from the interaction of the independent variables in the study, $d.f._{ab}$ is the number of degrees of freedom from the interaction of the independent variables in the study, and $d.f._e$ is the number of degrees of freedom from the error term in the two-way analysis of variance
$\chi^2_{df=1}$ (one degree of freedom)	$r = \sqrt{\dfrac{\chi^2}{n}},$ where n is the number of events in the study
z	$r = \sqrt{\dfrac{z^2}{n}},$ where n is the number of events in the study
d (when sample sizes are unequal)	$r = \sqrt{\dfrac{d^2}{d^2 + \frac{1}{pq}}},$ where $p = \dfrac{n_e}{n_e + n_c}$ and $q = 1 - p$; n_e is the number of events in the experimental group; and n_c is the number of events in the comparison group
d (when sample sizes are equal)	$r = \sqrt{\dfrac{d^2}{d^2 + 4}}$
g	$r = \sqrt{\dfrac{g^2 n_e n_c}{g^2 n_e n_c + ([n_e + n_c] * [n_e + n_c - 2])}}$

*Compare with η (eta) (see Chapter 8).

> ### Special Discussion 12.1
>
> Correcting for Attenuation in Measurement
>
> Measurement imperfections produce difficulties in estimating population characteristics accurately. The use of corrections for attenuation has some advantages. First, the distribution of relationships tends toward normality when unreliability in measurement is removed as another source of variation. Second, the actual correlation between variables is arbitrarily reduced by the imperfections in measurement. Hence, any associations with other theoretically important variables may go undetected simply due to limitations of measurement.
>
> Fortunately, a formula exists to correct a correlation for attenuation:
>
> $$\hat{r}_{xy} = \frac{r_{xy}}{\sqrt{r_x}\sqrt{r_y}}.$$
>
> In this treatment, $\hat{r}_{xy}$ is the correlation between variables x and y after correction for attenuation. In addition, r_{xy} is the observed correlation between variables x and y. The reliability of the measurement for independent variable x is identified as $\sqrt{r_x}$. Reliability for measurement of the dependent variable y is symbolized as $\sqrt{r_y}$. To find reliability of measures, researchers need only look at such measures as Cronbach's coefficient alpha or reports of split-half reliability. In the case of experimental variables where the variables are manipulated, rather than measured, researchers regularly presume that no measurement error was involved and assign a reliability coefficient of 1.0.
>
> It should be mentioned that some researchers believe that corrections for attenuation are problematic. First, they believe that such corrections may introduce biases that artificially benefit the researcher. Second, because the correction for attenuation causes the correlation to jump more for research involving low-reliability measures than for research involving high-reliability ones, some researchers suspect that it may reward the use of relatively weak measurement. Finally, it should be mentioned that statistical inference tools for correlations corrected for attenuation do not yet exist, and, hence, researchers still find it necessary to report results for both corrected and uncorrected correlations.

Computing Average Effect Sizes

Once the researcher has decided how to measure effects and whether to weight studies by sample sizes, effect sizes may be computed. As Table 12.6 shows, computing mean effect sizes depends on the initial type of measurement the authors use. These methods are similar in many ways because they use Fisher's Z transformation (Z_{Fisher}). In some cases, analyses are completed and then the results are transformed back to other "untransformed" scores for interpretation. For instance, researchers comparing standardized differences often transform their coefficients into equivalent correlations to complete analyses, but for interpretations they transform the average Z_{Fisher} back to equivalent difference scores.

Because effect sizes from large samples carry less sampling error than effect sizes based on small samples, researchers usually (but not universally) consider it helpful to compute a mean effect size. It often is helpful to give some weight to different studies based on their sample sizes. A simple way is to attach a weight to each effect size based on each study's sample size. A generally preferred approach involves use the inverse variance weight

Table 12.6   Computation of Mean Effects

Combined Measures	Weighted Means	Unweighted Means
Probabilities from significance levels	$$\bar{z} = \frac{\sum w_j z_j}{\sqrt{\sum w_j^2}}$$	$$\bar{z} = \frac{\sum z_j}{J}$$

where

$\bar{z}$ is the mean of the z values of one-tailed significance tests (e.g., $p = .05$ has a corresponding z value of 1.645),

w_j is the sample size weight for study j, and

J is the number of studies

| Standardized differences or correlations (Note: For these analyses, standardized differences are expressed as correlations using the appropriate formula from Table 12.4) | $$\bar{Z}_{\text{Fisher}} = \frac{\sum w_j Z_{\text{Fisher}\,j}}{\sum w_j}$$ | $$\bar{Z}_{\text{Fisher}} = \frac{\sum Z_{\text{Fisher}\,j}}{J}$$ |

where

$\bar{Z}_{\text{Fisher}}$ is the mean of the Z_{Fisher} transformations of the difference values (d or g if standardized differences; r or $G_{(r)}$ if expressed as correlations),

w_j is the sample size weight for study j,

Zz_{Fisher} is the z transformation of the difference values transformations (d or g if standardized differences, r or $G_{(r)}$ if expressed as correlations) from study j, and

J is the number of studies

NOTE: There are two weighting systems.

- The weighting by sample size involves setting w_j to the individual study sample size.
- The inverse variance weight (the generally preferred method) involves setting w_j to individual study sample size minus 3.

(Sánchez-Meca & Marín-Martínez, 1998), a method that gives increasing weight to effect sizes that are most likely to be estimated reliably. The standard error of the effect size is used to compute this degree of precision. As Table 12.6 indicates, the inverse variance weight method involves using the following weight:

$$w = \frac{1}{se^2}.$$

Because the standard error of the effect for the Z-transformed correlation coefficient is

$$se = \sqrt{\frac{1}{n-3}},$$

the weight becomes

$$w = \frac{1}{\left(\frac{1}{n-3}\right)},$$

which is equivalent to $w_j = n_j - 3$, the individual study sample size minus 3.[4]

Interpreting Effect Sizes

Meta-analysts often look for ways to interpret average effect sizes. Most scholars agree that theory and past research are the soundest sources of guidance. For instance, if other meta-analyses have been completed in the researcher's area, it makes sense to contrast those results with the newly completed one. It is also the case that there have been some interpretive aids developed over the years. For instance, J. Cohen (1992) suggests that effects may be interpreted as "small," "medium," or "large." For correlations, a minimum correlation of .10 is considered small, .30 is considered medium, and .50 is considered large. For standardized differences, a minimum of .2 is small, .5 is medium, and .8 is large. Such popular guidelines, combined with the advice previously given in this book (see Table 5.1's guidelines for interpreting correlations of at least .80 as "highly dependable," .60–.79 as "moderate to marked," .40–.59 as "fair," .20–.39 as "slight," and any correlation below .2 as a "negligible or chance relationship"), give the meta-analyst much advice to interpret the practical meaning of effects.

Sometimes, as mentioned in Special Discussion 5.1 in Chapter 5 ("Misleading Correlation Magnitudes and the Binomial Effect Size"), even modest effect sizes can be meaningful. The "binomial effect size display" is useful to make such interpretations. Researchers may wish to look to this interpretive aid to understand the full meaning of their results.

Coding Studies for Qualitative Differences

Sometimes meta-analysis is criticized either for failing to recognize the different quality of studies or for failing to account for the differences in different designs. In fact, one of the

---

[4]The formula for the weight is

$$w_j = \frac{1}{\left(\frac{1}{n_j-3}\right)}.$$

Of course,

$$1 \div \frac{1}{n_j - 3}$$

is equal to

$$1 * \frac{n_j - 3}{1},$$

which is $n_j - 3$.

most intriguing of elements in meta-analyses, coding for qualitative differences, allows exactly for such assessments. Researchers must code the ways that studies differ. Though the specific categories vary from one research topic to another, there are some general categories that must be coded. These categories include the following.

Categories for Coding Differences

- *Year of Study.* Some researchers suspect that the early studies in a field tend to be the most primitive. These studies might find different sorts of effects than might be observed in the studies completed as a research area matures. Furthermore, groups of subjects from one era might not reflect the general trend across time. By comparing the years of publication, these suspicions may be tested directly.
- *Number of Independent Variables in Each Study.* When computing effect sizes, there can only be 100% of the variance. But if there are many independent variables, the contribution made by the chief independent variable of interest to the meta-analyst may be smaller than it would be in a study with few independent variables. To check if increasing the number of independent variables has whittled down the effect size of a particular variable, the researcher probably should code these differences for later comparisons.
- *Field or Laboratory Studies.* Because field studies rarely control for many naturally occurring variables, differences in effects might be expected between laboratory and field studies.

Some rating systems require researchers to collect a group of experts (rarely more than five or six) who complete some coding of study qualities. It is important for the researchers to take time to train the expert coders on the use of check sheets and coding devices. Then comparisons across independent ratings may be checked for reliability. Though one cannot state that the results of such ratings are objective, they are **intersubjective** in that they are matters where common agreement exists among expert thinking despite admittedly different perspectives on many issues. Coding systems may be developed either as categories or—most commonly when using expert raters—on some continuous rating scale. Some common elements for group coding include the following.

- *Ratings of Study Quality.* Meta-analysts often find a group of scholars who have an understanding of a research area and ask them to rate the general quality of studies on some scale (such as a 0-to-10 scale with 0 indicating no real quality to the work and 10 indicating the highest possible quality). In addition to obtaining general ratings, researchers might have experts complete a rating scale based on a category system for rating the merit of research and scholarly articles (see Isaac & Michael, 1981, pp. 220–225). The reliability of codings then may be assessed by using such a device as Cohen's kappa or Scott's pi.
- *Strength of Independent Variable Manipulations.* Sometimes studies are criticized for using experimental variables that are weaker than those found in other settings. Using even a subjective rating scale, it is possible for researchers to examine the merits of such criticism.
- *Moderator Variables.* Meta-analysts find that searching for moderator variables makes a great difference in interpreting results from different collections of studies. To develop lists of moderators, researchers look at differences in studies based on methods (such as differences in samples, procedures, and use of specific control variables), basic design (experiments, surveys, etc.), and theoretic differences.

Checking Reliability of Coding

One might imagine that the obvious way to check reliability is to compare different sets of ratings. For measures on continuous variables (such as 0-to-10 scales used to rate study quality), the coefficient of concordance (W) could be used to check on ratings. Table 12.7 shows how such a computation is made. For instance, in the data in Table 12.7, four raters provided evaluations of the quality of 10 studies. The coefficient of concordance was .913, indicating high reliability among the ratings.[5]

Table 12.7

	Study 1	Study 2	Study 3	Study 4	Study 5	Study 6	Study 7	Study 8	Study 9	Study 10
Rater 1	4	4	5	5	6	6	7	8	9	9
Rater 2	5	5	5	6	7	6	8	9	8	9
Rater 3	6	6	6	5	7	7	8	9	9	8
Rater 4	5	6	6	6	6	7	7	8	8	9

[5]There is a way to use coefficient alpha to compute reliability ratings of continuous measures. This method is a variation of the typical pattern. Instead of asking if there is consistency among the ratings of items by raters, the researcher asks if there is consistency among the raters, with each study treated as a separate case. When using SPSS, the raters' assessments for the different studies may be entered in a fashion such as found in the table below.

	Rater 1	Rater 2	Rater 3	Rater 4
Study 1	4	5	6	5
Study 2	4	5	6	6
Study 3	5	5	6	6
Study 4	5	6	5	6
Study 5	6	7	7	6
Study 6	6	6	7	7
Study 7	7	8	8	7
Study 8	8	9	9	8
Study 9	9	8	9	8
Study 10	9	9	8	9

As the resulting output reveals, a coefficient alpha of .96 is reported. The "N of items" is the number of raters, rather than studies. The output is shown below.

```
Item-total Statistics

                  Scale        Scale      Corrected
                  Mean         Variance   Item-           Alpha
                  if Item      if Item    Total           if Item
                  Deleted      Deleted    Correlation     Deleted

     RATER1       20.7000      16.0111      .9689          .9368
     RATER2       20.2000      18.6222      .9286          .9397
     RATER3       19.9000      21.2111      .8820          .9555
     RATER4       20.2000      22.1778      .9098          .9544


Reliability Coefficients

N of Cases =      10.0              N of Items =   4

Alpha =      .9602
```

For ratings of categorical variables, the measure of intercoder reliability employs such measures as Scott's pi. As noted in Chapter 6, simply taking the number of times raters agree is misleading because the number of categories and the number of times a category is used can artificially affect the reliability coefficients. Scott's pi controls for both these difficulties. The computational formula for Scott's pi is found in Table 6.1.

Conducting the Analysis

The formal meta-analysis steps involve combining effect sizes, assessing variability, and completing any focused comparisons. Each step will be considered in turn.

Combining Effect Sizes

After reporting the weighted and unweighted mean effect sizes (as differences in either effects or correlations), researchers must decide if they wish to report a significance test for the average effect sizes. For instance, for a simple r, the formula for t often is used:

$$t = \frac{r\sqrt{n-2}}{\sqrt{1-r^2}}.$$

This formula would permit the researchers (after transforming $\bar{Z}_{\text{Fisher}}$ back into its equivalent r)[6] to know if the average effect size is significantly different from zero. Though it is common for researchers to report an omnibus significance test for the difference between the average correlation and zero, not much information is supplied by such a test. The large sample sizes involved in summing sample sizes from all the studies virtually ensure that any average effect size will be statistically significant. Because significance testing reveals only how unlikely an observed relationship is to be found as a result of random sampling error, and because sampling error is reduced with large sample sizes, there is little doubt that collecting large samples across studies usually will reveal "statistical significance," even when such a claim reveals little about the size of differences (Kotiaho & Tomkins, 2002). Furthermore, a vital criticism has been made that the assumptions underlying the use of significance testing for a primary statistic may not be satisfied by collections of studies (see Hedges & Olkin, 1985; Mullen, 1989; Rosenthal, 1991; Strube & Hartmann, 1983).

---

[6]To transform Fisher's Z back to r, the formula is

$$r = \frac{e^{2Z_{\text{Fisher}}} - 1}{e^{2Z_{\text{Fisher}}} + 1},$$

where e is the natural logarithm.

Interpreting the average effect size based on some criterion (such as Cohen's guidelines of small, medium, and large effects) usually reveals the important information for the researcher. Nevertheless, it is common for a significance test of the average effect size to be reported using F or t.

Reporting results is aided by the use of a chart, such as a stem-and-leaf display. In the study shown in Table 12.8, the plot of Fisher's Z scores (Z_r in the table) would show a distribution as follows.

Table 12.8

.5	
.4	2 9
.3	3 4 5 7
.2	0 2 6 9
.1	
.0	

The first column shows the first digit of the Z score. As can be seen, there were no effects with Z scores beginning with .0, .1, or .5. The distribution of scores was relatively compact. The median effect was between .33 and .34 (or .345). The researcher also might find it helpful to report such characteristics of distributions as skew (.30 in this case) and kurtosis (−.35 in this case).

Researchers also are invited to examine the study effects to identify any outliers that are part of different populations of studies. These outliers may be caused by any number of exceptional circumstances ranging from peculiar samples to nonstandard methods. If outliers can be explained, the studies may be excluded because, by definition, they are not from the same population of events as the rest of the studies. If no argument can be made to explain the outlier, the researcher cannot automatically exclude it.

Assessing Variability

In addition to looking at the average study effects, the meta-analyst also must look at dispersion of effects around the mean. If the dispersion is relatively normal and free of outliers, researchers have some reason to believe that the collection shows relative consistency, reflective of studies from one population. But if the dispersion shows great variability, the researcher knows that the studies reflect more than random variation around a mean. In short, great diversity indicates that there are differences between study effects as a result of at least one moderator variable.

To investigate whether the dispersion of study effects is greater than would have been expected at random, a **diffuse comparison test** may be computed.

- To complete a diffuse comparison of significance levels, the following formula is used:

$$\chi^2_{n-1} = \sum (Z_j - \overline{Z})^2,$$

where

Z_j is the one-sided Z score that corresponds to the significance test of study j,

$\overline{Z}$ is the mean Z score, and

n is the number of significance tests assessed in the meta-analysis.

If the test statistic is greater than the critical value of the chi-square distribution with $n - 1$ degrees of freedom, the null hypothesis that the study effects are homogeneous is rejected. If the test statistic does not fall in the critical region of the chi-square distribution, the assumption that the study effects are not significantly different from each other continues to hold.

- To complete a diffuse comparison of effect sizes expressed as Fisher's Z scores based either on d or r coefficients, the following formula is used:

$$\chi^2_{n-1} = \sum ([n_j - 3] * [Z_{\text{Fisher}j} - \overline{Z}_{\text{Fisher}}])^2,$$

where

n is the number of events in study j,

$Z_{\text{Fisher}j}$ is the Fisher Z for the effect from study j, and

$\overline{Z}_{\text{Fisher}}$ is the mean Fisher Z score.

An example of computing this test statistic may be found in Table 12.9 on page 338.

If either of these test statistics is statistically significant, the researcher knows that the effect sizes are inconsistent in the studies. This evidence tells the researcher that some studies are systematically different from the others. Thus, the researcher knows that at least two universes of study effects have been mixed in the data set, even thought they are fundamentally different from each other in some way. But what makes them different universes of effects? The search for the appropriate moderators must be included. This stage of the inquiry leads to completion of **focused comparisons**. Put another way, statistically significant diffuse comparisons suggest the presence of one or more moderating variables. Thus, specific focused comparisons need to be completed with each of the candidates as a significant moderator variable. Then, if the diffuse comparison tests of homogeneous effect sizes still are significant when effects are grouped according to the moderator variable, the researchers may eliminate that moderator from the list of candidates and move the search to another possible moderator. If researchers have hypothesized differences in effects from different groups of

Table 12.9 Computing the Diffuse Comparison

From the study data in Table 12.1, a researcher was interested in determining if the effect sizes were significantly different. Though these data are from effects sizes expressed as correlations, the same formula may be applied to situations in which the effects are expressed as differences that are transformed into Fisher's Z transformations.

r	Z_{Fisher}	n
0.28	0.29	60
0.40	0.43	50
0.35	0.37	60
0.45	0.49	56
0.20	0.20	100
0.25	0.26	60
0.32	0.33	76
0.22	0.23	80
0.33	0.35	50
0.34	0.36	60

The formula for the diffuse comparison is

$$\chi^2_{n-1} = \sum([n_j - 3] * [Z_{Fisher_j} - \bar{Z}_{Fisher}])^2.$$

When applied to these data, the formula becomes

$$
\begin{aligned}
&= ([60 - 3] * [.29 - .33]^2) + ([50 - 3] * [.43 - .33]^2) + ([60 - 3] * [.37 - .33]^2) \\
&\quad + ([56 - 3] * [.49 - .33]^2) \\
&\quad + ([100 - 3] * [.20 - .33]^2) + ([60 - 3] * [.26 - .33]^2) + ([76 - 3] * [.33 - .33]^2) \\
&\quad + ([80 - 3] * [.22 - .33]^2) + ([50 - 3] * [.34 - .33]^2) + ([60 - 3] * [.35 - .33]^2) \\
&= (57 * [-.04]^2) + (47 * .09^2) + (57 * .04^2) + (53 * .16^2) + (97 * [-.13]^2) \\
&\quad + (57 * [-.07]^2) + (73 * .00^2) \\
&\quad + (77 * [-.11]^2) + (47 * .01^2) + (57 * .02^2) \\
&= .0912 + .3807 + .0912 + 1.3568 + 1.6393 + .2793 + .0000 + .9317 + .0047 + .02 \\
&= 4.7977.
\end{aligned}
$$

Because at the .05 significance level with nine degrees of freedom the critical chi-square value is 16.919, the test statistic is not statistically significant. Hence, the researcher concludes that the effect sizes are homogeneous.

studies, researchers should complete focused comparison tests even if the diffuse comparison test is statistically insignificant.

Conducting Focused Comparisons

Writers have given many pieces of advice on how to assess the potential role of moderator variables. Different suggestions emerge, depending on whether the data are continuous measures or categorical variables.

In the case of continuous measures, some (e.g., Mullen & Miller, 1991, p. 445) have suggested that researchers code moderator variables and correlate these ratings with the effect sizes. Because it is not appropriate to test for the statistical significance of such a correlation, researchers need to avoid claims of "statistically significant" influences or predictors when interpreting their results. Yet, looking at correlations may be instructive. In the example reviewed in Table 12.10, for instance, a group of expert raters provided information about the judged quality of the research. When the size of the effect was revealed by a correlation of −.602, the results showed that a moderate to marked, strong, or large inverse effect existed. The higher the study quality was, the smaller the effect it reported.

As with most things, a certain amount of common sense should be applied in examining moderator variables. In fact, researchers should report if there are high intercorrelations among moderator variables (DeCoster, 2005, p. 45). Rather than presuming that separate moderator variables make unique contributions, researchers must be poised to recognize that several moderators may be different faces of the same underlying influence.

An alternative approach involves using focused comparisons to make assessments of *differences* in group means. There are three general steps to conduct a focused comparison.

First, potential moderator variables must be coded to identify the presence of potentially important influences from other variables. The nature of this coding sometimes can be completed by a single researcher, but sometimes a team of raters must look at the research studies and determine their assessments.

Second, the comparison may be made of statistical significance or effect sizes expressed as correlations. For researchers interested in testing the nature of significance levels, the appropriate formula is

$$Z = \frac{\sum \lambda_j Z_j}{\sqrt{\sum \lambda_j^2}},$$

where λ_j (lambda) is the weight of the contrast associated with the comparison involving study j and Z_j is the Z value associated with the one-tailed significance test for the hypothesis test in study j. If the observed Z value falls within the critical region of the test (with alpha risk of .05, the one-tailed critical region of Z begins at 1.645 and the two-tailed critical region of Z begins at 1.96), a statistically significant difference may be claimed. A statistically significant difference means that the research has found that the exact probabilities associated with the hypothesis test differ by more than a random amount between the groups of the moderator variable candidate.

(Text continues on page 342)

Table 12.10 Focused Comparisons With Effect Sizes Transformed into Fisher's Z Scores

In the diffuse comparison based on data from Table 12.2, several moderator variables might be considered. In this case, the researcher has considered the date of publication, the number of independent variables in the study, and whether the study happened to be a field or laboratory study.

r	n	Direction of Relationship	date	N of IVs	quality	Field or Lab	Population r	Zr
0.28	60	"+"	1984	2	8	1	0.2822636	0.2901
0.4	50	"+"	1991	2	5	1	0.4035745	0.4279
0.35	60	"+"	1992	2	7	1	0.3526941	0.3685
0.45	56	"+"	1996	3	3	1	0.4533856	0.489
0.2	100	"+"	1999	4	7	2	0.2009897	0.2038
0.25	60	"+"	2000	2	7	2	0.2520559	0.2576
0.32	76	"+"	2001	3	8	1	0.3219673	0.3338
0.22	80	"+"	2001	2	6	2	0.2213594	0.2251
0.33	50	"+"	2002	2	4	1	0.3331283	0.3463
0.34	60	"+"	2003	3	7	1	0.3426377	0.3571
							Ave Z=	0.2837
				0 to 10	1 if lab, 2 if field			

These ratings could be obtained by looking at the studies directly. The rating of study quality, on the other hand, is the result of a jury of experts who provided their ratings on a 0-to-10 scale (with 10 indicating the best quality possible). Of course, this example is presented only to illustrate the method. Because the diffuse comparison failed to observe significant differences among the study effects, most researchers would not have felt obligated to complete focused comparisons.

The focused comparison uses weights derived from the linear trends of the table of orthogonal polynomials. This table's contrast coefficients are most often used when completing trend analysis (see Chapter 8), and the linear effect is most useful here. In fact, the researchers actually compute a trend analysis to explore the influence of mediating variables. A portion of Appendix C.9 is found here.

Number of Group Means	Type of Trend	Coefficients (c_j) for Each Mean												$\sum c_j^2$
		1	2	3	4	5	6	7	8	9	10	11	12	
3	Linear	−1	0	1										2
	Quadratic	1	−2	1										6
10	Linear	−9	−7	−5	−3	−1	1	3	5	7	9			330

Because there are 10 groups, researchers enlist the linear contrast coefficients (λ) to contrast 10 means. The researchers might wish to compare those studies that were completed early and those that were completed recently. To do so, they would arrange the studies according to dates of publication. Then the orthogonal polynomial weights would be included. In this case, there is a tie, with two articles published in the same year. Hence, researchers would take the mean of the two contrast coefficients involved in the "tie" and assign both of them to the weights of the study effects. In this case, the seventh- and eighth-ranked studies would have taken on the coefficients of +3 and +5. Because there is no way to decide which gets preference, the average of the two coefficients (+4) is applied to each. The contrast (carrying out computations to the fourth decimal place) involves the formula

$$Z = \frac{\sum \lambda_j Z_{\text{Fisher}_j}}{\sqrt{\sum \frac{\lambda_j^2}{n_j - 3}}}$$

$$\sum \lambda_j Z_{\text{Fisher}_j} = (-9 * .2901) + (-7 * .4279) + (-3 * .489) + (-1 * .2038) + (1 * .2576)$$

$$+ (4 * .3338) + (4 * .2251) + (7 * .3463) + (9 * .3571) = -.9883$$

$$\sqrt{\sum \frac{\lambda_j^2}{n_j - 3}} = \sqrt{\begin{array}{c} \dfrac{-9^2}{60 - 3} + \dfrac{-7^2}{50 - 3} + \dfrac{-5^2}{60 - 3} + \dfrac{-3^2}{56 - 3} + \dfrac{-1^2}{100 - 3} + \dfrac{1^2}{60 - 3} + \dfrac{4^2}{76 - 3} \\[3mm] + \dfrac{4^2}{80 - 3} + \dfrac{7^2}{50 - 3} + \dfrac{9^2}{60 - 3} \end{array}}$$

$$= \sqrt{\frac{81}{57} + \frac{49}{47} + \frac{25}{57} + \frac{9}{53} + \frac{1}{97} + \frac{1}{57} + \frac{16}{73} + \frac{16}{77} + \frac{49}{47} + \frac{81}{57}}$$

$$= \sqrt{5.9906} = 2.4476$$

$$Z = \frac{\sum \lambda_j Z_{\text{Fisher}_j}}{\sqrt{\sum \frac{\lambda_j^2}{n_j - 3}}} = \frac{-.9883}{2.4476} = -.4038.$$

The negative sign of the coefficient indicates that the early studies tended to have greater effect sizes than the recent studies. Because the Z value does not fall into the critical region of Z (beginning at −1.645 for a one-tailed test or −1.96 for a two-tailed test), the trend is not statistically significant. Hence, the null hypothesis that the study effect sizes showed no decline over the years could not be rejected.

The difference between field studies and laboratory studies was instructive here. The formula produced a Z of 1.7084. For a one-tailed test in which the researcher hypothesized that laboratory studies produced greater effects than field studies, this result would be statistically significant. For a two-tailed test, however, it would not be statistically significant. Following a statistically significant focused comparison test, researchers follow-up by completing diffuse comparisons to see if each of the groups of studies had homogeneous differences. In this case, for the laboratory studies, the results were not statistically significant ($\chi^2 = 2.4406$, *d.f.* = 6, critical value = 12.592, $p > .05$). For the field studies the diffuse test also was not statistically significant ($\chi^2 = .1043$, *d.f.* = 2, critical value = 5.991, $p > .05$). Hence, it seems that any heterogeneity eliminated by distinguishing the field and laboratory studies results in homogeneous effect sizes in each category. If researchers, however, had found other significant differences in the diffuse test, it would indicate that the search for moderator variables had not yet been completely successful.

For effect sizes, the formula for a focused comparison is

$$Z = \frac{\sum \lambda_j Z_{\text{Fisher}\,j}}{\sqrt{\sum \frac{\lambda_j^2}{n_j - 3}}},$$

where

λ_j is the weight of the contrast associated with the comparison involving study j,

$Z_{\text{Fisher}\,j}$ is the Fisher's Z transformation of the value associated with the effect size found in study j, and

n_j is the number of events in study j.

Table 12.10 shows an example of computing the focused comparison test.

USING COMPUTER TECHNIQUES TO PERFORM META-ANALYSIS

Computerized meta-analysis has been dominated by spreadsheets and dedicated programs. At the present time, SPSS does not include subroutines for meta-analysis, though this situation may change with future versions.

Dedicated Tools for Completing Meta-Analyses

Several programs for completing meta-analyses are available. Some are marketed commercially, and others are supported by specific universities and organizations. Freeware tools such as EasyMA and META are DOS-based programs. Of the two, META is the more comprehensive and the more popular. With this program, researchers may choose to analyze exact probabilities (p values), effect sizes (d scores), or relationship effect sizes (r). For links to download these programs, you may go to the Web site for this chapter.

Commercial programs also are available but will not be reviewed here, though links to them may be found on the Web site for this chapter. These packages have many advantages, such as employing fairly standard data editors, but they also require learning a separate command language, and, it goes without saying, they require payment for use. Nevertheless, for a scholar who plans to do many meta-analyses, they are helpful tools to automate work.

Excel

Though Excel has no built-in meta-analysis functions, this spreadsheet contains elements that allow researchers to complete meta-analyses with a minimum of effort. To use Excel, researchers need to prepare the data and use macros.

Revisiting Criticism of Meta-Analysis

Many criticisms of meta-analysis seem illusory when the tool actually is understood. Some attacks on meta-analyses describe what happens in poor meta-analysis, rather than what occurs when the method is used properly. When one looks at the fundamental criticism of meta-analysis, much of it resides in the claim that the method lumps together studies that are not really comparable. As can be seen, however, coding potential moderator variables permits researchers to track differences in studies, rather than assuming that they are comparable in every way. Differences in study methods and theoretic orientations may be contrasted in focused comparisons.

One writer (DeCoster, 2005) has noted that many criticisms may be overcome by proper use of meta-analysis. Three of these charges and their answers follow.

Meta-analysis is a garbage-in, garbage-out procedure. . . . [S]ince the specific content of meta-analyses is always presented, it should be easier to detect poor meta-analyses than it would be to detect poor narrative reviews.

Meta-analysis cannot draw valid conclusions because only significant findings are published. Meta-analyses are actually less affected by this bias than narrative reviews, since a good meta-analysis actively seeks unpublished findings. Narrative reviews are rarely based on an exhaustive search of the literature.

Meta-analysis only deals with main effects. The effects of interactions are examined through moderator analyses. (DeCoster, 2005, p. 3)

Preparing Data for Meta-Analyses

In the spreadsheet that appears on the Web site for this chapter, data have been entered that may be replaced with your own. In this case, the data are expressed as the equivalent of *r*. Thus, if researchers are concerned with tests involving significance testing, other transformations must be used.

Each row of data represents a different case or study. Though this initial spreadsheet includes 10 studies in Rows 3 through 12, the researcher easily could insert additional cases. (For formatting purposes, studies are most easily inserted at Row 7 on the spreadsheet.) Column A includes the equivalent *r* for each study. These numbers are not corrected for attenuation, but if the researcher wishes to do so, the corrected correlations should be entered. The second column represents the number of events (not the degrees of freedom) in the study. Additional columns include matters that may or may not be used by the specific meta-analyst. For instance, in the example shown on the right, Column C includes the direction of the relationship.

Though a simple *r* reveals such directions, when relationships are computed from other measures

	A	B	C	D	E	F	G	H
1	r	n	Direction of	date	N of IVs	quality	Field	Populati
2			Relationship				or Lab	
3	0.28	60	"+"	1984	2	8	1	0.2822(
4	0.4	50	"+"	1991	2	5	1	0.4035
5	0.35	60	"+"	1992	2	7	1	0.3526(
6	0.45	56	"+"	1996	3	3	1	0.4533(
7	0.2	100	"+"	1999	4	7	2	0.2009(
8	0.25	60	"+"	2000	2	7	2	0.2520(
9	0.32	76	"+"	2001	3	8	1	0.3219(
10	0.22	80	"+"	2001	2	6	2	0.2213(
11	0.33	50	"+"	2002	2	4	1	0.3331
12	0.34	60	"+"	2003	3	7	1	0.3426(
13		1.06049005						
14						0 to 10	1 lab, 2 field	

(such as *eta* or *d*), the coefficient may represent the size of the relationship, but not its direction. The use of simple + or − signs may indicate this relationship. It also may be helpful to code the study date, the number of independent variables in a study, ratings of the quality of the study, and any other moderators that may have practical or theoretical significance. In this case, it was helpful to see if the studies were laboratory or field studies. In this example, if a study involved laboratory research, the number 1 was inserted into Column G. If the example were a field study, the number 2 was used. Other possible mediators may be inserted by adding columns to list codes. It might be mentioned that unlike examples used to illustrate computation in this chapter, the Excel template does not round initial numbers. Hence, the spreadsheet illustration here shows slightly different results from those reported elsewhere in this chapter.

Templates for Meta-Analyses

After data have been inserted, the assessment automatically computes the fail-safe number (based on effect sizes with an alpha risk of .05), weighted and unweighted effect sizes, and a diffuse test complete with a test of statistical significance.

	A	B	C	D	E	F	G	H	I	J	K	L	M
1	r	n	Direction of	date	N of IVs	quality	Field	Population r	Zr	Zj	unweighted Z(F)		
2			Relationship				or Lab						
3	0.28	60	"+"	1984	2	8	1	0.2822636	0.29	2.190508	0.287682072	(Sum Zj)^2	640.8729
4	0.4	50	"+"	1991	2	5	1	0.4035745	0.43	2.933614	0.42364893	Zp^2	2.706025
5	0.35	60	"+"	1992	2	7	1	0.3526941	0.37	2.782244	0.365443754		
6	0.45	56	"+"	1996	3	3	1	0.4533856	0.49	3.559637	0.484700279	Fail Safe Number	226.8319
7	0.2	100	"+"	1999	4	7	2	0.2009897	0.2	2.00684	0.202732554		
8	0.25	60	"+"	2000	2	7	2	0.2520559	0.26	1.94489	0.255412812	Mean Unweighted Effect Size	0.327184
9	0.32	76	"+"	2001	3	8	1	0.3219673	0.33	2.852334	0.331647109	Mean Weighted Effect Size	0.316406
10	0.22	80	"+"	2001	2	6	2	0.2213594	0.23	1.975114	0.223656109	Mean Raw Correlation Effect Size	0.314
11	0.33	50	"+"	2002	2	4	1	0.3331283	0.35	2.374408	0.342828254	Mean Raw Weighted Correlation	0.301871
12	0.34	60	"+"	2003	3	7	1	0.3426377	0.36	2.69588	0.354092529	Weighted Diffuse Test	4.689657
13			1.06049005								640.8729	degrees of freedom	9
14						0 to 10	1 lab, 2 field					Critical chi square value at p=.05	16.91896
15												p =	0.860479

After completing focused comparisons and correlations to determine the influence of moderator variables, the researcher may analyze each group of studies by deleting the remaining studies from the spreadsheet and checking diffuse test statistics. If the test statistic is statistically significant, the researcher knows that the differences in effect sizes have not yet been fully explained by the moderator. The combination of spreadsheet and dedicated meta-analysis programs can make the work of meta-analysis increasingly efficient for modern researchers.

Chapter 13

MULTIPLE REGRESSION CORRELATION

Multiple regression correlation is one of the most versatile tools for modern communication researchers. Multiple regression correlation actually is both an extension of correlation methods and a tool equivalent to analysis of variance. The use of this method is suitable for entire courses and books (and it has been the subject of both); this abbreviated treatment will consider how multiple regression correlation differs from simple bivariate correlation, the elements of multiple correlations, and the steps to be followed when completing a study that uses multiple regression correlation. The next chapter will examine follow-up methods to check the adequacy of models, use of hierarchical models, use of various other forms of variables (dummy and effects coding), and nonlinear effects.

CONTRASTING BIVARIATE CORRELATION AND MULTIPLE REGRESSION CORRELATION

A simple bivariate correlation deals with the association between two variables. **Multiple correlation** (sometimes called **multiple regression correlation** or **multiple linear correlation**) is an extension of linear correlation that permits researchers to correlate a set of independent (or **predictor**) variables with a single dependent (or **criterion**) variable. To symbolize this type of correlation, the researcher uses a capital R rather than a lowercase r. In a strict sense, **multiple regression** is a method to predict the value of a dependent variable "Y from two or more optimally combined independent variables" (Glass & Hopkins, 1984, p. 131). It uses the types of equations found in Special Discussion 13.1. On the other hand, **multiple correlation** refers to the overall association based on predictions from the optimal combination of more than one independent variable.

Several assumptions underlie multiple regression correlation.

- Dependent variable scores are normally distributed all along the line of best fit (also known as a line of regression). Thus, the assumption is made that residuals are normally distributed. Residuals are the differences between observed and predicted values of the dependent variable (given the multiple regression correlation model).
- There is a linear relationship between observed and predicted values of the dependent variable. This assumption also means that the residuals have a mean of zero.
- The variability of the residuals is the same through the entire range of values for the independent variables.

Multiple regression has some advantages over simple correlations. First, curvilinear effects can be tested by adding terms that are raised to different powers of the original variables. Second, interaction effects can be tested. Third, researchers may learn how much variation in the dependent variable is explained by one set of variables as opposed to another. An advantage that multiple regression correlation shares with simple linear correlation is that the relative importance of each variable can be identified. In addition, multiple regression correlation shares the assumptions of simple linear correlation.

Special Discussion 13.1

The Regression Model

The regression equation is designed to predict the individual scores of the data.

Conceptually, a **bivariate regression model** is an equation that identifies the relationship between an independent and a dependent variable. The bivariate model may be expressed as

$$Y = \beta_0 + \beta_1 X_1 + \varepsilon,$$

where

Y is the predicted value of the dependent variable;

β_0 is the Y-intercept, the point at which the regression line crosses the x-axis;

X_1 is the raw score value of the first independent or predictor variable;

β_1 is the slope of the regression line for the first variable; and

ε (lower case epsilon) is the error in prediction.

The **multiple regression model** illustrates the relationship between the dependent variable and a linear combination of independent variables and an error term. With two predictor variables, the model is illustrated as $Y = \beta_0 + \beta_1 X_1 + \beta_2 X_2 + \varepsilon$.

The **multiple regression equation** is a "mathematical equation relating the expected value or mean value of the dependent variable to the values of the independent variables" (D. R. Anderson, Sweeney, & Williams, 2003, p. 683). With two predictors, the equation is

$$E(Y) = \beta_0 + \beta_1 X_1 + \beta_2 X_0,$$

where

$E(Y)$ is the expected value or mean value of the dependent variable,

X_1 is the raw score value on the first independent or predictor variable,

X_2 is the raw score value on the second independent or predictor variable,

β_0 is the Y-intercept, and

β_1 and β_2 are the standardized regression coefficients that "enable researchers to compare the size of the influence of the independent variables measured using different metrics of scale of measurement" (Vogt, 2005, p. 24). These weights are expressed as standard scores (that is, scores are represented as units under the standard normal curve with a mean of zero and a standard deviation of 1).

The **estimated multiple regression equation** is a mathematical estimate of the multiple regression equation based on sample data using the method of least squares. With two predictors, the formula is

$$\hat{Y} = b_0 + b_1 X_1 + b_2 X_2,$$

where

$\hat{Y}$ is the estimated value of the dependent variable,

X_1 is the raw score value on the first independent or predictor variable,

X_2 is the raw score value on the second independent or predictor variable,

b_0 is the Y-intercept, and

b_1 and b_2 are the unstandardized regression coefficients.

COMPONENTS OF MULTIPLE CORRELATIONS

The multiple correlation is composed of many elements. It may be helpful to identify the special use of these elements in multiple correlation.

Predictor Variables

In multiple regression correlation, **predictor variables** are the independent variables used by the researcher. Though researchers often select predictor variables that reflect data snooping, their choices usually reflect some serious thinking. Predictor variables may produce different sorts of effects, similar to those found in analysis of variance.

Additive Effects

Additive effects are the influences of each predictor variable separately. For instance, a multiple correlation study might attempt to predict student motivation from knowledge of a student's communication apprehension and the degree to which the teacher uses nonverbal immediacy behaviors with students. The researchers may believe that the predictor variables produce influences primarily one at a time rather than as special combinations. Their influences, therefore, would be "additive." With **additive effects**, "the effects of the independent variables on a dependent variable can simply be added together to find their total effect" (Vogt, 2005, p. 4). Additive effects are identified in the multiple correlation equation $E(Y) = \beta_0 + \beta_1 X_1 + \beta_2 X_2$ by such terms as $\beta_1 X_1$ and $\beta_2 X_2$. The variation may be added together to produce an estimate of overall effects.

Interaction Effects

Interaction effects are the influences of predictor variables taken in combinations. Because multiple linear regression does not deal with interaction terms directly, researchers may create additional variables that are interactions among predictor variables. Then, the created variables may be entered into the multiple correlation to test if the observed R shows an increase. Sometimes these interactions are considered **moderator effects** because "the interacting third variable which changes the relation between two original variables is a moderator variable which moderates the original relationship" (Garson, 2003, ¶ 10). The next chapter presents information about the details of creating variables to identify interaction effects, along with the procedures for testing them. When a multiple regression correlation model does not include interaction terms, it often is called a main effect model.

The Need to Avoid Multicollinearity

It is important for predictor variables to be uncorrelated. **Multicollinearity** (also called **collinearity**) is the problem that exists when "two or more independent variables are highly

Special Discussion 13.2

Testing Differences in Multiple Correlations With Different Groups

Communication researchers often find that they need to make comparisons of groups of subjects. For instance, a researcher might wonder if the relationship between willingness to communicate with people of different cultures and communication competence differs depending on whether people are from individualistic or collectivist cultures. There is more than one option. Provided that the same measures were used, the researcher could do one of the following:

- Test the difference between unstandardized regression coefficients (Hardy, 1993, ¶ 52) with a test such as the following:

$$t = \frac{b_{Y1} - b_{Y2}}{s_{b_1 - b_2}} = \frac{b_{Y1} - b_{Y2}}{\sqrt{s_{b_1}^2 + s_{b_2}^2 - 2\text{Cov}_{b_1, b_2}}}.$$

- Use the Chow test and create a new variable that is dummy variable coded to identify the two groups of data. The researcher then uses the omitted variables F test to determine if the groups produce differences in R values. Some researchers prefer to create variables that carry the interaction of the grouping variables with other predictor variables.
- Use the Chow sum of squares test that compares the residuals sums of squares. The unrestricted sum of squares is computed as the sum of the residual sums of squares for the different groups. For all the data, the restricted sums of squares is computed. The difference between the two is tested with the following statistic:

$$F_{k, n-2k} = \frac{\dfrac{\text{restricted residual sums of squares} - \text{unrestricted residual sums of squares}}{k}}{\dfrac{\text{unrestricted residual sums of squares}}{n - 2k}},$$

where k is the number of parameters (including the intercept) and n is the number of events.

correlated; this makes it difficult if not impossible to determine their separate effects on the dependent variable" (Vogt, 2005, p. 198). The failure to maintain uncorrelated predictor variables creates three types of problems (after J. Cohen and Cohen, 1983, pp. 115–116).

- Interpretation of the actual impact of predictor variables may become difficult. If there are highly correlated predictor variables, it becomes impossible to determine each one's unique contribution. When the individual predictor variables do not produce statistically significant effects, some researchers mistakenly fail to check on multicollinearity.

  This is false reasoning. Multicollinearity increases the standard errors of the b coefficients. Increased standard errors in turn means [*sic*] that coefficients for some independent variables may be found not to be significantly different from 0, whereas without multicollinearity and with lower standard errors, these same coefficients might have been found to be significant and the researcher may not have come to null findings in the first place. (Garson, 2003, ¶ 91)

- Sampling stability is jeopardized. Partial coefficients become unstable, and the standard error of the regression weights increases when predictor variables are highly multicollinear. This latter effect occurs because the standard error of the regression coefficients increases as the correlations rise among the remaining predictors.[1] Because at least some of these standard error terms are larger than they would be with uncorrelated predictors, "any given sample may yield relatively poor estimates of the population regression coefficient" (J. Cohen & Cohen, 1983, p. 109).
- Computations are troubled. Rockwell (1975) explains that mathematically *uncorrelated* predictor variables are necessary to obtain a solution for the regression equation.

If this correlation matrix is singular [in this case, showing high intercorrelation among variables] no inversion is possible. Unlike the violation of such other assumptions as that of homoscedasticity, the regression analysis mathematically cannot proceed. . . ." (p. 309)

Elements of the Model

The multiple regression model includes several elements. Many items have been given various names in the literature, and specialized notation often has been used.

---

[1] The following is a formula for the standard error of the regression coefficient for any X_i (J. Cohen & Cohen, 1983, p. 109):

$$SE_{B_i} = \frac{sd_Y}{sd_i} \sqrt{\frac{1 - R_Y^2}{n - k - 1}} \sqrt{\frac{1}{1 - R_i^2}}$$

Hence, it is clear that the standard errors for some regression weights increase as the intercorrelation among remaining predictor variables with X_i grows. For beta weights, the first term in this formula becomes unity, and the formula for the standard error becomes

$$SE_{\beta_i} = \sqrt{\frac{1 - R_Y^2}{n - k - 1}} \sqrt{\frac{1}{1 - R_i^2}}.$$

In both cases, as the intercorrelation among predictors increases, the standard error increases, which means that some beta weights are reduced.

Intercept or Constant

The **intercept** is the value of the dependent variable Y when all values of the independent variables are equal to 0. Thus, "in multiple regression, the y intercept is the mean value of the dependent variable for a case with a value of zero on all the independent variables" (Vogt, 2005, p. 155). It represents the point where the line of best fit crosses the y-axis. This value sometimes is expressed with the symbols c (for *constant*) or a. The intercept is identified as β_0 in the multiple regression model and the multiple regression equation. The intercept is identified as b_0 in the estimated multiple regression equation. When looking at nonlinear patterns, the location of the intercept can be very important. The intercept can be tested to determine if its difference from zero is statistically significant.

Regression Weights

Estimates of the contributions made by each of the predictor variables are made by **regression weights**. These regression coefficients identify slopes associated with the variables of interest. Researchers examine two kinds of weights. Symbolized by b, an unstandardized regression weight "represents an estimate of the change in y corresponding to a 1-unit change in x_i when all other independent variables are held constant" (D. R. Anderson et al., p. 652). A measure called **level-importance** is the regression coefficient multiplied by the mean of the predictor variable. Adding all the level-importance values to the intercept value produces the dependent variable mean.

> Achen (1982: 72) notes that the b coefficient may be conceived as the "potential influence" of the independent on the dependent, while level importance may be conceived as the "actual influence." This contrast is based on the idea that the higher the b, the more y will change for each unit increase in b, but the lower the mean for the given independent, the fewer actual unit changes will be expected. By taking both the magnitude of b and the magnitude of the mean value into account, level importance is a better indicator of expected actual influence of the independent on the dependent. (Edari, 2004, ¶ 15)

In multiple regression correlation, **beta weights** (sometimes called standardized regression coefficients or standardized partial regression coefficients)[2] are regression coefficients that have been standardized so as to represent data from a distribution with a mean of zero and a standard deviation of 1. As a result, "the beta coefficient indicates the difference in a dependent variable associated with an increase (or decrease) of one standard deviation in an independent variable—when controlling for the effects of other independent variables" (Vogt, 2005, pp. 23–24).

One might wonder why it may be necessary to use the beta weight rather than the raw regression coefficient. When all the variables are from the same measurement scale (for instance, if each of the variables is a 5-point scale), interpreting the unstandardized regression coefficient is the most direct approach. Some scholars (see Achen, 1982) warned that researchers often over-rely on standardized regression coefficients (β) when they should

---

[2]A certain amount of confusion exists concerning the language. On one hand, betas (βs) in the multiple regression model "refer to the theoretical parameters of the population equation in raw score form" (Kachigan, 1991, p. 183). On the other hand, the computed beta weights "are actually empirical 'beta estimates' of the corresponding coefficients of the population equation in standardized z score form. Nonetheless, through common usage they have come to be called simply beta coefficients or beta weights . . ." (Kachigan, 1991, p. 183).

primarily examine unstandardized regression weights (*b*). As general advice, interpreting unstandardized regression coefficients is preferred "when: 1. you want to make a definitive prediction (e.g., the dollars of a person's salary or someone's GRE score) or 2. when you want to compare two groups (e.g., predicting the salaries for men and women in two separate regression equations)" (Losh, 2003, ¶¶ 58–60).

When variables are measured on different ranges of scores, it makes sense to standardize scores to create comparable measures. For instance, if one variable is a person's age and another is the person's communicator competence score, the unstandardized measures have completely different measurement continua. Furthermore, researchers may wish to rely on beta weights if they want to know the relative contribution each predictor variable makes in the multiple correlation equation as well as the influence of each predictor on the dependent variable.

The Correlation Coefficient

The **multiple correlation coefficient** *R* "is the measure of association between a dependent variable and an optimal combination of two or more" independent variables (J. Cohen & Cohen, 1983, p. 86). Unlike the bivariate correlation coefficient, which can range from –1.0 to +1.0, multiple correlation coefficients range from 0 to 1.0. A zero correlation shows the complete absence of a relationship between the predictors and the dependent variable, whereas 1.0 shows a perfect relationship. R^2 (similar to r^2) is sometimes called the **multiple coefficient of determination** and reports the proportion of variance in the dependent variable that is explained by knowledge of the optimal combination of two or more predictor variables.

A small *R* could mean many things. As in bivariate correlation, coefficient sizes may be reduced by using variables that show little variability. In addition, lack of perfect reliability limits the size of correlation coefficients that may be observed. Another reason that effect sizes could be relatively small is that the dependent variable and predictor variables are part of a nonlinear relationship. Because "multiple *linear* correlation" assumes that relationships are best approximated by a straight line, a curvilinear relationship could produce much smaller correlation coefficients than might be expected. Thus, researchers often are advised to check plots of data and to use methods to identify potential nonlinear relationships.

Sample multiple correlations may not equal population multiple correlations. In addition to random sampling error, "the optimizing procedures involved in obtaining the multiple regression equation cause the correlation $r_{y\hat{y}}$ to tend to be systematically higher that the corresponding parameter $\rho_{y\hat{y}}$" (Glass & Hopkins, 1984, p. 139). Not surprisingly, "*R* and R^2 typically overestimate their corresponding population values, especially with small samples" (Mertler & Vannatta, 2002, p. 177). The reason is that adding another predictor variable naturally increases the size of *R* as an artifact, even though the increase is not meaningful. Indeed, the expected R^2 is $\frac{k}{n-1}$, even if the actual multiple correlation coefficient is 0 (Morrison, 1976). Hence, if a researcher uses a sample of 10 with two predictor variables, a smallest observable R^2 would be .222, equivalent to a correlation coefficient *R* of .47). One response is to correct the multiple correlation for **shrinkage**, which attempts to eliminate influences of "error fitting" by taking into account sample size and the number of predictor variables. By doing so, the shrinkage formula attempts to identify the amount of variation in the dependent variable that "would be accounted for if we had derived the prediction equation in the population from which the sample was drawn" (J. P. Stevens, 2002, pp. 113–114) by suggesting the "tendency for the strength of prediction in a regression or correlation study to decrease in subsequent studies" (Vogt, 2005, p. 294). Yet, the common correction for shrinkage "does not indicate how well the derived equation will predict other samples from the sample population" (J. P. Stevens, 2002, p. 114). Indeed, Schmitt and Ployhart (1999) found that the correction for shrinkage provides "gross overestimates of cross-validity and should not be used as such" (p. 50). Though with large sample sizes, the correction for shrinkage makes very little difference, with small samples the correction has been known to reduce the R^2 to a negative coefficient (a theoretically meaningless number). Another option to reduce inflated Rs is to avoid using automated "stepwise" and "forward selection" methods to select a final set of predictor variables. Such stepwise and forward selection approaches tend to inflate the overall multiple correlation coefficient because they select predictors based on the size of correlations with the dependent variable rather than selecting variables based on some theoretic rationale.

HOW TO DO A MULTIPLE REGRESSION CORRELATION STUDY

Multiple correlation studies involve many steps. Of course, the steps listed here may be considered *guidelines*, rather than rules for completing such a study. It should be mentioned that researchers using multiple regression correlation usually find that after checking assumptions and residuals, they must make some revisions a complete the steps in the analyses again.

Select Predictor Variables

The first step in a study using multiple regression correlation involves choosing the variables that should predict outputs. Many researchers are tempted to start with a very long list of potential predictors, but there are reasons that such an approach is not very sensible. First, it is generally accepted in empirical research that—all other things being equal—an explanation that involves few variables to predict effects is superior to one that involves many variables. As the number of independent variables increases, the required sample size also grows. Second, multiple correlation models with many variables can prove difficult to interpret.

To select independent variables, researchers should be guided by several criteria.

- First, variables should have theoretic significance.
- Second, predictor variables should be derived from past research with the dependent variable.
- Third, variables that are highly correlated with each other should be avoided.

This last criterion involves the multicollinearity problem. When multicollinearity is high,[3] the order in which variables are entered into the equation affects the weights for each predictor variable. The regression weights for *whichever* variables are entered first will

---

[3]Defining what involves a "high" intercorrelation is not always clear. Heise (1969) explains that intercorrelations among predictor variables are acceptable provided, "The correlations between variables are not extremely large in absolute magnitude" (p. 57). Some guidelines suggest that multicollinearity problems exist if any simple intercorrelation is greater than .80. Others (e.g., Dizney & Gromen, 1967) have found that a correlation between predictors as low as .58 prevented accurate identification of the influence of both predictor variables.

account for the greatest proportion of variance (J. P. Stevens, 2002, pp. 119–121). Thus, it becomes difficult to interpret the actual comparative importance of the predictor variables.

Predictor variables may take several forms. Without attempting to categorize the forms of variables by some grand system, it may be said that predictor variables may include at least three major forms.

Continuous Predictors

Not surprisingly, **continuous predictors** are variables measured on the interval (or quasi-interval) or ratio levels of measurement. Traditional multiple regression correlation focuses on these sorts of variables.

Dummy or Indicator Predictors

Categorical variables that are coded to represent categorical or qualitative elements are called **dummy** or **indicator predictors**. The next chapter covers the details of such coding, but it is enough at this point to state that if a researcher wants to know if exposure to a message with previews enhances comprehension more than a message without the previews does, dummy variable coding could be used. Every person hearing the message with the previews could receive a score of 1, and every person not hearing the previews would receive a score of 0. If a control group is one of the two conditions, it should be coded as 0 and the treatment condition would be identified as 1.

Lagged Predictors

Lagged predictors are measures at one time that predict delayed dependent variable values at another time. Though the dependent variable actually lags after the predictor variables, the independent variables often are labeled "lagged variables." For instance, suppose a researcher wants to know how much influence on attitudes toward a political candidate is produced by the number of mailings (X_1) and the number of speeches political candidates give (X_2) during the last 3 months of the campaign. One might think that each month's attitudes toward the political candidate (Y) could be correlated with the number of speeches and mailings for that month, but there is a problem. Voters cannot be influenced by all the communication directed their way until *after* receiving the information. Hence, it might make sense to delay collecting dependent variable data until the next month. This type of sampling could be repeated for another few months. The multiple regression model for the lagged variable situation is

$$Y = \beta_0 + \beta_1 X_{1t-1} + \beta_2 X_{1t-2} + \beta_3 X_{1t-3} + \beta_4 X_{2t-1} + \beta_5 X_{2t-2} + \beta_6 X_{2t-3} + e,$$

where

Y is the dependent variable (attitudes toward the political candidate held by likely voters),

X_1 is the number mailings in a month,

X_2 is the number of speeches political candidates give in a month,

$t-1$ is 1 month previous to the time that the dependent variable is measured,

$t-2$ is 2 months previous to the time that the dependent variable is measured, and

$t-3$ is 3 months previous to the time that the dependent variable is measured.

Researchers have to be careful when using lagged variables. First, there should be some rationale for the number of "lags" that are involved. Adding large numbers of lags requires increased sample sizes, which may not be practical. Second, lagged variables tend to be highly correlated with each other. Thus, the interpretation of regression and beta weights must be done very carefully. To decide on the number of lags, Ott and Hildebrand (1983) suggest that researchers use a modified process of "trial and error." They recommend starting with a 1-month lag and computing the multiple R. Then, a 2-month lag may be added. If the multiple R does not substantially increase, then the additional lagged variable (and further lags) may be omitted. In addition, if the standard error of estimate is not reduced, adding lags may be ceased.

Gather an Adequate Sample

Multiple correlation requires a sample that is, well, ample. Though some writers (e.g., Allison, 1999, pp. 58–60) warn of researchers who use samples so large that even trivial correlations are detected as meaningful, most of the time, the chief concern involves what minimum sample sizes are acceptable. One guideline advises researchers to have 104 events plus the number of independent variables if they wish to test regression coefficients (Tabachnick & Fidell, 2001, p. 117). Another popular rule of thumb is that a sample must include *at least* 15 events per predictor variable (J. P. Stevens, 2002, p. 143). But the size of the population multiple correlation coefficient (ρ^2) makes a difference. The smaller the population multiple correlation coefficient is, the greater the number of events that is required for each predictor (S. A. Green, 1991). One study (C. Park & Dudycha, 1974) found that the sample size required to keep R^2 from deviating from R^2 corrected for shrinkage increases as the population ρ^2 to be detected decreases. For instance, with four predictor variables (assuming that shrinkage is no more than .05 with a high probability of .90), when the population ρ^2 is .50, the required sample is 66 (which equals 16.5 events per predictor variable). Similarly, when the population ρ^2 is .25, the required sample is 93 (which equals 23.25 events per predictor variable). Thus, researchers probably should use the 15 events per predictor as a minimum to be exceeded more often than not.

When the number of events is small, the observed R^2 tends to increase. As the number of predictor variables approaches the number of events in the sample, the R^2 also nears 1.0 even if the associations actually are nonexistent. Hence, researchers using multiple regression correlation with small samples may mislead themselves into thinking that they have identified substantial effects when, in fact, their large R coefficients are largely artifacts.[4]

---

[4]It is important to attempt to keep sample sizes equal across the measurement of all variables. Sometimes, however, individuals do not respond to all measures and imbalance occurs. This problem can make the calculations difficult.

> In addition to more difficult computational formulas, designs with unequal group sample sizes may be threatened by a number of validity problems depending on how the unequal samples came about. The term "unbalanced" is used to refer to designs with unequal sample sizes per group. In unbalanced designs, variables that might have been independent or uncorrelated with each other may become related or nonorthogonal. For dummy coding, this has no impact. For other contrast and comparison procedures, however, unequal sample sizes may affect the analysis. For effect coding, unequal sample sizes produce a change in the interpretation of the betas. The intercept, B_0, no longer represents the grand mean but the unweighted total mean (the mean of the group means). Similarly, the B_i for each effect vector is no longer a comparison of the group mean to the grand mean, but of the group mean to the unweighted total mean. (J. J. Stevens, 1999, ¶ 30)

Compute Multiple Regression Coefficients

Computers usually are employed to calculate multiple regressions coefficients. For purposes of illustration here, a simple case involving two predictor variables will be illustrated. The computations involve identifying the multiple correlation coefficient and the regression weights.

Computing R

Though the multiple correlation coefficient R may be reported, researchers often prefer to rely on R^2, mostly for conceptual reasons. For two predictor variables, R^2 may be computed as

$$R^2_{Y \cdot 12} = \frac{r^2_{Y1} + r^2_{Y2} - 2r_{Y1}r_{Y2}r_{12}}{1 - r^2_{12}},$$

where

$R^2_{Y \cdot 12}$ is the proportion of variance in the dependent variable Y that is shared with the optimal combination of the independent variables 1 and 2,

r^2_{Y1} is the squared correlation (coefficient of determination) of the dependent variable Y with independent variable 1,

r^2_{Y2} is the squared correlation (coefficient of determination) of the dependent variable Y with independent variable 2, and

r^2_{12} is the squared correlation (coefficient of determination) of the two independent variables with each other.

As this formula suggests, the overall R will be at least as large as the absolute value of the smallest correlation between the predictors and the dependent variable. An example using this formula is found in Table 13.1.

To test if the observed multiple correlation coefficient is different from zero, the researcher computes a test of statistical significance using the F distribution. The null hypothesis is H_0: $R = 0$. Computationally, the test is made easy by using the following formula:

$$F_{m,n-m-1} = \frac{R^2}{1 - R^2} * \left(\frac{n - m - 1}{m} \right),$$

where

R^2 is the squared multiple correlation coefficient,

m is the number of predictor variables, and

n is the number of events in the study.

For the numerator term, degrees of freedom are equal to m (the number of predictor variables). For the denominator, degrees of freedom are equal to n (the number of events in the study)

(Text continues on page 359)

Table 13.1 Multiple Regression Correlation Example

A researcher wanted to see if social attraction could be predicted from some characteristics of messages exchanged during conversations. A group of 53 people held conversations with others of the same sex whose conversations they rated on measures of lexical diversity (use of different words in conversation) and general assertiveness. Then, they rated the social attraction they felt toward the other person. In each case, the variables were continuous measures on the interval level.

Table of Correlations	Lexical Diversity X_1	General Assertiveness X_2	Social Attraction Y	Standard Deviation
Lexical diversity (X_1)	1.0	.274	.627	10.0
General assertiveness (X_2)		1.0	.437	7.8
Social attraction (Y)			1.0	6.8

The formula for multiple correlation with two predictor variables is

$$R^2_{Y \cdot 12} = \frac{r^2_{Y1} + r^2_{Y2} - 2r_{Y1}r_{Y2}r_{12}}{1 - r^2_{12}}.$$

When the values are inserted into the formula, the result is

$$R^2_{Y \cdot 12} = \frac{(.627)^2 + (.437)^2 - 2(.627 * .437 * .274)}{1 - (.274)^2}$$

$$R^2_{Y \cdot 12} = \frac{.393 + .191 - 2(.075)}{1 - .075} = \frac{.434}{.925} = .469.$$

To test the null hypothesis that the multiple correlation coefficient is zero (H_0: $R = 0$), the following formula may be used:

$$F_{m, n-m-1} = \frac{R^2}{1 - R^2} * \left(\frac{n - m - 1}{m} \right),$$

which becomes

$$F = \frac{.469}{1 - .469} * \left(\frac{53 - 2 - 1}{2} \right) = .883 * 25 = 22.075.$$

With alpha risk of .05, the table of critical values of F is entered with m degrees of freedom in the numerator and $n - m - 1$ degrees of freedom in the denominator. In this case, the degrees of freedom are 2 ($m = 2$ predictor variables) and 50 (53 − 2 − 1), which means that the critical value is 3.183. Because the test statistic is greater than the critical value, the researcher concludes that the multiple correlation coefficient is beyond what would have been expected to occur by random sampling error.

(Continued)

Table 13.1 (Continued)

To correct R^2 for shrinkage, the following formula is used:

$$R^2 = 1 - \left[(1 - R^2) * \left(\frac{n-1}{n-m-1} \right) \right].$$

Inserting the numbers into the formula, the adjusted correlation becomes

$$R^2 = 1 - \left[(1 - .469) * \left(\frac{53 - 1}{53 - 2 - 1} \right) \right] = 1 - (.531 * 1.04) = .448.$$

To compute beta weights in the case involving two predictor variables, the following formulae are used.

$$\beta_1 = \frac{r_{Y1} - r_{Y2}r_{12}}{1 - r_{12}^2} = \frac{.627 - (.437 * .274)}{1 - .075} = \frac{.507}{.925} = .548$$

$$\beta_2 = \frac{r_{Y2} - r_{Y1}r_{12}}{1 - r_{12}^2} = \frac{.437 - (.627 * .274)}{1 - .075} = \frac{.265}{.925} = .286$$

These beta weights indicate the amount of change in the dependent variable (attitude) associated with one standard deviation unit change in each predictor variable. To test if the beta weights are statistically significantly different from zero, an application of the t test is used.

The null hypothesis to be tested in each case is H_0: $\beta = 0$.

$$t = \frac{\beta}{s_\beta},$$

where β is the beta weight and s_β is the standard error of beta, and s_β may be computed from

$$s_\beta = \sqrt{\frac{1 - R^2}{n - k - 1}} \sqrt{\frac{1}{1 - R_i^2}},$$

where R^2 is the squared multiple correlation coefficient and R_i^2 is the squared multiple correlation coefficient of the predictor variable with the other predictor variables.

The t distribution is entered with $n - m - 1$ degrees of freedom, where n is the number of events in the study and m is the number of predictor variables.

Unstandardized regression coefficients may be obtained by the following formulae:

$$b_1 = \frac{\beta_1 * s_y}{s_1} = \frac{.548 * 6.8}{10} = .373, \quad \text{and}$$

$$b_2 = \frac{\beta_2 * s_y}{s_2} = \frac{.286 * 6.8}{7.8} = .249.$$

These unstandardized regression coefficients indicate how much of a change in the dependent variable attitude is associated with a one unit change in perceptions of message believability and ratings of source character when the other predictor variable is held constant.

minus m (the number of predictor variables) minus 1. A statistically significant F ratio indicates that the multiple correlation coefficient is unlikely to have been observed as a result of random sampling error. Thus, the null hypothesis may be rejected at the researcher's chosen alpha risk.

The correlation coefficient also is corrected for shrinkage, which adjusts for the sample size and the number of predictors in the regression equation. The most popular formula is suggested by Wherry (1931; see Herzberg, 1969):

$$R^2_{adj} = 1 - \left[(1 - R^2) * \left(\frac{n - 1}{n - m - 1} \right) \right],$$

where m is the number of predictor variables and n is the number of events in the study.

Assessing Components of Multiple Correlations

To assess the relative contribution of different predictor variables, standardized regression weights (beta weights) may be used. The formulae for beta weights take the following form in the case of two predictors:

$$\beta_1 = \frac{r_{Y1} - r_{Y2}r_{12}}{1 - r^2_{12}} \quad \text{and} \quad \beta_2 = \frac{r_{Y2} - r_{Y1}r_{12}}{1 - r^2_{12}}.$$

One also may compute beta weights from unstandardized regression coefficients and the standard deviations of the variables.[5]

To examine the statistical significance of the beta weights, the t test is enlisted to test the null hypothesis that the beta coefficient is not different from zero ($H_0: \beta_1 = 0$). The following formula is used:

$$t = \frac{\beta}{s_\beta},$$

where s_β is the standard error of the beta, computed as

$$s_\beta = \sqrt{\frac{1 - R^2}{n - k - 1}} \sqrt{\frac{1}{1 - R^2_i}},$$

where R^2 is the squared multiple correlation coefficient and R^2_i is the squared multiple correlation coefficient of the predictor variable with the other predictor variables.

---

[5]To calculate beta weights from regression coefficients, researchers may use

$$\beta = b * \frac{s_x}{s_y},$$

where b is the *un*standardized regression coefficient and s_x and s_y are the standard deviations of the predictor variable and the dependent variable, respectively.

The *t* test is entered with $n - m - 1$ degrees of freedom, where *n* is the number of events in the study and *m* is the number of predictor variables.

Beta weights identify individual contributions of predictor variables, but the overall *R* also reflects combinations of predictor variables. Hence, the beta weights often tell only part of the story about the influence of predictors. Thus, many researchers find it prudent to report both the zero-order correlations and the beta weights. In addition, as the next chapter illustrates, researchers may make direct examinations of interaction effects.

Unstandardized regression coefficients also may be examined. The coefficients may be computed directly or from the beta weights using the following general formula:

$$b_X = \frac{\beta_X * s_y}{s_X},$$

where

b_X is the regression weight for the predictor variable *x*,

s_Y is the standard deviation for the dependent variable *y*, and

s_X is the standard deviation for the predictor variable *x*.

This measure identifies the slope of the predictor.

Deciding on the Method to Select Entry of Variables

When there are more than two predictor variables, the researcher must decide how to enter the variables. First and foremost, any underlying theories and hypotheses should affect the decision. Those predictors for which there are theoretic reasons for inclusion should be the first to be entered. Otherwise, the researcher with a large number of predictors may find that independent variables that are not so theoretically meaningful may be the first to be retained in some methods. There are several options to enter variables.

Direct entry simply involves entering all variables into the multiple regression equation. This approach usually reflects a researcher's understanding of variables that are most important in the inquiry. Arguably, the greatest benefit of this approach is that direct entry methods make the researcher responsible for choices about the variables to examine.

Automatic selection methods include tools that permit predictor variables to be "sifted" based on statistical testing completed to include or remove predictors. Unlike the direct entry and hierarchical approaches, this set of methods tends not to reflect clear theory testing. Instead, researchers presume that their large numbers of predictors need to be reduced to a handful of meaningful variables by empirical methods alone. Several varieties exist for these tools.

- **Stepwise selection** is actually a *set* of methods. In fact, all the automated tools listed here could be called application of stepwise methods. In the approach popularly used (and employed by SPSS), predictor variables are subjected to a significance test, and the one with the smallest probability value is selected for the model. In subsequent steps, other variables are added if they meet the same criterion. At the same time, previously included variables that no longer are statistically significant predictors are removed.

- **Forward selection** is a method that begins by including the predictor variable that has the highest (absolute) correlation with the dependent variable. Then, a predictor with the highest remaining partial correlation with the dependent variable is entered next. Once an effect is entered, it is not excluded. The process continues until no new significant predictors in the multiple regression equation remain outside the model.
- **Backward elimination** is a method that enters all variables in one block and in subsequent steps eliminates variables that have the smallest partial correlation with the dependent variable.

In each of these cases, the researcher specifies the criteria for forward selection (usually $p <$ .05) and for backward elimination (usually $p > .10$).

Researchers usually find that the backward elimination method is most consistent with their desires to develop models and to reduce sources of error in prediction. With this method, the first entry is controlled by the researcher based on an understanding of theory and past research. Though the automatic methods of entering variables into multiple regression equations are convenient, some serious challenges have been raised to the casual use of stepwise selection methods. First, because stepwise entry uses statistical methods to maximize the size of multiple correlation coefficients, the overall Rs may overestimate the sizes of effects in the population. Second, with modest sample sizes, the use of stepwise selection will tend to capitalize on chance and sampling error (McIntyre, Montgomery, Srinivasan, & Weitz, 1983; Thompson, 1995). Third, in many cases stepwise methods will "not correctly identify the best variable set of a given size" (Thompson, 1995, p. 525). The method emphasizes selecting variables that produce significant contributions separately, rather than in combination or interactions with other variables. Furthermore, one study determined that "the number of authentic variables found in the final model subsets was always less than half the number of available authentic predictor variables" (Derksen & Keselman, 1992). Though the method certainly has its defenders (Lerner & Games, 1981), and many researchers find that the backward elimination approach is least likely to produce difficulties, there still is a reasonable preference for entering variables according to some rationale.

Using SPSS and Excel for Multiple Regression Correlation

Both SPSS and Excel have routines to complete multiple regression correlation. The SPSS options subroutines are most extensive and will be reviewed first.

SPSS

SPSS begins the multiple regression analysis of data with selection of *Regression* from the *Analysis* menu. Then, *Linear. . .* is chosen from the drop-down menu that appears. In the *Linear Regression* dialog box, the researcher highlights the dependent variable and moves it to the "Dependent:" field by using the arrow key. The predictor variables are highlighted and moved to the "Independent(s):" field. The *Method:* provides five options: "Enter" (in which all variables are entered at once), "Remove" (in which researcher-specified variables are removed from the full model as a block of variables), "Stepwise," "Backward," and "Forward." In this case, the researcher has chosen to use "Backward" elimination of statistically insignificant predictors after a multiple regression correlation analysis has been completed with all variables included.

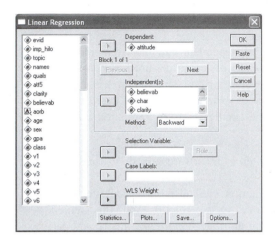

After clicking the *Continue* button, the researcher clicks the *Options. . .* button and opens the *Linear Regression: Options* dialog box. The criteria used for backward elimination may be examined to be sure that they are the ones desired. The default choices (.05 for entry of a variable and .10 for removal of a variable) may be changed if the researcher desires to do so. Clicking the *Continue* button, followed by *OK*, executes the regression routine.

After clicking on the *Statistics. . .* button, the *Linear Regression: Statistics* dialog box includes a number of alternative analyses that may be requested. It is important to check the "Model fit" box because this option requests the basics analyses (R and R^2, R^2 adjusted for shrinkage, standard error, and the F test for R).

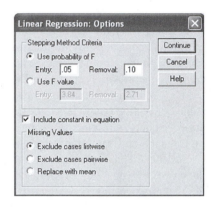

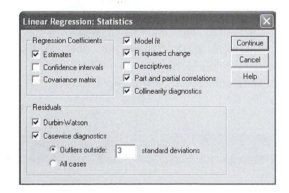

The output includes a list of the variables that composed each of the models, one before and one after backward elimination of statistically insignificant predictors. In this case, the second model removed the "message clarity" variable when testing effects. The results also provide information about the overall multiple regression correlation coefficient.

In addition, researchers will wish to request other information, such as the "R squared change" from one multiple regression correlation model to another. By checking appropriate boxes, the researcher can request information about "Part and partial correlations," which also includes a presentation of zero-order correlations of predictor with dependent variables. Multicollinearity information is also requested by checking the "Collinearity diagnostics" box. Additional information about "Residuals" also is requested. We will return to these latter topics later in this chapter.

Variables Entered/Removed[b]

Model	Variables Entered	Variables Removed	Method
1	clarity, char, believab[a]	.	Enter
2	.	clarity	Backward (criterion: Probability of F-to-remove >= 100).

a. All requested variables entered
b. Dependent Variable: attitude

Model Summary[b]

Model	R	R Square	Adjusted R Square	Std. Error of the Estimate	Change Statistics					Durbin-Watson
					R Square Change	F Change	df1	df2	Sig. F Change	
1	.647[a]	.419	.417	3.648	.419	206.620	3	860	.000	
2	.647[b]	.419	.417	3.646	.000	.098	1	860	.755	1.673

a. Predictors: (Constant), believab, char, clarity
b. Predictors: (Constant), believab, char
c. Dependent Variable: attitude

ANOVA[c]

Model		Sum of Squares	df	Mean Square	F	Sig.
1	Regression	8250.514	3	2750.171	206.620	.000[a]
	Residual	11446.820	860	13.310		
	Total	19697.333	863			
2	Regression	8249.213	2	4124.606	310.207	.000[b]
	Residual	11448.120	861	13.296		
	Total	19697.333	863			

a. Predictors: (Constant), believab, char, clarity
b. Predictors: (Constant), believab, char
c. Dependent Variable: attitude

Interestingly, in this case, when the statistically insignificant predictor variable was deleted, the overall R did not change. A test of statistical significance is provided in the analysis of variance table. For the reported F tests, a small statistical significance coefficient (*Sig.* usually below .05) indicates that R is different from zero.

Examination of regression weights is meaningful. The tests of beta weights in Model 1 (with all three predictors) show the message clarity variable to make a statistically insignificant contribution. After deletion of this variable from the second model, all remaining predictor variables were statistically significant (indicated by "*Sig.*" values below .05). It should be noted that the t tests used in SPSS are two-tailed tests. Researchers who have directional hypotheses will wish to *halve* the reported significance level to complete their tests. The "unstandardized coefficients" are used to create the estimated multiple regression model.

Coefficients[a]

Model		Unstandardized Coefficients		Standardized Coefficients	t	Sig.	Coefficients			Collinearity Statistics	
		B	Std. Error	Beta			Zero-order	Partial	Part	Tolerance	VIF
1	(Constant)	5.083	.671		7.581	.000					
	char	.228	.037	.185	6.074	.000	.437	.203	.158	.726	1.378
	clarity	−.012	.040	−.011	−.313	.755	.418	−.011	−.008	.568	1.760
	believab	.403	.025	.546	15.870	.000	.627	.476	.413	.570	1.753
2	(Constant)	5.070	.669		7.581	.000					
	char	.225	.036	.183	6.211	.000	.437	.207	.161	.779	1.284
	believab	.399	.022	.541	18.363	.000	.627	.530	.477	.779	1.284

a. Dependent Variable: attitude

The partial correlation listed for each predictor variable shows the correlation with the dependent variable when the effects of the other variables are excluded.

Excel

Excel also includes a multiple regression correlation function. The process begins by choosing *Data Analysis...* from the *Tools* menu. From the dialog box, the researcher selects *Regression...* and then clicks on the *OK* button (see page 364).

In the *Regression* dialog box, the researcher identifies the column and range of values in which the dependent variable is found and lists it in the "Input Y Range:" field. The columns where the predictor variables (two in this example) are found and their ranges are inserted into the "Input X Range:" field.

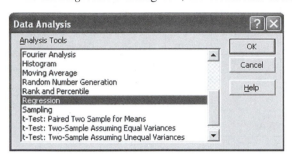

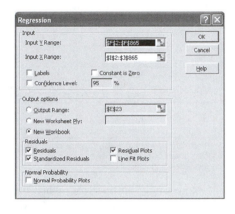

Excel requires researchers to place all independent variables in adjacent columns, but the dependent variable may be located in any column. If the variable names are located in the first row of each column of variable values, the researcher checks the labels box. Various *Residuals* analyses may be requested along with normal probability plots. Afterward, the researcher clicks *OK* to complete the computations. The results appear as the following output shows.

SUMMARY OUTPUT									
Regression Statistics									
Multiple R	0.6471464								
R Square	0.418798464								
Adjusted R Square	0.417448402								
Standard Error	3.646410164								
Observations	864								
ANOVA									
	df	*SS*	*MS*	*F*	*Significance F*				
Regression	2	8249.212936	4124.60647	310.2069201	3.4887E-102				
Residual	861	11448.1204	13.2963071						
Total	863	19697.33333							
	Coefficients	*Standard Error*	*t Stat*	*P-value*	*Lower 95%*	*Upper 95%*	*Lower 95.0%*	*Upper 95.0%*	
Intercept	5.069797019	0.668789141	7.58056121	8.89867E-14	3.757150261	6.382443777	3.757150261	6.382443777	
X Variable 1	0.398842565	0.021719682	18.3631865	8.3044E-64	0.356212881	0.441472249	0.356212881	0.441472249	
X Variable 2	0.224646119	0.036168346	6.21112504	8.17905E-10	0.153657732	0.295634505	0.153657732	0.295634505	

This analysis is based on direct entry of all variables. The R, R^2, and *Adjusted* (for shrinkage) R^2 are reported, and the overall R is tested for statistical significance. The values in the *Coefficients* column are the unstandardized regression coefficients, rather than the beta weights. The tests of statistical significance in this case all show p levels below .05. (The notation "E-102" means that the decimal point actually is 102 places to the left of its present location; "E-14" means that the decimal point is actually located 14 places to the left; "E-72" means that the decimal point is actually located 72 places to the left.)

Special Discussion 13.3

The Other Kinds of Correlations

The use of correlations involving more than one variable has been an object of some interest. Three of the most prominent options have been part correlation, partial correlation, and second-order partial correlation, but others exist.

Part Correlation. Researchers frequently complete studies where people are tested for some variable, given a treatment, and tested again. If researchers observe gains in scores, they may have some difficulty. "Such a posttest-minus-pretest measure, $X_2 - X_3$, is contaminated by the regression effect . . .—the gain scores, $X_2 - X_3$, would correlate negatively with pretest scores X_3" (Glass & Hopkins, 1984, p. 129) unless the correlation between the posttest and the pretest is 1.0. This condition is a problem because the amount of change should not necessarily correlate negatively with pretest status.

A better method to measure gain or change is to predict posttest scores ($\hat{X}_2$) from pretest scores (X_3) and use the deviation $X_2 - \hat{X}_2$ [also known as a **residual change score**] as a measure of gain above and beyond what is predictable from the pretest. (Glass & Hopkins, 1984, p. 129)

Sometimes called **semipartial correlation**, the **part correlation** (or semipartial correlation) is a form of "multiple correlation in which a variable is partialed out, but only from one of the other variables" (Vogt, 2005, p. 228). The formula for part correlation is

$$r_{1(2.3)} = \frac{r_{12} - r_{13}r_{23}}{\sqrt{1 - r_{23}^2}}.$$

Partial Correlation. This option is a "correlation between two variables after the researcher statistically subtracts or removes (controls for, holds constant, or "partials out") the linear effect of one or more other variables" (Vogt, 2005, p. 228). Partial correlations are symbolized with subscripts used to identify the correlation of variables. For instance, $r_{12.3}$ represents a partial correlation between variables 1 and 2 while partialing out the effects of variable 3. An example of the formula for this correlation is

$$r_{12.3} = \frac{r_{12} - r_{13}r_{23}}{\sqrt{(1 - r_{13}^2) * (1 - r_{23}^2)}}.$$

Second-Order Partial Correlation. This form of correlation is an extension of semipartial correlation that controls for two variables while examining the relationship between two others. An example of such a correlation is

$$r_{12.34} = \frac{r_{12.3} - r_{14.3}r_{24.3}}{\sqrt{(1 - r_{14.3}^2) * (1 - r_{24.3}^2)}}.$$

In theory, the levels of such extensions can continue. To identify the level of control for other variables, researchers use a certain kind of language.

- A **zero-order correlation** does not control for other variables.
- A **first-order correlation** controls for one other variable.
- A **second-order correlation** controls for two other variables.

Check on the Adequacy of the Regression Model

It is important to know that the assumptions underlying the use of multiple regression correlation have been met. Several matters deserve attention: assessment of residuals, autocorrelation, and multicollinearity.

Analysis of Residuals

By looking at plots and examining residuals, it is possible to check the assumption that residuals are normally distributed. **Residuals** are the differences between the observed and predicted values of the dependent variable (given the multiple regression correlation model). This characteristic is a reflection of the assumption of **homoscedasticity**, which means that variability in scores of one variable is stable through the entire range of the other variable and is homogeneous at all points along the line of best fit (line of regression). When this assumption is met, residuals between predicted and actual values should be randomly distributed and uncorrelated. If homoscedasticity cannot be assumed, "conventionally computed confidence intervals and conventional t-tests for OLS [ordinary least squares] estimators can no longer be justified" (Berry, 1993, p. 81). There may be several causes for this difficulty. There may be outliers in the data that have thrown off constant error variance. There may be subjects-by-conditions interactions created by outside variables that are introducing nonrandom variation into the data (in other words, there may be an important variable that has been left out of the model). There may be some predictor variables that have strong skew.

To identify this problem, residuals may be examined directly. SPSS and Excel both provide reports of residuals. Inspecting a residual plot of the predicted values (on the horizontal axis) with the residual values (on the vertical axis) can be instructive. To use SPSS for this purpose, the researcher selects *Regression* from the *Analysis* menu. Then,

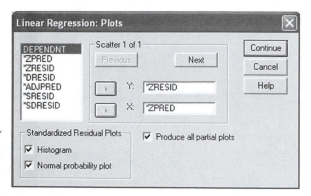

Linear... is chosen from the drop-down menu that appears. In the *Linear Regression* dialog box, after the researcher has indicated the dependent and independent variables, the *Plots...* key is clicked. To select a plot, the researcher must identify the axes for examination. The most common are the standardized residuals (*ZRESID) on the vertical (Y) axis and the standardized predicted values on the horizontal (X) axis. These choices may be inserted in appropriate fields.

The standardized scores are values subtracted from their means and divided by their standard deviations. Other options include residual and predicted values that are adjusted, studentized, or based on deleted cases. Summary statistics are presented in the form of standardized predictor and residual values.

The result of this request for a plot includes a chart such found on the next page, right. As can be seen, aside from two points that have been circled, the pattern seems generally random.

Nor is there strong evidence of heteroscedasticity. Yet, outliers might bear investigation. If the two outliers can be explained as coming from populations fundamentally different from the rest of the sample, they may be deleted. Sometimes, outliers are discovered to be the result of simple data entry errors.

Naturally, an outlier can be an extreme item on the vertical axis, on the horizontal axis, or both. Different statistical tools are available to detect different sources of deviation. To detect outliers on the vertical axis (that is, higher or lower than predicted), the Weisberg test may be used (though extensions permit its use in other ways as well). For the variables on the horizontal axis (that is, further to the right or left than predicted), the most popular tools combine use of Mahalanobis' Distance and Cook's *D*.

Both Cook's *D* and Mahalanobis' Distance may be tested by SPSS subroutines. To assess outliers, the researcher clicks the *Save* button from the *Linear Regression* dialog box. In the *Linear Regression: Save* dialog box, the researcher requests that various values be saved as new variables in the data file. Among requests made for unstandardized and standardized predicted and residual values, Cook's *D* and Mahalanobis' Distance are requested.

After clicking the *Continue* and *OK* buttons, the data file receives this information. In the output that appears, the residuals are examined statistically.

Detecting outliers from the vertical axis invites use of Weisberg's t_i (Weisberg, 1980). For each case, the following statistic is computed:

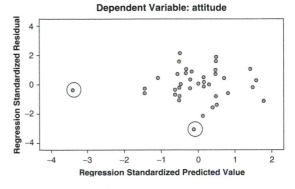

$$t_i = r_i * \sqrt{\frac{n - p' - 1}{n - p' - r_i^2}},$$

where

r_i is the standardized residual value (sometimes called Pearson residuals) for the case,

p' is the number of regression coefficients including the intercept, and

n is the number of events in the sample.

Though SPSS does not include this statistic, it supplies r_i (calling it the "standardized residual") and inserts it into the data set under the label "ZRE_1." This r_i value is the residual divided by an estimate of its standard deviation, which yields values with a mean of 0 and a standard deviation of 1. Armed with this information, researchers can compute Weisberg's t_i

from the formula on page 367. To determine if any of these values newly added to the data indicate outliers on the vertical axis, the table in Appendix C.13 may be consulted. A portion of it appears below.

| | Weisberg's t_i Critical Values at Alpha Risk = .05 *Number of Regression Coefficients Including the Intercept* | | | | Mahalanobis' Distance Critical Values at Alpha Risk = .05 *Number of Predictor Variables* | | | | Cook's Distance Guidelines *Number of Regression Coefficients Including the Intercept* | | | |
Number of Events	3	4	5	6	2	3	4	5	3	4	5	6
6	10.89	76.39	—	—	4	4.14	—	—	.89	.94	.98	1.00
7	6.58	11.77	89.12	—	4.71	5.01	5.12	—	.87	.93	.96	.98
500	3.92	3.92	3.92	3.92	18.12	20.75	23.06	25.21	.79	.84	.87	.89

In the example used here, there are three predictor variables and the intercept. Thus, the "Number of Regression Coefficients Including the Intercept" is equal to 4. Because the sample size exceeds 500, this number of events is used to enter the distribution. At alpha risk of .05, the critical value is 3.92. If the absolute value of the computed Weisberg t_i is greater than 3.92, the distance for the outlier is statistically significant (the outlying difference as large as this one on the vertical axis could be found by random sampling error fewer than 5 times out of 100). In the example of the outliers in the diagram, the absolute value Weisberg t_i value is 4.23,[6] which is greater than the critical value. Hence, the circled outlying point at the bottom of the chart of outliers is statistically significant, indicating its presence as an actual outlier on the vertical axis.

Detecting outliers on the horizontal axis (too far to the right or the left of the distribution) invites use of Mahalanobis' Distance and Cook's *D*.

- *Mahalanobis' Distance* (symbolized as D^2) shows how much the scores of a case differ from an estimate of the mean scores of all the variables. The reasoning is that if there is a multidimensional space defined by the predictor variables, the mean of all the data points could be plotted. This weighted mean of all the dimensions is called a **centroid** (Vogt, 2005, p. 41). Mahalanobis' Distance is the difference between the centroid and a target score in the multidimensional space.

---

[6]Though it was computed by using a recode function in SPSS, as an illustration of Weisberg's t_i, it may be mentioned that the outlying point was computed as follows:

$$t_i = r_i * \sqrt{\frac{n - p' - 1}{n - p' - r_i^2}}$$

$$t_i = -4.185 * \sqrt{\frac{864 - 4 - 1}{864 - 4 - (-4.185^2)}} = -4.18501 * \sqrt{\frac{864 - 4 - 1}{864 - 4 - (-4.185^2)}}$$

$$= -4.185 * \sqrt{\frac{859}{860 - 17.514}} = -4.185 * 1.01 = -4.23.$$

- *Cook's* D identifies the influence of suspected outliers on regression coefficients by examining regression coefficients that would exist if the outlier were deleted.[7]

In the SPSS output, the following summary report of residual statistics is supplied. Ideally, the distances should be approximately equal, but as can be seen, the analysis reveals that the Mahalanobis' Distance scores range from .051 to 25.032. Cook's *D* also shows a range extending from 0 to .0.50. To interpret the meaning of these distances, the table of Mahalanobis' Distance critical values may be referenced. With three predictor variables and a sample size such as this study's, the minimum distance value for a statistically significant outlier at alpha risk of .05 is 20.75. Because the maximum D^2 is 25.032 (larger than the critical value), there is at least one statistically significant outlier.

To see if the outliers have significant influences on the study's regression coefficients, Cook's *D* should be examined. For Cook's *D*, the general rule is that distance is statistically significant if it exceeds the *median value* of *F* (equivalent of $F_{p,\ n-p}$ with alpha risk of .5) with degrees of freedom equal to *p* (the number of regression coefficients including the intercept) for the numerator term and *n – p* (the number of events in the sample minus the number of regression coefficients including the intercept) for the term in the denominator for the *F* ratio

Residuals Statistics[a]

	Minimum	Maximum	Mean	Std. Deviation	N
Predicted Value	10.74	28.20	20.39	3.092	864
Std. Predicted Value	–3.121	2.525	.000	1.000	884
Standard Error of Predicted Value	.127	.634	.238	.078	884
Adjusted Predicted Value	10.84	28.29	20.39	3.093	884
Residual	–15.268	8.621	.000	3.642	884
Std. Residual	–4.185	2.363	.000	.998	884
Stud. Residual	–4.208	2.378	.000	1.001	884
Deleted Residual	–15.439	8.732	.002	3.664	864
Stud. Deleted Residual	–4.250	2.385	.000	1.003	884
Mahal. Distance	.051	25.032	2.997	2.989	884
Cook's Distance	.000	.050	.002	.005	884
Centered Leverage Value	.000	.029	.003	.003	864

a. Dependent Variable: attitude

---

[7]The formula for Cook's *D* is

$$CD_i = \frac{1}{k+1} r_i^2 \frac{h_{ii}}{1 - h_{ii}},$$

where

k is the number of predictor variables,

r_i is the standardized residual for the point, and

h_{ii} is the *i*th diagonal element from a matrix $\mathbf{X} (\mathbf{X'X})^{-1} \mathbf{X'}$ where $\mathbf{X}$ is a matrix of scores for the predictors.

These h_{ii} values are found in SPSS by choosing *Regression* from the *Analyze* menu, then clicking the *Save* button on the *Linear Regression* dialog box. By checking *Leverage Values* from the *Linear Regression: Save* dialog box, the h_{ii} values are inserted into the data file with the variable name "LEV_1." The centered leverage coefficient can take values ranging from zero (indicating no influence on the model) to $\frac{n-1}{n}$.

(McDonald, 2002, p. 127).[8] The table of values from Appendix C.13 shows that with four regression coefficients (three predictors and the intercept) and a sample size exceeding 500, the critical value for Cook's D is .84. Because the highest Cook's D statistic is .05, the outlier does not appear to reveal a statistically significant influence. Thus, despite their outlier status, it is not necessary to delete these points unless the researcher already has clear evidence that they are not really part of the population of the rest of the sample. As can be seen, with very large samples, the influence of an outlier on regression weights is not likely to be great (as indicated by the lack of a meaningful Cook's D).

What should a researcher do when faced with outliers? There two major options.

- Transformations of the data often can bring outliers closer to the centroids. Square root, logarithmic, and reciprocal transformations often can reduce the effects of outliers. As was explained in Chapter 4, the square root transformation can move the data toward a normal distribution even when there is initially moderate positive skew. The logarithmic transformation can be used when the data show strong positive skew and great variability. The reciprocal transformation is most useful when the data have positive skew and increases in variance after a specific threshold value is reached.
- Removing the outliers may be attempted. In this case, after the outliers were deleted, the resulting model produced a change in R^2 from .419 to .424. When corrected for shrinkage and rounded to the first decimal point, the R^2s did not change.

Model Summary[c]

Model	R	R Square	Adjusted R Square	Std. Error of the Estimate	R Square Change	F Change	df1	df2	Sig. F Change	Durbin-Watson
					Change Statistics					
1	.651[a]	.424	.422	3.623	.424	209.984	3	857	.000	
2	.651[b]	.424	.422	3.622	.000	.152	1	857	.697	.371

a. Predictors: (Constant), char, clarity, believab
b. Predictors: (Constant), char, believab
c. Dependent Variable: attitude

After the deletion, the tests did not detect outliers, but the process does not always work so neatly. Sometimes, researchers can remove outliers only to find that the new calculations show yet other outliers. One scholar explains, "They remove more observations and the cycle starts all over again. By the time they are done, many observations are set aside, no one is quite sure why, and no one feels very good about the final model" (Dallal, 2003, ¶ 11). Though "feelings" are not major influences in statistical testing, the fact is that removing outliers needs to be done with care.

---

[8]Another rule is that if D_i is greater than 1, the point is influential on the regression coefficients (Chatterjee, Hadi, & Price, 2000, p. 104). Because this "rule" diverges from the median of the $F_{p,\ n-p}$ guide, especially when large samples are involved, an alternative rule is that "for datasets with $n > 15$, we can consider points as influential: if $D_i > 0.7$ for $p = 2$, (one predictor); if $D_i > 0.8$ for $p = 3$, (two predictors); and if $D_i > 0.85$ for $p > 3$, (more than [two] predictors)" (McDonald, 2002, p. 127).

Check on Autocorrelation

Autocorrelation (sometimes called "serial correlation") is "a correlation of the values of a variable with the values of the same variable lagged one or more time periods back" (Aczel, 1989, p. 571). It tends to be reflected in cyclical activity when plots are examined. Because an assumption of multiple correlation is that the errors in prediction are independent, highly correlated errors are cause for concern. Autocorrelation often occurs in time-series analyses, where effects of some variables continue to be observed over time, even though the independent variables may change. The problem with autocorrelation is that it creates conditions where the seeming "fit" to the data is exaggerated. Because the standard errors become smaller than they ordinarily would be, the overall multiple R coefficients tend to be inflated. Thus, researchers may believe they have meaningful results when, in reality, they do not.

There are two types of autocorrelation. **Positive autocorrelation** involves a positive or negative residual to be followed by another of the same sign. Hence, the groups of positive and negative residuals tend to be in groups across time. Negative autocorrelation involves following a positive or negative residual with another of a different sign. Hence, over time a positive residual tends to be followed by a negative residual, and a negative residual tends to be followed in time by a positive residual. Figure 13.1 illustrates these plots.

Figure 13.1 Durbin-Watson Statistics With Autocorrelation Examples

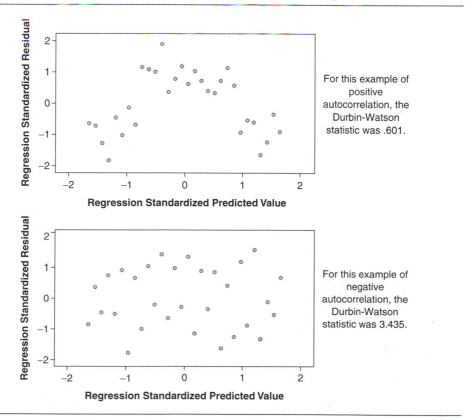

For this example of positive autocorrelation, the Durbin-Watson statistic was .601.

For this example of negative autocorrelation, the Durbin-Watson statistic was 3.435.

Model Summary[b]

Model	R	R Square	Adjusted R Square	Std. Error of the Estimate	Change Statistics						Durbin-Watson
					R Square Change	F Change	df1	df2	Sig. F Change		
1	.560[a]	.314	.289	2.08155	.314	12.814	1	28	.001		.601

a. Predictors: (Constant), time

b. Dependent Variable: confident

To identify if there is autocorrelation, the Durbin-Watson test may be enlisted. This test examines the null hypothesis H_0: $\rho = 0$, that there is no autocorrelation. In setting an alpha risk for the test, the researcher must realize that there may be either a directional or a nondirectional test. If one wishes to test for either positive or negative autocorrelation, a one-sided test may be used. But if the researcher wishes to know only if there is *some kind* of autocorrelation, a nondirectional test may be completed.

To obtain a plot of results, from the *Linear Regression* dialog box, the researcher clicks the *Plots* button. Then, the standardized residuals for the Y (vertical) axis may be identified and moved to the "*Y:*" field. The standardized residuals for the X (horizontal) axis may be identified and moved to the "*X:*" field.

The Durbin-Watson test uses the statistic

$$d = \frac{\sum_{t=2}^{n} (e_t - e_{t-1})^2}{\sum_{t=1}^{n} e_t^2},$$

where

e is the residual,

t is the time of the observation (thus, e_t is the residual at a given time, and e_{t-1} is the residual at the previous time), and

n is the number of events.

The Durbin-Watson test may be secured through SPSS by checking the *Durbin-Watson* test from the *Residuals* field in the *Linear Regression: Statistics* dialog box. After clicking the *Continue* button and the *OK* button, the test is reported as part of the *Model Summary* output. As Figure 13.1 shows, very small Durbin-Watson statistics are associated with positive autocorrelation, and very large statistics are linked to negative autocorrelation.

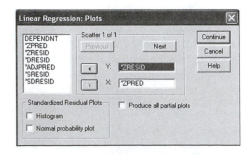

After clicking the *Continue* and *OK* buttons, the output is revealed. This output includes plots of

standardized residual and predictor variables. Though not strictly required to examine autocorrelation, the charts using standardized and unstandardized scores are very similar. Hence, researchers often can avoid using the separate SPSS *Chart* subroutines to produce a scatterplot of the residuals and time.

For a directional test examining evidence for a positive autocorrelation, the null hypothesis is H_0: $\rho = 0$, and the alternative research hypothesis is H_1: $\rho > 0$.

- If the Durbin-Watson test coefficient is below the lower limit (d_L) identified from the table of critical values, the one-tailed test is statistically significant. A portion of that table from Appendix C.14 appears below.

Critical Values of the Durbin-Watson Test at One-Tailed Alpha Risk of .05 and Two-Tailed Alpha Risk of .05 (in Bold in Parentheses)

Number of Events in Study	Upper and Lower Limits	Number of Independent (Predictor) Variables				
		1	*2*	*3*	*4*	*5*
15	Lower Limit of *d*	1.08 (**.95**)	.95 (**.83**)	.82 (**.71**)	.69 (**.59**)	.56 (**.48**)
	Upper Limit of *d*	1.36 (**1.23**)	1.54 (**1.40**)	1.75 (**1.61**)	1.97 (**1.84**)	2.21 (**2.09**)
30	Lower Limit of *d*	1.35 (**1.25**)	1.28 (**1.18**)	1.21 (**1.12**)	1.14 (**1.05**)	1.07 (**.98**)
	Upper Limit of *d*	1.49 (**1.38**)	1.57 (**1.46**)	1.65 (**1.54**)	1.74 (**1.63**)	1.83 (**1.73**)

Because the example of the positive autocorrelation is based on a sample of 30 events, a researcher making a directional (one-tailed) test with one independent variable would find that the *lower limit of* d is 1.35. Because the Durbin-Watson test is .601, the researcher would conclude that the residuals show evidence of positive autocorrelation.

- Traditionally, if the test statistic falls within the upper and lower limits (in this case, 1.35 and 1.49), the researcher accepts that the test is not conclusive on the matter.
- If the test statistic is greater than the *upper limit of* d, the researcher concludes that there is no evidence for claims of positive autocorrelation.

For a directional test examining evidence for negative autocorrelation, the null hypothesis is H_0: $\rho = 0$, and the alternative research hypothesis is H_1: $\rho < 0$. The range of the Durbin-Watson statistic is from 0 to 4. So, to use the same set of critical values, the researcher engages in some reversing of values.

- A statistically significant negative autocorrelation is claimed if the Durbin-Watson test statistic is greater than 4 minus the lower limit of *d* (d_L). In the example of negative autocorrelation in Figure 13.1, the Durbin-Watson test statistic was 3.435. With alpha risk of .05 (one-tailed), one independent variable, and a sample of 30 events, the *lower limit of* d found in the table of critical values (Appendix C.14) is 1.35. Carrying out the computations, 4 − 1.35 is 2.65. Because the observed value of 3.435 is greater than the minimum critical value, the researcher would conclude that there is evidence of negative autocorrelation.

- When the Durbin-Watson test statistic is between $4 - d_L$ (d_L represents the lower limit of d) and $4 - d_U$ (d_U represents the upper limit of d), the test is inconclusive.
- When the Durbin-Watson test statistic d is greater than $4 - d_L$, the researcher concludes that there is evidence of negative first-order error autocorrelation. When d is between $4 - d_U$ and $4 - d_L$, the test is inconclusive, and when d is below $4 - d_U$ (d_U represents the upper limit of d), there is no evidence of negative first-order autocorrelation of the errors.

For a nondirectional test examining evidence for a positive autocorrelation, the null hypothesis remains H_0: $\rho = 0$, and the alternative research hypothesis is H_1: $\rho \neq 0$. The researcher must remember, however, to use the *two-tailed* Durbin-Watson values from the table in Appendix C.14. The null hypothesis is rejected if the Durbin-Watson test coefficient is

- *Either* below $4 - d_U$ (indicating positive autocorrelation) *or*
- Above $4 - d_L$ (indicating negative autocorrelation).

For instance, suppose a researcher observes a Durbin-Watson statistic of 2.9 in a study involving a sample of 30 with two independent variables. With alpha risk of .05 (two-tailed), the two-tailed lower limit of d is 1.18 and the upper limit of d is 1.46. In these computations, $4 - d_L$ is 2.82 ($4 - 1.18 = 2.82$). Because the Durbin-Watson test coefficient of 2.9 is greater than $4 - d_L$, the researcher concludes that there is negative autocorrelation.

If autocorrelation is suspected, "Ideally, an autocorrelation model for the error terms should be adopted" (Ott & Hildebrand, 1983, p. 541). One simple error model is the **first-order autoregressive model**

$$\varepsilon_t = u_t + \rho u_{t-1},$$

where the u values are independent and ρ is a model parameter; $\rho > 0$ yields positive autocorrelation. If this model is correct and if (miraculously) ρ is known, then it can be proven that

$$Y_t - \rho Y_{t-1} = \beta_0(1 - \rho) + \beta_1(X_{t1} - \rho X_{t-1,1}) \ldots \beta_\kappa(X_{tk} - \rho X_{t-1,\kappa}) + \varepsilon_i - \rho \varepsilon_{t-1,1})$$

is a model satisfying the independent error assumption (Ott & Hildebrand, 1983, p. 541).

Unfortunately, researchers rarely know the value of ρ. One solution is to assume that $\rho = 1$. Then, the researcher may complete multiple regression analysis based on differences ($Y_t - Y_{t-1}$ and $X_t - X_{t-1}$). These differences often tend to eliminate the influences of autocorrelation.

In passing, it might be mentioned that the Durbin-Watson test is designed to identify first-order autocorrelation. Though details are beyond the scope of this book, there can be higher-order autocorrelations (second-order or third-order, for instance) without the presence of first-order autocorrelation. In such cases, rare though they are, the Durbin-Watson test is not helpful in identifying the autocorrelation forms.

Because autocorrelation often means a cyclical pattern exists, some (e.g., Ott & Hildebrand, 1983, p. 541) suggest that this effect might be added as a new predictor variable. One variable could be divided into two categories (1 representing the negative residuals and 2 representing the positive residuals). A warning is in order, of course. Variables added into the multiple regression equation require increased sample sizes. Furthermore, adding predictors without some theoretic rationale is not generally advised.

Check on Multicollinearity

Researchers have many tools to check for multicollinearity among predictor variables. In SPSS, some statistics are produced by researchers' checking *Collinearity diagnostics* in the *Linear Regression: Statistics* dialog box when running the *Regression* subroutine. The results include a section reporting a set of *Collinearity Statistics*. Two related statistics are presented.

Coefficients[a]

Model		Unstandardized Coefficients B	Unstandardized Coefficients Std. Error	Standardized Coefficients Beta	t	Sig.	Correlations Zero-order	Correlations Parital	Correlations Part	Collinearity Statistics Tolerance	Collinearity Statistics VIF
1	(Constant)	5.083	.671		7.581	.000					
	char	.228	.037	.185	6.074	.000	.437	.203	.158	.726	1.378
	clarity	−.012	.040	−.011	−.313	.755	.418	−.011	−.008	.568	1.760
	believab	.403	.025	.548	15.870	.000	.627	.476	.413	.570	1.753
2	(Constant)	5.070	.669		7.581	.000					
	char	.225	.036	.183	6.211	.000	.437	.207	.161	.779	1.284
	believab	.399	.022	.541	18.363	.000	.627	.530	.477	.779	1.284

a. Dependent Variable: attitude

- **Tolerance** is "the proportion of the variability in one independent variable not explained by the other independent variables" (Vogt, 2005, p. 325). It is computed by taking $1 - R^2$, with the individual variable treated as the dependent variable and the other variables treated as predictor variables. A tolerance approaching zero indicates a problem with multicollinearity, because it means that the variable in question contributes very little unique information to the overall model. In this case, the tolerances are fairly high (the possible range is 0 to 1). Hence, no multicollinearity problems are claimed.

- VIF, or the **variance inflation factor**, is $\dfrac{1}{\text{tolerance}}$.

  Hence, it reveals much of the same information as the tolerance. Computed with actual values to the second decimal point, the range of scores is from 1 to 100. Large VIF coefficients indicate that the regression coefficient variance is increasing, suggesting instability associated with multicollinearity problems. Not unexpectedly, the data presented in the example used here have small coefficients, indicating no great problems with multicollinearity.

To aid interpretation, other information is supplied in the *Collinearity Diagnostics* table.

Collinearity Diagnostics[a]

Model	Dimension	Eigenvalue	Condition Index	Variance Proportions			
				(Constant)	char	clarity	believab
1	1	3.918	1.000	.00	.00	.00	.00
	2	.039	9.965	.28	.09	.54	.03
	3	.022	13.201	.14	.65	.10	.48
	4	.020	14.057	.57	.26	.35	.49
2	1	2.952	1.000	.00	.00		.00
	2	.026	10.572	.29	.15		.98
	3	.022	11.685	.70	.85		.01

a. Dependent Variable: attitude

Eigenvalues are statistics used "to indicate how much of the variation in the original group of variables is accounted for by a particular factor" (Vogt, 2005, pp. 103–104). Though this term will be revisited in another chapter, it may be said here that eigenvalues indicate how many dimensions underlie a group of predictor variables. When many eigenvalues are near 0, the matrix becomes an *ill-conditioned cross-product matrix*, suggesting a multicollinearity problem. Though eigenvalues may be used to assess multicollinearity, they are most helpful here when used to create the **condition index**, which is the square root of the largest eigenvalue divided by each smaller eigenvalue. Though there is no test of statistical significance, a general rule of thumb is that a condition index above 15 indicates possible multicollinearity, and a condition index above 30 indicates severe multicollinearity. In each of the models listed in the example, the largest eigenvalue is associated with the intercept. The condition index values show that variables do not show strong intercorrelations.

Another part of the output deals with *Excluded Variables* that have been removed from the model. In this case, the message clarity variable was removed and a multiple correlation was completed. In addition to the contribution made by the variable to the multiple regression equation, the *Tolerance* and *VIF* show what these values would be if the excluded variable were included.

Excluded Variables[b]

Model		Beta in	t	Sig.	Partial Correlation	Collinearty Statistics		
						Tolerance	VIF	Minimum Tolerance
2	clarity	−.011[a]	−.313	.755	−.011	.568	1.760	.568

a. Predictors in the Model: (Constant), believab, char
b. Dependent Variable: attitude

A test of statistical significance to identify multicollinearity is called Haitovsky's test (Haitovsky, 1969). This test examines the null hypothesis that the matrix of correlations among independent variables is singular with a determinant of zero, the situation that would occur if the predictor variables were perfectly correlated with each other. A **determinant** "represents the *generalized* variance for several variables. That is, it characterizes in a single number how much variability is present on a set of variables" (J. P. Stevens, 2002, p. 64).[9] A nonsingular (or "regular" or "invertible") matrix is one that has an inverse, a quality that is essential for computing multiple correlation. As one scholar put it, .

> At the purely mathematical level, the assumption of nonsingularity is required in order that we may invert the correlation matrix of explanatory variables and thus obtain a solution for the regression equation. If this correlation matrix is singular no inversion is possible. Unlike the violation of such other assumptions as that of homoscedasticity, the regression analysis mathematically cannot proceed if the correlation matrix is singular. (Rockwell, 1975, p. 309)

In multiple correlation, a nonsingular matrix of intercorrelations is one that shows relatively low intercorrelations among the predictor variables. A nonsingular matrix has a determinant that is close to 1.0. Thus, examining the determinant can help identify if multicollinearity is a problem.

Specifically, the formula for Haitovsky's test is

$$\chi_h^2 = \left(1 + \frac{2p + 5}{6} - N\right) * \ln(1 - |\mathbf{X}^\mathsf{T}\mathbf{X}|),$$

---

[9] For a 2 × 2 matrix of predictor variables, such as the following illustrating total multicollinearity, the determinant for the table is computed by $|\mathbf{A}| = AD - BC = 1 * 1 - (1 * 1) = 0$.

	X_1	X_2
X_1	1 (Cell A)	1 (Cell B)
X_2	1 (Cell C)	1 (Cell D)

This matrix is, of course, a singular matrix of predictor variables. In a situation in which there is no multicollinearity at all, such as in the following table, the determinant is 1.

	X_1	X_2
X_1	1 (Cell A)	0 (Cell B)
X_2	0 (Cell C)	1 (Cell D)

This example is, of course, nonsingular and indicates a theoretically ideal set of predictors for multiple regression correlation.

where

p is the number of predictor variables,

N is the number of elements in the sample, and

$|X^TX|$ is the determinant of the correlation matrix of independent variables.

The degrees of freedom to enter the chi-square distribution are computed by $\dfrac{p * (p - 1)}{2}$.

If the test shows a statistically significant difference, it shows that multicollinearity is *not* a problem because the correlation matrix of predictor variables is *not* singular. Thus, researchers using multiple regression correlation desire that the Haitovsky test is statistically significant.

SPSS provides more than one way to identify the determinant. Among the easiest is to choose *Data Reduction* from the *Analyze* menu. Then *Factor. . .* may be selected. From the *Factor Analysis* dialog box, the researcher may highlight the independent variables and use the arrow key to move them into the "Variables:" field.

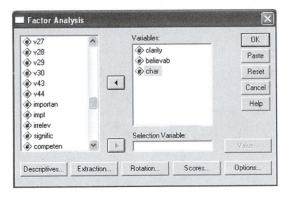

Then, the *Descriptives . . .* button may be clicked. In the *Factor Analysis: Descriptives* dialog box, the researcher checks the "Coefficients" and "Determinant" boxes. Then, the *Continue* button is clicked, followed by *OK* in the *Factor Analysis* dialog box.

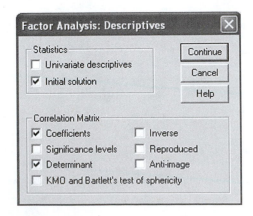

A portion of the output reveals the following information. Beneath the correlation matrix is the determinant. In this case, the determinant of the correlation matrix of predictor variables is .442.

Correlation Matrix[a]

		clarity	believab	char
Correlation	clarity	1.000	.625	.474
	believab	.625	1.000	.470
	char	.474	.470	1.000

a. Determinant = .442

To apply Haitovsky's test to the data, the following computations may be completed:

$$\chi_h^2 = \left(1 + \frac{2p + 5}{6} - N\right) * \ln(1 - |\mathbf{X^T X}|)$$

$$= \left(1 + \frac{(2 * 3) + 5}{6} - 864\right) * \ln(1 - .442)$$

$$= (1 + 1.83 - 864) * \ln(.558) = . - 861.17 * -.58 = 499.48.$$

Degrees of freedom are equal to

$$\frac{p * (p - 1)}{2},$$

which are 3 in this case

$$\left(\frac{3 * (3 - 1)}{2} = \frac{6}{2} = 3\right).$$

The critical chi-square value with 3 degrees of freedom and alpha risk of .05 is 7.81. Because the test statistic far exceeds the critical value, the researcher concludes that the correlation matrix among predictor variables is not singular. Hence, the researcher is able to claim that multicollinearity is not a statistically significant problem in the research.

What would happen if Haitovsky's test were not statistically significant? The presence of multicollinearity would be indicated. Yet, it is helpful to note that "collinearity does not affect the ability of a regression equation to predict the response. It poses a real problem if the purpose of the study is to estimate the contributions of individual predictors" (Dallal, 2001, ¶ 9). Thus, multicollinearity affects the regression weights much more than the overall *R*. Nevertheless, when there is multicollinearity, researchers normally attempt some form of data reduction. Sometimes researchers use factor analysis (which attempts to identify the number and nature of dimensions underlying a number of measures) to reduce the number of measures. As an alternative, sometimes researchers select a variable to represent the entire collection of highly intercorrelated predictors. This step has the effect of throwing out some other predictor variables, however, and may not be suitable to all researchers' purposes. Sometimes researchers simply discard offending predictor variables, but such a method may be troublesome because sometimes it may deny the importance of theory in guiding choices for constructing useful models. Garson (2003, ¶ 95) offers this list of additional possible reactions to multicollinearity:

1. Increasing the sample size is a common first step since when sample size is increased, the standard error decreases (all other things equal). This partially offsets the problem that high multicollinearity leads to high standard errors of the b and beta coefficients.

2. Use **centering**: transform the offending independents by subtracting the mean from each case. The resulting centered data may well display considerably lower multicollinearity. You should have a theoretical justification for this consistent with the fact that a zero b coefficient will now correspond to the independent being at its mean, not at zero, and interpretations of b and beta must be changed accordingly. . . .

3. [S]ubstitute [the] . . . crossproduct as an interaction term, or in some other way combine the intercorrelated variables. This is equivalent to respecifying the model by conceptualizing the correlated variables as indicators of a single latent variable. . . .

4. Leave one intercorrelated variable as is but then remove the variance in its covariates by regressing them on that variable and using the residuals.

5. Assign the common variance to each of the covariates by some probably arbitrary procedure.

6. Treat the common variance as a separate variable and decontaminate each covariate by regressing them on the others and using the residuals. That is, analyze the common variance as a separate variable. . . .

7. [Use ridge regression.] Ridge regression is an attempt to deal with multicollinearity through use of a form of biased estimation in place of OLS [ordinary least squares]. The method requires setting an arbitrary "ridge constant" which is used to produce estimated regression coefficients with lower computed standard errors. However, because picking the ridge constant requires knowledge of the unknown *population* coefficients one is trying to estimate, Fox (1991: [p.] 20) and others recommend against its use in most cases. SPSS has no ridge regression procedure, but its macro library has the macro ridge_regression.sps.

Chapter 14

EXTENSIONS OF MULTIPLE REGRESSION CORRELATION

Multiple regression correlation is a highly versatile family of tools. This chapter provides information about some additional ways multiple regression correlation may be used to deal with categorical independent variables, to examine interactions, and to explore forms of nonlinear effects.

USING CATEGORICAL PREDICTORS

Although multiple regression correlation typically uses predictor variables that are continuous measures, the method also may employ categorical predictors. For instance, researchers may use such variables as sex of participants, whether people are exposed to experimental or control conditions, or the types of message strategies people use in attempts at compliance gaining.

Dummy or Indicator Predictors

Dummy or indicator predictors are ways of coding categorical variables to represent nominal or qualitative variables. For instance, if researchers want to know if exposure to a message with previews enhances comprehension more than exposure to a message without the previews, they could use dummy variable coding. Every person who hears the message with the previews could be identified with a score of 1 on a variable called MESSAGE, and every person who does not hear the previews would receive a score of 0. If a control group is one of the two conditions, it should be coded as 0.

If there are three or more nominal categories involved, dummy variable coding typically adds variables (coded 0 or 1) to represent the presence or absence of additional categories. Suppose a researcher wishes to compare source competence ratings from three conditions where participants hear a persuasive message with reporting evidence, statistical evidence, or opinion evidence. A new variable (perhaps called EVID1) would be coded as 1 if participants are exposed to reporting evidence and 0 otherwise. A new variable (perhaps called EVID2) would be coded as 1 if participants are exposed to statistical evidence and 0 otherwise. The third condition is not represented by a third dummy variable because there can only be $g - 1$ (groups minus 1) aspects to test. Although it may not be immediately obvious, all three aspects of the conditions are fully described by two independent dummy variables. For example, identifying males and females in a sample only requires one variable (coded 0 and 1) to cover both categories. For three categories, only two dummy variables are needed because the third category is "represented implicitly: all cases falling in this category have X_1, X_2, and X_3 scores of 0, 0, 0" (J. Cohen & Cohen, 1983, p. 184). In fact, if a researcher includes a third dummy variable, there would be severe multicollinearity among predictors:

> If the analyst mistakenly fails to omit one category of the nominal variable from a regression which includes the intercept term, the correlation matrix is singular [the redundant third variable would be a simple linear function of the first two dummy variables]. If the category has very low frequency, the correlation matrix approaches singularity. This occurs even in the typical situation in which all simple correlations of dummy variables with other variables are minute. (Rockwell, 1975, pp. 312–313)

Thus, in our example the third category has not disappeared at all. It is the one condition receiving 0 on all the dummy variables.[1]

---

[1] Some advice about dummy variable coding is often given. First, if there is a true control group, it is recommended that this condition be the last group in the coding. Second,

> It's usually desirable, however, to choose an omitted category with a fairly large number of cases. If the omitted category has a small number of cases, the coefficients for the included categories will have large standard errors.
>
>   When representing a categorical variable by a set of dummy variables, it's desirable to perform a global test of whether all the dummies have coefficients of 0. This test does not depend on which category is chosen as the omitted category. (Allison, 1999, p. 172)

Third, "when group g has been assigned 0's arbitrarily, it is usually appropriate to run an additional regression analysis in which group g is now assigned 1's in a new dummy vector to obtain the relevant statistics and tests for group g" (J. J. Stevens, 1999, ¶ 8).

Special Discussion 14.1

Suppressor Variables

Researchers often find that relationships that should emerge seem elusive. Sometimes the difficulty is that there are suppressor variables operating in nonrandom ways. For multiple regression correlation studies, suppressors may be a particular concern. A **suppressor variable** is defined as a variable that conceals "or reduces (suppresses) a relationship between other variables. It may be an independent variable unrelated to the dependent variable but correlated with one or more of the other independent variables" (Vogt, 2005, p. 318). For instance, as a hypothetical example, a researcher may suspect that as people mature from adolescence, their assertiveness levels increase, but an individual's self-monitoring behavior also may increase with age and, if it does, the relationship between age and assertiveness would be reduced. Hence, self-monitoring would be a suppressor variable of the relationship between age and assertiveness. By itself, it would correlate lowly and inversely with the dependent variable, though it would have a moderate to high direct correlation with the other predictor variable. Failure to include the suppressor variable would result in underestimation of the size of coefficients in the model. Furthermore, the correlation of the suppressor variable with the dependent variable emerges only when other predictor variables are controlled.

The variable entry method used by researchers may cause difficulty for researchers. If researchers use the "forward" or "stepwise" selection methods, predictor variables are entered according to their relationship with the dependent variable (using assessments of relationship size or statistical significance probabilities). But with a suppressor variable, the statistically significant relationship with the dependent variable is clear only when controlling for other predictor variables. A suppressor variable probably would not be identified as a significant predictor when these methods are used.

When suggesting how to prevent missing important suppressor variables, J. P. Stevens (2002, p. 124) references Lord and Novick (1968) as recommending that when selecting predictor variables, researchers should

1. Choose variables that correlate highly with the criterion but that have low intercorrelations.

2. Add other variables to those selected above, such that these new variables have low correlations with the criterion but have high correlations with the other predictors.

Though the second piece of advice initially may sound silly, it is a reminder to pay attention to the possibility of suppressor variables in the data set.

When the new variables EVID1 and EVID2 are included in the multiple regression model, the regression weight b_0 for the intercept or constant is the dependent variable mean for all dummy variables coded as 0 (in short, it is the mean of the last evidence condition, dealing with opinion evidence effects on source competence ratings). Each regression weight reports the comparison of the group coded as 1 with the group coded as 0 on all dummy variables (regardless of coefficients of variables carrying interactions). A positive value for the regression coefficient b means that the group scores are higher than those for the group coded as 0 on all dummy variables. A negative value for the regression coefficient means that the group scores are lower than the group coded as 0 on all dummy variables. It should be understood that these interpretations apply to situations where the researcher has used only one independent variable whose levels have been dummy variable coded into separate variables. When there are other predictor variables in the multiple correlation equation, b_0 includes the value of the dependent variable when *all* predictor variables are equal to zero. The individual regression coefficient for the dummy-variable-coded variable reveals the difference between the variable category coded 1 "and all those coded 0 on the vector, while controlling for all other variables in the equation" (J. J. Stevens, 1999, ¶ 9). This use of multiple regression correlation illustrates an additional way that multiple regression correlation and analysis of variance may be considered equivalent methods.

Effects Coding

Sometimes called "deviation coding," **effects coding** identifies groups of participants on a new categorical variable, rather than using dummy variable coding. Effects coding uses values beyond 0 and 1 to code two or, most often, more than two categories. For instance, a researcher was interested in predicting communication adaptability (the degree to which a communicator adjusts interaction goals and behaviors in appropriate ways) of roommates from knowledge of the roommate's academic major: the fine arts, social sciences, business, natural sciences and mathematics, and other fields. Because it generally is believed that majors in the natural sciences and mathematics show the lowest levels of communication adaptability, they would be considered the candidates for lowest effects coding ratings. Hence, the natural sciences and mathematics majors would serve as a control group of responses. To code these effects, four variables are created and coded, as shown in Table 14.1.

Table 14.1

	X_1	X_2	X_3	X_4
Fine arts and humanities	1	0	0	0
Social sciences	0	1	0	0
Business	0	0	1	0
Other	0	0	0	1
Natural sciences and mathematics	−1	−1	−1	−1

To effects code the levels of the categorical variable representing different groups, $k - 1$ (with k as the number of categories) new variables are created. The sum of effects for each column is zero. Similar to dummy variable coding, the last group is included as the group receiving the effects code "−1" on all the variables. The regression coefficient b_0 for the intercept identifies the grand mean. A significant effect for variable X_1 indicates a primary difference between communication adaptability scores of fine arts and humanities majors on one hand, and natural sciences and mathematics majors on the other, while the influences of the three remaining majors are minimized.[2] The effects-coded variable X_2 primarily distinguishes between communication adaptability scores of social sciences majors and natural sciences and mathematics majors, while the influences of the three remaining majors are minimized. Because the regression coefficient for the intercept identifies the grand mean, other regression coefficients indicate the differences between one group when compared with the collection of all the others. In contrast, dummy variable coding suggests the influence of the presence or absence of a variable level in contrast to a single control condition.

When analyses are completed, researchers examine t tests to see if a given mean has a statistically significant difference from the grand mean. The direction of regression weights reveals something about the influence of a group or condition. For any group represented by an X variable, a positive regression coefficient indicates that the group's mean is higher than the grand mean of all groups. Because the other "effects-coded" variables include all comparison groups, no redundant direct comparison is made between the grand mean and the group coded with all -1 coefficients. Because researchers usually are interested in differences between group means, further interpretations of the sizes of beta weights are not usually given prominent attention.

Contrast Coding

Sometimes called "orthogonal contrast coding" or just "orthogonal coding," **contrast coding** "compares one linear combination of groups with a second linear combination of groups" (Bernstein, 1988, p. 126). Though the logic may be used to contrast two groups, contrast coding is particularly useful in situations where a researcher has more than two groups, such as when an experimenter exposes participants to messages from lowly, moderately, and highly credible sources. Although there is more than one way to compose contrast coefficients, when a predictor variable has more than two categories representing an underlying continuum, the values assigned to these conditions often may be drawn

Number of Group Means	Type of Trend	Coefficients (c_j) for Each Mean								
		1	2	3	4	5	6	7	8	9
3	Linear	−1	0	1						
	Quadratic	1	−2	1						
4	Linear	−3	−1	1	3					
	Quadratic	1	−1	−1	1					
	Cubic	−1	3	−3	1					

conveniently from the table of orthogonal polynomials in Appendix C.9, a portion of which is shown above. For situations where the groups are not from a continuum, but simple nominal

---

[2]Unlike dummy variable coding, where 0 and 1 are used, effects coding places no value between conditions coded −1 and +1. As J. Cohen and Cohen (1983) explain, "The minimum influence of the 0-coded groups on r_y is literally nil whenever $n_i = n_g$, that is, the sample sizes for the group coded 1 and the group coded −1 are equal" (p. 198). They observe that "*raw variables* sound like the *partialled* variables in dummy-variable analysis, and for equal n_i, they are" (p. 198).

In effects coding, the partialled X_1 produces a contrast between G_i and *all* the groups in the sample or, because the total sample includes G_i, one can think of the partialled effects-coded X_1 as a contrast between G_i and the remaining groups. In fact, the term *effects* comes from the AV [analysis of variance], where the sample effect of an experimental Treatment i on some dependent variable is the difference between that treatment group's mean $\bar{Y}_i$, and the unweighted mean of *all* the sample means of the observations $\bar{\bar{Y}}$ (i.e., the effect of Treatment i on Y is $\bar{Y}_i - \bar{\bar{Y}}$). (pp. 200–201)

categories (such as when researchers code four types of evidence used in persuasive messages), the researcher is careful to form contrasts that are consistent with hypotheses.

In the case of comparing three means arranged in order, the linear contrast coefficients are relevant. For instance, consider the case of a study in which a researcher examines the believability of a message attributed to sources with three levels of credibility (low, moderate, and high). The researcher might have two hypotheses:

H_1: Participants exposed to a persuasive message from a highly credible source show greater attitude change than participants exposed to a persuasive message from a lowly credible source.

H_2: Participants exposed to a persuasive message from a highly credible source show greater attitude change than participants exposed to a persuasive message from either a moderately or a lowly credible source.

The number of contrasts that can be tested is limited to the number of groups minus 1. Thus, in this example, two new variables are added to create the contrasts. Because the first hypothesis states that the high-credibility group differs from the low-credibility group, the linear trend coefficients may be used. As Table 14.2 shows, for the newly created X variable,

the low-credibility group is assigned a value of −1,

the high credibility group is assigned a value of +1, and

the moderate credibility group is assigned a value of 0.

For the second hypothesis, the high-credibility group is predicted to have higher message believability scores than members of the remaining two groups. Consistent with this hypothesis, the trend coefficients for the quadratic term may be used (1, −2, 1). Because the high-credibility condition is hypothesized to have message believability scores different from those of the other two groups, the high-credibility condition is given the polynomial that is different from the others. By the way, the same multiple correlation coefficient results would emerge if the signs of the contrast coefficients were reversed. The same multiple correlation information would appear, and the regression and beta weights (along with the t tests) would have the same values. The sign of the regression, beta, and t values would change, but this fact would not alter the results of the rest of the multiple regression correlation. So, if the researcher wishes, it is acceptable to reverse the signs of the coefficients to −1, 2, and −1. Each

Table 14.2

	X_1	X_2	Contrast Products
Low credibility	−1	1	−1
Moderate credibility	0	1	1
High credibility	1	−2	−2
			$\sum$ contrast products = −2

contrast-coded variable, thus, is a test of a different research hypothesis. The variables may be introduced into the multiple regression correlation to explore whether the results show significant effects related to the hypotheses.

One might think that the use of orthogonal contrast coefficients means that *contrasts* are orthogonal, and they are. If one adds the contrast coefficients for each hypothesis, the sum of the coefficients is 0. But to determine if the *hypotheses* also are orthogonal, the contrast coefficients for each group may be multiplied and added together. If the sum of these contrast products is not equal to zero, as is the case here, the hypothesized contrasts are not orthogonal. Common sense would also suggest that the hypotheses overlap, because *each* states that the high-credibility condition differs from another group on the amount of message believability produced. Hence, the same groups are repeatedly used to make comparisons. This fact increases the chances of Type I error beyond the alpha risk set by the researcher. When the hypothesized contrasts are not orthogonal, many (Bernstein, 1988, p. 135) suggest making some adjustment of the alpha risk used for each test of significance of beta weights. The level of each test's alpha risk, α', may be set by computing $\alpha' = 1 - (1 - \alpha)^{\frac{1}{k}}$, where k is the number of nonorthogonal hypothesis tests. In this case, because there are two new variables creating the nonorthogonal hypotheses represented by contrast-coded variables, the testwise alpha risk should be set at .0253 to maintain an overall alpha risk at .05. If there were three nonorthogonal hypothesis tests, *each* test's alpha risk would have to be set at .017 to ensure an experimentwise overall alpha risk of .05.

When using contrast coefficients, orthogonality also depends on equal sample sizes. If the sample sizes are unequal, a computational factor that provides weights for different sample sizes actually diminishes orthogonality further (G. Wolf & Cartwright, 1974). Thus, researchers using contrast coding are advised to take steps to ensure equal sample sizes.[3]

After the contrast coding is completed, the multiple regression correlation is completed with the new contrast-coded variables entered into the multiple regression equation in the same step. The researcher inspects the regression and the beta coefficients. The intercept is the weighted mean of scores on the dependent variable. The sizes of the regression weights indicate the influence of the contrasts in the newly created variables. The *t* tests of the beta weights indicate the statistical significance of the difference of the means of the two linear combinations involved in the contrasts for each hypothesis test. Yet, the comparative assessment of beta weights against each other may be difficult to make when the contrasts are not orthogonal.

---

[3]It is important to attempt to keep sample sizes equal across the measurement of all variables. Sometimes, however, participants do not respond to all measures and imbalance occurs. This problem can make the calculations difficult.

> In addition to more difficult computational formulas, designs with unequal group sample sizes may be threatened by a number of validity problems depending on how the unequal samples came about. The term "unbalanced" is used to refer to designs with unequal sample sizes per group. In unbalanced designs, variables that might have been independent or uncorrelated with each other may become related or nonorthogonal. For dummy coding, this has no impact. For other contrast and comparison procedures, however, unequal sample sizes may affect the analysis. For effect coding unequal sample sizes produce a change in the interpretation of the betas. The intercept, B_0, no longer represents the grand mean but the unweighted total mean (the mean of the group means). Similarly, the B_i for each effect vector is no longer a comparison of the group mean to the grand mean, but of the group mean to the unweighted total mean. (J. J. Stevens, 1999, ¶ 30)

CONTRASTING FULL AND REDUCED MODELS: HIERARCHICAL ANALYSIS

Researchers often want to know if the overall R changes when they add key variables. For instance, in examining curvilinear relationships, researchers add variables that carry the nonlinear elements. Then, they check to see if the overall R changes. One application of this approach is **hierarchical analysis**, in which "independent variables are entered into the regression equation in a sequence specified by the researcher in advance" (Vogt, 2005, p. 142). For instance, a researcher might enter a set of variables (sometimes a called "**block**") and look at the R^2 that results. Then, the researcher might add a variable that is an interaction effect among those variables. By comparing the R^2s, the researcher would be able to determine if a main effect or interaction effect explanation were the most useful way to understand the data.

In a typical procedure, the researcher enters variables identified from theory or previous experience with the variables. At each step, the overall R is computed and compared to R values for other models. The result is that

> [t]he R^2 for all h sets [of predictor variables] can thus be analyzed into increments in the proportion of Y variance due to the addition of each new set of IVs [independent variables] in the hierarchy. These increments in R^2 are, in fact, squared multiple semipartial correlation coefficients. . . . (J. Cohen & Cohen, 1983, p. 137)

Sometimes the researcher may not, in fact, find it useful to attempt to look at the comparative influences of all predictor variables. As will be seen subsequently, given the way the nonlinear trends are fit to the data, the comparisons of linear and nonlinear influences are most helpfully examined by looking at overall jumps in the size of R.

To see if the two correlations are different beyond the limits of random sampling error, researchers test a null hypothesis that the population multiple correlation for a model with a large number of predictors is equal to the population multiple correlation for a model with fewer predictors: H_0: $\rho^2_{Y.12...m_2} = \rho^2_{Y.12...m_1}$. The null hypothesis is appropriate when the number of predictors m_2 is greater than the number of predictors m_1. After setting an alpha risk for testing this null hypothesis, the following formula is used (Glass & Hopkins, 1984, p. 315):

$$F = \frac{\dfrac{R^2_{Y.12...m_2} - R^2_{Y.12...m_1}}{m_2 - m_1}}{\dfrac{1 - R^2_{Y.12...m_2}}{n - m_2 - 1}},$$

where:

$R^2_{Y.12...m_2}$ is the larger of the two correlations, with the larger number of predictors (m_2) in the comparison (in essence, the full[er] model);

$R^2_{Y.12...m_1}$ is the smaller of the two correlations, with the smaller number of predictors (m_1) in the comparison (in essence, the partial model);

n is the number of events;

degrees of freedom for the numerator are equal to $m_2 - m_1$ (the difference between the number of predictors in the two compared multiple regression correlations); and

degrees of freedom for the denominator are equal to $n - m_2 - 1$.

If the test statistic F is greater than the critical value at a given alpha risk, the difference between the two R_s is judge to be greater than would have been expected as a result of random sampling error.

INTERACTION EFFECTS

Interaction effects are the influences of variables taken in combinations. Because multiple linear regression correlation does not deal with interaction terms directly, researchers may create additional variables that carry the interactions. Then, they enter the newly created variables into the multiple correlation equation to test if R values show an increase. Sometimes these interactions are considered **moderator effects** because "the interacting third variable which changes the relation between two original variables is a moderator variable which moderates the original relationship" (Garson, 2003, ¶ 10). As already mentioned in the previous chapter, when multiple regression correlation models do not include interaction terms, they sometimes are called main effect models.

As a matter of language, researchers say that an interaction between two variables u and v "is '*carried by*,' not '*is*' the uv product" because "[o]nly when u and v have been linearly partialled from uv does it, in general, become the interaction IV [independent variable] we seek" (J. Cohen & Cohen, 1983, p. 305). Similar language is used when describing nonlinear effects. Though there are some detailed steps to be followed to include terms carrying interactions, generally speaking, the researcher multiplies the variables involved in the interaction to accomplish the task.

As an illustration, interaction effects may be included in multiple regression with two predictor variables as the following model shows: $Y = \beta_0 + \beta_1 X_1 + \beta_2 X_2 + \beta_3 X_1 X_2 + \varepsilon$. The term carrying the interaction source of variation is identified as $\beta_3 X_1 X_2$, which is the last set of terms in the model before the error term ε. As can be seen, interactions are examined in multiple correlation by including a new variable that is the product of the interacting variables. In this case, a third variable is created by multiplying Variable 1 by Variable 2 ($X_1 * X_2$).[4] Many, but certainly not all, scholars suggest the wisdom of standardizing scores first so that a zero point may be included.[5] You will notice that when the interaction is included, the full model is presented, including *both* the main effects and the interaction effect. Eventually, the impact of any interaction effect is detected by comparing Rs from multiple regression equations that include the interaction with others that do not.

---

[4]Some other options have been suggested to examine interactions (see Jaccard & Turrisi, 2003). A predictor variable could be classified into two groups based on a mean or median split (in the case of continuous variables) or on the basis of dichotomies from dummy or effects coding. Then, separate multiple regression correlation analyses could be completed on separate samples that were each restricted to one group level. The unstandardized regression weights represent slope. Hence, a comparison of the differences in slope would indicate the presence or absence of an interaction. A statistically significant difference would indicate an interaction.

[5]Standardizing scores (transforming them into z scores) by subtracting them from their means and dividing by the standard deviations has the advantage of creating values that have the same metric. Thus, some (e.g., Garson, 2003, ¶ 12) recommend that scores on continuous variables involved in interactions should be standardized before they are multiplied by other variables (dummy, effects, or contrast coded) to create variables carrying interaction effects. Others note that the practical influence of such standardizing rarely changes the size of observed R values since in computing correlations, variable data already are represented as z scores prior to taking the mean of their products for each event in the sample. Even so, because variables carrying interaction effects often create multicollinearity problems, using *centered variables* (values from which the mean is subtracted) may be useful because such centering often helps reduce multicollinearity.

The addition of an interaction can be substantial in its effects. For instance, a researcher was interested in predicting the relationship between interpersonal attraction from a knowledge of source credibility and perceived similarity of the source with the receiver. Variables were continuous measures from readily available scales. The multiple correlation coefficient R^2 based on a sample of 60 people was .395. Yet, the regression weights revealed that perceived similarity was not a statistically significant predictor. If the process had stopped there, the researcher might have concluded that similarity did not play much of a role in the process of interpersonal attraction. Rather than giving up, the researcher created a variable to carry an interaction effect by multiplying these two continuous measures by each other. This second model was tested, and the overall R^2 jumped to .602. Such a result suggested that the interaction of perceived similarity with credibility is an important factor in interpersonal attraction.

Model Summary

Model	R	R Square	Adjusted R Square	Std. Error of the Estimate	Change Statistics				
					R Square Change	F Change	df1	df2	Sig. F Change
1	.628[a]	.395	.374	3.28411	.395	18.600	2	57	.000
2	.776[b]	.602	.561	2.67042	.207	29.162	1	56	.000

a. Predictors: (Constant), similar, credib
b. Predictors: (Constant), similar, credib, interact

One might wish to examine the relative influence of different predictors (and all are statistically significant in Model 2). But there is a difficulty. Because the tolerance is quite low, it suggests that there is a problem with multicollinearity among predictors. Such a state of affairs is quite common in studies that include interactions. Hence, the testing of regression weights should not be a part of the process of examining influences.

Coefficients[a]

Model		Unstandardized Coefficients		Standardized Coefficients	t	Sig.	Coefficients			Collinearity Statistics	
		B	Std. Error	Beta			Zero-order	Partial	Part	Tolerance	VIF
1	(Constant)	−32.132	8.627		−3.725	.000					
	credib	22.887	6.765	1.290	3.383	.001	.598	.409	.349	.073	13.700
	similar	−11.318	5.999	−.719	−1.886	.064	.523	−.242	−.194	.073	13.700
2	(Constant)	676.423	131.399		5.148	.000					
	credib	−122.121	27.417	−6.885	−4.454	.000	.598	−.511	−.375	.003	336.232
	similar	−171.414	30.050	−10.896	−5.704	.000	.523	−.606	−.481	.002	513.548
	interac	32.750	6.065	18.188	5.400	.000	.573	.585	.455	.001	1596.554

a. Dependent Variable: Y

On balance, looking at interactions can make meaningful contributions to communication studies, but a word of warning is appropriate. Thoughtlessly adding interaction (and even nonlinear) effects can lead to capitalizing on chance and "overfitting" multiple regression correlation models. Researchers should have some reasoning or theoretic justifications behind the choice to add interactions.

Creating Interaction Terms

The ways that terms carrying interactions may be constructed depend on how predictor variables are measured and coded. When there are two variables involved in an interaction:

- If both individual predictor variables are continuous measures, the term carrying the interaction is simply the product of the two predictor variables. A full multiple regression model including two main additive effects ($\beta_1 X_1$ and $\beta_2 X_2$) and an interaction between two continuous or quantitative measures ($\beta_3 X_1 X_2$) is shown as $Y = \beta_0 + \beta_1 X_1 + \beta_2 X_2 + \beta_3 X_1 X_2 + \varepsilon$. In this case, a third predictor variable carrying the interaction is created by multiplying Variable 1 by Variable 2 ($X_1 * X_2$). The interaction effect is detected by comparing the multiple regression correlation equation that includes the interaction with an equation that excludes the interaction term. A statistically significant difference in R values is taken as evidence of a significant interaction effect.
- If the predictors carrying the interaction are both dummy or effects-coded variables representing simple dichotomous predictor variables, a "new" variable (such as X_3) also is created.[6] The X_3 variable carrying the interaction is simply the cross product of the two indicator variables in the interaction. That is, its values are the products of the X_1 and X_2 dummy variable values.[7] When more than two categories for the independent

---

[6]When the qualitative variable categories are used to examine a continuous dependent variable, the method actually is analysis of variance. In multiple regression correlation, however, the regression equation controls for sources of variation from additional variables. This method is known as analysis of covariance.

[7]Though they admit that the results are the same if dummy variables are coded 0 and 1, J. Cohen and Cohen (1983, pp. 212–214) also recommend that values for the variable carrying the interaction $X_1 X_2$ be created by using effects coding with contrast coefficients. To identify an interaction between two variables of two levels each, the researcher starts by creating an orthogonal contrast with two levels for each variable. For variable X_1, the low level (or control condition) is coded as $-\frac{1}{2}$ and the high (or treatment condition) is coded as $+\frac{1}{2}$. The second predictor variable (X_2) is coded in the same way. Then, a "new" variable (X_3) is created to carry the interaction. Its values are each condition's products of the X_1 and X_2 contrast values.

	Contrast Coefficient	$X_1 (-)$ $-\frac{1}{2}$	$X_1 (+)$ $+\frac{1}{2}$
$X_2 (-)$	$-\frac{1}{2}$	$+\frac{1}{4}$	$-\frac{1}{4}$
$X_2 (+)$	$+\frac{1}{2}$	$-\frac{1}{4}$	$+\frac{1}{4}$

As can be seen, both the main and interaction contrast coefficients sum to zero, maintaining orthogonal contrasts. For instance, for individuals in the condition where X_1 is low (−) and X_2 is low (−), the value for the interaction predictor (X_3) is $+\frac{1}{4}$ or .25; for individuals in the condition where X_2 is low (−) and X_1 is high (+), the value for the interaction predictor (X_3) is $-\frac{1}{4}$ or −.25, and so forth.

In general, overall model results are unaffected by the methods used for coding the categorical variables. In any of the procedures, the overall model tests whether group membership in general is related to the criterion, and how groups are "named" has no effect on this test. As a result, R, R^2, SS, MS, and F will all be the same regardless of coding method. Interpretation of the betas and other information associated with individual vectors or predictors depends completely on what coding method has been used and what vectors are included in the equation (J. J. Stevens, 1999, ¶ 29).

Though the two approaches give the same results on R, it is true that the regression coefficients and the beta weights are different for the two approaches. Thus, testing for the significance of the difference between the R without and R with the effect carrying the interaction is advisable.

variables are subjected to dummy variable coding, interpretations become increasingly complex, and researchers are directed to other sources for details (J. Cohen & Cohen, 1983, esp. chap. 8, and Kelly et al., 1969, esp. chap. 6). When the predictor carrying the interaction is added to the multiple regression correlation equation, a statistically significant interaction effect is identified by observing an increase in the size of R.

- If the two variables are contrast-coded predictors and the contrast coefficients are drawn from the table of orthogonal polynomials (Appendix C.9), the task of identifying interactions is simplified. By using the orthogonal polynomials, a term carrying the interaction is simply the product of the contrast coefficients from each level of the predictors involved in this interaction. For instance, in a situation where two predictors have three levels (a low, moderate, and high level), the linear orthogonal polynomials for each are −1, 0, and +1. The following arrangement would be involved:

Table 14.3

		X_1 *(low)*	X_1 *(moderate)*	X_1 *(high)*
	Contrast Coefficient	−1	0	+1
X_2 *(low)*	−1	1	0	−1
X_2 *(moderate)*	0	0	0	0
X_2 *(high)*	+1	−1	0	+1

A new variable (X_3) carrying the interaction variable would be created. Its values would be the products of the contrast coefficients. For instance, the value corresponding to the combination of X_1 at its low level and X_2 at is low level would be equal to 1 (X_1[low] with a value of 1 times X_2[low] with a value of 1 equals 1). In comparisons of multiple regression correlation equations with and without the variable carrying the interaction, the researcher would detect whether interaction effects are present by observing significant changes in R values.

- When one variable is continuous and the other is a dummy or effects-coded variable, the process of coding an interaction term must be done cautiously. The interaction would indicate different patterns from each level of the qualitative variable, not necessarily a statistically significant effect from *degrees* of the two predictor variables. Consider an interaction involving levels of a dummy or effects-coded variable and a continuous measure. In essence, the researcher describes different slopes at differently coded levels. Comparing slopes from each level of the qualitative variable is invited. The researcher multiplies the two variables involved in the interaction to create an indicator variable to carry in the interaction effect. When there are two predictor variables, therefore, the regression equation would include the two predictors (X_1 and X_2—whether standardized or not) and an indicator variable (X_3) carrying the interaction: $Y = \beta_0 + \beta_1 X_1 + \beta_2 X_2 + \beta_3 X_1 X_2 + \varepsilon$. The interaction is between a categorical and a continuous measure. In essence, this analysis explores whether the slope of the regression line is different when the dummy-coded variable is equal to 0 (or −1 for effects-coded variables) or when it is equal to 1. By examining different multiple regression correlations, the researcher identifies differences in slopes to understand the nature of interactions. In particular, with two predictor variables (one continuous and one dummy coded) and one indicator variable carrying the interaction (adapted from Aczel, 1989, pp. 537–538), the following interpretations are involved:

- o If the regression coefficients are all nonzero, there are two different lines of best fit with different slopes and different intercepts.
- o If β_2 is zero, there are two lines with the same intercept but a different slope.
- o If β_3 is zero, there is no interaction and the two lines are parallel.
- o If β_1 is not different from zero, there is no regression.

The figures below show some (but not the only) examples of the patterns that might appear under these interpretations. Directions of the regression weights, as usual, identify the direction of the slope. It might be reiterated that with interactions, it is not uncommon for multicollinearity effects to emerge. Furthermore, given the lack of continuous measures when one is using dummy or effects coding, statistical significance t tests are not involved in these interpretations of regression coefficients. Thus, when using dummy and effects coding variables in interactions, overall R values with and without terms carrying interaction effects may be preferred over the typical testing of the magnitude of standardized regression coefficients.

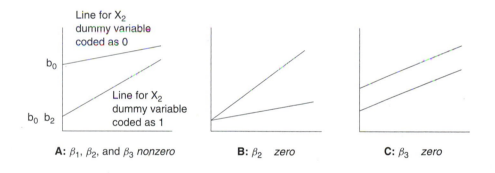

A: β_1, β_2, and β_3 *nonzero*   **B:** β_2 *zero*   **C:** β_3 *zero*

When the number of levels of dummy-coded or effects-coded variables go beyond two categories, additional indicator variables are created. The ways to design and interpret the emergent interaction terms also grow in detail. Such material goes beyond the scope of this introductory treatment; readers interested in interaction coding involving dummy and effects-coded variables with more than two levels are referred to the previously recommended works by Kelly et al. (1969, esp. chap. 6) and by J. Cohen and Cohen (1983, esp. chap. 8).

- If the two interacting predictor variables include a contrast-coded predictor and a continuous measure, there are different pieces of advice about coding. The contrast coefficients may be multiplied by the scores on the continuous measures. These continuous measures may take the form of raw scores, differences of the raw scores from their own means, or standard scores (z scores) of the continuous variable. Conceptually, using standard scores for the continuous variable might seem preferred because they ensure the presence of a zero point. But, in fact, the effects of using these different methods do not greatly affect R or mean square residual values, though there are noteworthy changes in regression coefficients and, of course, the intercept value.

Testing Interactions

To examine the size of the multiple R if an interaction exists, researchers find it most useful to compare two or more multiple regression correlation equations (depending on the number of interaction effects to be examined). The first equation contains only the predictor variables without the key interactions. After noting the size of the R, a second model is tested. This model includes the new variable carrying the interaction effect along with the main effect variables. For instance, consider a study involving the prediction of the amount of self-disclosure from two predictor variables: three levels of life stress (low, moderate, and high levels) and a sense of the individual's ability to deal successfully with stress. Stress may be coded using contrast coding, with linear coefficients drawn from the table of orthogonal polynomials in Appendix C.9. The measure of ability to deal successfully with stress may be assessed on the "denial of stress" scale, a continuous measure. The interaction term (called "intraw" here) is created by multiplying the contrast-coded stress levels with the continuous "denial of stress" measure. The results for the limited model are found below. The baseline model with two main effect predictors produces an R of .249.

Model Summary

Model	R	R Square	Adjusted R Square	Std. Error of the Estimate	Change Statistics R Square Change	F Change	df1	df2	Sig. F Change
1	.249[a]	.062	.051	5.254	.082	5.831	2	177	.004
2	.380[b]	.144	.130	5.032	.082	16.947	1	178	.000

a. Predictors: (Constant), stress, denial
b. Predictors: (Constant), stress, denial, intraw

When the residuals sums of squares (a measure of prediction error) are examined on the analysis of variance table, the residuals are 4,885.088. When the variable carrying the interaction effect is included, the multiple correlation coefficient R is .38. The sum of the residuals (a measure of prediction error) may be examined from the analysis of variance table. The residuals are 4,456.013, a number that is very similar to (though lower than) the partial model without the variable carrying the interaction effect. Hence, it does not seem that the new model has created noteworthy challenges to its fit to the data.

ANOVA[c]

Model		Sum of Squares	df	Mean Square	F	Sig.
1	Regression	321.862	2	160.931	5.831	.004[a]
	Residual	4885.088	177	27.599		
	Total	5206.950	179			
2	Regression	750.937	3	250.312	9.887	.000[b]
	Residual	4456.013	176	25.318		
	Total	5206.950	179			

a. Predictors: (Constant), stress, denial
b. Predictors: (Constant), stress, denial, intraw
c. Dependent Variable: amt_S_D

Examination of the regression coefficients for the models shows directions for the main and interaction effects. Though the denial of stress scale is a continuous measure for which use of the *t* test is appropriate, the remaining *t* tests should not be the basis of interpretations.

Coefficients[a]

Model		Unstandardized Coefficients		Standardized Coefficients	t	Sig.	Coefficients		
		B	Std. Error	Beta			Zero-order	Partial	Part
1	(Constant)	27.248	1.756		15.520	.000			
	denial	.325	.113	.209	2.864	.005	.209	.210	.209
	stress	.892	.480	.135	1.859	.065	.135	.138	.135
2	(Constant)	27.248	1.682		16.204	.000			
	denial	.325	.109	.209	2.991	.003	.209	.220	.209
	stress	−7.373	2.059	−1.119	−3.580	.000	.135	−.261	−.250
	intraw	.548	.133	1.287	4.117	.000	.196	.296	.287

a. Dependent Variable: amt_S_D

To test the significance of the difference between these two *R* values, the previously described formula is used.

$$F = \frac{\dfrac{R^2_{Y.12...m_2} - R^2_{Y.12...m_1}}{m_2 - m_1}}{\dfrac{1 - R^2_{Y.12...m_2}}{n - m_2 - 1}} = \frac{\dfrac{.144 - .062}{3 - 2}}{\dfrac{1 - .144}{180 - 3 - 1}} = \frac{\dfrac{0.82}{.856}}{\dfrac{}{176}} = \frac{.082}{.0049} = 16.73$$

Degrees of freedom for the numerator term are equal to $m_2 - m_1$ (the number of predictors in the full model minus the number of predictors in the partial model), or $3 - 2 = 1$. Degrees of freedom for the denominator term are equal to degrees of freedom for the residual term for the full model, or $n - m_2 - 1$ (the number of events in the study minus the number of predictors in the full model minus 1) or $180 - 3 - 1 = 176$. Appendix C.5 reveals that with alpha risk at .05 and degrees of freedom equal to 1 and 150, the critical value is 3.904. There are no degrees of freedom equal to 1 and 176 in this table, so the lower (and more conservative) value is used. The observed test statistic of 16.73 is far above the critical value of *F*. Therefore, the researcher concludes that the *R* of the full model, including the variable carrying the interaction effect, is significantly greater than the *R* of the main effects model. Hence, the presence of an interaction is detected, and the researcher attempts to describe it.

It is worth reiterating that when dummy and effects-coded variables are involved, *t* tests of individual regression weights should not be used. Instead, the collection of dummy and effects-coded variables should be entered as a group and the test of significance completed for the difference between overall R^2 values observed for competing models. Though separate *t* tests of beta weights are suitable for interval level independent variables, they are not appropriate for dummy and effects-coded variables. If all the dummy-coded variables represent levels of *one* independent variable, a simple test R^2 is appropriate. If there are additional predictor variables, a test of significance should compare the R^2 with the dummy variables to the R^2 that did not include the dummy-coded variables.

EXAMINING NONLINEAR EFFECTS

The versatility of multiple regression correlation includes adaptations that help detect nonlinear effects. This section will look into ways of identifying nonlinear patterns as well as ways to use SPSS to complete efficient curve fitting for the modern communication researcher.

Identifying Nonlinear Patterns

Though the multiple *linear* regression correlation is a linear correlation method, it may be used to explore nonlinear effects. For instance, consider this arrangement. The simple r is $-.2094$. Of course, as you can see, the association between the X and Y variables actually is nonlinear. Rather than rely on simple linear correlation alone, multiple regression correlation may be enlisted to provide a helpful alternative. Another predictor variable representing a curved (in this case, quadratic) function may be created and added to the formula. Then, a new correlation may be computed, including the linear and the nonlinear effects.

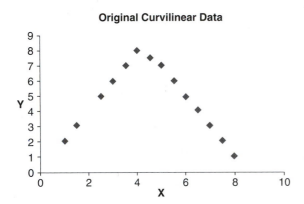

Original Curvilinear Data

To carry such nonlinear effects, a "new variable" would be created from the square of the original values. Then, two multiple regression correlation equations could be compared. Equation 1 would be

$$Y = b_0 + b_1 X_1.$$

Obviously, this model is just a bivariate correlation, because it has only one predictor. It might be noted that unstandardized weights are involved. The reason relates to the fact that the researcher is not interested in comparing the relative magnitudes of the contributions from the linear and nonlinear elements separately. Instead, comparison of the overall size of the correlation—with and without the nonlinear effect—is the chief interest. Furthermore, the researcher is not interested in predicting changes in the dependent variable based on knowledge of changes in one standard deviation of each predictor separately. A second equation model is constructed to permit identifying the nonlinear effect. Equation 2 would be

$$Y = b_0 + b_1 X_1 + b_2 X_1^2.$$

This second equation includes a "second" variable that is the square of the first predictor variable. Thus, a *quadratic* function of the independent variable is advanced to see if it adds a superior fit to the data. When this step is followed, the multiple R changes to .9683. One does not have to know the formula for computing the difference between multiple correlation coefficients to know that the difference in correlations from −.2094 to .9683 is statistically significant.

Some background regarding nonlinear relationships might be helpful. If a researcher wishes to identify a nonlinear form with one concave or convex curve, as shown in the scatterplot presented at the beginning of this section, an equation should be designed to include a quadratic trend. To illustrate how adding the square of scores can help identify a nonlinear relationship, it is helpful to look at the effect that adding such a squared element may have on actual data. In this case, a set of scores ranging from −8 to +8 is used to predict values on a vertical axis (y-axis) ($Y = X + X^2$). As can be seen in the diagram on the right, a curvilinear pattern is created.

X	Y
-8	56
-7	42
-6	30
-5	20
-4	12
-3	6
-2	2
-1	0
0	0
1	2
2	6
3	12
4	20
5	30
6	42
7	56
8	72

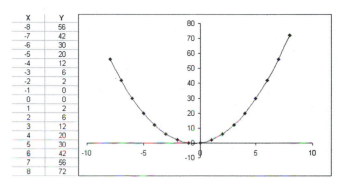

Consider a higher-order trend. A researcher might desire to explore a *cubic* trend featuring one point of inflection, where the curve changes its slope (in this case, from concave to convex). The effect of adding the cube of a variable whose scores range from −8 to +8 can be seen in the diagram on the right. To illustrate the impact of adding a cubic function to the equation, one might predict the value of the vertical (Y) variable with the equation $Y = X + X^2 + X^3$. By attempting to compare an equation that predicts these sorts of curvilinear relationships with actual data, it is possible to identify the specific contour of curvilinear relationships underlying the data.

X	Y
-8	-456
-7	-301
-6	-186
-5	-105
-4	-52
-3	-21
-2	-6
-1	-1
0	0
1	3
2	14
3	39
4	84
5	155
6	258
7	399
8	584

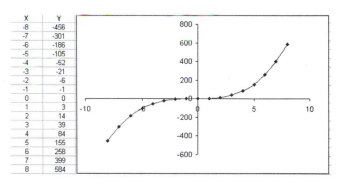

Though researchers may look for yet higher-order nonlinear effects, such as quartic and quintic effects, these patterns are rare in communication research. Hence, researchers may wish to limit searches for statistically significant nonlinear effects so that they avoid capitalizing on chance findings. Yet, there are ways to explore whether specific nonlinear trend fitting is indicated.[8]

---

[8]One approach involves examining partial regression plots. The researcher begins by creating a multiple regression correlation model with the linear predictor variables alone. Then the residuals are computed. In another step, the researcher takes a variable carrying a nonlinear effect (quadratic, to begin) as the dependent variable in a model that includes the linear predictor variables used in the previous analysis. After computing the residuals for this model, the researcher takes the residuals from each model and creates a plot of the Y residuals and the nonlinear term residuals. A visible pattern suggests that adding a nonlinear function of some sort would improve prediction. The contours of the plot would indicate whether the nonlinear effects should carry a quadratic, cubic, or even higher-order effect.

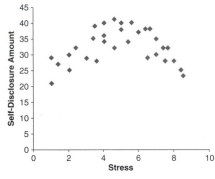

Looking at a scatterplot is useful. For instance, the following diagram shows the relationship between the amount of self-disclosure reported by 32 randomly selected people and the amount of life stress during a 3-month period. In this case, a bivariate linear correlation between the variables reveals a coefficient of $r = .066$ ($r^2 = .0044$). The researcher might conclude that there is no meaningful relationship between the variables. But if multiple regression correlation is used to detect a curvilinear relationship (by adding a second predictor that is the square of the first predictor), the resulting R^2 is .795 (corrected for shrinkage as .631).

Even without a plot, inspecting the intercept and the regression weights can reveal the nature of a relationship. Some general rules exist (Kelly et al., 1999, pp. 164–167) to guide interpretations (quotations drawn from p. 164):

- When b_2 is positive the curve has a U shape, but when b_2 is negative, the curve has an inverted U shape.
- The greater the size of b_2, the "more severe" is the curve.
- When b_1 and b_2 have the same sign, the curve is "displaced to the left. [With] . . . unlike signs the displacement is to the right."
- When b_1 is equal to "0, the curve will be symmetrical around" the y-axis.
- When the intercept is positive, the line of best fit crosses the y-axis above the horizontal axis.
- When the intercept is negative, the line of best fit crosses the y-axis below the horizontal axis.
- When the intercept is zero, the line of best fit crosses the y-axis at the horizontal axis.

In the study examining the relationship between life stress and the amount of self-disclosure communication, the intercept is 15.26, indicating that the line of best fit meets the y-axis above the horizontal axis. The regression weight for the life stress variable (b_1) is 8.881, and the squared life stress scores (b_2) regression coefficient is –.915. The fact that the regression weight for X_1 (the linear component carried by b_1) has a positive value indicates that the curve is displaced to the right of the vertical axis. The negative coefficient for b_2 indicates that the open end of the curve points down. Table 14.4 illustrates the appearance of these curved relationships.

To see if adding a nonlinear function enhances the multiple regression correlation coefficient, the null hypothesis that H_0: $\rho_{linear} = \rho_{nonlinear}$ may be tested. After setting an alpha risk (.05 for this case), the following test of significance is used:

$$F = \frac{\dfrac{R^2_{Y.12...m_2} - R^2_{Y.12...m_1}}{m_2 - m_1}}{\dfrac{1 - R^2_{Y.12...m_2}}{n - m_2 - 1}}$$

$$= \frac{\dfrac{.795 - .004}{2 - 1}}{\dfrac{.795}{32 - 2 - 1}} = \frac{.791}{0.27} = 29.296$$

Table 14.4 Detecting Nonlinear Trends in Multiple Regression Correlation

If Linear Component (b_1) Is	And If Nonlinear (Quadratic) Component (b_2) Is	If Intercept (b_0) Is		
		Negative (< 0)	*0*	*Positive (> 0)*
Negative (< 0)	*Negative (< 0)*			
	Positive (> 0)			
0	*Negative (< 0)*			
	Positive (> 0)			
Positive (> 0)	*Negative (< 0)*			
	Positive (> 0)			

The degrees of freedom are $m_2 - m_1$ ($2 - 1 = 1$) for the numerator and $n - m_2 - 1$ ($32 - 2 - 1$ = 29) for the denominator term. Appendix C.5 shows that with 1 degree of freedom for the term in the numerator (the between-groups term) and 29 degrees of freedom in the denominator (the within-groups term), the critical F value at alpha risk of .05 is 4.183. Hence, the researcher concludes that the model including a nonlinear trend has a significantly higher correlation coefficient than the linear model.

When using such a method, the researcher is not interested in the comparative influence of the quadratic or linear components. The important thing is to know if the overall R increases when variables representing curvilinear influences are added with the linear effect. Because the squared value of a variable is highly correlated with the original variable, there is high multicollinearity among predictor variables when variables carrying nonlinear trends are included. Thus, interpreting beta weights is problematic. Though beta .weights would be unstable, however, the R value would not be affected.

Curve Fitting Through SPSS

In addition to using hierarchical methods where the differences in two correlations are compared with a test of significance, sometimes shortcuts are possible. To use SPSS to fit curves to data, the researcher selects *Regression* from the *Analyze* menu and then chooses *Curve Estimation.* . . . In this example involving the relationship between life stress and the amount of self-disclosure, the researcher suspects the existence of an inverted U shape in the data.

To gather relevant information, the researcher highlights the dependent variable name and moves it to the "Dependent(s):" field by using the arrow key. The independent variable also is highlighted and moved to the "Independent" field. The researcher must identify that this element is a predictor. The alternative (indicated by clicking on the radio button) is to use

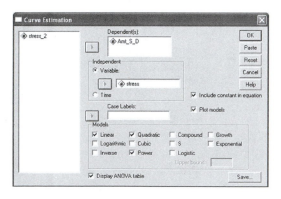

Time as the predictor variable as part of a time-series design. The researcher needs to check the "Display ANOVA table" box to make sure that the output includes F tests for R^2 coefficients. The researcher also must check the box to "Include constant in equation" so that information about the intercept will be part of the output. In this case, plots are requested to aid in interpreting results. The types of curves to be fit to the data may be checked. In this case, the researcher suspects a quadratic function. Hence, the quadratic box is checked, along with the lower-level trend (linear) and the next highest function (cubic, which is expected not to be statistically significant). If researchers use a term carrying the quadratic effect that is based on centered variables, the actual analysis is an application of orthogonal polynomials. Other curve estimation models also are available, including fitting a power curve, a compound model, a logarithmic model, an inverse model, an S curve, a logistic model, a growth model, and an exponential model.

Clicking on the *OK* button produces a set of output, a portion of which is the following comparison of the models. The first model deals with the linear effect. In this case, the model has a statistically insignificant R of .06582.

```
MODEL:   MOD_1.

Dependent variable.. Amt_Disc              Method.. LINEAR

Multiple R              .06582
R Square                .00433
Adjusted R Square      -.02886
Standard Error         5.48117

                  Analysis of Variance:

                  DF    Sum of Squares       Mean Square

Regression         1           3.92114          3.921139
Residuals         30         901.29761         30.043254

F =        .13052       Signif F =   .7204
```

The second model is the curvilinear model tested by including the quadratic function. Adding this element increases the *R* to a statistically significant .79462. Indeed, the "Signif F" is so small that the probability of finding these results by random sampling error is below one chance in 10,000.

```
Dependent variable.. Amt_Disc              Method.. QUADRATI

Multiple R              .79462
R Square                .63142
Adjusted R Square       .60601
Standard Error         3.39188

                  Analysis of Variance:

                  DF    Sum of Squares       Mean Square

Regression         2         571.57733        285.78867
Residuals         29         333.64142         11.50488

F =      24.84065       Signif F =   .0000

-------------------- Variables in the Equation --------------------

Variable                 B        SE B        Beta        T   Sig T

stress             8.881050    1.271153    3.682886    6.987   .0000
stress**           -.915123     .130280   -3.702741   -7.024   .0000
(Constant)        15.263578    2.751600                5.547   .0000
```

The regression weight for the intercept (called the constant) shows that it is positive, indicating that the fitted curve crosses the *y*-axis above the horizontal axis. The fact that the regression coefficients for the variables carrying the linear and nonlinear components have different signs reveals that the curve is displaced to the right of the vertical axis. Because the regression coefficient for the quadratic function is negative, the curve has an inverted U shape.

Adding the cubic function produces a multiple *R* of .80671, which is only .01209 different from that for the quadratic model. Thus, the researchers do not find support for a model with an additional point of inflection in the curve. Most researchers would conclude that higher-order effects also may be eliminated from the search. Although it is very rare, it is possible that a higher-order effect (such as quartic or quintic functions) might exist anyway.

To verify the nature of the relationships, the requested chart may be examined. As can be seen, the quadratic line is a close fit to the pattern of the data. It also is clear that the cubic trend provides information that is redundant to the quadratic trend. In sum, the curve-fitting subroutine from SPSS provides evidence to support the expectation that stress is curvilinearly related to the amount of self-disclosure people exhibit.

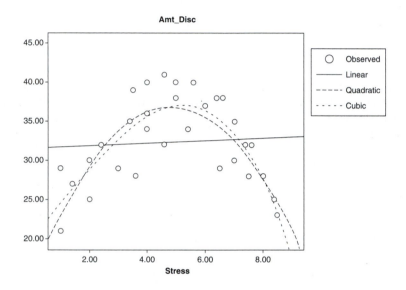

Chapter 15

EXPLORATORY FACTOR ANALYSIS

This chapter is designed to be a "consumer guide" to exploratory factor analysis as it is prominently used in communication studies. The chapter focuses on exploratory factor analysis in which there is no hypothesis to guide predictions of factor structures. The next chapter deals with confirmatory factor analysis in which hypotheses are made about the expected factor structures. For the most part, detailed calculations are ignored, both because they are complicated and because few, if any, modern communication scholars do these sorts of computations by hand. The integration of computer applications and the basic methods are the chief emphasis.

As a method, factor analysis attempts to identify highly intercorrelated groups of variables. When the number of variables is very small, it is possible to locate highly intercorrelated variables just by looking. As the number of variables increases, another approach is needed. Factor analysis attempts to help researchers find these underlying characteristics by looking for linear combinations of variables. Researchers often find this set of tools helpful when they have many scales to measure a variable and they wish to discover which scales are highly intercorrelated and seem to be measuring the same thing. Researchers then know which scale items reasonably may be combined into an index. Researchers also frequently wish to use this set of methods to help reduce the number of predictor variables in a study to a meaningful number of uncorrelated independent variables. Factor analysis also may be used as a step in the process of building predictive models.

FORMS OF FACTOR ANALYSIS

Factor analysis is a family of tools, rather than one statistic. There are two important varieties of factor analysis: exploratory factor analysis and confirmatory factor analysis.

In **exploratory factor analysis**, the "factors are defined in such a way as to meet certain mathematical considerations, without regard to any theory. The resulting factors are then named based on the variables that correlate most strongly with them and thereby contribute most heavily to their definition" (Bernstein, 1988, pp. 164–165). The purpose of this sort of work is discovering underlying dimensions "that influence the measured variables" (H. S. Park, Dailey, & Lemus, 2002, p. 563).

Confirmatory factor analysis, on the other hand, is a form of factor analysis in which dimensions "are defined according to the specification of a substantive theory" (Bernstein, 1988, p. 165). Instead of attempting to discover the existence and initial nature of dimensions underlying a number of measures, confirmatory factor analysis tests a hypothesis about the composition of factors. H. S. Park et al. (2002, p. 572) argue strongly that communication researchers should use confirmatory factor analysis (rather than exploratory factor analysis) when they have experience with measures or when they can rely on past theory about the expected factors that should emerge. Chapter 16 describes confirmatory factor analysis and introduces the Amos program to automate many of the mathematical operations involved. For now, it is enough to suggest that confirmatory factor analysis is used when there is a basis for making a hypothesis. Exploratory factor analysis is used for examining unhypothesized patterns.

THE NOTION OF MULTIVARIATE ANALYSES

The notion of multivariate analyses serves as the foundation of the family of tools involved in factor analysis. Hence, pausing to consider the meaning of some concepts in multivariate analysis is prudent. **Multivariate analysis** sometimes is defined as a set of statistical tools that use multiple dependent variables treated as a common set (Mertler & Vannatta, 2002, p. 342; J. P. Stevens, 2002, p. 2). Yet, this distinction is a fairly fluid one. Many books about multivariate statistics deal with topics ranging from multiple regression correlation (which has only one dependent variable at time) to factor analysis (which really does not distinguish between independent and dependent variables). Thus, common (and reasonable) treatments of these methods describe them in various terms as the "simultaneous investigation of two or more variable characteristics which are measured over a set of objects" (Kachigan, 1991, p. 1). This simultaneous investigation usually involves forming "linear combinations of the original variables . . . derived on the basis of some criterion of optimality" (Harris, 1975, p. 9) and "a simultaneous analysis of data on several variables" (Aczel, 1989, p. 895).

Uses of Multivariate Statistics in Research

Why would researchers care to treat data as some common set of information? Creative explanations could abound, but there are three practical reasons (see J. P. Stevens, 2002, p. 2).

- Variables often influence study participants in more than one way. These different "effects variables" might be overlooked if one looked at only one output variable.
- Communication may be appreciated as a complex process that involves more than one variable. Though many relationships involve one primary effect, many others involve more than one or two vital explanatory variables.
- Research may be efficient if several variables are examined at once, rather than by the process of trial and error involved in much experimentation.

It also might be mentioned that sometimes relationships involving two variables are clouded by much background variation. Though not unique to multivariate statistics, the process of partialing out the sources of variation can help reveal meaningful relationships among remaining primary variables of interest.

At one time, multivariate statistics were the domain of mathematical statisticians and highly specialized experts. Today, computer packages have made it possible for even neophyte researchers to use multivariate statistics if their research questions invite their use. When researchers notice that their problem questions and hypotheses refer to several related dependent variables, multivariate statistical tools seem invited. If the problem questions and hypotheses refer to several related independent variables, multivariate statistical tools still might bear a look. Regardless of the decisions made, the statistical tools may be chosen based on the problem questions and hypotheses, not the other way around.

Treating Data on Several Variables as a Single Element

The process of combining variables into a single score is a simple idea. After all, when researchers take three 7-point semantic differential–type attitude scale items (such as good-bad, wise-foolish, and positive-negative), they may add them together to make an attitude scale with a possible range of 3 to 21 points. These researchers are then representing separate measures as a common set. We do it all the time.

Actually, for all the seemingly mystical aspects of factor analysis, practically every time you take a test, what you receive are, in essence, factor scores. Suppose your instructor scores one point for each item you get correct on a multiple-choice or true-false test. Your score is the sum of the number of items you answer correctly; hence, it is a linear combination with equal weights called the *first centroid factor*. (Centroid factor analysis, which involves forming successive equally weighted sums, was an early form of factor analysis.) If, in contrast, you take an essay test with different weights for different questions, the resulting z scores would no longer be derived from the first centroid, since the weighting is unequal, but they would still be factor scores. (Bernstein, 1988, pp. 166–167)

As data become increasingly complicated, researchers may try to get information beyond simple totals of correct answers. Researchers may want to find evidence that different test items measure different underlying dimensions. Thus, the language changes accordingly. For instance, in a univariate test such as the *t* test, there is a comparison of two means. In multivariate analyses, there are more than two variables, so it becomes sensible to speak not of means but of mean vectors.

- A **vector** is a matrix with only one row (also known as a "row vector") or column (also known as a "column vector"), though it may be part of another matrix. Such vectors are ordered sets of scores, with each score representing a value on one of the multiple variables under analysis. As a matter of notation, "a column vector is symbolized by a lower case bold face letter but a column vector is symbolized by a lower case boldface letter and a prime ('), which allows it to be distinguished from a column vector" (Bernstein, 1988, p. 60).
- The scores in the vectors are called **elements**.
- The number of elements is called the vector's **dimension**.

In multivariate analyses, imagine that each vector is "a mathematical expression representing a subject's score on all the dependent variables" (Vogt, 2005, p. 338). Then, the "weighted combination of the observed dependent variables" (Vogt, 2005, p. 31) is called the **centroid**. When the question of interest is a comparison of means (as in the case of multivariate analysis of variance), "the mean of these individual vectors is the centroid" (Vogt, 2005, p. 338).[1] The **population centroid** consists of the weighted combination of the dependent variables of a population or distribution. The **sample centroid** is the weighted combination of the dependent variables in a sample for the variables in the analysis. The sampling distribution of the sample centroid is assumed to be multivariate normal. The **multivariate normal distribution** is an extension of the standard normal curve.

---

[1]Because data are summarized according to multiple properties, some of the standard elements expected in statistical analyses are routinely altered. For instance, in most discussions, the standard deviation is "replaced by its squared multivariate generalization of within variability, the sample covariance matrix **S**" (J. P. Stevens, 2002, pp. 198–199). Furthermore, the essential measures of differences and effect sizes also are changed as one moves from univariate to multivariate statistics, as the following table shows (J. P. Stevens, 2002, p. 198):

Measures of Effect Size	
Univariate	*Multivariate*
$d = \dfrac{\mu_1 - \mu_2}{\sigma}$	$D^2 = (\mu_1 - \mu_2)'\Sigma^{-1}(\mu_1 - \mu_2)$ Mahalanobis' distance
$\hat{d} = \dfrac{\bar{y}_1 - \bar{y}_2}{s}$	$\hat{D}^2 = (\bar{y}_1 - \bar{y}_2)'\Sigma^{-1}(\bar{y}_1 - \bar{y}_2)$ Hotelling's T^2 independent of sample size

USING EXPLORATORY FACTOR ANALYSIS

Factor analysis is a statistical method that helps "the researcher discover and identify the unities or dimensions, called factors, behind many measures" (Kerlinger, 1986, p. 138). It is most often identified as a data reduction technique in which many measures are interrelated, in that they happen to overlap in their measure of the same thing. In short, researchers have redundant information about the influence of variables. To remove the duplicate information in separate measures, researchers represent a large number of measures as different faces of a common construct, variously called a "latent variable," a "factor," a "hypothetical variable," or (a bit metaphorically) a "dimension." To do so, researchers look for a linear combination of variables that could permit one to summarize a collection of variables.

A difference exists between factor analysis and principal components analysis. **Principal components analysis** is designed to reduce a number of variables into the smallest number of possible components. Principal components analysis often is completed because researchers want to remove the influence of correlated predictor variables so that some advanced statistical tools may be used most appropriately. In reality, both common factor analysis and principal components analysis reduce the number of variables of interest. Even so, the differences between **common factor analysis** and principal components analysis can be noteworthy. First, common factor analysis divides variance into two components, common variance that is shared by many variables in the model and unique variance that is derived from a particular observed variable and its error component. Common factor analysis identifies the common variance rather than total variance. On the other hand, principal components analysis focuses attention on total variance only. The difference becomes increasingly apparent when the purposes are compared. Whereas common factor analysis attempts to account for correlations among variables, principal components analysis attempts to identify a minimum number of factors that account for total variance. Second, there are computational differences regarding the placement of terms in the diagonal elements of the matrix of correlations. Common factor analysis places what are called "communalities," rather than intercorrelations, in those locations.

Completing common factor analysis can be tricky. When attempting to reproduce the correlation matrices, there are more unknowns than there are equations. Unfortunately, "factor indeterminacy exists when one has *p* variables, and the *m* factors are not determinate" (Steiger, 1990, p. 42). Indeed, the problem of factor indeterminacy has challenged, but hardly eliminated, the routine use of common factor analysis (Velicer & Jackson, 1990). Though researchers using common factor analysis or principal components usually reach the same essential conclusions when applying their methods to common data sets (Velicer & Jackson, 1990, but also see Widaman, 1990), the theoretical problem of factor determinacy makes it seem that claims of alleged superiority of common factor analysis over principal components analysis "are largely illusory" (Steiger, 1990, p. 41). When it comes to efforts to identify reliable measures, Steiger (1996) concluded:

> Perhaps the simplest yet most telling messages common to the oft-conflicting work on indeterminacy are that high quality, well planned measurement procedures can alleviate indeterminacy problems. Ironically, such measures are in fact *components*, since the only truly determinate "factor" is one that is perfectly predictable from **Y**. It seems high-reliability linear composites are what the factor analytic communication has been looking for all along. . . . (pp. 549–550)

Now that we have recognized that there is a difference between common factor analysis and principal components analysis, this discussion will continue by looking at ways to help reduce data through factor analytic tools.

The Logic of Factor Analysis

Factor analysis attempts to reduce a number of observed or "manifest" variables into a smaller number of underlying unobserved or latent variables.[2]

> Factor analysis sets out to explain these correlations by introducing underlying factors f_1, f_2, . . . that account for the correlations. . . . One first asks the questions, Is there a factor f_1 such that if this is partialled out there remain no intercorrelations between the tests [called x_i through x_j]? If so, the *partial correlation* between any pair of tests x_i and x_j after f_1 has been eliminated must vanish. (Jöreskog, 1979b, p. 6)

If one could identify the factors, they could be used to represent many variables. After a common factor is recognized, the variables that define it may be correlated with the underlying dimensions.

To complete factor analyses, several assumptions must be made. The data must have

- Interval or ratio level of measurement,
- Independence of observations, and
- A bivariate normal distribution for each pair of variables.

In addition, there are some assumptions about the characteristics of factors that are extracted and defined. These latter matters, however, become most critical for confirmatory factor analysis, rather than exploratory factor analysis. One obvious assumption that underlies the

---

[2]According to Everitt (1987, p. 59),

> The factor analysis model postulates that the set of observed or *manifest* variables, $x_1, . . . , x_p$, are linear functions of a number of unobservable *latent* variables or factors plus a residual term; in algebraic terms the model may be written

$$x_1 = \lambda_{11}f_1 + \lambda_{12}f_2 + \cdots + \lambda_{1k}f_k + \mu_1,$$

$$.$$
$$.$$
$$.$$

$$x_p = \lambda_{p1}f_1 + \lambda_{p2}f_2 + \cdots + \lambda_{pk}f_k + \mu_p$$

> where $f_1, . . . , f_k$ represent the k latent variables or *common factors* and $\mu_1, . . . , \mu_p$ the residual terms.

Using various mathematic optimization methods to maximize or minimize some function is beyond the scope of this book. But it is enough to say here that λ values are affected by the methods used to identify linear combinations of variables.

use of all factor analyses is that there really are unobserved common dimensions that may be enlisted to account for the correlations among observed variables.[3] In fact, this assumption is the reason that factor analysis is meaningful. It may be examined by using such tools as the Kaiser-Meyer-Olkin measure of sampling adequacy and Bartlett's test of sphericity.

Along with these assumptions flow several others:

1. both common and unique factors have means of zero,

2. variances of common factors are equal to 1, and

3. common factors are uncorrelated with each other.

Elements of the Model

Factor analyses produce several elements of interest. The language of these matters makes a difference of which researchers should be aware.

Factors are the "unobserved variables" underlying a larger set of observed variables. There are different statistical ways to "extract" variables, but in the standard tool known as principal components analysis, the number of factors initially identified is equal to the number of variables in the analysis. Then, the factors that are common to several measures are called **common factors**. Because the remaining factors "are unique to each observed variable, they may be referred to as unique factors" (Kim & Mueller, 1978, pp. 12–13).

Factor loadings "represent the degree to which each of the variables correlates with each of the factors. In fact, these factor loadings are nothing more than the correlation coefficients between the original variables and the newly derived factors, which are themselves variables" (Kachigan, 1991, p. 243). Though the term "factor loading" sometimes is confused with other terms such as "factor pattern coefficients," "factor scores," and "factor structure coefficients," the meanings of these terms are different. Because factor loadings are correlations with possible values ranging from –1.0 to +1.0, they have many of the interpretable qualities of correlation coefficients generally.[4]

Eigenvalues also are called "characteristic values," "characteristic roots," "latent roots," and "invariant roots." In fact, eigenvalues are measures of the variance explained by factors.

---

[3]The use of factor analysis, principal components analysis, cluster analysis, and multidimensional scaling has caused some confusion. Whereas factor analysis is applied to correlation or covariance data, cluster analysis and multidimensional scaling are applied to other sorts of ratings, such as common groups or the similarity of message sources. Cluster analysis is a multivariate analysis tool that is "designed to determine whether individuals (or other units of analysis) are similar enough to fall into groups or clusters" (Vogt, 2005, p. 46). Multidimensional scaling is "a method of using space on a graph to indicate statistical similarity and difference" (Vogt, 2005, p. 198).

[4]Kim and Mueller (1979) explain:

The correlation between any two observed variables will be given by the multiplication of the two relevant factor loadings: $r_{ij} = (b_{iF})(b_{jF})$. This in turn implies that the residual correlation between X_i and X_j will be zero if the effect of the common factor is controlled: $r_{ij.F} = 0$. (p. 21)

In the language of linear algebra, "eigenvalues are the roots of determinantal equations" (Aczel, 1989, p. 952). Computationally, the eigenvalues are the total squared loadings of items on a factor. This notion becomes important when making decisions on ways to select the numbers of factors for analysis and interpretation.

The **communality** is "the *common factor variance* of each variable, i.e., the proportion of variance that is treated as systematic" (Bernstein, 1988, p. 163). Often symbolized as h^2, a commonality "of an observed variable is simply the square of the factor loadings for that variable (or the square of the correlation between that available and the common factor)" (Kim & Mueller, 1978, p. 21). In contrast, with a communality, the **uniqueness** of a variable is $1 - h^2$ and indicates the proportion of variance for a variable that is unassociated with the common factor variance.

An example of exploratory factor analysis is found in Table 15.1 and will serve as an illustration throughout the rest of this discussion. As can be seen, the descriptive analyses include information about the tenability of the initial assumptions underlying factor analysis.

The major assumption of factor analysis is that there really are underlying intercorrelations sufficient to suggest meaningful dimensions or factors. The suitability of one's data for this assumption may be tested by two particularly useful tools. articularly when sample sizes are modest, looking at these two measures becomes critical. As part of the descriptive output, the report on the left appeared.

KMO and Bartlett's Test[a]

Kaiser-Meyer-Olkin Measure of Sampling Adequacy.		.657
Bartlett's Test of Sphericity	Approx. Chi-Square	1140.116
	df	55
	Sig.	.000

a. Based on correlations

- The Kaiser-Meyer-Olkin measure of sampling adequacy reveals the proportion (or percentage, if you move the decimal point) of common variance in the data set. A large KMO value indicates that the data are suitable for use of factor analysis tools. There is no test of statistical significance with this tool, but by convention, researchers usually conclude that factor analysis will not be beneficial if KMO values are below .50.
- Bartlett's test of sphericity reports a statistical significance test of the null hypothesis that the population correlation matrix is an identity matrix of uncorrelated variables. If the null hypothesis for this test cannot be rejected, the variables under analysis are unrelated and there is little reason to complete factor analysis. A statistically significant effect (indicated by a small p, or probability value, typically below .05) suggests that factor analysis is suitable because the data show intercorrelations. Other assessments of distributions and homoscedasticity have been described in other chapters and will not be reviewed again here. For the data set presented here, both the KMO measure and Bartlett's tests suggest the suitability of the data for factor analysis.

Sample Size Concerns

Factor analysis requires a reasonable sample size. Indeed, the most popular tool, principal components analysis, tends to give biased parameter estimates when small samples are used (Snook & Gorsuch, 1989). Different guidelines have been suggested. One review

Table 15.1   An Exploratory Factor Analysis Example

The researcher obtained a random sample of 219 participants and had them listen to speeches with and without internal organizers. Then 10 scales were completed. In this case, the researcher was interested in exploring if there were any consistent underlying dimensions to a set of 10 five-point Likert-type scales used to measure general reaction to a message's basic composition. The items were as follows:

Scale Item	Strongly Disagree	Disagree	Neither Agree nor Disagree	Agree	Strongly Agree
11. The message was sensible	1	2	3	4	5
12. The message was logical	1	2	3	4	5
*13. The message was boring	1	2	3	4	5
14. The message was interesting	1	2	3	4	5
*15. The message was dull	1	2	3	4	5
16. The message was well structured	1	2	3	4	5
17. The message was reasonable	1	2	3	4	5
19. The message was clear	1	2	3	4	5
20. The message was well organized	1	2	3	4	5
*21. The message was confusing	1	2	3	4	5

Note: Item 18 was a measure of test-taking behavior and is not included in this table.

*Reverse scored (the observed value was subtracted from 6).

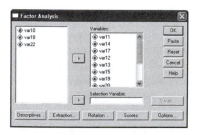

To complete the exploratory factor analysis of these scales, the researcher used SPSS. The researcher chose *Data Reduction* from the *Analyze* menu. From the submenu that appeared, the researcher selected *Factor...* , which called up the *Factor Analysis* dialog box. At this point, the researcher highlighted the critical variables for factor analysis (*var11* through *var21* in this example) and moved them to the "Variables:" field. To select some initial statistics, the researcher clicked the *Descriptives...* button and made a selection of descriptive statistics from the *Factor Analysis: Descriptives* dialog box. In this case, the researcher selected the *Univariate descriptives* (means, standard deviations, and number of events) and, of course, the *Initial solution* (communalities, eigenvalues, and percent of variance).

(Kieffer, 1999) argues that at least 300 cases should be used in factor analysis. In another early work, McCroskey and Young (1979) recognize that sample size did not affect factor analysis computations, but suggest a sample of approximately 200 for generalizable studies using factor analyses. Onwuegbuzie and Daniel (2003) review a tradition of advice and suggest "using 5 participants per variable as the bare minimum, although at least 10 participants per variable is much more desirable" (p. 28).

In reality, the desired sample size depends on the sizes of communalities, the sizes of factor loadings, and the numbers of items loaded on a factor. One influential study of the matter (Hakstian, Rogers, & Cattell, 1982) found that with sample sizes of 250, accurate numbers of factors were extracted using the traditional rules, provided that factors were defined by items with mean communalities of .60 or above. In some circumstances, it seems that large factor loadings may compensate for reduced sample sizes. A Monte Carlo study (Guadagnoli & Velicer, 1988) found that balancing sample sizes with factor loadings is critical, but the rules about the number of events needed for each variable could not be supported. Instead, the ratio of variables to factors is important.

- With nearly any sample size, dimensions are reliable if they have at least four loadings with absolute values above .60. Another inference that could be drawn is that "any component with at least three loadings above .80 will be reliable" (J. P. Stevens, 2002, p. 395).
- With sample sizes above 150, dimensions are reliable if they have more than nine items loading above .40.
- With sample sizes above 300, dimensions are reliable even if they have three or more low factor loadings.

Extraction of Factors

All factor analysis methods involve some choices in deciding data forms, selecting methods to extract factors, and choosing factors to be objects of interpretation. These matters will be reviewed in turn.

Data Form: Correlations or Covariances

Factor analysis may be completed with either correlations or covariances among observed variables. When the measures are all on the same continuum (for instance, if they are all 5-point Likert-type scales), it often is suggested that researchers use covariances (Morrison, 1976, p. 222). But when the measures are on different metrics (such as comparing 5-point scales with measures of intelligence that may range from below 50 to above 160), it usually is recommended that researchers use correlation matrices. In this way, "Using correlations rather than covariances amounts to standardizing the x's using their sample standard deviations, and this ensures that changing the scale of the x's has no effect on the analysis" (Bartholomew, 1987, p. 48).

The correlation coefficients have some advantages that covariances do not. In particular, a distribution of correlation coefficients remains multinomial[5] even when the underlying

---

[5]A multinomial distribution is an extension of the binomial distribution (Upton & Cook, 2002, p. 242). It represents "a probability distribution used to calculate the probabilities of entire frequency distributions" (Vogt, 2005, p. 199).

population distributions are not normal (Steiger & Hakstian, 1982). The same thing cannot be said for distributions of covariances. Unfortunately, the result is a certain amount of bias. Yet, if distributions are relatively normal and scaling is consistent across all measures, it may make sense to use the covariance matrix rather than the correlation matrix. Although the different coefficients rarely lead the researcher to draw fundamentally different interpretations about factor structures, it is the case that "the joint distribution of the correlation coefficients is not the same as that of the covariances and so it is not obvious that the estimators [computed by a form of maximum likelihood estimation] . . . will be true maximum likelihood estimators" (Bartholomew, 1987, p. 48). Not surprisingly, most factor analyses are completed on correlation matrices (Bartholomew, 1987, p. 48).

Deciding on Solutions

There are several approaches to exploratory factor analysis. In turn, each one may use different solutions. The most typical technique is called **R factor analysis**, and it uses covariances or correlations among observed variables to estimate factor structures underlying the variables themselves. Up to this point, this chapter has examined R factoring examples.

A second technique is called **Q factor analysis**, in which respondents or data elements—rather than variables—are grouped into sets that share common meaning. Q factor analysis is completed not on variables, but on cases. In communication, these cases may be people, newspapers, television sources, or the like. When using SPSS, most researchers place the variables in columns and list cases in each row. In Q factor analysis, the cases or subjects are placed in the columns (as variables) as follows.

	Tom	Dick	Harry	Larry	Moe	Curly	Shemp	Manny	Jack
1	1.0	1.00	4.00	1.00	1.00	1.00	3.00	1.00	2.00
2	3.0	3.00	1.00	2.00	4.00	1.00	5.00	4.00	4.00
3	4.0	3.00	4.00	4.00	4.00	3.00	3.00	4.00	3.00
4	3.0	3.00	1.00	2.00	4.00	1.00	5.00	4.00	4.00

The result of this analysis is the isolation of factors that represent cases or subjects that share common characteristics. One could imagine the value of such a tool for directors of forensics programs who might wish to identify critic-judges who give the same kinds of ratings for debating teams in intercollegiate competition. Researchers may identify such dimensions that describe patterns of respondents rather than patterns of variables.

In addition, there are forms of factor analysis that involve relating variables, persons, and occasions. For instance, **P analysis** factor analyzes variables across samples that are occasions or situations (similar to R type factor analysis). Similarly, **O analysis** completes factor analyses of occasions across variables (somewhat similar to Q factor analysis). Instead of variables, S and T factor analyses relate occasions to persons. In particular, **S analysis** completes a factor analysis of persons, with occasions of observations serving as the cases. **T analysis** factor analyzes occasions, with persons as the cases.

There are several different ways to extract factors. Each one has its own approach that could be attractive to the researcher. Given that the mathematics involved in factor analyses can be complex (and labor-intensive), few researchers complete them by hand. In SPSS, exploratory factor analysis tools permit completing factor analysis in rather short work. Among the most common methods supported by SPSS are the following:

- *Principal Components Analysis.* As previously described, this approach assesses all variance as common variance, with no unique variance. This method is the default option in SPSS, as well as in most other factor analysis programs.

Common factor analysis may be completed by any of the methods described below.

- *Unweighted Least Squares Factor Analysis.* This method extracts factors so that the sum of squared differences between observed and reproduced correlations is a minimum value. The diagonal elements of the matrix are ignored in unweighted least squares.
- *Generalized Least Squares.* This approach gives weights to intercorrelations between pairs of variables by using the inverse of the uniqueness of the variables $\left(\frac{1}{1-h^2}\right)$. Variables with low uniqueness receive the greatest weight.
- *Maximum Likelihood Factor Analysis (MLE).* This method extracts factors based on an optimizing method that estimates "parameters most likely to have resulted in observed sample data. . . . MLE chooses as the estimate of the parameter the value for which the probability of the observed scores is the highest" (Vogt, 2005, p. 188). This choice has an additional advantage of providing a goodness-of-fit measure with the SPSS output.
- *Principal Axis Factor Analysis.* After R^2 values from the correlation matrix are placed in the diagonals of the correlation matrix, extraction of factors is completed. After new communalities are computed, iterations continue, with new communalities replacing the previous ones until the convergence criterion for the factor analysis is met.
- *Alpha Factor Analysis.* This approach emphasizes alpha reliability of the factors by analyzing variables as a sample of measures from a larger population.
- *Image Factor Analysis.* This solution performs factor analysis based on the multiple linear regression correlation of variables with the collection of other variables, rather than relying on some function with underlying dimensions. This common variance of the variable is called its partial image.

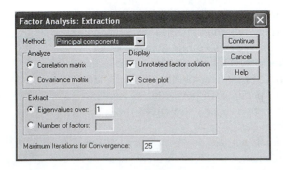

In SPSS, selecting a method for the factor analysis solution is a simple matter of clicking the *Extraction. . .* button. In this example, the researcher requests a *Principal components* solution. As described previously, this method extracts linear combinations of variables that are uncorrelated. The factors extracted begin with the factor associated with the largest portion of variance and continue through those with lower and lower proportions.

The researcher also must identify whether a correlation or covariance matrix will be analyzed as the raw data. Although a covariance matrix could have been selected, we will follow the default selection of the correlation matrix because it is most commonly used. A comparison with an analysis of covariance matrices also will be shared.

Deciding on Factors to Interpret

Two popular tools can be used to help select the number of factors to be extracted. The first approach is known as the Kaiser-Guttman rule, which states that factors should be extracted if they have eigenvalues greater than 1.0. As previously described in this chapter, eigenvalues measure the variance explained by factors and are the sum of squared loadings on a factor. If a factor has at least one item perfectly identified with it, the item's factor loading would be 1.0, which when squared also would be 1.0. Thus, the eigenvalue for a factor that perfectly identifies one variable would be at least 1.0. Of course, it rarely happens that an item is perfectly correlated with a factor, but several variables might be moderately or highly correlated with the factor. Their squared loadings easily could sum to an eigenvalue greater than one. The reasoning is that any factor that cannot identify the equivalent of at least one perfectly loaded variable is not much of a factor. Hence, factors with eigenvalues below 1.0 probably do not reveal much of interest to the researcher.

Of course, this rule often leads to extraction of more factors than really deserve attention. But the researcher has other ways to screen out meaningless factors. As it is, the Kaiser-Guttman guideline works best for principal components analyses.

> In a common factor analysis, communality estimates are inserted in the main diagonal of the correlation matrix. Therefore, for *p* variables, the variance to be decomposed into factors is less than *p*. It has been suggested that the latent root (eigenvalues) criterion should be lower and around the average for the initial communality estimates. (Information Technology Services, 1995, ¶ 21)

In the example used here, the researcher has selected a principal components solution with the minimum eigenvalue criterion of 1.0 for factor extraction. The output below shows that the principal components analysis produced two factors with eigenvalues greater than 1.0.

Total Variance Explained

Component	Initial Eigenvalues			Extraction Sums of Squared Loadings			Rotation Sums of Squared Loadings		
	Total	% of Variance	Cumulative %	Total	% of Variance	Cumulative %	Total	% of Variance	Cumulative %
1	4.301	43.011	43.011	4.301	43.011	43.011	3.008	30.079	30.079
2	1.600	16.004	59.016	1.600	16.004	59.016	2.894	28.937	59.016
3	.970	9.697	68.713						
4	.786	7.865	76.577						
5	.663	6.627	83.204						
6	.482	4.816	88.020						
7	.469	4.688	92.709						
8	.338	3.382	96.090						
9	.245	2.449	98.539						
10	.146	1.461	100.000						

Extraction Method: Principal Component Analysis.

Another approach is to use the "scree" plot to determine isolation of factors. "Scree" refers to the rocks and debris that are found at the bottom of a cliff. In a scree plot, the eigenvalues are plotted from the highest to the lowest. The result is that the factors that account for the greatest portions of total variance are identified as the ones that are part of a steep downward slope. On the other hand, those eigenvalues that are part of a shallow slope usually may be deleted. Checking the box for *Scree plot* produces the output to the left for this example.

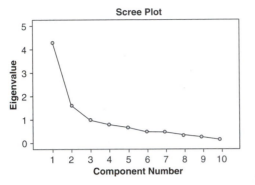

If one draws line segments between points to represent the steepness of slope, it becomes clear that only the first two factors show a steep slope. Eigenvalues associated with remaining factors show a fairly modest downward slope. The following chart shows what happens when lines are drawn to highlight these patterns. This chart reveals a clear intersection of two lines. The two eigenvalues showing steep slopes suggest two factors worth keeping. The eigenvalues that are part of the shallow slope (representing components 3 through 10) play minor roles and, hence, can be dropped from the final selection of variables.

In the SPSS box dedicated to *Factor Analysis: Extraction*, the researcher also wants to select the "Unrotated factor solution" box to obtain a component matrix of effects. After clicking the *Continue* button, the rest of the factor analysis procedure may be completed. In this case, two matters of interest in the output are critical, the table of communalities and the "Component Matrix" of unrotated factor loadings.

The values in the *Initial* communalities column equal 1.0 when principal components analysis is used to examine a correlation matrix. For analysis of covariance matrices, the initial communalities contain the variances of each of the variables. The *Extraction* communalities are the h^2 values that reveal the amount of variance in each variable that is explained by the factors. A large h^2 value for a variable suggests that the item is strongly associated with the factor structure. Low h^2 values help identify items that may be candidates for deletion in final interpretations.

Communalities

	Initial	Extraction
var11	1.000	.626
var14	1.000	.581
var17	1.000	.585
var12	1.000	.490
var13	1.000	.399
var15	1.000	.595
var19	1.000	.726
var20	1.000	.733
var16	1.000	.703
var21	1.000	.463

Extraction Method: Principal Component Analysis.

The *component matrix* is an essential part of factor analysis results. The sum of the squared loadings is equal to the eigenvalue for the factor. Hence, Component 1 (or factor I) accounts for the largest portion of the variance, and Component 2 (or factor II) accounts for the second largest portion of the variance. Furthermore, with principal components analysis, each component is uncorrelated with the others. Interpreting a component matrix is difficult when there is more than one factor involved. Hence, as an aid to interpretation, the factors may be rotated.

Component Matrix [a]

	Component	
	1	2
var11	.775	.157
var14	.675	.354
var17	.746	.171
var12	.680	.166
var13	.330	.539
var15	.559	.531
var19	.540	−.659
var20	.698	−.496
var16	.799	−.252
var21	.621	−.278

Extraction Method: Principal Component Analysis.
a. 2 Components extracted.

Rotation of Factors

With the method of principal components, the first factor accounts for the largest proportion of variance, and subsequent factors account for less and less variance. Unfortunately, this fact means that variables tend to load most heavily on the first factor and less so on others. If there were only one factor, the situation would be different, and the component matrix would tell the whole story without much difficulty in interpretation. But the presence of more than one factor causes difficulty. The numbers in the table do not show many high loadings, above .60, on the second factor. One might think that the second factor does not reveal much, but this interpretation would be mistaken. As an aid to interpretation, components or factors are *rotated* to help researchers interpret factors.

The Purpose of Factor Rotation

"The purpose of the rotation is to find the best distribution of the factor loadings in terms of the meaning of the factors" (Aczel, 1989, p. 95). The step is accomplished by rotating the angles of the axes so that the factor loadings end up being close to either 1.0 or .00 on each factor.

The goal of factor rotation is to find the "best" best factor loadings to give meaning to the extracted factors. It does not change the relationships among the variables one bit. Rotation of factors simply makes it increasingly easy for the factors to reveal their structures. In another sense, rotation is an effort to associate some of the variables with a factor that represents an underlying attribute that some of the variables share in common. This step uses methods that maximize the loadings of items on each factor while minimizing the loadings on others—all without changing the structure of the relations among variables.

There are different forms of rotation, but for purposes of our example, we will illustrate the most popular method, called varimax orthogonal rotation. To keep factors uncorrelated with each other, the rotation maintains axes at 90 degree angles. To understand the meaning of this statement, the diagrams shown on page 418 may be helpful. In the example used in this section of this chapter, the unrotated loadings may be plotted with Component 1 on the horizontal axis and Component 2 on the vertical axis. Rotation does not rotate the variables, but it rotates the *axes* used to identify relationships. The diagram below, left shows how the variables seem to cluster, but the matter may be made clear by sending another set of vertical and horizontal axes through the sets of variables. In fact, when the method known as varimax rotation is used for these data, the result is shown in the diagram below, right. As you can see, these new axes maximize loadings on one factor while minimizing them on others. Within each factor and for each variable, the variances and the communalities do not change, but the correlation of items with underlying factors becomes increasingly clear.

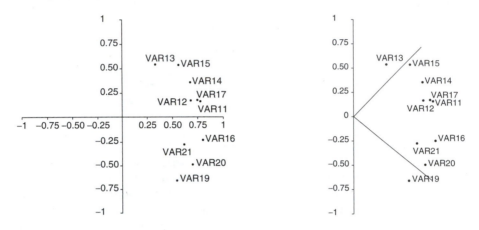

The final step of the rotation process involves "uprighting" the axes. The diagram below shows how this process looks for the message response measures in our example. These new

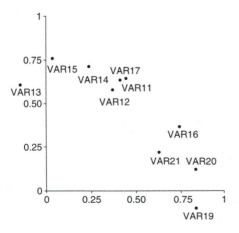

loadings are reported in a rotated component matrix. It bears repeating that although rotation of factors does not change basic relationships among variables, with varimax rotation "the *maximum variance property* of the original components is destroyed. . . . Thus, the first rotated factor will no longer necessarily account for the maximum amount of variance" (J. P. Stevens, 2002, p. 392). Researchers often reexamine the sum of squared loadings on factors to see how variance is partitioned. Furthermore, for solutions involving more than two factors, the rotation grows complicated, and visualizing rotations in two-dimensional space becomes a challenge. Instead, it makes sense to realize that the mathematics of the rotation simply extend basic rotation notions for additional factors.

Forms of Rotation

There are two general forms for rotations. One type is called an **orthogonal rotation** (also called "**rigid rotation**"), in which the axes are set at a 90 degree angle for every pair of factors. This form of rotation ensures that the linear combination of variables in the rotated matrix also will remain uncorrelated with each other. Three popular forms of orthogonal rotation include the following.

- **Varimax** orthogonal rotation attempts to maximize the variance on factors (as its name suggests) by minimizing the number of variables loading highly on the separate factors (Kaiser, 1958). This process is the default in SPSS and has become the most popular rotation method. The method normalizes the loadings on pairs of factors prior to rotation and tends to promote finding simple structures in which loadings are high on one factor and near zero on others. Varimax rotation inhibits researchers from interpreting results as consistent with single general factors. Researchers often find that when there *actually is* one underlying factor, varimax orthogonal rotation produces loadings that are difficult to interpret.

  > Items can also correlate poorly even though they measure the same thing, because their distributions differ in shape. . . . If I asked you "Do you eat ice cream at least twice a day?," I would be measuring the same thing as if I asked you if you eat it at least once a month, yet the proportion of "yes" answers on the two questions would clearly be different, which may lead the two questions to load on different factors. *Difficulty* factors . . . are factors in which loadings reflect similarity of response distribution rather than similarity of content. Consequently such factors are essentially artifacts. (Bernstein, 1988, p. 184)

  So, what are researchers supposed to do if past research or theory leads them to expect a strong general factor? One bit of advice recommends *not* using varimax rotation. The reason is that among rotation systems, "varimax assumes that there is no general factor in the data" (Gorsuch, 1966, p. 308). When applied to a general factor, varimax rotation attempts to maximize the variance of loadings of items on each extracted factor. By so doing, varimax rotation scatters portions of the general factor among the extracted factors, and a simple structure becomes difficult to achieve. While examining the trouble created by the extraction of too few factors, Wood, Tataryn, and Gorsuch (1996) found that overextraction followed by varimax rotation "can result in factor splitting when a general factor is present and there are no unique variables in the data set" (p. 354). To detect factors in which one is a general factor, varimax rotation is not as satisfactory as various other rotation systems (Tenopyr & Michael, 1964). In rotating factors containing a general factor, researchers generally prefer to use oblique rotation and check for the presence of a factor that often has the largest proportion of variance in the factor analysis (in some cases, even surpassing all other factors combined).

  Although difficult to complete with SPSS, another piece of advice suggests that if there is reason to expect that there may be one general factor accompanied by one or more uncorrelated secondary factors, researchers may "leave the first factor as it is and rotate all subsequent factors to varimax. The first factor will thus be a general factor and the remaining factors will have the requisite group structure" (Bernstein, 1988, p. 184).

- **Quartimax** orthogonal rotation attempts to make each row of factor loadings either as large or as small as possible (Neuhaus & Wrigley, 1954). The result is that the method produces a minimum number of interpretable factors required to explain the variables.[6] Because this rotation method is compatible with the expectation of a general factor, it often is invited when such expectations are prominent.

- **Equamax** is an orthogonal rotation combining varimax and quartimax methods to produce a simplification of variables on factors with maximum variance. Both the number of variables and the number of factors are minimized.

A second form of rotation is known as **oblique** or **non-rigid** rotation. This form of analysis does not fix the angle of rotation at 90 degrees. Thus, some correlation among factors exists. In fact, the purpose of oblique rotation is to redefine factor loadings so that researchers may find "the *best association* between factors and variables that are included in them, regardless of whether the factors are independent of each other" (Aczel, 1989, p. 953). Deciding to use orthogonal or oblique rotations of variables requires thinking beyond statistical materials. On one hand, orthogonal rotations often are preferred because they promote clear interpretations of factors. On the other hand, McCroskey and Young (1979) argue that accepting correlations among factors is the most realistic way to look at communication phenomena in general. Hence, they recommend the widespread use of oblique factor rotations. Yet, some writers discourage routine use of oblique rotations in exploratory factor analysis. One author declared:

> Because the factor intercorrelations represent additional free variables, there are more possibilities for strange things to happen in oblique than in orthogonal solutions. For example, two tentative factors may converge on the same destination during an interactive search, as evidenced by the correlation between them becoming high and eventually moving toward 1.00—this cannot happen if factors are kept orthogonal. Despite their real theoretical metrics, oblique solutions tend to be more expensive to compute, more vulnerable to idiosyncrasies in the data, and generally more likely to go extravagantly awry than orthogonal ones. (Loehlin, 1987, p. 164)

---

[6]It is not immediately clear why the method would be called quartimax. The reason is that the method uses the sum of the fourth powers of the factor loadings b from the component matrix. Responding to positions taken by Ferguson (1954) and others, Bernstein (1988) explains the fundamental reasoning behind the quartimax method:

[S]ince the sum of squared factor loadings across rows is invariant $h^2 = \sum b^2$ this equality holds for all variables individually and, therefore, collectively. One may square both sides of the equation, leading to a sum of h^4 values on the left-hand side of the equation. The right-hand side consists of two types of expressions. One is the sum of fourth powers of b (b^4). The other consists of cross products of b^2 values for a given variable on pairs of factors. The result is nothing other than an expansion of $(X + Y)^2$ into $X^2 + Y^2 + 2XY$. The first two terms (X^2 and Y^2) represent the b^4 terms and $2XY$ corresponds to cross products of b^2 terms for different factors.

In quartimax, the b^4 terms are maximized, which is equivalent to minimizing the squared cross-product terms, as the two terms add to a constant. Maximizing b^4 accomplishes the objective of making the absolute values of loadings across rows as large or as small as possible. (pp. 182–183)

Still others believe that different rotation methods do not usually matter. For instance, two scholars stated:

Our advice to the user is that one should not be unduly concerned about the choice of the particular rotation method. If identification of the basic structuring of variables into theoretically meaningful subdimensions is the primary concern of the researcher, as is often the case in an exploratory factor analysis, almost any readily available method of rotation will do the job. Even the issue of whether factors are correlated or not may not make much difference in the exploratory stages of analysis. (Kim & Mueller, 1978, p. 50)

Two popular methods of oblique rotation include direct Oblimin and Promax.

- **Direct Oblimin** oblique rotation (Jennrich & Sampson, 1966) involves selecting a factor called delta or w (for weight) that determines

  the degree to which correlations among the factors is encouraged. If $w = 0, \ldots$ it tends to result in solutions with fairly substantial correlations among the factors. By making the weight w negative, high correlations among factors are penalized. Most often, zero weights or modest negative weights (e.g., $w = -0.5$) will work best. Large negative weights (e.g., $w = -10$) will yield essentially orthogonal factors. Positive weights (e.g., $w = 0.5$) tend to produce overoblique and often problematic solutions. (Loehlin, 1987, p. 164)

  In addition to direct Oblimin, there is a form called indirect Oblimin, which is not supported by SPSS. This approach uses the weight w to examine a different matrix. The process of using direct Oblimin involves more than one pass through the data with different delta values. Researchers look for solutions that involve the fewest number of iterations.

- **Promax** completes analyses by conducing a varimax rotation followed by calculations that further reduce loadings that are close to zero (Hendrickson & White, 1964). The varimax loadings are raised to some higher power, such that the low loadings become smaller and smaller. Yet, the reduced high loadings still remain high enough for interpretation. "The second step of a Promax solution is a variant of a procedure called Procrustes (Hurley & Cattell, 1962), which forces a factor pattern matrix to a best least squares fit to a predesignated target matrix. It gets its name from the legendary Greek who forced travelers to fit his guest bed by stretching or lopping them as necessary" (Loehlin, 1987, p. 166).

There are some warnings about oblique rotations. First, "though oblique rotation preserves the communalities of the variables" (Norušis, 1988, p. 146), the total proportions of variance for factors cannot be computed by summing the individual squared variable loadings (see Bernstein, 1988, p. 185). Second, interpreting obliquely rotated factors may become difficult. "An oblique rotation will likely produce two correlated factors with less-than-obvious meaning, that is, with many cross-loadings" (StatSoft, 2003c, ¶ 30). Hence, two other matrices need to be examined.

1. Factor pattern matrix—the elements here are analogous to standardized regression coefficients from a multiple regression analysis. That is, a given element indicates the importance of that variable to the factor, with the influence of the other variables partialed out.

2. Factor structure matrix—the elements here are the simple correlations of the variable with the factors; that is, they are the factor loadings.

For orthogonal factors these two matrices are the same (J. P. Stevens, 2002, p. 393).

When oblique rotation is used, the pattern matrix shows factor loadings for the communalities whose range is not limited to be from −1.0 to 1.0 (Norušis, 1988, p. 147). The pattern matrix presents the partial correlation coefficients between the factor and the variables. These loadings are the bases for subsequent factor labeling and interpretations. When data are analyzed in the form of covariances rather than correlations, both original and rescaled coefficients (standardized to be on the same measurement scale) are reported.

The factor structure matrix reports the critical information (the actual correlations between factors and variables) for the typical researcher using oblique rotations. The structure matrix is less affected by sampling error than is the pattern matrix—regardless of whether the rotation is completed by orthogonal or oblique rotation (Bernstein, 1988, p. 177). On the other hand, the pattern matrix has the advantage of adjusting the loadings on one factor to account for the remaining factors.

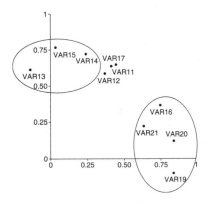

In the example used in this chapter, a varimax orthogonal rotation was used. Following this rotation, the arrangement shown on the left was found. The circles were added to identify variables on the message reception scales that seem to measure the same things. The actual rotated factor matrix appears in the next section of this chapter, on factor interpretation issues.

Interpreting Factors

Understanding what the factor analysis has revealed involves making some artistic judgments about the meaning of the variable loadings on factors. This process involves both defining factors and using some care when interpreting factors.

Defining Factors

The items that load highly on a factor define that factor. Deciding which items load on a factor, however, is not always simple. One tradition uses a minimum loading of .3 to identify a variable that is relevant to defining a factor (Bernstein, 1988, p. 177). Another approach takes its reasoning from the judgment that statistically significant factor loadings should account for at least 15% of the variance on the factor. J. P. Stevens (2002, p. 394) suggests that loadings of at least .40 should be required for interpretation. This sort of reasoning is fairly common in many communities in the social sciences, but others have found this loading criterion rather anemic. It often is the case that items have coefficients above .40 on more than one factor. In communication studies, the standards for identifying variables with factors tend to be on the conservative side, yet many factor analyses in communication studies tend to hold up surprisingly well over successive efforts at validation and cross-validation. As far back as 1979, McCroskey and Young explained:

> We, and several other factor analysts, have been plagued with the issue of what to do with the items that contribute significant variance on two or more factors. We have employed in many instances the *a priori* criterion that for the loading of an item to be considered significant it must have a primary loading on one factor of at least .60, and no secondary loading on another factor with a value above .40. It has been charged that this criterion for item significance is very conservative, for, in fact, we may be discarding items that are contributing variance to the factor model. We agree. In our use of factor analysis, we have been primarily interested in instrument development. We have sought items that are "pure" measures of a given factor and have used orthogonal (varimax) rotation procedures to increase the purity. . . . If, however, one has *a priori* grounds for hypothesizing that certain items will load on certain factors, or even that they will contribute variance to several factors, the .60–.40 criterion would be of little value. In exploratory investigation of a construct, we would suggest the utilization of a more liberal criterion. Similarly, when any rotation method other than varimax is employed, the .60–.40 criterion is meaningless. (p. 380)

There is no "law" on the matter, however, and this rule is not universally accepted. Yet, it remains influential, and for the rest of this discussion, we will adopt these conservative guidelines proposed by McCroskey and Young (1979).

In the example dealing with message reception scales, the rotated factor matrix is shown on the right below. In each case where an item is judged to be loaded on a factor, the loading is circled. It might be helpful to look at variables without circles.

- Some items fail to load on a factor because their loadings are too low. Variable 12 does not have any loadings of .60 or greater (though the loading of .590 on factor 2 comes close).
- Some items fail to load on a factor because the secondary loadings are too high. Variable 11 has a loading of .650 on the second factor, but because it also has a loading above .40 on the first factor, it is not considered to define a factor clearly. Variable 17 has the same defect (the secondary loading is .420, which is above the maximum for a secondary loading).

Rotated Component Matrix[a]

	Component	
	1	2
var11	.451	.650
var14	.243	(723)
var17	.420	.640
var12	.376	.590
var13	−.135	(618)
var15	.036	(770)
var19	(.846)	−.102
var20	(.847)	.125
var16	(.752)	.371
var21	(.641)	.229

Extraction Method: Principal Component Analysis.
Rotation Method: Varimax with Kaiser Normalization.
a. Rotation converged in 3 iterations.

By convention, a factor usually is not considered to be defined unless at least two variables load on it. If a factor has only one item, the "factor" is just the variable alone, not some underlying dimension. Hence, it makes little sense to speak of a factor with only one item. If a factor has no variables clearly loaded on it, the factor would be identified as an artifact and would be discarded by prudent researchers. In this case, each factor is defined by three or more items. As a result, the researcher would conclude that the two factors are underlying dimensions of the initial collection of measures.

But what is the nature of each dimension? To answer this question, the researcher looks at the variables on each factor and makes an argument about the underlying construct that seems to be identified. This matter is not statistical so much as it is an exercise in inductive logic.[7] In essence, the researcher develops a name for the factors according to some common property they share. In the example developed at length in this chapter, the first factor is defined by four variables:

Variable 16: The message was well structured.

Variable 19: The message was clear.

Variable 20: The message was well organized.

Variable 21: The message was confusing (reverse scoring).

These variables all seem to deal with the content and organizational clarity of the message. Hence, the dimensions might be labeled "Message Clarity" by the researcher.

The second dimension is composed of the following variables:

Variable 13: The message was boring (reverse scoring);

Variable 14: The message was interesting; and

Variable 15: The message was dull (reverse scoring).

Because all these scales seem to deal with the degree of interest in the message, the dimension might be labeled "message interestingness" or "interest" for short. Of course, the researcher must have a rationale for choosing labels for factors.

After identifying factors, the researcher may want to create an index from the items on the same dimensions. There are some variations in the methods researchers use. The most common approach takes items that define a dimension and adds the values from each variable to create an index or composite scale. A second approach is to compute the mean value of all of the variables on the dimension. A third approach involves multiplying the variable values by some value, such as communalities, before summing their values. In reality, there are few differences in the effects observed in using these alternatives. Thus, it probably makes the most

---

[7]Researchers do not ignore the item loadings in this step. Sometimes researchers look at the variable with the highest loading on a factor to detect if its qualities indicate what a dimension really is about. For instance, if a researcher noted that the highest loading on a dimension were the Likert-type scale "The source is trustworthy," the researcher might consider the possibility that the dimension deals with communicator trust generally.

sense to select the simplest and immediately justifiable option, that of adding the items. Of course, the new scales should be examined for reliability before using them in statistical analyses.

Warnings About Interpreting Effects in Factor Analysis

The convenient use of computers has made factor analysis available to nearly anyone who wishes to use the method. But factor analysis can produce some effects that can mislead researchers.

"Phantom" factors exist when a factor includes a set of variables with moderate to high positive loadings, whereas another factor includes the same items with a set of moderate to high *negative* loadings. Such a condition is a likely indicator that only one underlying factor actually exists. The "two factors" actually are just mirrors of each other created by measurement from different ends of the same continuum.

Intercorrelations of final measured factors can occur even with identification of orthogonal factors. When researchers reduce the number of variables in an effort at data reduction, they often drop unwanted measures, or they create new measures that are indices of subsets of variables. It is wise to check to ensure that these new representative measures or new indices are uncorrelated, especially if the factor analysis had been completed to help prevent multicollinearity effects. One may wonder how such a thing is possible if researchers use orthogonal rotation. After all, orthogonal rotation means that the factors will remain uncorrelated. The existence of orthogonal factors, however, means only that each factor's *linear combination of variables* is uncorrelated with the others. But after conducting factor analyses, researchers use the information to delete items from consideration, sum selected variables into new scales, and to perhaps identify one or two representative variables to represent the factor. In short, researchers hardly ever use measures that are composed of the *entire linear combination* of one factor that is orthogonal to the *entire linear combination* of another factor. Thus, scores on these final measures may, in fact, be correlated, even if they were derived from orthogonally rotated factors. Researchers should examine the intercorrelations of their final measures to ensure that all their research requirements (such as avoidance of multicollinearity) have been met.

Misidentification of factors can occur several different ways, but one of the most common errors is to attempt to use factor analysis to identify philosophic *categories* or to define *varieties* of concepts. The methods of factor analysis describe underlying patterns in the ways variables are used and related. Put simply, factor analysis reveals only how measures are correlated with each other. If the measures are drawn from people, the factors reveal how people tend to use the measures. The factors themselves are different dimensions of the ways measures are interrelated, *not different philosophic types* of things. Thus, factor analysis cannot answer philosophical questions, such as the mind-body duality, categories of arguments, or the types of love that exist. Instead, factor analysis may reveal the ways individuals use measures to respond to concepts (such as the notion of existence or of love). In an appropriate interpretation of factor analysis, a researcher might examine scales designed to measure student perceptions of teachers. The researcher might find three factors, such as immediacy, competence, and goodwill. These factors would be faces of teacher perception (similar in many ways to "teacher credibility"). The factors, however, are not *types* of teachers or types of credibility, but ways that students use scales to structure their perceptions of teachers.

Thus, it should be possible to find a teacher who is high in all three dimensions, or a teacher who is high in one and low in the others, or any combination. The dimensions may apply to *any* teachers, but they do not identify *types* of teachers. In an example of an inappropriate interpretation of factor analysis, suppose a researcher asked participants to complete scales regarding perceptions of types of arguments. After finding four factors in a standard R factor analysis," the researcher might conclude that there were four types of arguments: arguments showing bias, arguments drawing analogies, arguments from morality, and deductive arguments. But R factor analysis could not identify types of arguments, though it could reveal dimensions of scaled perceptions of *any* type of evidence. The error becomes obvious because it would be impossible for a given argument to score highly on all types of argument factors. For instance, an argument could not be an argument from analogy and a deductive argument at the same time. Obviously, the researcher has misidentified what the factors actually reveal. Researchers use R factor analysis to examine dimensions of correlated measures, not as solutions to philosophic or taxonomic questions.

Chapter 16

CONFIRMATORY FACTOR ANALYSIS THROUGH THE AMOS PROGRAM

Unlike exploratory factor analysis, which usually is not guided by theory to predict the composition of factors, confirmatory factor analysis involves some hypothesizes to predict the composition of underlying factors. This tool has become increasingly popular in recent years as computer programs have made it accessible to researchers. Our discussion is focused predominantly on the ways that today's researchers actually use this approach. Rather than stressing computations, the use of the Amos[1] program is emphasized because it is now widely available through SPSS and because it is among the easiest confirmatory factor analysis programs to use. In particular, this chapter examines the basic idea of confirmatory factor

---

[1]Amos is a registered trademark of Amos Development Corporation.

analysis and then explains the use of the Amos program to conduct the actual statistical work for confirmatory factor analysis models.

THE NOTION OF CONFIRMATORY FACTOR ANALYSIS

Confirmatory factor analysis is "factor analysis conducted to test hypotheses (or confirm theories) about the factors one expects to find. It is a subtype of structural equation modeling . . ." (Vogt, 2005, p. 56). To understand this approach, then, researchers must define additional terms. A **structural equation** is "an equation representing the strength and nature of the hypothesized relations among (the 'structure' of) sets of variables in a theory" (Vogt, 2005, p. 313). In turn, **structural equation modeling** consists of "models made up of more than one structural equation; models that describe causal relations among latent variables and include coefficients for endogenous variables" (Vogt, 2005, p. 313). The notions of causal analysis and modeling are covered in Chapter 17; it is enough for now to state that an **endogenous variable** is one that is predicted by other elements in a causal system.

Purposes of Confirmatory Factor Analysis

Confirmatory factor analysis investigates *hypothesized* linear combinations of variables. Yet, the distinctions between simple exploratory and confirmatory methods can be fluid.

> For instance, it is possible that the researcher may specify that there will be, say, two factors but may not anticipate exactly what variables will represent each. Or, to illustrate one of the numerous strategies that can be employed, the researcher may use one half of the sample to explore the possible factor structure, and then use the other half of the sample to test the factorial hypothesis that was developed from the examination of the first half. . . . [This method] is often used as a heuristic device. For example, assume the researcher is certain that on the basis of previous research or strong theory there are two separate dimensions of liberalism—one mainly concerned with the economic issues and the other with civil rights issues. This researcher is interested primarily in constructing a scale of economic liberalism (to be used as a variable in further analysis, but uncertain whether the opinion about providing financial aid to unwed mothers reflects the dimension of economic liberalism, or is better subsumed under the civil rights dimension). Here factor analysis may be used as a means of checking out the meaning of a particular variable or variables. (Kim & Mueller, 1978, p. 10)

Researchers find that confirmatory factor analysis may involve more than simply examining hypothesized factor structures.

One of the most prominent purposes involves testing whether a set of measures continues to exhibit the same factor structure as hypothesized. For instance, researchers often use scales that were previously developed for other research. They often wish to revalidate their work. Many other researchers may want to use previously established scales for their own studies. Though most researchers rely on a combination of exploratory factor analysis followed by assessing the continued reliability of the measure, others have suggested the wisdom of using confirmatory factor analysis. In fact, H. S. Park et al. (2002, p. 572) have urged communication researchers to use confirmatory factor analysis routinely when revalidating measures.

Another purpose for confirmatory factor analysis is its role in constructing a causal model. Such programs as Amos, LISREL, and EQS employ confirmatory factor analysis to develop the measurement model that underlies the causal modeling. Thus, confirmatory factor analysis plays an important role in many efforts to engage in advanced modeling.

Some other purposes may be served by confirmatory factor analysis (after Bernstein, 1988, pp. 203–208). Though not exhaustive, this list suggests some of the most popular purposes.

- *Comparing Alternative Solutions From the Data.* Researchers using one method of factor extraction or one type of factor rotation could attempt to compare different factor scores.
- *Comparing Alternative Solutions From Different Individuals.* One of the most popular reasons for conducting confirmatory factor analysis involves examining whether different sets of subjects provide different solutions. Whether the researcher wishes to cross-validate a set of scales with different samples, or whether the researcher simply wishes to know if the past pattern of variable use continues to hold with new samples, confirmatory factor analysis may be used. "The basic issue would then be one of *replication*. If, conversely, there is a systematic difference, such as in gender, then the fundamental issue is one of *invariance* or *robustness*" (Bernstein, 1988, p. 206).
- *Factor Matching.* One effort involves exploring ways to transform two sets of factors into structures that most strongly resemble each other. Based on work completed by Cliff (1966), the method extends notions of orthogonal rotation by rotating a factor set so that it is highly similar to a second set.

> Factor matching is useful in allowing one to recognize that the overall *structure* of two solutions can be quite similar even if individual factors are somewhat dissimilar. For example, suppose that one solution produced two factors, *A* and *B*, and that another solution produced two factors of the form $C = (A + B)$ and $D = (A - B)$. [If] it can be shown that the individual correlations between pairs of factors from the two studies, such as *A* and *C*, will be .7071 in absolute magnitude, . . . *B* and *D* will correlate −.7071. *A* and *C* will correlate as highly as *B* and *C*. However, the major point is that a suitable . . . rotation of either solution . . . will bring the two into complete congruence. (Bernstein, 1988, p. 208)

It may be recalled from Chapter 15 that two factors that are mirror images of each other usually are interpreted as indicating the presence of one underlying factor. Factor matching permits researchers to identify such similarities in factor structures despite apparent differences.

Another purpose for confirmatory factor analysis reflects an effort to enlist this method as a way to complete analyses that are similar to other multivariate statistical tools. In particular, confirmatory factor analysis may be useful for *comparing alternative solutions with different variables from the same individuals.* Though it may sound a bit unusual, researchers sometimes are interested in exploring whether one set of interrelated variables is compatible with another set of interrelated variables. For instance, a researcher might factor analyze k_a variables involving whether a collection of students came from collectivist cultures, their ability to speak English fluently, and whether they were international students. Then, the researcher could examine a set of k_b communication orientations such as interpersonal communication competence, communication apprehension, and empathic listening skills. The

Special Discussion 16.1

Comparing Factor Solutions From Different Samples

The scaling matrices are represented by the symbol $\mathbf{D}$. The factor score weight matrices are symbolized as $\mathbf{W}$. The correlation matrices are symbolized as $\mathbf{R}$. Thus, for the first sample group, the scaling factor matrix is symbolized as $\mathbf{D}_a$, the factor score weight matrix is $\mathbf{W}_a$, and the correlation matrix is $\mathbf{R}_a$. The corresponding matrices for the second group are $\mathbf{D}_b$, $\mathbf{W}_b$, and $\mathbf{R}_b$. "Regardless of whether the group differences are random or systematic, the similarity of the two sets of factor scores within a set A is given by . . . $\mathbf{R}_{ab \cdot a} = \mathbf{S}'_a \mathbf{R}_a \mathbf{S}_b$ (Bernstein, 1988, p. 206). "The similarity of factor scores within set B is given by . . . $\mathbf{R}_{ab \cdot b} = \mathbf{S}'_a \mathbf{R}_b \mathbf{S}_b$ (Bernstein, 1988, p. 206).

The coefficient of congruence (Burt, 1948; Tucker, 1951; Wrigley & Neuhaus, 1955) was developed to identify consistency of pattern matrices. If there were pattern matrices $\mathbf{b}$ from two samples, a and b, the congruency coefficient would be

$$c = \frac{\mathbf{b}_{ia}\mathbf{b}_{jb}}{\sqrt{\mathbf{b}_{ia}^2}\sqrt{\mathbf{b}_{jb}^2}},$$

where ia is point i in configuration a and jb is point j in configuration b.

In essence, this measure indicates the distances between the points i and j in the compared configurations. An alternative raw score formula is

$$\frac{\sum_i x_i y_i}{\sqrt{\sum_i x_i^2 \sum_i y_i^2}},$$

where x_i and y_i are the loadings on the compared factor configurations.

This second formula bears a striking similarity to the formula for the Pearson product-moment correlation. In fact, when the data input "are derived from standardized components . . . , the coefficient of congruence equals the factor correlation" (Bernstein, 1988, p. 207). As one guideline, a congruence coefficient of at least .78 has been suggested before a claim of "a match" between factor structures may be claimed (Schneewind & Cattell, 1970).

researcher might use confirmatory factor analysis to examine how highly correlated the factor scores of the background variables are with the factor scores for the communication disposition factors. This method shares a similarity with canonical correlation, in which a set of dependent variables is correlated with a set of independent variables.

Types of Confirmatory Factor Analysis

The confirmatory factor analysis approach itself goes back over half a century. There are two general traditions that fall under the heading of confirmatory factor analysis.

Traditional confirmatory factor analysis uses a combination of hypotheses about factors and general factor analysis methods. Rather than employing principal components solutions, traditional confirmatory factor analysis relies on principal axis factoring. The researcher looks for factor loadings that are consistent (or inconsistent) with hypothesized loadings. As explained in Chapter 15, principal axis factor analysis places R^2 values from the correlation matrix in the diagonals of the correlation matrix and makes an initial extraction of factors. Then, after new communalities are computed, the process is repeated with the new communalities replacing the previous ones until the convergence criterion for the factor analysis is met. This repeated process of factor analysis permits the researcher to compare the predicted model against the specifics of the data. Where differences from the predicted model emerge, they can be identified early, and the researcher often finds it possible to develop improved alternative models. Though this method *may* use statistical tools that test the "macro" fit of the factor structure to the hypothesized model, the emphasis is placed on "micro" examination of exceptionally large or small factor loadings.

Use of structural equation modeling to complete confirmatory factor analysis is the most popular method for completing confirmatory factor analyses, and it is the method described for the rest of this chapter. In this approach, confirmatory factor analysis is the "measurement model" for a system in which the factors are identified as latent variables in a larger predictive model. Because the structural equation model is hypothesized in advance, the factors are predicted from the researcher's model of the structures underlying manifest variables. Unlike the traditional confirmatory factor analysis model, in which individual loadings are reexamined in detail, the structural equation model approach also enlists general tests of the fit of the model to the data, such as the likelihood ratio chi-square test (despite its limitations), examination of residuals (a form of microanalysis), and more than a score of other general tests.

Data Characteristics and Assumptions of Confirmatory Factor Analysis

To make predictions of factors, researchers identify parameters for which some values are known and for which others are to be estimated.

> [P]arameters are of three kinds: (a) *fixed parameters* that have been assigned given values, (b) *constrained parameters* that are unknown, but equal to one or more other parameters, and (c) *free parameters* that are unknown and not constrained to be equal to any other parameter. The advantage of such an approach is the great generality and flexibility obtained by the various specifications that may be imposed. (Jöreskog, 1979a, p. 47)

Several assumptions underlie the use of confirmatory factor analysis. Naturally, many of these matters are shared with all varieties of factor analyses. A major assumption tested by the modeling process is that there really are unobserved common dimensions that may be enlisted to account for the correlations among observed variables. Another assumption is made that the data themselves are measured on the interval or ratio level. As noted in Chapter 15, confirmatory factor analysis also makes some assumptions—at least initially— about the characteristics of extracted factors: Both common and unique factors have means of zero, variances of common factors are equal to 1, and common factors are uncorrelated with each other.

In the approach using structural equation modeling, several other assumptions apply. As with multiple regression correlation, it is assumed that residuals (differences between the observed and predicted values of the dependent variable) are normally distributed, show the same pattern of relationship through the entire range of the variables (homoscedasticity), are independent of each other, and are independent of the exogenous variables. Also consistent with multiple regression correlation is the assumption that there is a linear relationship between observed and predicted values of the dependent variable. Although it is not immediately obvious, this assumption also means that the residuals have a mean of zero.

Unless researchers explicitly command that different methods be used, maximum likelihood estimation typically is employed to compute estimates of parameters. To ensure that the estimates *actually are* maximum likelihood estimates (or generalized least squares estimates, if that option is selected), the researcher must assume a couple of things.

- Independence of observations is assumed. Though measures may be from the same participants, this assumption means that participants or events are chosen independently from the population.
- Observed variables must have a multivariate normal distribution. This multivariate normal distribution is an extension of the logic of the standard normal curve to multiple variables.[2] Among other things, if researchers know that this assumption is not tenable, standard chi-square statistics related to model fit should probably be replaced by interpreting the *Satorra-Bentler scaled chi-square* test, which adjusts the chi-square value for nonnormal distributions.

Though other families of statistics often require underlying normal distributions and independence of observations, satisfying these assumptions alone (and ignoring multivariate

---

[2]This approach avoids a technical definition beyond the scope of this book, but it may be said that a multivariate normal distribution can be shown to be an extension of the standard normal curve. The standard normal curve density function for a random variable is

$$f(x) = \frac{1}{(2\pi\sigma)^{\frac{1}{2}}} e^{-\frac{(x-\mu)^2}{2\sigma^2}}.$$

In contrast, when this distribution is extended to multiple variables, the density function for the multivariate normal distribution becomes

$$f(\mathbf{x}_1, \mathbf{x}_2 \ldots, \mathbf{x}_k) = \frac{1}{(2\pi)^{\frac{k}{2}} |\Sigma|^{\frac{1}{2}}} e^{-\frac{1}{2}(\mathbf{x}-\mu)' \Sigma^{-1} (\mathbf{x}-\mu)},$$

where

$\mathbf{x}$ is the vector random variable,

μ is the vector of means,

Σ is a variance-covariance matrix,

$|\Sigma|$ is the determinant of the variance-covariance matrix, and

k is the number of events.

normal distributions) may not be enough for prudent researchers. In structural equation modeling programs, "meeting these requirements leads only to asymptotic conclusions (i.e., conclusions that are approximately true for large samples)" (Arbuckle & Wothke, 1999, p. 79).

Another assumption underlying computations is that the covariance matrix is positive definite. In positive definite matrices, all eigenvalues are above zero.[3] If the covariance matrix is not positive definite, Amos ceases data processing, and complete output is not presented.

It should be mentioned that when using structural equation modeling, one commonly rejects distributional assumptions. When such distribution problems are found (which is a frequent enough situation), the researcher would be wise to identify reasons and to solve them, if possible. Often, but not always, researchers need only increase their sample sizes to find that their data approximate an underlying multivariate normal distribution with other distribution assumptions also satisfied.

When direct remedies are not sufficient to deal with violation of distribution assumptions, there can be some difficulty obtaining meaningful solutions. In such circumstances, violations of distribution assumptions often are handled by accepting a certain amount of compromise, such as accepting correlated common factors or correlated error terms, or fixing some initial parameters. In fact, sometimes researchers claim to have good reasons to justify violating some assumptions.

Sometimes researchers are not as greatly concerned about distributional assumptions as they are at other times. For instance, when using maximum likelihood estimation methods,

if some exogenous variables are fixed (i.e., they are either known beforehand or measured without error), their distribution may have *any shape* [italics added], provided that:

- For any value pattern of the fixed variables, the remaining (random) variables have a (conditional) normal distribution.
- The (conditional) variance-covariance matrix of the random variables is the same for every pattern of the fixed variables.
- The (conditional) expected values of the random variables depend linearly on the values of the fixed variables. (Arbuckle & Wothke, 1999, p. 78)

As long as the observed variables are normally distributed for each level of the fixed variables, and have the same conditional variance-covariance matrices, confirmatory factor analysis may be completed with correlated factors.

Researchers also can—and often do—explore models that do not meet the assumptions of uncorrelated error terms and uncorrelated factors. In fact, researchers often find that good cases can be made for models that do not make these initial assumptions. Thus, modifications sometimes are made in the model to permit examining factor structures that violate these initial assumptions. This matter will be revisited in this chapter's section on "Measurement Adequacy and Considering Modifications."

---

[3]Furthermore, a positive definite matrix is symmetric $\mathbf{A}$ where the quadratic form $\mathbf{x}^H\mathbf{A}\mathbf{x}$ is greater than zero for all nonzero vectors $\mathbf{x}$.

USING THE AMOS PROGRAM FOR CONFIRMATORY FACTOR ANALYSIS

Confirmatory factor analysis has been given a prominent place in the Amos program. This program is widely available through SPSS and, hence, has become a program of choice for increasing numbers of researchers interested in both confirmatory factor analysis and structural equation modeling. The letters in Amos are an abbreviation of "**A**nalysis of **MO**ment **S**tructures." As do other programs, such as LISREL, EQS, and EZPath, this program combines confirmatory factor analysis with causal modeling. Causal modeling will be covered in the next chapter. The present treatment introduces the basics of using Amos as well as its application to confirmatory factor analysis. In particular, this section introduces the nomenclature of Amos, explains the operation of the program, and shows how to interpret the results of an actual analysis.

The Initial Language of Amos

For confirmatory factor analysis, the chief question is whether a group of observed variables converges to identify the underlying factor or latent variable in some hypothesized way.

- An *observed variable* (also called a manifest variable) is one that is measured on a given item or scale.
- An *unobserved variable* (also called a latent variable or a factor) is one that is not observed directly. This factor is composed of observed variables.
- A *model* is a predicted pattern of relationships among the types. In a broad sense, a model is "a simple description of a probabilistic process that may have given rise to observable data" (Upton & Cook, 2002, p. 234). In this context, the description exhibits relationships among observed (manifest) variables and underlying factors (unobserved or latent variables), as well as error terms.
- The *parameters* are coefficients expressing relationships among elements of the model. As previously noted, these parameters may be fixed, constrained, or free.

Measures (observed variables) converge on underlying constructs (unobserved variables) in a *measurement* model.

Beginning Amos and Entering Data

Amos permits researcher to enter and analyze data in several ways. On one hand, those who wish to exercise the controls of programming languages may use Amos Basic to undertake programming in the Sax Basic Language[TM],[4] which is similar to Microsoft Visual Basic and is also compatible with Microsoft Visual Basic for Applications.[5] On the other hand, the easiest way to use the powerful tools of Amos is to start the *Amos Graphics* program. This latter approach is described here.

---

[4]Sax Basic Language is a registered trademark of Polar Engineering and Consulting.

[5]Visual Basic and Visual Basic for Applications are registered trademarks of the Microsoft Corporation.

Operation of the Program

To introduce how Amos is used for confirmatory factor analysis, an example of measurement model construction will be used in the remainder of this chapter. In this case, a researcher was interested in using confirmatory factor analysis to examine the nature of scales designed to measure source credibility. There is, of course, quite a bit of theory and research on the subject. The researcher wanted to tap two dimensions of credibility, source character and source competence ratings. Based on past experience and a research tradition, the researcher designed some 7-point semantic differential–type scales to measure these dimensions. The source character dimension was to be measured by two scales bounded by bipolar adjectives: trustworthy/untrustworthy and honest/dishonest. The source competence factor was tapped by three scales: expert/inexpert, knowledgeable/unknowledgeable, and competent/incompetent. Two hundred participants completed the scales. The number of observed variables is kept small for purposes of illustration. In reality, researchers usually employ more than two items to measure an underlying or latent dimension.

When running Amos from a personal computer, the researcher begins by selecting *Amos (5.0)* from the *All Programs* section of the *Start* menu. A drop-down menu appears with several options: *Amos Basic*, *Amos Graphics*, *File Manager*, *Graphics Automated Demo*, *Seed Manager*, *Text Output*, *View Data*, and *View Path Diagrams*. The researcher chooses *Amos Graphics* to use the graphic display method to construct a model. These models may be measurement models, as is the case here, or structural models, as discussed in the next chapter. The following layout appears:

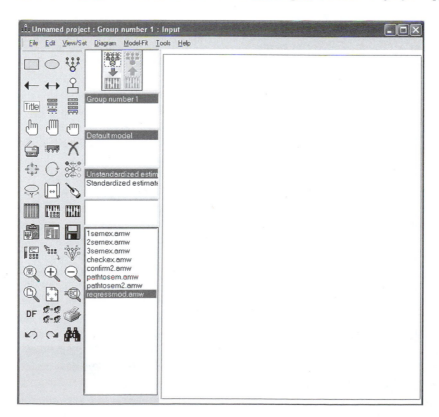

The menu items allow the researcher to command the layout, analysis, and presentation of the Amos modeling approach. The main window contains toolbar icons that are shortcuts to essential commands. The large blank area is the *drawing area*, where symbols and variables are placed. To load a data file for analysis, the researcher clicks the *Select Data Files* icon ▦ or types the *Control-D* combination. This step opens a *Data Files* dialog box, and the researcher clicks on the *File Name* button to begin a search for the location of the data file.

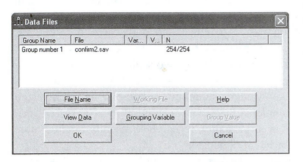

Data may be imported from dBase, Excel, FoxPro, Lotus 123, MS Access, or ordinary text files. In this case, the researcher used an SPSS data file. To ensure that the data have been loaded, the researcher might wish to click the *View Data* button and verify the transfer of the file. In this case, the *SPSS Data Editor* was active, and clicking the appropriate icon permitted the researcher to make a selection. Once the proper file was selected, the researcher clicked on the *OK* button to load the data.

Constructing the Diagram

The Amos Graphics program permits the researcher to use an intuitive diagrammatic approach to prepare models. Diagrams simply are inserted into the drawing field. Because there are two unobserved variables (or latent variables), they were placed on the drawing first. The researcher clicked on the oval icon, which activated the *Draw unobserved variables* tool. While this icon was still active, the researcher placed the mouse cursor at the top of the drawing area. By holding the left mouse button, the researcher controlled the size of the oval to be used for the unobserved variable. Two ovals were placed in the middle of the page, one for the character dimension and one for the competence dimension. To deactivate this tool, the *Draw unobserved variables* icon was clicked again. To add two measured variables for each of the latent variables, the *Draw indicator variable* icon ⚇ was clicked. This shortcut is very useful because it sets initial parameters for the researcher. After highlighting the icon, every time the left mouse button is clicked over an unobserved (or latent) variable oval, a manifest (or observed) variable is attached. Furthermore, a place for its error term also is attached. In the example here, the researcher added two indicator variables to the unobserved variable that is to be used for the "character" dimension. Three indicator variables were added to the unobserved variable used for the "competence" dimension. When finished adding these paths, the researcher clicked the *Draw indicator variable* button to deactivate it. Because the *Draw indicator variable* tool adds the indicator variables *above* the ovals, the researcher decided to rotate the model's graphic image. The researcher clicked the ◔ button to activate the *Rotate the indicators of a latent variable* tool. Clicking an oval moves the indicator variables by 90 degrees. Thus, the following model was drawn.

If the rectangles or ovals need to be moved, the researcher may click on the *Move objects* icon ![icon], which will permit moving any item that is highlighted. Numbers have been inserted into some paths. The reason is that to identify the model, the scale of the unobserved or latent variable must be defined. The step may be accomplished by setting the variance of the path coefficient from an unobserved variable (an underlying factor) to an observed variable at some positive value. In this case, the *Draw indicator variable* tool has automated this task by constraining a parameter at 1.

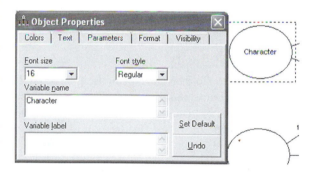

The researcher also wanted to insert variable names into the boxes and ovals. Double-clicking on any box or oval produces a dialog box that permits identification of variables. In this case, the researcher double-clicked each of the boxes and ovals to enter names. For the unobserved variables or factors indicated in ovals, the researcher needed to insert new labels. In this case, the researcher labeled the first factor or latent variable "character." For the manifest or observed variables of which this unobserved variable (or factor) is composed, the researcher assigned the variables from the variable list. To identify variables from the data set to the model, the researcher may click on the *List variables in dataset* icon ![icon]. This step activates the *Variables in Dataset* dialog box, which lists all the variables in the data file. The researcher may move any of these variables to the correct location by clicking on the variable name and dragging it (by depressing the left mouse button) to the desired rectangle. In this case, the researcher placed the observed variables called TRUST and HONEST in the rectangles connected by paths to the "character" unobserved variable. When Amos brings files from SPSS, it truncates the variable names into labels of no more than eight characters. Thus, it is a good idea for researchers to make sure that the original variable names do not duplicate each other in their first eight characters. The process

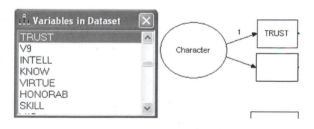

was followed for the second unobserved variable (located in an oval), which was labeled "Competence." Because this factor was hypothesized to be composed of three variables, rectangles for them were provided. Similarly, the variables called EXPERT, KNOWLEDG, and COMPETEN each were placed in one of the rectangles adjacent to the oval for the "Competence" factor.

The error terms must be labeled as well. Their labels are matters of convenience, but many researchers prefer to use the terms that are familiar to those using LISREL (delta [δ] for the error terms associated with the exogenous indicators, and epsilon [ε] for error terms associated with latent endogenous variables). Nevertheless, keeping track of information supplied on the output can be confusing if only cryptic symbols are used. In this case, the first part of the label was indicated as "e_" to symbolize that it was an error term. The last part of the label included the first letter of the observed indicator variable. Thus, "e_t" was used for the error term of the "*TRUST*" indicator variable, "e_h" was used for the error term of the "*HONEST*" indicator variable, and so forth.

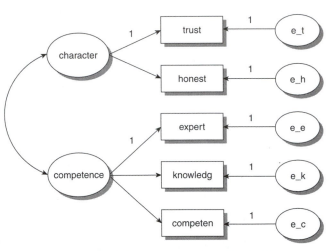

Confirmatory Factor Analysis for Credibility Scales

Arrows appear from the unobserved variables (the factors) to their observed indicator variables. To indicate a relationship between the two unobserved variables or factors, a curved double arrow must be added. To accomplish this task, the researcher clicks on the double arrow icon ↔ and depresses the left mouse button when drawing an arrow from one unobserved variable to the other. The diagram looks similar to the one found here.

This diagram represents the measurement model in the form of "a single multiple factor confirmatory factor analysis" (Loehlin, 1987, p. 78). As can be seen, the relationship between the emergent unobserved factors is a free parameter to be determined. In addition, because all the observed variables have only one error term, these paths are constrained to equal 1. Though one of the parameters from each factor is constrained at 1, the others are free parameters.

Examining Model Parameters

As with any form of factor analysis, Amos uses optimizing methods such as maximum likelihood estimation to identify relationships between observed and unobserved variables. For confirmatory factor analysis, maximum likelihood estimation methods are most frequently used as optimizing techniques (see Jöreskog, 1969), though other methods are available (for a review of other methods, see Everitt, 1987). Suffice it to say for this introductory treatment, when conducting the analysis, the researcher needs to request specific output elements. Clicking on the *Analysis properties* icon ▦ produces a dialog box of output options.

On the *Estimation* tab, the researcher finds several options to minimize discrepancies in the model's estimates.[6] These elements boil down to three major choices: some variation of ordinary least squares (which is the basis of so many correlation tools), generalized least squares, and maximum likelihood estimation. Maximum likelihood is the default, and for estimating model parameters, it has the advantages of consistency, normality as sample size increases, and efficiency (Keeping, 1995, p. 123). Although covering the details of maximum likelihood estimation is beyond this scope of this book, it may be said that when using maximum likelihood criteria, population parameters are estimated by a function in which a "to choose as estimator of a [population] parameter θ is chosen such that "a function based on the sample of observations which will, when substituted for θ, make the probability of the sample a maximum. In other words, for this value of θ the observed sample is also the most likely sample" (Keeping, 1995, p. 123). Maximum likelihood and generalized least squares also have another property that makes them particularly useful in structural equation modeling. "For ML and GLS, the value of the criterion at the point of best fit, multiplied by $N - 1$, where N is the number of subjects, yields a quantity that, under appropriate conditions, approximately follows the χ^2 distribution" (Loehlin, 1987, p. 57). Thus, if a researcher wishes to use chi-square tests of the fit of the model to data, such alternatives to ordinary least squares can be particularly helpful.

---

[6]The relationship among ordinary least squares (OLS), generalized least squares (GLS), and maximum likelihood (ML) may be expressed as follows (following Loehlin, 1987, p. 54):

$$\text{OLS} = \text{trace } (\mathbf{S} - \mathbf{C})^2$$
$$\text{GLS} = \tfrac{1}{2} \text{ trace } [(\mathbf{S} - \mathbf{C}) \, \mathbf{S}^{-1}]^2$$
$$\text{ML} = \ln |\mathbf{C}| - \ln |\mathbf{S}| + \text{trace } \mathbf{S}\mathbf{C}^{-1} - m,$$

where

S is a matrix of observed correlations or covariances (|**S**| is the determinant of a matrix of observed correlations or covariances),

C is a matrix of implied correlations or covariances (|**C**| is the determinant of a matrix of implied correlations or covariances),

m is the number of variables (diagonal elements),

trace is the sum of the diagonal elements of the matrix, and

1n is the natural logarithm, and raising a value to the power of –1 indicates taking the inverse of the values.

Thus, the ordinary least squares are simply the sum of the squared differences. The generalized least squares is similar, but the differences are multiplied by the inverse of the observed values before the squaring of differences is computed. For maximum likelihood criteria, the difference between the natural logs of the determinants of the observed and implied correlations or covariances is computed (if the observed and implied correlations or covariances matrices are equal, the differences between the logs of the determinants will be zero). Then, the researcher computes the trace of the inverse of the products of the observed and the implied correlations or covariances minus the number of variables (if the observed and implied correlations or covariances matrices are equal, $\mathbf{S}\mathbf{C}^{-1}$ is an identity matrix and subtracting *m* will result in a value of 0). Therefore, as differences between the **S** and the **C** matrices increase, maximum likelihood value increases in positive value.

On the *Output* tab, the researcher finds a series of choices. The most commonly selected (and selected in this example) include the following:

- *Minimization history:* reports summarizing steps in the minimization of the discrepancy function using convergence criteria
- *Sample moments:* reports the covariance matrix for the sample
- *Implied moments:* reports the covariance matrix for the values of the observed variables
- *Residual moments:* reports differences between the sample and implied covariance matrices
- *Modification indices:* reports modification indices (Jöreskog & Sörbom, 1986, pp. III.18–III.22) that conservatively estimate what effect on discrepancy would occur if the constraints on each parameter were removed. When modification indices are requested, an entry must be placed in the *Threshold for modification indices* field. Most of the time, researchers put the number 4 in this location. The reasoning is that for a modification index to reduce the statistically significant chi-square value, it should do so by an amount equal to the minimum required to produce statistical significance at alpha risk of .05. Because at alpha risk of .05 and one degree of freedom the critical chi-square value is 3.84 (which rounds to 4), it is decided that any improvement in modification indices worth noticing should reduce the chi-square statistic by at least this amount. The chi-square difference statistic measures the statistical significance of the difference between two structural equation models of the same data, in which one model is a nested subset of the other. Specifically, chi-square difference is the standard test statistic for comparing a modified model with the original one. If chi-square difference shows no significant difference between the unconstrained original model and the nested, constrained modified model, then the modification is accepted. Even so, some common sense should be used in the interpretation of such matters. The chi-square difference also is affected by sample size. With large sample sizes, even very small differences may be identified as statistically significant. It should be observed that the modification procedures are computed only if they would produce *threshold for modification indices* greater than 4. It also should be noted that the modification indices in Amos involve the effects of *adding* paths to the model. To determine if paths should be deleted, the researcher needs to reason through a process of elimination.

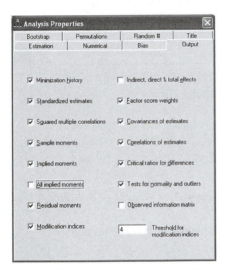

- *Factor score weights:* provides a report of the regression weights from observed to unobserved variables
- *Covariances of estimates:* reports a matrix of the covariances for all parameter estimates
- *Correlations of estimates:* reports a matrix of the correlation coefficients for all parameter estimates
- *Critical ratios for differences:* reports a test of the null hypothesis that the values for each pair of population parameters are equal

- *Tests for normality and outliers:* reports of statistics to examine multivariate normality assumed for observed variables. This section includes univariate assessments of skew and kurtosis as well as Mardia's coefficient of multivariate kurtosis (Mardia, 1970, 1974). Following a statistically significant coefficient of multivariate kurtosis, a check for outliers becomes critical, and a table of outliers (based on Mahalanobis' distance) is examined.

After the desired analyses are identified, clicking the icon that resembles an abacus ▦ executes the *Calculate estimates* command. To detect information about the results, one may examine two buttons at the top center of the page ▨▨. When the button on the left is clicked, it activates the *View the input path diagram (model specification)* command and shows the diagram the researcher has "drawn." When the button on the right is clicked, the *View the output path diagram* is active and the diagram shows the set of paths, complete with coefficients. In this example, the researcher clicked the button on the right. The table shown here includes a set of unstandardized estimates of parameters. The researcher who wishes to copy a diagram for insertion into other text materials may do so rather easily. From the *Edit* menu, the researcher clicks on the *Copy (to clipboard)* option. Then, from within another document, the researcher may use the paste command (Control-V) to insert the diagram as an object. By clicking on the *standardized estimate* statement in the middle column of the Amos control field, the researcher produced the same model, with paths showing standardized regression coefficients (beta weights). In addition, the model reflected setting the intercept at zero, using uncorrelated error terms, and measurement errors of 0 for individual exogenous variables. **Exogenous variables** are ones that are not predicted by other influences. The resulting diagram may be seen on the immediate right.

To see the entire output, the researcher clicked on the *View text* icon ▦. This output requires the *Text Output* subprogram to be operating. If it is not, the researcher must start the *Text Output* subprogram from the *Programs* submenu of the *Start* menu. In this case, the output

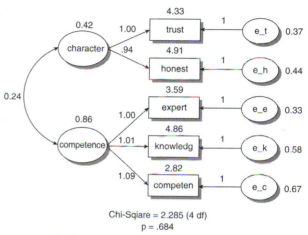

Confirmatory Factor Analysis for Credibility Scales

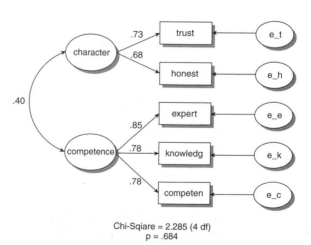

Confirmatory Factor Analysis for Credibility Scales

(shown in Table 16.1) began with an *Analysis Summary*. Next, a *Variable Summary* report listed and identified all the variables. Error terms and the two factors of credibility were listed under the category of "unobserved, exogenous variables." The five scale items (abbreviated names trust, honest, expert, knowledg, and competen) were listed as observed, endogenous variables. **Endogenous variables** are predicted from others. Though the language may seem odd, in this case, the model shows the scale items to be "predicted" from the unobserved factors, character and competence.

A *Parameter Summary* included the number of parameters that are fixed, labeled, or unlabeled. A table also reported whether the parameters involved weights, covariances, variances, means (there were none in this application of confirmatory factor analysis), or intercepts. Because it was requested, assessment of normality materials was presented, as shown in Table 16.2. The minimum and maximum values for each of the observed variables were presented. The sample skewness statistic was presented for each variable. Only one variable, the competence scale, had a skew beyond ±1. The remaining univariate distributions seemed within normal bounds. The kurtosis is computed by a formula that identifies a standard normal curve as a kurtosis of 0. Thus, an absolute value of kurtosis greater than 1 would indicate deviations from normality. The kurtosis values for at least two variables (competence and honest) were beyond what may have been expected in a normal distribution of scores. As an aid to interpretation, critical ratio columns (marked c.r.) were inserted. The critical ratios were created by dividing the skewness or kurtosis by the standard error values for each variable. These values may be interpreted as z scores, which, in turn, may be examined to assess the probability of observing these skew or kurtosis values by random sampling error. These statistics, however, are univariate estimates of whether a variable's deviation from normal distribution is statistically significant. The last row included a test of multivariate normality using Mardia's (1970, 1974) coefficient of multiple kurtosis. The critical ratio value appeared in the last column. It might be mentioned that deviations from normality are believed to affect Type I error rates more than some other elements of statistical analyses. Because there is very little significance testing involved in factor analysis, such information provides mostly supplemental descriptive information about the sample.

In addition, a table (Table 16.3) was produced to include information about multivariate outliers in the data set. Values that were farthest from the

Table 16.1

Notes for Group (Group number 1)
The model is recursive.
Sample size = 200

Table 16.2

Assessment of Normality (Group number 1)						
Variable	*min*	*max*	*skew*	*c.r.*	*kurtosis*	*c.r.*
competen	1.000	7.000	1.069	6.171	1.091	3.150
knowledg	1.000	7.000	−.743	−4.291	.780	2.252
expert	1.000	6.000	.357	2.063	−.091	−.264
honest	2.000	7.000	−.068	−.395	1.069	3.087
trust	2.000	7.000	.044	.255	.151	.435
Multivariate					3.193	2.698

Table 16.3

Observations Farthest From the Centroid (Mahalanobis' Distance) (Group number 1)			
Observation number	*Mahalanobis' d-squared*	*p1*	*p2*
44	18.893	.002	.332
155	17.974	.003	.120
32	17.169	.004	.053
100	17.151	.004	.011

centroid were listed in order. To compute the degrees of outlier status, Mahalanobis' distance is used. In addition, two columns reported probabilities assuming underlying normal distributions. A column identified as *p1* reported the probability of the given event exceeding the distance of the observation. The *p2* column revealed the probability of any event exceeding the distance of the observation. Put another way, for case 44, the probability of any event exceeding 18.893 was .002. The probability was .332 that the largest distance would exceed 18.893. Low probabilities in the *p2* column show that cases are far from the centroid. In general, when both the *p1* and *p2* values are low (below .05, for instance), the case is a candidate for deletion (see Bollen, 1987).

The next output section (Table 16.4) included sample moments, including information about covariances among observed variables. A report of the **condition number** for the matrix of covariances was provided.[7] This number is created by dividing the smallest eigenvalues into the largest eigenvalues. A small determinant suggests that there is a linear dependency of variables and that standard errors may be inflated. When the statistics were based on correlations, the condition number was 8.989. When confirmatory factor analysis is used on measures with the same possible range of scores (as was the case here, where each measure was a 7-point scale), analyses should be based on the variance-covariance matrix instead of the correlation matrix (Thompson & Daniel, 1996). Only two eigenvalues were larger than 1, suggesting support for the hypothesized two-factor solution.

Table 16.4

	competen	knowledg	expert	honest	trust
Sample Covariances (Group number 1)					
competen	1.691				
knowledg	.949	1.450			
expert	.934	.873	1.192		
honest	.268	.217	.223	.812	
trust	.300	.190	.253	.394	.789

Condition number = 8.989
Eigenvalues
3.458 1.046 .617 .428 .385
Determinant of sample covariance matrix = .368

Notes for Model (Default model) is a section that provides critical information about model composition and identification. As shown in Table 16.5, the estimated parameters were fewer than the number of "distinct sample moments." The likelihood ratio chi-square test is a global measure of fit that was not statistically significant. In this case, with alpha risk of .05, the critical value of chi-square was 11.14. The observed test statistic did not exceed this critical value. Thus, the null hypothesis that the confirmatory factor analysis model does not differ from the data was not rejected. Other measures of fit also may be used and, as will be seen, in this case there were no differences in them either.

Table 16.5

Computation of Degrees of Freedom (Default model)

Number of distinct sample moments:	20
Number of distinct parameters to be estimated:	16
Degrees of freedom (20 − 16):	4

Result (Default model)
Minimum was achieved
Chi-square = 2.285
Degrees of freedom = 4
Probability level = .684

---

[7]Amos reports the condition number of the sample covariance matrix often symbolized as $\mathbf{S}^{(g)}$. Some other structural equation programs report the condition number of the raw data matrix, symbolized as $\mathbf{X}$, for which the columns are scaled to produce $\mathbf{S}^{(g)} = \mathbf{X}'\mathbf{X}$. The condition number reported by Amos is the square of this alternative condition number.

The *Estimates* output (regression weights, shown in Table 16.6) reports tables that reveal the unstandardized and the standardized parameter estimations for the model. These values are the same as those that appear on the model diagrams. The C.R. is computed for any unconstrained parameter (any parameter not initially set at 1). The C.R. is the estimate divided by the standard error (S.E.), which standardizes this value with a mean of 0 and a standard deviation of 1. Thus, this value may permit the researcher to examine the null hypothesis that the population parameter is significantly different from zero.

Table 16.6

Regression Weights (Group number 1—Default model)		Estimate	S.E.	C.R.	P	Label
trust	<--- character	1.000				
honest	<--- character	.939	.258	3.636	***	par_1
expert	<--- competence	1.000				
knowledg	<--- competence	1.007	.092	10.931	***	par_2
competen	<--- competence	1.091	.100	10.957	***	par_3

C.R. values greater than 1.96 indicate that a difference from 0 as large as that found in this parameter would be expected to occur by random sampling error no more than 5 times out of 100. As can be seen, the unconstrained parameters were different form zero. Thus, it appeared that the items loaded on the factors beyond loadings expected by chance. The assessment of critical ratios is not provided for examining correlation coefficients or standardized regression weights, or when unweighted least squares or scale-free least squares estimation methods are used. Because with one degree of freedom, chi-square is the square of z, squaring the C.R. for an item suggests the approximate quantity that the likelihood ratio chi-square statistic would rise if that item's parameter were set at 0. In addition, the standardized regression weights most commonly included in reports of confirmatory factor analyses were presented (as shown in Table 16.7).

Table 16.7

Standardized Regression Weights (Group number 1—Default model)		Estimate
trust	<--- character	.729
honest	<--- character	.675
expert	<--- competence	.851
knowledg	<--- competence	.776
competen	<--- competence	.779

The covariances and correlations among the unobserved variables also were reported. In this case, the output showed the covariance at .242 and they correlation at .402. When these values are reported on the actual diagram, they are rounded. Hence, they covariance is identified at .24 and the correlation is listed as .40. These values were found on the diagrams, but because these diagrams rarely appear in presentations of confirmatory factor analysis, other reports in the text of a report are most common. Other estimates included implied variances and covariances, residual covariances, and standardized residual covariances. Inspecting the residual covariances can be instructive. This matrix is created by subtracting the actual covariances from the implied covariances for each pair of observed variances. A sound measurement model should reveal residual covariances close to zero. In this example, the differences were quite small, with the largest difference only –.053 (between knowledg and trust; see Table 16.8). To interpret these results, the standardized residual covariances are created by dividing the residual covariance for each pair of observed variables by the standard error. Thus, values lower than 1.96 indicated the absence of statistically significant differences from what would be expected by random sampling error. In fact, for these data, there were no standardized residual covariances that met that threshold. As can be seen, this examination of standardized residual covariances is a form of microanalysis that structural equation modeling shares with traditional confirmatory factor analysis. Though requested, no modification index results were reported because none of the parameter changes would have reduced the likelihood ratio chi-square by the default threshold value of 4.

Examining Measurement Model Fit Indices

Though the likelihood ratio chi-square test is heavily used in assessing confirmatory factor analysis results, it tends to reject otherwise tenable models when large sample sizes (more than 200) are involved (Schumacker & Lomax, 1996, p. 125). Thus, alternative measures of model fit also are reported. Amos produces more than 20 model fit indices. There is no universally accepted single index of measurement model fit. Hence, in addition to the popular chi-square test, other tests often are recommended in confirmatory factor analysis reports.[8] Some of the popular tests reported in the output will be described here. Some other tests that are tangential to confirmatory factor analysis assessment are included in the output, though they are not reviewed here.

Table 16.8

Residual Covariances (Group number 1—Default model)

	competen	knowledg	expert	honest	trust
competen	.000				
knowledg	.002	.000			
expert	−.006	.005	.000		
honest	.020	−.012	−.004	.000	
trust	.036	−.053	.011	.000	.000

Standardized Residual Covariances (Group number 1—Default model)

	competen	knowledg	expert	honest	trust
competen	.000				
knowledg	.018	.000			
expert	−.052	.041	.000		
honest	.239	−.147	−.060	.000	
trust	.429	−.684	.157	.000	.000

- *Chi-Square–Based Measures of Discrepancy:* These measures examine the difference between sample data and predicted patterns in the data and include variations of the chi-square likelihood ratio tests. In this case, the output shown in Table 16.9 was obtained.

Table 16.9

Model	NPAR	CMIN	DF	P	CMIN/DF
Default model	16	2.285	4	.684	.571
Saturated model	20	.000	0		
Independence model	10	323.918	10	.000	32.392

NPAR is not a test, but the number of parameters in the model. A comparison was made between the default model, which was designed by the researcher, and the saturated model that

---

[8]It is, of course, unwise to follow the chi-square test of significance in a mechanical way. This test assumes that the observed variables have a multivariate normal distribution, which sometimes is not the case. Furthermore, the chi-square statistic "is based on the assumption that the model holds exactly in the population . . . this may be an unreasonable assumption in most empirical research" (Jöreskog, 1993, p. 309).

included all possible relationships among variables and, hence, had a "perfect fit" to the data. The independence model is so restricted that it is unrealistic to expect a fit of this model to actual data sets. The measures listed here included the following:

CMIN: The minimum discrepancy $\hat{C}$ is distributed as chi-square and is the same as the chi-square test previously reported in the section on *Notes for Model (Default model)*. A statistically significant difference (indicated by a probability level no greater than .05) suggests that the model does not fit the data. This model seemed to fit the data.

CMIN/DF: The minimum discrepancy $\hat{C}$ is divided by its degrees of freedom in an attempt to adjust for model complexity. For a tenable model, the value should be close to 1. One writer explains, "a $\frac{\chi^2}{d.f.}$ ratio greater than 2.00 represents an inadequate fit" (Byrne, 1989, p. 55). As indicated by a value below 2.0, this model appeared to fit the data. Neither the CMIN χ^2 test nor the CMIN/DF test suggested a significant deviation of the models from the data.

- *Baseline Model Comparisons:* These measures attempt to contrast some baseline model (not always a null hypothesis model) with another measurement model of interest. Such output as shown in Table 16.10 was produced by the Amos program.

Table 16.10

Baseline Comparisons					
Model	*NFIDelta1*	*RFIrho1*	*IFIDelta2*	*TLIrho2*	*CFI*
Default model	.993	.982	1.005	1.014	1.000
Saturated model	1.000		1.000		1.000
Independence model	.000	.000	.000	.000	.000

NFI: As an alternative to chi-square, the normed fit index (also called the Bentler-Bonett normed fit index) uses a statistic known as Delta1. Computationally, NFI divides the model's minimum discrepancy $\hat{C}$ by the minimum discrepancy of the baseline model $\hat{C}_b$ and then subtracts this value from 1. Values above .8 or .9 are recommended for claims of model fit, and 1.0 indicates a perfect fit of the model to the data. Though it tends to compensate for chi-square's upward bias with large sample sizes, it may be biased against models based on small sample sizes. For the measurement model in our example, the value of .993 showed evidence of acceptable fit.

RFI: The relative fit index (rho1) permits scores to vary beyond the range of zero and 1. In computations, RFI adjusts the NFI by dividing discrepancy values by the degrees of freedom for hypothesized and baseline models. Then, this value is subtracted from zero. Coefficients close to 1 are considered desirable. The RFI of .982 in our measurement model example suggests strong fit to the data.

IFI: The incremental fit index (Delta2) can range above 1.0, though acceptable fit is judged to be close to 1.0 and above .90. The IFI is computed as

$$\frac{\hat{C}_b - \hat{C}}{\hat{C}_b - d.f.},$$

where $\hat{C}_b$ is the minimum discrepancy of the baseline model, $\hat{C}$ is the minimum discrepancy for the hypothesized model (CMIN), and *d.f.* is the degrees of freedom for the hypothesized model. For the example provided in this illustration, the incremental adjustment for the measurement model was 1.005, which was consistent with acceptable fit of the model to the data.

TLI: The Tucker-Lewis Index, or rho2, minimizes the influence of sample size on obtained values and adjusts NFI by the complexity of the model. The TLI is computed as

$$\frac{\dfrac{\hat{C}_b - \hat{C}}{d_b - d}}{\dfrac{\hat{C}_b}{d_b} - 1}.$$

Though the value of the TLI is not limited to a 0-to-1 range, values close to 1.0 are taken as evidence of acceptable fit of the model to the data. For the measurement model in our example, the TLI of 1.014 was within the bounds of an acceptable model.

CFI: Similar to the NFI, the Bentler (1990) comparative fit index (except for its failure to control for sample size) contrasts the covariance matrix of the hypothesized model against an independence model where latent variables are assumed to be uncorrelated. The CFI indicates the percentage to which the data covariance can be reproduced by the hypothesized model. For sound models, the CFI should be above .90, which was the case in this example.

- *Parsimony Adjusted Fit Measures:* This family of measures attempts to compensate for the complexity of models. These measures reduce the overall size of the measures of fit by a constant known as the "parsimony ratio" (PRATIO). The PRATIO (Mulaik et al., 1989) is computed as $\frac{d}{d_0}$, in which the degrees of freedom for the hypothesized model d are divided by the degrees of freedom for the independence model d_0. When NFI and the CFI are multiplied by the PRATIO, the reduced values are called the PNFI (parsimony normed fit index) and PCFI (parsimony comparative fit index), respectively. Though there are no hard-and-fast rules for interpreting these coefficients, the closer they are to 1.0, the stronger (and more parsimonious) the model fit is claimed to be. In the case of the example used here (see Table 16.11), the parsimony adjusted measures all were below .50, which often is taken as indicating an invitation to reconsider the model's construction. Yet, the small number of defining variables for each dimension contributed to

Table 16.11

Parsimony-Adjusted Measures			
Model	*PRATIO*	*PNFI*	*PCFI*
Default model	.400	.397	.400
Saturated model	.000	.000	.000
Independence model	1.000	.000	.000

ratios that greatly reduced the overall parsimony adjusted measures more than would have been the case with a typical example involving a higher number of measures.

- *RMSEA Measures:* The *Root Mean Square Error* of *Approximation* takes the square root of the F_0 values[9] that have been divided by the number of degrees of freedom for testing the model. This approach "can be interpreted as a root mean square standardized measure of badness of fit of a particular model ..." (Steiger, 1998, p. 413). To accept a model, a general rule of thumb is that the RMSEA should be below .05 or .06 (Hu & Bentler, 1999). In this case, the RMSEA was .037 (see Table 16.12), which indicated that the model was within the bounds of a tenable model.

Table 16.12

RMSEA				
Model	*RMSEA*	*LO 90*	*HI 90*	*PCLOSE*
Default model	.037	.000	.129	.492
Independence model	.432	.392	.474	.000

- *PCLOSE:* The PCLOSE statistic is a transformation of the RMSEA into a test of statistical significance. The null hypothesis is that the population RMSEA is no greater than .05. A statistically significant test (indicated by a small probability level) indicates that the RMSEA is greater than .05. In this case, the probability value of .492 was produced, indicating no statistically significant difference between the observed RMSEA and an RMSEA $\leq$ .05.

A note about the interpretation of the indices of fit should be made. The fact that *a lot of indices* point to an acceptable model (as is the case with the measurement model reported here) does not mean that we have *lots of evidence* of fit. Most of the statistics are variations of other statistics. Hence, most of the information is not corroboration, but redundancy in reporting the same information.[10] So, what information about fit should the researcher report? There is conflicting advice. Nearly all researchers report the chi-square-based measures of discrepancy including CMIN, the likelihood ratio chi-square test, and CMIN/DF. Similarly, the RMSEA almost always is reported. For any further descriptions of fit, some writers (e.g., Jaccard & Wan, 1996, p. 87) suggest supplementing this list with one test from the "baseline model comparisons" and "parsimony adjusted fit measures."

Measurement Adequacy and Considering Modifications

Following a successful confirmatory factor analysis, indicators may be treated as different faces of the same measure, and researchers may average them or add them together (or weight

---

[9]F_0 is $\frac{NCP}{n}$, where $NCP = \max(\hat{C} - d, 0)$; $\hat{C}$ is the minimum discrepancy value CMIN, and d is the degrees of freedom for the hypothesized model.

[10]One that is not the same as the others is the Bayesian information criterion (BIC), which uses Bayes's theorem in an attempt to recognize parsimonious models. The BIC adjusts the chi-square statistic for the number of parameters, the number of observed (manifest) variables, and the sample size. A negative value for the BIC emerges when the model has more support than a just-identified model (which would have a coefficient of 0). In comparing models, a difference in BIC value of 5 or greater is "strong evidence" and 10 is "conclusive evidence" for one model's superiority (Raftery, 1995).

them by some system) to form a common index. Then, such standard tools as Cronbach's coefficient alpha may be used to obtain a reliability score that summarizes the internal consistency of the measure. Though this step may seem unnecessary, the fact is that a measure of model fit may show acceptable fit simply because the model has paths with small coefficients. Hence, even though a measurement model may show acceptable fit by the various tests used, it may be revealed to have low reliability when Cronbach's coefficient alpha is applied to it. In addition, as an effort at cross-validation, different subgroups in the sample might be compared to identify the measurement invariance of the factor solution.

Confirmatory factor analysis does not always yield a sound model in one pass through the data. If tests of the model's fit indicate that the factor structure is not as hypothesized, there is a certain amount of tension regarding the choices to be made. On one hand, because the researcher examined a hypothesized factor structure, a simple conclusion would be that the hypothesis must be rejected. The researcher might wish to reconsider the conceptual foundation of the confirmatory factor analysis model and return to the drawing board. Hence, if anything, exploring modifications may create a conservative bias against the researcher's search for a model with acceptable fit. If the researcher decides to complete model modifications, the researcher may explore alternatives such as considering measurement models that do not meet all initial assumptions or exploring alternative paths.

Examining Models That Do Not Meet All Initial Assumptions

Though confirmatory factor analysis assumes uncorrelated common factors and uncorrelated measurement error terms, researchers might have legitimate reasons to examine models that do have correlations. In fact, they might include correlated common factors as part of their initial set of hypothesized factors. Fortunately, the Amos program permits researchers to explore models with such correlated terms. Garson (2004) explains the matter in some useful detail:

> [M]easurement error terms represent causes of variance due to unmeasured variables as well as random measurement error. Depending on theory, it may well be that the researcher should assume unmeasured causal variables will be shared by indicators or will correlate. . . . That is, including correlated measurement error in the model tests the possibility that indicator variables correlate not just because of being caused by a common factor, but also due to common or correlated unmeasured variables. This possibility would be ruled out if the fit of the model specifying uncorrelated error terms . . . [were] as good as the model with correlated errors specified. (¶ 15)

Thus, the presence of additional variables creating nonrandom influences may be revealed by correlated error terms. Even admitting the influence of such additional variables, the researcher still may wish to test the hypothesized factor structure. Thus, the researcher may wish to accept some correlated error terms in the factor model.

Sometimes researchers wish to permit correlations among common factors. Indeed, if there is a theoretic basis behind the choice, a logical argument can justify this exception to the data assumption. Of course, the presence of two highly correlated factors may indicate that there really is only one underlying factor. To examine the matter empirically, the researcher may compare the fit of the originally hypothesized factor structure model with the fit of a measurement model in which the correlations among the factors are constrained to be equal to 1.00. "If the constrained model is not significantly worse than the unconstrained one, the researcher concludes that a one-factor model would fit the data as well as a multi-factor one and, on the principle of parsimony, the one-factor model is to be preferred" (Garson, 2004, ¶ 16).

Exploring Alternative Paths

When researchers find models that do not have adequate fit, one response involves inspecting the modification index section of the output to search for paths that may be added to the model to improve its fit. It bears repeating that the Amos output section dealing with modification indices explores only the effects of *adding* paths. Deleting paths also are reasonable options that must be explored through a process of elimination.

There is more than one strategy about deciding which modifications to include. Two common guidelines are as follows:

- Construct a new model that includes a parameter path with the largest modification index. Then, the fit of the new model to the data is checked by use of tests of fit, such as those using the chi-square distribution. If the new model improves fit, it may be retained.
- Construct a new model that includes all paths with parameters that had modification index scores over 100. Then, following similar advice as previously described, the adequacy of the new model would be examined by specific tests of fit.

Though such modifications may seem obvious repairs, they come at a price. Unless there is some conceptual or theoretic reason to add paths or correlated error terms, new models may not survive when efforts are made to replicate them. The more compromises are made, especially those without substantive reasons behind them, the more the confirmatory factory analysis will not hold up to future scrutiny.

Chapter 17

MODELING
COMMUNICATION BEHAVIOR

The language of modeling reflects different research traditions. Hence, many scholars lump together path models, structural equation models, causal models, and the like. A modern trend is to call these things *models* or *causal models* in general. The models all share a common focus in examining the flow of suspected mediating variables that may explain important phenomena.

The phrase "path analysis" can be traced back at least as far as 1921, when Sewell Wright (1921, 1934) illustrated how to identify complex models based on information revealed from correlations. Over the years, at least two general categories of models have been developed.

- **Path analysis** is "a kind of multivariate analysis in which causal relations among several variables are represented by graphs (path diagrams) showing the 'paths' along which causal influences travel" (Vogt, 2005, p. 230). In this sort of model, all the variables are **observed variables**, also known as **manifest variables**.
- **Structural equation models** "describe causal relationships among latent variables and include coefficients for endogenous variables" (Vogt, 2005, p. 281). As stated in Chapter 16, **latent variables** are underlying factors or dimensions that are not observed directly. These latent variables are also known as unmeasured variables, constructs, or factors. Structural equation models are "a melding of factor analysis and path analysis into one comprehensive statistical methodology" (Kaplan, 2000, p. 3). These structural equation models (SEM for short) actually have two models, a **measurement model** that identifies the ways individual measures are related to latent variables (often considered basic constructs under investigation), and a **structural model** that illustrates and tests the hypothesized relationships among variables.

Researchers often combine the methods to examine a structural equation model that is composed of a combination (or "hybrid") of observed and latent variables. Different approaches often are divided into two categories: traditional path models and structural equation models. Although structural equation modeling was originally developed to analyze latent composite variables (e.g., Bentler, 1980; Jöreskog, 1973), most modeling in communication research has been restricted to studies of observed variables only. In fact, a content analysis of structural equation model studies in communication from 1995 through 2000 found that fewer than 7% of the structural equation models involved latent composite variables only (Holbert & Stephenson, 2002). Slightly more than 35% of the studies involved models with combinations of latent and observable variables. Thus, standard path analysis with observed variables remains a popular tool for modern communication researchers.

THE GOALS OF MODELING

Structural equation modeling and path modeling are elegant ways to examine many hypotheses. Rather than rely on hypotheses that are stated in words alone, the models *exhibit* relationships of interest.

Presentation of a Map of Relationships

The first part of a path model involves a diagram of relationships. Models may show both direct and indirect effects. In multiple regression analysis, a single output measure is identified (in the absence of interactions or suppressor variables) as a result of direct paths from predictors. In essence, multiple regression correlation is a form of path modeling. Yet, when there are moderating variables, it makes sense to consider increasingly complicated models, called path models. Researchers often find it efficient to describe relationships with a picture, rather than as a series of propositions (though propositions may be derived from any model). For instance, if there were a model with five variables, there could be one comprehensive picture of the process, or the researcher could make potentially 10 separate statements about the relationships of variables taken a pair at a time (computed as $\frac{p(p-1)}{2}$, where p is the number of variables).

Of course, identifying and picturing paths may be easier said than done. First, past research that has used modeling has proven notorious for failure to cross-validate. Studies that take data at one point in time to obtain a random draw of events across conditions are called **cross-sectional** studies. As a general rule, cross-sectional studies (which are most common in communication studies) do not provide evidence for the cross-validation for models. Second, it may be difficult to form a picture of many relationships among variables because the past research has produced unclear results. Third, it may be difficult to form a picture of relationships because there may be a bewilderingly large number of causes for many communication phenomena. None of these limitations, however, should stop thoughtful researchers. Preparing models that can be tested is justification enough to explore this approach. Sometimes just imagining possible causal relationships can be helpful to stimulate thinking in productive directions.

Predictions From Causal Ordering of Variables

Researchers often hypothesize about causal order among relationships. When researchers advance problem questions that deal with multiple variables arranged in some sort of cause-and-effect arrangement, modeling may be particularly invited. For causal claims, the "cause" variables should precede the others that are identified as effects. But this stipulation does not mean that models are simply time-series analyses in which the same variable is measured at different time periods.

A comment about causality is appropriate here. Although structural equation modeling is frequently associated with the label "causal modeling" (Asher, 1983), most models are based on simple associations, and the term "cause" is used to define types of models that attempt to specify order, rather than assertions of ultimate causes. There are no assumptions of strict deterministic causality or exact predictions. For those interested in drawing hard-and-fast causal relationships, it is wise to be warned that "conclusions drawn from causal modeling with correlational data must be confined to the following limitation: The results of causal modeling are valid and unbiased only if the assumed model adequately represents the real causal processes" (Mertler & Vannatta, 2002, p. 199, citing Tate, 1992). Causal modeling is

Special Discussion 17.1

Assessing Cause

In his effort to assess causal relationships as a form of inductive reasoning, John Stuart Mill developed five ways that observations could be examined to discover whether the relationship between them is causal or accidental. Called Mill's canons of causality, they include these elements that are suitable to help assess whether correlations reported in path models really are evidence of causality in "causal modeling."

The Method of Agreement: "*If two or more instances of the phenomenon under investigation have only one circumstance in common, the circumstance in which alone all the instances agree is the cause (or effect) of the given phenomenon*" (Mill, 1872/1959, p. 255). Hence, if the path coefficients come from experiments that share only one common independent variable, the common element is likely to be the cause.

The Method of Difference: "*If an instance in which the phenomenon under investigation occurs, and an instance in which it does not occur, have every circumstance in common save one, that one occurring only in the former: the circumstances in which alone the two instances differ is the effect, or the cause, or an indispensable part of the cause, of the phenomenon*" (Mill, 1872/1959, p. 256). If the path coefficients come from experiments where the effect occurred in the presence of the experimental variable and not when the experimental variable was absent, the common independent variable is likely to be the cause. This method is the basis of causal claims from experiments.

The Joint Method of Agreement and Difference: "*If two or more instances in which the phenomenon occurs have only one circumstance in common, while two or more instances in which it does not occur have nothing in common save the absence of that circumstance, the circumstance in which alone the two sets differ is the effect, or cause, or an indispensable part of the cause, of the phenomenon*" (Mill, 1872/1959, p. 259). The method combines the first two methods to make strong assertions of causality.

The Method of Residues: "*Subduct from any phenomenon such part as is known by previous inductions to be the effect of certain antecedents, and the residue of the phenomenon is the effect of the remaining antecedents*" (Mill, 1872/1959, p. 260). If all the alternative pathways to a variable can be eliminated as causes on the basis of other proof, the remaining path suspected as causal is the cause.

The Method of Concomitant Variation: "*Whatever phenomenon varies in any manner whenever another phenomenon varies in some particular manner, is either a cause or an effect of that phenomenon, or is connected with it through some fact of causation*" (Mill, 1872/1959, p. 263). In path analysis, this canon indicates that a high path coefficient means that some causal forces are operating.

Though these canons are helpful, there are some difficulties with this form (and any form) of inductive reasoning. Inductive reasoning can only lead to conclusions that have a high probability of being true. Furthermore, the methods work best when careful control is practiced and when all the possible antecedent circumstances are controlled or otherwise carefully taken into account. In essence, the cause cannot be identified until the researcher already knows all of the possible causes. Researchers may not be ready to make such claims.

best considered a search for "proximate" causes in which variables that trigger others can be found. There is no search for final causes. Instead, the "causal modeling techniques examine whether a pattern of intercorrelations among variables 'fits' the researcher's underlying theory of which variables are causing other variables" (Mertler & Vannatta, 2002, p. 199).

Despite such concerns, however, there are occasions when causal patterns can be inferred even though one has correlational data. First, if a variable suspected of being a cause occurs first in a sequence, then it is possible that it is a cause of other effects. If variables occur simultaneously, it is difficult to argue that one is the cause and another is an effect. Thus, researchers constructing causal models feel increasingly confident if they can submit that causal variables occurred before the effect variables. Second, if it is clearly impossible for a variable to have been the cause of another, it can be eliminated as a competing path. For instance, sex of the subject cannot be the effect of one's level of communication apprehension; communication apprehension does not determine whether a person is male or female. Third, if **spurious correlations** ("nonsense" correlations between variables that appear related but are, in fact, not causally associated) can be eliminated from the list of possible causal forces, a remaining causal claim may become viable.

HOW TO DO A MODELING STUDY

Many steps are involved in examining structural equation or path models. Although the process can be elaborate, only the major steps are listed here.

Step 1: Develop a Theoretically or Conceptually Based Ordering of Variables

The order of variables should be developed based on past research, theory development, or conceptualizations based in research. Ultimately, the purpose of any model is to predict dependent variables. These models may be most useful when researchers take into account some mediating processes.

In these models, variables are of two forms:

- **Exogenous variables** (also known as "prior variables") are variables that have no predictors. Their values are dependent on systems "from outside the system being studied. A causal system says nothing about its exogenous variables. Their values are given, not analyzed" (Vogt, 2005, p. 110). Their values are assumed to be measured without error.
- **Endogenous variables** are predicted by other variables. Their variability is assumed to be explained by their predictors. A dependent variable is sometimes distinguished as a special form of endogenous variable that is the final object of prediction in the model.

Researchers selecting variables for their models must take into account the potential difficulty created by multicollinearity, or high levels of interrelationship among independent predictor variables.

Multicollinearity is literally built into a set of structural equations. If X_1 causes X_2 and X_2 causes X_3, it is all but inevitable that X_1 and X_2 are correlated. If X_1 is a strong cause of X_2, it may be difficult, if not impossible, to disentangle the causal effects of X_1 and X_2 on X_3 with a small sample. (Kenny, 1979, p. 85)

If two predictors have intercorrelations greater than the average of their reliabilities, no claims of discriminant validity can be made for the measurements (Campbell & Fiske, 1959). Thus, the usefulness of redundant multiple indicators for the same cause is greatly limited.

Special Discussion 17.2

Causal Analysis Through Corresponding Regressions

The search for causality using the method of concomitant variation has stimulated some researchers to look for traces left by corresponding regressions. One interesting and controversial approach was initiated by Chambers (1986), who started with the observation that although causally related variables should have high positive correlations, not all the scores in a distribution would share that pattern. When dependent variables' scores were divided into high, moderate, and low scores, it was found that moderate scores were associated with either high or low values of the independent variable. Furthermore, Monte Carlo studies revealed that when a causal relation is present, the variance of the dependent variable scores associated with moderately scoring independent variables is lower than the variance of the independent variable scores associated with the moderately scoring dependent variables.

This information led Chambers (1991) to suggest a way to infer a presence of a causal relationship: When there are two variables, the researcher may run two regressions, with the first variable as independent in the first and the second as dependent, and then with independent and dependent variables switched in the second regression. For each case, the researcher follows these steps:

1. The residuals in the dependent variable predicted scores are computed for each event in the study.
2. The deviations of the independent variable around its mean are identified for each event in the study.
3. The deviations are correlated.
4. The first three steps are repeated with the independent and dependent variables reversed.
5. The two correlations may be compared. When the actual cause of dependent variable effects is the independent variable, the correlation should be higher than when the noncausal factor is the independent variable. The reason is that the moderate dependent variable values should be more closely associated with moderate independent variable values when the actual cause is used as a predictor. The overall correlations should be inverse because when predictor variable scores are extreme, dependent variable residuals should decline (increased variability occurs among moderate scores). In an application of this method to an example in the social sciences, Chambers (1991, p. 66) recommended that researchers faced with the absence of any inverse correlations assume that there are no causal relationships among the chief variables of interest.

This approach assumes the following: bivariate causality in which one of the measured variables is the cause, moderate sample sizes of at least 50 events, correlations in the range of .2 to .9, and additivity of error terms in determining the dependent variable. These assumptions (especially the first one) are not casual ones, and the approach is not universally accepted.

Although some researchers do not include hypotheses in their exploration of path models, they eventually find themselves engaging in statistical hypothesis testing nonetheless. Hence, a typical hypothesis in a modeling study posits that one variable affects another. For instance, in the causal model shown on the left, researchers might examine if there is a significant regression of variable X_4 on variables X_2 and X_3.

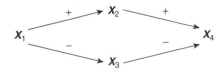

Such a hypothesis might be stated verbally as

H$_1$: X_2 increases X_4 or H$_1$: $\rho_{42} > 0$.

The null hypothesis to be tested would be

H$_0$: $\rho_{42} \leq 0$, which states that the relationship between variables X_4 and X_2 is equal to 0 or some negative value below 0.

Other hypotheses include the following statements:

H$_2$: X_3 decreases X_4, or H$_2$: $\rho_{43} < 0$. The null hypothesis would be

H$_0$: $\rho_{43} \geq 0$, which states that the relationship between variables X_4 and X_3 is equal to 0 or some positive value above 0.

H$_3$: X_1 decreases X_2, or H$_3$: $\rho_{21} < 0$. The null hypothesis would be

H$_0$: $\rho_{21} \geq 0$, which states that the relationship between variables X_2 and X_1 is equal to 0 or some positive value above 0.

H$_4$: X_1 increases X_3, or H$_1$: $\rho_{31} > 0$. The null hypothesis would be

H$_0$: $\rho_{31} \leq 0$, which states that the relationship between variables X_3 and X_1 is equal to 0 or some negative value below 0.

For path models, some sources (Causality Lab, 2004) recommend that researchers present hypotheses in a single graphic display. The path parameters and their directions (indicated by positive and negative signs to indicate direct and inverse relationships) may receive special attention. Hypothesis testing may be completed by conducting statistical tests of the fit of the model to the data. Unlike some other hypothesis tests, the researchers are *not* hoping for statistically significant differences. In this situation, researchers actually speculate that the model does *not* deviate from the data. Rejecting this null hypothesis would mean rejection of the model.

Step 2: Construct the Model

Path models start with a structural equation. As has been seen, the paths themselves are part of a causal model that is expressed diagrammatically. Although it is not strictly required that a diagram be displayed, there are many advantages in doing so, not the least of which is an economy of presentation.

Many computer programs contain protocols for labeling model elements. Some of the most frequently used symbols are identified here.

- *X*s identify observed or measured variables. In many structural equation modeling programs, these measured variables are placed in boxes.
- *z*s often are used to identify observed or measured variables. These *z* symbols indicate that the variable is in the form of a standard score or *z* score with a mean of 0 and a

standard deviation of 1. Representing variables as z scores can make the process of understanding predictive equations increasingly clear. In this chapter, Xs are used to indicate both variables and variable values.

- Latent variables are identified by variables placed in circles or ovals.

Identify Predictive Links

Models are drawn to identify direct and indirect effects. **Direct effects** are indicated by straight arrows drawn from a variable (assumed to be a cause) to another variable (which is the effect). These paths may lead from an exogenous variable, but not to one. If there is more than one exogenous variable, a curved line (often with arrows) $\subset$ is drawn to identify that there is no causal relationship. Curved arrows also may be drawn to indicate relationships among covariances for which causality is not claimed. Naturally, exogenous variables are initially presumed to be uncorrelated, but if there is reason for expressing an association between them, it would be indicated in the statement of the coefficients.

Indirect effects are influences on variables as mediated by the presence of another endogenous variable. Sometimes the mediating variable is called an "intervening variable" (though that term has some extra meaning of its own), sometimes it is called a "moderator variable," and sometimes it is not given a special name at all. Nevertheless, the ability to be isolated for indirect effects is one of the great advantages of using structural equation modeling techniques. A mediated path (indicated by the absence of a direct path between two variables) to other exogenous variables does not mean that there is no relationship. At the very most, it indicates that a partial relationship is absent when other predictors with direct paths are held constant. As an illustration, at one time it was theorized that evidence produced attitude change in persuasive messages by increasing the credibility of the source, which in turn affected attitude change. The model (Evidence Use → Source Credibility → Attitude Change) predicted an indirect effect of evidence on attitude change.

The simple model previously shown has one exogenous variable (X_1) and three endogenous variables (X_4 also may be known as a dependent variable). The directions of the relationships are indicated by the plus and minus signs representing direct and inverse relationships, respectively. Although the arrows indicate direct effects (not to be confused with "direct relationships") between pairs of variables, the X_2 and X_3 endogenous variables also reveal that there are indirect paths between X_1 and X_4. Once all the effects are diagramed, it becomes easy to report total effects.

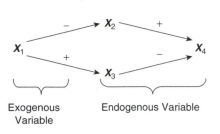

Exogenous
Variable

Endogenous Variable

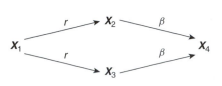

The **path coefficients**, p coefficients, or structural coefficients are links between the variables involved in direct effects. The paths are symbolized by such terms as p_{34}, p_{31}, p_{42}, and so forth. As a matter of tradition, the variable predicted is listed first because this variable is the one that is *regressed* against the predictor variables. When there is one predictor of an exogenous variable, the path coefficient is the zero-order correlation (r) between variables. When a variable has two or more predictors, the paths are in the form of beta weights. As the diagram at the left shows, these path coefficients are simply applications of regression analyses. These paths may be interpreted as the amount of change in one variable that is associated with a standard deviation change in the other.

Although models may be categorized in several ways, two basic forms of models are recursive and nonrecursive. In **recursive models**, all paths move in one direction only (e.g., A → B). There are no feedback loops (no A⇌B) and no reciprocal patterns between pairs of variables (no A ⟵⟶ B). To fit a nonrecursive model to the data, "ordinary least squares regression will provide good estimates of the parameters when the necessary assumptions are made about the properties of the residual terms" (Asher, 1983, p. 15). For other models, including nonrecursive models, estimation methods beyond ordinary least squares must be enlisted.

In a path diagram, other symbols typically are used, with specific meanings.

- An arrow → with a single direction indicates the direct effect of one variable on another.
- A curved line indicates the covariance or correlation between pairs of error terms or the correlation between a pair of exogenous variables. A curved line indicates that a causal interpretation is not invited for the relationship.

Some rules generally are followed for constructing models (Mertler & Vannatta, 2002, p. 207). First, a path may pass through a given variable only once. Second, "no path may go backward on an arrow after going forward on another arrow (although it is acceptable to go forward on an arrow after *first* going backward" (p. 207). Third, only one bidirectional arrow can appear on a single path.

Specify Error Terms

In addition to the observed and latent variables, some measure of residual error in prediction also has to be included. By implication, this error term reveals the influence of other direct predictors not in the model. For path models, error terms reveal the absence of predictability for each R^2 or r in the model. In structural equation models, the error terms also are called **disturbances** (and the disturbance term is the residual term described in Chapter 13). Error terms are symbolized as arrows (sometimes with dotted lines) connected to the predicted endogenous variables. These terms usually are identified with numbered subscripts as e_1, e_2, e_3, or e_4 to indicate that they are involved in predicting values for particular predicted variables. Because these terms deal with prediction error and not measurement error, they are not presented for exogenous variables. Because each endogenous variable has a disturbance term, the implication is drawn that each structural equation has a disturbance or error term.

Several assumptions are made about the error terms:

- That residuals (differences between the observed and predicted values of the dependent variable) are normally distributed.
- That variability of the residuals holds the same relationship pattern through the entire range of the variables.
- That residuals are independent of the exogenous variables and from each other.
- That there is a linear relationship between observed and predicted values of the dependent variable (this assumption also means that the residuals have a mean of zero).

Naturally, the assumptions can be assessed rather than just presumed.

Step 3: Gather Reliable Data of Relationships Related to Theory

Because structural equation modeling extends multiple regression correlation, it stands to reason that the requirements of sampling adequacy also apply here. In the first place, the sampling should be a random sample of adequate size. With nonrandom samples, selection bias may jeopardize the model's overall validity (Muthen & Jöreskog, 1983). Traditional advice recommends sample sizes of at least 104 events plus the number of independent variables (Tabachnick & Fidell, 2001, p. 117). Other guidelines have advised at least 15 events per predictor variable (J. P. Stevens, 2002, p. 143). For structural equation modeling, increased sample sizes are routinely advised. Various experts advise 100 events with highly reliable measures and 200 with moderately reliable measures (Hoyle & Kenny, 1999), 150 (J. C. Anderson & Gerbing, 1988), and 200 (Chou & Bentler, 1995).

Step 4: Test the Model

Much of the statistical work in structural equation modeling involves checking assumptions, assessing variance explained, and assessing the model's fit to the data.

Check Assumptions

In addition to assumptions previously mentioned, several routinely tested assumptions underlie the use of structural equation models.

- Variability of the residuals is assumed to hold the same relationship pattern through the entire range of the variables (homoscedasticity).
- Data are assumed to be sampled independently of each other; with independence, residuals are independent of the exogenous variables and from each other (thus, the covariances of errors are zero).
- A linear relationship between observed and predicted values of the dependent variable is assumed. This assumption also means that the residuals have a mean of zero.

The assumptions of homoscedasticity and of independence of residuals can be examined by looking at charts of data distributions. Furthermore, because of the use of least squares methods, the residuals are, in fact, uncorrelated with the exogenous variables.

In structural modeling, this result requires that the disturbances be uncorrelated with the causes of the endogenous variables . . . the assumption of uncorrelated errors implies that: 1. The endogenous variable must not cause any of the variables that cause it; that is, there is no reverse causation. 2. The causal variables must be measured without error and with perfect validity. 3. None of the unmeasured causes must cause any of the causal variables; that is, there are no common causes, or third variables. (Kenny, 1979, p. 65)

Although modest violations of homoscedasticity may not greatly affect statistical test results, violating the independence assumption can make a great difference. Independence can be ensured by taking care in the sampling process; hence, researchers are well advised to explain how their sampling ensured independence of observations. Avoiding reverse causation can be addressed by design choices and ruling out arrangements that could result in a reverse sequence.[1]

"Perfect" measurement may not be completely possible, but it may be very closely approximated. For instance, when a variable is an experimental manipulation, such as the number of deliberate repetitions used by a speaker, the measurement may be assumed (aside from some philosophic nit-picking) to have reliability of 1. Measurement of such variables as participant age, sex, and academic major may be very close to reliability of 1.0. Observed correlation coefficients may be corrected for attenuation of measurement (see Schmidt & Hunter, 1996). Not only does the correction permit researchers to address the question of measurement reliability, but "correction for attenuation due to error of measurement produces a point estimate closer to the population value of the population corrected effect size" (Boster, 2002, p. 483).

Under specific circumstances, two other assumptions may be added.

- When hypotheses about regression equations are involved, the assumption of normal distribution of errors (residuals) is included (Kenny, 1979, p. 62). Although statistical tests are robust to violations of this assumption, it may be checked by consulting charts of residuals, much as is ordinarily done in multiple regression analysis.
- When variables are studied in a single cross-section analysis, the **equilibrium** assumption is made that "if X_1 is assumed to cause X_2 with a lag of k units, and if X_1 and X_2 are contemporaneously measured at time t, equilibrium exists if $X_1 = X_2$; that is, X_1 did not change between times $t - k$ and t" (Kenny, 1979, p. 66). In short, the cross section is assumed to capture the causality if the causal variable has not shown change from one time to another. Except for cross-validation studies, this assumption typically remains untested.

Depending on the specific tools at work, the researcher may find that there are other assumptions that must be made. Sometimes assumptions about unidirectional causation and independent errors require examining subsets ("blocks") of endogenous variables and their associated errors. Such a model is called block recursive.

Variance Explained

Researchers typically report the overall effect sizes for each exogenous variable. Because the SEM approach is an extension of multiple regression correlation, it makes sense to use that option to get the job done. Both corrected and uncorrected R^2 coefficients usually are reported.

Check Deviations From Predicted Expectations

Testing the fit of a structural equation model involves both inspecting parameters and applying specific statistical tools such as confidence intervals, goodness-of-fit tests, and various indices. Other tests involve looking at deviations from expectations.

---

[1]Obviously, lack of reverse causation, perfect measurement, and lack of common causes are rather stringent assumptions. Reverse causation can be ruled out by theory or logic; for example, variables measured at one point in time do not cause variables measured earlier in time. "If reverse causation cannot be ruled out, however, a nonhierarchical model must be specified, the parameters of which cannot be estimated by an ordinary regression analysis. . . ." The common cause problem can be solved by measuring the third variables (although these variables must be perfectly measured), but it is still logically impossible to demonstrate that all third variables have been excluded if the multiple correlation is less than one. (Kenny, 1979, p. 66)

Sound models tend to have relatively small residual errors. Thus, researchers often look at these errors to check whether the model has disturbances that suggest the operation of other forces. Bollen (2002, p. 617) explains:

> Some authors describe ε_i [the disturbance term or residual error] as a random variable that has three components: (a) an inherent, unpredictable random component present in virtually all outcomes, (b) a component that consists of a large number of omitted variables that influence Y_i, and (c) random measurement error in Y_i (e.g., Johnston, 1984, pp. 14–15; Maddala, 1983, p. 32).

Other authors would add a fourth component, such as would occur if a researcher assumes a linear relation when a curvilinear one is more appropriate (e.g., Hanushek & Jackson, 1977, pp. 12–13; Weisberg, 1980, p. 6). Thus, researchers often look at the disturbance terms early in assessing model fit because they may provide circumstantial evidence that the model has omitted other, important variables.[2]

Many statistical tools for testing goodness of fit have been developed for use in structural equation modeling. As reviewed in Chapter 16, there are many approaches. These tools attempt to examine whether models have "verisimilitude," or the appearance of truth (see review in Meehl & Waller, 2002). The most popular tool used to assess fit is an application of chi-square called the **likelihood ratio test** and the GFI (goodness-of-fit index). These models, it should be remembered, are only estimates of relationships. As one author (Cudeck, 1991) explains, "A 'correctly specified model' is, always has been, and always will be a fiction. . . . All that can be hoped is that a model captures some reasonable approximation to the truth" (p. 261). Hence, instead of alleging "proof" for their models, researchers claim that their models are "supported" or are "found tenable."

Step 5: Revise the Model

Among articles in communication journals from 1995 to 2000, models using observed variables alone failed to fit the data 20.5% of the time. Of models involving combinations of observed and latent variables, 79.5% failed to fit the data (Holbert & Stephenson, 2002). Thus, researchers often revisit their models to see if other specifications make sense.

On other occasions, the question is not whether the model fits, but which of several competing models best fits the data (J. C. Anderson & Gerbing, 1988). Sometimes researchers find that a model can be improved by adding a direct path between variables that have higher correlations than is predicted for them. Sometimes variables can be deleted as a way to improve a model. Other guidelines have been suggested over the years. To create equivalent models with improved fit, researchers may examine the possibility of inverting the order of variables or permitting residuals to be correlated (Stelzl, 1986). In addition, for "just-identified" models (a term to be defined subsequently), a replacing rule may be applied to permit interchanging direct paths, reciprocal paths, and correlated residuals when there are direct paths leading to other variables in the model (Lee & Hershberger, 1990, 1991).

---

[2]Bollen (2002, pp. 617–619) suggests that increases in disturbances may indicate latent variables that exhibit nonrandom influences. Although there are some technical difficulties with calling observed disturbances indications of latent variables, there is little doubt that large residuals may indicate that variables not included in a model exhibit nonrandom influences.

PATH MODELS

Although the term "path model" is often used interchangeably with any modeling, we already have identified it as part of the tradition that examines structural equation modeling with observed or manifest variables. Although structural equation model testing has been streamlined by computer programs, it is helpful to remember that no computer (yet) can construct a path model; so path modeling requires some serious thinking about causes for phenomena. Path models are most concerned with the roles of moderator variables and indirect or mediated paths.

Designing of Models

For any path model that describes data, the researcher expects relationships between moderator and dependent variables (identified as endogenous variables that are last in a sequence) to be greater than relationships between exogenous and dependent variables. Furthermore, adjacent variables should have larger relationships than variables that are mediated by several endogenous variables. An illustration might make this process increasingly understandable. The model identified as "Figure 17.1: Path Model 1" hypothesizes that receivers' levels of communication apprehension influence their levels of interpersonal trust with acquaintances. Yet, this communication apprehension effect occurs by inversely influencing perceptions of interpersonal solidarity with others, which affects the amount of self-disclosure they share with their acquaintances. A model of these relationships may be found in Path Model 1 shown below. Pearson product moment correlations have been placed above each direct path.

Figure 17.1   Path Model 1

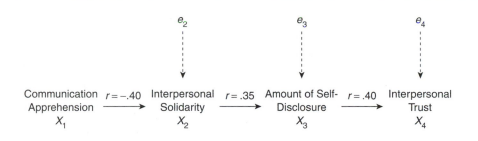

Starting with the interpersonal trust variable, the size of the correlation coefficients between it and other variables should decline as one moves to the variables further and further to the left. A moderator variable should be more closely associated with the dependent variable than an exogenous variable is. In fact, the dependent variable's association with the exogenous variable would be considered spurious. In this simple path model, the theoretically expected correlations between any two variables are simply the products of all the paths between them in addition to any error terms. Thus, Table 17.1 shows how the predicted paths for this simple model would be computed. The diagram shows terms e_1, e_2, and e_3. As will be explained subsequently, these elements are the disturbance (or residual error) terms for predicting each endogenous variable. Diagrams typically omit disturbance terms for exogenous variables because they involve measurement error rather than prediction error.

Table 17.1

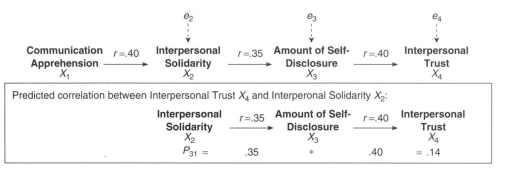

Computing Coefficients and Testing Models

After a model is selected for examination, researchers specify the nature of the causes within the model for each variable. This information permits computing the theoretically expected path coefficients among variables in the model. To illustrate a path model where each variable is not predicted by one variable alone, consider the case of the researcher using the previously identified variables. As shown in Figure 17.2, the researcher might hypothesize a different arrangement with two exogenous variables, interpersonal solidarity and interpersonal attraction. These two variables are assumed to be uncorrelated, even though the actual correlation coefficient between them is .09.

Computing Path Coefficients

Defining structural equations that identify the source of variation for each variable is essential to computing path coefficients. The two exogenous variables, interpersonal solidarity and interpersonal attraction, are not predicted by other variables but are caused by e, the error or disturbance term, which is assumed to equal zero. As mentioned previously, disturbance terms for exogenous variables indicate measurement error, rather than prediction error; hence, it is not necessary to insert error terms for the exogenous variables on path diagrams. Because X_1 is explained by no variables except elements outside the model, its predicted values may be symbolized as $z_1 = e_1$. This statement is called the **structural equation** for variable X_1. Because interpersonal attraction X_2 also is an exogenous variable, its structural equation is $z_2 = e_2$.

For the amount of self-disclosure, variable X_3, there are two paths (one each from X_1 and X_2) forming the prediction. Hence, the structural equation for X_3 is $z_3 = p_{32}z_2 + p_{31}z_1 + e_3$. Because the interpersonal trust variable, X_4, is predicted by only variable X_3, the structural equation for variable X_4 is $z_4 = z_3 + e_4$. To figure out what path coefficients are expected to be, researchers apply either of two rules.

- The so-called first law of path analysis states that to derive the correlation of any variable with an endogenous variable Y,

$$r_{YZ} = \sum p_{YXi} r_{XiZ},$$

where

   p_{YXi} is the path from variable X_i to Y and

   p_{XiZ} is the path indicating the correlation between X_i and Z, and the set of X_i variables that includes all the causes of variable Y (from Kenny, 1979, p. 36).

   In other words, the correlation between two variables is obtained by adding the products of each structural parameter for every variable that causes the effects on the endogenous variables. "A simple procedure to employ is to write all the path coefficients of the endogenous variable including the disturbance. Next to each path write the correlation of the exogenous variable of that path with the variable Z. Multiply each path and correlation and sum the products" (Kenny, 1979, p. 36).

- The **tracing rule** states that the correlation of any variable with an endogenous variable Y is equal to the sum of all the products of the paths between the two variables. All traced paths between the two variables are included, provided that (a) no variable is entered more than once and (b) no variable is entered in one direction and exited in the same direction (Kenny, 1979, pp. 37–42).

The two rules produce the same results and, hence, researchers may view them as convenient substitutes for each other. Even so, the tracing rule approach is more prone to clerical errors on the part of the researcher than is the approach using the first law of path analysis.

As an example, consider how the predicted correlations can be found for Path Model 2 in Figure 17.2. Because there are no reciprocal causes or feedback loops, the model is clearly

Figure 17.2   Path Model 2

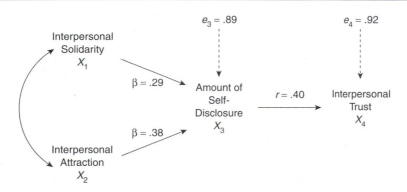

recursive.[3] A friendly word of advice: The material in the rest of this section is really pretty easy, but you have to follow it slowly—one step at a time—to see the common sense that is involved.

- For the relationship between interpersonal solidarity (X_1) and the amount of self-disclosure in the relationship (X_3), there is a direct path. But X_3 has two predictors, which must be taken into account. To compute the expected correlation, one multiplies structural equations. You may remember from Chapter 5 that to compute a population correlation using the original z score method, one takes the average of the products of the z scores for all the events in the sample, $\dfrac{\sum z_x z_y}{N}$ or $\dfrac{1}{N}\sum z_x z_y$. Thus, to find the value of this predicted equation, one multiplies the structural equation values together for each event and then divides by N. In this case, the correlation is predicted as $\dfrac{1}{N}\sum z_1 z_3$.

  Because the error terms are uncorrelated with other elements in the model, their coefficients are 0 and the structural equation for z_3 simplifies to $p_{32}z_2 + p_{31}z_1$. Once this element is substituted, the formula for the predicted correlation between X_1 and X_3 becomes $\dfrac{1}{N}\sum z_1(p_{32}z_2 + p_{31}z_1)$. When the terms are multiplied out, the equation becomes

$$\frac{\sum p_{32}z_2 z_1}{N} + \frac{\sum p_{31}z_1^2}{N},$$

which is equivalent to

$$\left(\frac{\sum p_{32}}{N} * \frac{\sum z_2 z_1}{N}\right) + \left(\frac{\sum p_{32}}{N} * \frac{\sum z_1^2}{N}\right).$$

---

[3] Another way to isolate whether a model is recursive is to take all the structural equations for the model and place them in a matrix, with any residual error terms placed on the right. If a matrix of zeros appears in the upper or lower diagonal (depending on the form of notation used), the model is recursive (see Asher, 1983, pp. 88–89). For instance, a model to be presented shortly includes the following structural equations: $X_6 = p_{65}z_5 + e_6$; $X_5 = p_{54}z_4 + e_5$; $X_4 = p_{43}z_3 + p_{42}z_2 + p_{41}z_1 + e_4$; $X_3 = p_{32}z_2 + p_{31}z_1 + e_3$; $X_2 = e_2$; and $X_1 = e_1$. Inserting them into a matrix of coefficients yields the pattern shown below. Because all the entries in the upper diagonal are 0, the system is recursive.

X_1	X_2	X_3	X_4	X_5	X_6	e
1	0	0	0	0	0	e_1
0	1	0	0	0	0	e_2
$-p_{31}z_1$	$-p_{32}z_2$	1	0	0	0	e_3
$-p_{41}z_1$	$-p_{42}z_2$	$-p_{43}z_3$	1	0	0	e_4
0	0	0	$-p_{54}z_4$	1	0	e_5
0	0	0	0	$-p_{65}z_5$	1	e_6

At this point, you may notice that $\frac{\sum z_2 z_1}{N}$ is the formula for the Pearson product-moment correlation r between variables X_2 and X_1.[4]

You also may notice that $\frac{\sum z_1^2}{N}$ is the average of squared standard scores. Because the standard scores already are deviations from a mean of zero, the squared z values also are the squared deviations of z scores from their means. The mean of the sum of these values is also known as the population variance of z scores. The population variance of z is 1 because z scores have standard deviations of 1. Thus, this term in the formula becomes a constant equal to 1.

Thus, the equation further simplifies to

$$\left(\frac{\sum p_{32}}{N} * r_{21}\right) + \left(\frac{\sum p_{32}}{N} * 1\right).$$

In addition, if all the values of p_{32} or p_{31} are the same (as they are when using the same path scores), the average of the paths is equal to the original path coefficients. Therefore, the predicted path coefficient formula reduces to $p_{31} = p_{32}r_{12} + p_{31}$. Inserting the appropriate numbers, the coefficient becomes $(-.38 * .09) + .29 = .26$.

---

[4]Here is the idea. The chapter on correlations (Chapter 5) explained that the earliest formula for correlation is the mean of the products of the z scores for the two variables. So, for variable X and variable Y, the formula is $\rho_{XY} = \frac{\sum z_X z_Y}{N}$. This formula is a population formula because the standard deviation used to compute z scores has N in the denominator. With sample standard deviations used, the formula here divides not by N, but by $n - 1$. If the path equation for Variable 4 (z_4) is inserted in place of z_y, the formula becomes

$$\rho_{X4} = \frac{\sum z_X (p_{43} z_x + e_4)}{N}.$$

This formula translates to

$$\rho_{X4} = \frac{\sum (p_{43} z_x z_x + e_4 z_x)}{N} = \frac{\sum p_{43} z_X^2}{N} + \frac{\sum e_4 z_x}{N}.$$

But an assumption of the model is that there is no correlation between z and e. So, the formula becomes

$$\frac{\sum p_{43} z_X^2}{N} + 0.$$

In addition, the population variance of $\left(z \frac{\sum z_X^2}{N}\right)$ is 1 because z scores have standard deviations of 1.

The term $\frac{\sum p_{43} z_X^2}{N}$ is equivalent to $\frac{\sum p_{43}}{N} * \frac{\sum z_X^2}{N}$, which means that the formula becomes:

$$\left(\frac{\sum p_{43}}{N} * \frac{\sum z_X^2}{N}\right) + 0.$$

Hence, the formula may be cast as $\rho_{X4} = \left(\frac{\sum p_{43}}{N} * 1\right) + 0$. Because the path ($p_{43}$) is constant, the sum of these elements divided by N also is the value of the path, which simplifies to $p_{X4} = p_{43}$. Thus, when there is only one predictor for a variable, the expected path is the correlation between the two variables.

- The predicted correlation between interpersonal attraction (X_2) and amount of self-disclosure (X_3) is computed from the product of the two structural equations for variables X_2 $(z_2 = e_2)$ and X_3 $(z_3 = p_{32}z_2 + p_{31}z_1 + e_3)$. Using methods similar to those described to identify the correlation for the relationship between X_1 and X_3, one may take the average of the products of the z scores for all the events in the sample, $\frac{1}{N}\sum z_x z_y$ or $\frac{1}{N}\sum z_2 z_3$. As we have seen, because the error terms are uncorrelated with other elements in the model, their coefficients are 0 and the structural equation for z_3 simplifies to $p_{32}z_2 + p_{31}z_1$. After substitutions, the formula for the predicted correlation between X_2 and X_3 becomes $\frac{1}{N}\sum z_1(p_{32}z_2 + p_{31}z_1)$. When the terms are multiplied, the equation becomes

$$\frac{\sum p_{32}z_2^2}{N} + \frac{\sum p_{31}z_1 z_2}{N} = \left(\frac{\sum p_{32}}{N} * \frac{\sum z_2^2}{N}\right) + \left(\frac{\sum p_{31}}{N} * \frac{\sum z_1 z_2}{N}\right),$$

  which is equivalent to $p_{32} = p_{32} + p_{31}r_{12}$. Inserting the numbers, the coefficient becomes $-.38 + (.09 * .29) = -.35$.

- For the predicted correlations between interpersonal solidarity (X_1) and interpersonal trust (X_4), one multiplies each of the paths by the path between Variable 3 and Variable 4. Because the intermediate formulae already have been computed, the process simplifies to $p_{41} = p_{34}(p_{32}r_{12} + p_{31}) = p_{34}p_{32}r_{12} + p_{34}p_{31}$. Inserting the values, this path is revealed to be $(.40 * -.38 * .09) + (.40 * .29) = .10$.

- For the predicted correlations between interpersonal attraction (X_3) and interpersonal trust (X_4), one multiplies each of the paths by the path between Variable 3 and Variable 4. Because the intermediate formulae already have been computed, the process simplifies to $p_{42} = p_{34}p_{32} = p_{34}(p_{32} + p_{31}r_{12}) = p_{34}p_{32} + p_{34}p_{31}r_{12}$. Inserting the values, this path is revealed to be $(.40 * -.38) + (.40 * .29 * .09) = -.14$.

The results of these predictions may be placed in a table such as Table 17.2. A cursory look at the table shows relatively small differences between the observed and predicted equations. You will notice that when a path consists of a single predictor, the predicted direct path is constrained to equal its predicted value.

Table 17.2

Lower Diagonal: Predicted Correlations[a]	Upper Diagonal: Observed Correlations			
	X_1	X_2	X_3	X_4
X_1: Interpersonal solidarity	1	.09	.29	.11
X_2: Interpersonal attraction	.00(.09)	1	−.35	−.03
X_3: Amount of self-disclosure	.26(.03)	−.35(.00)	1	.40
X_4: Interpersonal trust	.10(.01)	−.14(.11)	.40(.00)[b]	1

a. Absolute differences between observed and predicted values in parentheses.

b. The predicted correlation is constrained to equal its observed value.

Computing **R** *and Residuals for Each Predicted Variable*

Researchers regularly report the percentage of variance explained for both the dependent variable and the other endogenous variables. Variance explained is not a test of the fit of the model to the data, because models that fit the data well may not account for large portions of variance (Bielby & Hauser, 1977). Nevertheless, it is a piece of descriptive information that reveals the usefulness of the model. In the case of endogenous variables with multiple predictors, the multiple regression correlation term, R^2, is most typically reported. For endogenous variables with single predictors, the simple r^2 is reported because it is equivalent to R^2 in these circumstances. Thus, in Path Model 2, the R for the prediction of interpersonal trust is equal to the Pearson product-moment r of .40 which, when transformed into a coefficient of determination (r^2), indicates that 16% of the variance in trust can be explained by a knowledge of the amount of self-disclosure. In this case, R for the prediction of the amount of self-disclosure is .45, whose coefficient of determination R^2 is .20, indicating that 20% of the variance in the amount of self-disclosure could be explained by a knowledge of interpersonal solidarity and interpersonal attraction ratings.

To compute disturbance terms in predicting each endogenous variable, the formula $\sqrt{1 - R^2}$ may be used. These values may be placed on a path model diagram next to the e symbols near the predicted variables. Disturbance terms are omitted for the exogenous variables because this residual error value identifies prediction error, not measurement error.

Checking Fit of the Model to the Data

Once the predicted path coefficients have been computed, some steps have to be made to ensure that they are comparable to the actual correlations among variables. There are several options (see Bollen & Long, 1993).

Perhaps the most direct way involves constructing confidence intervals around observed correlations and examining whether the predicted correlations fall within that range. If the differences are smaller than the confidence interval, the observed correlation is within the limits of random sampling error of the predicted correlation. Hence, the prediction is said to fit the data. This method permits researchers to target specific details about the location of any predictive shortcomings. The formula for a two-tailed 95% confidence interval around a correlation coefficient is $\pm \frac{1.96}{\sqrt{n}}$. If observed and predicted correlations differ by more than $\frac{1.96}{\sqrt{n}}$ (in either direction, because it is a two-tailed test), then the model does not fit the data.

Other tests rely on a global examination of fit. Although very popular, they may leave the researcher knowing that there is a misspecification in the model, but not knowing where.[5] Inspecting other modification indices may help, however. Two of the most popular tools for traditional path modeling are the likelihood ratio chi-square test and the root mean square approximation RMSEA. Other related tools, such as the goodness-of-fit index, are associated

---

[5]In different—but instructive—research, a comparison of several techniques was examined to determine if error variances of misspecified models could be detected when using a z test, a Wald test, a likelihood ratio chi-square test, a Lagrangian multiplier test, and confidence intervals. Researchers found that "the use of confidence intervals as well as four other proposed tests yielded similar results when testing whether the error variance was greater than or equal to zero" (Chen, Bollen, Paxton, Curran, & Kirby, 2001, p. 468).

with the measures supported by specific programs (e.g., Amos, LISREL, EQS) designed for the analysis of covariance matrices.

The likelihood ratio chi-square test is a global test and takes the form $\chi^2 = N\,\Phi$ where Φ is equal to $ln\ |C^*| - ln\ |S| + trace\ (SC^{*-1}) - m$ (where C^* is the maximum likelihood estimate of the population covariance matrix, assuming the null hypothesis; S is the covariance matrix of the sample). The trace is the sum of the diagonal elements of a matrix. Though it seems most suitable for models involving 75 to 200 events, for moderate to small samples it leads to excessive rejection of null hypotheses (and hence, false claims that a model does not fit) (see Neill & Dunn, 1975; Steiger, 1980, p. 248). Others observe that as samples grow beyond 200 events, the test "is almost always statistically significant. Chi square is also affected by the size of the correlation in the model: the larger the correlations, the poorer the fit" (Kenny, 2003, ¶ 2).

The **root mean square error of approximation (RMSEA)** is most often reserved for analysis of covariance matrices, but it also has applications when correlations are used. This measure is based on the RMR (root mean square residual), which is the square root of the average squared amount by which the observed and expected sample variances and covariances differ. But such estimates do not adjust for the number of paths in the model. The RMSEA takes the square root of the F_0 values that have been divided by the number of degrees of freedom for testing the model. Taking the square root of the resulting ratio gives the population root mean square error of approximation, or RMSEA (though its developers [Steiger & Lind, 1980] referred to it as RMS). This approach "can be interpreted as a root mean square standardized measure of badness of fit of a particular model . . ." (Steiger, 1998, p. 413). To accept a model, a general rule of thumb is that the RMSEA should be below .05 or .06 (Hu & Bentler, 1999). The RMSEA coefficient is *not* a probability statement. Indeed, one of its developers (Steiger, 2000) chided others who use it as a form of statistical hypothesis testing.

When path models have troubled fit to data, researchers sometimes rely on repairs of convenience regardless of whether there is a theoretic justification for doing so. For instance, a researcher with a sample of 200 participants examined the tenability of Path Model 3. Structural equations were defined and predicted correlations were computed.[6] It might be

---

[6]With this complex model, the structural equations were $z_6 = z_5 + e_6$; $z_5 = z_4 + e_5$; $z_4 = p_{41}z_1 + p_{42}z_2 + p_{43}z_3 + e_4$; $z_3 = p_{31}z_1 + p_{32}z_2 + e_3$; $z_2 = e_2$; and $z_1 = e_1$. Thus, the predicted correlations for X_6 and X_5 as well as for X_5 and X_4 were equal to their observed values. That is, $p_{65} = r_{65}$ and $p_{54} = r_{54}$. Other paths also were computed:

$$p_{64} = p_{65}p_{54}.$$

Because multiple sources predict Variable 4 and Variable 3, and because the tracing rule requires each variable to be entered only once and that no variable is both entered and exited through an arrowhead on the path, the path analyst must take care not to violate these rules preventing inappropriate duplications.

$$p_{63} = p_{65}p_{54}p_{43} + p_{65}p_{54}p_{42}r_{23} + p_{65}p_{54}p_{41}r_{13};$$
$$p_{62} = p_{65}p_{54}p_{42} + p_{65}p_{54}p_{43}r_{23} + p_{65}p_{54}p_{41}r_{12};$$
$$p_{61} = p_{65}p_{54}p_{41} + p_{65}p_{54}p_{43}r_{13} + p_{65}p_{54}p_{42}r_{12};$$
$$p_{53} = p_{54}p_{43} + p_{54}p_{42}r_{23} + p_{54}p_{41}r_{13};$$
$$p_{52} = p_{54}p_{42} + p_{54}p_{43}r_{23} + p_{54}p_{41}r_{12};$$
$$p_{51} = p_{54}p_{41} + p_{54}p_{43}r_{13} + p_{54}p_{42}r_{12};$$
$$p_{43} = p_{43} + p_{41}r_{13} + p_{42}r_{12};$$
$$p_{42} = p_{42} + p_{41}r_{12} + p_{43}r_{32};$$
$$p_{41} = p_{41} + p_{43}r_{13} + p_{42}r_{12};$$
$$p_{32} = p_{32} + p_{31}r_{12};\ \text{and}$$
$$p_{31} = p_{31} + p_{32}r_{12}.$$

mentioned that some path analysts believe that examining predicted relationships with direct paths do not help test model fit, since the predicted correlations are simply the direct paths after accounting for spurious correlations. These predicted values involving direct paths always are close to the observed correlations. In this example, such instances are identified on Figure 17.3 as predicted correlations including a direct path. Other cases, where an endogenous variable is predicted from only one variable, are identified as predicted correlations that are constrained to equal their observed values.

Figure 17.3   Path Model 3

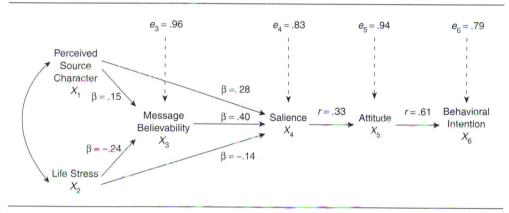

For this model, confidence intervals revealed that one observed correlation was much higher than predicted. The 95% confidence interval was $\pm \dfrac{1.96}{\sqrt{n}} = \pm \dfrac{1.96}{\sqrt{200}} = \pm .138 \approx .14$.

As Table 17.3 shows, the difference between the predicted and the observed correlations between life stress (X_2) and behavioral intentions (X_4) was larger (though inverse) than the confidence interval.

Table 17.3

Lower Diagonal: *Predicted Correlations*[a]	*Upper Diagonal: Observed Correlations*					
	X_1	X_2	X_3	X_4	X_5	X_6
X_1: Source character	1	.05	.14	.33	.10	.16
X_2: Life stress	.00 (.05)	1	−.23	−.22	−.09	−.20
X_3: Message believability	.14[c](.00)	−.23[c](.00)	1	.47	.26	.04
X_4: Topic salience	.33[c](.00)	−.22[c](.00)	.47[c](.00)	1	.33	.24
X_5: Attitude	.11 (.01)	−.07 (.02)	.16 (.10)	.33[b]	1	.61
X_6: Behavioral intention	.07 (.09)	−.04 (.16)	.09 (.05)	.20(.04)	.61[b]	1

a. Absolute differences between observed and predicted values in parentheses.
b. The predicted correlation is constrained to equal its observed value.
c. Predicted correlation includes a direct path between varriables.

There also was a sizable difference between the observed and predicted correlations for the relationship between message believability (X_3) and attitudes (X_5). Furthermore, the source character ratings showed a somewhat odd pattern. Rather than coefficients declining as they moved further away from adjacent variables, there sometimes was a jump in predicting behavioral intentions. The researcher would have to reject the model. The RMSEA was .11, and the χ^2 value was 35.67 with 8 degrees of freedom ($p < .05$; critical value 15.51).

Some researchers might fiddle with the model in hopes of making it work. For instance, direct paths could be added between message believability and attitude, and between life stress and behavior intentions. But there are two difficulties with this strategy. First, the two predictor variables of attitude (believability and salience) had a higher correlation with each other than with the attitude measure. The beta weights would be .27 from the salience measure and .14 from the belivevability measure. Second, as shown below, it makes no theoretic sense, even if it worked.

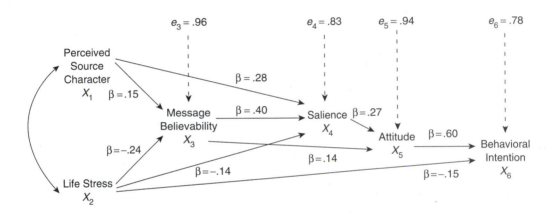

Furthermore, it did not really work in this case. Enlisting the Amos program for further analysis, the chi-square likelihood ratio was 21.622, which, with 6 degrees of freedom, was statistically significant. Furthermore, in this revised model the predicted correlation between believability and behavioral intentions became too high (.20) to fit the data (the observed correlation was .04; the deviation was .16). Another direct path could be added, of course, but the model would soon become so unwieldy that its usefulness in summarizing relationships would become doubtful. By reducing the number of indirect effects that may be examined, the process rapidly becomes a model of direct effects that do not require modeling at all.

Overfitting

Researchers sometimes force a model to fit by including so many direct and mediated paths that little predictive error is possible to identify. This problem is called **overfitting** (and should not be confused with overidentification, which is not a defect in path analysis). This tendency often leads to developing path models that do not cross-validate and that fail to advance understanding. There is more than one reason such a condition emerges. The researcher may capitalize on chance findings, especially when small samples are used. Furthermore, measurement imperfections may prevent clear isolation of relationships.

Researchers frequently find evidence to support more than one path model to describe a data set. Experience with path analysis usually reveals that models with small numbers of paths tend to cross-validate more often than complex models. There are some guidelines to decide which models deserve the most serious attention. First, if competing models fit the data equally well, the one that accounts for the greatest variation in predicted variables should be preferred. Second, if two fitting models account for roughly the same proportions of variance in predicted variables, the one that is simplest should be advanced.

Identification of the Model

Path analysis estimates of the structural model (not the measurement model) cannot be completed for models that are not identified. A parameter that can be predicted or estimated to have one unique (deliberate redundancy here) value is said to be **identified**. Hence, models composed of identified equations also are considered to be identified. A parameter that cannot be predicted or estimated to have one value is said to be **unidentified** or **underidentified.** Naturally, the model with which it is associated also is considered unidentified or underidentified. A problem of identification exists when there are more unknown elements than can be estimated from the available (known) data. "In other words, it occurs when there are too many unknowns in a causal model for a solution to be possible" (Vogt, 2005, p. 149). Any sound path model must be identified such that the unknown parameters can be shown as unique functions of the identified elements of the model. There are three types of models.

- An **underidentified model** is composed of one or more unidentified equations. Underidentification exists when it is impossible to provide a unique identification for all parameters. For instance, imagine that there is a correlation of .64 between source attractiveness and perceived similarity. If the researcher suggests a reciprocal relationship between these variables, the model is in good shape *if* the researcher has separate correlations for each of the paths. If the researcher does not have such information, there is a problem. A correlation of .64 could be attributable to the product of two correlations (one from source attractiveness and one from perceived similarity), each one of which is .80 (.80 * .80 = .64). Or the correlation of .64 could be the product of a correlation of .91 and another of .70. Or the correlation of .64 could be the product of a correlation of .852 and another of .752. There is no single best answer to identify the parameter. Thus, the model remains underidentified. Structural equations for underidentified models cannot be estimated.

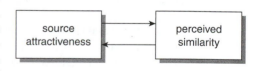

- A **just identified** (or "exactly identified") model is one for which there are as many known as unknown parameters. A model is *just identified* if the number of structural equations in the model matches the number of correlations (or covariances). So, a solution may be found for each parameter. The possible number of correlations between pairs of variables is equal to $\frac{p(p-1)}{2}$, where p is the number of variables in the model.

As an example of a just identified model, consider Path Model 4 (Figure 17.4). Interestingly, this just identified model has a path between every pair of variables. There are direct effects for each variable except for the one exogenous variable. There is only one estimate of a parameter available to the researcher. Because there are no indirect paths to explore, the researcher might find this model of limited interest.

Figure 17.4 Path Model 4

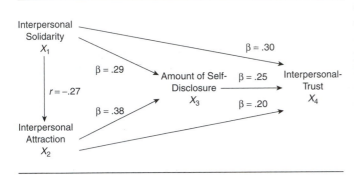

- An **overidentified model** is one for which an unknown parameter can be solved (or predicted) in more than one way. Though different equations could be used to estimate parameters, as far back as 1960, Wright solved this challenge by recommending the use of multiple regression methods that remain in use today. Researchers find that overidentified models are most valuable because

> over identifying restrictions also increase the efficiency of parameter estimation (Goldberger, 1973). If there are two estimates of the same parameter, those estimates can be pooled to obtain a new estimate whose variance is less than or equal to the variance of either original parameter estimate. (Kenny, 1979, p. 45)

To assess identification, researchers compare two numbers. The first number is the possible number of correlations between pairs of observed variables; the second is the actual total of model parameters. This sum is produced by adding the number of observed paths, the number of correlations between pairs of exogenous variables (computed as $\frac{\text{number of exogenous variables} * (\text{number of exogenous variables} - 1)}{2}$), and any correlations between pairs of errors, excluding the paths to error terms.

- If the actual total model parameters are greater than the possible number of correlations between pairs of observed variables, the model is underidentified.
- If the actual total model parameters are smaller than the possible number of correlations between pairs of observed variables, the model is overidentified.
- If the actual total model parameters are the same as the possible number of correlations, the model may be just identified (provided that the pattern of underidentification and overidentification of other variables does not lead to underidentification for the model).

In the examples examined in this chapter, Path Model 3 has 7 paths, 1 correlation between exogenous variables, and 0 correlations among error terms, for total model parameters of 8. The total possible number of correlations is 15. Because the total possible correlations are greater than the total model parameters, Path Model 3 is overidentified. Path Model 4 has

6 paths, 0 correlations between exogenous variables, and 0 correlations among error terms, for total model parameters of 6. The total possible number of correlations is 6. Because the total possible correlations equals the total model parameters, Path Model 4 may be "just identified."

USING THE AMOS PROGRAM

Amos[7] (**A**nalysis of **MO**ment **S**tructures) was introduced in the last chapter as a method to complete confirmatory factor analysis. Amos also permits creating and testing general structural equation models, which is the primary focus of attention here. The comprehensiveness of AMOS combined with the convenience of its wide availability through SPSS (which has now dropped LISREL) surely will contribute to the further popularity of AMOS and structural equation modeling.

The Approach of Amos

Amos allows researchers to use diagrams or programming in the Sax Basic Language,[8] which is compatible with the language known as Visual Basic for Applications[TM].[9] The graphical approach will be emphasized in this discussion because of its obvious efficiency.

The details of using the drawing area and handling basic commands were explained in Chapter 16 and will not be reviewed here. Amos also allows researchers to create diagrams and prepare path models for analysis, testing, and even presentation. Once a diagram has been drawn of the model, Amos develops simultaneous equations among variables by use of optimizing methods such as maximum likelihood estimation. Structural relationships may be between observed variables (manifest variables) or unobserved variables (latent variables). In traditional path modeling, observed variables are explored and their measurement properties are established separately. In contrast, Amos encourages exploring relationships among latent variables or constructs whose measurement composition is verified as part of the model. Because Amos involves confirmatory factor analysis methods, it is most properly considered to be a theory-testing method, rather than a theory exploration tool.

As described in Chapter 16, structural equation models in general, and Amos in particular, assume multivariate normal distributions. Although this assumption is not necessary when considering exogenous variables that are measured without error, it applies to all latent variables, as well as to measurement errors for observed exogenous variables and to endogenous variables. Though imperfect, Mardia's coefficient of multivariate kurtosis (Mardia, 1970, 1974) is included in Amos output.

---

[7]Amos is a registered trademark of the Amos Development Corporation.

[8]Sax Basic Language is a registered trademark of Polar Engineering and Consulting.

[9]Visual Basic and Visual Basic for Applications are registered trademarks of the Microsoft Corporation.

Phases of Model Development With Amos

Amos requires researchers to define the forms of the variables in the study. In particular, they must specify whether a variable is

- an observed variable that is a measurement on a given item or scale,
- a latent variable or underlying factor that is not observed directly, or
- a term to identify error terms.

After the researcher has identified such information, a model may be sketched out and contrasted with the data.

To illustrate how this process is completed, an example will be explored. In this case, a researcher suspected that the credibility of the message and the perceptions of source character would be good predictors of whether women would take some action to help lower their risks of breast cancer. In the study, women participants rated the character of a well-known public figure and then read a message attributed to that source. Afterward, participants completed scales to assess message credibility. Finally, two 5-point Likert-type scales ("I intend to learn more about breast cancer" [learnabo] and "I intend to complete a breast cancer self-examination" [selfexam]) were completed to measure individuals' intentions to acquire additional medical information about breast cancer. The message credibility scales were "the message was believable" (believe) and "the message content was accurate" (acconten). Source credibility scales were "the source of the message is trustworthy" (trust) and "the source of the message is virtuous" (virtue).[10]

After starting the *Amos Graphics* program (the *Amos Basic* program could have been used if the researcher wished to use Amos Basic programming language), the researcher began to enter a path model on the drawing area. The researcher clicked the *Select Data Files* icon ▦ to select a data file for active use, following the same steps as used in the confirmatory factor analysis setup described in Chapter 16. In SPSS, input may be in the form of raw data or matrices of covariances or correlations. If a correlation matrix is input, the types of variables are identified in a column marked "rowtype," and the variable names are listed in available columns and in the "varname" column. Using this format also required including the sample size, means, and standard deviations for the variables.

	rowtype	varname	believe	acconten	learnabo	selfexam	trust	virtue
1	n		280.00	280.00	280.00	280.00	280.00	280.00
2	corr	believe	1.00					
3	corr	acconten	.60	1.00				
4	corr	learnabo	.52	.37	1.00			
5	corr	selfexam	.40	.32	.59	1.00		
6	corr	trust	.15	.12	.42	.40	1.00	
7	corr	virtue	.17	.08	.28	.33	.63	1.00
8	stddev		1.59	1.35	1.23	1.43	1.70	1.86
9	mean		4.53	4.92	5.21	4.85	4.09	5.24

---

[10]The number of observed variables is kept small for purposes of illustration. In reality, most researchers would have more than two items to measure an underlying or latent dimension.

Constructing the Diagram

Because there were three latent or unobserved variables, they would be placed on the drawing by clicking on the oval *Draw unobserved variables* icon and drawing three ovals in the middle of the page (two on one row and one on another). Afterward, clicking the *Draw unobserved variables* icon would deactivate it. To add the two measured variables for each of the latent variables, the *Draw indicator variable* icon 🙄 was used, similar to the way it was described in the discussion of confirmatory factor analysis. Each time the left mouse button is clicked, a manifest (or observed) variable, along with a place for its error term, is attached. Two indicator paths were added to each latent variable. The diagrams may be rotated using the *Rotate the indicators of a latent variable* tool ◔ (each click on a parent oval moves the indicator variables by 90 degrees). Something resembling the diagram on the top right was drawn.

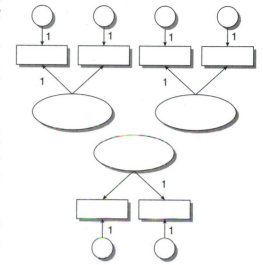

Any movement of objects could be completed by using the *Move objects* icon, 🚚 which, not surprisingly, moves a highlighted item. Numbers have been inserted into some paths. To identify the regression model, the scale of the unobserved or latent variable must be defined. This step may be accomplished by setting the variance of the path coefficient from a latent to an observed variable at some positive value. In this case, the *Draw indicator variable* tool automated this task by constraining a parameter at 1.

After clicking on the *List variables in dataset* icon, 📊, variable names were inserted into rectangles by clicking and dragging the desired names to the rectangles. For instance, the observed variable BELIEVE was highlighted and dragged to the first box, as shown in the middle on the right.

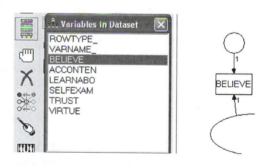

Latent variables were labeled by double-clicking on the ovals and making insertions in the "Variable names" field of the *Object Properties* dialog box. In this case, the "behavior intentions" latent variable was identified as composed of LEARNABO and SELFEXAM. The other two latent variables were labeled "message credibility" (composed of BELIEF and ACCONTEN scales) and "source credibility" (composed of TRUST and VIRTUE scales).

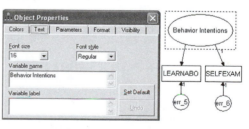

The error terms were labeled as well. Some researchers prefer to use labels that are familiar to LISREL users (delta [δ] for the error terms associated with the exogenous indicators, epsilon [ε] for error terms associated with latent endogenous variables, and zeta [ζ] terms for structural disturbances). In this example, however, the researcher simply numbered error terms from "err_1" through "err_8."

Special Discussion 17.3

LISREL* is a clever program that combines confirmatory factor analysis and path modeling using the language of structural equation modeling. In the past, because of its support by SPSS, it was the tool of choice by structural equation modelers in academic life. Other programs, particularly Amos, have begun to eclipse its popularity.

There are two fundamental equations in LISREL (Jöreskog & Sörbom, 1986, p. I.6). The first is the structural equation model, and the second is the measurement model. Each will be considered in turn.

$$\text{Structural Equation Model: } \eta = B\eta + \Gamma\xi + \zeta$$

where

η (eta) is "the names of all the endogenous concepts in a column vector" (Hayduk, 1987, pp. 90–91) of $m \times 1$ dimension, where m is the number of endogenous concepts;

$B\eta$ is an $(m \times m)$ matrix containing the structural coefficients (β) multiplied by the η $(m \times 1)$ matrix;

Γ (uppercase gamma) is an $(m \times n)$ matrix containing the structural coefficients (γ [lowercase gamma]), which is multiplied by the ξ (xi, pronounced "ksi" and rhymes with "sigh") $(n \times 1)$ vector of exogenous concepts; and

ζ (zeta) is an $m \times 1$ vector of exogenous concepts.

In addition,

the covariances among exogenous concepts are an $n \times n$ matrix Φ (phi);

the covariances among the residual errors (ε) in the conceptual model are an $m \times m$ vector ψ (psi, pronounced "sigh");

y is "a vector of observed endogenous indicators" (Hayduk, 1987, p. 91) of $p \times 1$ dimension, where p is the number of endogenous indicators;

Λ_y (lambda) is a $(p \times m)$ matrix containing the structural coefficients of y multiplied by the η $(m \times 1)$ vector of endogenous concepts; and

ε (epsilon) is a $p \times 1$ vector of errors in the measurement model for y.

In addition, θ_ε (theta sub epsilon) is a $(p \times p)$ vector of the covariances among the errors of exogenous concepts.

$$\text{Measurement Model for } x = \Lambda_x \xi + \delta$$
$$\text{Measurement Model for } y = \Lambda_y \eta + \varepsilon$$

where

x is "a vector of observed exogenous indicators" (Hayduk, 1987, p. 91) of $q \times 1$ dimension, where q is the number of exogenous indicators;

Λ_x (lambda) is a $(q \times n)$ matrix containing the structural coefficients of x multiplied by the ξ $(n \times 1)$ vector of exogenous concepts; and

δ (delta) is a $q \times 1$ vector of errors in the measurement model for x.

In addition, θ_δ (theta sub delta) is a $(q \times q)$ vector of the covariances among the errors of exogenous concepts.

*LISREL is a registered trademark of Scientific Software Inc.

Thus, to use LISREL, the researcher must identify the variables that are manifest (observed) and those that are latent. Then, the program is used to identify parameters and examine evidence of the fit of the model to the data. LISREL is best suited for the analysis of covariance structures yielding latent variables or factors, but it can be used for examining correlation structures. It also may be used to examine relations among manifest variables by substituting observable variables for the values of variables otherwise presumed to be latent. Furthermore, LISREL is strong when linking a set of latent *X* and *Y* variables. When a string of mediated paths is involved, the model is strained and routinely produces rejection of sound models. An example of such a model may be found in the figure shown below. One might imagine that LISREL requires data at the interval or ratio level, but LISREL also supports a module called PRELIS, which is a set of alternative procedures for non-normal ordinal measures.

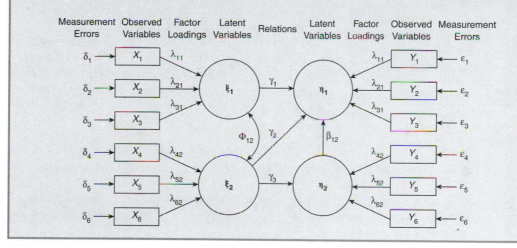

Clicking the arrow toolbar permitted the researcher to draw the arrows between any two endogenous latent variables. The researcher was interested in a direct path (an arrow with a single point) from source credibility to message credibility and another path to behavior intentions. Furthermore, a direct path is predicted from message credibility to behavior intentions.

Each endogenous variable predicted by another endogenous variable must have an error term. In this example, there were two endogenous variables predicted by other endogenous variables, "message believability" and "behavior intentions." To add such error terms, the researcher clicked on the *Add a unique variable to an existing variable* icon. While this button was active, clicking on the "message credibility" oval added another latent variable for the error term. Unfortunately, it was placed next to the other manifest variables associated with this variable. Hence, the researcher may have needed to move it using the *Move objects* icon. When completed, the model looks similar to the figure on the right.

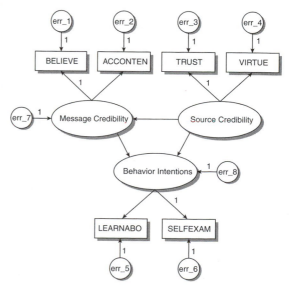

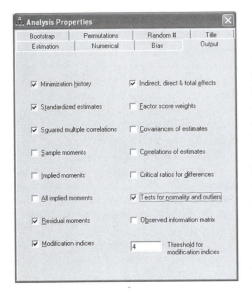

Examining Model Characteristics and Parameters

Specific output was requested for the example we are describing. Clicking on the *Analysis properties* icon [icon] produced a dialog box to control output. On the *Estimation* tab, the researcher found several options to minimize discrepancies in the model's estimates. Maximum likelihood estimation is the default for computing model parameters. This approach has the advantages of consistency, efficiency, and normality as sample size increases (Keeping, 1995, p. 123). Furthermore, likelihood ratio chi-square tests of model fit usually are presented, and the use of a maximum likelihood solution is most often recommended.

On the *Output* tab, the researcher found another series of choices. In addition to the ones selected for confirmatory factor analysis in the last chapter, several other output options usually are considered. Some of the boxes include the following categories of options.

- *Squared multiple correlations:* multiple correlations (when multiple predictors are involved) and correlations (when multiple predictors are involved) among endogenous variables and their predictor variables.
- *Residual moments:* differences between the sample and implied covariance matrices or the differences between sample and implied means (if means and intercepts are included in the model).
- *Indirect, direct & total effects:* all effects divided into categories (when the *Standardized estimates* box also is checked, the standardized as well as the unstandardized direct, indirect, and total effects are included).

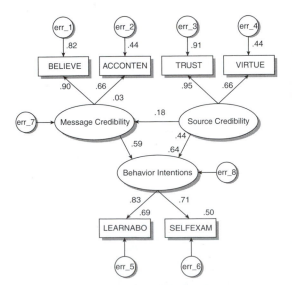

Afterward, the researcher clicked the *Calculate estimates* icon [icon]. Examining the output model by clicking on the *View the output path diagram* involved clicking the right button at the top center of the page [icon]. The diagram appeared with a complete set of coefficients. Depending on whether the researcher clicked the *standardized estimate* statement in the middle column of the Amos control field, these parameter estimates may be unstandardized or standardized, as is shown in the diagram to the left.

The paths shown on the diagram revealed standardized regression coefficients (beta weights). In addition, because standardizing the output sets the intercept at zero, error terms are uncorrelated, and exogenous variables have measurement errors of 0.

Clicking the *View text* icon ▦ revealed the output divided into sections, though the *Text Output* subprogram must be operating to display it. After an *Analysis Summary* listing the type of model and the sample size, a *Variable Summary* report lists all the variables in the model and classifies them as observed or unobserved (latent) and endogenous or exogenous. Error terms are listed under the category of "unobserved, exogenous variables." A *Parameter Summary* includes the number of parameters that are fixed, labeled, or unlabeled. A table also reports whether the parameters involve covariances, variances, means, or intercepts.

The next section includes *Notes for Model (Default model)*, which reports critical information about model composition and identification. The section for this model is found in Table 17.4.

In this case, the estimated parameters were fewer than the number of "distinct sample moments." Hence, the model was overidentified and was suitable for structural equation modeling. In short, the model could be tested. In contrast, a "just identified" model would always show perfect fit as an artifact. If the model were underidentified or unidentified, a warning would appear and the researcher would receive information about the sort of parameter estimation problems that are present. The output also states that the estimation method successfully achieved a local minimum value. The likelihood ratio chi-square test was not statistically significant. In this case, with alpha risk of .05, the critical value of likelihood ratio chi-square was 12.59. The observed test statistic (9.016) was not greater than this value. Thus, the null hypothesis that the model does not differ from the data set could not be rejected. Unlike most statistical significance testing, path modelers do *not* want to find significant differences between the paths and the data. Hence the model may be accepted. Of course, model fit actually means that the model *permits* reproducing the correlation or covariance matrix. In this case, that assumption continues to hold. Other measures of fit also were used, and, as will be seen, they revealed the same patterns.

The *Estimates* output provided tables of the unstandardized and the standardized parameter estimations for the model. The unstandardized values (except for those whose values are constrained) were tested to see if their diffences from zero were statistically significant. In this case, all of them were, as indicated by *p* values below .05. When the exact probability is lower than .000, three asterisks are placed in the column for *p* values. The standardized regression weights are among the most important to examine. These paths are most typically placed on

Table 17.4

Computation of Degrees of Freedom (Default model)

Number of distinct sample moments: 21
Number of distinct parameters to be estimated: 15
Degrees of freedom (21 - 15):   6

Result (Default model)

Minimum was achieved
Chi-square = 9.016
Degrees of freedom = 6
Probability level = .173

Table 17.5

Regression Weights (Group number 1—Default model)

			Estimate	S.E.	C.R.	P	Label
Message Credibility	<---	Source Credibility	.162	.063	2.582	.010	
Behavior Intentions	<---	Message Credibility	.418	.063	6.664	***	
Behavior Intentions	<---	Source Credibility	.277	.052	5.339	***	
TRUST	<---	Source Credibility	1.000				
VIRTUE	<---	Source Credibility	.757	.108	6.978	***	
BELIEVE	<---	Message Credibility	1.000				
ACCONTEN	<---	Message Credibility	.625	.077	8.164	***	
LEARNABO	<---	Behavior Intentions	1.005	.096	10.512	***	
SELFEXAM	<---	Behavior Intentions	1.000				

published path models. The standardized regression weights for this model are found in Table 17.6.

Table 17.6

Standardized Regression Weights (Group number 1—Default model)			
			Estimate
Message Credibility	<---	Source Credibility	.183
Behavior Intentions	<---	Message Credibility	.591
Behavior Intentions	<---	Source Credibility	.442
TRUST	<---	Source Credibility	.955
VIRTUE	<---	Source Credibility	.660
BELIEVE	<---	Message Credibility	.903
ACCONTEN	<---	Message Credibility	.664
LEARNABO	<---	Behavior Intentions	.830
SELFEXAM	<---	Behavior Intentions	.711

Table 17.7 reports the variances, standard errors, and critical ratios of parameters, and the probability of differences of observed variances being explicable by random sampling error.

The R^2 for the prediction of (other than exogenous) variables also was reported. As a measure of behavioral intentions about breast cancer health care, this model predicted 64% of the shared variance (see Table 17.8).

Table 17.7

Variances (Group number 1—Default model)					
	Estimate	S.E.	C.R.	P	Label
Source Credibility	2.624	.411	6.381	***	
err_7	1.985	.293	6.772	***	
err_8	.370	.088	4.185	***	
err_1	.465	.216	2.153	.031	
err_2	1.014	.119	8.499	***	
err_3	.256	.333	.770	.441	
err_4	1.946	.251	7.739	***	
err_6	1.009	.115	8.808	***	
err_5	.468	.087	5.399	***	

Table 17.8

Squared Multiple Correlations (Group number 1—Default model)	
	Estimate
Message Credibility	.033
Behavior Intentions	(.640)
LEARNABO	.689
SELFEXAM	.505
VIRTUE	.436
TRUST	.911
ACCONTEN	.441
BELIEVE	.815

Examining Model Fit

The standardized residual covariances also were reported because the researcher checked the *Request residual moments* option. These residuals appear in Table 17.9. Ideally, these standardized residuals should reflect a standard normal distribution. As a rule, the values should be below 1.96 in a tenable model. A difference greater than 1.96 indicates that the residuals are beyond a chance expectation at a decision rule of .05. The modification indices were not computed because

Table 17.9

Standardized Residual Covariances (Group number 1—Default model)					
	LEARNABO	*SELFEXAM*	*VIRTUE*	*TRUST*	*ACCONTEN*	*BELIEVE*
LEARNABO	.000					
SELFEXAM	.000	.000				
VIRTUE	−.346	1.163	.000			
TRUST	−.248	.418	.000	.000		
ACCONTEN	−.009	.046	−.003	.067	.000	
BELIEVE	.244	−.475	1.013	−.126	.000	.000

there was no significant deviation from acceptable fit and because any changes would not reduce the chi-square value by the minimum of 4.0. If a model fails to fit the data, the modification indices indicate which paths, if altered by relaxing initial assumptions, would lead to greatest changes in the value of the likelihood ratio chi-square test.

This section ended with minimization history followed by indices of model fit. The Amos program produces more than 20 model fit indices, though the development of such tests is active and there may be as many as 100 different tests available. Only a handful will be interpreted here to explore the health model. Many of these tests were described in Chapter 16 and will not be reviewed again here. The fit of the model to the data is revealed in Table 17.10.

Table 17.10

Model	NPAR	CMIN	DF	P	CMIN/DF
Default model	15	9.016	6	.173	1.503
Saturated model	21	.000	0		
Independence model	6	559.603	15	.000	37.307

Model	RMR	GFI	AGFI	PGFI
Default model	.063	.990	.965	.283
Saturated model	.000	1.000		
Independence model	.777	.559	.382	.399

Model	RMSEA	LO 90	HI 90	PCLOSE
Default model	.042	.000	.096	.524
Independence model	.361	.335	.387	.000

- CMIN is the minimum discrepancy $\hat{C}$ and is an application of the chi-square test. Because no statistically significant difference was noted, the breast cancer health model seemed to fit the data.
- CMIN/DF adjusts CMIN for model complexity. A value below 2 indicates acceptable fit. This model clearly fit the data, as indicated by a value of 1.503.
- RMR is the root mean square residual, described in this chapter's section on "Checking Fit of the Model to the Data." Ideal fit is indicated by RMR values approaching zero. Though it is a judgment call, a value below .08 (which was found in this example) is considered acceptable fit. This measure is not available for models with manifest variables only.
- GFI is the *Goodness of Fit Index*, which is computed as $GFI = 1 - \dfrac{\hat{F}}{\hat{F}_b}$, where $\hat{F}$ is the minimum value of the discrepancy function and $\hat{F}_b$ is the discrepancy function for the null model where all parameters except for the variances have values set at 0. The

highest GFI is 1.0, indicating a perfect fit of the model to the data. The GFI for the health model was .99, a value that suggested strong fit. GFI is not available to assess models with manifest variables only.

- AGFI is the *Adjusted Goodness of Fit Index*, which adjusts the GFI for the degrees of freedom for the hypothesized model. It is computed as $AGFI = 1 - (1 - GFI)\frac{d_b}{d}$, where $d_b = \sum_{g=1}^{G} p^{*(g)}$. The most positive value indicating perfect fit is 1.0, but values may go below zero. The breast cancer health model had a very high AGFI (.965) and, hence, the evidence of fit seemed consistent with other measures. The AGFI is not available to assess models with manifest variables only.

It might be mentioned that the measures just identified have been criticized for being biased upward with increasing sample sizes. Hence, other measures have been recommended.

- PGFI is the *Parsimony Goodness of Fit Index*, which adjusts the GFI for the degrees of freedom for the null model. The PGFI is computed as $PGFI = GFI\frac{d}{d_b}$, where d is degrees of freedom for the hypothesized model and $d_b = \sum_{g=1}^{G} p^{*(g)}$ is the degrees of freedom for the null model, called the *baseline* model. The PGFI differs from the AGFI in whether the null or hypothesized degrees of freedom are used to standardize comparison values. In this case, the value of .283 suggested reasonable fit to the data. The PGFI is not available for assessing models with manifest variables only.
- RMSEA, as previously described in this chapter, is the *Root Mean Square Error of Approximation*. As previously described, values below .05 are taken as support for claims of fit of the model to the data. In this case, the RMSEA was .042, which was within acceptable limits.
- PCLOSE is a statistical significance test of the RMSEA. Rejecting the null hypothesis asserts that the population RMSEA is greater than .05. In this case, the probability value of .524 indicated no statistically significant difference between the observed RMSEA and an RMSEA ≤ .05. Thus, the model was supported.

As explained in Chapter 16, these measures of fit often are based on the same statistical approach. Hence, when the health communication model "passes" 20 tests, it does not mean we have 10 times as much proof as for a model that "passes" 2 tests. Thus, the tests of fit should be taken as imperfect indicators of model fit to the data, especially because many seem to report variations of the same basic information.

Using Amos for Models With Observed Variables Only

Amos is a versatile program that also analyzes models with observed variables only, without much difficulty. As an example, the path model dealing with source character and life stress may be analyzed using this program. After inputting the diagram from the previously described model, the result was as is shown on page 485. As the model indicated, all key variables were placed in rectangles to indicate that they were observed variables. Only error terms for each of the endogenous variables were placed in ovals. The two exogenous variables were assumed to be unrelated. Thus, the curved line between the exogenous variables indicated this lack of association.

After clicking on the *Analysis properties* icon 🖼, the researchers selected options for output. Some output is provided for models composed of latent variables only. Some other measures of model fit are omitted because they apply to covariance matrices for unobserved variables. Clicking the *Calculate estimates* icon 🎹 produced the formal analysis. To secure a diagram with parameters included, the researcher clicked the *View the output path diagram* button, which is located on the right side of the pair of buttons at the top of the page 🖫. As shown on the right, clicking on the *Standardized estimated* bar on the parameter format field produces

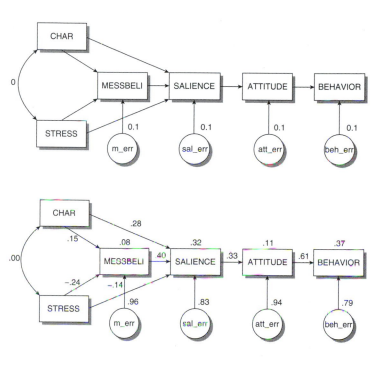

a diagram with standardized parameters included. Within the limits of rounding error, the results mirrored the analysis of these data using traditional path modeling methods. The numbers above the rectangles were the r^2 or R^2 coefficients for each endogenous variable. These elements also were reported in the text version of the output, as shown in Table 17.11. In addition to the description of the model, the results showed a statistically significant chi-square likelihood ratio test (as indicated by a probability level below .05). Thus, the model did not seem to fit the data.

The modification indices examine the parameters that are constrained to equal a constant value and estimate the amount by which the chi-square test of model discrepancy would be reduced if the constraints on the parameter were removed. Additional modification indices are computed for paths that are not

Table 17.11

Notes for Model (Default model)

Computation of Degrees of Freedom (Default model)

Number of distinct sample moments:	27
Number of distinct parameters to be estimated:	19
Degrees of freedom (27 − 19):	8

Result (Default model)

Minimum was achieved
Chi-square = 35.674
Degrees of freedom = 8
Probability level = .000

part of the model, except for paths that would require making an exogenous variable into an endogenous variable or that would make an indirect path from a variable back to itself (creating a nonrecursive model). As Table 17.12 shows, the modification indices revealed some interesting results. The first box reports on the effects of relaxing assumptions about the parameters constrained to be zero (including the assumption of uncorrelated error terms). The second box reports on the impact of other nonexistent paths. In particular, examining the modification indices reported for parameters constrained to be zero, the largest modification index was 13.589, indicating that the chi-square test statistic would decrease by at least this amount if the covariance between the error terms for behavior and

Table 17.12

			M.I.	Par Change
m_err	<---	beh_err	13.589	−.221
STRESS	<---	beh_err	9.355	−1.521
CHAR	<---	beh_err	4.355	.485
			M.I.	Par Change
STRESS	<---	beh_err	9.355	−1.521
CHAR	<---	beh_err	4.355	.485
MESSBELI	<---	beh_err	13.589	−1.370
BEHAVIOR	<---	m_err	13.589	−.061

message believability were allowed to take a nonzero value. The column marked "Par Change" indicates the estimated amount by which the parameter value would drop (−.221) if this path were permitted (because the original value was constrained to equal zero, the reported "Par Change" also is the actual estimated covariance). Even if this change were made, however, the chi-square test statistic still would have been statistically significant. So, the changes would have made little difference. Examining the unpredicted paths, some changes might produce changes in chi-square values, but none of them would make sense given the theoretic foundation of the model. Hence, the examination of the modification indices revealed little evidence that the model could be saved by relaxing assumptions or adding paths.

The indices of fit showed the model's inadequacy (see Table 17.13). Not only was the CMIN (the chi-square likelihood ratio) test statistically significant, but the CMIN/DF measure was far above 2. The RMSEA was greater than .05, and the PCLOSE test revealed that the RMSEA was beyond the .05 threshold for acceptable models. In general, when an apparently unacceptable model is found, the Hoelter's critical N can be instructive. This statistic reveals the sample size at which the model would have been accepted (at the .05 or

Table 17.13

Model	NPAR	CMIN	DF	P	CMIN/DF
Default model	19	35.674	8	.000	4.459
Saturated model	27	.000	0		
Independence model	12	323.724	15	.000	21.582

Model	RMSEA	LO 90	HI 90	PCLOSE
Default model	.111	.076	.150	.003
Independence model	.272	.246	.298	.000

Model	HOELTER .05	HOELTER .01
Default model	122	158
Independence model	22	27

.01 level). Because most measures of fit are sensitive to sample size, this statistic reveals how large the sample would be *just below* the point at which the model would have been rejected by statistics based on comparisons with random sampling error. The stronger the model, the larger this number is. In this case, the model would have been rejected with any sample above 122. Given the recommendation by Hoelter (1983) that a critical N of at least 200 is expected of acceptable models, the researcher must reject the model.

As can be seen, employing Amos for models with all observed variables can be quite useful. In this case, an unacceptable model was identified both with traditional path analysis and with Amos's use of structural equation modeling. As a revision of the model, the researcher might add paths or delete troublesome variables. In this case, if the behavioral intentions measure were removed, the model's fit to the data would improve substantially. In fact, when this step was taken, the CMIN chi-square likelihood ratio dropped to a statistically insignificant 5.173 with 4 degrees of freedom. Furthermore, all tests of fit were supportive of the revised model.

APPENDIX A

Using Excel XP[†] to Analyze Data

Excel XP is sometimes also called Excel 10 and Excel 2002. But regardless of labels, this spreadsheet has emerged as a dominant spreadsheet program that is useful for researchers and others keeping track of numerical data. The use of a set of built-in statistical analysis functions has made this program a popular one among many researchers. It is readily available as part of the Microsoft Office suite of programs, and many colleges and institutions support its use with a full range of consulting services. Yet, the program is intuitively appealing and not particularly complicated for modern students. Excel uses a spreadsheet format to handle data sets and statistically analyze many types of data. This discussion will consider ways to get statistical functions operating in Excel. Then, this guide takes a blunt, "survival skills" approach to giving you quick information so that you may get up and running with Excel.

To use this guide, you should first have some knowledge of the Microsoft Windows XP operating system (or, at least, general Windows operating systems). If you need to refresh yourself on the ways to run such a system, you should feel free to use the assistance provided on the "Windows Basics" review. To use this guide, you may go to the **Start** menu and click on **Help and Support**. On the full set of menu options that appear, select **Windows Basics**. It also is assumed that you know the ways to start a computer, insert CDs and DVDs, and operate a mouse. It might go without saying—but it rarely does—that it is important for you to understand how to **Save** and **Open** files, and the importance of saving files often.

GETTING READY TO RUN STATISTICS WITH EXCEL

Excel XP has a number of built-in statistical analysis subroutines. But you will need to see if they are currently installed. Click on the **Tools** menu to see if the **Data Analysis** options are available. If this set of options is not present, you will need to install them. It is a

---

[†]Excel XP, Excel, Windows XP, and Windows are registered trademarks of the Microsoft Corporation.

simple task. From the **Tools** menu, click on **Options.** Then, click on **Add-ins.** On the menu that appears, check the **Analysis ToolPak** choice. Then click on the **OK** button.

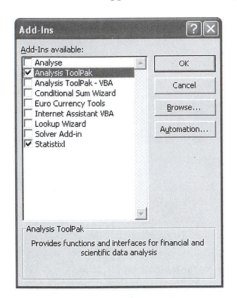

These options consist of 19 different collections of statistical tests, including correlations, *t* tests, analyses of variance, histograms, and the like. Many of these tools also are handled separately in the built-in statistical functions.

It also should be mentioned that there are add-in programs that provide additional support for advanced statistical tools not supported by the basic Excel program. Some of these statistical tools are also found in macros that are supplied on the Web site for this book. Others are from commercially available sources. Though there are several, two of the most useful are *StatistiXL* and *Analyze-It.* Other versatile programs are from *Unistat, NAG* (Numerical Algorithms Group), and *StatTools.* These sources are commercially available, but there are academic sources that feature shareware or freeware add-ins and macros that can help streamline processing of statistical data. A partial list of these sources and their links is located on the Web site for this chapter in the book.

For all its popularity, one must remember that Excel is not a program dedicated to statistical analyses. Many advanced tools are not included with built-in functions, and it is not as flexible as other programs that focus on statistical analysis of data. But creative researchers often find ways to complete advanced calculations that are not currently included.

HANDLING DATA

Excel begins with a blank spreadsheet. Clicking on the blank space in the corner between A and 1 highlights the whole spreadsheet. Any changes in ranks or sorting of any variable will affect the order of the events in the whole spreadsheet. The columns of an Excel spreadsheet are identified as A, B, C, and so forth. The rows are prenumbered 1, 2, 3, and so forth. Specific cells are identified by these combinations of row numbers and column letters. For instance, B1 is the cell in the second column of the first row. To enter data or a formula, you simply click on a cell to make it active and start typing. After clicking a cell, whatever is entered is also listed in the *formula bar* at the top of the page. Clicking *Return* or moving to another cell by use of an arrow key keeps an entry in the cell. Formula statements or functions also may be entered into a cell.

The most immediate step for the analysis of data, of course, is to *have* some for study. You begin by entering data or opening a data file. The name for each variable is identified at the top of the column. The scores from each case of data may be inserted a row at a time. Excel has no automated ways to deal with missing values. Hence, researchers should attempt to include complete data sets.

Researchers often have to complete computations and create new variables that are combinations of others. Excel makes this process rather simple. For instance, researchers might have several measures of interpersonal solidarity that are determined to measure the same underlying dimension. To create a composite index, the scales might be added to create a score. The researcher moves to a blank cell and clicks on it to make it active. If the researcher wishes to add six variables into a common scale, the first step involves placing an equal sign (=) in the highlighted cell. This equal sign also appears on the formula field that begins with the function sign *fx*. If the equal sign is omitted, the formula, rather than the result of the formula, appears in the cell and in the formula field. The second step involves identifying the first cell to be added by clicking on it (its cell identification is also placed in the formula field). The third step involves entering a plus by making an appropriate keystroke. Then, this process is continued by clicking on another cell to enter its identification, followed by another plus sign, and so forth until the formula is completed. Entering *Return* causes the result of the formula to be placed in the target cell. The researcher usually leaves the first row blank so that a label may be entered. Yet, the addition is completed only for the first case (the first row) of data.

To create the same effect for each row of data, the researcher highlights the cell with the formula to be copied for other cases. Then, the researcher selects **Copy** from the **Edit** menu. The highlighted cell features a border that begins to flash. To copy this function, the researcher holds down the left mouse button and moves down the column through all the data rows. The cells in the column are highlighted to indicate that they are now active as well. Entering *Return* causes the highlighted cells to have completed the same addition for their own scores.

Automatically, the cell identifiers have been changed to produce the same addition as used for the first row of data. But the data to be added are restricted to each row, a condition that is what most researchers wish when using this function.

The symbols used to create a formula are shared by most spreadsheet programs and by SPSS. In addition, researchers may use parentheses to define processes further in their construction of a formula. The standard operators used in Excel are as follows:

FINV   ✕ ✓ *fx* =A2+B2+C2+D2+E2+F2

	A	B	C	D	E	F	G	H
1	X1	X2	X3	X4	X5	X6	solidarity	
2	1	2	3	3	3	2	=A2+B2+C2+E2+F2	
3	4	4	5	4	3	2		
4	5	3	3	5	5	6		
5	3	3	4	3	5	7		
6	6	5	5	3	3	4		
7	7	7	3	5	6	7		
8	7	7	6	7	7	6		
9	3	3	7	7	7	6		
10	4	5	7	3	3	4		
11	5	3	3	3	5	3		
12	3	4	5	4	5	6		

G2   *fx* =A2+B2+C2+D2+E2+F2

	A	B	C	D	E	F	G
1	X1	X2	X3	X4	X5	X6	solidarity
2	1	2	3	3	3	2	14
3	4	4	5	4	3	2	
4	5	3	3	5	5	6	
5	3	3	4	3	5	7	
6	6	5	5	3	3	4	
7	7	7	3	5	6	7	
8	7	7	6	7	7	6	
9	3	3	7	7	7	6	
10	4	5	7	3	3	4	
11	5	3	3	3	5	3	
12	3	4	5	4	5	6	

	A	B	C	D	E	F	G
1	X1	X2	X3	X4	X5	X6	solidarity
2	1	2	3	3	3	2	14
3	4	4	5	4	3	2	22
4	5	3	3	5	5	6	27
5	3	3	4	3	5	7	25
6	6	5	5	3	3	4	26
7	7	7	3	5	6	7	35
8	7	7	6	7	7	6	40
9	3	3	7	7	7	6	33
10	4	5	7	3	3	4	26
11	5	3	3	3	5	3	22
12	3	4	5	4	5	6	27

- arithmetic operators: + (addition), − (subtraction), * (multiplication), / (division), % (percent), and ∧ (exponents)
- comparison operators: = (equal to), > (greater than), < (less than), >= (greater than or equal to), <= (less than or equal to), and <> (not equal to)

- text operator: & (adjoins text), for example Jill&Paul become JillPaul
- reference operators: ":" (colon) means through all cells listed (i.e., G2:G12 includes all cells in column G from row 2 through row 12), "," (comma) means that some cells are selected from a series (i.e., "G2, G5" means only the cells G2 and G5 are involved in the process)

Operators ordinarily are executed in a set order. But the use of parentheses can control the sequence in which the order is executed. Percents are computed first, exponents second, multiplication and division third, and finally addition and subtraction. If researchers are not aware of this priority, they sometimes can get results that do not meet their expectations or needs.

USING THE MENU BAR

The *menu bar* includes items that make Excel look and operate as it does. The menu bar is a list of words that call up drop-down menus with instructions for Excel. The *toolbar* includes a host of symbols to control frequently used commands. A *worksheet* is a page of cells contained within a workbook. A *workbook* is an Excel file that contains one or more worksheets. These worksheets may contain input data, output, or even graphics, such as charts. Whenever a workbook is opened, these linked workbooks also are made available.

Ordinarily, the menu bar has nine different words. If you add a program such as *Statistics XL,* another menu of items will be added. You may either click on the menu bar to open a menu or you may type "Alt" and a letter that stands for the first letter of the item from the menu bar. Once a menu is opened, if a word has an underlined letter you may type this

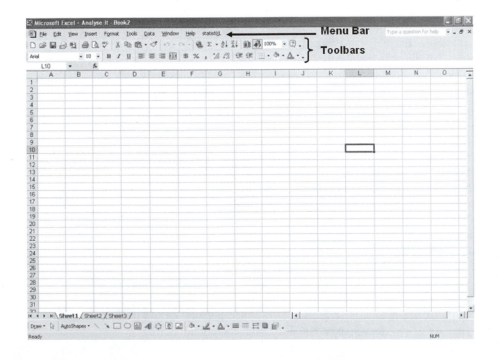

letter and the menu or window will be opened. If the items do not have key letters underlined, pressing the "Alt" button will turn on these indicators. This section will define the various menus on Excel XP.

The *File* menu includes a large number of commands:

- *New:* opens a new workbook file
- *Open:* opens a workbook file that already exists
- *Close:* concludes work on an open workbook file (you will be prompted to save your file)
- *Save:* saves the file that currently is open
- *Save As:* saves the open file with a different file name or file format
- *Save As Web Page:* saves the open file in HTML (Hypertext Markup Language) format for use in Internet applications
- *Save Workspace:* saves multiple workbooks as a Workspace, with all associated workbooks within the Workspace opened when the Workspace is reopened
- *Search:* searches for files to open based on the presence of certain information or words
- *Web Page Preview:* shows the appearance of the Excel XP file as a publication on a Web page
- *Page Setup:* shows available printing features for open files and worksheets
- *Print Area:* permits selecting only selected cells for printing (completed by highlighting the field for printing)
- *Print Preview:* shows the way the workbook or worksheet would look if printed with current specifications
- *Print:* displays options to control printing the open workbook or the displayed worksheet (including selecting the Print range: *All* pages or *Pages listed From-To, Number of copies,* and *Print what,* a highlighted *Selection, Active sheets,* or *Entire workbook*)
- *Send To:* sends a workbook or worksheet by e-mail
- *Properties:* stores information about the file (including *General, Summary, Statistics, Contents,* and *Custom* categories of information)
- *Recent Documents:* lists recently used or favorite files
- *Exit:* ends Excel XP session

The *Edit* menu focuses on controlling information and organizing data. In addition, it has a couple of tools that help control commands during the session.

- *Undo* [of several actions]: reverses the last action taken (also accomplished by the reverse arrow key ↰); this command also is accompanied by an alternate *Can't Undo* command
- *Repeat:* causes the last action to be repeated
- *Cut:* removes a selected item and places a copy on the clipboard where it may be pasted to another location
- *Copy:* keeps the selected items on the worksheet, and also places a copy on the clipboard where it may be pasted to another location
- *Office Clipboard. . . :* displays a window that includes a list of all the items currently on the clipboard
- *Paste:* applies contents from the clipboard to an active location

- *Paste Special. . . :* permits pasting a portion of a cell's contents to an active location
- *Paste As Hyperlink:* permits pasting a hyperlink to a Web site to an active location
- *Fill:* permits filling cells with data that are on the clipboard
- *Clear:* deletes contents of highlighted active cells
- *Delete. . . :* removes highlighted cells and determines how the remaining cells are to be adjusted as a result of the deletions
- *Delete Sheet:* removes the currently displayed worksheet from the workbook
- *Move or Copy Sheet. . . :* permits you to move or copy an entire worksheet to a different location or to a different workbook
- *Find. . . :* searches for text, characters, or values within a worksheet
- *Replace. . . :* replaces cell contents with different text, characters, or values
- *Go To. . . :* permits displaying a worksheet within a workbook
- *Links. . . :* opens a window to update or change links in a workbook
- *Object:* permits editing objects in a workbook

The *View* menu controls the different ways that toolbars, menu items, and worksheets are formatted:

- *Normal:* displays worksheets in standard (default) format
- *Page Break Preview:* shows locations of page breaks
- *Task Pane:* controls (by use of a check box) whether a window remains open, identifying the status of searches, new workbooks, clip art used, and clipboard content
- *Toolbars:* displays a submenu with 21 families of toolbars available for display (check boxes determine which ones are actively displayed)
- *Formula Bar:* check box allows control of whether the formula bar is or is not displayed
- *Status Bar:* check box allows control of whether the status bar is or is not displayed
- *Header and Footer. . . :* opens a dialog box to control any placement of headers or footers on each page
- *Comments:* views comments associated with specific cells
- *Custom Views:* opens the dialog box to control custom view options and handling of hidden fields
- *Full Screen:* fills the monitor screen with the current document
- *Zoom:* opens a dialog box that controls magnification of the display

The *Insert* menu allows the addition of objects and elements to the worksheet:

- *Cells. . . :* opens a dialog box to insert cells and control the locating of other cells, rows, and columns around them
- *Rows:* inserts a row before the specified row location
- *Columns:* inserts a column before the specified column location
- *Worksheet:* inserts a worksheet into a workbook
- *Chart. . . :* opens *Chart Wizard* to create charts (often works best if the researcher highlights columns and rows of data first)
- *Symbol:* opens a dialog box that lists symbols, including math and Greek alphabet symbols

- *Page Break:* inserts a page break to end at a certain line at the location needed
- *Function. . . :* opens a window with categories of functions, including statistical functions (also accessed by the ƒ)
- *Name:* a submenu controlling labeling of cell ranges
- *Comment:* opens a file into which a comment may be inserted into a cell
- *Picture:* opens a drop-down menu to control inserting pictures, clip art, or graphics into the worksheet
- *Diagram. . . :* opens the *Diagram Gallery* to guide development of organizational, cyclical, radial, pyramid, Venn, and target diagrams
- *Object. . . :* opens a dialog box to allow inserting an object created with any of 59 other applications
- *Hyperlink. . . :* opens a dialog box to control inserting hyperlinks to Web sites

The *Format* menu controls the different ways of displaying information in the worksheet:

- *Cells. . . :* opens a dialog box to control the way information is handled in cells, including the types of numbers to be used, alignment in cells, fonts, borders, patterns to fill cells, and protection of worksheets
- *Row:* opens a submenu to specify control of row height, methods of fitting data in rows, and whether the rows will be hidden or unhidden
- *Column:* opens a submenu to determine column-width methods of fitting data in columns, and whether the columns will be hidden or unhidden
- *Sheet:* opens a submenu that controls the renaming of the worksheet, the background color of the worksheet, and whether the sheet is to be treated as hidden or unhidden
- *AutoFormat. . . :* opens a dialog box to guide the design of the worksheet in choices from 17 different basic formats
- *Conditional Formatting. . . :* opens a dialog box that permits highlighting some cells for contrast with others
- *Style. . . :* records style settings for a worksheet for importation elsewhere

The *Tools* menu features options that are useful in statistical analysis of data. This list is one of the "growth areas" of the various versions of Excel, with each version adding selections to this set of options.

- *Spelling:* conducts a spell check for the worksheet
- *Error Checking. . . :* conducts a check for computation and logic errors on the worksheet
- *Speech:* moves to drop-down menus that use Microsoft Office voice recognition interfaces (*Speech Recognition. . .* check box configures the microphone and prepares to recognize the user's spoken voice with a set vocabulary; *Show Text to Speech Toolbar. . .* check box places the *Language Toolbar* on the topic of the spreadsheet allowing control of dictation and voice commands as well as handwriting and drawing pad input)
- *Share Workbook. . . :* produces a dialog box that allows different users to work on the same worksheet or workbook at the same time

- *Track Changes:* opens a drop-down menu that permits the user to highlight, accept, or reject changes made to the worksheet or workbook
- *Compare and Merge Workbooks. . . :* collects information from separate workbooks and compares the differences for efficient editing
- *Protection:* a set of options for controlling access to portions or all of worksheets or workbooks
- *Online Collaboration:* choices from drop-down menus permit users to work with other users by scheduling online meetings and hosting discussions on the Web
- *Goal Seek. . . :* when preparing worksheets that can be completed by others, this family of commands limits the values that are acceptable input
- *Scenarios. . . :* uses values from other workbooks typically to aid forecasting
- *Formula Auditing:* opens a drop-down menu that traces precedents and dependent cells to reveal interconnections, and permits checking the flow of computations in a specified formula
- *Tools on the Web. . . :* by using an open interface to the Internet, this set of tools permits adding programs and special support tools for Excel XP operations
- *Macro:* opens dialog boxes that examine, edit, and protect macros (routine sets of instructions that are repeated in spreadsheet operations) written in the Excel XP format; this selection also includes options to open the *Visual Basic Editor* and the *Microsoft Script Editor* for development of dedicated macros using those languages
- *Add-Ins:* opens an *Add-Ins* dialog box that permits installing supplemental programs and functions
- *AutoCorrect:* opens a dialog box that automates the correction of misspellings, Internet and network tags, and various smart tags for e-mail
- *Customize. . . :* opens a dialog box to control display of toolbar items and commands
- *Options. . . :* opens a dialog box with 13 file folders that control procedures such as automatic saving of files and ways to handle spell checks
- *Data Analysis. . . :* opens the previously described *Data Analysis* dialog box permitting use of the statistical analysis tools from the Analysis ToolPak

The *Data* menu characterizes ways to deal with and to record data.

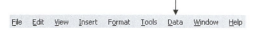

- *Sort. . . :* opens a dialog box to sort columns or rows in ascending or descending order. If only a column is sorted, the entire set of cases is not sorted as well (although highlighting the whole spreadsheet before sorting will cause the entire set of cases to be sorted), and blanks are treated as text data
- *Filter:* attaches a control to variables to specify cases that are to be included in the final data set
- *Form. . . :* opens a dialog box to monitor and control automating or simplifying data entry into spreadsheet cells
- *Subtotals. . . :* opens a dialog box to create a target cell to contain subtotals
- *Validation. . . :* opens a *Data Validation* dialog box to control the "validity" of input values, as well as displaying text messages and error alert messages
- *Table. . . :* opens a dialog box to define a set of cells as a table, which can be treated separately from the rest of the spreadsheet

- ***Text to Columns. . . :*** opens the *Text to Columns Wizard,* which guides the user through processes to format data from a single cell (perhaps imported from a text file containing data recorded in a word-processing format)
- ***Consolidate. . . :*** opens a dialog box to combine data into one set for use
- ***Group and Outline:*** opens submenus that allow users to group or ungroup highlighted cells, and to control the automatic creation of outlines isolated before or after a given point
- ***PivotTable and PivotChart Report. . . :*** opens the *PivotTable and PivotChart Wizard* to specify data sets and to create Pivot Tables and Pivot Charts
- ***Import External Data:*** opens submenus that control import data from other files, database systems, and Internet sources
- ***Refresh Data:*** controls updating existing worksheet files based on newly imported data
- ***Dataset. . . :*** opens a *Dataset Properties* dialog box that controls the layout and format of newly opened data sets

The ***Window*** menu enables the creation and opening of windows along with ways to identify characteristics of windows. At the bottom of the drop-down menu that appears, a list of open windows is provided. By clicking on any of these labels, the user is taken to that Excel XP window and it becomes active. The specific commands include the following items.

File   Edit   View   Insert   Format   Tools   Data   Window   Help   statistiXL

- ***New Window:*** opens a new window that initially appears to duplicate the current active window (changes then can be made without altering the basic structure or format of the worksheet)
- ***Arrange:*** opens a dialog box that controls the ways all Excel XP windows are displayed on the screen (tiles, horizontal, vertical, cascade) at the same time
- ***Hide:*** controls whether a highlighted cell's content is hidden
- ***Unhide:*** controls whether a cell's content (hidden by the ***Hide*** command) is revealed
- ***Split:*** divides the active window into two parts that may be edited separately
- ***Freeze Pane:*** creates panes of the worksheet that are visible when scrolling elsewhere in the sheet
- ***Unfreeze Pane:*** reverses the ***Freeze Pane*** command

The ***Help*** menu features a host of sources of information for users. It is extensive in advanced versions of Excel. The *Office Assistant* takes the form of an icon that floats on the spreadsheet during sessions. It provides prompts and guidance through some functions that Excel believes may be challenging for users. Although it can be turned off, this assistant often is useful to have handy when the user is in the process of getting familiar with Excel. The ***Help*** menu includes a powerful help function in ***Microsoft Excel Help***. Clicking this option causes a Microsoft Excel Help dialog box to emerge with tabs to help users get information through an *Answer Wizard;* an *Index* that allows specific words to be used as a basis for searching for information; and *Contents,* which helps secure information by guiding users through a user's manual organized by topics. In addition to these sources of information, the ***Help*** menu also includes the following:

File   Edit   View   Insert   Format   Tools   Data   Window   Help

- *Show Office Assistant:* keeps the Office Assistant icon on the spreadsheet
- *Hide Office Assistant:* removes the Office Assistant icon from the spreadsheet, although pressing F1 activates the Office Assistance help menu
- *What's This?:* creates a question mark symbol that may be attached to any location on the spreadsheet to check for further information from Help messages
- *Office on the Web:* uses open Internet connections to link to the Excel Web site
- *Lotus 1-2-3 Help:* provides guides for those who wish to use the family of Lotus 1-2-3 for conversions to Excel XP
- *Detect and Repair:* attempts to provide limited corrections and repairs of corrupted files and to provide some program corrections
- *About Microsoft Excel:* provides basic documentation from Microsoft involving program licenses, versions, system information, available technical support, and items that have been disabled to permit Excel XP to operate efficiently

TOOLBARS

Toolbars provide icons or pictures to run Excel XP commands. The toolbars that actually are shown are chosen from a long list, and displaying all of them would result in a researcher

having very little room to display data. So, to control the tool space that is used, the *View* menu is chosen.

Then the *Toolbars . . .* option is selected. The drop-down menu that appears shows a large (and growing) list of toolbars you could place on the worksheet. Clicking on the selection makes the toolbar immediately visible on the top of the spreadsheet beneath the menu bar. Once icons are displayed on the spreadsheet, clicking on one will activate a set of commands. If the cursor is placed over an icon, a brief statement of the meaning of the icon will be presented.

HOW TO RUN STATISTICS FROM THE ANALYSIS TOOLPAK

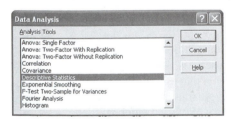

One might suppose that there is not much more to running statistical analyses than taking data that are on one worksheet and going to the *Data Analysis* section of the *Tools* menu. And to some extent, you would be correct in this assumption. To use the *Data Analysis* tools, the researcher goes to the *Tools* menu and clicks on the *Data Analysis* command.

These tools include these statistical collection options:

- *ANOVA: Single Factor:* one-way ANOVA of differences among means of two or more samples
- *ANOVA: Two-Factor With Replication:* standard two-way analysis of differences from two independent variables with at least two levels each (requires equal sample sizes)
- *ANOVA: Two-Factor Without Replication:* a random effects ANOVA (two-way analysis of variance with only one sample element per group)

- *Correlation:* Pearson product-moment correlation
- *Covariance:* the unstandardized correlation coefficient showing the covariation of two variables
- *Descriptive Statistics:* for selected variables, analyses include means, standard errors, medians, modes, standard deviations, variances, kurtosis estimates, skews, ranges, minimums, maximums, sums, counts, and confidence intervals
- *Exponential Smoothing:* trend line from forecast data adjusted for the error in prior forecasts (the smoothing constant determines how strongly forecasts respond to errors in the prior forecast)
- *F-Test Two-Sample Variance:* test of homogeneity of variance (with F at .025, one-tailed; this statistic also is known as Hartley's H)
- *Fourier Analysis:* linear equation solving via the Fast Fourier Transform and/or its inverse
- *Histogram:* a form of bar chart with variables on both the X and Y axes representing continuous measures
- *Moving Average:* trend line from forecast data adjusted for the mean of previous periods
- *Random Number Generation:* random numbers from normal, uniform, discrete, Bernoulli, binomial, Poisson, or patterned distributions
- *Rank and Percentile:* tables of rank and percentile ranks for the values in the data set
- *Regression:* multiple regression correlation that uses the least squares method to identify a line of best fit for a data set involving one dependent variable (called Input Variable Y) and multiple independent variables (called Variables X)
- *Sampling:* selects a sample from the entire data set
- *t Test: Paired Two-Sample for Means:* t tests for pairs of scores from the same events measured more than once
- *t Test: Two-Sample Assuming Equal Variances:* t tests for the means of two independent groups of events
- *t Test: Two-Sample Assuming Unequal Variances:* t tests for the means of two independent groups of events when the variances are unequal and a single variance estimate of within-groups error must be used
- *z Test: Two-Sample for Means:* use of the z test for differences between means where population variances are known and samples are not relatively small

Individual examples of the use of these tools are found in the book's chapters that deal with specific statistics. Naturally, when a researcher is interested in finding additional information or definitions of these tools, there are some options. One of the most useful is to highlight the statistic in question. Clicking on the right mouse button produces a prompt that asks *"What's This?"* Clicking on this prompt with the left mouse button provides a *Help* window that describes the tools in question and provides further definitions. Another source of useful information is found on the *Help* menu. After selecting *Microsoft Excel Help*, a dialog box appears into which the researcher may type the specific tool by name to seek information about the statistic of interest.

Using the *Data Analysis* functions involves more than simply highlighting some columns and clicking on a statistical option. The data often must be prepared. For instance, it should be noted that Excel often requires special arrangements of data, such as requiring that multiple independent variables be located in adjacent columns. Furthermore, Excel does not make it possible to use files with missing data.

USING FUNCTIONS

The researcher can select a cell and insert a preset function. The list is a long one that includes more than 450 specific options. To access them, the researcher who has selected a cell has some choices. One option involves going to the ***Insert*** menu and selecting 𝑓ₓ. A second option involves clicking 𝑓ₓ from the toolbars. A third option involves clicking the down arrow next to the sigma sign Σ ⁻ on the toolbar. The drop-down menu includes simple sums of scores, averages, counts of the number of events, minimum observed values, and maximum observed values. Then the ***More Functions. . .*** option that follows these functions may be selected to obtain a full list of choices. Regardless of the method used, the functions are found in an *Insert Function* dialog box. The functions are categorized according to whether they are functions useful in financial reporting, date and time assessment, mathematical and trigonometry applications, statistical tools, lookup and reference management options, database operations, text manipulation, logical relations, tools to assess information about data being processed, engineering functions, or user-defined functions.

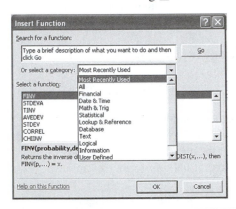

The functions list a name for an operation and then include information about the ways to identify the data to be included.

As an example to illustrate how all functions operate, suppose a researcher wishes to obtain the standard deviation of a set of scores for a variable. Selecting *Statistics* from the drop-down menu of the ***Insert Function*** dialog box produces a series of options. By selecting the *STDEV* function, the researcher can call for a sample standard deviation. Clicking on the *OK* button produces another dialog box that controls identification of the data for analysis.

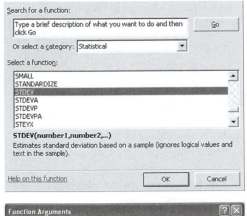

In this case, the researcher may click on the 🖻 as well as 🔢 to return to the worksheet and highlight rows or columns of data, which are copied into the *Function Arguments* box as shown here.

When the 🖻 as well as 🔢 are clicked, the data set is defined and the ***Function Arguments*** dialog box completed. Clicking the OK button places the answer to these calculations in the specified cell of the worksheet as shown on the left.

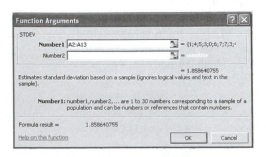

In the formula field on the menu, the actual statement of the function is presented. This formula may be copied and pasted as part of other analyses. In many cases, the researcher may wish to enter a direct statement of a function into a cell. The pattern for these functions is relatively common. It includes a name for the function (in abbreviated form) followed by a list of the cell range where the data are located. So, square root is called with the command SQRT(A2:A13). This statement means that the square root is to be taken of the data in the range extending from column A, row 2, all the way through column A, row 13.

In addition to square root, some of the most common basic functions include sums, means, and absolute values. As illustrations, these functions may be called as follows:

- SUM is the total of a host of scores, such as in the formula field example, "=SUM(E2: F13)." This formula results in adding all the data values extending from row 2 through row 13 of both columns E and F.
- AVERAGE is the arithmetic mean of a total of a set of scores, such as in the formula field statement "=AVERAGE(A3:A13)." This statement commands that the mean be taken of the values in rows 3 through 13 of column A.
- ABS is the absolute value of a score, even if that score is another function. For instance, the researcher could enter the value "ABS(AVERAGE(A3:A13))." This statement yields the absolute value of the mean of scores located in rows 3 through 13 of column A.

Sometimes, such as when analysis of variance or multiple regression correlation is computed, the output requires more space than a cell or two. Hence, researchers often find it useful to specify output at locations that are beyond the range of rows of data.

A word of warning is appropriate. Although the situation is improving, in some cases involving detailed analyses, getting data analyzed can be troublesome in Excel XP. For instance, to compute a chi-square test of independence, the researcher must use a function call after making sure that the data are in the form of observed counts and expected counts. Thus, researchers find that Excel XP may require a little data preparation to complete some assessments of interest.

APPENDIX B

Using SPSS[†] 12 for Windows[††]

SPSS 12 is a collection of statistical subroutines that permit you to use personal computers to analyze research data. SPSS (short for "Statistical Package for the Social Sciences" when it began in the late 1960s) initially ran on mainframe computers. The current version is designed to run on the Windows operating system. Version 12 is especially designed for such operating systems as Windows XP.[††]

This guide is designed to give you enough information to get you started with entering your own data and understanding what is involved in using the SPSS system. Sections deal with how to enter and screen your own data in SPSS, how to create indexes from scales, the commands in the SPSS system, how to deal with output, and alternative menu systems.

HOW TO ENTER AND SCREEN YOUR OWN DATA IN SPSS

When you open SPSS 12 for Windows, you will see a spreadsheet that looks very similar to others that are arrayed in rows and columns. If you have a data file you wish to use, you will be prompted to open it. If you wish to use an Excel spreadsheet, current versions of SPSS permit you to use it with no particular effort. If you wish to enter your own data, SPSS provides you with a blank form, such as that seen on page 504. This window is called the *Data Editor,* and there are several different fields of interest. The *Menu Bar* has a set of words that, when clicked open, provides menus of options. The *Tool Bar* has a series of buttons that are shortcuts to frequently used options that can be entered from the menu bar items. You do not have to show any toolbars if you wish.

[†]SPSS is a registered trademark of the SPSS Corporation.

[††]Windows, Windows XP, Excel, Powerpoint, and Equation Editor are registered trademarks of Microsoft Corporation.

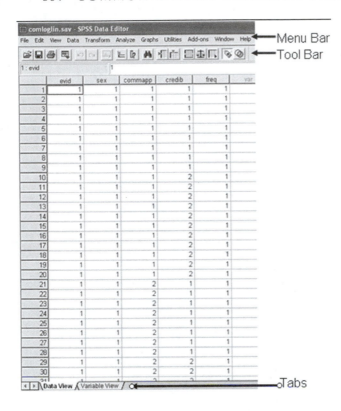

At the bottom of the spreadsheet are two folder *Tabs,* much like the tabs on a file folder. When you click different tabs, you move back and forth from the ***Data View*** to the ***Variable View.*** The Data View shows a spreadsheet with each case in a separate row. The columns identify the variables on which measures are taken.

Entering Data

You may place values in any cell to enter data, although most researchers enter data one case at a time. To see how the data are identified, you may click on the Variable View tab. In the Variable View below, one can see data that have different sorts of variables (numeric and string) and use different sorts of alignments. Furthermore, some variables (i.e., GPA) have numbers that are placed behind the decimal point, whereas others do not. Some variables are from a continuous "scale," and one (i.e., AORB) is a nominal-level measure with simple names of categories. To change any of these forms, the researcher needs only to click on a field and make the desired changes.

	Name	Type	Width	Decimals	Label	Values	Missing	Columns	Align	Measure
1	evid	Numeric	11	0		None	None	8	Right	Scale
2	imp_hilo	Numeric	11	0		None	None	8	Right	Scale
3	topic	Numeric	11	0		None	None	8	Right	Scale
4	names	Numeric	11	0		None	None	8	Right	Scale
5	quals	Numeric	11	0		None	None	8	Right	Scale
6	attitude	Numeric	11	0		None	None	8	Right	Scale
7	att5	Numeric	8	0		None	None	8	Right	Scale
8	clarity	Numeric	11	0		None	None	8	Right	Scale
9	believab	Numeric	11	0		None	None	8	Right	Scale
10	aorb	String	1	0		None	None	1	Left	Nominal
11	age	Numeric	11	0		None	None	8	Right	Scale
12	sex	Numeric	11	0		None	None	8	Right	Scale
13	gpa	Numeric	11	1		None	None	8	Right	Scale
14	class	Numeric	11	0		None	None	8	Right	Scale
15	v1	Numeric	11	0		None	None	8	Right	Scale

If the researcher finds a cell in which the data need to be replaced, the cell may be clicked and the new data value may be substituted. Unlike standard spreadsheet programs, a researcher cannot insert a formula into a cell of data. If you enter data in a cell outside the boundaries of the defined data file, the data rectangle is extended to include any rows and/or columns between that cell and the file boundaries. There are no "empty" cells. For numeric variables, blank cells are treated as missing values. For string variables, however, a blank is considered a valid value.

To enter your own data, it is important to start with a blank or *New* spreadsheet from the *File* menu. Then, select *Data* to produce a grid of cells. You must then identify and name your variables. You may click on the *Variable View* tab and then go to the cell in the top left column, which is located under *Name.* Then, names of variables may be provided. Researchers can choose any descriptive labels, but they must not be longer than eight characters and must not include special characters such as periods or blanks.

Initially, all the variables are assumed to be numeric variables of a maximum of 11 digits and no places behind the decimal point. But if a researcher wishes to make a change, clicking the Numeric field brings up a *Variable Type* dialog box that permits the researcher to specify the type of variable from eight options. In addition, the number of places behind the decimal point may be specified.

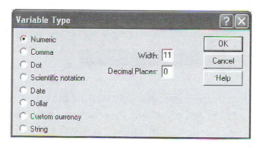

Clicking other columns introduces chances to change the ways variables are treated. Clicking on

- *Widths:* increases or decreases the data display width
- *Decimals:* adds or subtracts the number of decimal places in the data
- *Label:* specifies a name for a variable that should be used in output (this label may be more than eight characters but fewer than 121 characters)

- *Values:* are labels of no more than 60 characters that are to be assigned to each number of a variable (for a sex variable, for instance, 1 might be labeled "male" and 2 might be labeled "female").

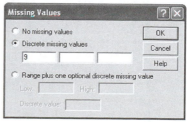

- *Missing:* data may be identified by using a value for a variable (e.g., researchers using 7-point scales may use 0 or 9 to represent missing responses). When these values are found for a variable, the response is viewed as missing, rather than as an actual numeric response.

As the dialog box shows, more than one missing value may be used.

- *Columns:* options allow the researcher to control the width of the display of the variable in the *Data View* without changing the values in each cell. Researchers also can click and drag the borders of columns to adjust widths.
- *Align:* options permit researchers to display the cell data with the values placed in the *Center,* flush to the *Right,* and flush to the *Left.*
- *Measure:* identifies the variable's level of measurement on the *Nominal, Ordinal,* or *Scale* (i.e., interval or ratio) levels.

If the same choices are to be shared from one variable to another, the cells making the choices may be copied (either by use of the *Copy* function from the *Edit* menu or by using the Control-C keyboard combination) and then pasted to the cells of other variables copied (either by use of the *Paste* function from the *Edit* menu or by using Control-V keyboard combination).

By clicking the *Data View* tab, the researcher can see the arrangement of variables in columns of the spreadsheet. Data from each respondent may be put on each row. If you find that you have left out a variable, you may add a variable by selecting *Insert Variable* from the *Data* menu.

A new variable labeled VAR00001 will be inserted and you may define the variable by clicking on the *Variable View* tab and identifying the characteristics you prefer. If you wish to insert a piece of data, you may go to the end of the data and enter information (after clicking on the *Data View* tab). Or, if you wish to insert a case at a particular location, you may click on a row to highlight it. Then, selecting *Insert Case* from the *Data* menu creates a blank row above the highlighted row. New case data may be added at this point. To delete a case, one need only highlight the row and press the delete key. To delete a variable, the researcher highlights the column of interest and then uses the delete key.

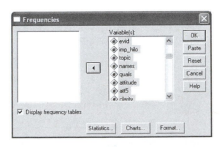

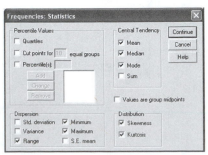

Data Screening

To verify that the data make sense, it is helpful for the researcher to screen the data to ensure that keystroke errors are not present. One way is to complete a descriptive analysis output. This matter may be handled easily from the *Analyze* menu; the researcher simply selects *Descriptive Statistics* followed by *Frequencies. . . .* From the *Frequencies* dialog box, the researcher may highlight all the variables in the first box and use the arrow button to transfer them to the *Variable(s):* field.

After clicking on the *Statistics. . .* button, the researcher may select statistics that are likely to reveal whether erroneous scores have been entered. The researcher would probably select the mean, median, mode, skewness, and kurtosis, but particularly revealing would be the range and minimum and maximum scores.

HOW TO ENTER DATA FROM A WORD PROCESSOR

Sometimes, researchers have data in word-processing or ASCII files. Rather than reentering the lines of data, SPSS permits them to use the files as data files, but there are some steps that must be taken to accomplish this task. In particular, the word-processing file must be saved as a text file (with the suffix "txt").

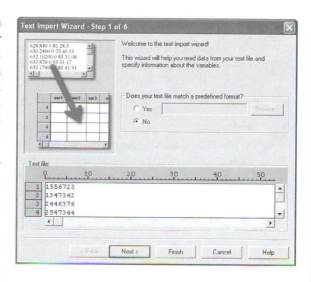

From the *File* menu, select *Read Text Data.* The researcher then is prompted to find the "txt" file location and to select it. This step transfers the researcher to the Text Import Wizard, where the data are identified in a "text file:" window in the same format in which they were in the word-processing program. By following instructions, the transfer may be made.

In the Text Import Wizard, researchers are prompted to insert "break points" that separate one variable's scores from another's. As shown on the right, these break points are inserted by clicking in the spaces between the scores that come from different variables. If these separations are not included, SPSS assumes that all the numbers in the row represent scores of one variable. If you place spaces between the variables in the original text file, the Text Import Wizard will assume that they are located to separate variables. Then, the researcher will be prompted to verify that this practice is the case.

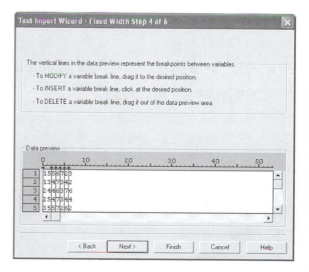

Variable names may be added by the Text Import Wizard or through the SPSS Variable View folder. Either way, at the end, the researchers have produced an SPSS data file ready for editing, analyzing, and saving.

	age	good	wise	positive	benefic	appropri
1	15.00	5.00	6.00	7.00	2.00	3.00
2	13.00	4.00	7.00	3.00	4.00	2.00
3	24.00	4.00	6.00	3.00	7.00	6.00
4	25.00	4.00	7.00	3.00	4.00	4.00
5	35.00	5.00	7.00	2.00	6.00	2.00
6	32.00	3.00	6.00	7.00	3.00	5.00

If any mistaken scores were present, this analysis probably would reveal them. For instance, if the researcher used 5-point scales and finds a maximum score of 8 on some measure, a likely keystroke error has been identified. After selecting these statistics, the researcher would click on the *Continue* button. In the *Frequencies* dialog box, the researcher then would click on the *Charts. . .* button. In the *Frequencies: Charts* dialog box, the researchers will find it most useful to select the option to have *Histograms* of each variable produced.

SPSS for Windows Viewer or the *Output* **Window.** Researchers often call this element the Output since SPSS uses that shorthand when the window is minimized on a computer screen. A nice quality of the Windows Viewer is that objects displayed there can be copied and inserted as needed into other work. In addition, some editing of tables and charts can be completed in this window. Another valuable feature of the Output window presentation is that researchers can "right click" (use the right button on the mouse) to highlight output and then receive guidance about the interpretation of results by selecting *Results Coach* from the dialog box that appears. Although help does not exist on every topic, it does exist for many of the most complicated statistical issues.

HOW TO CREATE INDEXES FROM SCALES

Researchers find it important to develop a set of measures that can be verified as sound and then used in subsequent analysis. Individual scales may be compared with others to determine reliability. Then, indexes that are composites of these scales may be used in the final studies.

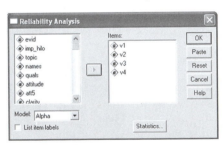

Researchers start by identifying scales that are alleged to measure common things. Sometimes, researchers complete factor analyses of scales (see Chapters 15 and 16) to identify the underlying dimensions of several scales. But regardless of the method, researchers eventually compute reliability estimates. One of the most common ways to determine reliability is Cronbach's coefficient alpha (see Chapter 6). From the *Analyze* menu, the researcher selects *Scale* and then *Reliability Analysis. . . .* In the resulting dialog box, the scales that are believed to form a composite index are highlighted and moved to the *Items:* field.

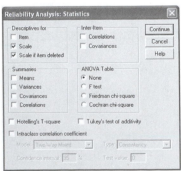

The researcher then clicks on the *Statistics. . .* button to select statistics for the analysis of the four scale items. In the Statistics dialog box, the researcher should select (at minimum) *Scale,* and *Scale if item deleted.* Although other statistics could be selected, this minimum is enough to illustrate the process of using basic SPSS here.

Then, the researcher will click the **Continue** button followed by the **OK** button. The output for the analysis below reveals that the four scales combine to produce one measure with an overall reliability coefficient alpha of .8646. In addition, deleting any item results in coefficients that are lower than the combined reliability coefficient. Hence, the researcher would conclude that the four items (identified here only as V1, V2, V3, and V4) may be added to create an index.

```
R E L I A B I L I T Y A N A L Y S I S - S C A L E (A L P H A)
N of

Statistics for      Mean        Variance    Std Dev     Variables
SCALE               20.5579     22.5297     4.7465      4

Item-total Statistics
                Scale         Scale        Corrected
                Mean          Variance     Item-          Alpha
                if Item       if Item      Total          if Item
                Deleted       Deleted      Correlation    Deleted
        V1      15.1563       13.9327      .7091          .8300
        V2      15.3079       12.3130      .8159          .7835
        V3      15.4896       13.4252      .6972          .8336
        V4      15.7199       13.3096      .6424          .8582

Reliability Coefficients
N of Cases  =  .864.0    N of Items  =  4
Alpha  =  .8646
```

To create an index, researchers must use at least one of the operations from the **Transform** menu:

Transform is a set of tools that create composite scales, score data, and recode elements.

- **Compute** permits a new variable score to be created by adding, subtracting, multiplying, and dividing other variables. In the example considered here, a composite attitude measure called ATTITUD may be created by the **Compute** function. After selecting **Compute** from the **Transform** menu, the researcher may create a new variable by adding the four scale items V1, V2, V3, and V4. As can be seen, ATTITUD is identified in the **Target Variable:** field as the name of the new variable. The actual computation involving preexisting variables is inserted in the **Numeric Expression** field. When the researcher clicks the **OK** button, the new variable is inserted at the end of the list of variables. Researchers create basic measures early in the process of their research projects and use transformations to automate the process.

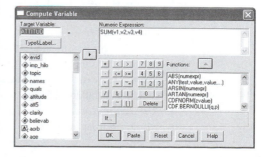

There are other options that may be used in the **Transform** family of tools, such as the following:

- **Recode** changes scores from their original numbers to new values. For instance, a researcher might wish to reverse values before adding negatively phrased scale items into a scale. When using **Recode** commands, researchers must decide if they wish to recode values **Into Same Variables** or whether they wish to recode **Into Different Variables**

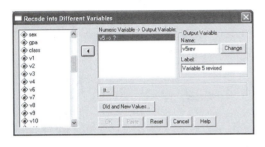

(in which case a new variable is created with the revised values). In a typical case, researchers might wish to recode a negatively phrased scale. To do so, the researcher selects the negative item and then selects **Recode** from the **Transform** menu. Most researchers transform variables into different variables because it is difficult to get back to original values if a mistake is made along the way. To transform into different variables, entries are made as shown in the dialog box to the left. To complete this recoding process, the researcher must insert a new name in the field marked **Output Variable, Name.** A variable label also may be added to help the researcher keep track of the changes. When the recodes are to occur under specific circumstances, the researcher clicks the **If. . .** button.

To insert the changed values, the researcher clicks the button identified as **Old and New Values. . .** or **Recode into Different Variables: Old and New Values.** The process

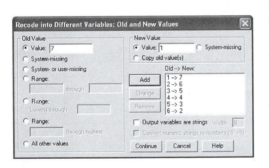

involves identifying the current value in the **Old Values** field and inserting the revised value in the **New Value** field. The researcher keeps adding recodes until all desired changes are made.

If researchers wish (and it often is desirable), missing values may identified by selecting the **System- or user-missing** radio button and providing information about the values or the range of values to be treated as missing. Clicking **Continue** and **OK** buttons completes the recoding process and, if it has been desired, a new variable is located at the end of existing columns of variables.

Although other **Transform** options are available, most researchers find that they rely most on **Compute** and **Recode.** Other transforms include the following:

- **Visual Bander**: a set of tools that creates new variables that group existing variables according to common values to create ordinal or categorical values from existing variable scores
- **Count**: a transform that creates a new variable that is a count of the number of times a particular value appears in the data for a variable
- **Rank Cases**: a transform that creates a new variable that is some form of rank (simple ranks, normal and Savage scores, and percentiles of existing variables)
- **Automatic Recode**: a transform that changes numeric and string variables into successive whole-number integers. String variables are categories (1, 2, 3, etc.) based on alphabetic order.

- ***Create Time Series:*** a transform that creates new variables based on modifications of existing variables. Transform options often used in time-series analyses feature differences between successive values in the series; seasonal differences; centered moving averages (averages of values around a current value); prior moving averages (averages of preceding values around a current average); running medians (medians of values surrounding and including the current value); cumulative sums of values; lag (values of preceding cases based on lag orders); leads (values of subsequent cases, based on the specified lead order, that are based on the number of cases following the current case); and smoothing (values based on major data smoothers).
- ***Replace Missing Values:*** a transform used mostly in time series analyses (where missing values are problematic) that substitutes otherwise "missing values" with the mean or median of nearby points, linear interpolations, or linear trend at point methods
- ***Random Number Seed:*** an option that allows the researcher to set the starting value of the pseudo-random number generator so that a specific sequence of random numbers can be used again
- ***Run Pending Transforms:*** a command that permits the researcher to execute transforms

COMMANDS IN THE SPSS SYSTEM

Not to be confused with different editors, there are two major ways that researchers may issue commands in SPSS. One is to use the Syntax Editor, and the other is to use the Data Editor.

The Syntax Editor

At one time, SPSS consisted of a series of commands that were entered into control lines in a "mini program" designed by the researcher. Though most of the commands now are handled through the menus and dialog boxes, sometimes researchers wish to rely on direct commands (and sometimes the only way to accomplish the researcher's objectives is to use the command language).

To determine what command language syntax is available, after selecting a procedure, the researcher may click on the *Help* button. In the dialog box that appears, clicking a *Syntax* button produces a listing of the command line options for that procedure, as shown on page 512.

The command syntax may be copied to other files and used to guide specific analyses. If you have a command file already written, it may be imported and opened from the ***File*** menu by selecting ***Open*** and ***Syntax. . .*** from the options that follow. In these cases, the new file is opened in the Syntax Editor.

In reality, most researchers find that when they have occasion to use the Syntax Editor, they need to change only a few things. Hence, it makes sense to let the program create many of the data lines, which can be modified or copied to another file for subsequent use. To access the command lines created by a procedure, the researcher looks for the Paste button on a procedure dialog box. This button opens a list of commands that may be copied and pasted to a command file for editing. The researcher then may modify the file as needed. Sometimes, researchers find it useful to include the data in the list of command lines. These lines are identified by a "BEGIN DATA" line with an "END DATA" line after the last line of data.

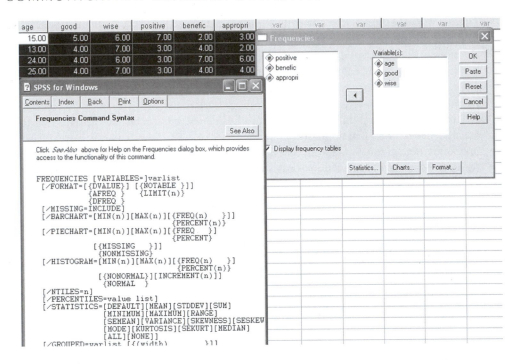

Commands in the Data Editor

In the Data Editor, the basic commands are menu driven, although toolbars are available to help researchers use shortcuts to many of these menu options. Aside from the *Analyze* commands that have been covered in the textbook proper, and the *Transforms* tools that already have been covered, the menu items not previously listed will be identified here.

On the menu bar, families of operations are identified in words that, when clicked, reveal a host of other options, choices, and actions for the researcher. In addition, these words have critical letters that are underscored. When a researcher holds down the "ALT" key and types the first letter of the menu item, the menu is activated and a drop-down menu of choices appears.

The menu for *File* contains the following options:

- *New,* which creates a new file of some sort. In drop-down menus, researchers indicate whether they wish to create *Data, Syntax, Output, Draft Output,* or *Script* windows.
- *Open,* which opens a file that already exists. In drop-down menus, researchers indicate what types of files they wish to open. *Data* opens data files of different formats, including SYSTAT, Excel, SPSS portable, Lotus, SYLK, dBase, and text files. *Syntax* opens syntax editor files in standard SPSS (.sps, .spo [viewer document]), draft viewer (.rtp), and SPSS Script (.sbs) formats. *Output* opens files in SPSS (.sps, .spo), draft viewer (.rtp), and SPSS Script (.sbs) formats. *Script* opens SPSS Script (similar to Visual Basic Script) from SPSS (.sps, .spo), draft viewer (.rtp), and SPSS Script (.sbs) formats. *Other* opens file types including SPSS (.sps, .spo), draft viewer (.rtp), and SPSS Script (.sbs) and, well, "other" formats.

- *Open Database,* which calls up the Database Capture Wizard and facilitates use of established data sets
- *Read Text Data,* which imports text files as data sets and uses the Text Import Wizard to identify characteristics of the data
- *Save,* which saves a copy of the active file to some storage device
- *Save As,* which lets the researcher save that active file with a new name or file format (including ASCII with or without tab delimiters, previous versions of SPSS, Excel, 123-REL, SYLK, and versions of dBase)
- *Mark As Read Only,* which allows the researcher to save a file as "read only" to prevent the accidental corruption or deletion of original data files
- *Display Data Info,* which presents details about the file's format and variable structure, called a "data dictionary"
- *Cache Data,* which creates a data cache in the researcher's computer so that subsequent analyses can be completed without reading all the data from the file anew
- *Stop Processor,* which interrupts processing of data
- *Switch Server,* which adds or changes operations to a different server for any network in use (switching servers causes closing of all open windows)
- *Print Preview,* which displays the way printed output will appear on final copy
- *Print*, which controls printing the window or material or selected items
- *Recently Used Data,* which uses a submenu listing data files that have been used in the recent past
- *Recently Used Files,* which uses a submenu listing nondata files that have been used in the recent past
- *Exit,* which ends the SPSS session

The menu for *Edit* has the following commands:

- *Undo,* which reverses a command (also may be activated by pressing the *Control* and *Z* keys or clicking on the reverse arrow button)
- *Redo,* which changes back a mistaken *Undo* command (also may be activated by pressing the curved arrow button key)
- *Cut,* which deletes a highlighted item in a cell and stores it on the system clipboard (also may be activated by pressing the *Control* and *X* keys)
- *Copy,* which stores a highlighted item in a cell on the system clipboard without deleting the original cell material (also may be activated by pressing the *Control* and *C* keys)
- *Paste,* which places an item from the system clipboard into a highlighted cell (also may be activated by pressing the *Control* and *V* keys)
- *Paste Variables,* which pastes characteristics from one variable to a newly created variable identified on the *Variable View* tab
- *Clear,* which removes data from highlighted cells
- *Find,* which permits researchers to search for specific values or words in a worksheet (also may be activated by pressing the *Control* and *F* keys)
- *Options,* which are ways that SPSS operations may be modified to meet the desires of the researchers. When clicking this selection, a dialog box with 10 folder tabs is identified. As with any tab page, to get a change recorded, the researcher must press the *Apply* button before clicking on the *OK* button.

The options found on the *General* tab page are the following:

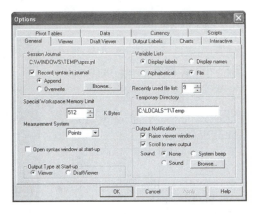

– **Session Journal:** In the *General* tab, researchers may click on the box to **Record syntax in journal.** At the beginning of each session a record will be kept of all commands (those run from syntax windows and commands created by menu-drive selections) from a session.

– **Special Workspace Memory Limit:** This option identifies the amount of working memory to execute commands. Although the default is 512K, if the researcher gets a message indicating a need to change workspace or that the system is "out of memory," this default value may be changed.

– **Measurement System:** The system used for identifying spacing and location on charts, tables, and cells is indicated in points, inches, or centimeters.

– **Open Syntax Window at Start-Up:** To open the SPSS session with the command Syntax Window, the appropriate box may be selected. If it is not checked, the menu-drive system that relies on dialog boxes will be the default.

– **Variable Lists:** This option controls how names of variables will be displayed. Researchers who wish variable labels to be displayed may specify this option in preference to variable names. Displays of names in the worksheet may be in alphabetical order or file order (the order that the variables actually were entered and added to the list).

– **Recently Used Files List:** A limit is set on the number of recently used files that will be shown in the dialog box when **Recently used files list** is selected from the *File* menu.

– **Temporary Directory:** The drive and folder where temporary files used in the SPSS runs are to be stored.

– **Output Type at Start-Up:** The viewer initially used for scanning output is identified. The choices include "The Viewer," which handles pivot tables (that may be edited and modified after data analyses are completed), and "The Draft Viewer," which treats pivot tables as text output and treats charts as metafiles (metafiles have all the fonts and border styles of the original table output).

– **Output Notification:** The notice that SPSS has executed a program and that output is available may be provided automatically or excluded.

In addition to the tabs for *General* Options, other options exist for **View, Draft Viewer, Output Labels, Charts, Interactive** features, **Pivot Tables, Data, Currency,** and **Scripts.** Detailed options are available with each.

The *View* menu provides control over worksheet appearance and use of toolbar shortcuts:

- **Status Bar:** This menu choice removes or reinstates the status bar at the bottom of the worksheet (a checkmark reinstates it, and removing the checkmark removes the status bar).
- **Toolbars:** This choice produces a menu with all possible toolbars for display. The researcher may choose those that he or she wishes to include and remove those that are

not desired for display. Nine toolbar families are possible, and options exist for using large or small buttons to identify them.

- *Grid Lines:* This selection controls whether grid lines are included on the worksheet.
- *Value Labels:* This selection toggles back and forth to display variable value labels or suppress them from displays.
- *Variables:* This section toggles back and forth from *Data* and *Variable* views.

The *Data* menu permits the researcher to controls the way data are handled in the worksheet. The dialog boxes produced by selecting this menu item contain the following:

File Edit View Data Transform Analyze Graphs Utilities Add-ons Window Help

- *Define Variable Properties:* This selection begins a scan of data to identify the types of scores that are in the data set for variables of interest. The option is especially valuable for cleaning data.
- *Copy Data Properties:* This selection initiates a "wizard" to copy data set properties from an external file.
- *Define Dates:* This selection identifies how dates will be identified consistently in the data file (a step often vital for researchers planning time series analyses).
- *Insert Variable:* This choice inserts a new column on the far left of the worksheet, identified by such a label as "var00001." Researchers may supply variable names and other crucial information by clicking on the *Variable View* tab and filling in appropriate fields.
- *Insert Case:* After highlighting a row in the worksheet, this option inserts a row of blank cells immediately above and permits the researcher to add new data.
- *Go to Case:* Choosing this option opens a dialog box that sends the researcher to a specific case number.
- *Sort Cases:* This selection sorts data by ascending or descending values of a particular variable (numerically or alphabetically).
- *Transpose:* This selection switches the rows and columns on the worksheet and saves the result as a new file.
- *Restructure:* This selection initiates the "Restructure Data Wizard" that restructures multiple variables into single variables. The approach may structure existing variables into cases or cases into variables, or may transpose variables into cases of a new variable.
- *Merge Files:* Variables or data from another file are combined with an open file (often the changes involve updating files of data examined over time).
- *Aggregate:* This selection allows researchers to combine groups of cases into a single summary based on the value of a grouping variable (often useful in creating data for command lines analyzing categorical data).
- *Orthogonal Design:* This selection can either *Generate. . .* a display of the orthogonal main effects of several variables or factors or *Display. . .* the effects. This process is completed without testing all combinations of variable levels as part of interaction terms.
- *Split File:* This choice produces a dialog box that defines ways to split data files into subgroups based on the values of a specific variable. Then, depending on the choices of the researcher, the results may compare the groups or treat them as separate elements of output.
- *Select Cases:* A dialog box prompts the researcher to make a selection of a subset of the data file for statistical analyses to follow. The selection may be based on satisfying

requirements specified by an "If" statement, a random sample of cases, a sampling based on time or case range, or a sampling based on the values of a "filter" variable that identifies the cases to be included.

- **Weight Cases:** This selection gives cases different weights, often as preparation for analysis of "count" data.

Analyze is a set of statistical subroutines that makes up SPSS. There are more than 100 statistics in the system, and this book has included ways to employ these routines and to interpret them. Hence, the details of these tools will not be included here. It might be noted, however, that many descriptions of the statistics can be found in some detail through the **Help** menu.

File   Edit   View   Data   Transform   Analyze   Graphs   Utilities   Add-ons   Window   Help

The **Graphs** menu moves the researcher to dialog boxes that take variables from the data set and complete graphic displays popularly requested in scholarly work. Seventeen families of graphs include bars, lines, areas, pies, and high-low charts. Although drawn from the realm of manufacturing work, rather than

File   Edit   View   Data   Transform   Analyze   Graphs   Utilities   Add-ons   Window   Help

communication studies, Pareto diagrams and control charts for different sorts of data are included. In addition, the options include boxplots and error bars that often are used in social science research. The routines also include scatterplots, histograms, P-P charts, Q-Q charts, sequence charts, ROC graphs, and examinations of time series data (including autocorrelation, cross-correlation, and spectral analyses).

The **Utilities** menu permits researchers to inspect details of data sets, manage menus, and control additional programming environments. There are seven options on this menu.

File   Edit   View   Data   Transform   Analyze   Graphs   Utilities   Add-ons   Window   Help

- **Variables** includes a dialog box that permits the researcher to identify characteristics about specific variables. Such matters as missing values, value labels, and variable formats are provided for each variable. Although these variable definitions cannot be changed in these dialog boxes, researchers can go to specific variables and identify related syntax for variables.
- **OMS Identifiers** provides a set of terms and subroutine syntax for use of the Output Management System command language that permits researchers to use SPSS command language and to write output in SPSS, XML, HTML, or text formats.
- **Data File Comments** inserts comments about data files and permits these comments to be included in output.
- **Define Sets** identifies a selection of variables to be considered in various analyses. Defining and labeling a set of variables can improve speed of processing when there are large numbers of variables. Called a "set," these collections of variables can be called forth by their unique names.
- **Use Sets** opens a dialog box that permits the researcher to use the sets from past definitions. Two "default" sets already are included: "ALLVARIABLES" (a set with all variables in the file—in essence, no subset of variables at all) and "NEWVARIABLES" (a set with only newly created variables). Although other sets may be included, no sets will be used if the "ALLVARIABLES" set is retained in the "Sets in Use" list.
- **Run Script** allows the researcher to call up a programming environment. Using the dialog box editors and object browsers, researchers may insert programs from the Sax BASIC.

- *Menu Editor* presents the researcher with a dialog box that permits control over the way menus and submenus are displayed. The researcher may insert menu items that run command syntax files or other applications, or that send data to Excel, Lotus 123, SYLK, and dBASE programs. In addition, menu items can be used to call up user-defined scripts.

Add-ons consist of a menu of information about auxiliary programs that can be run as part of the SPSS platform, even though they are not currently part of the basic SPSS system. Dialog boxes guide readers to information about supplemental programs available through SPSS, such as SPSS Maps, SPSS Exact Tests, and SPSS Complex Samples (including "Sampling Plan Wizard," "Complex Sample Selection," "Analysis Plan Wizard," "Complex Sample Descriptives" statistics, and use of "Complex Sample Tabulate" displays). *Add-ons* include a menu of 13 *Applications,* including AMOS. The other applications are Answer Tree, Clementine, Decision Time, Sample Power, SigmaPlot, SigmaStat, SmartViewer Web Server, SPSS Data Entry, SPSS ReportWriter, SPSS Server, TextSmart, and WebApp. A *Services* menu permits registered SPSS users to seek consulting and training assistance.

Window allows the researcher to transition from one open screen to another. The *Window* list includes *Minimize all Windows,* a command that minimizes all open windows (without closing them).

The *Help* menu is a system of sources of assistance to the researcher. There are eight options on the *Help* menu.

- *Topics* allows the researcher to get an explanation of information about SPSS and statistics in the form of a list of *Contents* organized in chapter form, a detailed and searchable *Index,* and a detailed *Find* tab identifying families of information.
- *Tutorial* includes instructional information organized by content lessons. In addition, searchable *Index* and *Find* tabs permit finding guidance on specific activities.
- *Case Studies* are extended tutorial slide presentations that illustrate program operations in base, advanced models, and multiple regression applications.
- *Statistics Coach* is a tutorial on the ways that appropriate statistics may be selected to analyze different sorts of data.
- *Command Syntax Reference* opens a file to review SPSS command language.
- *SPSS Home Page* sends the researcher to the home page of SPSS (provided that a browser is available and that an Internet link is open). This source has many detailed descriptions of methods and answers to many questions about challenges involved in using SPSS.
- *About. . .* provides information about the SPSS version and license you are using.
- *Register Product. . .* allows the user to go online to register the software.

DEALING WITH OUTPUT

In the Output Window, SPSS users have a host of choices to copy and edit materials for insertion in other reports. For researchers, these choices are quite helpful in preparing research papers. There are several ways that such information can be handled. The major tools mentioned in this brief review include the *Output View Editor* and *Editing Pivot Tables*.

Output View Editor

Although the *Output View Editor* appears to duplicate the function of the *SPSS Data Viewer,* there are some big differences. This treatment considers commands that are different from those options available on the *SPSS Data Viewer* set of menus. The *Output Area* is divided into an *Outline Area* (also known as the Information Area) and a *Content Area* (which, in turn, is a place where many other "editable" fields may be found). By clicking on fields in the *Content Area,* different menu options become active and the researcher may complete editing steps.

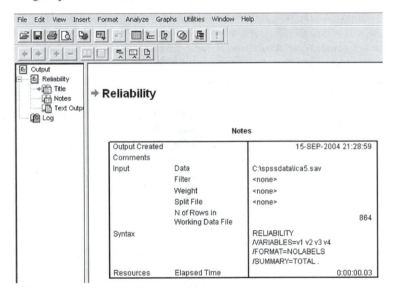

The first menu with some unique commands is the *Edit* menu.

Although the use of *Undo* (⤺), *Cut,* *Copy,* and *Options* is duplicated in both the *Data* and *Output* views, other commands are distinct to the *Output Viewer.* These commands are as follows:

- *Copy Objects:* After a section of the Content Window is highlighted, selecting the *Copy Objects* command places a copy of the selection on the clipboard. Unlike the ordinary *Copy* command, this option keeps all the original formatting and spacing. In contrast, the simple *Copy* command places the text of the selected material on the clipboard, but does not keep all the formatting.
- *Paste After:* Despite its different label, *Paste After* means the same as the general *Paste* command.
- *Paste Special:* After an object is saved to the clipboard by *Copy* or *Cut* commands, the *Paste Special* command permits the researcher to paste the selected material into the *Output Viewer* as an SPSS Output Navigator Object or as a picture (metafile).

- *Delete:* After an object is selected, this command eliminates the object.
- *Select All:* This option results in highlighting all objects in the *Output Viewer*'s content pane.
- *Select:* This option allows the researcher to identify some output from the entire content pane. Because output often contains several analyses, the researcher often finds this option useful to manage output.
- *Outline:* This option allows the researcher to manipulate the structure of elements in the outline pane.
- *Links:* This option is conditional on whether links are open. The command controls such links with active files.
- *Objects:* Once an object in the content pane is highlighted, this option transforms into a menu called *SPSS Pivot Table Object*. A pivot table is an object of information that SPSS permits the researcher to use to create other objects such as graphs. The menu options include *Edit* (which allows the researcher to alter the way information is presented graphically or, to some extent, analytically) or *Open* (which allows the researcher to change format or presentation form). The *Open* command opens a window with an *SPSS Pivot Table* menu.

The second menu with unique elements is *View*, which contains a series of choices that permits researchers to control the ways that output information is revealed.

In addition to the *Status Bar* and *Toolbar* commands, some unique alternatives are available on the *View* menu.

- *Expand* or *Collapse:* After selecting outline elements, the content area may alternatively show them in their full form or limit their display.
- *Show* and *Hide:* After selecting outline elements, the content area may alternatively show or fail to show the elements. The objects are not deleted, but their display is controlled in the content pane.
- *Outline Size:* The size of the display in the information area is controlled.
- *Outline Font:* The appearance of materials in the outline is controlled.

The third menu with unique elements is *Insert*, which contains a series of choices that permits researchers to modify the objects that are displayed and to use other subprograms to create additional displays. Selecting the *Insert* menu opens a long list of choices and dialog boxes.

- *Page Break* and *Clear Page Break:* This choice permits researchers to control where they wish printing on a new page to begin. Previously chosen options may be reversed by the *Clear Page Break* command.
- *New Heading:* This selection adds another section to the outline.
- *New Title, New Page Title*, or *New Text:* This selection inserts another heading, title, or text box into the display of the *Content* pane. These options change the display of toolbars to include controls for fonts and commonly used terms in SPSS.

- *Interactive **2**-D Graph* and *Interactive **3**-D Graph:* This selection switches the researcher to dialog boxes dealing with subprograms that produce two-dimensional graphs and three-dimensional (sometimes called "exploded") graphs.
- *Old **G**raph:* This selection opens a dialog box to open a saved chart file.
- *New **M**ap:* When appropriate objects are selected, this option permits inserting geographic maps to display data relationships.
- *Text **F**ile . . . :* Text files in the LST format may be opened and imported into the output window.
- *Object . . . :* This choice opens a dialog box that permits the researcher to insert objects from any of more than 30 formats, including Excel, Powerpoint, and Microsoft Equation Editor.

The fourth menu with unique elements is ***F**ormat.*

Commands are provided to take objects in highlighted *Content* area objects and align elements to the left, center, or right.

Pivot Table Editing

Most of the output objects may be identified as standard tables. Yet researchers sometimes find it necessary to make modifications in such materials to enhance clear presentations of reports. SPSS permits output tables to be reformatted and greatly modified by use of a series of commands. To activate the *Pivot Table Editor*, researchers begin by selecting a table object from the *Content* pane. Then, the researcher chooses *SPSS Pivot Table Object* from the *Edit* menu.

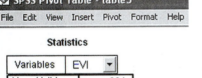

Then the researcher chooses *Open*. In the dialog box that appears, researchers find unique commands permitting them to control what appears in tables. Both content and data display portions are fair game. As seen in the dialog box at the left, there are six menu items and a seventh category dedicated to *Help* (which deposits the researcher at the general help resources for SPSS, rather than help specifically related to editing pivot tables).

The remaining menus are dedicated to the following areas.

- *File:* The *File* menu is limited to one command, *Close*.
- *Edit:* The *Edit* menu includes several commands that are generic to lists of *Edit* options, including *Cut, Copy, Paste*, and *Paste Special*. Some other commands are unique to the *Pivot Table Editor:*
  - *Group* or *Ungroup:* Highlighted items in a table may be grouped or ungrouped to permit common or separate treatments.
  - *Drag to Copy:* This control toggles on and off to control moving elements of the display from one location to another.

- *Create to Graph:* The researcher may take data and select any of seven forms of graphs (bar, dot, line, ribbon, drop-line, area, and pie) to display the table information.

- *View:* The *View* menu controls a number of commands including whether or not to show the Edit Pivot Table Toolbar, and whether to *Hide* or *Show* all or part of the pivot table. In addition, whether or not to show gridlines for editing purposes is included.
- *Insert:* This menu permits researchers to add another title, caption, or footnote to the table object.
- *Pivot:* This menu system allows major reformatting of tables and gives the pivot table system much of the reason for its name. The commands deal with several matters of interest to researchers.
  - *Bookmarks:* To save a format for a table, researchers "bookmark" a view of the table. Researchers often find this feature of editing pivot tables to be especially good insurance against mistakes. Researchers label the table form and may save all elements of the table.
  - *Transpose Rows and Columns:* After selecting *Table* or *Table Body* (if one does not wish to change locations of table titles as well) from the *Edit* menu, the researcher who chooses *Transpose Rows and Columns* will find the "row" and "column" elements switched.
  - *Move Layers to Rows* and *Move Layers to Columns:* These commands take levels on a table and represent them either in row or column divisions.
  - *Reset Pivots to Defaults:* To return to the original table setup, the researcher may select this reset option.
  - *Pivoting Trays:* To change the identification of items, pivoting trays are used to move editing icons to each tray in the order that the researcher wants the items displayed (left to right or top to bottom). To use these tools, *Pivoting Trays* must be turned on from the *Pivot* menu. This step creates a dialog box that permits movement of icons to different locations in pivoting trays to arrange elements of the table.
  - *Go to Layer:* Short for *Go to Layer Category*, this option permits researchers to control editing locations by layers.
- *Format:* This set of commands controls fonts, number format, cell widths, and scores of table presentation elements by use of eight commands and six dialog boxes of specific options.

It also should be mentioned that right-clicking on the mouse will result in a drop-down menu of commonly used commands that researchers may access. In addition, shortcuts are available through the toolbar system controlled by the *View* menu.

ALTERNATIVE EDITING ENVIRONMENTS

There are many editing environments and accompanying menu systems in SPSS. Some have developed from past versions of SPSS and remain incorporated into current versions. In addition to the *Data Editor*, *Output Editor*, and *Pivot Table Editor*, some of the most prominent are the following:

Draft Viewer Window: Researchers may choose to present output as text materials instead of objects and pivot tables. The menus become important in the Draft Viewer because much of the initial formatting of output is not retained. In particular, the *Insert* menu is important to identify necessary page breaks. The *Format* menu includes many changes in the ways text is highlighted.

Chart Editor Window: Researchers may modify high-resolution charts. Yet this form of editing does not recalculate statistics. Any changes made in the chart are not automatically reflected in other chart elements. Changes typically are restricted to alterations in fonts, changes in axes, and forms. As a shortcut to these methods, the researcher may double-click the chart in the *Output Navigator* and then may click on specific chart elements to select items, followed by double-clicking to open a dialog box to guide researchers through chart-editing processes. To change chart types, the researcher may use the *Gallery* drop-down menu from the *Graphs* menu.

Script Editor: Because the SPSS command syntax can use scripts written in Sax BASIC, an editing window for this form is made available. This form permits debugging of such scripts as the major function of the window.

Appendix C

Tables

APPENDIX C.1

Standard Normal Curve

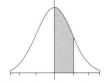

Z	.00	.01	.02	.03	.04	.045	.05	.06	.07	.08	.09
0.0	.0000	.0040	.0080	.0120	.0160	.0179	.0199	.0239	.0279	.0319	.0359
0.1	.0398	.0438	.0478	.0517	.0557	.0576	.0596	.0636	.0675	.0714	.0753
0.2	.0793	.0832	.0871	.0910	.0948	.0968	.0987	.1026	.1065	.1103	.1141
0.3	.1179	.1217	.1255	.1293	.1331	.1350	.1368	.1406	.1443	.1480	.1517
0.4	.1554	.1591	.1628	.1664	.1700	.1718	.1736	.1772	.1808	.1844	.1879
0.5	.1915	.1950	.1985	.2019	.2054	.2071	.2088	.2123	.2157	.2190	.2224
0.6	.2257	.2291	.2324	.2357	.2389	.2405	.2422	.2454	.2486	.2517	.2549
0.7	.2580	.2611	.2652	.2673	.2704	.2719	.2734	.2764	.2794	.2823	.2852
0.8	.2881	.2910	.2939	.2967	.2995	.3009	.3023	.3051	.3078	.3106	.3133
0.9	.3159	.3186	.3212	.3238	.3264	.3277	.3289	.3315	.3340	.3365	.3389
1.0	.3413	.3438	.3461	.3485	.3508	.3520	.3531	.3354	.3577	.3599	.3621
1.1	.3643	.3665	.3686	.3708	.3729	.3739	.3749	.3770	.3790	.3810	.3830
1.2	.3849	.3869	.3888	.3907	.3925	.3934	.3944	.3962	.3980	.3997	.4015
1.3	.4032	.4049	.4066	.4082	.4099	.4107	.4115	.4131	.4147	.4162	.4177
1.4	.4192	.4207	.4222	.4236	.4251	.4258	.4265	.4279	.4292	.4306	.4319
1.5	.4332	.4345	.4357	.4370	.4382	.4388	.4394	.4406	.4418	.4429	.4441
1.6	.4452	.4463	.4474	.4484	.4495	.4500	.4505	.4515	.4525	.4535	.4545
1.7	.4554	.4564	.4573	.4582	.4591	.4695	.4599	.4608	.4616	.4625	.4633
1.8	.4641	.4649	.4656	.4664	.4671	.4675	.4678	.4686	.4693	.4699	.4706
1.9	.4713	.4719	.4726	.4732	.4738	.4741	.4744	.4750	.4756	.4761	.4767
2.0	.4772	.4778	.4783	.4788	.4793	.4796	.4798	.4803	.4808	.4812	.4817
2.1	.4821	.4826	.4830	.4834	.4834	.4840	.4842	.4646	.4850	.4854	.4857
2.2	.4861	.4864	.4868	.4871	.4875	.4876	.4878	.4881	.4884	.4887	.4890
2.3	.4893	.4896	.4898	.4901	.4904	.4905	.4906	.4909	.4911	.4913	.4916
2.4	.4918	.4920	.4922	.4925	.4927	.4928	.4929	.4931	.4932	.4934	.4936
2.5	.4938	.4940	.4941	.4943	.4945	.4945	.4946	.4948	.4949	.4951	.4952
2.6	.4953	.4955	.4956	.4857	.4959	.4959	.4960	.4961	.4962	.4963	.4964
2.7	.4965	.4966	.4967	.4968	.4969	.4970	.4070	.4971	.4972	.4973	.4974
2.8	.4974	.4975	.4976	.4977	.4977	.4978	.4978	.4978	.4979	.4980	.4981
2.9	.4981	.4982	.4982	.4983	.4984	.4983	.4984	.4985	.4985	.4986	.4986
3.0	.4987	.4987	.4987	.4988	.4988	.4988	.4989	.4989	.4989	.4990	.4990
3.1	.4990	.4991	.4991	.4991	.4992	.4992	.4992	.4992	.4992	.4993	.4993
3.2	.4993	.4993	.4994	.4994	.4994	.4994	.4994	.4994	.4995	.4995	.4995
3.3	.4995	.4995	.4995	.4996	.4996	.4996	.4996	.4996	.4996	.4996	.4997
3.4	.4997	.4997	.4997	.4997	.4997	.4997	.4997	.4997	.4997	.4997	.4998
3.5	.4998	.4998	.4998	.4998	.4998	.4998	.4998	.4998	.4998	.4998	.4998
3.6	.4998	.4998	.4999	.4999	.4999	.4999	.4999	.4999	.4999	.4999	.4999
3.7	.4999	.4999	.4999	.4999	.4999	.4999	.4999	.4999	.4999	.4999	.4999
3.8	.4999	.4999	.4999	.4999	.4999	.4999	.4999	.4999	.4999	.4999	.4999
3.9	.49998										
4.0	.49998										
4.5	.499998										
4.9	.4999998										

APPENDIX C.2

Random Numbers

127	275	054	576	974	438	900	773	118	682
796	457	043	782	012	309	372	298	196	698
095	455	550	524	819	058	014	199	949	847
228	863	271	236	910	833	700	573	719	231
842	383	636	766	831	864	542	183	042	796
674	678	109	730	366	215	433	586	153	534
653	827	572	299	517	272	659	733	673	206
542	623	153	786	346	447	217	030	590	711
761	710	300	306	807	246	310	961	636	478
596	175	814	445	258	601	440	767	143	951
238	926	598	917	871	951	353	221	534	385
790	882	297	397	417	204	838	593	615	127
571	881	757	783	330	383	247	024	319	225
386	286	878	109	080	415	011	244	938	579
048	291	144	996	614	209	054	138	448	680
347	555	866	566	414	178	097	199	764	428
074	541	390	979	888	867	438	795	074	186
798	670	590	394	355	470	424	587	721	171
983	751	929	285	232	156	055	097	630	330
464	070	999	196	531	398	088	971	412	073
332	057	513	121	925	443	899	850	610	161
750	249	882	478	053	867	222	260	410	781
456	462	780	709	165	738	848	557	402	871
149	685	439	475	476	491	322	623	251	202
582	807	358	720	144	815	414	491	347	402
259	617	413	875	680	814	441	759	818	939
084	070	685	080	846	585	493	333	419	523
378	778	041	130	067	120	702	158	913	333
377	225	351	227	024	924	238	184	887	221
667	317	063	331	910	580	849	377	549	230
216	956	403	907	744	680	922	601	260	987
227	543	141	072	075	248	938	511	733	479
471	001	359	154	666	876	904	455	819	162
251	519	874	249	439	820	579	969	803	827
196	391	552	616	994	043	014	335	461	826
416	249	353	949	080	699	160	827	984	820
314	167	980	553	253	605	145	747	542	756
199	258	445	602	933	988	131	611	495	379
285	435	241	339	361	793	911	808	165	372
963	054	289	968	594	201	876	642	152	009
694	169	084	903	328	051	193	915	335	339
303	129	291	977	391	128	908	411	710	163
886	002	792	679	485	807	207	429	012	393
593	931	466	042	632	096	541	424	757	234
039	726	335	784	096	154	810	492	480	588

(Continued)

(Continued)

789	672	690	538	084	730	984	653	383	738
547	862	153	293	750	054	903	383	800	497
921	702	614	034	291	052	271	143	355	899
465	219	616	928	523	981	851	914	149	967
243	331	866	040	565	031	761	377	917	297
567	010	517	185	042	075	896	604	429	688
441	270	425	106	177	892	553	269	037	558
068	200	076	546	886	040	564	631	571	115
330	161	970	234	919	781	364	735	985	632
049	913	635	446	750	301	215	183	457	704
551	903	563	958	913	428	280	471	856	708
433	665	276	838	108	037	386	503	875	698
137	047	946	783	600	128	560	196	302	902
769	833	584	195	548	944	073	077	705	432
146	491	054	084	292	875	482	525	432	698
434	148	824	027	469	666	402	167	903	051
200	807	646	152	718	811	665	681	995	662
896	231	634	785	897	174	659	733	522	396
369	759	806	990	466	311	010	891	442	431
616	170	216	888	947	550	939	025	674	343
270	965	817	420	127	257	254	753	457	197
778	337	593	722	112	628	373	580	013	278
333	418	864	751	759	926	303	615	991	105
213	803	316	122	259	425	633	498	765	116
947	993	891	061	885	800	545	209	915	550
057	814	403	705	164	938	738	741	973	734
595	332	884	551	503	702	185	759	209	534
339	406	504	965	254	724	684	361	990	763
673	451	995	377	236	746	828	944	835	103
864	726	234	435	157	438	840	926	633	826
297	226	089	734	701	404	875	040	868	028
543	642	089	613	563	893	401	965	155	595
619	354	423	599	436	300	363	131	725	213
635	043	923	434	508	044	192	870	233	631
786	718	328	043	011	461	477	033	741	837
336	337	470	015	686	831	370	768	692	101
523	677	250	708	492	811	129	993	890	916
805	119	522	573	594	497	557	174	475	435
787	262	808	813	604	620	455	217	827	067
596	351	329	922	934	772	252	871	296	854
363	996	621	488	290	522	055	463	344	862
378	750	236	123	021	873	686	802	648	890
431	350	130	643	004	607	238	842	537	022
842	219	819	227	695	744	051	115	795	040
857	662	701	369	052	108	596	333	212	574
691	459	506	701	208	411	203	884	961	482
155	669	110	069	624	702	848	635	363	542
810	174	127	440	491	190	770	730	983	553

792	654	063	795	294	263	207	516	279	171
363	954	474	250	863	193	079	187	432	387
667	537	353	737	990	866	715	967	138	315
055	125	100	458	134	348	701	707	121	589
167	959	157	335	100	240	523	428	136	140
978	524	307	170	403	005	852	249	266	905
212	114	567	656	799	291	347	071	550	925
515	646	052	639	960	550	496	854	097	939
665	170	836	418	325	050	819	732	661	404
265	782	389	010	499	197	554	962	725	770
522	396	635	622	235	826	687	911	958	451
512	086	502	530	822	351	777	499	360	041
119	787	020	891	636	833	339	039	730	891
779	279	550	949	290	509	891	947	485	239
770	368	592	287	771	738	736	167	238	354
706	955	836	551	509	765	715	351	899	477
384	967	851	944	762	654	330	941	535	046
516	104	238	975	257	232	970	496	584	833
791	589	485	744	864	756	175	519	670	998
290	413	056	169	026	219	971	062	834	014
769	079	983	491	605	198	850	402	489	640
946	632	758	760	105	639	896	486	029	752
706	497	839	014	598	464	058	904	091	590
442	843	355	152	356	635	475	303	752	001
231	292	519	416	815	743	556	054	482	630
332	328	363	090	507	431	218	210	648	409
250	434	231	430	942	037	605	321	205	100
051	604	200	257	272	794	450	041	316	566
426	589	282	904	999	399	275	941	259	782
834	490	448	380	172	161	870	984	074	123
184	331	050	540	944	803	323	467	216	781
477	638	823	110	694	546	721	535	303	526
066	516	899	275	750	826	147	235	648	916
796	472	987	435	342	991	469	343	208	794
477	822	179	552	417	003	004	993	091	818
535	431	039	486	646	589	121	650	814	613
559	055	391	565	115	539	405	686	426	206
878	769	172	027	275	862	097	116	784	288
132	104	764	380	687	666	413	298	718	773
889	102	276	494	579	965	684	771	744	412
048	787	270	851	102	524	987	828	930	465
166	006	851	474	423	064	487	838	547	794
141	107	475	428	192	270	037	650	885	570
564	016	229	675	147	015	191	151	713	313
426	219	484	281	417	513	929	826	181	354
160	189	311	090	886	267	545	207	266	537
678	437	235	286	621	254	377	999	583	442
810	241	804	933	359	763	461	929	509	206

(Continued)

(Continued)

211	577	192	861	821	336	217	920	950	620
237	728	835	913	079	135	430	868	894	754
832	568	763	883	529	126	566	746	004	889
110	711	448	356	061	701	287	778	367	454
849	770	615	658	507	619	695	223	034	382
233	306	994	178	848	454	177	150	013	882
373	776	922	799	307	936	919	976	847	952
632	516	883	455	137	944	423	824	011	727
678	627	104	772	163	892	945	938	277	928
012	241	953	504	849	569	676	959	856	653
872	832	818	473	387	452	286	004	489	883
484	340	985	347	701	232	119	416	901	017
974	646	128	059	045	947	679	998	392	877
342	927	913	093	979	052	928	492	145	132
811	766	248	510	050	577	745	017	851	745
786	447	406	292	284	084	465	136	718	952
355	595	313	117	238	147	119	164	835	335
094	713	308	563	534	342	239	911	151	867
059	554	244	452	912	116	304	078	515	024
966	088	868	263	362	475	129	996	900	112
507	624	786	274	801	123	624	210	944	585
416	848	929	898	536	249	528	781	756	080
039	503	969	788	723	083	422	789	066	652
226	255	042	496	302	512	175	193	217	884
864	719	621	167	759	168	987	795	178	988
171	299	677	820	426	441	684	432	664	675
451	166	539	344	542	102	583	313	707	051
683	886	117	124	776	152	374	172	720	447
016	620	411	209	184	585	011	921	801	266
798	186	998	998	373	262	604	797	738	277
106	602	252	022	057	983	256	867	352	331
866	200	946	143	324	237	884	102	783	603
133	263	003	393	018	195	865	510	312	823
052	080	188	949	072	458	486	499	038	047
552	380	772	268	642	109	498	850	006	515
908	004	897	860	971	942	523	128	277	411
013	641	487	946	035	551	777	778	932	352
155	941	073	034	645	835	751	521	993	367
681	012	918	592	691	088	120	621	729	046
574	702	365	690	636	950	727	613	095	848
349	831	105	165	621	685	056	694	680	727
859	962	400	709	869	506	156	927	735	546
593	010	603	479	967	374	502	647	471	043
076	004	200	248	284	344	929	182	917	425
560	557	486	226	309	967	398	751	967	481
191	485	214	546	282	256	731	479	687	261
708	489	156	431	904	187	667	885	216	744
423	382	884	666	885	716	782	266	771	647

271	705	954	475	708	172	311	676	668	577
637	381	518	478	707	032	345	499	731	963
590	343	697	645	821	298	854	276	693	347
772	765	957	899	007	974	786	346	752	364
012	143	059	305	384	375	669	900	139	263
253	185	679	780	230	239	812	232	138	791
515	754	700	283	327	293	534	834	484	393
512	655	228	157	308	623	877	286	449	392
078	357	936	091	196	903	766	631	997	939
130	692	557	282	851	595	080	884	002	954
131	491	782	601	556	035	778	034	472	670
165	589	714	839	710	595	471	945	802	928
419	517	909	976	391	967	481	924	230	329
909	382	918	206	468	418	660	444	944	598
547	657	131	027	824	214	301	513	032	207
843	876	078	614	735	289	610	395	720	024
450	300	251	913	798	331	606	664	122	079
369	635	522	328	184	397	417	694	266	922
985	356	609	552	222	645	458	367	483	675
166	058	700	187	341	560	302	178	663	232
651	297	795	823	076	151	344	833	916	998
665	739	924	344	721	921	396	061	406	995
141	316	821	500	682	139	962	609	024	674
166	717	108	101	468	769	789	388	264	078
863	581	401	767	487	408	866	151	029	292
028	770	529	127	200	969	551	035	303	811
644	178	705	532	348	028	522	872	148	081
384	630	325	018	659	153	953	401	339	128
806	467	832	329	594	357	813	577	623	309
542	213	533	142	703	182	872	503	306	499
327	726	971	226	720	368	059	937	852	228
814	369	882	863	504	565	642	666	077	339
894	575	668	461	181	602	855	247	155	217
085	396	065	615	208	004	729	816	976	223
629	116	521	646	187	077	434	708	440	079
185	499	155	134	481	081	124	804	263	497
281	207	511	428	324	583	409	678	358	967
214	563	937	912	359	333	203	398	326	605
767	056	359	388	328	601	095	588	699	450
932	631	642	575	372	753	916	845	488	210
082	515	403	970	053	950	471	702	935	249
130	966	233	163	746	957	563	775	613	324
280	061	453	189	337	112	895	112	217	144
079	727	354	240	496	106	103	193	923	065
127	296	366	558	752	124	834	285	105	519
783	199	309	597	366	161	074	622	429	203
124	415	255	664	430	162	633	960	435	365
913	657	315	211	797	319	359	427	313	775

(Continued)

(Continued)

675	325	067	970	890	719	377	789	985	671
050	694	118	650	135	551	760	339	947	873
406	959	744	580	905	555	505	809	306	692
528	447	369	982	169	231	368	014	615	170
998	810	799	090	738	614	270	657	065	296
738	596	556	812	182	905	271	559	378	264
600	870	530	277	286	117	189	702	002	096
732	925	260	857	235	510	640	919	146	531
596	126	929	337	729	025	248	566	317	317
170	211	850	523	695	273	098	060	063	297
911	305	078	748	200	456	241	552	140	599
143	563	768	398	999	128	477	485	425	633
825	579	288	507	671	508	635	946	533	785
229	857	855	243	852	662	797	770	386	110
964	191	790	524	987	498	132	430	241	046
708	416	581	026	371	072	496	971	994	396
461	696	989	894	827	335	320	848	984	173
599	059	834	732	918	570	050	742	386	918
119	376	840	504	351	508	889	742	544	099
940	970	955	243	806	647	783	335	535	421
291	927	150	784	771	945	245	749	653	511
555	686	341	613	888	730	609	822	759	032
780	220	591	861	939	704	351	485	377	357
770	617	598	053	021	587	438	739	848	527
704	563	287	299	150	414	233	530	532	835
883	964	011	666	804	204	039	599	377	202
216	048	600	547	949	704	584	365	565	215
293	144	841	441	886	473	933	163	210	333
197	555	770	980	741	181	986	881	722	499
814	863	280	371	850	923	942	666	688	469
227	126	103	173	697	474	662	690	571	924
704	958	311	423	207	183	944	922	076	756
600	271	463	205	046	033	189	710	602	440
298	642	130	357	015	733	514	206	746	286
574	309	165	054	112	596	901	657	990	222
806	388	272	989	194	401	117	898	748	583
230	524	571	371	041	859	301	073	254	919
783	283	555	324	990	730	503	932	205	356
768	291	929	653	196	608	856	475	016	557
003	052	068	907	762	471	807	446	245	015
335	139	022	380	937	063	746	442	986	127
945	310	865	812	750	840	738	838	290	149

APPENDIX C.3

Minimum Correlations for
Significance at Different Sample Sizes

Number of Events in Sample	Minimum Correlation for Significance at p = .10 (two tailed) p = .05 (one tailed)	Minimum Correlation for Significance at p = .05 (two tailed) p = .025 (one tailed	Minimum Correlation for Significance at p = .02 (two tailed) p = .01 (one tailed)	Minimum Correlation for Significance at p = .01 (two tailed) p = .005 (one tailed)
3	.988	.997	.9995	.9999
4	.900	.950	.980	.990
5	.805	.878	.934	.959
6	.729	.811	.882	.917
7	.669	.754	.833	.875
8	.621	.707	.789	.834
9	.582	.666	.750	.798
10	.549	.632	.715	.765
11	.521	.602	.685	.735
12	.497	.576	.658	.708
13	.476	.553	.634	.684
14	.458	.532	.612	.661
15	.441	.514	.592	.641
16	.426	.497	.574	.623
17	.412	.482	.558	.606
18	.400	.468	.542	.590
19	.389	.456	.528	.575
20	.378	.444	.516	.561
21	.369	.433	.503	.549
22	.360	.423	.492	.537
23	.352	.413	.482	.526
24	.344	.404	.472	.515
25	.337	.396	.462	.505
26	.330	.388	.453	.496
27	.323	.381	.445	.487
28	.317	.374	.437	.479
29	.311	.367	.430	.471
30	.306	.361	.423	.463
32	.296	.349	.409	.449
34	.287	.339	.397	.436
36	.279	.329	.386	.424
38	.271	.320	.376	.413
40	.264	.312	.367	.403

(Continued)

Appendix C.3 (Continued)

Number of Events in Sample	Minimum Correlation for Significance at p = .10 (two tailed) p = .05 (one tailed)	Minimum Correlation for Significance at p = .05 (two tailed) p = .025 (one tailed	Minimum Correlation for Significance at p = .02 (two tailed) p = .01 (one tailed)	Minimum Correlation for Significance at p = .01 (two tailed) p = .005 (one tailed)
45	.248	.294	.346	.380
50	.235	.279	.328	.361
60	.214	.254	.300	.330
70	.198	.235	.278	.306
80	.185	.220	.260	.286
90	.174	.207	.245	.270
100	.165	.197	.232	.256
120	.151	.179	.212	.234
150	.135	.160	.190	.210
180	.123	.146	.173	.192
200	.117	.139	.164	.182
300	.095	.113	.134	.149
400	.082	.098	.116	.128

APPENDIX C.4

Critical Values of t

	.10	.05	.025	.01	.005	← *Alpha risk for **one-tailed** tests*
	.20	.10	.05	.02	.01	← *Alpha risk for **two-tailed** tests*

Degrees of Freedom

1	1.078	6.314	12.706	31.821	63.657	Degrees of freedom are computed by
2	1.886	2.920	4.303	6.965	9.925	taking the number of events in
3	1.638	2.353	3.182	4.541	5.841	the study and subtracting the number
4	1.533	2.132	2.776	3.747	4.604	of population parameters estimated
5	1.476	2.015	2.571	3.365	4.032	by sample statistics in the numerator
6	1.440	1.943	2.447	3.143	3.707	of the formula for t.
7	1.415	1.895	2.365	2.998	3.499	
8	1.397	1.860	2.306	2.896	3.355	
9	1.383	1.833	2.262	2.821	3.250	For instance, for the one-sample
10	1.372	1.812	2.228	2.764	3.169	t test, the formula is
11	1.363	1.796	2.201	2.718	3.106	
12	1.356	1.782	2.179	2.681	3.055	
13	1.350	1.771	2.160	2.650	3.012	
14	1.345	1.761	2.145	2.624	2.977	$$t = \frac{\bar{X} - \mu}{\frac{s}{\sqrt{n}}}.$$
15	1.341	1.753	2.131	2.602	2.947	
16	1.337	1.746	2.120	2.583	2.921	
17	1.333	1.740	2.110	2.567	2.898	Because there is one $\bar{X}$ in the
18	1.330	1.734	2.101	2.552	2.878	numerator in the formula, degrees of
19	1.328	1.729	2.093	2.539	2.861	freedom are the number of events
20	1.325	1.725	2.086	2.528	2.845	minus 1.
21	1.323	1.721	2.080	2.518	2.831	
22	1.321	1.717	2.074	2.508	2.819	
23	1.319	1.714	2.069	2.500	2.807	
24	1.318	1.711	2.064	2.492	2.797	For the independent samples
25	1.316	1.708	2.060	2.485	2.787	t test, the formula is
26	1.315	1.706	2.056	2.479	2.779	
27	1.314	1.703	2.052	2.473	2.771	
28	1.313	1.701	2.048	2.467	2.763	$$t = \frac{\bar{X}_1 - \bar{X}_2}{sp * \sqrt{\frac{1}{n_1} + \frac{1}{n_2}}}.$$
29	1.311	1.699	2.045	2.462	2.756	
30	1.310	1.697	2.042	2.457	2.750	
31	1.309	1.696	2.040	2.453	2.744	
32	1.309	1.694	2.037	2.449	2.738	Since there are two $\bar{X}$s in the
33	1.308	1.692	2.035	2.445	2.733	numerator in the formula, degrees of
34	1.307	1.691	2.032	2.441	2.728	freedom are the number of events
35	1.306	1.690	2.030	2.438	2.724	minus 2.
40	1.303	1.684	2.021	2.423	2.704	
50	1.299	1.676	2.009	2.403	2.678	
55	1.297	1.673	2.004	2.396	2.668	
60	1.296	1.671	2.000	2.390	2.660	
65	1.295	1.669	1.997	2.385	2.654	
70	1.294	1.667	1.994	2.381	2.648	
75	1.293	1.665	1.992	2.377	2.643	
80	1.292	1.664	1.990	2.374	2.639	
90	1.291	1.662	1.987	2.368	2.632	
100	1.290	1.660	1.984	2.364	2.626	
150	1.290	1.655	1.976	2.352	2.609	
200	1.286	1.652	1.972	2.345	2.601	
500	1.283	1.648	1.965	2.334	2.586	
1000	1.282	1.646	1.962	2.330	2.581	
∞	1.282	1.645	1.960	2.326	2.576	

APPENDIX C.5

F Distribution

.05

between groups variancedegress of freedom
within groups variancedegress of freedom

		1	2	3	4	5	6	7	8	9	10	11	12	13
2	.05	18.513	19.000	19.164	19.247	19.296	19.329	19.353	19.371	19.385	19.396	19.405	19.412	19.419
	.025	38.506	39.000	39.166	39.248	39.298	39.331	39.356	39.373	39.387	39.398	39.407	39.415	39.421
	.01	98.502	99.000	99.164	99.251	99.302	99.331	99.357	99.375	99.39	99.397	99.408	99.419	99.422
3	.05	10.128	9.552	9.277	9.117	9.013	8.941	8.887	8.845	8.812	8.785	8.763	8.745	8.729
	.025	17.443	16.044	15.439	15.101	14.885	14.735	14.624	14.54	14.473	14.419	14.374	14.337	14.305
	.01	34.116	30.816	29.457	28.71	28.237	27.911	27.671	27.489	27.345	27.228	27.132	27.052	26.983
4	.05	7.709	6.944	6.591	6.388	6.256	6.163	6.094	6.041	5.999	5.964	5.936	5.912	5.891
	.025	12.218	10.649	9.979	9.604	9.364	9.197	9.074	8.98	8.905	8.844	8.794	8.751	8.715
	.01	21.198	18.000	16.694	15.977	15.522	15.207	14.976	14.799	14.659	14.546	14.452	14.374	14.306
5	.05	6.608	5.786	5.409	5.192	5.050	4.950	4.876	4.818	4.772	4.735	4.704	4.678	4.655
	.025	10.007	8.434	7.764	7.388	7.146	6.978	6.853	6.757	6.681	6.619	6.568	6.525	6.488
	.01	16.258	13.274	12.06	11.392	10.967	10.672	10.456	10.289	10.158	10.051	9.963	9.888	9.825
6	.05	5.987	5.143	4.757	4.534	4.387	4.284	4.207	4.147	4.099	4.060	4.027	4.000	3.976
	.025	8.813	7.260	6.599	6.227	5.988	5.820	5.695	5.600	5.523	5.461	5.410	5.366	5.329
	.01	13.745	10.925	9.780	9.148	8.746	8.466	8.260	8.102	7.976	7.874	7.790	7.718	7.657
7	.05	5.591	4.737	4.347	4.120	3.972	3.866	3.787	3.726	3.677	3.637	3.603	3.575	3.550
	.025	8.073	6.542	5.890	5.523	5.285	5.119	4.995	4.899	4.823	4.761	4.709	4.666	4.628
	.01	12.246	9.547	8.451	7.847	7.460	7.191	6.993	6.840	6.719	6.620	6.538	6.469	6.410
8	.05	5.318	4.459	4.066	3.838	3.688	3.581	3.500	3.438	3.388	3.347	3.313	3.284	3.259
	.025	7.571	6.059	5.416	5.053	4.817	4.652	4.529	4.433	4.357	4.295	4.243	4.200	4.162
	.01	11.259	8.649	7.591	7.006	6.632	6.371	6.178	6.029	5.911	5.814	5.734	5.667	5.609
9	.05	5.117	4.256	3.863	3.633	3.482	3.374	3.293	3.230	3.179	3.137	3.102	3.073	3.048
	.025	7.209	5.715	5.078	4.718	4.484	4.320	4.197	4.102	4.026	3.964	3.912	3.868	3.831
	.01	10.562	8.022	6.992	6.422	6.057	5.802	5.613	5.467	5.351	5.257	5.178	5.111	5.055
10	.05	4.965	4.103	3.708	3.478	3.326	3.217	3.135	3.072	3.020	2.978	2.943	2.913	2.887
	.025	6.937	5.456	4.826	4.468	4.236	4.072	3.950	3.855	3.779	3.717	3.665	3.621	3.583
	.01	10.044	7.559	6.552	5.994	5.636	5.386	5.200	5.057	4.942	4.849	4.772	4.706	4.650
11	.05	4.844	3.982	3.587	3.357	3.204	3.095	3.012	2.948	2.896	2.854	2.818	2.788	2.761
	.025	6.724	5.256	4.630	4.275	4.044	3.881	3.759	3.664	3.588	3.526	3.474	3.430	3.392
	.01	9.646	7.206	6.217	5.668	5.316	5.069	4.886	4.744	4.632	4.539	4.462	4.397	4.342
12	.05	4.747	3.885	3.490	3.259	3.106	2.996	2.913	2.849	2.796	2.753	2.717	2.687	2.660
	.025	6.554	5.096	4.474	4.121	3.891	3.728	3.607	3.512	3.436	3.374	3.321	3.277	3.239
	.01	9.330	6.927	5.953	5.412	5.064	4.821	4.640	4.499	4.388	4.296	4.220	4.155	4.100
13	.05	4.667	3.806	3.411	3.179	3.025	2.915	2.832	2.767	2.714	2.671	2.635	2.604	2.577
	.025	6.414	4.965	4.347	3.996	3.767	3.604	3.483	3.388	3.312	3.250	3.197	3.153	3.115
	.01	9.074	6.701	5.739	5.205	4.862	4.620	4.441	4.302	4.191	4.100	4.025	3.960	3.905
14	.05	4.600	3.739	3.344	3.112	2.958	2.848	2.764	2.699	2.646	2.602	2.565	2.534	2.507
	.025	6.298	4.857	4.242	3.892	3.663	3.501	3.380	3.285	3.209	3.147	3.095	3.050	3.012
	.01	8.862	6.515	5.564	5.035	4.695	4.456	4.278	4.140	4.030	3.939	3.864	3.800	3.745

		1	2	3	4	5	6	7	8	9	10	11	12	13
15	.05	4.543	3.682	3.287	3.056	2.901	2.790	2.707	2.641	2.588	2.544	2.507	2.475	2.448
	.025	6.200	4.765	4.153	3.804	3.576	3.415	3.293	3.199	3.123	3.060	3.008	2.963	2.925
	.01	8.683	6.359	5.417	4.893	4.556	4.318	4.142	4.004	3.895	3.805	3.730	3.666	3.612
16	.05	4.494	3.634	3.239	3.007	2.852	2.741	2.657	2.591	2.538	2.494	2.456	2.425	2.397
	.025	6.115	4.687	4.077	3.729	3.502	3.341	3.219	3.125	3.049	2.986	2.934	2.889	2.851
	.01	8.531	6.226	5.292	4.773	4.437	4.202	4.026	3.890	3.780	3.691	3.616	3.553	3.498
17	.05	4.451	3.592	3.197	2.965	2.810	2.699	2.614	2.548	2.494	2.450	2.413	2.381	2.353
	.025	6.042	4.619	4.011	3.665	3.438	3.277	3.156	3.061	2.985	2.922	2.870	2.825	2.786
	.01	8.400	6.112	5.185	4.669	4.336	4.101	3.927	3.791	3.682	3.593	3.518	3.455	3.401
18	.05	4.414	3.555	3.160	2.928	2.773	2.661	2.577	2.510	2.456	2.412	2.374	2.342	2.314
	.025	5.978	4.560	3.954	3.608	3.382	3.221	3.100	3.005	2.929	2.866	2.814	2.769	2.730
	.01	8.285	6.013	5.092	4.579	4.248	4.015	3.841	3.705	3.597	3.508	3.434	3.371	3.316
19	.05	4.381	3.522	3.127	2.895	2.740	2.628	2.544	2.477	2.423	2.378	2.340	2.308	2.280
	.025	5.922	4.508	3.903	3.559	3.333	3.172	3.051	2.956	2.880	2.817	2.765	2.720	2.681
	.01	8.185	5.926	5.010	4.500	4.171	3.939	3.765	3.631	3.523	3.434	3.360	3.297	3.242
20	.05	4.351	3.493	3.098	2.866	2.711	2.599	2.514	2.447	2.393	2.348	2.310	2.278	2.250
	.025	5.871	4.461	3.859	3.515	3.289	3.128	3.007	2.913	2.837	2.774	2.721	2.676	2.637
	.01	8.096	5.849	4.938	4.431	4.103	3.871	3.699	3.564	3.457	3.368	3.294	3.231	3.177
21	.05	4.325	3.467	3.072	2.840	2.685	2.573	2.488	2.420	2.366	2.321	2.283	2.250	2.222
	.025	5.827	4.420	3.819	3.475	3.250	3.090	2.969	2.874	2.798	2.735	2.682	2.637	2.598
	.01	8.017	5.780	4.874	4.369	4.042	3.812	3.640	3.506	3.398	3.310	3.236	3.173	3.119
22	.05	4.301	3.443	3.049	2.817	2.661	2.549	2.464	2.397	2.342	2.297	2.259	2.226	2.198
	.025	5.786	4.383	3.783	3.440	3.215	3.055	2.934	2.839	2.763	2.700	2.647	2.602	2.563
	.01	7.945	5.719	4.817	4.313	3.988	3.758	3.587	3.453	3.346	3.258	3.184	3.121	3.067
23	.05	4.279	3.422	3.028	2.796	2.640	2.528	2.442	2.375	2.320	2.275	2.236	2.204	2.175
	.025	5.750	4.349	3.750	3.408	3.183	3.023	2.902	2.808	2.731	2.668	2.615	2.570	2.531
	.01	7.881	5.664	4.765	4.264	3.939	3.710	3.539	3.406	3.299	3.211	3.137	3.074	3.020
24	.05	4.260	3.403	3.009	2.776	2.621	2.508	2.423	2.355	2.300	2.255	2.216	2.183	2.155
	.025	5.717	4.319	3.721	3.379	3.155	2.995	2.874	2.779	2.703	2.640	2.586	2.541	2.502
	.01	7.823	5.614	4.718	4.218	3.895	3.667	3.496	3.363	3.256	3.168	3.094	3.032	2.977
25	.05	4.242	3.385	2.991	2.759	2.603	2.490	2.405	2.337	2.282	2.236	2.198	2.165	2.136
	.025	5.686	4.291	3.694	3.353	3.129	2.969	2.848	2.753	2.677	2.613	2.560	2.515	2.476
	.01	7.770	5.568	4.675	4.177	3.855	3.627	3.457	3.324	3.217	3.129	3.056	2.993	2.939
26	.05	4.225	3.369	2.975	2.743	2.587	2.474	2.388	2.321	2.265	2.220	2.181	2.148	2.119
	.025	5.659	4.265	3.670	3.329	3.105	2.945	2.824	2.729	2.653	2.590	2.536	2.491	2.452
	.01	7.721	5.526	4.637	4.140	3.818	3.591	3.421	3.288	3.182	3.094	3.021	2.958	2.904
27	.05	4.210	3.354	2.960	2.728	2.572	2.459	2.373	2.305	2.250	2.204	2.166	2.132	2.103
	.025	5.633	4.242	3.647	3.307	3.083	2.923	2.802	2.707	2.631	2.568	2.514	2.469	2.429
	.01	7.677	5.488	4.601	4.106	3.785	3.558	3.388	3.256	3.149	3.062	2.988	2.926	2.872
28	.05	4.196	3.340	2.947	2.714	2.558	2.445	2.359	2.291	2.236	2.190	2.151	2.118	2.089
	.025	5.610	4.221	3.626	3.286	3.063	2.903	2.782	2.687	2.611	2.547	2.494	2.448	2.409
	.01	7.636	5.453	4.568	4.074	3.754	3.528	3.358	3.226	3.120	3.032	2.959	2.896	2.842
29	.05	4.183	3.328	2.934	2.701	2.545	2.432	2.346	2.278	2.223	2.177	2.138	2.104	2.075
	.025	5.588	4.201	3.607	3.267	3.044	2.884	2.763	2.669	2.592	2.529	2.475	2.430	2.390
	.01	7.598	5.420	4.538	4.045	3.725	3.499	3.330	3.198	3.092	3.005	2.931	2.868	2.814

(Continued)

(Continued)

between groups variance degress of freedom
within groups variance degress of freedom

		1	2	3	4	5	6	7	8	9	10	11	12	13
30	.05	4.171	3.316	2.922	2.690	2.534	2.421	2.334	2.266	2.211	2.165	2.126	2.092	2.063
	.025	5.568	4.182	3.589	3.250	3.026	2.867	2.746	2.651	2.575	2.511	2.458	2.412	2.372
	.01	7.562	5.390	4.510	4.018	3.699	3.473	3.305	3.173	3.067	2.979	2.906	2.843	2.789
35	.05	4.121	3.267	2.874	2.641	2.485	2.372	2.285	2.217	2.161	2.114	2.075	2.041	2.012
	.025	5.485	4.106	3.517	3.179	2.956	2.796	2.676	2.581	2.504	2.440	2.387	2.341	2.301
	.01	7.419	5.268	4.396	3.908	3.592	3.368	3.200	3.069	2.963	2.876	2.803	2.740	2.686
40	.05	4.085	3.232	2.839	2.606	2.449	2.336	2.249	2.180	2.124	2.077	2.038	2.003	1.974
	.025	5.424	4.051	3.463	3.126	2.904	2.744	2.624	2.529	2.452	2.388	2.334	2.288	2.248
	.01	7.314	5.178	4.313	3.828	3.514	3.291	3.124	2.993	2.888	2.801	2.727	2.665	2.611
50	.05	4.034	3.183	2.790	2.557	2.400	2.286	2.199	2.130	2.073	2.026	1.986	1.952	1.921
	.025	5.340	3.975	3.390	3.054	2.833	2.674	2.553	2.458	2.381	2.317	2.263	2.216	2.176
	.01	7.171	5.057	4.199	3.720	3.408	3.186	3.020	2.890	2.785	2.698	2.625	2.563	2.508
60	.05	4.001	3.150	2.758	2.525	2.368	2.254	2.167	2.097	2.040	1.993	1.952	1.917	1.887
	.025	5.286	3.925	3.343	3.008	2.786	2.627	2.507	2.412	2.334	2.270	2.216	2.169	2.129
	.01	7.077	4.977	4.126	3.649	3.339	3.119	2.953	2.823	2.718	2.632	2.559	2.496	2.442
70	.05	3.978	3.128	2.736	2.503	2.346	2.231	2.143	2.074	2.017	1.969	1.928	1.893	1.863
	.025	5.247	3.890	3.309	2.975	2.754	2.595	2.474	2.379	2.302	2.237	2.183	2.136	2.095
	.01	7.011	4.922	4.074	3.600	3.291	3.071	2.906	2.777	2.672	2.585	2.512	2.450	2.395
80	.05	3.960	3.111	2.719	2.486	2.329	2.214	2.126	2.056	1.999	1.951	1.910	1.875	1.845
	.025	5.218	3.864	3.284	2.950	2.730	2.571	2.450	2.355	2.277	2.213	2.158	2.111	2.071
	.01	6.963	4.881	4.036	3.563	3.255	3.036	2.871	2.742	2.637	2.551	2.478	2.415	2.361
90	.05	3.947	3.098	2.706	2.473	2.316	2.201	2.113	2.043	1.986	1.938	1.897	1.861	1.830
	.025	5.196	3.844	3.265	2.932	2.711	2.552	2.432	2.336	2.259	2.194	2.140	2.092	2.051
	.01	6.925	4.849	4.007	3.535	3.228	3.009	2.845	2.715	2.611	2.524	2.451	2.389	2.334
100	.05	3.936	3.087	2.696	2.463	2.305	2.191	2.103	2.032	1.975	1.927	1.886	1.850	1.819
	.025	5.179	3.828	3.250	2.917	2.696	2.537	2.417	2.321	2.244	2.179	2.124	2.077	2.036
	.01	6.895	4.824	3.984	3.513	3.206	2.988	2.823	2.694	2.590	2.503	2.430	2.368	2.313
120	.05	3.920	3.072	2.680	2.447	2.290	2.175	2.087	2.016	1.959	1.910	1.869	1.834	1.803
	.025	5.152	3.805	3.227	2.894	2.674	2.515	2.395	2.299	2.222	2.157	2.102	2.055	2.014
	.01	6.851	4.787	3.949	3.480	3.174	2.956	2.792	2.663	2.559	2.472	2.399	2.336	2.282
150	.05	3.904	3.056	2.665	2.432	2.274	2.160	2.071	2.001	1.943	1.894	1.853	1.817	1.786
	.025	5.126	3.781	3.204	2.872	2.652	2.494	2.373	2.278	2.200	2.135	2.080	2.032	1.991
	.01	6.807	4.749	3.915	3.447	3.142	2.924	2.761	2.632	2.528	2.441	2.368	2.305	2.251
180	.05	3.894	3.046	2.655	2.422	2.264	2.149	2.061	1.990	1.932	1.884	1.842	1.806	1.775
	.025	5.109	3.766	3.189	2.858	2.638	2.479	2.359	2.263	2.185	2.120	2.065	2.018	1.976
	.01	6.778	4.725	3.892	3.425	3.120	2.904	2.740	2.611	2.507	2.421	2.348	2.285	2.230
200	.05	3.888	3.041	2.650	2.417	2.259	2.144	2.056	1.985	1.927	1.878	1.837	1.801	1.769
	.025	5.100	3.758	3.182	2.850	2.630	2.472	2.351	2.256	2.178	2.113	2.058	2.010	1.969
	.01	6.763	4.713	3.881	3.414	3.110	2.893	2.730	2.601	2.497	2.411	2.338	2.275	2.220
400	.05	3.865	3.018	2.627	2.394	2.237	2.121	2.032	1.962	1.903	1.854	1.813	1.776	1.745
	.025	5.062	3.723	3.149	2.818	2.598	2.440	2.319	2.224	2.146	2.080	2.025	1.977	1.936
	.01	6.699	4.659	3.831	3.366	3.063	2.847	2.684	2.556	2.452	2.365	2.292	2.229	2.175

		14	15	16	17	18	19	20	21	22	23	24	25	30
2	.05	19.424	19.429	19.433	19.437	19.440	19.443	19.446	19.448	19.45	19.452	19.454	19.456	19.463
	.025	39.427	39.431	39.436	39.439	39.442	39.446	39.448	39.450	39.452	39.455	39.457	39.458	39.465
	.01	99.426	99.433	99.437	99.441	99.444	99.448	99.448	99.451	99.455	99.455	99.455	99.459	99.466
3	.05	8.715	8.703	8.692	8.683	8.675	8.667	8.660	8.654	8.648	8.643	8.638	8.634	8.617
	.025	14.277	14.253	14.232	14.213	14.196	14.181	14.167	14.155	14.144	14.134	14.124	14.115	14.081
	.01	26.924	26.872	26.826	26.786	26.751	26.719	26.690	26.664	26.639	26.617	26.597	26.579	26.504
4	.05	5.873	5.858	5.844	5.832	5.821	5.811	5.803	5.795	5.787	5.781	5.774	5.769	5.746
	.025	8.684	8.657	8.633	8.611	8.592	8.575	8.560	8.546	8.533	8.522	8.511	8.501	8.461
	.01	14.249	14.198	14.154	14.114	14.079	14.048	14.019	13.994	13.97	13.949	13.929	13.911	13.838
5	.05	4.636	4.619	4.604	4.590	4.579	4.568	4.558	4.549	4.541	4.534	4.527	4.521	4.496
	.025	6.456	6.428	6.403	6.381	6.362	6.344	6.329	6.314	6.301	6.289	6.278	6.268	6.227
	.01	9.770	9.722	9.680	9.643	9.609	9.580	9.553	9.528	9.506	9.485	9.466	9.449	9.379
6	.05	3.956	3.938	3.922	3.908	3.896	3.884	3.874	3.865	3.856	3.849	3.841	3.835	3.808
	.025	5.297	5.269	5.244	5.222	5.202	5.184	5.168	5.154	5.141	5.128	5.117	5.107	5.065
	.01	7.605	7.559	7.519	7.483	7.451	7.422	7.396	7.372	7.351	7.331	7.313	7.296	7.229
7	.05	3.529	3.511	3.494	3.480	3.467	3.455	3.445	3.435	3.426	3.418	3.410	3.404	3.376
	.025	4.596	4.568	4.543	4.521	4.501	4.483	4.467	4.452	4.439	4.426	4.415	4.405	4.362
	.01	6.359	6.314	6.275	6.240	6.209	6.181	6.155	6.132	6.111	6.092	6.074	6.058	5.992
8	.05	3.237	3.218	3.202	3.187	3.173	3.161	3.150	3.140	3.131	3.123	3.115	3.108	3.079
	.025	4.130	4.101	4.076	4.054	4.034	4.016	3.999	3.985	3.971	3.959	3.947	3.937	3.894
	.01	5.559	5.515	5.477	5.442	5.412	5.384	5.359	5.336	5.316	5.297	5.279	5.263	5.198
9	.05	3.025	3.006	2.989	2.974	2.960	2.948	2.936	2.926	2.917	2.908	2.900	2.893	2.864
	.025	3.798	3.769	3.744	3.722	3.701	3.683	3.667	3.652	3.638	3.626	3.614	3.604	3.560
	.01	5.005	4.962	4.924	4.890	4.860	4.833	4.808	4.786	4.765	4.746	4.729	4.713	4.649
10	.05	2.865	2.845	2.828	2.812	2.798	2.785	2.774	2.764	2.754	2.745	2.737	2.730	2.700
	.025	3.550	3.522	3.496	3.474	3.453	3.435	3.419	3.403	3.390	3.377	3.365	3.355	3.311
	.01	4.601	4.558	4.520	4.487	4.457	4.430	4.405	4.383	4.363	4.344	4.327	4.311	4.247
11	.05	2.739	2.719	2.701	2.685	2.671	2.658	2.646	2.636	2.626	2.617	2.609	2.601	2.570
	.025	3.359	3.330	3.304	3.282	3.261	3.243	3.226	3.211	3.197	3.184	3.173	3.162	3.118
	.01	4.293	4.251	4.213	4.180	4.150	4.123	4.099	4.077	4.057	4.038	4.021	4.005	3.941
12	.05	2.637	2.617	2.599	2.583	2.568	2.555	2.544	2.533	2.523	2.514	2.505	2.498	2.466
	.025	3.206	3.177	3.152	3.129	3.108	3.090	3.073	3.057	3.043	3.031	3.019	3.008	2.963
	.01	4.052	4.010	3.972	3.939	3.910	3.883	3.858	3.836	3.816	3.798	3.780	3.765	3.701
13	.05	2.554	2.533	2.515	2.499	2.484	2.471	2.459	2.448	2.438	2.429	2.420	2.412	2.380
	.025	3.082	3.053	3.027	3.004	2.983	2.965	2.948	2.932	2.918	2.905	2.893	2.882	2.837
	.01	3.857	3.815	3.778	3.745	3.716	3.689	3.665	3.643	3.622	3.604	3.587	3.571	3.507
14	.05	2.484	2.463	2.445	2.428	2.413	2.400	2.388	2.377	2.367	2.357	2.349	2.341	2.308
	.025	2.979	2.949	2.923	2.900	2.879	2.861	2.844	2.828	2.814	2.801	2.789	2.778	2.732
	.01	3.698	3.656	3.619	3.586	3.556	3.529	3.505	3.483	3.463	3.444	3.427	3.412	3.348
15	.05	2.424	2.403	2.385	2.368	2.353	2.340	2.328	2.316	2.306	2.297	2.288	2.280	2.247
	.025	2.891	2.862	2.836	2.813	2.792	2.773	2.756	2.740	2.726	2.713	2.701	2.689	2.644
	.01	3.564	3.522	3.485	3.452	3.423	3.396	3.372	3.350	3.330	3.311	3.294	3.278	3.214

(Continued)

(Continued)

between groups variance degress of freedom
within groups variance degress of freedom

		14	15	16	17	18	19	20	21	22	23	24	25	30
16	.05	2.373	2.352	2.333	2.317	2.302	2.288	2.276	2.264	2.254	2.244	2.235	2.227	2.194
	.025	2.817	2.788	2.761	2.738	2.717	2.698	2.681	2.665	2.651	2.637	2.625	2.614	2.568
	.01	3.451	3.409	3.372	3.339	3.310	3.283	3.259	3.237	3.216	3.198	3.181	3.165	3.101
17	.05	2.329	2.308	2.289	2.272	2.257	2.243	2.230	2.219	2.208	2.199	2.190	2.181	2.148
	.025	2.753	2.723	2.697	2.673	2.652	2.633	2.616	2.600	2.585	2.572	2.560	2.548	2.502
	.01	3.353	3.312	3.275	3.242	3.212	3.186	3.162	3.139	3.119	3.101	3.083	3.068	3.003
18	.05	2.290	2.269	2.250	2.233	2.217	2.203	2.191	2.179	2.168	2.159	2.150	2.141	2.107
	.025	2.696	2.667	2.640	2.617	2.596	2.576	2.559	2.543	2.529	2.515	2.503	2.491	2.445
	.01	3.269	3.227	3.190	3.158	3.128	3.101	3.077	3.055	3.035	3.016	2.999	2.983	2.919
19	.05	2.256	2.234	2.215	2.198	2.182	2.168	2.155	2.144	2.133	2.123	2.114	2.106	2.071
	.025	2.647	2.617	2.591	2.567	2.546	2.526	2.509	2.493	2.478	2.465	2.452	2.441	2.394
	.01	3.195	3.153	3.116	3.084	3.054	3.027	3.003	2.981	2.961	2.942	2.925	2.909	2.844
20	.05	2.225	2.203	2.184	2.167	2.151	2.137	2.124	2.112	2.102	2.092	2.082	2.074	2.039
	.025	2.603	2.573	2.547	2.523	2.501	2.482	2.464	2.448	2.434	2.420	2.408	2.396	2.349
	.01	3.130	3.088	3.051	3.018	2.989	2.962	2.938	2.916	2.895	2.877	2.859	2.843	2.778
21	.05	2.197	2.176	2.156	2.139	2.123	2.109	2.096	2.084	2.073	2.063	2.054	2.045	2.010
	.025	2.564	2.534	2.507	2.483	2.462	2.442	2.425	2.409	2.394	2.380	2.368	2.356	2.308
	.01	3.072	3.030	2.993	2.960	2.931	2.904	2.880	2.857	2.837	2.818	2.801	2.785	2.720
22	.05	2.173	2.151	2.131	2.114	2.098	2.084	2.071	2.059	2.048	2.038	2.028	2.020	1.984
	.025	2.528	2.498	2.472	2.448	2.426	2.407	2.389	2.373	2.358	2.344	2.332	2.320	2.272
	.01	3.019	2.978	2.941	2.908	2.879	2.852	2.827	2.805	2.785	2.766	2.749	2.733	2.667
23	.05	2.150	2.128	2.109	2.091	2.075	2.061	2.048	2.036	2.025	2.014	2.005	1.996	1.961
	.025	2.497	2.466	2.440	2.416	2.394	2.374	2.357	2.340	2.325	2.312	2.299	2.287	2.239
	.01	2.973	2.931	2.894	2.861	2.832	2.805	2.780	2.758	2.738	2.719	2.702	2.686	2.620
24	.05	2.130	2.108	2.088	2.070	2.054	2.040	2.027	2.015	2.003	1.993	1.984	1.975	1.939
	.025	2.468	2.437	2.411	2.386	2.365	2.345	2.327	2.311	2.296	2.282	2.269	2.257	2.209
	.01	2.930	2.889	2.852	2.819	2.789	2.762	2.738	2.716	2.695	2.676	2.659	2.643	2.577
25	.05	2.111	2.089	2.069	2.051	2.035	2.021	2.007	1.995	1.984	1.974	1.964	1.955	1.919
	.025	2.441	2.411	2.384	2.360	2.338	2.318	2.300	2.284	2.269	2.255	2.242	2.230	2.182
	.01	2.892	2.850	2.813	2.780	2.751	2.724	2.699	2.677	2.657	2.638	2.620	2.604	2.538
26	.05	2.094	2.072	2.052	2.034	2.018	2.003	1.990	1.978	1.966	1.956	1.946	1.938	1.901
	.025	2.417	2.387	2.360	2.335	2.314	2.294	2.276	2.259	2.244	2.230	2.217	2.205	2.157
	.01	2.857	2.815	2.778	2.745	2.715	2.688	2.664	2.642	2.621	2.602	2.585	2.569	2.503
27	.05	2.078	2.056	2.036	2.018	2.002	1.987	1.974	1.961	1.950	1.940	1.930	1.921	1.884
	.025	2.395	2.364	2.337	2.313	2.291	2.271	2.253	2.237	2.222	2.208	2.195	2.183	2.133
	.01	2.824	2.783	2.746	2.713	2.683	2.656	2.632	2.609	2.589	2.570	2.552	2.536	2.470
28	.05	2.064	2.041	2.021	2.003	1.987	1.972	1.959	1.946	1.935	1.924	1.915	1.906	1.869
	.025	2.374	2.344	2.317	2.292	2.270	2.251	2.232	2.216	2.201	2.187	2.174	2.161	2.112
	.01	2.795	2.753	2.716	2.683	2.653	2.626	2.602	2.579	2.559	2.540	2.522	2.506	2.440
29	.05	2.050	2.027	2.007	1.989	1.973	1.958	1.945	1.932	1.921	1.910	1.901	1.891	1.854
	.025	2.355	2.325	2.298	2.273	2.251	2.231	2.213	2.196	2.181	2.167	2.154	2.142	2.092
	.01	2.767	2.726	2.689	2.656	2.626	2.599	2.574	2.552	2.531	2.512	2.495	2.478	2.412

		14	15	16	17	18	19	20	21	22	23	24	25	30
30	.05	2.037	2.015	1.995	1.976	1.960	1.945	1.932	1.919	1.908	1.897	1.887	1.878	1.841
	.025	2.338	2.307	2.280	2.255	2.233	2.213	2.195	2.178	2.163	2.149	2.136	2.124	2.074
	.01	2.742	2.700	2.663	2.630	2.600	2.573	2.549	2.526	2.506	2.487	2.469	2.453	2.386
35	.05	1.986	1.963	1.942	1.924	1.907	1.892	1.878	1.866	1.854	1.843	1.833	1.824	1.786
	.025	2.266	2.235	2.207	2.183	2.160	2.140	2.122	2.105	2.089	2.075	2.062	2.049	1.999
	.01	2.639	2.597	2.560	2.527	2.497	2.470	2.445	2.422	2.401	2.382	2.364	2.348	2.281
40	.05	1.948	1.924	1.904	1.885	1.868	1.853	1.839	1.826	1.814	1.803	1.793	1.783	1.744
	.025	2.213	2.182	2.154	2.129	2.107	2.086	2.068	2.051	2.035	2.020	2.007	1.994	1.943
	.01	2.563	2.522	2.484	2.451	2.421	2.394	2.369	2.346	2.325	2.306	2.288	2.271	2.203
50	.05	1.895	1.871	1.850	1.831	1.814	1.798	1.784	1.771	1.759	1.748	1.737	1.727	1.687
	.025	2.140	2.109	2.081	2.056	2.033	2.012	1.993	1.976	1.960	1.945	1.931	1.919	1.866
	.01	2.461	2.419	2.382	2.348	2.318	2.290	2.265	2.242	2.221	2.202	2.183	2.167	2.098
60	.05	1.860	1.836	1.815	1.796	1.778	1.763	1.748	1.735	1.722	1.711	1.700	1.690	1.649
	.025	2.093	2.061	2.033	2.008	1.985	1.964	1.944	1.927	1.911	1.896	1.882	1.869	1.815
	.01	2.394	2.352	2.315	2.281	2.251	2.223	2.198	2.175	2.153	2.134	2.115	2.098	2.028
70	.05	1.836	1.812	1.790	1.771	1.753	1.737	1.722	1.709	1.696	1.685	1.674	1.664	1.622
	.025	2.059	2.028	1.999	1.974	1.950	1.929	1.910	1.892	1.876	1.861	1.847	1.833	1.779
	.01	2.348	2.306	2.268	2.234	2.204	2.176	2.150	2.127	2.106	2.086	2.067	2.050	1.980
80	.05	1.817	1.793	1.772	1.752	1.734	1.718	1.703	1.689	1.677	1.665	1.654	1.644	1.602
	.025	2.035	2.003	1.974	1.948	1.925	1.904	1.884	1.866	1.850	1.835	1.820	1.807	1.752
	.01	2.313	2.271	2.233	2.199	2.169	2.141	2.115	2.092	2.070	2.050	2.032	2.015	1.944
90	.05	1.803	1.779	1.757	1.737	1.720	1.703	1.688	1.675	1.662	1.650	1.639	1.629	1.586
	.025	2.015	1.983	1.955	1.929	1.905	1.884	1.864	1.846	1.830	1.814	1.800	1.787	1.731
	.01	2.286	2.244	2.206	2.172	2.142	2.114	2.088	2.065	2.043	2.023	2.004	1.987	1.916
100	.05	1.792	1.768	1.746	1.726	1.708	1.691	1.676	1.663	1.650	1.638	1.627	1.616	1.573
	.025	2.000	1.968	1.939	1.913	1.890	1.868	1.849	1.830	1.814	1.798	1.784	1.770	1.715
	.01	2.265	2.223	2.185	2.151	2.120	2.092	2.067	2.043	2.021	2.001	1.983	1.965	1.893
120	.05	1.775	1.750	1.728	1.709	1.690	1.674	1.659	1.645	1.632	1.620	1.608	1.598	1.554
	.025	1.977	1.945	1.916	1.890	1.866	1.845	1.825	1.807	1.790	1.774	1.760	1.746	1.690
	.01	2.234	2.191	2.154	2.119	2.089	2.060	2.035	2.011	1.989	1.969	1.950	1.932	1.860
150	.05	1.758	1.734	1.711	1.691	1.673	1.656	1.641	1.627	1.614	1.602	1.590	1.580	1.535
	.025	1.955	1.922	1.893	1.867	1.843	1.821	1.801	1.783	1.766	1.750	1.736	1.722	1.665
	.01	2.203	2.160	2.122	2.088	2.057	2.029	2.003	1.979	1.957	1.937	1.918	1.900	1.827
180	.05	1.747	1.722	1.700	1.680	1.661	1.645	1.629	1.615	1.602	1.589	1.578	1.567	1.523
	.025	1.940	1.907	1.878	1.852	1.828	1.806	1.786	1.767	1.750	1.734	1.720	1.706	1.649
	.01	2.182	2.140	2.102	2.067	2.036	2.008	1.982	1.958	1.936	1.915	1.896	1.879	1.805
200	.05	1.742	1.717	1.694	1.674	1.656	1.639	1.623	1.609	1.596	1.583	1.572	1.561	1.516
	.025	1.932	1.900	1.870	1.844	1.820	1.798	1.778	1.759	1.742	1.726	1.712	1.698	1.640
	.01	2.172	2.129	2.091	2.057	2.026	1.997	1.971	1.947	1.925	1.905	1.886	1.868	1.794
400	.05	1.717	1.691	1.669	1.648	1.630	1.613	1.597	1.582	1.569	1.556	1.545	1.534	1.488
	.025	1.899	1.866	1.836	1.810	1.786	1.763	1.743	1.724	1.707	1.691	1.676	1.662	1.603
	.01	2.126	2.084	2.045	2.011	1.979	1.951	1.925	1.900	1.878	1.857	1.838	1.820	1.745

APPENDIX C.6

Critical Values of the Dunn-Šidák Multiple Range Test

Within-Groups Degrees of Freedom		Number of Comparisons												
		2	3	4	5	6	7	8	9	10	15	20	25	30
2	.05	6.164	7.582	8.774	9.823	10.77	11.64	12.45	13.21	13.93	17.07	19.72	22.05	24.16
	.01	14.07	17.25	19.93	22.2	24.41	26.37	28.2	29.91	31.53	38.62	44.6	49.87	54.63
3	.05	4.156	4.826	5.355	5.799	6.185	6.529	6.842	7.128	7.394	8.505	9.387	10.13	10.78
	.01	7.447	5.656	9.453	10.20	10.85	11.44	11.97	12.45	12.90	14.80	16.30	17.57	18.68
4	.05	3.481	3.941	4.290	4.577	4.822	5.036	5.228	5.402	5.562	6.214	6.714	7.127	7.480
	.01	5.594	6.248	6.751	7.166	7.520	7.832	8.112	8.367	8.600	9.556	10.29	10.90	11.42
5	.05	3.152	3.518	3.791	4.012	4.197	4.385	4.501	4.630	4.747	5.219	5.573	5.861	6.105
	.01	4.771	5.243	5.599	5.888	6.133	6.346	6.535	6.706	6.862	7.491	7.968	8.355	8.684
6	.05	2.959	3.274	3.505	3.690	3.845	3.978	4.095	4.200	4.296	4.675	4.956	5.182	5.372
	.01	4.315	4.695	4.977	5.203	5.394	5.559	5.704	5.835	5.954	6.428	6.782	7.068	7.308
7	.05	2.832	3.115	3.321	3.484	3.620	3.736	3.838	3.929	4.011	4.336	4.574	4.764	4.923
	.01	4.027	4.353	4.591	4.782	4.941	5.078	5.198	5.306	5.404	5.791	6.077	6.306	6.497
8	.05	2.743	3.005	3.193	3.342	3.464	3.569	3.661	3.743	3.816	4.105	4.316	4.482	4.621
	.01	3.831	4.120	4.331	4.498	4.637	4.756	4.860	4.953	5.038	5.370	5.613	5.807	5.969
9	.05	2.677	2.923	3.099	3.237	3.351	3.448	3.532	3.607	3.675	3.938	4.129	4.280	4.405
	.01	3.688	3.952	4.143	4.294	4.419	4.526	4.619	4.703	4.778	5.072	5.287	5.457	5.598
10	.05	2.626	2.860	3.027	3.157	3.264	3.355	3.434	3.505	3.568	3.813	3.989	4.128	4.243
	.01	3.580	3.825	4.002	4.141	4.256	4.354	4.439	4.515	4.584	4.852	5.046	5.199	5.326
11	.05	2.586	2.811	2.970	3.094	3.196	3.283	3.358	3.424	3.484	3.715	3.880	4.010	4.117
	.01	3.495	3.726	3.892	4.002	4.129	4.221	4.300	4.371	4.434	4.682	4.860	5.001	5.117
12	.05	2.553	2.770	2.924	3.044	3.141	3.224	3.296	3.359	3.416	3.636	3.793	3.916	4.017
	.01	3.427	3.647	3.804	3.927	4.029	4.114	4.189	4.256	4.315	4.547	4.714	4.845	4.953
13	.05	2.526	2.737	2.886	3.002	3.096	3.176	3.245	3.306	3.361	3.571	3.722	3.839	3.935
	.01	3.374	3.582	3.733	3.850	3.946	4.028	4.099	4.162	4.218	4.438	4.595	4.718	4.819
14	.05	2.503	2.709	2.854	2.967	3.058	3.135	3.202	3.261	3.314	3.518	3.662	3.775	3.867
	.01	3.324	3.528	3.673	3.785	3.878	3.956	4.024	4.084	4.138	4.347	4.497	4.614	4.710
15	.05	2.483	2.685	2.827	2.937	3.026	3.101	3.166	3.224	3.275	3.472	3.612	3.721	3.810
	.01	3.285	3.482	3.622	3.731	3.820	3.895	3.961	4.019	4.071	4.271	4.414	4.526	4.618
16	.05	2.467	2.665	2.804	2.911	2.998	3.072	3.135	3.191	3.241	3.433	3.569	3.675	3.761
	.01	3.251	3.443	3.579	3.684	3.771	3.844	3.907	3.963	4.013	4.206	4.344	4.451	4.540

Within-Groups Degrees of Freedom		\multicolumn{13}{c}{*Number of Comparisons*}
		2	3	4	5	6	7	8	9	10	15	20	25	30
17	.05	2.452	2.647	2.783	2.889	2.974	3.046	3.108	3.163	3.212	3.399	3.532	3.634	3.718
	.01	3.221	3.409	3.541	3.644	3.728	3.799	3.860	3.914	3.963	4.150	4.284	4.387	4.472
18	.05	2.439	2.631	2.799	2.869	2.953	3.024	3.085	3.138	3.186	3.370	3.499	3.599	3.681
	.01	3.195	3.379	3.508	3.609	3.691	3.760	3.820	3.872	3.920	4.102	4.231	4.332	4.414
19	.05	2.427	2.617	2.750	2.852	2.934	3.004	3.064	3.116	3.163	3.343	3.470	3.569	3.649
	.01	3.173	3.353	3.479	3.578	3.658	3.725	3.784	3.835	3.881	4.059	4.185	4.283	4.363
20	.05	2.417	2.605	2.736	2.836	2.918	2.986	3.045	3.097	3.143	3.320	3.445	3.541	3.620
	.01	3.152	3.329	3.454	3.550	3.629	3.695	3.752	3.802	3.848	4.021	4.144	4.239	4.317
24	.05	2.385	2.566	2.692	2.788	2.866	2.931	2.988	3.037	3.081	3.249	3.366	3.457	3.531
	.01	3.089	3.257	3.375	3.465	3.539	3.601	3.654	3.702	3.744	3.905	4.019	4.107	4.179
30	.05	2.354	2.528	2.649	2.742	2.816	2.878	2.932	2.979	3.021	3.180	3.291	3.376	3.445
	.01	3.029	3.188	3.298	3.384	3.453	3.511	3.561	3.605	3.644	3.794	3.900	3.981	4.048
40	.05	2.323	2.492	2.608	2.696	2.768	2.827	2.878	2.923	2.963	3.113	3.218	3.298	3.363
	.01	2.970	3.121	3.225	3.305	3.370	3.425	3.472	3.513	3.549	3.689	3.787	3.862	3.923
60	.05	2.294	2.456	2.568	2.653	2.721	2.777	2.826	2.869	2.906	3.049	3.148	3.223	3.284
	.01	2.914	3.056	3.155	3.230	3.291	3.342	3.386	3.425	3.459	3.589	3.679	3.749	3.805
120	.05	2.265	2.422	2.529	2.610	2.675	2.729	2.776	2.816	2.852	2.987	3.081	3.152	3.209
	.01	2.859	2.994	3.087	3.158	3.215	3.263	3.304	3.340	3.372	3.493	3.577	3.641	3.693
∞	.05	2.237	2.388	2.491	2.569	2.631	2.683	2.727	2.766	2.300	2.928	3.016	3.083	3.137
	.01	2.806	2.934	3.022	3.089	3.143	3.186	3.226	3.260	3.289	3.402	3.480	3.539	3.587

APPENDIX C.7

Dunnett's *tD'* Table

Within-Groups Degrees of Freedom	Two-Tailed Alpha Risk Comparisons	One-Tailed Alpha Risk Comparisons	Number of Groups Including Control Group								
			2	3	4	5	6	7	8	9	10
5	.10	.05	2.02	2.44	5.68	2.85	2.98	3.08	3.16	3.24	3.03
	.05	.025	2.57	3.03	3.29	3.48	3.62	3.73	3.82	3.90	3.97
	.02	.01	3.36	3.90	4.21	4.43	4.60	4.73	4.85	4.94	5.03
	.01	.005	4.03	4.63	4.98	5.22	5.41	5.56	5.69	5.80	5.89
6	.10	.05	1.94	2.34	2.56	2.71	2.83	2.92	3.00	3.07	3.12
	.05	.025	2.45	2.86	3.10	3.26	3.39	3.49	3.57	3.64	3.71
	.02	.01	3.14	3.61	3.88	4.07	4.21	4.33	4.43	4.51	4.59
	.01	.005	3.71	4.21	4.51	4.71	4.87	5.00	5.10	5.20	5.28
7	.10	.05	1.89	2.27	2.48	2.62	2.73	2.82	2.89	2.95	3.01
	.05	.025	2.36	2.75	2.97	3.12	3.24	3.33	3.41	3.47	3.53
	.02	.01	3.00	3.42	3.66	3.83	3.96	4.07	4.15	4.23	4.30
	.01	.005	3.50	3.95	4.21	4.39	4.53	4.64	4.74	4.82	4.89
8	.10	.05	1.86	2.22	2.42	2.55	2.66	2.74	2.81	2.87	2.92
	.05	.025	2.31	2.67	2.88	3.02	3.13	3.22	3.29	3.35	3.41
	.02	.01	2.90	3.29	3.51	3.67	3.79	3.88	3.96	4.03	4.09
	.01	.005	3.36	3.77	4.00	4.17	4.29	4.40	4.48	4.56	4.62
9	.10	.05	1.83	2.18	2.37	2.50	2.60	2.68	2.75	2.81	2.86
	.05	.025	2.26	2.61	2.81	2.95	3.05	3.14	3.20	3.26	3.32
	.02	.01	2.28	3.19	3.40	3.55	3.66	3.75	3.82	3.89	3.94
	.01	.005	3.25	3.63	3.85	4.01	4.12	4.22	4.30	4.37	4.43
10	.10	.05	1.81	2.15	2.34	2.47	2.56	2.64	2.70	2.76	2.81
	.05	.025	2.23	2.57	2.76	2.89	2.99	3.07	3.14	3.19	3.24
	.02	.01	2.71	3.11	3.31	3.45	3.56	3.64	3.71	3.78	3.83
	.01	.005	3.17	3.53	3.74	3.88	3.99	4.08	4.16	4.22	4.28
11	.10	.05	1.80	2.13	2.31	2.44	2.53	2.60	2.67	2.72	2.77
	.05	.025	2.20	2.53	2.72	2.84	2.94	3.02	3.08	3.14	3.19
	.02	.01	2.72	3.06	3.25	3.38	3.48	3.56	3.63	3.69	3.74
	.01	.005	3.11	3.45	3.65	3.79	3.89	3.98	4.05	4.11	4.16
12	.10	.05	1.78	2.11	2.29	2.41	2.50	2.58	2.64	2.69	2.74
	.05	.025	2.18	2.50	2.68	2.81	2.90	2.98	3.04	3.09	3.14
	.02	.01	2.68	3.01	3.19	3.32	3.42	3.50	3.56	3.62	3.67
	.01	.005	3.05	3.39	3.58	3.71	3.81	3.89	3.96	4.02	4.07
13	.10	.05	1.77	2.09	2.27	2.39	2.48	2.55	2.61	2.66	2.71
	.05	.025	2.16	2.48	2.65	2.78	2.87	2.94	3.00	3.06	3.10
	.02	.01	2.65	2.97	3.15	3.27	3.37	3.44	3.51	3.56	3.61
	.01	.005	3.01	3.33	3.52	3.65	3.74	3.82	3.89	3.94	3.99
14	.10	.05	1.76	2.08	2.25	2.37	2.46	2.53	2.59	2.64	2.69
	.05	.025	2.14	2.46	2.63	2.75	2.84	2.91	2.97	3.02	3.07
	.02	.01	2.62	2.94	3.11	3.23	3.32	3.40	3.46	3.51	3.56
	.01	.005	2.98	3.29	3.47	3.59	3.69	3.76	3.83	3.88	3.93

Within-Groups Degrees of Freedom	Two-Tailed Alpha Risk Comparisons	One-Tailed Alpha Risk Comparisons	Number of Groups Including Control Group								
			2	3	4	5	6	7	8	9	10
15	.10	.05	1.75	2.07	2.24	2.36	2.44	2.51	2.57	2.62	2.67
	.05	.025	2.13	2.44	2.61	2.73	2.82	2.89	2.95	3.00	3.04
	.02	.01	2.60	2.91	3.08	3.20	3.29	3.36	3.42	3.47	3.52
	.01	.005	2.95	3.25	3.43	3.55	3.64	3.71	3.78	3.83	3.88
16	.10	.05	1.75	2.06	2.23	2.34	2.43	2.50	2.56	2.61	2.65
	.05	.025	2.12	2.42	2.59	2.71	2.80	2.87	2.92	2.97	3.02
	.02	.01	2.58	2.88	3.05	3.17	3.26	3.33	3.39	3.44	3.48
	.01	.005	2.92	3.22	3.39	3.51	3.60	3.67	3.73	3.78	3.83
17	.10	.05	1.74	2.05	2.22	2.33	2.42	2.49	2.54	2.59	2.64
	.05	.025	2.11	2.41	2.58	2.69	2.78	2.85	2.90	2.95	3.00
	.02	.01	2.57	2.86	3.02	3.14	3.23	3.30	3.36	3.41	3.45
	.01	.005	2.90	3.19	3.36	3.47	3.56	3.63	3.69	3.74	3.79
18	.10	.05	1.73	2.05	2.21	2.32	2.41	2.48	2.53	2.58	2.62
	.05	.025	2.10	2.40	2.56	2.68	2.76	2.83	2.89	2.94	2.98
	.02	.01	2.55	2.84	3.01	3.12	3.21	3.27	3.33	3.38	3.42
	.01	.005	2.88	3.17	3.33	3.44	3.53	3.60	3.66	3.71	3.75
19	.10	.05	1.73	2.03	2.20	2.31	2.40	2.47	2.52	2.57	2.61
	.05	.025	2.09	2.39	2.55	2.66	2.75	2.81	2.87	2.92	2.96
	.02	.01	2.54	2.83	2.99	3.10	3.18	3.25	3.31	3.36	3.40
	.01	.005	2.86	3.15	3.31	3.42	3.5	3.57	3.63	3.68	3.72
20	.10	.05	1.72	2.03	2.19	2.30	2.39	2.46	2.51	2.56	2.60
	.05	.025	2.09	2.38	2.54	2.65	2.73	2.80	2.86	2.9	2.95
	.02	.01	2.53	2.81	2.97	3.08	3.17	3.23	3.29	3.34	3.38
	.01	.005	2.85	3.13	3.29	3.40	3.48	3.55	3.60	3.65	3.69
24	.10	.05	1.71	2.01	2.17	2.28	2.36	2.43	2.48	2.53	2.57
	.05	.025	2.06	2.35	2.51	2.61	2.70	2.76	2.81	2.86	2.90
	.02	.01	2.49	2.77	2.92	3.03	3.11	3.17	3.22	3.27	3.31
	.01	.005	2.80	3.07	3.22	3.32	3.40	3.47	3.52	3.57	3.61
30	.10	.05	1.70	1.99	2.15	2.25	2.33	2.40	2.45	2.50	2.54
	.05	.025	2.04	2.32	2.47	2.58	2.66	2.72	2.77	2.82	2.86
	.02	.01	2.46	2.72	2.87	2.97	3.05	3.11	3.16	3.21	3.24
	.01	.005	2.75	3.01	3.15	3.25	3.33	3.39	3.44	3.49	3.52
40	.10	.05	1.68	1.97	2.13	2.23	2.31	2.37	2.42	2.47	2.51
	.05	.025	2.02	2.29	2.44	2.54	2.62	2.68	2.73	2.77	2.81
	.02	.01	2.42	2.68	2.82	2.92	2.99	3.05	3.10	3.14	3.18
	.01	.005	2.70	2.95	3.09	3.19	3.26	3.32	3.37	3.41	3.44
60	.10	.05	1.67	1.95	2.10	2.21	2.28	2.35	2.39	2.44	2.48
	.05	.025	2.00	2.27	2.41	2.51	2.58	2.64	2.69	2.73	2.77
	.02	.01	2.39	2.64	2.78	2.87	2.94	3.00	3.04	3.08	3.12
	.01	.005	2.66	2.90	3.03	3.12	3.19	3.25	3.29	3.33	3.37
120	.10	.05	1.66	1.93	2.08	2.18	2.26	2.32	2.37	2.41	2.45
	.05	.025	1.98	2.24	2.38	2.47	2.55	2.60	2.65	2.69	2.73
	.02	.01	2.36	2.60	2.73	2.82	2.89	2.94	2.99	3.03	3.06
	.01	.005	2.62	2.85	2.97	3.06	3.12	3.18	3.22	3.26	3.29
∞	.10	.05	1.64	1.92	2.06	2.16	2.23	2.29	2.34	2.38	2.42
	.05	.025	1.96	2.21	2.35	2.44	2.51	2.57	2.61	2.65	2.69
	.02	.01	2.33	2.56	2.68	2.77	2.84	2.89	2.93	2.97	3.00
	.01	.005	2.58	2.79	2.92	3.00	3.06	3.11	3.15	3.19	3.22

APPENDIX C.8

Critical Values of the Studentized Range Statistic

Within-Groups Degrees of Freedomm		2	3	4	5	6	7	8	9	10	11	12	16	20
							Number of Groups Compared							
2	.05	6.085	8.331	9.798	10.88	11.73	12.44	13.03	13.54	13.99	14.39	14.75	15.91	16.77
	.01	14.04	19.02	22.29	24.72	26.63	28.20	29.53	30.68	31.69	32.59	33.40	36.00	37.95
3	.05	4.501	5.910	6.825	7.502	8.037	8.478	8.853	9.177	9.462	9.717	9.946	10.69	11.24
	.01	8.261	10.62	12.17	13.33	14.24	15.00	15.64	16.20	16.69	17.13	17.53	18.81	19.77
4	.05	3.927	5.040	5.757	6.287	6.707	7.053	7.347	7.602	7.826	8.027	8.208	8.794	9.233
	.01	6.512	8.120	9.173	9.958	10.58	11.10	11.55	11.93	12.27	12.57	12.84	13.73	14.40
5	.05	3.635	4.602	5.218	5.673	6.033	6.330	6.582	6.802	6.995	7.168	7.324	7.828	8.208
	.01	5.702	6.976	7.804	8.421	8.913	9.321	9.669	9.972	10.24	10.48	10.70	11.40	11.93
6	.05	3.461	4.339	4.896	5.305	5.628	5.895	6.122	6.319	6.493	6.649	6.789	7.244	7.587
	.01	5.243	6.331	7.033	7.556	7.973	8.318	8.613	8.869	9.097	9.301	9.485	10.08	10.54
7	.05	3.344	4.165	4.681	5.060	5.359	5.606	5.815	5.998	6.158	6.302	6.431	6.852	7.170
	.01	4.949	5.919	6.543	7.005	7.373	7.679	7.939	8.166	8.368	8.548	8.711	9.242	9.646
8	.05	3.261	4.041	4.529	4.886	5.167	5.399	5.597	5.767	5.918	6.054	6.175	6.571	6.870
	.01	4.746	5.635	6.204	6.625	6.960	7.237	7.474	7.681	7.863	8.027	8.176	8.659	9.027
9	.05	3.199	3.949	4.415	4.756	5.024	5.244	5.432	5.595	5.739	5.867	5.983	6.359	6.644
	.01	4.596	5.428	5.957	6.348	6.658	6.915	7.134	7.325	7.495	7.647	7.784	8.232	8.573
10	.05	3.151	3.877	4.327	4.654	4.912	5.124	5.305	5.461	5.599	5.722	5.833	6.194	6.467
	.01	4.482	5.270	5.769	6.136	6.428	6.669	6.875	7.055	7.213	7.356	7.485	7.906	8.226
11	.05	3.113	3.820	4.256	4.574	4.826	5.028	5.202	5.353	5.487	5.605	5.713	6.062	6.326
	.01	4.392	5.146	5.621	5.970	6.247	6.476	6.672	6.842	6.992	7.128	7.250	7.649	7.952
12	.05	3.082	3.773	4.199	4.508	4.751	4.950	5.119	5.265	5.395	5.511	5.615	5.953	6.209
	.01	4.320	5.046	5.502	5.836	6.101	6.321	6.507	6.670	6.814	6.943	7.060	7.441	7.731
13	.05	3.055	3.735	4.151	4.453	4.690	4.885	5.049	5.192	5.318	5.431	5.533	5.862	6.112
	.01	4.260	4.964	5.404	5.727	5.981	6.192	6.372	6.528	6.667	6.791	6.903	7.269	7.548
14	.05	3.033	3.702	4.111	4.407	4.639	4.829	4.990	5.131	5.254	5.364	5.463	5.786	6.029
	.01	4.210	4.895	5.322	5.634	5.881	6.085	6.258	6.409	6.543	6.664	6.772	7.126	7.395
15	.05	3.014	3.674	4.076	4.367	4.595	4.782	4.940	5.077	5.198	5.306	5.404	5.720	5.958
	.01	4.168	4.836	5.252	5.556	5.796	5.994	6.162	6.309	6.439	6.555	6.660	7.003	7.264
16	.05	2.998	3.649	4.046	4.333	4.557	4.741	4.897	5.031	5.150	5.256	5.352	5.662	5.897
	.01	4.131	4.786	5.192	5.489	5.722	5.915	6.079	6.222	6.349	6.462	6.564	6.898	7.152
17	.05	2.984	3.623	4.020	4.303	4.524	4.705	4.858	4.991	5.108	5.212	5.307	5.612	5.842
	.01	4.099	4.742	5.140	5.430	5.659	5.847	6.007	6.147	6.270	6.381	6.480	6.806	7.053
18	.05	2.971	3.609	3.997	4.277	4.495	4.673	4.824	4.956	5.071	5.174	5.267	5.568	5.794
	.01	4.071	4.703	5.094	5.379	5.603	5.788	5.944	6.081	6.201	6.310	6.407	6.725	6.968
19	.05	2.960	3.593	3.977	4.253	4.469	4.645	4.794	4.924	5.038	5.140	5.231	5.528	5.752
	.01	4.046	4.670	5.054	5.334	5.554	5.735	5.889	6.022	6.141	6.247	6.342	6.654	6.891
20	.05	2.950	3.578	3.958	4.232	4.445	4.620	4.768	4.896	5.008	5.108	5.199	5.493	5.714
	.01	4.024	4.639	5.018	5.294	5.510	5.688	5.839	5.970	6.087	6.191	6.285	6.591	6.823
24	.05	2.919	3.532	3.901	4.166	4.373	4.541	4.684	4.807	4.915	5.012	5.099	5.381	5.594
	.01	3.956	4.546	4.907	5.168	5.374	5.542	5.685	5.809	5.919	6.017	6.106	6.394	6.612
28	.05	2.898	3.517	3.882	4.145	4.439	4.515	4.657	4.778	4.885	4.980	5.066	5.344	5.554
	.01	3.934	4.516	4.871	5.128	5.33	5.495	5.635	5.757	5.865	5.961	6.048	6.33	6.544
30	.05	2.888	3.486	3.845	4.102	4.302	4.464	4.602	4.720	4.824	4.917	5.001	5.271	5.475
	.01	3.889	4.455	4.799	5.048	5.242	5.401	5.536	5.653	5.756	5.849	5.932	6.203	6.407
40	.05	2.858	3.442	3.791	4.039	4.232	4.389	4.521	4.635	4.735	4.854	4.904	5.163	5.358
	.01	3.825	4.367	4.696	4.931	5.114	5.265	5.392	5.502	5.599	5.686	5.764	6.017	6.207
60	.05	2.829	3.399	3.737	3.977	4.163	4.314	4.441	4.550	4.646	4.732	4.808	5.056	5.241
	.01	3.762	4.282	4.595	4.818	4.991	5.133	5.253	5.356	5.447	5.528	5.601	5.837	6.015
120	.05	2.800	3.356	3.685	3.917	4.096	4.241	4.363	4.468	4.560	4.641	4.714	4.950	5.126
	.01	3.702	4.200	4.497	4.709	4.872	5.005	5.118	5.214	5.299	5.375	5.443	5.662	5.827
∞	.05	2.772	3.314	3.633	3.858	4.030	4.170	4.286	4.387	4.474	4.552	4.622	4.845	5.012
	.01	3.643	4.120	4.403	4.603	4.757	4.882	4.987	5.078	5.157	5.227	5.290	5.493	5.645

APPENDIX C.9

Table of Orthogonal Polynomials

Number of Group Means	Type of Trend	Coefficients (c_j) for Each Mean												$\sum c_j^2$
		1	2	3	4	5	6	7	8	9	10	11	12	
3	Linear	−1	0	1										2
	Quadratic	1	−2	1										6
4	Linear	−3	−1	1	3									20
	Quadratic	1	−1	−1	1									4
	Cubic	−1	3	−3	1									20
5	Linear	−2	−1	0	1	2								10
	Quadratic	2	−1	−2	−1	2								14
	Cubic	−1	2	0	−2	1								10
	Quartic	1	−4	6	−4	1								70
6	Linear	−5	−3	−1	1	3	5							70
	Quadratic	5	−1	−4	−4	−1	5							84
	Cubic	−5	7	4	−4	−7	5							180
	Quartic	1	−3	2	2	−3	1							28
	Quintic	−1	5	−10	10	−5	1							252
7	Linear	−3	−2	−1	0	1	2	3						28
	Quadratic	5	0	−3	−4	−3	0	5						84
	Cubic	−1	1	1	0	−1	−1	1						6
	Quartic	3	−7	1	6	1	−7	3						154
	Quintic	−1	4	−5	0	5	−4	1						84
8	Linear	−7	−5	−3	−1	1	3	5	7					168
	Quadratic	7	1	−3	−5	−5	−3	1	7					168
	Cubic	−7	5	7	3	−3	−7	−5	7					264
	Quartic	7	−13	−3	9	9	−3	−13	7					616
	Quintic	−7	23	−17	−15	15	17	−23	7					2,184
9	Linear	−4	−3	−2	−1	0	1	2	3	4				60
	Quadratic	28	7	−8	−17	−20	−17	−8	7	28				2,772
	Cubic	−14	7	13	9	0	−9	−13	−7	14				990
	Quartic	14	−21	−11	9	18	9	−11	−21	14				2,002
	Quintic	−4	11	−4	−9	0	9	4	−11	4				468
10	Linear	−9	−7	−5	−3	−1	1	3	5	7	9			330
	Quadratic	6	2	−1	−3	−4	−4	−3	−1	2	6			132
	Cubic	−42	14	35	31	12	−12	−31	−35	−14	42			8,580
	Quartic	18	−22	−17	3	18	18	3	−17	−22	18			2,860
	Quintic	−6	14	−1	−11	−6	6	11	1	−14	6			780
11	Linear	−5	−4	−3	−2	−1	0	1	2	3	4	5		110
	Quadratic	15	6	−1	−6	−9	−10	−9	−6	−1	6	15		858
	Cubic	−30	6	22	23	14	0	−14	−23	−22	−6	30		4,290
	Quartic	6	−6	−6	−1	4	6	4	−1	−6	−6	6		286
	Quintic	−3	6	1	−4	−4	0	4	4	−1	−6	3		156
12	Linear	−11	−9	−7	−5	−3	−1	1	3	5	7	9	11	572
	Quadratic	55	25	1	−17	−29	−35	−35	−29	−17	1	25	55	12,012
	Cubic	−33	3	21	25	19	7	−7	−19	−25	−21	−3	33	5,148
	Quartic	33	−27	−33	−13	12	28	28	12	−13	−33	−27	33	8,008
	Quintic	−33	57	21	−29	−44	−20	20	44	29	−21	−57	33	15,912

APPENDIX C.10

Table of Critical Values of Chi-Square

Alpha Risk Identifying the Proportion of the Chi-Square Distribution to the Right of the Listed Critical Value

Degrees of Freedom	.99	.95	.90	.10	.05	.025	.01	.005	.001
1	0.0002	0.0039	0.0158	2.71	3.84	5.02	6.63	7.88	10.88
2	0.0201	0.1026	0.2107	4.61	5.99	7.38	9.21	10.6	13.82
3	0.1148	0.3519	0.5844	6.25	7.81	9.35	11.34	12.84	16.27
4	0.2971	0.7107	1.06	7.78	9.49	11.14	13.28	14.86	18.47
5	0.5543	1.15	1.61	9.24	11.07	12.83	15.09	16.75	20.51
6	0.8721	1.64	2.204	10.64	12.59	14.45	16.81	18.55	22.46
7	1.24	2.17	2.83	12.02	14.07	16.01	18.48	20.28	24.32
8	1.65	2.73	3.49	13.36	15.51	17.54	20.09	21.95	26.13
9	2.09	3.33	4.17	14.68	16.92	19.02	21.67	23.59	27.88
10	2.56	3.94	4.87	15.99	18.31	20.48	23.21	25.19	29.59
11	3.05	4.57	5.58	17.28	19.68	21.92	24.73	26.76	31.26
12	3.57	5.23	6.3	18.55	21.03	23.34	26.22	28.3	32.91
13	4.11	5.89	7.04	19.81	22.36	24.74	27.69	29.82	34.53
14	4.66	6.57	7.79	21.06	23.68	26.12	29.14	31.32	36.13
15	5.23	7.26	8.55	22.31	25	27.49	30.58	32.8	37.7
16	5.81	7.96	9.31	23.54	26.3	28.85	32	34.27	39.25
17	6.41	8.67	10.09	24.77	27.59	30.19	33.41	35.72	40.79
18	7.01	9.39	10.86	25.99	28.87	31.53	34.81	37.16	42.31
19	7.63	10.12	11.65	27.2	30.14	32.85	36.19	38.58	43.82
20	8.26	10.85	12.44	28.41	31.41	34.17	37.57	40	45.31
21	8.9	11.59	13.24	29.62	32.67	35.48	38.93	41.4	46.8
22	9.54	12.34	14.04	30.81	33.92	36.78	40.29	42.8	48.27
23	10.2	13.09	14.85	32.01	35.17	38.08	41.64	44.18	49.73
24	10.86	13.85	15.66	33.2	36.42	39.36	42.98	45.56	51.18
25	11.52	14.61	16.47	34.38	37.65	40.65	44.31	46.93	52.62
26	12.2	15.38	17.29	35.56	38.89	41.92	45.64	48.29	54.05
27	12.88	16.15	18.11	36.74	40.11	43.19	46.96	49.65	55.48
28	13.56	16.93	18.94	37.92	41.34	44.46	48.28	50.99	56.89
29	14.26	17.71	19.77	39.09	42.56	45.72	49.59	52.34	58.3
30	14.95	18.49	20.6	40.26	43.77	46.98	50.89	53.67	59.7
40	22.16	26.51	29.05	51.81	55.76	59.34	63.69	66.77	73.4
60	37.48	43.19	46.46	74.4	79.08	83.3	88.38	91.95	99.61
80	53.54	60.39	64.28	96.58	101.88	106.63	112.33	116.32	124.84
100	70.06	77.93	82.36	118.5	124.34	129.56	135.81	140.17	149.45

APPENDIX C.11

Table of Critical Values of the Kolmogorov-Smirnov One-Sample Test

N	Minimum D Values Associated With Alpha Risk		
	.10	**.05**	**.01**
2	.776	.842	.929
3	.642	.708	.829
4	.564	.624	.734
5	.510	.563	.669
6	.470	.519	.617
7	.438	.483	.576
8	.411	.454	.542
9	.388	.430	.513
10	.368	.409	.489
11	.352	.391	.468
12	.338	.375	.449
13	.325	.361	.432
14	.314	.349	.418
15	.304	.338	.404
16	.295	.327	.392
17	.286	.318	.381
18	.278	.309	.371
19	.272	.301	.361
20	.264	.294	.352
21	.259	.287	.344
22	.253	.281	.337
23	.247	.275	.330
24	.242	.269	.323
25	.238	.264	.317
26	.233	.259	.311
27	.229	.254	.305
28	.225	.250	.300
29	.221	.246	.295
30	.218	.242	.290
35	.202	.224	.269
40	.189	.210	.252
45	.179	.198	.238
50	.170	.188	.226
60	.155	.172	.207
70	.144	.160	.192
80	.134	.150	.179
90	.127	.141	.169
100	.121	.134	.161

For samples greater than 100, compute critical D values as $\frac{1.22}{\sqrt{n}}$ for $\alpha = .10$, $\frac{1.358}{\sqrt{n}}$ for $\alpha = .05$, and $\frac{1.628}{\sqrt{n}}$ for $\alpha = .01$.

APPENDIX C.12

Table of Critical Values of the Lilliefors Test

N	Minimum Differences Associated With Alpha Risk		
	.10	.05	.01
4	.352	.381	.417
5	.315	.337	.405
6	.294	.319	.364
7	.276	.300	.348
8	.261	.285	.331
9	.249	.271	.311
10	.239	.258	.294
11	.230	.249	.284
12	.223	.242	.275
13	.214	.234	.268
14	.207	.227	.261
15	.201	.220	.257
16	.195	.216	.250
17	.189	.206	.245
18	.184	.200	.239
19	.179	.195	.235
20	.174	.190	.231
25	.165	.180	.203
30	.144	.161	.187
35	.136	.150	.174
40	.127	.14	.163
45	.120	.132	.154
50	.114	.125	.146
55	.109	.119	.139
60	.104	.114	.133
65	.100	.110	.128
70	.096	.106	.123
75	.093	.102	.119
80	.090	.099	.115
85	.087	.096	.112
90	.085	.093	.109
95	.083	.091	.106
100	.081	.089	.103
125	.072	.079	.092
150	.066	.072	.084
175	.061	.067	.078
200	.057	.063	.073

For samples greater than 200, compute critical values as $\frac{.805}{\sqrt{n}}$ for $\alpha = .10$, $\frac{.886}{\sqrt{n}}$ for $\alpha = .05$, and $\frac{1.031}{\sqrt{n}}$ for $\alpha = .01$.

APPENDIX C.13

Table of Values of Weisberg's t_i, Mahalanobis' Distance, and Cook's D Tests of Outliers

Number of Events	Weisberg's t_i Critical Values at Alpha Risk = .05[1] *Number of Regression Coefficients Including the Intercept*				Mahalanobis' Distance Critical Values at Alpha Risk = .05[2] *Number of Predictor Variables*				Cook's Distance Guidelines *Number of Regression Coefficients Including the Intercept*			
	3	*4*	*5*	*6*	*2*	*3*	*4*	*5*	*3*	*4*	*5*	*6*
6	10.89	76.39	—	—	4	4.14	—	—	.89	.94	.98	1.00
7	6.58	11.77	89.12	—	4.71	5.01	5.12	—	.87	.93	.96	.98
8	5.26	6.9	12.59	101.9	5.32	5.77	6.01	6.11	.86	.91	.95	.97
9	4.66	5.44	7.18	13.36	5.85	6.43	6.80	7.01	.85	.91	.94	.96
10	4.32	4.77	5.60	7.45	6.32	7.01	7.50	7.82	.85	.90	.93	.95
12	3.96	4.17	4.49	4.98	7.10	7.99	8.67	9.19	.84	.89	.92	.94
14	3.79	3.91	4.07	4.30	7.70	8.78	9.61	10.29	.83	.88	.91	.94
16	3.68	3.77	3.87	4.00	8.27	9.44	10.39	11.20	.82	.88	.91	.93
18	3.62	3.68	3.75	3.83	8.73	10.00	11.06	11.96	.82	.87	.90	.93
20	3.58	3.62	3.67	3.73	9.13	10.49	11.63	12.62	.82	.87	.90	.92
25	3.53	3.55	3.58	3.61	9.94	11.48	12.78	13.94	.81	.86	.89	.92
30	3.51	3.52	3.54	3.56	10.58	12.24	13.67	14.95	.81	.86	.89	.91
35	3.50	3.51	3.52	3.54	11.10	12.85	14.37	15.75	.80	.86	.89	.91
40	3.50	3.51	3.52	3.53	11.53	13.36	14.96	16.41	.80	.85	.89	.91
45	3.51	3.52	3.53	3.54	11.90	13.80	15.46	16.97	.80	.85	.88	.90
50	3.51	3.52	3.53	3.55	12.23	14.18	15.89	17.45	.80	.85	.88	.90
100	3.60	3.60	3.61	3.61	14.22	16.45	18.43	20.26	.79	.84	.88	.90
200	3.73	3.73	3.73	3.73	15.99	18.42	20.59	22.59	.79	.84	.87	.89
500	3.92	3.92	3.92	3.92	18.12	20.75	23.06	25.21	.79	.84	.87	.89

1. Values for Weisberg's test are taken in part from Weisberg (1985).
2. Values for Mahalanobis's Distance are taken in part from Barnett and Lewis (1978).

APPENDIX C.14

Table of Critical Values of the Durbin-Watson Test at One-Tailed Alpha Risk of .05 and Two-Tailed Alpha Risk of .05 (in Bold in Parentheses)

Number of Events in Study	Upper and Lower Limits	Number of Independent (Predictor) Variables				
		1	*2*	*3*	*4*	*5*
15	Lower Limit of *d*	1.08 (**.95**)	.95 (**.83**)	.82 (**.71**)	.69 (**.59**)	.56 (**.48**)
	Upper Limit of *d*	1.36 (**1.23**)	1.54 (**1.40**)	1.75 (**1.61**)	1.97 (**1.84**)	2.21 (**2.09**)
16	Lower Limit of *d*	1.10 (**.98**)	.98 (**.86**)	.86 (**.75**)	.74 (**.64**)	.62 (**.53**)
	Upper Limit of *d*	1.37 (**1.24**)	1.54 (**1.40**)	1.73 (**1.59**)	1.93 (**1.80**)	2.15 (**2.03**)
17	Lower Limit of *d*	1.13 (**1.01**)	1.02 (**.90**)	.90 (**.79**)	.78 (**.68**)	.67 (**.57**)
	Upper Limit of *d*	1.38 (**1.25**)	1.54 (**1.40**)	1.71 (**1.58**)	1.90 (**1.77**)	2.10 (**1.98**)
18	Lower Limit of *d*	1.16 (**1.03**)	1.05 (**.93**)	.93 (**.82**)	.82 (**.72**)	.71 (**.62**)
	Upper Limit of *d*	1.39 (**1.26**)	1.53 (**1.40**)	1.69 (**1.56**)	1.87 (**1.74**)	2.06 (**1.93**)
19	Lower Limit of *d*	1.18 (**1.06**)	1.08 (**.96**)	.97 (**.86**)	.86 (**.76**)	.75 (**.66**)
	Upper Limit of *d*	1.40 (**1.28**)	1.53 (**1.41**)	1.68 (**1.55**)	1.85 (**1.72**)	2.02 (**1.90**)
20	Lower Limit of *d*	1.20 (**1.08**)	1.10 (**.99**)	1.00 (**.89**)	.90 (**.79**)	.79 (**.70**)
	Upper Limit of *d*	1.41 (**1.28**)	1.54 (**1.41**)	1.68 (**1.55**)	1.83 (**1.70**)	1.99 (**1.87**)
21	Lower Limit of *d*	1.22 (**1.10**)	1.13 (**1.01**)	1.03 (**.92**)	.93 (**.83**)	.83 (**.73**)
	Upper Limit of *d*	1.42 (**1.30**)	1.54 (**1.41**)	1.67 (**1.54**)	1.81 (**1.69**)	1.96 (**1.84**)
22	Lower Limit of *d*	1.24 (**1.12**)	1.15 (**1.04**)	1.05 (**.95**)	.96 (**.86**)	.86 (**.77**)
	Upper Limit of *d*	1.43 (**1.31**)	1.54 (**1.42**)	1.66 (**1.54**)	1.80 (**1.68**)	1.94 (**1.82**)
23	Lower Limit of *d*	1.26 (**1.14**)	1.17 (**1.06**)	1.08 (**.97**)	.99 (**.89**)	.90 (**.80**)
	Upper Limit of *d*	1.44 (**1.32**)	1.54 (**1.42**)	1.66 (**1.54**)	1.79 (**1.67**)	1.92 (**1.80**)
24	Lower Limit of *d*	1.27 (**1.16**)	1.19 (**1.08**)	1.10 (**1.00**)	1.01 (**.91**)	.93 (**.83**)
	Upper Limit of *d*	1.45 (**1.33**)	1.55 (**1.43**)	1.66 (**1.54**)	1.78 (**1.66**)	1.90 (**1.79**)
25	Lower Limit of *d*	1.29 (**1.18**)	1.21 (**1.10**)	1.12 (**1.02**)	1.04 (**.94**)	.95 (**.86**)
	Upper Limit of *d*	1.45 (**1.34**)	1.55 (**1.43**)	1.66 (**1.54**)	1.77 (**1.65**)	1.89 (**1.77**)
26	Lower Limit of *d*	1.30 (**1.19**)	1.22 (**1.12**)	1.14 (**1.04**)	1.06 (**.96**)	.98 (**.88**)
	Upper Limit of *d*	1.46 (**1.35**)	1.55 (**1.44**)	1.65 (**1.54**)	1.76 (**1.65**)	1.88 (**1.76**)
27	Lower Limit of *d*	1.32 (**1.21**)	1.24 (**1.13**)	1.16 (**1.06**)	1.08 (**.99**)	1.01 (**.91**)
	Upper Limit of *d*	1.47 (**1.36**)	1.56 (**1.44**)	1.65 (**1.54**)	1.76 (**1.64**)	1.86 (**1.75**)
28	Lower Limit of *d*	1.33 (**1.22**)	1.26 (**1.15**)	1.18 (**1.08**)	1.10 (**1.01**)	1.03 (**.93**)
	Upper Limit of *d*	1.48 (**1.37**)	1.56 (**1.45**)	1.65 (**1.54**)	1.75 (**1.64**)	1.85 (**1.74**)
29	Lower Limit of *d*	1.34 (**1.24**)	1.27 (**1.17**)	1.20 (**1.10**)	1.12 (**1.03**)	1.05 (**.96**)
	Upper Limit of *d*	1.48 (**1.38**)	1.56 (**1.45**)	1.65 (**1.54**)	1.74 (**1.63**)	1.84 (**1.73**)
30	Lower Limit of *d*	1.35 (**1.25**)	1.28 (**1.18**)	1.21 (**1.12**)	1.14 (**1.05**)	1.07 (**.98**)
	Upper Limit of *d*	1.49 (**1.38**)	1.57 (**1.46**)	1.65 (**1.54**)	1.74 (**1.63**)	1.83 (**1.73**)
31	Lower Limit of *d*	1.36 (**1.26**)	1.30 (**1.20**)	1.23 (**1.13**)	1.16 (**1.07**)	1.09 (**1.00**)
	Upper Limit of *d*	1.50 (**1.39**)	1.57 (**1.47**)	1.65 (**1.55**)	1.74 (**1.63**)	1.83 (**1.72**)

Number of Events in Study	Upper and Lower Limits	Number of Independent (Predictor) Variables				
		1	2	3	4	5
32	Lower Limit of d	1.37 (**1.27**)	1.31 (**1.21**)	1.24 (**1.15**)	1.18 (**1.08**)	1.11 (**1.02**)
	Upper Limit of d	1.50 (**1.40**)	1.57 (**1.47**)	1.65 (**1.55**)	1.73 (**1.63**)	1.82 (**1.71**)
33	Lower Limit of d	1.38 (**1.28**)	1.32 (**1.22**)	1.26 (**1.16**)	1.19 (**1.10**)	1.13 (**1.04**)
	Upper Limit of d	1.51 (**1.41**)	1.58 (**1.48**)	1.65 (**1.55**)	1.73 (**1.63**)	1.81 (**1.71**)
34	Lower Limit of d	1.39 (**1.29**)	1.33 (**1.24**)	1.27 (**1.17**)	1.21 (**1.12**)	1.15 (**1.06**)
	Upper Limit of d	1.51 (**1.41**)	1.58 (**1.48**)	1.65 (**1.55**)	1.73 (**1.63**)	1.81 (**1.70**)
35	Lower Limit of d	1.40 (**1.30**)	1.34 (**1.25**)	1.28 (**1.19**)	1.22 (**1.13**)	1.16 (**1.07**)
	Upper Limit of d	1.52 (**1.42**)	1.58 (**1.48**)	1.65 (**1.55**)	1.73 (**1.63**)	1.80 (**1.70**)
36	Lower Limit of d	1.41 (**1.31**)	1.35 (**1.26**)	1.29 (**1.20**)	1.24 (**1.15**)	1.18 (**1.09**)
	Upper Limit of d	1.52 (**1.43**)	1.59 (**1.49**)	1.65 (**1.56**)	1.73 (**1.63**)	1.80 (**1.70**)
37	Lower Limit of d	1.42 (**1.32**)	1.36 (**1.27**)	1.31 (**1.21**)	1.25 (**1.16**)	1.19 (**1.10**)
	Upper Limit of d	1.53 (**1.43**)	1.59 (**1.49**)	1.66 (**1.56**)	1.72 (**1.62**)	1.80 (**1.70**)
38	Lower Limit of d	1.43 (**1.33**)	1.37 (**1.28**)	1.3 (**1.23**)	1.26 (**1.17**)	1.21 (**1.12**)
	Upper Limit of d	1.54 (**1.44**)	1.59 (**1.50**)	1.66 (**1.56**)	1.72 (**1.62**)	1.79 (**1.70**)
39	Lower Limit of d	1.43 (**1.34**)	1.38 (**1.29**)	1.33 (**1.24**)	1.27 (**1.19**)	1.22 (**1.13**)
	Upper Limit of d	1.54 (**1.44**)	1.60 (**1.50**)	1.66 (**1.56**)	1.72 (**1.63**)	1.79 (**1.69**)
40	Lower Limit of d	1.44 (**1.35**)	1.39 (**1.30**)	1.34 (**1.25**)	1.29 (**1.20**)	1.23 (**1.15**)
	Upper Limit of d	1.54 (**1.45**)	1.60 (**1.51**)	1.66 (**1.57**)	1.72 (**1.63**)	1.79 (**1.69**)
45	Lower Limit of d	1.48 (**1.39**)	1.43 (**1.34**)	1.38 (**1.30**)	1.34 (**1.25**)	1.29 (**1.21**)
	Upper Limit of d	1.57 (**1.48**)	1.62 (**1.53**)	1.67 (**1.58**)	1.72 (**1.63**)	1.78 (**1.69**)
50	Lower Limit of d	1.50 (**1.42**)	1.46 (**1.38**)	1.42 (**1.34**)	1.38 (**1.30**)	1.34 (**1.26**)
	Upper Limit of d	1.59 (**1.50**)	1.63 (**1.54**)	1.67 (**1.59**)	1.72 (**1.64**)	1.77 (**1.69**)
55	Lower Limit of d	1.53 (**1.45**)	1.49 (**1.41**)	1.45 (**1.37**)	1.41 (**1.33**)	1.38 (**1.30**)
	Upper Limit of d	1.60 (**1.52**)	1.64 (**1.56**)	1.68 (**1.60**)	1.72 (**1.64**)	1.77 (**1.69**)
60	Lower Limit of d	1.55 (**1.47**)	1.51 (**1.44**)	1.48 (**1.40**)	1.44 (**1.37**)	1.41 (**1.33**)
	Upper Limit of d	1.62 (**1.54**)	1.65 (**1.57**)	1.69 (**1.61**)	1.73 (**1.65**)	1.77 (**1.69**)
65	Lower Limit of d	1.57 (**1.49**)	1.54 (**1.46**)	1.50 (**1.43**)	1.47 (**1.40**)	1.44 (**1.36**)
	Upper Limit of d	1.63 (**1.55**)	1.66 (**1.59**)	1.70 (**1.62**)	1.73 (**1.66**)	1.77 (**1.69**)
70	Lower Limit of d	1.58 (**1.51**)	1.55 (**1.48**)	1.52 (**1.45**)	1.49 (**1.42**)	1.46 (**1.39**)
	Upper Limit of d	1.64 (**1.57**)	1.67 (**1.60**)	1.70 (**1.63**)	1.74 (**1.66**)	1.77 (**1.70**)
75	Lower Limit of d	1.60 (**1.53**)	1.57 (**1.50**)	1.54 (**1.47**)	1.51 (**1.45**)	1.49 (**1.42**)
	Upper Limit of d	1.65 (**1.58**)	1.68 (**1.61**)	1.71 (**1.64**)	1.74 (**1.67**)	1.77 (**1.70**)
80	Lower Limit of d	1.61 (**1.54**)	1.59 (**1.52**)	1.56 (**1.49**)	1.53 (**1.47**)	1.51 (**1.44**)
	Upper Limit of d	1.66 (**1.59**)	1.69 (**1.62**)	1.72 (**1.65**)	1.74 (**1.67**)	1.77 (**1.70**)
85	Lower Limit of d	1.62 (**1.56**)	1.60 (**1.53**)	1.57 (**1.51**)	1.55 (**1.49**)	1.52 (**1.46**)
	Upper Limit of d	1.67 (**1.60**)	1.70 (**1.63**)	1.72 (**1.65**)	1.75 (**1.68**)	1.77 (**1.71**)
90	Lower Limit of d	1.63 (**1.57**)	1.61 (**1.55**)	1.59 (**1.53**)	1.57 (**1.50**)	1.54 (**1.48**)
	Upper Limit of d	1.68 (**1.61**)	1.70 (**1.64**)	1.73 (**1.66**)	1.75 (**1.69**)	1.78 (**1.71**)
95	Lower Limit of d	1.64 (**1.58**)	1.62 (**1.56**)	1.60 (**1.54**)	1.58 (**1.52**)	1.56 (**1.50**)
	Upper Limit of d	1.69 (**1.62**)	1.71 (**1.65**)	1.73 (**1.67**)	1.75 (**1.69**)	1.78 (**1.71**)
100	Lower Limit of d	1.65 (**1.59**)	1.63 (**1.57**)	1.61 (**1.55**)	1.59 (**1.53**)	1.57 (**1.51**)
	Upper Limit of d	1.69 (**1.63**)	1.72 (**1.65**)	1.74 (**1.67**)	1.76 (**1.70**)	1.78 (**1.72**)

REFERENCES

Achen, C. H. (1982). *Interpreting and using regression.* Thousand Oaks, CA: Sage.

Aczel, A. (1989). *Complete business statistics.* Homewood, IL: Irwin.

Ahlgrim-Delzell, L. (2001, April 19). Measures of association for cross-tabulations. In *Sociology 4156: Quantitative analysis.* Retrieved July 12, 2004, from University of North Carolina, Charlotte, Web site: www.uncc.edu/laahlgri/chapter7.htm

Allison, P. D. (1999). *Multiple regression: A primer.* Thousand Oaks, CA: Pine Forge Press.

Alsawalmeh, Y. M., & Feldt, L. S. (1994). A modification of Feldt's test of the equality of two dependent alpha coefficients. *Psychometrika, 59,* 49–57.

Anastasi, A. (1968). *Psychological testing* (3rd ed.). New York: Macmillan.

Anderson, D. R., Sweeney, D. J., & Williams, T. A. (2003). *Modern business statistics with Microsoft® Excel.* Cincinnati, OH: South-Western.

Anderson, J. C., & Gerbing, D. W. (1988). Structural equation modeling in practice: A review and recommended two-step approach. *Psychological Bulletin, 10,* 411–423.

Anderson, T. W., & Darling, D. A. (1954). A test of goodness of fit. *Journal of the American Statistical Association, 49,* 765–769.

Arbuckle, J. L. (2003). Condition number (of the sample covariance matrix). *Amos 5.0.1 (Build 5151).* Chicago, IL: SmallWaters Corp.

Arbuckle, J. L., & Wothke, W. (1999). *Amos 4.0 user's guide.* Chicago: SmallWaters Corp.

Ashenfelter, O., Harmon, C., & Oosterbeek, H. (1999). A review of estimates of the schooling/earnings relationship, with tests for publication bias. *Labour Economics, 6,* 453–470.

Asher, H. B. (1983). *Causal modeling* (2nd ed.). Beverly Hills, CA: Sage.

Assunçào, R., & Reis, E. A. (1999). A new proposal to adjust Moran's I for population density. *Statistics in Medicine, 18,* 2147–2161.

Bachrach, A. J. (1981). *Psychological research: An introduction* (4th ed.). New York: Random House.

Baker, B. O., Hardyk, C. D., & Petrinovich, L. F. (1966). Weak measurement vs. strong statistics: An empirical critique of S. S. Stevens' proscriptions on statistics. *Educational and Psychological Measurement, 26,* 291–309.

Barchard, K. A., & Hakstian, A. R. (1997). The effects of sampling model on inference with coefficient alpha. *Educational and Psychological Measurement, 57,* 893–905.

Bardo, J. W., & Yeager, S. J. (1982a). Consistency of response style across types of response formats. *Perceptual and Motor Skills, 55,* 307–310.

Bardo, J. W., & Yeager, S. J. (1982b). Note on reliability of fixed-response formats. *Perceptual and Motor Skills, 54,* 1163–1166.

Bardo, J. W., Yeager, S. J., & Klingsporn, M. J. (1982). Preliminary assessment of format-specific control tendency and leniency error in summated rating scales. *Perceptual and Motor Skills, 55,* 227–234.

Barlow, D. H., & Hersen, M. (1984). *Single case experimental designs: Strategies for studying behavior change* (2nd ed.). New York: Pergamon.

Bartholomew, D. (1987). *Latent variable models and factor analysis*. Oxford, UK: Oxford University Press.

Barnett, V., & Lewis, T. (1978). *Outliers in statistical data*. Chichester, UK: Wiley.

Baxter, L. (1975, November). *The independent effects of seating position on the frequency and direction of small group interaction*. Paper presented at the Western Speech Communication Association Convention, Seattle, WA.

Beatty, M. J. (2002). Do we know a vector from a scalar? Why measures of association (not their squares) are appropriate indices of effect. *Human Communication Research, 28,* 605–611.

Begg, C. B., & Mazumdar, M. (1994). Operating characteristics of a rank correlation test for publication bias. *Biometrics, 50,* 1088–1101.

Bentler, P. M. (1980). Multivariate analysis with latent variables: Causal modeling. *Annual Review of Psychology, 31,* 419–456.

Bentler, P. M. (1990). Comparative fit indexes in structural models. *Psychological Bulletin, 107,* 238–246.

Berger, B. A., & McCroskey, J. C. (1982). Reducing communication apprehension in pharmacy students. *American Journal of Pharmaceutical Education, 46,* 132–136.

Bernstein, I. H. (1988). *Applied multivariate analysis*. New York: Springer-Verlag.

Berry, W. D. (1993). *Understanding regression assumptions*. Thousand Oaks, CA: Sage.

Bielby, W. T., & Hauser, R. M. (1977). Structural equation models. *Annual Review of Sociology, 3,* 137–161.

Bollen, K. A. (1987). Outliers and improper solutions: A confirmatory factor analysis example. *Sociological Methods and Research, 15,* 375–384.

Bollen, K. A. (2002). Latent variables in psychology and the social sciences. *Annual Review of Psychology, 53,* 605–634.

Bollen, K. A., & Long, J. S. (Eds.). (1993). *Testing structural equation models*. Newbury Park, CA: Sage.

Boneau, C. A. (1960). The effects of violations of assumptions underlying the *t* test. *Psychological Bulletin, 57,* 49–64.

Bonnett, D. G. (2003). Sample size requirements for testing and estimating coefficient alpha. *Journal of Educational and Behavioral Statistics, 27,* 335–340.

Borgatta, E. F., & Bohrnstedt, G. W. (1980). Level of measurement: Once over again. *Sociological Methods and Research, 9,* 147–160.

Boster, F. J. (2002). On making progress in communication science. *Human Communication Research, 28,* 473–490.

Box, G. E. P. (1950). Problems in the analysis of growth and wear curves. *Biometrics, 6,* 362–389.

Burgoon, M., Hall, J., & Pfau, M. (1991). A test of the "messages-as-fixed-effect fallacy" argument: Empirical and theoretical implication of design choices. *Communication Quarterly, 39,* 18–34.

Burt, C. W. (1948). The factorial study of temperamental traits. *British Journal of Psychology (Statistical Section), 1,* 178–203.

Byrne, B. M. (1989). *A primer of LISREL: Basic applications and programming for confirmatory factor analytic models*. New York: Springer-Verlag.

Calkins, K. G. (2002, October 1). What does he mean? In *An introduction to statistics*. Retrieved February 26, 2003, from www.andrews.edu/~calkins/math/webtexts/stat04.htm

Calzada, M. E., & Scariano, S. M. (2002, October 31–November 4). Visual EDFSoftware to check the normality assumption. In *Electronic Proceedings of the International Conference on Technology in Collegiate Mathematics,* Orlando, FL.

Camilli, G., & Hopkins, K. D. (1978). Applicability of chi square to 2 × 2 contingency tables with small expected cell frequencies. *Psychological Bulletin, 85,* 163–167.

Camilli, G., & Hopkins, K. D. (1979). Testing for the association in 2 × 2 contingency tables with very small sample sizes. *Psychological Bulletin, 86,* 1011–1114.

Campbell, D. T. (1960). Recommendations for the APA test standards regarding construct, trait, and discriminant validity. *American Psychologist, 15,* 546–553.

Campbell, D. T., & Fiske, D. W. (1959). Convergent and discriminant validation by the multitrait-multimethod matrix. *Psychological Bulletin, 56,* 81–105.

Canary, D., & Spitzberg, B. H. (1987). Appropriateness and effectiveness perceptions of conflict strategies. *Human Communication Research, 14,* 93–118.

Card, D., & Krueger, A. B. (1995). Time series minimum-wage studies: A meta-analysis. *American Economic Review, 85,* 238–243.

Causality Lab. (2004, June 14). Constructing hypotheses. In *Carnegie Mellon curriculum on causal and statistical reasoning.* Retrieved August 9, 2004, from www.phil.cmu.edu/projects/causality-lab/tutorials/hyp_demo1/hyp_demo1.html

Chambers, W. V. (1986). Inferring causality from corresponding variances. *Perceptual and Motor Skills, 63,* 475–478.

Chambers, W. V. (1991). Inferring formal causation from corresponding regressions. *The Journal of Mind and Behavior, 12,* 49–70.

Champion, D. J. (1970). *Basic statistics for social research.* Scranton, PA: Chandler.

Chang, L. (1994). A psychometric evaluation of 4-point to 6-point Likert-type scales in relation to reliability and validity. *Applied Psychological Measurement, 18,* 205–216.

Charter, R. A. (1996). Note on the underrepresentation of the split-half reliability formula for unequal standard deviations. *Perceptual and Motor Skills, 82,* 401–402.

Charter, R. A. (2001). It is time to bury the Spearman-Brown "prophecy" formula for some common applications. *Educational and Psychological Measurement, 61,* 690–696.

Chatterjee, S., Hadi, A. S., & Price, B. (2000). *Regression analysis by example* (3rd ed.). New York: Wiley.

Chen, F., Bollen, K. A., Paxton, P., Curran, P. J., & Kirby, J. B. (2001). Improper solutions in structural equation models: Causes, consequences, and strategies. *Sociological Methods & Research, 29,* 468–508.

Chou, C. P., & Bentler, P. M. (1995). Estimates and tests in structural equation modeling. In R. H. Hoyle (Ed.), *Structural equation modeling* (pp. 37–59). Thousand Oaks, CA: Sage.

Churchill, G. A., & Peter, J. P. (1984). Research design effects on the reliability of rating scales: A meta-analysis. *Journal of Marketing Research, 21,* 360–375.

Cicchetti, D. V., Showalter, D., & Tryer, P. J. (1985). The effect of number of rating scale categories on levels of interrater reliability: A Monte Carlo investigation. *Applied Psychological Measurement, 9,* 31–36.

Clark, H. H. (1973). The language-as-fixed-effect fallacy. *Journal of Verbal Learning & Verbal Behavior, 12,* 335–339.

Cliff, N. R. (1966). Orthogonal rotation to congruence. *Psychometrika, 31,* 33–42.

Cochran, W. G. (1954). Some methods for strengthening the common χ^2 test. *Biometrics, 10,* 417–451.

Cohen, J. (1960). A coefficient of agreement for nominal scales. *Educational and Psychological Measurement, 20,* 37–46.

Cohen, J. (1988). *Statistical power analysis for the behavioral sciences* (2nd ed.). Hillsdale, NJ: Lawrence Erlbaum.

Cohen, J. (1992). A power primer. *Psychological Bulletin, 112,* 155–159.

Cohen, J., & Cohen, P. (1983). *Applied multiple regression/correlation analysis for the behavioral sciences* (2nd ed.). Hillsdale, NJ: Lawrence Erlbaum.

Cohen, M. E. (2001). Analysis of ordinal dental data: Evaluation of conflicting recommendations. *Journal of Dental Research, 80,* 309–313.

Cohen, P. R. (1995). *Empirical methods for artificial intelligence.* Cambridge, MA: Bradford Books, Massachusetts Institute of Technology Press.

Collier, R. O., Baker, F. B., Mandeville, C. K., & Hayes, T. F. (1967). Estimates of test size for several test procedures on conventional variance ratios in repeated measures design. *Psychometrika, 32,* 339–353.

Conover, W. J. (1974). Some reasons for not using the Yates' continuity correction on 2×2 contingency tables. *Journal of the American Statistical Association, 69,* 374–382.

Copas, J. (1998). What works? Selectivity models and meta-analysis. *Journal of the Royal Statistical Society* (Series A), *162,* 95–109.

Cox, D. R., & Wermuth, N. (1996). *Multivariate dependencies: Models, analysis and interpretations.* London: Chapman and Hall.

Cozby, P. C. (1989). *Methods of behavioral research* (4th ed.). Mountain View, CA: Mayfield.

Cronbach, L. J. (1946). Response sets and test validity. *Educational and Psychological Measurement, 6,* 475–494.

Cronbach, L. J. (1950). Further evidence on response sets and test design. *Educational and Psychological Measurement, 10,* 3–31.

Cronbach, L. J. (1951). Coefficient alpha and the internal structure of tests. *Psychometrika, 16,* 297–334.

Crown, J. S. (2000). Percentage points for directional Anderson-Darling goodness-of-fit tests. *Communications in Statistics: Simulation and Computation, 29,* 523–532.

Cudeck, R. (1991). Comments on "Using causal models to estimate indirect effects." In L. M. Collins & J. L. Horn (Eds.), *Best methods for the analysis of change: Recent advances, unanswered questions, future directions* (pp. 260–263). Washington, DC: American Psychological Association.

Cummins, R. A., & Gullone, E. (2000). Why we should not use 5-point Likert scales: The case for subjective quality of life measurement. *Proceedings, Second International Conference on Quality of Life in Cities* (pp. 74–93). Singapore: National University of Singapore.

Dahle, T. L., & Monroe, A. H. (1961). The empirical approach. In C. W. Dow (Ed.), *An introduction to graduate study in speech and theatre* (pp. 173–200). East Lansing: Michigan State University Press.

Dallal, G. E. (2001). *Collinearity.* Retrieved March 10, 2004, from Tufts University Web site: www.tufts.edu/~gdallal/collin.htm

Dallal, G. E. (2003). *Regression diagnostics.* Retrieved March 10, 2004, from Tufts University Web site: www.tufts.edu/~gdallal/diagnose.htm

D'Andrade, R., & Dart, J. (1990). The interpretation of r versus r_2 or why percent of variance accounted for is a poor measure of size of effect. *Journal of Quantitative Anthropology, 2,* 47–59.

DeCoster, J. (2001, May 14). *Notes on transforming and restructuring data.* Retrieved March 30, 2005, from Department of Social Psychology, Free University Amsterdam Web site: www.stat-help.com/struct.pdf

DeCoster, J. (2005, June 29). *Meta-analysis notes.* Amsterdam: Department of Social Psychology, Free University Amsterdam, the Netherlands. Retrieved November 28, 2005, from http://artemis.austincollege.edu/acad/psych/lbrown/meta.pdf

de Finetti, B. (1981). Funzione caratteristica di un fenomeno aleatorio. In *Scritti [1926–1930].* Padova, Italy: Cedam. (Reprinted from *Memorie della Reale Accademia dei Lincei, 6,* 86–133, 1930)

Delaware Student Testing Program. (1999, November 9). *Notes on reliability and validity of the Delaware Student Testing Program.* Retrieved May 14, 2003, from Delaware Department of Education Web site: www.doe.state.de.us/aab/rel_val_19991109.html

DeLong, B., & Lang, K. (1992). Are all economic hypotheses false? *Journal of Political Economy, 100,* 1257–1272.

de Moivre, A. (1756). *The doctrine of chances or, A method of calculating the probability of events in play* (3rd ed.). London: Millar.

Derksen, S., & Keselman, H. J. (1992). Backward, forward and stepwise automated subset selection algorithms: Frequency of obtaining authentic and noise variables. *British Journal of Mathematical and Statistical Psychology, 45,* 265–282.

Diefenbach, M. A., Weinstein, N. D., & O'Reilly, J. (1993). Scales for assessing perceptions of health hazard susceptibility. *Health Education Research, 8,* 181–192.

Dixon, W. J. (1954). Power under normality of several non-parametric tests. *Annals of Mathematical Statistics, 25,* 610–614.

Dixon, W. J., & Tukey, J. W. (1968). Approximate behavior of the distribution of winsorized t (trimming/winsorization 2). *Technometrics*, 10, 83–98.

Dizney, H., & Gromen, L. (1967). Predictive validity and differential achievement on three MLA comparative language foreign language tests. *Educational and Psychological Measurement, 27,* 1127–1130.

Draper, D., Hodges, J. S., Mallows, C. L., & Pregibon, D. (1993). Exchangeability and data analysis. *Journal of the Royal Statistical Society* (Series A), *156,* 9–37.

Duhachek, A., & Iacobucci, D. (2004). Alpha's standard error (ASE): An accurate and precise confidence interval estimate. *Journal of Applied Psychology, 89,* 792–808.

Dunnett, C. W. (1964). New tables for multiple comparisons with a control. *Biometrics, 20,* 482–491.

Duvall, S. J., & Tweedie, R. L. (2000a). A non-parametric "trim and fill" method of assessing publication bias in meta-analysis. *Journal of the American Statistical Association, 95,* 89–98.

Duvall, S. J., & Tweedie, R. L. (2000b). Trim and fill: A simple funnel-plot-based method of testing and adjusting for publication bias in meta-analysis. *Biometrics, 56,* 455–463.

Edari, R. S. (2004). *Multiple regression.* Retrieved June 10, 2004, from University of Wisconsin, Milwaukee, Web site: http://66.102.7.104/search?q=cache:icke9LdT3X4J:www.uwm.edu/~edari/methstat/regress.htm+%22multiple+regression%22+edari&hl=en

Ender, P. (2003, June). Applied categorical & nonnormal data analysis: Introduction. In *Education 231C.* Retrieved December 5, 2003, from the UCLA Graduate School of Education and Information Studies Web site: www.gseis.ucla.edu/courses/ed231c/intro.html

Everitt, B. S. (1987). *Introduction to optimization methods and their application in statistics.* London: Chapman and Hall.

Fagley, N. S., & McKinney, I. J. (1983). Reviewer bias for statistically significant results: A reexamination. *Journal of Counseling Psychology, 30,* 298–300.

Feldt, L. S. (1969). A test of the hypothesis that Cronbach's alpha or Kuder-Richardson coefficient twenty is the same for two tests. *Psychometrika, 34,* 363–373.

Feldt, L. S. (1980). A test of the hypothesis that Cronbach's alpha reliability coefficient is the same for two tests administered to the same sample. *Psychometrika, 45,* 99–105.

Feldt, L. S., & Brennan, R. L. (1989). Reliability. In R. L. Linn (Ed.), *Educational measurement* (3rd ed., pp. 105–146). Washington, DC: American Council on Education.

Feldt, L. S., & Qualls, A. L. (1996). Bias in coefficient alpha arising from heterogeneity of test content. *Applied Measurement in Education, 9,* 277–286.

Feldt, L. S., Woodruff, D. J., & Salih, F. A. (1987). Statistical inference for coefficient alpha. *Applied Psychological Measurement, 11,* 93–103.

Ferguson, G. A. (1954). The concept of parsimony in factor analysis. *Psychometrika, 19,* 281–290.

Fleiss, J. L. (1971). Measuring nominal scale agreement among many raters. *Psychological Bulletin, 76,* 378–382.

Fox, J. (1991). *Multiple and generalized nonparametric regression.* Thousand Oaks, CA: Sage.

Franke, R. H., & Kaul, J. D. (1978). The Hawthorne experiments: First statistical interpretation. *American Sociological Review, 43,* 623–643.

Frankfort-Nachmias, C., & Leon-Guerrero, A. (2002). *Social statistics for a diverse society* (3rd ed.). Thousand Oaks, CA: Pine Forge Press.

Frey, L. R., Botan, C. H., & Kreps, G. L. (2000). *Investigating communication: An introduction to research methods* (2nd ed.). Boston: Allyn & Bacon.

Garson, G. D. (2003). *Multiple regression.* Retrieved December 10, 2003, from the North Carolina State University Web site: http://www2.chass.ncsu.edu/garson/pa765/regress.htm

Garson, G. D. (2004). *Structural equation modeling.* Retrieved May 5, 2004, from the North Carolina State University Web site: http://www2.chass.ncsu.edu/garson/pa765/structur.htm

Givens, G. H., Smith, D. D., & Tweedie, R. L. (1997). Publication bias in meta-analysis: A Bayesian data-augmentation approach to account for issues exemplified in the passive smoking debate. *Statistical Science, 12,* 221–250.

Glaser, S. R., Zamanou, S., & Hacker, K. (1987). Measuring and interpreting organizational culture. *Management Communication Quarterly, 1,* 174–198.

Glass, G. V (1976). Primary, secondary, and meta-analysis of research. *Educational Researcher, 5,* 3–8.

Glass, G. V, & Hopkins, K. D. (1984). *Statistical methods in education and psychology* (2nd ed.). Englewood Cliffs, NJ: Prentice-Hall.

Glass, G. V, & Hopkins, K. D. (1995). *Statistical methods in education and psychology* (3rd ed.). Englewood Cliffs, NJ: Prentice-Hall.

Glass, G. V, Peckham, P. D., & Sanders, J. R. (1972). Consequences of failure to meet assumptions underlying the fixed effects analysis of variance and covariance. *Review of Educational Research, 42,* 237–288.

Gleser, L. J., & Olkin, I. (1996). Models for estimating the number of unpublished studies. *Statistical Medicine, 15,* 2493–2507.

Goldberger, A. S. (1973). Efficient estimation in overidentified models: An interpretive analysis. In A. S. Goldberger & O. D. Duncan (Eds.), *Structural equation models in the social sciences* (pp. 131–152). New York: Seminar Press.

Goodman, L. A. (1954). Kolmogorov-Smirnov tests for psychological research. *Psychological Bulletin, 51,* 160–168.

Goodman, S. N., & Berlin, J. A. (1994). The use of predicted confidence intervals when planning experiments and the misuse of power when interpreting results. *Annals of Internal Medicine, 121,* 200–206.

Görg, H., & Strobl, E. (2000). *Multinational companies and productivity spillovers: A meta-analysis with a test for publication bias* (Research Paper 17). Nottingham: Centre for Research on Globalisation and Labour Markets, School of Economics, University of Nottingham [UK]. Available from www.nottingham.ac.uk/economics/leverhulme/research_papers/00_17.pdf

Görg, H., & Strobl, E. (2001). Multinational companies and productivity spillovers: A meta-analysis with a test for publication bias. *Economic Journal, 111,* 723–739.

Gorsuch, R. L. (1966). The general factor in the test anxiety questionnaire. *Psychological Reports, 19,* 308.

Grant, E. L., & Leavenworth, R. S. (1996). *Statistical quality control* (7th ed.). New York: McGraw-Hill.

Green, S. A. (1991). How many subjects does it take to do a multiple regression analysis? *Multivariate Behavioral Research, 26,* 499–510.

Green, S. B., Lissitz, R. W., & Mulaik, S. A. (1977). Limitations of coefficient alpha as an index of test unidimensionality. *Educational and Psychological Measurement, 37,* 827–838.

Greenhouse, S. W., & Geisser, S. (1959). On methods in the analysis of profile data. *Psychometrika, 24,* 95–112.

Grizzle, J. E. (1967). Continuity correction in the chi-square test for 2×2 tables. *American Statistician, 21*(4), 28–32.

Guadagnoli, E., & Velicer, W. (1988). Relation of sample size to the stability of component patterns. *Psychological Bulletin, 103,* 265–275.

Haitovsky, Y. (1969). Multicollinearity in regression analysis: A comment. *Review of Economics and Statistics, 51,* 486–489.

Hakstian, A. R., & Barchard, K. A. (2000). Toward more robust inferential procedures for coefficient alpha under sampling of both subjects and conditions. *Multivariate Behavioral Research, 35,* 427–456.

Hakstian, A. R., Rogers, W. D., & Cattell, R. B. (1982). The behavior of number-of-factors rules with simulated data. *Multivariate Behavioral Research, 17,* 193–219.

Hakstian, A. R., & Whalen, T. E. (1976). A *k*-sample significance test for independent alpha coefficients. *Psychometrika, 41,* 219–231.

Hanushek, E. A., & Jackson, J. E. (1977). *Statistical methods for social scientists.* New York: Academic Press.

Hardy, M. A. (1993). *Regression with dummy variables.* Newbury Park, CA: Sage.

Harris, R. J. (1975). *A primer of multivariate statistics.* New York: Academic Press.

Hart, A. (2001). Mann-Whitney test is not just a test of medians: Differences in shape can be important. *British Medical Journal, 323,* 391–393.

Hayduk, L. A. (1987). *Structural equation modeling with LISREL: Essentials and advances.* Baltimore, MD: Johns Hopkins University Press.

Hecht, M. L. (1978). The conceptualization and measurement of interpersonal communication satisfaction. *Human Communication Research, 4,* 253–264.

Hedges, L. V., & Olkin, I. (1985). *Statistical methods for meta-analysis.* New York: Academic Press.

Heise, D. R. (1969). Problems in path analysis and causal inferences. In E. F. Borgatta (Ed.), *Sociological methodology* (pp. 38–73). San Francisco: Jossey-Bass.

Helberg, C. (1995, June). *Pitfalls of data analysis (or how to avoid lies and damned lies).* Paper presented at the Third International Applied Statistics in Industry Conference, Dallas, TX. Retrieved July 10, 2003, from www.execpc.com/~helberg/pitfalls/

Hemphill, J. F. (2003). Interpreting the magnitudes of correlation coefficients. *American Psychologist, 58,* 78–80.

Hendrickson, A. E., & White, P. O. (1964). Promax: A quick method for rotation to oblique simple structure. *British Journal of Mathematical and Statistical Psychology, 17,* 65–70.

Henson, R. K. (2002). Understanding internal consistency reliability estimates: A conceptual primer on coefficient alpha. *Measurement and Evaluation in Counseling and Development, 34,* 177–189.

Herzberg, P. A. (1969). The parameters of cross-validation. *Psychometrika* (Monographs uppl. 16).

Hodges, J., & Lehmann, E. L. (1956). The efficiency of some nonparametric competitors of the *t* test. *Annals of Mathematical Statistics, 27,* 324–335.

Hoelter, J. W. (1983). The analysis of covariance structures: Goodness-of-fit indices. *Sociological Methods and Research, 11,* 325–344.

Hoenig, J. M., & Heisey, D. M. (2001). The abuse of power: The pervasive fallacy of power calculations for data analysis. *The American Statistician, 55,* 19–24.

Holbert, R. L., & Stephenson, M. T. (2002). Structural equation modeling in the communication sciences, 1995–2000. *Human Communication Research, 28,* 531–551.

Hopkins, W. G. (2000a, December 18). Calculations for reliability. In *A new view of statistics.* Retrieved April 23, 2003, from www.sportsci.org/resource/stats/relycalc.html

Hopkins, W. G. (2000b). Measures of reliability in sports medicine and science. *Sports Medicine, 30,* 1–15.

Hopkins, W. G. (2000c, June 16). Summarizing data: Precision of measurement. In *A new view of statistics.* Retrieved April 23, 2003, from www.sportsci.org/resource/stats/precision.html

Hoyle, R. H., & Kenny, D. A. (1999). Sample size, reliability, and tests of statistical mediation. In R. H. Hoyle (Ed.), *Statistical strategies for small sample research* (pp. 195–222). Thousand Oaks, CA: Sage.

Hsu, T. C., & Feldt, L. S. (1969). The effect of limitations on the number of criterion score values on the significance of the *F* test. *American Educational Research Journal, 6,* 515–527.

Hu, L., & Bentler, P. M. (1999). Cutoff criteria for fit indexes in covariance structure analysis: Conventional criteria versus new alternatives. *Structural Equation Modeling, 6,* 1–55.

Huck, S. W. (2003). Misconceptions. In *Reading statistics and research* (chap. 4). Retrieved May 14, 2003, from www.readingstats.com/fourth/misconceptions4.htm

Huff, D. (1954). *How to lie with statistics.* New York: Norton.

Hunter, J. E., & Schmidt, F. L. (1990). *Methods of meta-analysis: Correcting error and bias in research findings.* Newbury Park, CA: Sage.

Hurley, J. R., & Cattell, R. B. (1962). The Procrustes program: Producing direct rotation to test a hypothesized factor structure. *Behavioral Science, 7,* 258–274.

Huynh, H. (1978). Some approximate tests for repeated measurement designs. *Psychometrika, 43,* 161–175.

Huynh, H., & Feldt, L. S. (1970). Conditions under which mean square ratios in repeated measurement designs have exact *F* distributions. *Journal of the American Statistical Association, 65,* 1582–1589.

Huynh, H., & Feldt, L. S. (1976). Estimation of the Box correction for degrees of freedom from sample data in the randomized clock and split plot designs. *Journal of Educational Statistics, 1,* 69–82.

Hyman, H. (1955). *Survey design and analysis.* Glencoe, IL: Free Press.

Infante, D. A., & Rancer, A. S. (1982). A conceptualization and measure of argumentativeness. *Journal of Personality Assessment, 46,* 72–80.

Information Technology Services. (1995, June 26). *Factor analysis using SAS PROC FACTOR.* Retrieved December 25, 2004, from University of Texas at Austin Statistical Services Web site: www.utexas .edu/cc/docs/stat53.html

Isaac, S., & Michael, W. B. (1981). *Handbook in research and evaluation* (2nd ed.). San Diego: EdITS.

Jablin, F. M. (1978). Message-response and "openness" in superior-subordinate communication. In B. D. Ruben (Ed.), *Communication yearbook 2* (pp. 293–310). New Brunswick, NJ: Transaction Books.

Jaccard, J., & Turrisi, R. (2003). *Interaction effects in multiple regression* (2nd ed.). Thousand Oaks, CA: Sage.

Jaccard, J., & Wan, C. K. (1996). *LISREL approaches to interaction effects in multiple regression.* Thousand Oaks, CA: Sage.

Jackson, S., Brashers, D. E., & Massey, J. E. (1992). Statistical testing in treatment by replication designs: Three options reconsidered. *Communication Quarterly, 40,* 211–238.

Jackson, S., & Jacobs, S. (1983). Generalizing about messages: Suggestions for the design and analysis of experiments. *Human Communication Research, 9,* 169–191.

Jackson, S., O'Keefe, D. J., & Jacobs, S. (1988). The search for reliable generalizations about messages: A comparison of research strategies. *Human Communication Research, 15,* 127–141.

Jackson, S., O'Keefe, D. J., Jacobs, S., & Brashers, D. (1989). Messages as replications: Toward a message-centered design strategy. *Communication Monographs, 56,* 364–384.

Jaeger, R. M. (1990). *Statistics: A spectator sport* (2nd ed.). Newbury Park, CA: Sage.

Jenkins, G. D., & Taber, T. D. (1977). A Monte Carlo study of factors affecting three indices of composite scale reliability. *Journal of Applied Psychology, 62,* 392–398.

Jennrich, R. I., & Sampson, P. F. (1966). Rotation for simple loadings. *Psychometrika, 31,* 313–323.

Johnson, D. H. (1995). Statistical sirens: The allure of nonparametrics. *Ecology, 76,* 1998–2000.

Johnston, J. (1984). *Econometric methods.* New York: McGraw-Hill.

Jöreskog, K. G. (1969). A general approach to confirmatory maximum likelihood factor analysis. *Psychometrika, 34,* 183–220.

Jöreskog, K. G. (1973). A general method for estimating a linear structural equation system. In A. S. Goldberger & O. D. Duncan (Eds.), *Structural equation models in the social sciences* (pp. 85–112). New York: Seminar Press.

Jöreskog, K. G. (1979a). Analyzing psychological data by structural analysis of covariance matrices. In K. G. Jöreskog, D. Sörbom, & J. Magidson (Eds.), *Advances in factor analysis and structural equation models* (pp. 45–100). Lanham, MD: University Press of America.

Jöreskog, K. G. (1979b). Basic ideas of factor and component analysis. In K. G. Jöreskog, D. Sörbom, & J. Magidson (Eds.), *Advances in factor analysis and structural equation models* (pp. 5–20). Lanham, MD: University Press of America.

Jöreskog, K. G. (1993). Testing structural equation models. In K. A. Bollen & J. S. Long (Eds.), *Testing structural equation models* (pp. 294–316). Newbury Park, CA: Sage.

Jöreskog, K. G., & Sörbom, D. (1986). *LISREL 6.* Mooresville, IN: Scientific Software.

Kachigan, S. K. (1991). *Multivariate statistical analysis: A conceptual introduction* (2nd ed.). New York: Radius Press.

Kaiser, H. F. (1958). The varimax criterion for analytic rotation in factor rotation. *Psychometrika, 23,* 187–200.

Kaplan, D. (2000). *Structural equation modeling: Foundations and extensions.* Thousand Oaks, CA: Sage.

Keeping, E. S. (1995). *Introduction to statistical inference.* New York: Dover.

Kelly, F. J., Beggs, D. L., & McNeil, K. A. (1969). *Research design in the behavioral sciences: Multiple regression approach.* Carbondale: Southern Illinois University Press.

Kenny, D. A. (1979). *Correlation and causality.* New York: John Wiley.

Kenny, D. A. (2003, October 26). *Measuring model fit.* Retrieved February 10, 2004, from http://davidakenny.net/cm/fit.htm

Kerlinger, F. N. (1986). *Foundations of behavioral research* (3rd ed.). New York: Holt, Rinehart and Winston.

Keselman, H. J., Rogan, J. C., Mendoza, J. L., & Breen, L. L. (1980). Testing the validity conditions of repeated measures *F* tests. *Psychological Bulletin, 87,* 479–481.

Keselman, R. C., & Zumbo, B. (1997). Specialized test for detecting treatment effects in the two-sample problem. *Journal of Experimental Education, 65,* 355–366.

Kieffer, K. M. (1999). An introductory primer on the appropriate use of exploratory and confirmatory factor analysis. *Research in the Schools, 6,* 410–416.

Kim, J.-O., & Mueller, C. W. (1978). *Introduction to factor analysis: What it is and how to do it.* Newbury Park, CA: Sage.

Kirk, R. E. (1982). *Experimental design: Procedures for the behavioral sciences* (2nd ed.). Belmont, CA: Brooks/Cole.

Koenker, R. (1961). *Simplified statistics.* Bloomington, IL: McKnight & McKnight.

Komaroff, E. (1997). Effects of simultaneous violations of essential tau-equivalence and uncorrelated error on coefficient alpha. *Applied Psychological Measurement, 21,* 337–348.

Kotiaho, J. S., & Tomkins, J. L. (2002). Meta-analysis, can it ever fail? *Oikos, 96,* 551–553.

Lee, S., & Hershberger, S. (1990). A simple rule for generating equivalent models in covariance structure modeling. *Multivariate Behavioral Research, 25,* 313–334.

Lee, S., & Hershberger, S. (1991). "A simple rule for generating equivalent models in covariance structure modeling": Erratum. *Multivariate Behavioral Research, 26,* 198.

Leedy, P. D. (1989). *Practical research: Planning and design* (4th ed.). New York: Macmillan.

Lenth, R. V. (2001). Some practical guidelines for effective sample size determination. *American Statistician, 55,* 187–193.

Lerner, J. V., & Games, P. A. (1981). Maximum R^2 improvement and stepwise multiple regression as related to over-fitting. *Psychological Reports, 48,* 979–983.

Levine, M., & Ensome, M. H. (2001). *Post hoc* power analysis: An idea whose time has passed? *Pharmacotherapy, 21,* 405–409.

Levine, T. R., & Banas, J. (2002). One-tailed *F*-tests in communication research. *Communication Monographs, 69,* 132–143.

Levine, T. R., Bresnahan, M. J., Park, H. S., Lapinski, M. K., Wittenbaum, G. M., Shearman, S. M., et al. (2003). Self construal scales lack validity. *Human Communication Research, 29,* 210–252.

Levine, T. R., & Hullett, C. R. (2002). Eta squared, partial eta squared, and misreporting of effect size in communication research. *Human Communication Research, 28,* 612–625.

Light, R., Singer, J., & Willett, J. (1990). *By design.* Cambridge, MA: Harvard University Press.

Lilliefors, H. W. (1967). On the Kolmogorov-Smirnov test for normality with mean and variance unknown. *Journal of the American Statistical Association, 64,* 399–402.

Lipsey, M. W., & Wilson, D. B. (2001). *Practical meta-analysis.* Thousand Oaks, CA: Sage.

Lissitz, R. W., & Green, S. B. (1975). Effect of the number of scale points on reliability: A Monte Carlo approach. *Journal of Applied Psychology, 60,* 10–13.

Lix, L. M., & Keselman, R. C. (1998). To trim or not to trim: Tests of location equality under heteroscedasticity and nonnormality. *Educational and Psychological Measurement, 58,* 409–429.

Loehlin, J. C. (1987). *Latent variable model: An introduction to factor, path, and structural analysis.* Hillsdale, NJ: Lawrence Erlbaum.

Lord, F. M. (1955). Sampling fluctuations resulting from the sampling of test items. *Psychometrika, 20,* 1–22.

Lord, F. M., & Novick, M. R. (1968). *Statistical theories of mental test scores.* Reading, MA: Addison-Wesley.

Losh, S. C. (2003, July 15). *Guide 8: More technical aspects of regression.* Retrieved March 10, 2004, from the Florida State University Web site: http://edf5400-01.su04.fsu.edu/Guide8.html

Losh, S. C. (2004, June 21). *Guide 5: Bivariate associations and correlation coefficient properties.* Florida State University. Retrieved August 25, 2004, from the Florida State University Web site: http://edf5400-01.su04.fsu.edu/Guide5.html

Lunney, G. H. (1970). Using analysis of variance with a dichotomous dependent variable: An empirical study. *Journal of Educational Measurement, 7,* 263–269.

Maddala, G. S. (1983). *Limited-dependent and qualitative variables in econometrics.* New York: Macmillan.

Mardia, K. V. (1970). Measures of multivariate skewness and kurtosis with applications. *Biometrika, 57,* 519–530.

Mardia, K. V. (1974). Applications of some measures of multivariate skewness and kurtosis in testing normality and robustness studies. *Sankhya* (Series B), *36,* 115–128.

Marwell, G., & Schmitt, D. R. (1967). Dimensions of compliance gaining behavior: An empirical analysis. *Sociometry, 30,* 350–364.

Mason, R. D. (1970). *Programmed learning aid for business and economic statistics.* Homewood, IL: Learning Systems.

Matell, M. S., & Jacoby, J. (1971). Is there an optimal number of alternatives for Likert scale items? Study I: Reliability and validity. *Educational and Psychological Measurement, 31,* 657–674.

McCroskey, J. C. (1975, November). *Critique.* Paper presented at the Western Speech Communication Association Convention, Seattle, WA.

McCroskey, J. C., Beatty, M. J., Kearney, P., & Plax, T. G. (1985). The content validity of the PRCA-24 as a measure of communication apprehension across communication contexts. *Communication Quarterly, 33*(3), 165–173.

McCroskey, J. C., & Young, T. J. (1979). The use and abuse of factor analysis in communication research. *Human Communication Research, 5,* 375–382.

McDonald, B. (2002). A teaching note on Cook's distance—a guideline. *Research Letters in the Information and Mathematical Sciences, 3,* 127–128.

McIntyre, S. H., Montgomery, D. B., Srinivasan, V., & Weitz, B. A. (1983). Evaluating the statistical significance of models developed by stepwise regression. *Journal of Marketing Research, 20,* 1–11.

McKelvie, S. J. (1978). Graphic rating scales—how many categories? *British Journal of Psychology, 69,* 185–202.

Meehl, P. E., & Waller, N. G. (2002). The path analysis controversy: A new statistical approach to strong appraisal of verisimilitude. *Psychological Methods, 7,* 283–300.

Mertler, C. A., & Vannatta, R. A. (2002). *Advanced and multivariate research methods* (2nd ed.). Los Angeles: Pyrczak Publishing.

Mill, J. S. (1872). *A system of logic: Ratiocinative and inductive* (8th ed.). New impression, 1959. London, UK: Longmans.

Miller, G. R., Boster, F. J., Roloff, M., & Seibold, D. (1977). Compliance-gaining message strategies: A typology of some findings concerning the effects of situational differences. *Communication Monographs, 44,* 37–51.

Minium, E. W. (1970). *Statistical reasoning in psychology and education.* New York: Wiley.

Møller, A. P., & Jennions, M. D. (2001). Testing and adjusting for publication bias. *TRENDS in Ecology & Evolution, 16,* 580–586.

Morrison, D. F. (1976). *Multivariate statistical methods.* New York: McGraw-Hill.

Moses, L. E. (1952). A two-sample test. *Psychometrika, 17,* 239–247.

Moss, P. A. (1994). Can there be validity without reliability? *Educational Researcher, 23,* 5–12.

Mulaik, S. A., James, L. R., Van Alstine, J., Bennett, N., Lind, S., & Stilwell, C. D. (1989). Evaluation of goodness-of-fit indices for structural equation models. *Psychological Bulletin, 105,* 430–445.

Mullen, B. (1989). *Advanced basic meta-analysis.* Hillsdale, NJ: Erlbaum.

Mullen, B., & Miller, N. (1991). Meta-analysis. In C. M. Judd, E. R. Smith, & L. H. Kidder (Eds.), *Research methods in social relations* (6th ed., pp. 425–449). Fort Worth, TX: Holt, Rinehart and Winston.

Muthen, B., & Jöreskog, K. G. (1983). Selectivity problems in quasi-experimental studies. *Evaluation Review, 7,* 139–174.

National Center for Educational Statistics. (2002). Subject: Statistical analysis, inference and comparison. In *Statistical standards: Analysis of data/production of estimates or projections.* Retrieved May 5, 2003, from the National Center for Education Statistics Web site: http://nces.ed.gov/statprog/ 2002/std5_1.asp

Neill, J. J., & Dunn, O. J. (1975). Equality of dependent correlation coefficients. *Biometrics, 31,* 531–543.

Nelson, L. S. (1998). The Anderson-Darling test for normality. *Journal of Quality Technology, 30,* 298–299.

Neuhaus, J. O., & Wrigley, C. (1954). The quartimax method: An analytic approach to orthogonal simple structure. *British Journal of Statistical Psychology, 7,* 81–91.

Nevill, A. M., & Atkinson, G. (1997). Assessing agreement between measurement recorded on a ratio scale in sports medicine and sports science. *British Journal of Sports Medicine, 31,* 314–318.

Norušis, M. J. (1988). *SPSS-X advanced statistics guide* (2nd ed.). Chicago: SPSS.

Nunnally, J. (1978). *Psychometric theory* (2nd ed.). New York: McGraw-Hill.

Onwuegbuzie, A. J., & Daniel, L. G. (2003, February 19). Typology of analytical and interpretational errors in quantitative and qualitative educational research. *Current Issues in Education, 6*(2). Retrieved March 1, 2004, from http://cie.ed.asu.edu/volume6/number2/

Osburn, H. G. (2000). Coefficient alpha and related internal consistency reliability coefficients. *Psychological Methods, 5,* 343–355.

Ott, L., & Hildebrand, D. K. (1983). *Statistical thinking for managers.* Boston: Duxbury.

Ozer, D. J. (1985). Correlation and the coefficient of determination. *Psychological Bulletin, 97,* 307–315.

Park, C., & Dudycha, A. (1974). A cross validation approach to sample size determination for regression models. *Journal of the American Statistical Association, 69,* 214–218.

Park, H. S., Dailey, R., & Lemus, D. (2002). The use of exploratory factor analysis and principal components analysis in communication research. *Human Communication Research, 28,* 562–577.

Pearson, K. (1893). Asymmetrical frequency curves. *Nature, 48,* 615–616.

Pearson, K. (1905). Das fehlergesetz und seine verallgemeinerungen durch Fechner und Pearson. A rejoinder. *Biometrika, 4,* 169–212.

Pedhazur, E. J., & Schmelkin, L. P. (1991). *Measurement, design, and analysis: An integrated approach.* Hillsdale, NJ: Lawrence Erlbaum.

Pfaffenberger, R. C., & Patterson, J. H. (1977). *Statistical methods for business and economics.* Homewood, IL: Irwin.

Plonsky, M. (1997). *Psychological statistics: Nonparametric statistics.* Retrieved March 10, 2004, from www.uwsp.edu/psych/stat/14/nonparm.htm

Raftery, A. E. (1993). Bayesian model selection in structural equation models. In K. A. Bollen & J. S. Long (Eds.), *Testing structural equation models* (pp. 163–180). Newbury Park, CA: Sage.

Raftery, A. E. (1995). Bayesian model selection in social research. *Sociological Methodology, 25,* 111–196.

Rand Corporation. (1955). *A million random digits with 100,000 normal deviates.* New York: Free Press.

Raykov, T. (1998). Coefficient alpha and composite reliability and interrelated nonhomogeneous items. *Applied Psychological Measurement, 22,* 375–385.

Reinard, J. C. (2001). *Introduction to communication research* (3rd ed.). Boston: McGraw-Hill.

Reinard, J. C., & Arsenault, D. J. (2000). The impact of strategic and nonstrategic *voir dire* questions on jury decisions. *Communication Monographs, 67,* 158–177.

Reinard, J. C., Fu, P.-W., Hoover, G., Barr, D., Bybee, K., Corralejo, E. A., et al. (2002, February). *Speed versus accuracy: A content analysis of media report veracity and the alacrity hypothesis.* Paper presented at the Western States Communication Association Convention, Long Beach, CA.

Rockwell, R. C. (1975). Assessment of multicollinearity: The Haitovsky test of the determinant. *Sociological Methods & Research, 3,* 308–320.

Rogan, J. C., Keselman, H. J., & Mendoza, J. L. (1979). Analysis of repeated measurements. *British Journal of Mathematical and Statistical Psychology, 32,* 269–286.

Roscoe, J. T., & Byars, J. A. (1971). An investigation of the restraints with respect to sample size commonly imposed on the use of the chi-square statistic. *Journal of the American Statistical Association, 66,* 755–759.

Rosenberg, M. S. (2005). The file-drawer problem revisited: A general weighted method for calculating fail-safe numbers in meta-analysis. *Evolution, 59,* 464–468.

Rosenthal, R. (1979). The "file drawer problem" and tolerance for null results. *Psychological Bulletin, 86,* 638–641.

Rosenthal, R. (1983). Assessing the statistical and social importance of the effects of psychotherapy. *Journal of Consulting and Clinical Psychology, 51,* 4–13.

Rosenthal, R. (1991). *Meta-analytic procedures for social research* (Rev. ed.). Newbury Park, CA: Sage.

Rosenthal, R., Rosnow, R. L., & Rubin, D. B. (2000). *Contrast and effect sizes in behavioral research: A correlational approach.* New York: Cambridge University Press.

Rosenthal, R., & Rubin, D. B. (1982a). Comparing effect sizes of independent studies. *Psychological Bulletin, 99,* 400–406.

Rosenthal, R., & Rubin, D. B. (1982b). A simple, general purpose display of magnitude of experimental effect. *Journal of Educational Psychology, 74,* 166–169.

Rouanet, H., & Lepine, D. (1970). Comparisons between treatments in a repeated measures design: ANOVA and multivariate methods. *British Journal of Mathematical and Statistical Psychology, 23,* 147–163.

Rubin, R. B. (1994). Interpersonal solidarity scale. In R. B. Rubin, P. Palmgreen, & H. E. Sypher (Eds.), *Communication research measures: A sourcebook* (pp. 223–225). New York: Guilford.

Rubin, R. B., Palmgreen, P., & Sypher, H. E. (Eds.). (2004). *Communication research measures: A sourcebook.* Mahwah, NJ: Erlbaum.

Salvucci, S., Walter, E., Conley, V., Fink, S., & Saba, M. (1997). *Measurement error studies at the National Center for Education Statistics.* Washington, DC: U.S. Department of Education.

Sampling. (2003). In *Community health research methods* (lesson 5). Retrieved April 12, 2003, from the Wellspring: An Online Community of Distance Educators Web site: http://wellspring.isinj.com/sample/communityhealth/research/page26.htm

Sánchez-Meca, J., & Marín-Martínez, F. (1998). Weighting by inverse-variance or by sample size in meta-analysis: A simulation study. *Educational and Psychological Measurement, 58,* 211–220.

Schmidt, F. L., & Hunter, J. E. (1996). Measurement error in psychological research: Lessons from 26 research scenarios. *Psychological Methods, 1,* 199–223.

Schmitt, N. (1996). Uses and abuses of coefficient alpha. *Psychological Assessment, 8,* 350–353.

Schmitt, N., & Ployhart, R. E. (1999). Estimates of cross-validity for stepwise regression and with predictor selection. *Journal of Applied Psychology, 84,* 50–57.

Schneewind, K., & Cattell, R. B. (1970). Zum problem der faktorindentification: Verteilungen and vertranensintervalle von congruentzkoeffizienten. *Psychologische Beiträge, 12,* 214–226.

Schumacker, R. E., & Lomax, R. G. (1996). *A beginner's guide to structural equation modeling.* Mahwah, NJ: Lawrence Erlbaum.

Scott, W. (1955). Reliability of content analysis: The case of nominal scale coding. *Public Opinion Quarterly, 17,* 321–325.

Shevlin, M., Miles, J. N. V., Davies, M. N. O., & Walker, S. (2000). Coefficient alpha: A useful indicator of reliability? *Personality and Individual Differences, 28,* 229–237.

Shojima, K., & Toyoda, H. (2002). Estimation of Cronbach's alpha coefficient in the content of item response theory. *Japanese Journal of Psychology, 73,* 227–233.

Sideridis, G. D. (1999). Examination of the biasing properties of Cronbach coefficient alpha under conditions of varying shapes of data distribution: A Monte Carlo simulation. *Perceptual and Motor Skills, 89,* 899–902.

Siegel, S. (1956). *Nonparametric statistics for the behavioral sciences.* New York: McGraw-Hill.

Snook, S. C., & Gorsuch, R. L. (1989). Principal component analysis versus common factor analysis: A Monte Carlo study. *Psychological Bulletin, 106,* 148–154.

Snuder, T. A. B., & Hagenaars, J. A. (2001). Guest editors' introduction to the special issue on causality at work. *Sociological Methods and Research, 30,* 3–10.

Song, F., Eastwood, A. J., Gilbody, S., Duley, L., & Sutton, A. J. (2000). Publication and related biases. *Health Technology Assessment, 4*(10), 1–115. Available from www.hta.nhsweb.nhs.uk/fullmono/mon410.pdf

Spinelli, J. J., & Stephens, M. A. (1987). Tests for exponentiality when origin and scale parameters are unknown. *Technometrics, 29,* 471–476.

Stanford-Binet Intelligence Scales, Fifth Edition: Features. (2004). Retrieved September 20, 2005, from the Riverside Publishing Company Web site: www.riverpub.com/products/clinical/sbis5/features.html

StatSoft. (2003a). *ANOVA/MANOVA.* Tulsa, OK: StatSoft. Retrieved November 5, 2003, from www.statsoft.com/textbook/stanman.html

StatSoft. (2003b). *Nonparametric statistics.* Tulsa, OK: StatSoft. Retrieved February 24, 2004, from www.statsoft.com/textbook/stnonpar.html

StatSoft. (2003c). *Principal components and factor analysis.* Tulsa, OK: StatSoft. Retrieved January 10, 2004, from www.rdagroup.com/researchers_toolbox/toolbox_est_facanalysis.asp

Steiger, J. H. (1980). Tests for comparing elements of a correlation matrix. *Psychological Bulletin, 87,* 245–251.

Steiger, J. H. (1990). Some additional thoughts on components, factors, and factor indeterminacy. *Multivariate Behavioral Research, 25,* 41–45.

Steiger, J. H. (1996). Dispelling some myths about factor indeterminacy. *Multivariate Behavioral Research, 31,* 539–550.

Steiger, J. H. (1998). A note on multiple sample extensions of the RMSEA fit index. *Structural Equation Modeling, 5,* 411–419.

Steiger, J. H. (2000). Point estimation, hypothesis testing, and interval estimation using the RMSEA: Some comments and a reply to Hayduk and Glaser. *Structural Equation Modeling, 7,* 149–162.

Steiger, J. H., & Hakstian, A. R. (1982). The asymptotic distribution of elements of a correlation matrix: Theory and application. *British Journal of Mathematical and Statistical Psychology, 35,* 208–215.

Steiger, J. H., & Lind, J. C. (1980, May 30). *Statistically-based tests for the number of common factors.* Paper presented at the Meeting of the Psychometric Society, Iowa City, IA.

Steiger, J. H., & Ward, L. M. (1987). Factor analysis and the coefficient of determination. *Psychological Bulletin, 10,* 471–474.

Stelzl, I. (1986). Changing causal relationships without changing the fit: Some rules for generating equivalent LISREL models. *Multivariate Behavioral Research, 21,* 309–331.

Stephens, M. A. (1974). EDF statistics for goodness of fit and some comparisons. *Journal of the American Statistical Association, 69,* 730–737.

Sternstein, M. (1994). *Statistics.* Hauppauge, NY: Barron's Educational Series.

Stevens, J. J. (1999). *Dummy, effect, and contrast coding.* Retrieved September 13, 2005, from http://commfaculty.fullerton.edu/jreinard/new_page_15.htm

Stevens, J. P. (2002). *Applied multivariate statistics for the social sciences* (4th ed.). Mahwah, NJ: Erlbaum.

Stiff, J. B. (1994). *Persuasion.* New York: Guilford.

Stoloff, P. H. (1967). Correcting for heterogeneity of covariance for repeated measures designs of the analysis of variance. *Educational and Psychological Measurement, 30,* 909–924.

Streiner, D. L. (2003a). Being inconsistent about consistency: When coefficient alpha does and doesn't matter. *Journal of Personality Assessment, 80,* 217–222.

Streiner, D. L. (2003b). Starting at the beginning: An introduction to coefficient alpha and internal consistency. *Journal of Personality Assessment, 80,* 99–103.

Strube, M. J., & Hartmann, D. P. (1983). Meta-analysis: Techniques, applications, and functions. *Journal of Consulting and Clinical Psychology, 51,* 14–27.

Student. (1908). On the probable error of the mean. *Biometrika, 6,* 1–25.

Tabachnick, B. G., & Fidell, L. S. (1996). *Using multivariate statistics* (3rd ed.). New York: HarperCollins.

Tabachnick, B. G., & Fidell, L. S. (2001). *Using multivariate statistics* (4th ed.). Needham Heights, MA: Allyn & Bacon.

Tanizaki, H. (1997). Power comparison of non-parametric tests: Small-sample properties from Monte Carlo experiments. *Journal of Applied Statistics, 24,* 603–632.

Task Force on Statistical Inference. (1996, December 14–15). Task Force on Statistical Inference initial report, Board of Scientific Affairs. *APA Online.* Retrieved February 17, 2003, from the American Psychological Association Web site: www.apa.org/science/tfsi.html

Tatsuoka, M. (1969). *Validation studies: The use of multiple regression equations.* Champaign, IL: Institute for Personality and Ability Testing.

Tenopyr, M. L., & Michael, W. B. (1964). The development of a modification in the normal varimax method for use with correlation matrices containing a general factor. *Educational and Psychological Measurement, 24,* 677–699.

Thompson, B. (1994a, February). The concept of statistical significance testing. *Measurement Update, 4*(1), 5–6. (ERIC Document Reproduction Services No. ED366654)

Thompson, B. (1994b). Guidelines for authors. *Educational and Psychological Measurement, 54,* 837–847.

Thompson, B. (1995). Stepwise regression and stepwise discriminant analysis need not apply here. A guidelines editorial. *Educational and Psychological Measurement, 55,* 525–534.

Thompson, B., & Daniel, L. G. (1996). Factor analytic evidence for the construct validity of scores: A historical overview and some guidelines. *Educational and Psychological Measurement, 56,* 197–208.

Towers, G. M. (2003). *Calculating full-range correlations for the mega test.* Retrieved March 22, 2003, from www.eskimo.com/~miyaguch/megadata/fullcorr.html

Trochim, W. M. K. (2002, June 29). *Reliability & validity.* Retrieved May 14, 2003, from www.socialresearchmethods.net/kb/rel&val.htm

Tucker, L. R. (1951). *A method for synthesis of factor analytic studies* (Personnel Research Section Report No. 984). Washington, DC: Department of the Army.

Tuckman, B. W. (1999). *Conducting educational research* (5th ed.). Fort Worth, TX: Harcourt.

Upton, G., & Cook, I. (2002). *Oxford dictionary of statistics.* Oxford, UK: Oxford University Press.

Velicer, W. F., & Jackson, D. N. (1990). Component analysis versus common factor analysis: Some issues in selecting an appropriate procedure. *Multivariate Behavioral Research, 25,* 1–28.

Velleman, P. F., & Wilkinson, P. F. (1993). Nominal, ordinal, interval, and ratio typologies are misleading. *The American Statistician, 47,* 65–72.

Vogt, W. P. (1999). *Dictionary of statistics & methodology: A nontechnical guide for the social sciences* (2nd ed.). Thousand Oaks, CA: Sage.

Vogt, W. P. (2005). *Dictionary of statistics & methodology: A nontechnical guide for the social sciences* (3rd ed.). Thousand Oaks, CA: Sage.

Watt, J. H., & van den Berg, S. A. (1995). *Research methods for communication science.* Boston: Allyn & Bacon.

Weisberg, S. (1980). *Applied linear regression.* New York: Wiley.

Weisberg, S. (1985). *Applied linear regression* (2nd ed.). New York: Wiley.

Weng, L. J. (2004). Impact of the number of response categories and anchor labels on coefficient alpha and test-retest reliability. *Educational and Psychological Measurement, 64,* 956–972.

Wheeless, L. R. (1978). A follow-up study of the relationships among trust, disclosure, and interpersonal solidarity. *Human Communication Research, 4,* 143–157.

Wherry, R. J. (1931). A new formula for predicting the shrinkage of multiple correlation. *Annals of Mathematical Statistics, 2,* 440–457.

Widaman, K. F. (1990). Bias in pattern loadings represented by common factor analysis and component analysis. *Multivariate Behavioral Research, 25,* 89–95.

Wilk, H. B., Shapiro, S. S., & Chen, H. J. (1965). A comparative study of various tests of normality. *Journal of the American Statistical Association, 63,* 1343–1372.

Wilkinson, L., & Task Force on Statistical Inference, APA Board of Scientific Affairs. (1999). Statistical methods in psychology journals: Guidelines and explanations. *American Psychologist, 54,* 594–604.

Wolf, G., & Cartwright, B. (1974). Rules for coding dummy variables in multiple regression. *Psychological Bulletin, 81,* 173–179.

Wolpert, R. L., & Mengersen, K. L. (2004). Adjusted likelihoods for synthesizing empirical evidence from studies that differ in quality and design: Effects of environmental tobacco smoke. *Statistical Science, 19*(3), 1–42.

Wood, J. M., Tataryn, D. J., & Gorsuch, R. L. (1996). Effects of under- and overextraction on principal axis factor analysis with varimax rotation. *Psychological Methods, 1,* 354–365.

Woodruff, D. J., & Feldt, L. S. (1986). Tests for equality of several alpha coefficients when their sample estimates are dependent. *Psychometrika, 51,* 393–413.

World at Work. (2000). *World at Work issue statement.* Retrieved February 20, 2003, from the World at Work Web site: www.worldatwork.org/pressroom/generic/html/press-issuestate.html

Wright, S. (1921). Correlation and causation. *Journal of Agricultural Research, 20,* 557–585.

Wright, S. (1934). The method of path coefficients. *Annals of Mathematical Statistics, 5,* 161–215.

Wrigley, C., & Neuhaus, J. O. (1955). The use of an electronic computer in principal axes factor analysis. *Journal of Educational Psychology, 46,* 31–41.

Wulder, M. (2002, December 30). *Homoscedasticity.* Retrieved April 29, 2003, from the Natural Resources Canada Web site: www.pfc.forestry.ca/profiles/wulder/mvstats/homosced_e.html

Young, D. M., & Seaman, J. W. (1990). A power comparison of eight test statistics for detecting univariate non-normality. *The Texas Journal of Science, 42,* 295–302.

Yuan, K. H., Guarnaccia, C. A., & Hayslip, B. (2003). A study of the distribution of sample coefficient alpha with the Hopkins Symptom Checklist: Bootstrap versus asymptotics. *Educational and Psychological Measurement, 63,* 5–23.

Yuen, K. K. (1974). The two-sample trimmed *t* for unequal population variances. *Biometrika, 61,* 165–170.

Zimmerman, D. W. (1998). Invalidation of parametric and nonparametric statistical tests by concurrent violation of two assumptions. *Journal of Experimental Education, 67,* 55–68.

Zimmerman, D. W., Zumbo, B. D., & Lalonde, C. (1993). Coefficient alpha as an estimate of test reliability under violation of two assumptions. *Educational and Psychological Measurement, 53,* 33–49.

INDEX